NEW YORK REVIEW BOOKS
CLASSICS

THE HALL OF USELESSNESS

SIMON LEYS is the pen name of Pierre Ryckmans, who was born in Belgium and settled in Australia in 1970. He taught Chinese literature at the Australian National University and was Professor of Chinese Studies at the University of Sydney from 1987 to 1993. Leys's writing has appeared in *The New York Review of Books*, *Le Monde*, *Le Figaro Littéraire*, and other periodicals. Among his books are *Chinese Shadows*, *The Death of Napoleon* (forthcoming from NYRB Classics), *Other People's Thoughts*, and *The Wreck of the Batavia & Prosper*. In 1996 he delivered the Australian Broadcasting Corporation's Boyer Lectures. His many awards include the Prix Renaudot, the Prix Femina, the Prix Guizot, and the Christina Stead Prize for Fiction.

THE HALL OF USELESSNESS

Collected Essays

SIMON LEYS

NEW YORK REVIEW BOOKS

New York

THIS IS A NEW YORK REVIEW BOOK
PUBLISHED BY THE NEW YORK REVIEW OF BOOKS
435 Hudson Street, New York, NY 10014
www.nyrb.com

Library of Congress Cataloging-in-Publication Data
Leys, Simon, 1935–
[Essays. Selections]
The hall of uselessness : collected essays / by Simon Leys.
    pages cm. — (New York Review Books classics)
Originally published: Collingwood, Vic. : Black Inc., 2011.
Includes bibliographical references and index.
ISBN 978-1-59017-620-7 (alk. paper)
I. Title.
AC25.L53 2013
824'.914—dc23

                        2012044121

ISBN 978-1-59017-620-7
Available as an electronic book; ISBN 978-1-59017-638-2

Printed in the United States of America on acid-free paper.
1 0   9   8   7   6   5

For Hanfang

CONTENTS

THE HALL OF USELESSNESS
(By Way of a Foreword)

> Everyone knows the usefulness of what is useful, but few know the usefulness of what is useless.
>
> —ZHUANG ZI

TRADITIONALLY, Chinese scholars, men of letters, artists would give an inspiring name to their residences, hermitages, libraries and studios. Sometimes they did not actually possess residences, hermitages, libraries or studios—not even a roof over their heads—but the existence or non-existence of a material support for a Name never appeared to them a very relevant issue. And I wonder if one of the deepest seductions of Chinese culture is not related to this conjuring power with which it vests the Written Word. I am not dealing here with esoteric abstractions, but with a living reality. Let me give you just one modest example, which hit me long ago, when I was an ignorant young student.

In Singapore, I often patronised a small movie theatre which showed old films of Peking operas. The theatre itself was a flimsy open-air structure planted in a paddock by the side of the road (at that time, Singapore still had a countryside): a wooden fence enclosed two dozen rows of seats—long planks resting on trestles. In the rainy season, towards the end of the afternoon, there was always a short heavy downpour, and when the show started, just after dark, the planks often had not yet had time to dry; thus, at the box-office, with your ticket, you received a thick old newspaper to cushion your posterior against the humidity. Everything in the theatre was shoddy and ramshackle—everything except the signpost with the theatre's name hanging above the entrance: two characters written in a huge and generous calligraphy, *Wen Guang*—which could be translated as "Light of Civilisation" or "Light of the Written-Word" (it is the same thing). However, later on in the show, sitting under the starry sky and watching on screen Ma Lianliang give his sublime interpretation of the part of the wisest minister of the Three Kingdoms (third century AD), you realised that—after all—this "Light of Civilisation" was no hollow boast.

Now, back to The Hall of Uselessness. It was a hut located in the heart of a refugee shantytown of Hong Kong (Kowloon side). To reach it at night, one needed an electric torch, for there were no lights and no roads—only a dark maze of meandering paths across a chaos of tin and plywood shacks; there were open drains by the side of the paths, and fat rats ran under the feet of passers-by. For two years I enjoyed there the fraternal hospitality of a former schoolmate, whom I knew from Taiwan—he was an artist (calligrapher and seal-carver) sharing a place with two postgraduate students, a philologist and a historian. We slept on bunks in a single common room. This room was naturally a complete mess—anywhere else it would have resembled a dismal slum, but here all was redeemed by the work of my friend: one superb calligraphy (in seal-script style) hanging on the wall—*Wu Yong Tang*, "The Hall of Uselessness." If taken at face value, it had a touch of tongue-in-cheek self-deprecation; in fact, it contained a very cheeky double-meaning. The words (chosen by our philologist companion, who was a fine scholar) alluded to a passage from *The Book of Changes*, the most ancient, most holy (and most obscure) of all the Chinese classics, which said that "in springtime the dragon is useless." This, in turn, according to commentaries, meant that in their youth the talents of superior men (promised to a great future) must remain hidden.

I spent two years in The Hall of Uselessness; these were intense and joyful years—when learning and living were one and the same thing. The best description of this sort of experience was given by John Henry Newman. In his classic *The Idea of a University*, he made an amazingly bold statement: he said that if he had to choose between two types of universities, one in which eminent professors teach students who come to the university only to attend lectures and sit for examinations, and the other where there are no professors, no lectures, no examinations and no degrees, but where the students live together for two or three years, he would choose the second type. He concluded, "How is this to be explained? When a multitude of young men, keen, open-hearted, sympathetic and observant as young men are, come together and freely mix with each other, they are sure to learn from one another, even if there be no one to teach them; the conversation of all is a series of lectures to each, and they gain for themselves new ideas and views, fresh matter of thought and distinct principles for judging and acting day by day."

I hope I have remained faithful to the memory of The Hall of Uselessness—not in the meaning intended by my friends (for I am afraid I am not exactly of the dragon breed!), but at least in the more obvious meaning of Zhuang Zi, quoted above. Yet is this second aspiration more humble, or more ambitious? After all, this sort of "uselessness" is the very ground on which rest all the essential values of our common humanity.

—S.L.

Canberra, March 2011

Part I
QUIXOTISM

THE IMITATION OF OUR LORD DON QUIXOTE

IN DEBATES, the word "quixotic" is nearly always meant as an insult—which puzzles me, since I can hardly think of a greater compliment. The way most people refer to Don Quixote makes you wonder if they have actually read the book. In fact, it would be interesting to find out whether *Don Quixote* is still as widely read as the universal popularity of the character would normally suggest. But it could be awkward to conduct such an enquiry—especially among educated people, one often encounters a strange misconception that there are a certain number of books one *should* have read, and it would be shameful to acknowledge that one has failed in this sort of cultural obligation. Personally, I disagree with such an attitude; I confess I read only for pleasure.

Of course, I am talking here about creative literature (fiction and poetry), not about the theoretical literature (information, documents) which scholars and professional people must master in order to perform competently within their respective disciplines. For instance, you would naturally expect that—let us say—a medical practitioner should have read some treatises of anatomy and pathology; but you cannot demand that he also be thoroughly conversant with all the short stories of Chekhov. (Though, as a wise doctor once remarked, between two doctors whose medical qualifications are otherwise equal, we should trust the one who reads Chekhov.)

Literary critics do fulfil a very important role (as I shall try to show in a moment), but there seems to be a problem with much contemporary criticism, and especially with a certain type of academic literary criticism. One has the feeling that these critics do not really like literature—they do not enjoy reading. Worse even, if they were actually to enjoy a book, they would suspect it to be frivolous. In their eyes, something that is amusing cannot be important or serious.

This attitude is unconsciously pervading our general view of literature. As a result, we tend to forget that until recently most literary masterpieces were designed as popular entertainment. From Rabelais, Shakespeare and Molière in the classical age, down to the literary giants of the nineteenth century—Balzac, Dumas, Hugo, Dickens, Thackeray—the main concern of the great literary creators was not so much to win the approval of the sophisticated connoisseurs (which, after all, is still a relatively easy trick) as to touch the man in the street, to make him laugh, to make him cry, which is a much more difficult task.

The notion of "literary classic" has a solemn ring about it. But *Don Quixote*, which is *the* classic *par excellence*, was written for a flatly practical purpose: to amuse the largest possible number of readers, in order to make a lot of money for the author (who needed it badly). Besides, Cervantes himself hardly fits the lofty image most people have in mind when they think of inspired writers who create immortal masterpieces: originally a soldier of fortune, he was wounded in action and remained a cripple; captured by pirates, he was sold as a slave in North Africa; when, after long years of captivity, he was finally able to return to Spain, it was only to fall into dire poverty; he was sent to jail several times; his life was a harrowing struggle for survival. He repeatedly attempted—always without success—to earn money with his pen: theatrical plays, pastoral novels. Most of these works have disappeared and the little that remains is not particularly impressive.

It was only at the very end of his career—he was already fifty-eight—with *Don Quixote* in 1605 that he finally hit the jackpot: the book was at once a runaway best-seller. And Cervantes died just one year after the publication of the second and final part of his book (1615). Since *Don Quixote* was rightly hailed as one of the greatest works of fiction of any age, in any language, it is interesting to note that it was also—quite literally—a pot-boiler concocted by a hopeless old hack, at the very end of his tether.

Furthermore, when we consider what set off Cervantes's imagination, our puzzlement increases: he had intended his entire book as a

machine de guerre directed against a very peculiar target—the literature of chivalry and knight errantry, a genre which had been in fashion for a while. This literary crusade now appears utterly irrelevant,
but for Cervantes it was an important cause that mobilised the best of
his intellectual energy; in fact, the relentless pursuit of this rather idle
quarrel provided the very backbone of his entire narrative. As we all
know, the overall structure of *Don Quixote* is very simple: the basic
premise of the story is set in the first few pages of Chapter One, and
the thousand pages that follow simply represent its applications to diverse situations—hundreds of variations on one theme.

Is it necessary to recall this premise here? Don Quixote, who is a
kind, wise and learned country gentleman with little money and
much leisure (always a dangerous combination for an imaginative person), develops an extraordinary addiction to the literature of chivalry.
In Cervantes's own words:

> This gentleman in the times when he had nothing to do—as
> was the case for most of the year—gave himself to the reading
> of books of knight errantry; which he loved and enjoyed so
> much that he almost entirely forgot his hunting, and even the
> care of his estate. So odd and foolish, indeed, did he grow on
> this subject that he sold many acres of corn-land to buy these
> books of chivalry to read ... [In the end], he so buried himself
> in his books that he spent the nights reading from twilight till
> daybreak and the days from dawn till dark; and so from little
> sleep and much reading, his brain dried up and he lost his wits.

As a consequence, he then decided to turn himself into a knight
errant—and out he went into the vast world, in the hope of illustrat-
ing his name for all time with noble and valiant deeds. But the problem, of course, was that knights errant belonged to another age, long
vanished. In the ruthless modern world, his obstinate quest for honour and glory was a grotesque anachronism. The conflict between his
lofty vision and a trivial reality could only lead to an endless series of
preposterous mishaps; most of the time, he ended up as the victim of
cruel and elaborate practical jokes. In the very end, however, he finally

wakes up from his dream, and realises that, all along, what he had chased with such absurd heroism was a ludicrous illusion. This discovery is his ultimate defeat. And he literally dies from a broken heart.

The death of Don Quixote in the last chapter is the climax of the entire book. I would challenge any reader, however tough and insensitive, to read these pages without shedding a tear. And yet, even at that crucial juncture, Cervantes is still pursuing his old obsession, and once again he finds the need to score a few more cheap points at the expense of some obscure books of chivalry. The intrusion of this futile polemic at that very moment is utterly anti-climactic—but then Cervantes has a perverse habit of ruining his own best effects, a practice that has infuriated many readers and critics (I shall return to this a little later). What I wish to underline here is simply this: it is bizarre to observe how a literary masterpiece which was to exert such universal appeal—transcending all barriers of language, culture and time—could, from the start, have been entirely predicated upon such a narrow, tedious and pointless literary quarrel. In order to appreciate fully the oddity of this situation, one should try to transpose it into modern terms: it is as if, for instance, Patrick White (let us say) were to have devoted his greatest creative effort to the single-minded debunking of some trash fiction published in *Women's Weekly* or *New Idea*.

But this, in turn, raises an interesting question. A little while ago, out of the blue, I inadvertently caught some critical flak for venturing to suggest in a nationally broadcast lecture (among a few other heresies) the notion (quite banal in fact) that creative literature, inasmuch as it is artistically valid, can carry no message. This view is not new, by the way, and should be self-evident. Hemingway, whom I quoted, had expressed it best to a journalist who was questioning him on "the messages" of his novels. He very sensibly replied: "There are no messages in my novels. When I want to send a message, I go to the post office."

Some critics reacted indignantly to my statement: "What? No messages in the masterpieces of world literature? And what about Dante's *Divine Comedy*? What about Milton's *Paradise Lost*?" Even more to the point, they could have added: "And what about Cervantes's *Don Quixote*?"

Of course, many poets and novelists *think* that they have messages to communicate, and most of the time they passionately believe in the momentous significance of their messages. But quite frequently these messages are far less important than their authors originally assumed. Sometimes they prove to be actually mistaken, or downright silly or even obnoxious. And often, after a while, they become simply irrelevant, whereas the works themselves, if they have genuine literary merit, acquire a life of their own, revealing their true, long-lasting meaning to later generations; but of this deeper meaning, the author himself was hardly aware. Most of Dante's most fervent readers today care very little for medieval theology; and virtually none of *Don Quixote*'s modern admirers have ever read—let alone heard the names of—most of the books of chivalry that Cervantes attacked with such fierce passion.

In fact, it is in this gap between the author's conscious intention (which may be merely incidental) and the deeper meaning of his work that the critic can find the only legitimate ground on which to exert his craft. Chesterton put it well, in one of the introductions he wrote to Dickens's novels:

> The function of criticism, if it has a legitimate function at all, can only be one function—that of dealing with the subconscious part of the author's mind which only the critic can express, and not with the conscious part of the author's mind, which the author himself can express. Either criticism is no good at all (a very defensible position) or else criticism means saying about an author the very things that would have made him jump out of his boots.

The closer a book comes to being a genuine work of art, a true creation with a life of its own, the less likely it is that the author had full control over and a clear understanding of what he wrote. D. H. Lawrence, who was an exceptionally perceptive critic, summed this up in a statement I have already quoted many times but which one should never tire of invoking: "Never trust the artist. Trust the tale. The proper function of a critic is to save the tale from the artist who created it."

This urge "to save the tale from the artist who created it" has proved particularly strong with the critics of *Don Quixote*. In fact, some of these critics have developed a most peculiar attitude: it is as if the more they come to love Don Quixote, the more they come to resent Cervantes. At first this paradox may seem far-fetched, but there is a logic to it.

Last century, when theatrical troupes went on tour in the country, performing romantic melodramas for unsophisticated village audiences, it often happened that the actor who had impersonated the villain of the play had to be protected after the show, since the local toughs would be waiting for him in order to beat him up, in punishment for all the evil deeds he had just committed so convincingly on stage. Similarly, it is because Don Quixote has become so intensely alive and real for them that some readers cannot forgive Cervantes for subjecting their hero to such a foul and savage treatment.

Or again, you can find another instance of this same phenomenon illustrated in a popular contemporary thriller. In Stephen King's *Misery* (I have not read the book; I only saw the film, which is horribly funny), a best-selling author is being held captive by a female fan; distressed and angered by the fictional death of her favourite heroine, this psychopathic reader tortures the hapless author and forces him to rewrite the ending of his novel.

Now, the four modern critics of Cervantes whose views I wish briefly to survey here rank among the best literary minds of our time, and therefore—needless to say—they should have very little in common with the psychotic freak in King's story, or with the country bumpkins who used to beat up stage villains at the back door of the theatre. And yet, as we shall see, both the sophistication of the former and the crude naïveté of the latter bear witness to the operative virtue of the same magic: *the reality of fiction*.

The first of the critics I shall consider is Vladimir Nabokov. Nabokov gave six lectures on *Don Quixote* when he was a visiting lecturer at Harvard during the early 1950s.[1] When preparing his course, at first he relied upon the memory he had retained of the novel, which he had enjoyed in his youth. Soon, however, he felt the need to go back to the text—but this time, he was appalled by the crudeness and the savagery of Cervantes's narrative. In the words of Brian Boyd, his biographer: "He detested the belly-laughs Cervantes wanted his readers to derive from his hero's discomfiture, and he repeatedly compared the vicious 'fun' of the book with Christ's humiliation and crucifixion, with the Spanish Inquisition, with modern bullfighting."

So much did he enjoy thundering against *Don Quixote* in front of a large student audience that he eventually upset a number of colleagues on the faculty, and he was solemnly warned: "Harvard thinks otherwise." When, some years later, he applied for a chair at Harvard, his candidacy was rejected, which was a bitter blow for him. Other factors were probably more significant but the *Don Quixote* lectures may well have had some part in this fiasco.

Nabokov always found particular enjoyment in challenging received opinions. On the subject of *Don Quixote*, his taste for the unconventional helped him to formulate at least one original and important observation: contrary to what most readers believe, the narrative of *Don Quixote* is not made up of one monotonous series of disasters. After a careful check, episode by episode, Nabokov was able to demonstrate that the issue of each adventure was actually quite unpredictable, and he even compiled the score of Don Quixote's victories and defeats as games in a tennis match, which remained full of suspense till the very end: "6–3, 3–6, 6–4, 5–7. But the fifth set will never be played. Death cancels the match."

His distaste for Cervantes's sadistic treatment of Don Quixote reached such a point that he eventually excluded the book from his regular lectures on foreign literature at Cornell: he could not bear to dwell on the subject any longer. But the corollary of his virulent hostility towards the writer was a loving admiration for his creature, which he expressed in a moving tribute:

> [Don Quixote] has ridden for three hundred and fifty years through the jungles and tundras of human thought—and he has gained in vitality and stature. We do not laugh at him any longer. His blazon is pity, his banner is beauty. He stands for everything that is gentle, forlorn, pure, unselfish, and gallant.

The second critic I wish to evoke here is Henry de Montherlant.[2] Montherlant, one of the most remarkable French writers of our century (a novelist, playwright and essayist), was deeply imbued with Spanish culture. He spent much time in Spain (he even learned and practised bullfighting); his fluent knowledge of Spanish enabled him to read *Don Quixote* in the original text.

He re-read the book four times during his life, and he too experienced an increasing irritation at Cervantes's coarse treatment of a sublime character. Besides, he felt that the book was much too long and that it contained too many tasteless and cruel jokes. But this objection could be turned against itself—is this not precisely a perfect definition of life itself? Come to think of it: a story that drags on much too long and is full of tasteless and cruel jokes ... Note that the worst accusations that can be directed against Cervantes always point in the end to the unique and disquieting power of his book to conjure reality.

Finally, what irked Montherlant most—what he could not forgive Cervantes for—was that, through the entire book, not *once* does the author express *one* word of compassion for his hero, or *one* word of blame for the vulgar bullies who relentlessly mock and persecute him. This reaction—very similar to that of Nabokov—once again reflects a paradox, now familiar to us. What infuriates the critics of Cervantes is precisely the main strength of his art: the secret of its lifelikeness. Flaubert (who, by the way, worshipped *Don Quixote*) said that a great writer should stand in his novel like God in his creation. He created everything and yet is nowhere to be seen, nowhere to be heard. He is everywhere and yet invisible, silent, seemingly absent and indifferent. We curse him for his silence and his indifference, which we take as evidence of his cruelty.

But if the author were to intervene in his narratives—if, instead of letting facts and actions speak for themselves, he were to speak in his own voice—the spell would be broken at once, we would be suddenly reminded that this is not life, this is not reality—it is merely a tale. When we reproach Cervantes for his lack of compassion, his indifference, his cruelty, for the brutality of his jokes, we forget that the more we hate the author, the more we believe in the reality of his world and his creatures.

This absolute reality of Don Quixote became an article of faith for the most powerful and most original of all his modern commentators—my third critic, Miguel de Unamuno. Unamuno (1864–1936) was a multiform genius: scholar, philosopher, novelist, essayist, poet—Basque, Spaniard, European, universal humanist. He wrote a book, *The Life of Don Quixote and Sancho Panza*,[3] in which he commented on the entire novel of Cervantes, chapter by chapter. His paraphrase of Cervantes is imaginative, paradoxical, profound—and also extremely funny.

His main argument, which he sustained, tongue in cheek, over more than four hundred pages, is that Don Quixote should be urgently rescued from the clumsy hands of Cervantes. Don Quixote is our guide, he is inspired, he is sublime, he is true. As for Cervantes, he is a mere shadow: deprived of Don Quixote's support, he hardly exists; when reduced to his own meagre moral and intellectual resources, he proved unable to produce any significant work. How could he ever have appreciated the genius of his own hero? He looked at Don Quixote from the point of view of the world—he took the side of the enemy. Thus, the task which Unamuno assigned to himself was to set the record straight—to vindicate at last the validity of Don Quixote's vision against the false wisdom of the clever wits, the vulgarity of the bullies, the narrow minds of the jesters—and against the dim understanding of Cervantes.

In order to appreciate fully Unamuno's essay, one must place it within the context of his own spiritual life, which was passionate and tragic. Unamuno was a Catholic for whom the problem of faith remained all his life *the* central issue: not to believe was inconceivable—and to believe was impossible. This dramatic contradiction was well expressed in one of his poems:

> . . . I suffer at your expense,
> Non-existing God, for if You were to exist,
> Me too, I would truly exist.[4]

In other words: God does not exist, and the clearest evidence of this is that—as all of you can see—*I* do not exist, either. Thus, with Unamuno, every statement of disbelief turns into a paradoxical profession of faith. In Unamuno's philosophy, faith ultimately creates the thing it contemplates—not as subjective and fleeting auto-suggestion, but as an objective and everlasting reality that can be transmitted to others.

And finally it is Sancho Panza—all the Sancho Panzas of this world—who will vouch for this reality. The earthy Sancho, who followed Don Quixote for so long, with scepticism, with perplexity, with fear, also followed him with fidelity. Sancho did not believe in what his master believed, but he believed in his master. At first he was moved by greed, finally he was moved by love. And even through the worst tribulations, he kept following him because he came to *like the idea*. When Don Quixote lay dying, sadly cured of his splendid illusion, ultimately divested of his dream, Sancho found that he had inherited his master's faith; he had acquired it simply as one would catch a disease—through the contagion of fidelity and love.

Because he converted Sancho, Don Quixote will never die.

Thus, in the madness of Don Quixote, Unamuno reads a perfect illustration of the power and wisdom of faith. Don Quixote pursued immortal fame and a glory that would never fade. To this purpose, he chose to follow what would appear to be the most absurd and impractical path: he followed the way of a knight errant in a world where chivalry had disappeared ages ago. Therefore clever wits all laughed at his folly. But in this long fight, which pitted the lonely knight and his faithful squire against the world, which side was finally befogged in illusion? The world that mocked them has turned to dust, whereas Don Quixote and Sancho live forever.

That Don Quixote proved ultimately to have been wise is a point which was persuasively developed by the last of my critics, Mark Van Doren, in his essay *Don Quixote's Profession*. This piece, now sadly out of print, urgently deserves to be rediscovered by all lovers of literature.[5]

Van Doren aptly characterises *Don Quixote* as a book of "mysterious simplicity": "The sign of its simplicity is that it can be summarised in a few sentences. The sign of its mysteriousness is that it can be talked about forever. It has indeed been talked about as no other story ever was. For a strange thing happens to its readers. They do not read the same book . . . There were never so many theories about anything, one is tempted to say, as there are about *Don Quixote*. Yet it survives them all, as a masterpiece must do, if it would live."

The entire essay begins with a paragraph which deserves to be quoted in full, for, in its luminous elegance, it affords a characteristic example of Van Doren's style:

> A gentleman of fifty, with nothing to do, once invented for himself an occupation. Those about him, in his household and his village, were of the opinion that no such desperate step was necessary. He had an estate and was fond of hunting; these, they said, were occupation enough, and he should be content with the uneventful routines it imposed. But the gentleman was not content. And when he set out in earnest to live an altogether different life he was thought by everybody, first at home and then abroad, to be either strange or mad. He went away three times, returning once of his own accord, but in the second and third cases being brought back by persons of the village who had pursued him for this purpose. He returned each time in an exhausted state, for the occupation he embraced was strenuous; and soon after his third homecoming he took to bed, made his will, confessed his sins, admitted that the whole enterprise had been an error, and died.

The central argument in Van Doren's essay is that (whatever Cervantes himself may have thought on the subject), Don Quixote was not mad. He became deluded only when he tried to assess the progress of his enterprise. And here, the hoaxes to which he fell victim played a fatal role: they gave him a false assurance that his undertaking was really feasible, they confirmed his mistaken hope that he might eventually succeed. Thus, these hoaxes artificially prolonged his career. Yet, at any time he could have abandoned his quest and returned home, had success not appeared to be within reach. Only the illusion which fed on the hoaxes gave him the courage to forge ahead. But he always remained free to decide whether to pursue or to desist. A real madman does not have such a choice: he is the prisoner of his madness; when it becomes unbearable he cannot drop out of it and simply go home to resume his previous way of life.

The occupation Don Quixote chooses for himself is that of knight errant. He is not under the delusion that he is a knight errant—no, he sets his mind on *becoming* one. He does not play at being someone else, as children do in their games; he is not pretending to be someone else, like an impostor, or impersonating a character, like an actor on stage. And he adopts the profession of knight after due reflection: it is the result of a deliberate choice. After having considered other options, he finally decides that the career of a knight errant would be the most rewarding, intellectually and morally.

But "How does one become a knight?" Van Doren asks. By acting like a knight—which is the very opposite of pretence, of make-believe. And to act the way Don Quixote does is more than to ape. To imitate as he does is a profound apprenticeship—the true way of learning and the key to understanding. "What is the difference between acting like a great man and being one? To act like a poet is to write poems; to act like a statesman is to ponder the nature of goodness and justice; to act like a student is to study; to act like a knight is to think and feel like one."

Had Don Quixote been simply and plainly mad, or had he indulged in a protracted game of self-deception and play-acting, we should not be talking of him now, Van Doren observes—"We are talking of him because we suspect that, in the end, he did become a knight."

"Man is a creature who makes pictures of himself, and then comes to resemble the picture." Iris Murdoch made this observation in a different context, but it accurately identifies a defining feature of human nature. It was most memorably exemplified by Don Quixote—which gave Cervantes's novel its universal relevance.

Unlike Don Quixote, however, most of us do not have the chance to select and decide for ourselves which characters we should apply ourselves to becoming. Circumstances of life do the casting; our roles are being imposed on us, other people dictate to us our lines and prompt our acting. A haunting illustration of this was provided in one of Rossellini's last films, *General della Rovere* (1959). A petty crook in Italy at the end of World War II is arrested by the Gestapo and forced by them to impersonate a prestigious figure of the Resistance, General della Rovere, so that they can extract information from political prisoners. But the con man performs his role so convincingly that the other prisoners come to worship him as their moral leader; thus he is progressively compelled to live above himself and to match the image created by their expectations. In the end, he refuses to betray their trust, he is put in front of a firing squad and dies the death of a hero. He has truly become General della Rovere.

As for us, life seldom offers such dramatic scripts. Usually the roles we have to play are more humble and banal—which does not mean that they are less heroic. We too have companions in captivity with extravagant expectations that can force us to act parts well beyond our natural abilities. Our parents expect us to be sons or daughters, our children expect us to be fathers and mothers, our spouses expect us to be husbands and wives; and none of these roles is light or easy. They are all fraught with risks and challenges, with trials, anguishes, humiliations, with victories and defeats.

To man's basic interrogation—Why is it that God never speaks to us openly or answers us directly with a clear voice? Why are we never allowed to see his face?—C. S. Lewis gave a striking answer: How can God meet us face to face, *till we have faces*?

When we first enter upon the stage of life, it is as if we were only given masks that correspond to our respective roles. If we act our part well enough, the mask eventually turns into our true face. Thus Don Quixote becomes a knight, Rossellini's petty crook becomes General della Rovere—and each of us, we can become at last who we were originally meant to be.

The famous multi-billionaire Ted Turner made a remarkable statement some years ago. He said he disliked Christianity, as he felt that it was "a religion of losers." How very true! What an accurate definition indeed!

The word "quixotic"—as I indicated at the very beginning—has entered the common language, with the meaning "hopelessly naïve and idealistic," "ridiculously impractical," "doomed to fail." That this epithet can be used now in an exclusively pejorative sense not only shows that we have ceased to read Cervantes and to understand his character, but more fundamentally it reveals that our culture has drifted away from its spiritual roots.

Make no mistake: for all its earthiness, its cynical jests, its bawdy and scatological realism, Cervantes's masterpiece is anchored in Christianity—more specifically, in Spanish Catholicism, with its strong mystical drive. In this very connection, Unamuno remarked that John of the Cross, Teresa of Avila and Ignatius of Loyola did not reject rationality, nor did they distrust scientific knowledge; what led them to their mysticism was simply the perception of *"an intolerable disparity between the hugeness of their desire and the smallness of reality."*

In his quest for immortal fame, Don Quixote suffered repeated defeats. Because he obstinately refused to adjust "the hugeness of his desire" to "the smallness of reality," he was doomed to perpetual failure. Only a culture based upon "a religion of losers" could produce such a hero.

What we should remember, however, is this (if I may thus paraphrase Bernard Shaw): The successful man adapts himself to the world. The loser persists in trying to adapt the world to himself. Therefore all progress depends on the loser.

AN EMPIRE OF UGLINESS

EIGHTEENTH-CENTURY literature developed the new literary genre of the epistolary novel; I wonder if it would not be legitimate for me to propose now a new form of book review, the epistolary criticism, in which arguments are developed through an exchange of letters between the reviewer and the author of the book under examination. Or perhaps I should not try to disguise the fact: what follows is not much of a book review. But then, what is being reviewed is not much of a book either.

We live in an age of hyperbole. Plumbers are now called "sanitation engineers," waiters have become "food and beverage attendants," barbers devote themselves to the cultivation of "creative coiffure stylism," garbage collectors are turned into "solid-waste disposal officers"—and Christopher Hitchens's own little piece of solid waste is called "a book" (*The Missionary Position: Mother Teresa in Theory and Practice*, London and New York: Verso, 1995).

In the latter's case, the use of this euphemism achieved one substantial result: the thing in question could be dignified with fully fledged book reviews in otherwise reputable magazines and journals; in fact, this is how I was first exposed to it. The *New York Review of Books* published a fairly considerate, earnest and detailed account of its contents, granting it pride of place in its issue of 11 July 1996. The article in question prompted me to send the following letter to this respected literary journal, which duly published it on 19 September:

> Bashing an elderly nun under an obscene label does not seem to
> be a particularly brave or stylish thing to do. Besides, it appears
> that the attacks which are being directed at Mother Teresa all

boil down to one single crime of hers: she endeavours to be a Christian, in the most literal sense of the word—which is (and always was, and will always remain) a most improper and unacceptable undertaking in this world.

Indeed, consider her sins:

1. *She occasionally accepts the hospitality of crooks, millionaires and criminals.* But it is hard to see why, as a Christian, she should be more choosy in this respect than her Master, whose bad frequentations were notorious and shocked all the Hitchenses of his time.

2. *Instead of providing efficient and hygienic services to the sick and dying destitutes, she merely offers them her care and her love.* When I am on my deathbed, I think I should prefer to have one of her sisters by my side, rather than a modern social worker.

3. *She secretly baptises the dying.* The material act of baptism consists in shedding a few drops of water on the head of a person, while mumbling a dozen simple ritual words. Either you believe in the spiritual effect of this gesture—and then you should dearly wish for it—or you do not believe in it, and the gesture is as innocent and well-meaningly innocuous as chasing a fly away with a wave of the hand. If a cannibal who happens to love you presents you with his most cherished possession—a magic crocodile tooth that should protect you forever—will you indignantly reject his gift for being primitive and superstitious, or will you gratefully accept it as a generous mark of sincere concern and affection?

Jesus was spat upon—but not by journalists, as there were none in his time. It is now Mother Teresa's privilege to experience this particular updating of her Master's predicament.

Mr. Hitchens replied at great length to this letter. His rejoinder, which was published in the *New York Review of Books* of 19 December, made essentially the following points:

1. Mother Teresa contradicted herself, on the one hand, by declaring (to the *Ladies Home Journal*) that her friend Princess

Diana would be "better off when free of her marriage," while on the other hand she advised the Irish to vote against the right to remarry after divorce.

2. He re-emphasised once more the fact that Mother Teresa had visited the Duvaliers in Haiti and accepted money from the notorious financial swindler Charles Keating, who had been convicted of defrauding hundreds of "small and humble savers."

3. He repeated his accusation that Mother Teresa attempts to proselytise the dying by surreptitiously baptising them. (How can you proselytise the comatose and the dying? He does not explain.)

4. He found no traces in the Gospels of Hitchenses being shocked by Jesus' unconventional behaviour.

5. He asks in what way the title of his book can be read as an obscenity.

These various points will be dealt with in a moment: at the time, I merely wrote a brief reply, which was published by the *New York Review of Books* in its issue of 9 January 1997:

If Mr. Hitchens were to write an essay on His Holiness the Dalai Lama, being a competent journalist, he would no doubt first acquaint himself with Buddhism in general and with Tibetan Buddhism in particular. On the subject of Mother Teresa, however, he does not seem to have felt the need to acquire much information on her spiritual motivations—his book contains remarkable howlers on elementary aspects of Christianity (and even now, in the latest ammunition he drew from the *Ladies Home Journal*, he displayed a complete ignorance of the position of the Catholic Church on the issues of marriage, divorce and remarriage).

In this respect, his strong and vehement distaste for Mother Teresa reminds me of the indignation of the patron in a restaurant who, having been served caviar on toast, complained that the jam had a funny taste of fish. The point is essential, but it deserves a development which would require more space and more time than can be afforded me here and now. (However, I am working on a review of his book, which I shall gladly forward to him once it comes out in print.)

Finally, Mr. Hitchens asked me to explain what made me say that *The Missionary Position* is an obscene title. His question, without doubt, bears the same imprint of sincerity and good faith that characterised his entire book. Therefore, I owe him an equally sincere and straightforward answer: my knowledge of colloquial English being rather poor, I had to check the meaning of this enigmatic title in *The New Shorter Oxford Dictionary* (Oxford University Press, 1993, two volumes—the only definition of the expression can be found in Vol. I, p. 1,794). But Mr. Hitchens, having no need for such a tool in the exercise of his trade, probably does not possess a copy of it. It will therefore be a relief for his readers to learn that his unfortunate choice of a title was *totally innocent*: when he chose these words, how could he possibly have guessed what they actually meant?

A few days after the publication of this rejoinder, I received a personal letter from Mr. Hitchens. In this private communication—which was naturally most amiable and good-humoured—Mr. Hitchens informed me of his address, so as to enable me to send him the book review, which I had rather recklessly committed myself to write (I say "recklessly," considering my innate and invincible indolence). Besides, he was keen to learn which exactly were the howlers I had hinted at in my rejoinder. He also informed me that he possessed a copy of *The Oxford English Dictionary*: he furthermore suggested that, should I peruse it, I would learn that there is a world of difference between an *obscenity* (which I had so flippantly accused him of) and the normal use of witty *double entendre*, which, he suggested, normally characterises his subtle and tactful writing.

Finally, for my entertainment, he attached to his letter a rather funny newspaper clipping (from the *Washington Times*) regarding a miraculous event that had recently taken place in the Bongo Coffee Shop in Nashville, Tennessee: a customer had found a likeness of Mother Teresa appearing in his breakfast cinnamon bun, which the manager of the shop subsequently enshrined in purple velvet, to be displayed to the pious veneration of the large crowds that soon came flocking to the lucky café. To this intriguing piece of news, Mr. Hitchens appended the comment: "Whatever may be the problems of unbelief, one would not exchange them for the problems of faith."

Courtesy naturally commanded a prompt acknowledgement of his letter. I immediately sent him the following reply:

Dear Mr. Hitchens,

Thank you for your letter. Now that I have your address, I shall certainly be able to send you the review, as promised—but it may still take a little while: I am a slow writer.

Regarding your insistence that the title of your book—when applied to an 86-year-old nun who serves the poor and made a vow of chastity nearly 70 years ago—cannot be read as an obscenity: if a schoolboy draws on the blackboard a cartoon of his teacher copulating with a goat, one may feel irritated by his immature prank, but at the same time, one must grudgingly acknowledge his spirited irreverence. If, however, this same schoolboy eventually insists tearfully that he did not do anything, that he did not mean to be cheeky, that he merely meant to draw an honest and plain zoology assignment, he simply cancels the only merit one could ever have credited him with. Forgive my frankness: in a way, your original offensiveness was more respectable than your present glosses and disclaimers.

Thank you for the newspaper clipping you sent me. I found it very amusing and will add it to my rich collection. But I would question the soundness of the distinction you make between "the problems of unbelief" and "the problems of faith." I am afraid you did not draw the demarcation line in the right spot. People who share Mother Teresa's faith are not likely to discover her face in cinnamon buns (or if they do, they would have a good laugh). When a man ceases to believe in God (as Chesterton said), the problem is not that he starts to believe in nothing, but that he will believe in *anything*. He may not believe that Christ is alive, but then he will believe that Elvis Presley is.

At one point in his little tract (page 66), Mr. Hitchens observes that Mother Teresa "must necessarily admit to being disqualified by inexperience" when she chooses "to speak on matters such as sexuality and reproduction." Nowadays a similar criticism is also often made of the Pope—once I even came across an intriguing variation on that theme: according to one particularly inspired critic, the pontiff's alleged incompetence in these matters was to be ascribed to his being merely "an old Polish bachelor." I have still not grasped in what way the fact of hailing from Poland should constitute a specific disability for someone who has to adjudicate on the issues of sexual morality.

By Mr. Hitchens's logic, only a cow should be truly qualified to run a dairy farm. Still, the notion that it is generally unwise to make pronouncements in areas that lie outside one's expertise remains a sound principle. I only wish that Mr. Hitchens himself would abide by it.

In the very first chapter of his pamphlet, before fully launching into his diatribe against Mother Teresa, Mr. Hitchens makes a fantastic reference to an episode in the life of Jesus Christ, which exposes an ignorance that is so staggering, it simply takes your breath away. In this new Gospel-according-to-Christopher, Jesus *himself* once broke a costly box of unguent on his own feet. (Presumably in homage to himself—another instance of his notorious sense of self-importance?) At this point, the innocent reader is positively hit by a sudden fit of dizziness and rubs his eyes in disbelief.

How should I describe this feeling? Imagine a new book, a critical essay on—let us say—some fundamental aspects of Western cultural history; the book in question is attracting much attention; it is controversial and has already provoked earnest debate. Yet, on the first page, you come across this statement: the Trojan horse was a famous stratagem invented by Joan of Arc at the siege of Orléans.

Mr. Hitchens goes on to blame Mother Teresa for not doing what she never intended to do in the first instance; and he finds it scandalous that she is doing precisely what she originally vowed to do. Yet she had stated her purpose with blinding clarity: "We can do no great things, only small things with great love."

The problem is: he takes it for granted that Mother Teresa should be some sort of philanthropist, whose aim in life is to distribute financial grants among the needy and to provide them with efficient social services and up-to-date medical care.

Mother Teresa is not a philanthropist. She is a Christian. A philanthropist is a person who has a fondness for anthropoids. A Christian is a person who loves Christ. Nay, this latter definition is still too bold (by its standard I myself would stand in great danger of being found abysmally wanting); the best definition was probably the one provided 1,900 years ago by a cool observer—a sceptical Roman bureaucrat, an official from the colonial service reporting to his superiors in Rome on the latest antics of some troublesome Jewish natives under his administration: these people were squabbling "about a dead man called Jesus, whom Paul declares to be alive."

This weird belief that a dead man called Jesus is still alive should command all the deeds and all the thoughts of a Christian. It is *the* key to understanding Mother Teresa's vocation. Surely it is not mere prejudice if we distrust music criticism written by the deaf, or art criticism written by the blind; and to assess literary works, you need to be literate. In the realm of the spirit, there is such a thing as spiritual literacy.

Make no mistake here: I am not claiming some sort of monopoly over enlightenment that should be the exclusive preserve of Christians—far from it. Spiritual illiterates are to be found everywhere; actually, we form quite a crowd every Sunday in church!

Since Mr. Hitchens found the Christianity of Mother Teresa mystifying and abhorrent, would he have more luck with a Hindu saint? I happen to have encountered one and was struck by the fact that his message was quite similar, though put in a different language. I met him in the pages of an obscure and long-forgotten book, dating back to the beginning of this century. The passage is long, but deserves to be quoted in full as I believe it to be directly relevant to the very heart of our discussion. The narrator, D. G. Mukerji, returning home to India after a long stay in the United States, describes his visit to the sage:

> On the floor were seated two young ladies, an old gentleman, their father, and a young monk in yellow, crouching before the Master, as though bowed by his sanctity. The Holy One bade me be seated.

"I am glad," he said, "that thy feet pain thee. That will start the easing of the pain in thy soul."... He turned to the others. "What was I talking about?... I remember: the hospital which is a punishment for doing good."

"How could that be, my Lord?" questioned the old gentleman.

"Even thou, an old man, dost ask me that question also? Well—it all began one day about eleven years ago. I, who was meditating with a brother disciple under a big tree, decided to stop meditating and care for a man who had fallen sick by the roadside. He was a lean moneylender from Marwar and he had come to Benares to make a rich gift to some temple in order to have his way to Heaven paved in solid gold. Poor fellow, he did not know that all the flowery good deeds done to catch the eye of God will in the end become the bitter fruits of desire.

"I ministered to him until he recovered and could return to Marwar, to lend more money, I suppose. But the rascal did me an evil turn. He spread the news all along the way that if people fell sick near my big tree, I took care of them. So very soon, two more people came and fell sick at the pre-arranged place. What else could my brother disciple and I do, but care for them? Hardly had we cured them when we were pelted with more sick folk. It was a blinding shower. I saw in it all a terrible snare: beyond doubt, I felt, if I went on tending the sick, by and by I would lose sight of God.

"Pity can be a ghastly entanglement to those who do not discriminate, and there I stood, with a wall of sick men between me and God. I said to myself: 'Like Hanuman, the monkey, leap over them and fling thyself upon the Infinite.' But somehow I could not leap and I felt lame. Just at that juncture, a lay disciple of mine came to see me: he recognised my predicament and, good soul that he was, he at once got hold of a doctor and an architect and set to work to build the hospital. Very strange though it seems, other illusions co-operated with that good man to help him—the moneylender, the first fellow I cured, sent an additional load of gold and built the day clinic. In six years the place was a solid home of delusion where men put their soul-evolution back by doing good. Shiva, Shiva!"

"But, Master, I notice that your own disciples, boys and young girls, work there?" I put in my question.

"Yes, like these two young ladies here, other young people come to me to serve God. Well, youth suffers from a delusion that it can do good. But I have remedied that somewhat; I let them take care of the sick as long as their outlook on God remains vivid and untarnished, but the moment any of my disciples show signs of being caught in the routine of good works—like the scavenger's cart that follows the routine of removing dirt every morning—I send that person off to our retreat in the Himalayas, there to meditate and purify his soul. When he regains his God-outlook to the fullest, if he wishes, I let him return to the hospital. Beware, beware: good can choke up a soul as much as evil."

"But if someone does not do it, how will good be done?" questioned the old gentleman in a voice full of perplexity.

"Live so," replied the Master in a voice suddenly stern, "live so that by the sanctity of thy life all good will be performed involuntarily."

Mother Teresa has occasionally hobnobbed with the wealthy, the powerful and the corrupt. In Mr. Hitchens's eyes this is a cause for deepest scandal. In his indignation and obsessive denunciations, I wonder if he is not the victim of a common syndrome, which was best diagnosed in the ancient parable of "The Crow and the Phoenix."

The phoenix is a rare and delicate bird, most fastidious in all its habits: it roosts only on the tallest branches of one certain species of tree, the lofty catalpa; it drinks nothing but the purest dewdrops; it eats nothing but the inner petals of precious orchids. Once, as the phoenix was circling above the forest at dusk, preparing to alight for the night on a tall catalpa, down below in the mud a crow that was busy gobbling up a rotten dead rat saw the shadow of the noble bird and lifting up its head screeched angrily at him: "Don't you dare steal my dinner!"

Mr. Hitchens's fierce indignation betrays a naïveté that is so touching, it almost brings tears to the eyes. Can he *really* believe that a person such as Mother Teresa is looking forward to eating dead rats in the company of millionaire vulgarians and tin-pot dictators? To be invited with the famous and the glamorous inside the palatial mansions of the criminally rich, or aboard their fabulous yachts, may perhaps present some seductive glitter to wretched mediocrities such as Mr. Hitchens or myself; but I doubt if it can hold much seduction for Mother Teresa. Not that I imagine her to be above all temptations. On the contrary: even the Prince of Angels was tempted and fell— but it was not for the dubious privilege of drinking an *apéritif* with "Baby Doc" Duvalier.

Still (you will say), the fact remains that she has occasionally shared the repasts of disreputable characters. Why?

When John Henry Newman gave up the exquisite sophistication of a congenial life of scholarship among his peers in Oxford and joined the Catholic Church—a church of uneducated workers and poor Irish servants—he found himself burdened with prosaic parish duties in the intellectual backwaters of Birmingham. A snobbish monsignor took pity on what he believed to be his painful predicament and wrote him a letter, inviting him to come to Rome, where he would find a more cultured milieu. Newman's curt reply is well-known: "I have received your letter inviting me to preach in your church at Rome to 'an audience more educated than could ever be the case in England.' However, *Birmingham people have souls*: and I have neither taste nor talent for the sort of work which you cut out for me: and I beg to decline your offer."

This is a reality which a reverse snobbery usually prevents us from perceiving (and which—let us admit it—runs against all visible evidence), but it remains nevertheless true: just like the people of Birmingham, the wealthy, the powerful and the corrupt *also have souls*.

Jesus knew this already. In Jericho, a man called Zacchaeus—the wealthiest crook in town, who was rightly detested and despised by all decent people—eagerly wanted to meet him. Being aware of this, Jesus invited himself into Zacchaeus's house, to the latter's delight. But this move provoked a scandal among the Pharisees and the Hitchenses. (The original text of the Gospel is traditionally translated as "the Pharisees and the Scribes." We are following here an emendation that seems justified by modern exegesis.)

All took it amiss. "He has gone in to lodge," they said, "with one who is a sinner." To which Jesus retorted: "He too is a son of Abraham. That is what the Son of Man has come for, to search out and save what was lost."

———

Once—many years ago—a minuscule incident afforded me a deeply upsetting revelation. I was writing in a café; I had been sitting there for a couple of hours already, comfortably settled at a table with my books and papers. Like many lazy people, I enjoy a measure of hustle and bustle around me while I am supposed to work—it gives me an illusion of activity—and thus the surrounding din of conversations and calls did not disturb me in the least. The radio that had been blaring in a corner all morning could not bother me either: pop songs, stockmarket figures, muzak, horseracing reports, more pop songs, a lecture on foot-and-mouth disease in cows—whatever: this audio-pap kept dripping like lukewarm water from a leaky faucet and nobody was listening anyway.

Suddenly a miracle occurred. For a reason that will forever remain mysterious, this vulgar broadcasting routine gave way without transition (or, if there had been one, it escaped my attention) to the most sublime music: the first bars of Mozart's clarinet quintet began to flow and with serene authority filled the entire space of the café, turning it at once into an antechamber of Paradise. But the other patrons who had been chatting, drinking, playing cards or reading newspapers were not deaf after all: this magical irruption of a voice from heaven provoked a general start among them—all faces turned round, frowning with puzzled concern. Yet, in a matter of seconds, to the huge relief of all, one customer resolutely stood up, walked straight to the radio, turned the tuning knob and cut off this disquieting *intermède*, switched to another station and restored at once the more congenial noises, which everyone could again comfortably ignore.

At that moment the realisation hit me—and has never left me since: true Philistines are not people who are incapable of recognising beauty; they recognise it all too well; they detect its presence anywhere, immediately, and with a flair as infallible as that of the most sensitive aesthete—but for them, it is in order to be able better to pounce upon it at once and to destroy it before it can gain a foothold in their universal empire of ugliness. Ignorance is not simply the absence of knowledge, obscurantism does not result from a dearth of light, bad taste is not merely a lack of good taste, stupidity is not a simple want of intelligence: all these are fiercely *active* forces, that angrily assert themselves on every occasion; they tolerate no challenge to their omnipresent rule. In every department of human endeavour, inspired talent is an intolerable insult to mediocrity. If this is true in the realm of aesthetics, it is even more true in the world of ethics. More than artistic beauty, moral beauty seems to exasperate our sorry species. The need to bring down to our own wretched level, to deface, to deride and debunk any splendour that is towering above us, is probably the saddest urge of human nature.

LIES THAT TELL THE TRUTH

In art truth is suggested by false means.
                                              —EDGAR DEGAS

Truth is only believed when someone has invented it well.
                                              —GEORGE SANTAYANA

To think clearly in human terms you have to be impelled by a
poem.
                                              —LES MURRAY

THIS ESSAY was originally an address to the annual conference of
the Supreme Court of New South Wales, where its title, at the request
of the organisers, was changed to "Historical and Other Truths"—
which was deemed more appropriate for such a serious audience. For
judges are supposed to be serious; indeed, don't they wear wigs and
gowns to convince us—and remind themselves—of their seriousness?
Serious people have little time for any form of fiction. With such a
flippant title, my talk was not likely to attract many listeners. Still, the
change left me slightly uneasy—since, strictly speaking, I am not a
historian—and I am glad to be able now to relinquish the false adver-
tisement of which I was somehow guilty.

My article carries three epigraphs. Most lectures, addresses—and
essays—are usually forgettable. Epigraphs should be memorable. My
readers will naturally forget this article, but they should remember
the epigraphs. The first one is by a painter, the second one by a philosopher, the third one by a poet.

Painters, philosophers, poets, creative writers—and also inventors and scientists—all reach truth by taking imaginative short-cuts. Let us consider some of these.

Plato's dialogues remain the cornerstone of all Western philosophy. Very often what we find at their core is not discursive reasoning but various myths—short philosophical parables. Myth is the oldest and richest form of fiction. It performs an essential function: "what myth communicates is not truth but reality; truth is always about something—reality is what truth is about" (C.S. Lewis).

At roughly the same time as Plato in the West, ancient Daoist thinkers in China also expressed their ideas in imaginative form. On the subject that occupies us here—how do our minds reach truth— there is one tale in Lie Zi that seems illuminating and fundamental.

In the time of the Warring States, horses were very important for military reasons. The feudal lords employed the services of experts to find good ones. Best of all was the super-horse (*qian-li ma*), an animal which could run a thousand miles a day without leaving tracks and without raising dust. Super-horses were most sought after, but they were also very rare and hard to detect. Hence the need for highly specialised experts; most famous among these was a man called Bole. Eventually Bole became too old to pursue his field trips prospecting for super-horses. Thus his employer, the Duke of Qin, asked him if he could recommend another expert to carry on with this task. "Yes," said Bole, "I have a friend, a pedlar of firewood in the market, who is quite a connoisseur of horses." Following Bole's advice, the duke dispatched this man on a mission to find a super-horse. Three months later, the man returned and reported to the duke: "I have found one; it is in such-and-such a place; it's a brown mare." The duke sent his people to fetch the animal, which proved to be a black stallion. The duke was not happy and summoned Bole: "That friend of yours—he does not seem to be much of an expert: he could not even get the animal's sex and colour right!" On hearing this, Bole was amazed:

> Fantastic! He is even better than myself, a hundred, a thousand times better than myself! What he perceives is the innermost nature of the animal. He looks for and sees what he needs to see. He ignores what he does not need to see. Not distracted by

external appearances, he goes straight to the inner essence. The
way he judges horses shows that he should be judge of more important things than horses.

And, needless to say, this particular animal proved to be a super-horse
indeed, a horse that could run a thousand miles a day without leaving
tracks and without raising dust.

In reflecting on the ways by which our minds apprehend truth, you
may feel that a 2,300-year-old Chinese parable is of only limited relevance. But if so, let us consider something closer to hand: the mental
processes followed by modern Western science.

Claude Bernard, the great pathologist whose research and discoveries were of momentous importance in the development of modern
medical science, one day entered the lecture hall where he was going
to teach and noticed something peculiar: various trays were on a table,
containing different human organs; on one of these trays, flies had
gathered. A common mind would have made a common observation,
perhaps deploring a lack of cleanliness in the room or instructing the
janitor to keep the windows shut. But Bernard's was not a common
mind: he observed that the flies had gathered on the tray which contained livers—and he thought, There must be sugar there. And he
discovered the glycogenic function of the liver—a discovery that
proved decisive for the understanding and treatment of diabetes.

I found this anecdote not in any history of medical science, but in
the diaries of the greatest modern French poet, Paul Claudel. And
Claudel commented: "This mental process is identical to that of *poetical* writing... The impelling motion is the same. Which shows that the
primary source of scientific thought is not reasoning, but the precise
verification of an association *originally supplied by the imagination*."

Note that when I refer to "poetry," I am taking this word in its
most fundamental sense. Samuel Johnson, in his monumental dictionary of the English language, assigns three definitions to the word
"poet," in decreasing order of importance: first, "an inventor"; second,
"an author of fiction"; and last, "a writer of poems."

Truth is grasped by an imaginative leap. This applies not only to
scientific thinking but also to philosophical thought. When I was a

naïve young student in the first year of university, our Arts course included the study of philosophy—a prospect that excited me much at first, though I was soon disappointed by the mediocrity of our lecturer. However, through family acquaintances I had the good fortune to know personally an eminent philosopher of our time, who happened to be also a kind and generous man. On my request, he drafted for me a list of basic readings: one handwritten page with bibliographic references of a selection of classic texts, modern works, histories of philosophy and introductions to philosophy. I treasured this document; yet, over the years, wandering round the world, I misplaced it and, like many other treasures, eventually lost it. Now, half a century later, I have long forgotten the actual items on the list. What I still remember is the postscript the great philosopher had inscribed at the bottom of that page—I remember it vividly because, at the time, I did not understand it and it puzzled me. The postscript said (underlined), "Most important of all, don't forget: do read a lot of novels." When I first read this note, as an immature student, it shocked me. Somehow it did not sound serious enough. For, naïvely, we tend to confuse what is *serious* with what is *deep*. (In the editorial pages of our newspapers, leading articles are serious, while cartoons are funny; yet quite often the cartoon is deep and the leader is vapid.) It took me a long time to appreciate the full wisdom of my philosopher's advice; now I frequently encounter echoes of it. And to the observation I have already quoted elsewhere, that one should prefer a medical practitioner who reads Chekhov, I would add that, if I commit a crime, I hope to be judged by a judge who has read Simenon.

Men of action—people who are totally involved in tackling what they believe to be real life—tend to dismiss poetry and all forms of creative writing as a frivolous distraction. Our great Polar explorer Mawson wrote in a letter to his wife some instructions concerning their children's education. He insisted that they should not waste their time reading novels, but should instead acquire factual information from books of history and biography.

This view—quite prevalent, actually—that there is an essential difference between works of imagination on the one hand, and records of facts and events on the other, is very naïve. At a certain depth or a certain level of quality, all writings tend to be creative writing, for they all partake of the same essence: poetry.

History (contrary to the common view) does not record events. It merely records echoes of events—which is a very different thing—and, in doing this, it must rely on imagination as much as on memory. Memory by itself can only accumulate data, pointlessly and meaning-lessly. Remember Jorge Luis Borges's philosophical parable "Funes the Memorious." Funes is a young man who, falling on his head from a horse, becomes strangely crippled: his memory hyper-develops, he is deprived of any ability to forget, he remembers everything; his mind becomes a monstrous garbage dump cluttered and clogged with irrel-evant data, a gigantic heap of unrelated images and disconnected in-stants; he cannot evacuate any fragment of past experiences, however trifling. This relentless capacity for absolute and continuous recollec-tion is a curse; it excludes all possibility of thought. For thinking re-quires space in which to forget, to select, to delete and to isolate what is significant. If you cannot discard any item from the memory store, you cannot *abstract* and generalise. But without abstraction and gen-eralisation, there can be no thought.

The historian does not merely record; he edits, he omits, he judges, he interprets, he reorganises, he composes. His mission is nothing less than "to render the highest kind of justice to the visible universe, by bringing to light the truth, manifold and one, underlying its every aspect." Yet this quote is not from a historian discussing history writ-ing; it is from a novelist on the art of fiction: it is the famous begin-ning of Joseph Conrad's preface to *The Nigger of the "Narcissus,"* a true manifesto of the novelist's mission.

The fact is, these two arts—history writing and fiction writing—originating both in poetry, involve similar activities and mobilise the same faculties: memory and imagination; and this is why it could rightly be said that the novelist is the historian of the present and the historian the novelist of the past. Both must invent the truth.

Of course, accuracy of data is the pre-condition of any historical work. But in the end, what determines the quality of a historian is the quality of his judgement. Two historians may be in possession of the same data; what distinguishes them is what they make of their common information. For example, on the subject of convict Australia, Robert Hughes gathered a wealth of material which he presented in his *Fatal Shore* in a vivid and highly readable style. On the basis of that same information, however, Geoffrey Blainey drew a conclusion that is radically different—and much more convincing. Hughes had likened convict Australia to the "Gulag Archipelago" of the Soviet Union, but Blainey pointed out that whereas the Soviet Gulag was a totally sterile machine designed solely to crush and destroy its inmates, in Australia, out of a convict system that was also brutal and ferocious, a number of individuals emerged full of vigour and ambition, who rose to become some of their country's richest citizens. In turn, they soon generated a dynamic society and, eventually, a vibrant young democracy. What matters most in the end is how the historian *reads* events—and this is where his judgement is put to the test.

To reach the truth of the past, historians must overcome specific obstacles: they have to gather information that is not always readily available. In this sense, they must master the methods of a specialised discipline. But to understand the truth of the present time, right in front of us, is not the preserve of historians; it is our common task. How do we usually cope with it? Not too well, it seems.

Let us consider just two examples—still quite close to us, and of colossal dimensions. The twentieth century was a hideous century, filled with horrors on a gigantic scale. In sheer magnitude, the terror perpetrated by modern totalitarianisms was unprecedented. It developed essentially in two varieties: Stalinist and Hitlerian.

When we read the writings of Soviet and East European dissidents and exiles, we are struck by one recurrent theme: their amazement, indignation and anger in the face of the stupidity, ignorance and indifference of Western opinion and especially of the Western intelligentsia, which remained largely incapable of registering the reality of their predicament. And yet the Western countries were spending huge resources, both to gather intelligence and to develop scholarly research on the communist world—all to very little avail. Robert Conquest, one of the very few Sovietologists who was clear-sighted from the start, experienced acute frustration in his attempts to share and communicate his knowledge. After the disintegration of the Soviet Union, his publisher proposed to reissue a collection of his earlier essays and asked him what title he would suggest. Conquest thought for one second and said, "How about *I Told You So, You Fucking Fools*?"

Interestingly enough, the name of one writer appears again and again in the writings of the dissidents from the communist world— they pay homage to him as the only author who fully perceived the concrete reality of their condition, down to its very sounds and smells—and this is George Orwell. Aleksandr Nekrich summed up this view: "Orwell is the only Western writer who really understood the essential nature of the Soviet world." Czesław Miłosz and many others made similar assessments. And yet, *Nineteen Eighty-Four* is a work of fiction—an imaginary projection set in the future of England.

The Western incapacity to grasp the Soviet reality and all its Asian variants was not a failure of information (which was always plentiful); it was a *failure of imagination*.

The horrors of the Nazi regime have long been fully documented: the criminals have been defeated and sentenced; the victims, survivors, witnesses have spoken; the historians have gathered evidence and passed judgement. Full light has been cast upon this entire era. The records fill entire libraries.

In all this huge literature, however, I would wish to single out one small book, extraordinary because of its very ordinariness: the prewar memoir of a young Berliner, Raimund Pretzel, who chose to leave his country in 1938 on purely moral grounds. Written under the pen-name of Sebastian Haffner, it carries a fittingly modest and unassuming title: *Geschichte eines Deutschen* (Story of a German), which was badly translated for the English edition as *Defying Hitler*. It was published posthumously only a few years ago by the author's son, who discovered the manuscript in his father's papers.

The author was a well-educated young man; the son of a magistrate, he himself was entering that same career; his future prospects were secure; he loved his friends, his city, his culture, his language. Yet, like all his compatriots, he witnessed Hitler's ascent. He had no privileged information; simply, like any other intellectual, he read the newspapers, followed the news, discussed current affairs with friends and colleagues. He clearly felt that, together with the rest of the country, he was being progressively sucked into a poisonous swamp. To ensure a reasonably smooth and trouble-free existence, small compromises were constantly required—nothing difficult nor particularly dramatic; everyone else, to a various extent, was similarly involved. Yet the sum total of these fairly banal, daily surrenders eroded the integrity of each individual. Haffner himself was never forced into participating in any extreme situation, was never confronted with atrocities, never personally witnessed dramatic events or political crimes. Simply, he found himself softly enveloped into the all-pervasive moral degradation of an entire society. Experiencing nothing more than what all his compatriots were experiencing, he faced the inescapable truth. Since he was lucky enough to have no family responsibilities, he was free to abandon his beloved surroundings and to forsake the chance of a brilliant career: he went into voluntary exile, first to France and then England—*to save his soul*. His short (unfinished), clear-sighted and sober memoir raises one terrifying question: all that Haffner knew at the time, many millions of people around him knew equally well. Why was there only one Haffner?

Earlier on, I suggested that artists and creative writers actually develop alternative modes of access to truth—all the short-cuts afforded by inspired imagination. Please do not misunderstand me: if I suggest that there are alternative approaches to truth, I do not mean that there are alternative truths. Truth is not relative; by nature it is within the reach of everyone, it is plain and obvious—sometimes even painfully so. Haffner's example illustrates it well.

At the time of the Dreyfus Affair—the most shameful miscarriage of justice in French modern history—one of the eminent personalities who came to Dreyfus's defence was a most unlikely figure. Maréchal Lyautey, being an aristocrat, monarchist, Catholic, third-generation military man, seemed naturally to belong to the other side—the side of rightist, anti-Semitic, clerical, militaro-chauvinistic bigots. He became a supporter of Dreyfus (who was falsely convicted of the crime of treason) for only one reason: he himself had integrity. The pro-Dreyfus committee gathered to discuss what to call itself;

most members suggested the name Alliance for Justice. "No," said Lyautey. "We must call it *Alliance for Truth*." And he was right, for one
can honestly hesitate on what is *just* (since justice must always take
into account complex and contradictory factors), but one cannot hesitate on what is *true*.

Which brings me to my conclusion. My conclusion is in fact my
unspoken starting point. When I was first invited to speak on the subject of truth, it was a few days before Easter. During the successive
days of the Christian Holy Week, we read in church the four Gospel
narratives of the last two days in the life of Christ. These narratives
each contain a passage on the trial of Jesus in front of the Roman governor, Pontius Pilate; the concept of truth appears there in a brief dialogue between judge and accused. It is a well-known passage; at that
time, it struck me in a very special way.

The high priests and the Sanhedrin had arrested Jesus, and they
interrogated him. In conclusion, they decided that he should be put to
death for blasphemy. But they were now colonial subjects of the Roman empire: they had lost the power to pronounce and carry out
death sentences. Only the Roman governor possessed such authority.

Thus they bring Jesus to Pilate. Pilate finds himself in a predicament. First, there is the problem inherent to his position: he is both
head of the executive and head of the judiciary. As supreme ruler, he is
concerned with issues of public order and security; as supreme judge,
he should ensure that the demands of justice are being met. Then
there is his own personal situation: the Jews naturally see him for
what he is—an odious foreign oppressor. And he distrusts and dislikes these quarrelsome and incomprehensible natives who give him
endless trouble. During his tenure, twice already there have been severe disturbances; the governor handled them badly—he was even
denounced in Rome. He cannot afford another incident. And this
time, he fears a trap.

The Jewish leaders present themselves as loyal subjects of Caesar.
They accuse Jesus of being a rebel, a political agitator who tells the
people not to pay taxes and who challenges Caesar's authority by
claiming that he himself is a king. Now, if Pilate does not condemn
him, Pilate himself would be disloyal to Caesar.

Pilate interrogates Jesus. Naturally, he finds Jesus' notion of a spiritual kingdom quite fanciful, but it seems also harmless enough. The accused appears to be neither violent nor fanatic; he has poise; he is articulate. Pilate is impressed by his calm dignity, and it quickly becomes obvious to him that Jesus is entirely innocent of all the crimes of which he has been accused. Pilate repeats it several times: "I can find no fault in this man." But the mob demands his death, and the Gospel adds that, hearing their shouts, "Pilate was more afraid than ever." Pilate is scared: he does not want to have, once again, a riot on his hands. Should this happen, it would be the end of his career.

In the course of his interrogation, as Pilate questions Jesus on his activities, Jesus replies: "What I came into the world for, is to bear witness of the truth. Whoever belongs to the truth, listens to my voice." To which Pilate retorts: "The truth! But what is the truth?" He is an educated and sophisticated Roman; he has seen the world and read the philosophers; unlike this simple man, this provincial carpenter from Galilee, he knows that there are many gods and many creeds under the sun . . .

However, beware! Whenever people wonder "What is the truth?" usually it is because the truth is just under their noses—but it would be very inconvenient to acknowledge it. And thus, against his own better judgement, Pilate yields to the will of the crowd and lets Jesus be crucified.

Pilate's problem was not how to ascertain Jesus' innocence. This was easy enough: it was obvious. No, the real problem was that, in the end—like all of us, most of the time—he found it more expedient to wash his hands of the truth.

Part II
LITERATURE

THE PRINCE DE LIGNE, OR THE EIGHTEENTH CENTURY INCARNATE

THE PRINCE de Ligne did not have a very high opinion of literary life in our Belgian provinces. Aware of the poverty and isolation of Jean-Jacques Rousseau (of whom he was a wholehearted admirer), he had visited him in order to offer him a refuge on his estate; when Jean-Jacques did not respond to this invitation, the Prince renewed his initiative, writing Rousseau a letter that has remained famous: "Consider my proposals. No one reads in my country; you will be neither admired nor persecuted."[1] So the Prince would no doubt be pleasantly surprised to know that, two hundred and fifty years later, here in Belgium, there is not only a witty and cultivated woman to celebrate his genius but also a Royal Academy of Literature to republish her exquisite book. Towards the end of his life, during his Viennese exile, he had already been overjoyed by the anthology of his writings compiled and presented by Madame de Staël (whose sometimes muddle-headed ideas he had once gently mocked). Women, and not only literate and intellectual women, were always full of kindness for him.

"The Prince de Ligne is the eighteenth century incarnate." Thus Paul Morand. So accurate is this characterisation that in his old age, which is to say during the first fifteen years of the nineteenth century, the Prince cut the figure of the last survivor of a bygone age. Today, by contrast, it is precisely to that anachronistic aspect that we feel the closest.

Ligne shares a good many traits with Mozart, apropos of whom George Bernard Shaw made a comment that it may be useful to quote here. Mozart's greatness, Shaw argued, lay not in innovation, but on

---

Preface to Sophie Deroisin, *Le Prince de Ligne*.

the contrary in his success in bringing a tradition to an unsurpassable perfection: "Many Mozart worshippers cannot bear to be told that their hero was not the founder of a dynasty. But in art the highest success is to be the last of your race, not the first. Anybody, almost, can make a beginning: the difficulty is to make an end, to do what cannot be bettered."

———

Gay and lively, always effervescent and unable to stay still, Ligne was ever on the move, traveling on horseback, by carriage, barge, galley or sleigh; he spent his life rushing from one end of Europe to the other. His prose has a breathless allegro quality that echoes this rollicking mobility. Despite the trials of life, the death of a beloved son, the failure of a military career brilliantly initiated only to be prematurely wrecked by a conspiracy of mediocrities—there was a deep source of joy and a grace in him that never ran dry. He was disarmingly thoughtless, yet astonishing in his psychological insight. His overdeveloped sensitivity tended easily to be concealed behind the mask of a buffoon; he never missed the chance to make a bad pun, for instance, or to play a practical joke. In this way he put idiots off the scent, but in the end they would get their own back. Wagner rebuked Mozart for a "lack of seriousness";[2] a similar reproach took its toll on Ligne: no sooner was he no longer dealing with the great intelligence of a Maria-Theresa of Austria or a Joseph II in Vienna, or of Catherine the Great in Russia, his own "lack of seriousness" concealed his genius from mediocre sovereigns who no longer dared employ him, thus condemning him to a premature semi-retirement.

But parallels with Mozart, no matter how illuminating, should not be overdone.[3] We must not forget, above all, that Ligne, as Prince of the Holy Roman Empire, Lord of Baudour, Chevalier of the Golden Fleece, Grandee of Spain, Seneschal of Hainaut, and Field-Marshal of the Imperial Armies, was first and foremost an aristocrat who assumed his high birth (going back to Charlemagne!) completely, and remained ever aware of the demanding ethic that it required of him. He wrote on this subject, defining nobility as "the obligation to do nothing ignoble," and it was by this yardstick that he measured and lucidly assessed his peers. At the same time he treated his subjects and subordinates with a courtesy that came from the heart: "I have made emperors and empresses wait for me, but never a soldier." So his vassals, like the simple troopers of his Ligne-Infanterie regiment with whom he shared the dangers and miseries of campaigning, made no mistake when they demonstrated such a fierce loyalty.

Like every true aristocrat, Ligne was basically a man without a profession. If he was a man of war, and indeed he was, as we shall see in a moment, it was by nature rather than by occupation. (Could one ever say of a poet, or a monk, that they practiced their calling *professionally*?) In the worlds of letters and of the arts (including the designing of gardens), Ligne was an amateur in the deepest, most complete and most fruitful sense of the word; free from considerations of utility, he pursued such disciplines for his own satisfaction, following his whims and at his leisure, with grace, nonchalance and detachment, ever guided by sudden inspiration. At bottom there is only one art that matters, and that is the art of life. Hired artisans can achieve great technical mastery, but they have no access to higher values of this kind, the pursuit of which embodies an exquisite *inexpertness* beyond the reach of the professional's virtuosity.

———

I am drawing here on the aesthetic discourse of traditional Chinese scholars, of which of course Ligne knew absolutely nothing; but had he encountered that approach, it would surely not have disconcerted him. After all, it was he who, apropos of the Ottoman Empire, addressed "observers, travellers, spectators" in the following terms: "Instead of thinking trivial thoughts about the nations of Europe, which are all for the most part alike, meditate rather on everything having to do with Asia if you would discover new, beautiful, great, noble, and very often reasonable things."

This open-mindedness made Ligne into one of the very first, and greatest, of truly modern Europeans. His Belgian birth predisposed him in this respect[4]: he described himself as a "Flemish gentleman" but "a Walloon in the army,"[5] and wrote that "I like my standing as a foreigner everywhere, French in Austria, Austrian in France, both of them in Russia. This is the way to succeed everywhere," for "one loses esteem in a country that one dwells in all the time." (This is profoundly true; Pascal had said roughly the same thing, in different words.)

Two passions, as noted earlier, dominated the life of the Prince de Ligne: he loved war and he loved women.

———

Warfare was the sole function of Ligne's caste, its very raison d'être, its honour and duty. For Ligne valour was the cardinal virtue, he preferred a country full of bandits to one full of petty criminals, for bandits at least display courage when they risk their lives in the exercise of their skills. War was the chief occupation of Ligne's life, and was accordingly the subject of a good portion of the thirty-four volumes of his collected works (*Mélanges militaires, littéraires et sentimentaires* [Military, Literary and Sentimental Miscellany]). An anecdote will serve to illustrate the odd intimacy that the Prince entertained with his military vocation. He cherished his son Charles more than any other being in the world, but no sooner was the boy of an age to ride a horse than he led him into action: "I set in motion a small vanguard engagement with the Prussians, and, charging on horseback alongside him I took his little hand in mine as we galloped, and when I had the first shot fired told him: 'how fine it would be, my Charles, should we suffer a slight wound together.'" (Eventually, some twenty years later, when Charles was thirty-three, he was decapitated by a French cannonball. At the news of his son's death the Prince passed out. He remained unconsolable.)[6]

———

As for women, the catalogue of his conquests (by no means all glorious) is longer and more varied that Don Giovanni's as sung by Leporello: his immense range extended from prostitutes to crowned heads. What kind of hunger drove him in this regard? He was, so to speak, in love with love: "In love only the beginning is delightful. I am not surprised that we get so much pleasure from beginning over and over again."

On this topic two remarks of Ligne's are worth mentioning. The first is a joke, but of course jokes can be more revealing than serious statements. In a letter, the Prince recalls a bantering conversation with the Emperor of Austria and the King of Prussia; the three were considering what one might most wish to be: "For my part, I told them that *I would like to be a pretty woman until the age of thirty*, then a very lucky and very able army general until sixty, and a cardinal until eighty." The second observation is a remarkable one, noted in Ligne's *Mes écarts*, and marks him off in a radical and surprising way from Don Juan as from his old friend and fellow-adventurer Casanova: "It is a real and abominable crime to interfere with a marriage of love. Since this is the highest of joys, he who would seek to deprive two loving spouses of it ought to be punished. Can anything else be worth the continual happiness enjoyed by two people who are made for each other?"

————

The Prince de Ligne had scant respect for what we would nowadays call academic knowledge: "I do not care for scholars unless they are scholars without wishing to be or without knowing it. There is nothing easier than becoming a scholar. To acquire learning, it suffices to lock oneself up in one's house for six months. It is far better to have a good imagination than a good memory." What would he have thought of those interminable and exhausting biographies, so fashionable today, produced by pen-pushers who, knowing everything and understanding nothing, pile up mountains of ponderous and insignificant data with which to bury some hapless poet, some fine artist or some other victim of their choosing? In stark contrast, Sophie Deroisin, with her intuitive approach and her light (but penetrating) touch, would seem to be well in harmony with the taste and disposition of her seductive subject.

Casanova, who knew his illustrious friend very well, offered him this insightful comment: "Your mind is of the kind which lends impetus to the minds of others." It is surely that same impetus which animates the pages you are about to read. Sophie Deroisin was a "sensitive soul" in the Stendhalian sense: she had as much heart as intelligence; she loved to admire, and she suffered joyfully from chronic enthusiasm. "Enthusiasm is the finest of faults," wrote the Prince de Ligne. "It is better to be wrong with enthusiasm than right in some other way." But enthusiasm certainly did not lead Sophie Deroisin astray, even if it may have shielded her from certain parts of the picture. Ligne is the incarnation of the eighteenth century, as we said at the outset, and Sophie Deroisin has an admirable grasp of the grace of that era, but she prefers not to see it in all its alarming ferocity, filth, cruelty, mud and blood. Ligne, however, had both feet firmly planted in all that (so did Mozart). On that the academic historians give us plenty of concrete detail. But their view, though perhaps more complete, is not necessarily more true. In his old age, in Vienna, a voluntary exile from his beloved Beloeil—which he was prevented from seeing only by "humour [i.e., mood], horror, and honour"— Ligne knew poverty. Contemporary witnesses describe him as a hirsute, wigless old man who "smelled very bad." Others report that he had an ass, a sheep and a goat which every morning jumped up on his bed begging for food. The two accounts, equally reliable, are by no means contradictory, but the scholarly biographies retain only the former, Sophie Deroisin only the latter. It seems to me that she was not wrong.

Emerson said that "books are for nothing but to inspire." There could be no better description of the worth of this one.

BALZAC

ARTHUR Waley said that he preferred to read Dickens in Chinese translation (Dickens's first Chinese translator was indeed an exquisite writer). I wonder if Balzac does not also belong to the category of writers who actually benefit from being translated. I suspect that his visionary imagination would remain unaffected by the transposition into another language, whereas it would be relatively easy for tactful translators to soften the jarring notes and straighten the blunders that, in the original, frequently jolt the reader or threaten, at the most dramatic moments, to set off anticlimactic laughter.

Balzac's prose is littered with ludicrous conceits, mixed metaphors, clichés and various manifestations of naïveté and bad taste. Mere haste and negligence cannot fully account for so much awkwardness; although his first drafts were often dashed off at astounding speed and in enormous creative bursts, Balzac was also a painstaking, obsessive —and notorious—re-writer. His revisions, corrections, re-corrections and corrections of re-corrections that swelled into the margins of his galley proofs, smothering the printed text under their exuberant growth, famously drove typesetters to fury and despair.

That such a great writer should have written so badly was a source of puzzlement for some of the best connoisseurs (who were also his warmest admirers), from Baudelaire to Flaubert. The paradox was aptly summed up by Flaubert himself: "What a man Balzac would have been had he known how to write! But that was the only thing he lacked. After all, an artist would never have accomplished so much, nor had such breadth."

Review of Graham Robb: *Balzac: A Biography* (London: Picador, 1994).

French literary taste always finds it difficult to deal with those aspects of genius that do not readily fit within a classical frame. An early illustration of this tendency was provided by Voltaire when he apologised for having foolishly introduced Shakespeare on the French stage: "I first showed the French a few pearls I had retrieved from his huge heap of dung...I did not realise at the time that I was actually trampling upon the laurels of Racine and Corneille in order to adorn the head of this barbaric play-actor."[1] Later on, native literary giants did not fare much better. Victor Hugo, who was Balzac's junior by only three years (but whose career lasted nearly twice as long), came to enjoy even greater popularity; yet, for all his triumphs, he never fully succeeded in disarming the reservations of the purists. In our own time, two comments that summarise, with cruel wit, the critical ambivalence that still persists towards Hugo would fit Balzac much better. On being asked who was the greatest French poet, André Gide replied: "Victor Hugo—alas!" And Jean Cocteau added: "Victor Hugo was a madman who believed he was Victor Hugo." Both in greatness and in lunacy, Balzac certainly scaled heights that were at least as spectacular.

Balzac's claim to the title of Greatest French Novelist of All Time can hardly be disputed: he simply bulldozed his way into that position, propelled by the sheer mass and energy of his production. The total cast of his *Comédie humaine* amounts to some 3,500 characters (including a few animals)—in all Western literature, only Shakespeare and Dickens approached such a bewildering fecundity.

To engage in a complete reading of his *Comédie humaine* is akin to climbing onto a raft and attempting the descent of a huge wild river: once you start, you cannot get off, you are powerless to stop, you are carried away into another world—more exciting, more intense, more *real* than the dull scene you left ashore. Everything is larger than life, loaded with energy. In Balzac's novels, Baudelaire observed, even doorkeepers have genius, and Oscar Wilde added:

> A steady course of Balzac reduces our living friends to shadows, and our acquaintances to the shadows of shades. His characters have a kind of fervent, fiery coloured existence. They dominate

us and defy scepticism … Balzac is no more a realist than Holbein was. He created life, he did not copy it.

If the ride is exhilarating, it can also be rough. At times you will
surge and soar, but you will also be bumped about and struck by ab-
surdities: "Children, said the old marquess, as he took *all three of them
by the hand*." You will have to swallow a ration of indigestible, insipid
or silly images: "She was more than a woman, she was a masterpiece!"
"Socrates, the pearl of mankind." Sometimes, however, the tasteless-
ness is relieved by grotesquerie: "The Countess's breasts, which were
lightly veiled by a translucid gauze, were devoured by the charmed
eyes of the young man, who could, in the silence of the night, hear the
murmur of these ivory globes." (In fact, women's breasts seem to have
fed some of Balzac's oddest inspirations. Elsewhere, he describes the
visual impact produced by a middle-aged woman's "low-cut dress":
"Mlle. Cormon's treasures were violently thrust out of their jewel-
cases.") In some passages the gap that usually separates literature from
cheap sentimental fiction is boldly bridged, for instance in this description of a loose actress falling passionately in love with a handsome young poet:

> Coralie took advantage of the darkness to bring to her lips Luc-
> ien's hand, and she kissed it, and wetted it with her tears. Lucien
> was moved, down to the very marrow of his bones. The humil-
> ity shown by a courtesan in love sometimes presents a moral
> splendour that could teach a lesson even to the angels.

Yet even popular women's magazines have their editorial standards, and one doubts if they would ever have been willing to publish
the passage in which Lucien is in his loge and Coralie is on stage, behind the curtain which is still down, and "suddenly the amorous light
flowing from her eyes *pierced the curtain* and flooded into Lucien's
gaze." These quotations (which I have translated directly from the
French)[2] all come from Balzac's mature masterpieces. If an aspiring
writer were to show such samples of his prose to a competent critic,
publisher or editor, the only sensible advice that could be given him

would be to renounce forever any literary ambition, never again to touch a pen; any activity would be preferable—instead of writing fiction, let him start a pineapple farm or go into the grocery business, sell manure, import railway sleepers from the Ukraine, dredge the Tiber for lost Roman antiquities or dig for gold in Brazil. In fact, these were some of the many enterprises that Balzac seriously contemplated; had he achieved a measure of success in any of them, he himself believed that he would have devoted his creative imagination entirely to business, and that he would have forsaken all literary endeavours. Or would he?

In his hugely entertaining new biography of Balzac (certainly the best of all those I have read), Graham Robb does not directly address the central paradox of Balzac's prodigious achievement: How was it possible that the greatest monument of European fiction was built by a man singularly devoid of literary taste? Although Robb takes a purely biographical and non-literary approach (the novels are not analysed but merely mentioned, as chronological stages in Balzac's career), he eventually provides most of the clues that may help to solve this riddle.

Balzac's mother was a cold and frivolous woman, who denied him her affection. This childhood wound never healed. He himself was later to say: "All my misfortune came from my mother: she destroyed me purposefully, for the fun of it." Georges Simenon—the poor man's Balzac of our time—recognised here his own predicament and commented:

> From the example of Balzac, I wish to show that a novelist's work is not an occupation like another—it implies renunciation, it is a vocation, if not a curse, or a disease … It is sometimes said that a typical novelist is a man who was deprived of motherly love … The fact is that the need to create other people, the compulsion to draw out of oneself a crowd of different characters, could hardly arise in a man who is otherwise happy and harmoniously adjusted to his own little world. Why should he so obstinately attempt to live other people's lives, if he himself were secure and without revolt?[3]

Balzac's first mistress, who considerably contributed to the refinement of his sensibility, was a few years older than his mother, and subsequently all the women who mattered in his life were, to some extent, substitute mothers. In an early letter, he wrote: "I have only two passions: love and glory"—and the purpose of the latter was to secure the former. He confessed that the primary motivation of his writing was to win the love of women, and in this he succeeded remarkably well: after his death, more than 10,000 letters from female admirers were found among his papers.

Countess Hanska was to become his last and greatest love—greatest, because it was essentially imaginary and literary, and was conducted for sixteen years mostly by correspondence. When they finally succeeded in getting back together and marrying, Balzac was a dying man. She had first entered Balzac's life as an anonymous correspondent; her passion was originally aroused simply by reading his novels in the backwoods of the Ukraine.

The seduction exerted by the great novelist's prose was so powerful that it could work even by proxy: it was once rumoured that "several men had obtained the favours of respectable women at the Opera ball by pretending to be Balzac." This might have seemed fairly easy, since he was short and fat, with common and vulgar looks, like a Daumier shopkeeper or butcher. But it would also have been difficult: his enormous head, beautiful and blazing eyes, generous laughter and boisterous spirits set him apart from the crowd. Perhaps Rodin caught best his paradoxical appearance: a sort of gigantic dwarf, a coiled-up spring of pure energy. By a cruel contradiction, however, if he wrote novels to win women, he also had to forsake women in order to write novels: he firmly believed that every man had at birth a finite store of vital fluid and that the secret of creative life was to hoard one's energy. Sperm was for him an emission of pure cerebral substance—once, having spent the night with an enchanting creature, he turned up at the house of a friend, crying: "I just lost a book!"[4]

Another central experience of Balzac's childhood was his exile to a Spartan boarding school at the tender age of eight. The brutalities of boarding school can routinely maim sensitive children for life; occasionally they may also breed a genius. Numbed by sorrow and fear, the child Balzac fell into a stupor; his teachers, unable to draw any intelligent response out of their lethargic pupil, bombarded him with punishments. Detention meant being locked for hours or even days on end in a tiny cell, and the little boy ended up spending up to four days a week in the solitary gloom of the school prison. To escape from this desolation, mere dreaming was not enough: he had to invent for himself another world, more real than this unbearable environment. Relying on his memory, he began to recreate in his mind scenes he had read about in books; he developed a visionary imagination that enabled him to conjure entire worlds, with near-hallucinatory power.

Later in life, he explained: "Whenever I like, I draw a veil over my eyes. Suddenly I go back into myself, and there I find a dark room in which all the accidents of Nature reproduce themselves in a form far purer than the form in which they appeared to my outer senses." He had learned to cultivate visions which fed not on fantasy but on truth, the truth of his own memory and observation, which he could summon up and modify at will.[5] Balzac would constantly resort to these "wilful hallucinations," not only to find material for his books but also as a refuge against unhappiness, or as an emergency escape whenever he found himself cornered by reality.

Of course, when the frontier between the mind's vision and reality becomes blurred, one may reach the edge of madness, but Balzac believed that this danger could be overcome if the vision was transformed into knowledge through the mediation of writing. His faith in the power of the written word to become objective truth was repeatedly confirmed by eerie experiences: his fiction contained startling premonitions. At times, events unfolded in his life as if they had already been mapped out in his writing; the printed word was producing reality instead of reflecting it. In his case, as Robb puts it, "The experience came *after* the writing." There was a complete inversion of roles between invention and reality, which culminated on his deathbed when he deliriously called for Dr. Bianchon, the fictional doctor of *La Comédie humaine*, who alone, he believed, would be able to save him. (The anecdote may be mythical but myths can hint at a deeper truth.)

The story of Balzac's literary beginnings is amazing; his must be the only example of a man who successfully willed himself into genius without any apparent talent at the start. At the age of sixteen, Robb tells us, he firmly set his mind on becoming Great and Famous; at twenty, he decided that literature should be the field where he would reap glory, love and wealth. The next ten years were dismal: he virtually chained himself to his desk, producing a long series of ridiculous tragedies and unreadable novels (for some of which he wrote no fewer than sixteen different beginnings). As Baudelaire described it:

Nobody could ever possibly imagine how clumsy, silly and STUPID that great man was in his youth. And yet he managed to acquire, to get for himself so to speak, not only grandiose ideas but also a vast amount of wit. But then he NEVER stopped working.

Finally, when he was thirty-one, he had a breakthrough with his first accomplished work, *La Peau de chagrin*, which was also an immediate commercial success. For the next twenty years—until he died, in fact—his great creations were to follow at a breathtaking pace (though even in his purest masterpieces, he never entirely succeeded in pruning his style of its original clumsiness). Literary success, however, proved to be a curse: in order to create, he virtually renounced living—it was as if, to inject life into *La Comédie humaine*, he had to die. Quite literally, his writing killed him.

At first, writing was for him a sort of asceticism. A passage in *La Muse du département* could be read as a manifesto for his method:

There is no great talent without great willpower. These twin forces are needed to build the huge monument of an individual glory. Superior men keep their brains in a productive state, just as the knights of old kept their weapons in perfect condition. They conquer laziness, they deny themselves all debilitating pleasures ... Willpower can and should be a just cause for pride, much more than talent. Whereas talent develops from the cultivation of a gift, willpower is a victory constantly won again over instincts, over inclinations that must be disciplined and repressed, over whims and all kinds of obstacles, over difficulties heroically surmounted.[6]

Soon, however, the discipline turned into an all-consuming obsession. Although he wore a monk's robe when writing, his frantic work had little in common with the quiet and regular pace of cloister life: it became an addiction, an orgy in reverse. At times he only slept two hours a night. He ate no solid food, fearing that digestion might slow down his mind, and sustained himself only with gallons of strong coffee. On finishing a novel, he would collapse, sleep continuously for some twenty hours, and then gorge himself like a camel arriving at an oasis. He had originally a powerful constitution, but with such a regimen he already began to have alarming symptoms of physical decay in his late thirties; since he never eased the pace of his demented activity his health continued to deteriorate. He turned into a premature invalid, and died at fifty-one.

It was not simply in order to meet publishers' deadlines that Balzac worked in such a suicidal fashion. His life was a long and desperate race to keep one step ahead of a pack of creditors. From an early age, he had gone heavily into debt; later on, the more money he earned (his novels achieved considerable commercial success, some even sold out the very day they appeared) the worse his financial situation became. His megalomaniacal appetites, wastefulness and recklessness cannot alone explain his state of chronic bankruptcy. (His basic theory was that spending money was the best way of paying off debts: when the tailor presents his bill, instead of paying, one should immediately order another dozen waistcoats.) Balzac was widely thought to be afflicted with acute financial ineptitude, but Robb shows that the reality was much more complex: "The schemes he came up with can be divided into two categories: practical ideas, which he never seriously thought of putting into practice, and impractical ones, which he did." In pursuing the impractical schemes he ensured his own ruin; but he allotted the practical ones to some of his characters, thus making plausible their fabulous fortunes. Robb writes:

Certainly a contemporary reader using *La Comédie humaine* as an investment guide would probably have made a handsome profit... Balzac steered his banker, Baron Nucingen, and the money-lender Magus to undreamt-of wealth by having them invest, for example, in the Orléans Railway, while he lost his own money on the Northern Railway.

There is no escaping the radical difference between the capacity for conception and that for execution: imagination and action are often at opposite poles. That is why novelists usually do not become millionaires, whereas millionaires do not even read novels. Serious people involved in weighty affairs have no time for the puerile games of artistic creation. A man who is entirely "adult" and totally healthy (the latter state, as Sterne warned us, is a most abnormal condition, one that should warrant constant caution) would certainly never contemplate playing the flute all day long, or telling idle tales, or acting and singing on a stage, or playing with clay, paints and brushes. "Genius," Baudelaire said, "is childhood recalled at will."

The paradox by which Balzac could be financially wise in his fiction while losing all his money in life was duplicated in various other matters. For instance, the very women who had been drawn to him by the penetrating intuition of the female heart that he showed in his novels were appalled to discover how insensitive, naïve and awkward the real man could be. (The same contradiction has characterised many creative people: for example, Mozart in his operas composed what is perhaps the only music endowed with acute psychological perception—and yet he was notoriously inept at handling, or even at understanding, the most basic human relations in his life.)

Balzac presents one of the purest examples of the creative genius: "pure" in the sense that he was largely free of extraneous virtues. What enables great artists and writers to create is not intelligence (theirs can sometimes be average, or even mediocre: Balzac, for instance, often had ideas of startling absurdity; not only was he lacking in elementary common sense, but at times he verged on insanity). It is not sensitivity (many people can "feel" with utter intensity without being necessarily able to express themselves). It is not a matter of education and taste (in the decor of his lodgings, Balzac displayed the aesthetic sense of a prosperous Caribbean pimp). The real source of all creation (as Baudelaire again pointed out) is imagination. Balzac's fiction originally sprang from an intuition he first discovered as a wretched little schoolboy locked in a dark closet at his boarding school—an intuition to which he remained faithful until death, and which enabled him to enlarge immeasurably the world of countless readers: life is a prison, and only imagination can open its windows.

VICTOR HUGO

Glory is like the bed of Louis XIV in Versailles; it is magnificent and there are bugs in it.

—Victor Hugo[1]

Early in his career, Henry James lived for some time in Paris. Since he needed money, he worked for a while as a correspondent for the *New York Tribune*.[2] In his dispatch of January 1876, he reported on Victor Hugo's latest political activities. The old poet *cum* prophet had been pleading with the representatives of all the municipalities of France for the restoration of Paris as the national capital—a status which the city had lost after the bloody suppression of the Commune by the Versailles government five years earlier. James wrote:

> The newspapers for the last fortnight have contained little else than addresses and programs from the candidates for the Senate and the Chambers. One of the most remarkable documents of this kind is a sort of *pronunciamento* from Victor Hugo ... It seems incredible that Victor Hugo's political vaticinations should have a particle of influence upon any human creature; but I have no doubt that they reverberate sonorously enough in some obscure *couches sociales*, and there is no reason indeed why the same influences which shaped Victor Hugo should not have produced a number of people who are like him in everything except in having genius. But in these matters genius does not

---

Review of Graham Robb: *Victor Hugo: A Biography* (New York: Norton, 1997).

count, for it is certainly absent enough from his address to the delegates of the communes of France. *It might have been believed that he had already given the measure of the power of the human mind to delude itself with mere words and phrases, but his originality in this direction is quite unequalled, and perhaps I did wrong to say that there was no genius in it. There is at any rate a genius for pure verbosity.** What he has to say to his brother delegates ... is that "upon this Paris which merited all venerations has been heaped all affronts ... In taking from her her diadem as the capital of France, her enemies have laid bare her brain as the capital of the world. This great forehead of Paris is now entirely visible, all the more radiant that it is discrowned. Henceforth the nations unanimously recognize Paris as the leading city of the human race." M. Hugo proceeds to summon his electors "to decree the end of abuses by the advent of truths, to affirm France before Germanism, Paris before Rome, light before night."[3] Whether or not as a nation the French are more conceited than their neighbours is a question that may be left undecided; a very good case on this charge might be made out against every nation. *But certainly France occasionally produces individuals who express the national conceit with a transcendent fatuity which is not elsewhere to be matched. A foreign resident in the country may speak upon this point with feeling; it makes him extremely uncomfortable. I don't know how it affects people who dislike French things to see their fantastic claims for their spiritual mission in the world, but it is extremely disagreeable for those who like them.* Such persons desire to enjoy in a tranquil and rational manner the various succulent fruits of French civilization, but they have no fancy for being committed to perpetual genuflections and prostrations. They read Victor Hugo's windy sublimities in the evening paper over their profanely well-cooked dinners, and probably on leaving the restaurant their course lies along the brilliantly illuminated boulevard. The aspect of the boulevards, on a fine mild evening, is as cheerful as you please,

---

*My italics.

but it exhibits a number of features which are not especially provocative of veneration . . .

(And more specifically, James continued, if the strolling foreigner were to watch one of the fashionable plays currently performed in the theatres of these same boulevards, he might ask himself "at what particular point of these compositions the brain of the capital of the world is laid bare. A good many other things are laid bare, but brain is not among them.")

There is a certain piquancy in watching Henry James engaged in upbraiding another writer for his verbosity; but it is not merely for the idle enjoyment of this paradox that I have quoted his Paris dispatch at such length. His comments are in fact highly revealing of an enduring and typical attitude towards Hugo, which to this very day seems to remain prevalent in the Anglo-Saxon world. For instance, only a few months ago, the distinguished art critic Robert Hughes reviewed with his usual flair and vigour a remarkable exhibition of Hugo's paintings in New York—but characteristically, the title given to his article was a straightforward translation into modern vernacular of James's suave sarcasm: "Sublime Windbag."[4]

Windbag? Hugo would not have disliked that word. Wind—Paraclete—breath—spirit—inspiration: the suggestive chain of etymologies and word associations that always fired and sustained his imagination would not have escaped him. Besides, *the wind* had inspired in him extraordinary pages (to find their match in the history of world literature, one would have to go back to the visionary writings of Zhuang Zi in China, 2,300 years ago). As regards Hugo's "transcendent fatuity," James was not the first to marvel at it: a number of French critics had already led the way. A fellow poet having said that Hugo was "as stupid as the Himalayas," the great man sensibly replied that a Himalayan stupidity was to be preferred to the plain variety. (One is reminded of Muhammad Ali's retort on failing the intelligence test in the army: "I have said that I am the greatest. Ain't nobody ever heard me say I was the smartest.")

Baudelaire—who sent fawning letters to Hugo and wrote adulatory reviews of his books—repeatedly disclosed in his private

correspondence his true opinion on the subject: "One can simultaneously possess a special genius and be a fool. Hugo provides us the best
evidence of this." And again (commenting on a newly published collection of Hugo's poetry): "[These poems] are dreadfully heavy. In
these things, I can only find further occasion to thank the Lord who
did not give me such stupidity." But the publication of Hugo's greatest
masterpiece, *Les Misérables*, incited Baudelaire's most ferocious verve:
the book with its angelic prostitutes and sentimental criminals redeemed by the power of kindness made him wince, and he even toyed
with the idea of writing a satirical *Anti-misérables*.[5]

Yet, when you call a man a fool, the epithet acquires a very special
dimension if you also happen to be his son and heir. Whereas the
Jamesian irony on the same subject sounds merely flippant—and ultimately irrelevant—Baudelaire's private outbursts have a *sacrilegious*
quality and should illuminate rather than obscure the close filiation
that links his poetry to that of Hugo. He himself knew all too well
that, without the triumphant breakthrough of Hugo's poetic revolution which opened the way and cleared the field, his own *Fleurs du
mal* could not have found ground on which to blossom. It is true that
today, the acute modernity of Baudelaire's voice still vibrates in our
lives, whereas the passing of time has cruelly battered the great monuments which Hugo built in verse, and few visitors still care to wander
amid these ruins. It is the distance between the two poets that strikes
us now; but if one is within the same tradition, one tends to be more
aware of the differences; in this respect, the perspective of a sensitive
outsider may sometimes be more penetrating. Thus, for instance, Joseph Brodsky, commenting on "the gaudiness and eloquence" of the
two writers within the French poetical "tradition of pathos and urgent statement," was right in his boldness: "Hugo, Baudelaire—for
me these are the same poet with two different names."[6] Some truths
are simply better perceived from a distance.

What has contributed to obscure Hugo's role as the decisive pio-
neer of modern French poetry—down to its most elitist and hermetic
twentieth-century expressions—is the vulgar institutionalisation of
his colossal fame that took place at the end of his life. In old age, he
literally became the object of a popular cult. His white beard, his huge

forehead pregnant with unfathomable visions, easily lent themselves to use as some kind of substitute image of God the Father—a god for the new secularised masses to which he preached the universal brotherhood of mankind and the forthcoming advent of a World Republic. (Meanwhile we have seen famous writers serving worse causes.)

When he died, the funeral procession that carried his remains into the Pantheon—thus completing the deification process—was followed by a million mourners. The flamboyant bad taste of the ceremony presented a farcical mixture of melodrama and carnival—well summarised by the poisonous pen of Edmond de Goncourt, who noted in his diary entry for 2 June 1885:

> The night before Hugo's funeral—this night of desolate wake of the entire nation—was celebrated with a gigantic copulation: brothels having closed for the circumstance, their women went to participate in a huge priapic orgy on the lawns of the Champs-Elysées—and our good policemen refrained from disturbing these republican unions...Another detail regarding the "f—ing" funeral of our great man—this information comes from police sources—for the last week, all the prostitutes have been performing their services with a black crêpe draped round their private parts—c—ts in mourning![7]

But the price of this popularity was a certain alienation from the intellectual and artistic elite. The intelligentsia usually leaves the frequenting of the National Monuments to country bumpkins, foreigners and tourists. Retired schoolteachers in the provinces may perhaps still be able to recite Hugo's verses, but the arbiters of literary elegance frown when hearing his name. Gide's notorious *bon mot* has remained memorable (I do not apologise for quoting it here once more; better than a long essay, it sums up the ambivalence of the critical Establishment on his subject). On being asked who was the greatest French poet, Gide replied: "Hugo, alas."

Indeed, for the sophisticated connoisseur, the greatness of Hugo is a bitter paradox: France's most famous writer is also the one who is most offensive to French taste. The French genius cultivates measure, lucidity and perfection—and Hugo is excessive, mad and flawed. In a tradition that values order, harmony and a sense of proportion, Hugo came to pitch the gaudy tent of his freak show: a nightmarish circus full of hunchbacks and dwarves and monsters, and fights to the death with crocodiles and giant octopuses, against a backdrop of dark sewers, Gothic ruins, stormy nights, fires, floods and shipwrecks... And the madness that accompanied him in life (both his brother and his daughter had to be confined till death in a lunatic asylum) constantly lurks in his works. As Graham Robb points out perceptively, there is evidence that, at times, Hugo was afraid of the outpourings from his own imagination, and would append reassuring conclusions to his most frightening poems: "Everyone is a lunatic in the privacy of their own mind, and considering the treasures in Hugo's unconscious, his apparent sanity is a far more remarkable phenomenon." Only in his paintings—most of which were not meant to be shown to the public—did Hugo (who was one of the most original graphic artists of his century, and of ours as well) dare fully to pursue some of his most disturbing visions.

At the end of the Hugolian century, the painter Degas once confessed his frustration to Mallarmé: "I have so many ideas for poems—if only I could write them down!" "My dear Degas," Mallarmé replied, "poems are not written with ideas, they are written with *words*."[8]

Inasmuch as modern poetry can be characterised by this awareness that poems are generated by words rather than by ideas—that it is the "linguistic impulse" that drives the poet—it reflects an attitude that can be traced back directly to Hugo. "Any more or less serious poet knows that he is writing because language is dictating to him." This statement is actually by Brodsky, but it could as aptly describe Hugo's revolution.[9]

With Hugo, for the first time, language is consciously put in command. He said, "Words are The Word, and The Word is God." He deliberately allowed himself to be led by words, for "words are the mysterious passers-by of the soul."[10] Being the guardian of words, the poet is vested with prophetic powers: he is the guide who will take mankind to the Truth.

Hugo's religion of language was built upon solid foundations; his mastery of words was unparalleled. This was a reflection of his innate talents much more than a result of his education. Son of a plebeian father who was a revolutionary soldier and became a general of Napoleon, and of a mother with vaguely aristocratic forebears, Hugo received a traditional yet rather basic schooling; with the exception of two memorable years spent in Italy and Spain (where General Count Hugo was sent on imperial missions), Victor grew up in Paris. By the age of fifteen, the stupendous precocity of his poetic genius was already showing—it received the official consecration of prestigious literary prizes, and under the Restoration, the young prodigy was soon rewarded with royal patronage.

A friend of the family recalled the claim he once heard him making: "There is only one classical writer in the century—only one, do you hear? Me. *I know the French language better than anyone else alive!*"[11]

This was no hollow boast: with the richest vocabulary since Rabelais, his linguistic keyboard presents the bewildering range of a grand organ—by turns solemn, familiar, thundering, whispering, screeching, bellowing, murmuring, roaring. He could improvise effortlessly in all forms of regular poetry; impeccable alexandrine meter was for him a native language. He was a fluent Latinist and had a good knowledge of Spanish; and though his English remained quite atrocious (even after twenty years of exile spent in the largely English-speaking Channel Islands), he constantly toyed with it (foreign idioms are magic when you do not really understand the language). Technical terms from all sorts of trades and crafts stirred his imagination; he explored in depth the slang of the underworld, the jargon of criminals and of jails; his mastery of the technical language of the sea (navigation, naval architecture, ships, riggings and sails, manoeuvre and seamanship) is exhaustive and astonishing—and professionally accurate.[12] During his travels, he collected in his notebooks all the strange words and bizarre or ridiculous names that caught his attention in the streets, on posters, public notices or on shop signs. Puns, in particular, fascinated him no end. ("A pun is the bird-dropping of a soaring spirit," says a character in *Les Misérables*.) Starting with multilingual variations on his own name ("Ego Hugo," "Hu(e)! Go!"[13]), he displayed in his diaries a manic compulsion for playing with words. But he went further; far from confining this activity to his private notebooks, he sometimes extended this sort of exercise to his most solemn and formal poetic creations. In his justly famous "Booz endormi" (Proust, and he is not alone in this opinion, considered it the greatest poem in the French language, placing it even above the works of his beloved Baudelaire[14]), Hugo, at a loss to find a rhyme to complete the poem, simply made it up with an impudent pun. This could easily appear as a crude schoolboyish prank, and in the majestic context of the poem, the effect of such an intrusion should be grotesque—but it is sublime.[15]

At such a point, the servant of the word has truly become its creator and master. Someone once reproached him (in another context) for having fabricated a word that did not exist in the dictionary: "This is not French!"

"Now it is," Hugo replied.[16]

———

Half of the misery in this world is caused by people whose only talent is to worm their way into positions for which they otherwise have no competence. Conversely, how many talented individuals remain forever in obscurity for the lack of one ability: self-promotion? Hugo presents the rare example of a prodigiously gifted man who was also the shrewd impresario of his own talent. From a very early age, he learned how to please influential people, and he also knew when, and how far, he could judiciously offend them. At the age of twenty, he was granted a pension from King Louis XVIII (in reward for a sycophantic poem), but seven years later, he cleverly declined another pension from Louis's successor, the most unpopular Charles X. During the 1840s, he cultivated fairly close and cordial relations with King Louis-Philippe, without ever compromising his independence or becoming a mere courtier. Thus, with a cunning mixture of respect and iconoclasm, he succeeded in securing the favours of the Establishment without alienating the enthusiastic devotion of his own young followers; he was simultaneously rewarded by the political and literary authorities, and idolised by poets with dishevelled hair and crimson waistcoats. He was made a chevalier of the *Légion d'honneur* at twenty-three—an exceptionally young age for such an honour. (Shortly after, on a journey, wearing the ribbon of this much coveted distinction, he was arrested by a gendarme who suspected him of impersonation!)

The tumultuous staging of his drama *Hernani* in 1830 consecrated his position as the guiding star of the Romantic movement—he was then twenty-eight. But being universally acknowledged as the leader of the literary revolution did not prevent him entering a few years later the prestigious fortress of literary conservatism, the French Academy. Neither did the political right penalise him for his fashionable anti-conformism: he was made a *pair de France* (more or less the equivalent of a life-peer in the British House of Lords). Thus, before reaching the middle of life, he had achieved all the goals and reaped all the honours which ambitious writers and politicians would normally take twice the time to obtain.

Trollope famously observed that "success is a necessary misfortune of human life, but it is only to the very unfortunate that it comes early." This is true, but only for most of us who make up the plodding majority. For a man like Hugo, who was *truly* ambitious (I mean, who desired *genuine* greatness), early success was a blessing: he got success out of his system—it freed his mind for better things. The frantic race for the wretched baubles that keeps us running on the social treadmill until we collapse of old age was already over for him while still young. Ribbons, honours, titles, prizes, medals—the paltry rewards, the laughable carrots which we docilely pursue on a lifelong chase—he won them all in the first part of his career; what would have been the point of slaving for another fifty years, merely to add a few more knick-knacks to his dusty collection?

Halfway through life, he found himself free—free to risk everything, free to become himself, to be idealistic, brave, generous, reckless and noble, free to take once and for all the side of Justice—this permanent "fugitive from the side of victory." In 1851, when Louis Bonaparte (Napoleon's nephew, "who stuffed the Eagle" with his "cadaverous face of a card sharp") staged his coup against the Republic and re-stored the Empire, turning himself into "Napoléon-le-Petit"—as Hugo was to call him, with lethal wit—the poet stood up against the despot (though he knew his cause was desperate) and lent his voice to the victims, the losers, the downtrodden, the *misérables*. He made a vain attempt to organise popular resistance against the usurper, but the secret police of Louis Bonaparte already had the situation under control. Overnight, Hugo had to forsake everything: his position, his public audience, his home, his country; he had to hide and to flee, he was a fugitive with a reward on his head—he was forced into perma-nent exile.

He escaped to Brussels, and from there went to the Channel Is-lands, first taking refuge in Jersey, then finally settling in Guernsey. His exile was to last nearly twenty years. Now he could say at last: "The literary revolution and the political revolution have effected their junction in me." What a liberation! Youth had suddenly burst into his life: "Those who become young late in life, stay young lon-ger."[17] He was to stay young till his death in 1885, at age eighty-three.

Hugo's writings are full of prophetic insights on his own destiny. Some twenty years earlier, commenting on the life of Rubens during a first visit to Belgium, he observed: "A great man is born twice. The first time as a man, the second as a genius."[18] Exile was to be Hugo's second birth—the chance of his life. And he had the wisdom to see this. Three years into his new life, he noted:

> I find increasingly that exile is good.
>
> It is as if, without their knowing it, the exiles were near some sort of sun: they mature quickly.
>
> These last three years, I feel that I am on the true peak of life; I can distinguish the real lineaments of all that people call facts, history, events, successes, catastrophes—the huge machinery of Providence.
>
> At least, for this reason alone, I should thank Mr. Bonaparte who exiled me, and God who chose me.
>
> Maybe I shall die in this exile, but I shall die a better man. All is well.

Five years later:

What a pity I was not exiled earlier! I could have achieved so many things which I fear I shall not have the time to complete.

Eight years later:

In exile, I said the word that explains my entire life: I grew.[19]

In his dashing early days in Paris, he had been the centre of an ebullient court of admirers, fellow writers, followers, idlers and parasites. His house was invaded by endless cohorts of visitors, he did not even have the time to answer his mail, and from dawn till night his door was simply left open. Now, however, not many of his fair-weather acquaintances would still find the courage to brave the mists and storms of the Channel to make a pilgrimage to the exile's rock, or be bold enough to run the gauntlet of the spies and secret police who kept Hugo's outside contacts under close surveillance. As a result, the poet found himself left with only two interlocutors—but with these at least, he felt on the same footing: God and the ocean.

No wonder these years of solitude and contemplation were the most productive of his life. They were also happy years—for himself at least, if not for his family. (His daughter Adèle went insane; his wife[20] and grown-up sons could not bear the loneliness and eventually moved back to Brussels, where Hugo would from time to time pay them a visit, on the way to one of his occasional continental jaunts.)

Most of his masterpieces date from this period, climaxing in 1862 with his monumental novel, *Les Misérables*—less a novel than an immense prose poem, perhaps the last and only genuine epic of modern times. Hugo's passion for language found here its hugest and wildest outlet. The book is like a foaming and thundering Niagara of words; it is also a dumbfounding patchwork in which philosophico-sociopolitical dissertations constantly interrupt the narrative. There are passages of comedy, of drama, of satire, of breathtaking action; there are tender elegies, realistic sketches, huge historic frescoes; there are essays on the most disparate topics, such as the linguistic structure of slang, the economics of sewage recycling—a prodigious display of encyclopaedic interests (which influenced Jules Verne)—and yet these heteroclite fragments are all swept together and eventually merge in one powerful poetic stream.

By its very nature, such a book should be untranslatable. And yet it was soon to become a part of all the main cultures of the world and to touch millions of readers in many different languages.[21] What is the power latent in the original that enables it to survive translation and to remain operative, even in a mutilated form? *Les Misérables* has a mythic dimension that directly taps into the deeper sources of our common humanity. It is popular literature in the same sense as Homer is popular literature: it addresses all mankind.

The book was first printed in Brussels (1 April 1862); other editions immediately followed, nearly simultaneously, in Paris, Madrid, London, Leipzig, Milan, Naples, Warsaw, Saint Petersburg, Rio de Janeiro.[22] From the start it exerted a universal appeal: the original publication was delayed at the printers by the tears of the typographers who were reading and composing the galley proofs. Their emotion and enthusiasm were soon to be shared by the most diverse readership—French and foreign, young and old, naïve and sophisticated. At the remotest end of Europe, Tolstoy secured without delay a copy of the book and was overwhelmed. One may say without exaggeration that *Les Misérables* triggered *War and Peace*.[23] Giants breed giants.

Hugo's prodigious creativity during the years of exile found another outlet—more intimate, but no less intense and powerful—in his pictorial activity. Though critics have not ignored it, it seems to me that this aspect of his genius has remained somehow underestimated. For instance, instead of talking of Hugo's drawings, it would be much more accurate to speak of his paintings—borrowing a concept from Chinese traditional aesthetics, which would be particularly appropriate in his case.[24] For the Chinese, all the graphic improvisations, or "ink-plays" which scholars and literary men execute during their leisure hours, simply using the basic tools they need for their daily writing (calligraphic brush, ink and paper) are not only considered as fully fledged paintings but, more than the large-scale, showy productions of professional artists, they achieve the very perfection of what a true painting should always aim at: they are a visible "imprint of the heart" of the painter.

Delacroix said that the highest feat for a painter is to inject reality into a dream.[25] Here lies precisely the haunting power of Hugo's visionary works: his imagination, however bold and wild, was always sustained by a technical proficiency acquired through a long practice of sketching. (During his early journeys through Belgium and Germany, Hugo recorded with vivid accuracy, in pen or pencil, monuments and scenic spots: his sketch books were to him what cameras have become for today's travellers.)

Hugo said that "every great artist, at his beginning, remakes the whole art to his own image." This is particularly true for Hugo's paintings. Most of these were not shown in his time, and for good reason: the public for such an art was not yet born. It is only now, through a familiarity with the developments of twentieth-century painting, that we are able at last to appreciate Hugo's graphic experiments.

Hugo's exile came to an end with the fall of the Second Empire. His return to France was triumphal, and the last fifteen years of his life were one long protracted apotheosis. He continued to produce: poems, political addresses, polemical essays (the eloquence and ferocity of *Histoire d'un crime*—1877—contributed to saving the Republic from the menace of a new coup), and one last magnificent novel, *Quatre-vingt-treize*. But not even death could put an end to his career: posthumous publication of his private papers (notebooks, drafts, prose and verse fragments, diaries, correspondence, etc., which equal the published works in quantity, and sometimes even exceed them in interest) have occupied another three-quarters of a century.

———

Four years ago, Graham Robb published a splendid biography of Balzac. He has now applied the same winning methods—sharp judgement, wit, lively style and vast information—to the writing of a new biography of Hugo. If his *Victor Hugo* does not afford the same delights as *Balzac*, it is, I think, through no fault of the biographer. It simply would be unfair, and foolish, of us to expect that the same methods applied to a different object may achieve identical results.

Balzac is an essentially endearing character. But if one had to characterise Hugo's multi-faceted personality, a hundred adjectives may come to mind, yet "endearing" would certainly not be one of them. In fact, it is precisely when dealing with figures such as Hugo that one feels obliged once again to question the desirability, if not the very feasibility, of literary biography.

It is not simply that giants do not bear close scrutiny (as Gulliver discovered to his utter discomfort when he had to climb into the bosoms of the court ladies of Brobdingnag) but, more essentially, there is this basic truth: the only thing that could justify our curiosity is precisely what must necessarily escape the biographer's analysis—the mystery of artistic creation. Hugo's long exile was the climax of his life, but these momentous twenty years could be described in merely one sentence: He stood in front of the ocean and he wrote.*

The thesis that literary biography is doomed to fail by its very nature is not new, and creative artists have expounded it most persuasively. Proust wrote an entire treatise on the subject, *Contre Sainte-Beuve*, and it would be rather fatuous for me to attempt rehashing it here. Closer to us, Malraux summed up the issue quite pointedly: "Our time is fond of unveiling secrets—first because we seldom forgive those whom we admire; secondly, because we vaguely hope that, amid these unveiled secrets, we may find the secret of genius. Under the artist, we wish to reach the man. But when you scrape a fresco, if you scrape it down to its shameful bottom layer, all you get in the end is mere plaster."[26] But well before him the indignation that a poet must experience before our indiscreet appetite for biographical information was most memorably expressed by Pushkin: "The mob reads confessions and notes, etc., so avidly because in their baseness they rejoice at the humiliations of the high and the weaknesses of the mighty. Upon discovering any kind of vileness they are delighted.

---

*Hugo used to write *standing* at a high desk.

He's little like us! He's vile like us! You lie, scoundrels: he is little and vile, but differently, not like you."[27]

Note that I am quite aware of my own contradictions. If my readers derive any enjoyment from this little article, they should also keep in mind that a great deal of its information was directly drawn from Robb's work. And even as I question the point of writing literary biographies, I know all too well that I shall continue to read them—especially when they are as intelligent and readable as this one.

VICTOR SEGALEN REVISITED THROUGH HIS COMPLETE CORRESPONDENCE

WHEN VICTOR Segalen died in 1919 at the age of forty-one, he had published only one book, *Les Immémoriaux* (1907), and two slim collections of poetry, *Stèles* (1912) and *Peintures* (1916), and he was barely known beyond a small circle of intimates.[1] His widow Yvonne—a devoted wife who had supported and loved him with intelligence and followed him with courage—strove to preserve his memory by arranging for posthumous publication of two manuscripts, *René Leys* (1922) and *Équipée* (Expedition, 1929). Despite her efforts, it was to be feared that the writings and even the name of the poet were doomed to oblivion.

In this connection I must ask the reader's forbearance if I now insert a personal parenthesis (rest assured, it will be the last). In 1971, when I published *The Chairman's New Clothes*,[2] I needed, at short notice and for trivial bureaucratic reasons, to sign the book with a pseudonym. If I was bold enough to borrow my false surname from Segalen's masterpiece, it was solely because at that time *René Leys* was completely out of print and had been impossible to find for over twenty years, so that the name had no resonance save in the memories of a handful of faithful admirers of Segalen, lovers of literature and somewhat smitten by things Chinese. It was to this happy few—my like, my brothers—that I was directing an innocent wink. Had I had the slightest notion at that time of how Segalen's work was to become the object of an extraordinary renewal of interest, I would have modestly chosen some other banal Flemish patronymic—Beulemans, say, or Coppenolle—but now it is rather too late for that.

As a matter of fact Segalen's triumphant return had been foreshadowed by Professor Henri Bouillier's magisterial biography *Victor*

Segalen (Paris: Mercure de France, 1961). The same Henri Bouillier has now given us the poet's correspondence.[3] Thirty years after Bouillier's biography, Gilles Manceron's *Segalen* appeared (Paris: Jean-Claude Lattès, 1991); so far from duplicating the earlier biography, it rounded it out admirably.

In the interim, thanks above all to the devoted efforts of Victor's daughter Annie Joly-Segalen (1912–1998), the issuing of unpublished manuscripts and posthumous fragments, reprints, selected works, popular editions, scholarly editions, collector's editions, commemorative exhibitions and international conferences all proliferated. Segalen became the subject of a steady flow of books, essays, studies and articles; as far away as the Antipodes, doctoral theses focused on him, while in Brest a university has now been named after him.[4]

As to the indefatigable activity of Madame Joly-Segalen, Bouillier is hardly exaggerating when he speaks of a "prodigious filial love from beyond the grave" and "the miraculous resurrection of a father by his daughter." But he is, I feel, on much less certain ground when he adds that "it was thanks to her" that "Segalen has become one of the century's greatest poets." In the previous century Rimbaud had only a sister (a blundering busybody to boot), while Laforgue had no one, and surely both these poets have endured solely by virtue of their poetry?

The three high points of Segalen's existence—the two years in Polynesia (1903–1905), his first great Chinese adventure (1909), and finally his anguished quest on the threshold of the beyond, in the last twelve months of his life—provide the finest and most intense pages of this enormous correspondence. The remainder (and the two volumes of letters, along with the supplemental *Repères* [Reference Guide] comprise 2,850 pages), though perhaps not always of burning interest, nevertheless serve to confirm John Henry Newman's dictum that "the true life of a man is in his letters."

Segalen's prime correspondents, from his adolescence up until his return from Polynesia and marriage, were his parents, especially his mother. Thereafter his wife became the soul mate to whom he wrote almost daily during his frequent and prolonged absences; his last letter to her was written on the eve of his death. His close friends—and

Segalen attached great importance to friendship—included his fellow naval officers (Henry Manceron, Jean Lartigue) but also admired elders, intellectuals and artists (Daniel de Monfreid, Debussy, Jules de Gaultier, Claudel, etc.).

Segalen was born in Brest into a modest middle-class family with deep Breton and Catholic roots. His father was a gentle and self-effacing civil servant and an amateur painter. His mother, somewhat musical—she played the church organ and the piano—was a formidable and frighteningly possessive person, and she long wielded tight control over her son (who as a twenty-one-year-old medical student was still obliged to write her, not only to justify his smallest expenditures but even to explain on one occasion what had prevented him from receiving Holy Communion at Mass, a tale-bearing chaplain having duly reported this misdemeanour to Madame Segalen).

———

Segalen's background was certainly narrow and smothering in many respects, but it is worth bearing in mind that this provincial bourgeoisie did know how to sacrifice for the education of its offspring. Thus Victor received a solid literary, classical and scientific education; he was also introduced in childhood to music and painting, which remained passions of his throughout his life. Nor must we overlook the essential: he benefited from what only the warm affection of a united family can supply, a happy childhood, which arms one to face life and, once adult, to eliminate the risk of losing time in some fatuous and vain quest for happiness.

But Segalen had a frail and nervous disposition, and he was prone all his life long to bouts of melancholy. At boarding school, far from home, he was laid low by depression. While he was a student at the Bordeaux School of Naval Medicine, his sister and mother had to come and support him during another attack. He needed his family, yet at the same time he longed to take wing. This desire for emancipation manifested itself in various ways—in his rejection of the organized Church as in his liaisons with young women (liaisons which he had to conceal from his mother—another source of anxiety).

True freedom from the family's grip came only, in the nature of things, with his great departure for Polynesia, his first overseas posting. But loving ties with his parents were maintained by letter well beyond that moment, and right up until his marriage. Thereafter, however, though still respectful and courteous, his communications became rare and more distanced. Five years before his death, Segalen confided to a very dear friend that "Nothing at all has been a disappointment to me except my mother (the reluctant affection I once felt for her perished long ago)." Two years before his death, in a letter to his wife concerning the education of their older son, in whom he wished to instil high standards, he remarked that "I feel that my parents were satisfied with mediocrity, and for that I shall never forgive them."

Segalen became a Navy doctor for simple practical reasons: his family could not have afforded extended study for him. In point of fact he liked neither the sea nor medicine. He suffered from seasickness, and he cursed the time-consuming demands of a profession that distracted him from his true passions. On both matters his correspondence is explicit.

The sea: "I find the open sea boring, nauseating and stupid." "My Pacific crossing was bleak, banal, and long." "Fifteen stupid days on this stupid sea. How horribly monotonous the South Pacific is as a mass of water!" "I shall relish with ever-renewed joy the charm of a night on land, cool and with no rolling." "Ah! How good the solid, fragrant earth is after five days on the high seas! Decidedly, the sea is beautiful only as seen from the coast, or framed by shores, beaches, and rocks. The open sea is paltry and odourless. . . . And the vast horizon shrinks and squeezes you like an iron ring." "Life at sea gives me the slightly stale feeling of a pious old maid in religious retreat. . . . The open sea is really and truly imbecilic. Its only virtue is that it conveys you 'elsewhere.'"

As for medicine, Segalen hardly ever speaks of it in any but exasperated terms: "For me medicine means oppressive and monotonous boredom." At one point he complains of "the vile butchery of medical practice" that prevents him from playing his piano; at another, he fancies that "Sinology, an exact science" might "save him once and for all from the vileness of medicine." It should be noted, nevertheless, that Segalen was a good doctor who combined competence with compassion. During the struggle against an outbreak of plague in northeast China he distinguished himself by his courage, devotion and organizational skill.

In any case, it was surely better to be a Navy doctor than a pharmacist in Brest, as his mother had originally wanted for him. And he had no reason for complaint with respect to the French Navy, which treated him generously, and underwrote the two most fruitful episodes in his career, namely the revelation of Polynesia and the revelation of China, which would successively inspire and nourish his entire literary output.

In Polynesia he discovered a paradise in agony and, simultaneously, the work of Gauguin, who had just died there. In the islands he experienced a kind of happiness—or was it perhaps simply the fact of being young, and released at long last from the oppressive bigotry of his provincial childhood? Many years later he could still write to a friend about that time: "I have told you that I was happy in the Tropics. That is violently true. For two years in Polynesia I slept badly from joy. I had awakenings in tears at the arriving light of day. . . . I felt gaiety coursing through my muscles. Thinking was itself a delight. . . . I had my work in hand, I was free, recovering, fresh, and sensually rather well practiced. The whole island came to me like a woman. And from women indeed I received gifts that more complete countries no longer offer. Apart from the traditional Maori wife with her sweet fresh skin, smooth hair, and muscular lips, I experienced caresses [etc.]."

———

This lyrical outpouring is no doubt partly due to the writer's distance in time from what he is recalling. His original letters from Tahiti tell a rather different story. Following the usual custom of officers at that time, he had indeed set out by taking a native mistress, but he seems to have tired of her rather quickly, as he confided in various somewhat caddish letters to an old pal of his: "For the time being I have left the full-blooded Tahitian vahine as being too far removed from our own race. They would be perfect, these brown-skinned girls with their long sleek hair, long eyelashes and velvet skin, if only, instead of launching a full-scale courting ritual, replete with palaver and haggling, they would comply with simple commands, just as they used to in the past.... They are dishonest, egoistic, and obviously not very intellectual or even intelligent. What is the use, then, of showing them the same respect as would be appropriate towards a lover very close to us, submissive, devoted, such as we are surer to find among female species less far removed from our own.... In six months, after experiencing the Tahitian, then the half-White, I came back to the White woman, and now from her too, willingly, I am drawing away...." Furthermore, "the sexual act is indifferent to me, it takes too long, and then those women who truly please me I would rather have as friends than as mistresses."

Clearly, for all his intelligence, all his heart, Segalen was also, willy-nilly, a child of the stupid nineteenth century. Later in the correspondence, moreover, there are more signs of this, no less distressing, in his reactions to China.

But at the same time he was too sensitive not to intuit, albeit confusedly, just how inadequate, vulgar and low his own world was. From Polynesia he brought back his first book, *Les Immémoriaux,* which is explicitly intended to counteract the literature of "colonial impressions" so much in favour at the time. In contradistinction to the writer-tourist, Segalen sets out to depict less the effect of the surroundings on the traveller than the effect of the traveller on the surroundings: "I am distinctly not one for the brief visions that delight Pierre Loti and thanks to which he in turn delights his female readers. I need to know, over and above the way a country appears, just what that country thinks...." Loti and Co. "have told what they saw, what they felt in the presence of unexpected things and people the shock of whose encounter they had sought out. But have they revealed what these things and people thought themselves, or what they thought of them, the visitors? For there is perhaps also a shock delivered by the traveller to the spectacle before him, a reverse shock that affects what the traveller sees."

This is a splendid program, but Segalen's letters from Polynesia reveal just how far short he fell of carrying it out. Among those vahines with their long hair and stunted ideas, did he really ever discover "what the country really thought"? And how do the superb evocations of Tahitian landscapes and atmospheres that lend so much life and colour to his letters truly differ from Loti's finest descriptions?

The same contradiction between the traveller's lofty ambitions and his disappointingly meagre achievements was to be repeated, and on a monumental scale, when he confronted China. At the same time China played a decisive part in Segalen's spiritual development. In the first place, it saved him from the dismal swamp of the "literary world" into which he had briefly been tempted to plunge. On his return from Polynesia, in fact, he very nearly turned into an *homme de lettres*: *Les Immémoriaux* appeared to have attracted the attention of the jury of the Prix Goncourt, and this prompted him to fling himself briefly into a round of literary and fashionable social events.[5] Thank heavens, Segalen's book garnered not a single vote, and he came to his senses. Had he won the Prix Goncourt, one may only imagine how long it would have taken him to rediscover his true path.

At this juncture, Segalen persuaded the Navy to post him to Peking as an interpreter in training. Before leaving, he wrote to Jules de Gaultier, his mentor and the inventor of *Bovarysme* ("the power granted man to conceive of himself as other than he is"): "I have started to learn Chinese. All in all, I expect a great deal from this apparently thankless task, for it can deliver me from a danger: in France, once my projects have been put into practice, what will there be left for me to do except 'literature'? I am afraid of the search for a 'subject.'...In China, tackling the most antipodal of matters, I expect a great deal from this extreme exoticism."

The "exoticism" that Segalen expected from China, and that was to remain the philosophical underpinning of his entire work, has nothing to do with the picturesque of impressionistic travel writing—it is the exact opposite. "Exotic knowledge" is a perception of difference that operates like a dike, blocking the flow of consciousness and thus raising its level and intensifying its energy. The "feeling of diversity," which is the source of all the savour of life, is threatened by habit, proximity, satiation, homogenization, and the nightmare of ultimate entropy, as prefigured by the universal degradation of anthropological diversity. According to Segalen, "exoticism is thus not adaptation, not the perfect understanding of an outside-oneself that one can embrace within oneself, but rather the acute and immediate perception of an eternal incomprehensibility. Let us start from such an acknowledgement of impenetrability. Let us not flatter ourselves by thinking that we can assimilate customs, races, nations, others; on the contrary, let us rejoice in our never being able to do so, and thus guarantee the enduring pleasure of experiencing Diversity."

Here a warning is in order: any reader who approaches Segalen in hopes of finding some sort of introduction to China is knocking at the wrong door. Segalen was certainly right to describe the Chinese universe as "the most antipodal of matters": China does indeed constitute, in the cultural sphere, "the other pole of human experience."

But the correct conclusion to be drawn from this observation was stated half a century later, by Professor Joseph Needham, the immensely erudite author of the monumental *Science and Civilization in China,* a veritable encyclopaedia of Chinese knowledge: "Chinese civilization presents the irresistible fascination of what is totally other, and only what is totally other can inspire the deepest love, together with a strong desire to know it." Segalen, by contrast, starting from the assumption that China was "impenetrable"—and that it was desirable that it stay that way—had gone straight down a dead end.

He spent five years in China (1909–1914), but it was the first six months of his stay that constituted its high point while at the same time defining its limits once and for all. Before embarking on the study of Chinese for which the Navy had sent him to Peking, he undertook, with his friend Auguste Gilbert de Voisins, a long expedition across the most ancient of Chinese lands, the provinces of the West and Southwest almost as far as the borders of Tibet, then back down the Yangtze from Sichuan to the coast. This long and exciting adventure, admirably described in the almost daily reports that Segalen composed for his wife when the travellers halted for the night, constitutes a great sporting feat; yet even though Segalen had studied and planned the itinerary with great care and intelligence, the two friends were engaged for six months in the equivalent of today's "safaris" for millionaires which take affluent tourists from one splendid site to another, all barely accessible to ordinary foreign visitors.

Voisins, who disposed of a vast fortune, financed the whole enterprise, which was mounted, armed and equipped on the grandest scale: five saddle horses, one pack horse, eleven mules, a donkey, and a whole retinue of helpers—intendant, interpreter, cook, two "boys," two ostlers, five muleteers; and with that a whole raft of furniture, tables and beds, guns, and provisions as if for a crossing of the Sahara. Nothing had been overlooked: they even had butter in cans and powdered yeast to raise Western-style bread (since the delicious *mantou*—the Chinese steamed buns commonly eaten in the provinces through which our travellers passed—were adjudged inedible...).

By way of contrast, one cannot help thinking of the Australian journalist Dr. G. E. Morrison, the legendary "Morrison of Peking" (1861–1920), a near contemporary of Segalen's, a doctor like him, whose destiny was likewise transformed by China.[6] Fifteen years before Segalen, Morrison had made an equally ambitious journey, though his was ultimately far more fruitful in terms of human experience. He went alone, on foot, from Shanghai to the Burmese frontier through the Chinese Southwest. He left with only eighteen pounds in his pocket (a budget a thousand times smaller than that of the later French travellers); all he had on his back was an ample Chinese robe and a simple umbrella of bamboo and oil paper; all along the way, he relied for food and lodging on the hospitality of local people, and by and large had no complaints....

As for Segalen, who also crossed an enormous swath of China, he seems, paradoxically, to have conversed with no Chinese people at all, with the sad exception of his own servants, who naturally could do nothing but endorse the clichés that all colonials, in every latitude, use to characterize the "natives"—calling them born liars, thieves, swindlers and cowards. Still, there is no denying that the two friends took real physical risks: it takes endurance and courage to ride for thousands of kilometres, braving every weather, following precipitous mountain paths and fording wild rivers.

But even though they bravely exposed themselves to all the hazards of their adventure, one gets the impression that they were traveling in a kind of hermetic cocoon isolated from the humanity around them. The fact that there were two of them—two very close friends speaking the same language, sharing the same passion for literature (Voisins was a novelist then enjoying a certain vogue; his works, mercifully, have since fallen into oblivion)—eventually transformed their bivouacs into a kind of countrified version of a Parisian *salon*.

Once back in Peking, where his wife soon joined him, with their older boy—a daughter and a second son would be born in China in the following years—Segalen turned to his study of Chinese. He seems to have focused on the classical language, which would serve him well in his archaeological and epigraphic researches. As for spoken Chinese, it is hard to know what level of competence he achieved, but the contempt he evinced for the study of it is hardly a good sign. Soon, sad to say, material considerations obliged him to abandon Sinology temporarily and resume medical practice, which had come to be an abomination for him, and, what was worse, he found himself forced to leave Peking, which he loved, and go and work in Tientsin, a sinister town where he rediscovered everything that he had fled: a hateful atmosphere of "Swiss or Belgian provincial mediocrity."

In 1914, just after he had at last succeeded, with his two friends Voisins and Lartigue, in mounting another expedition, more systematically archaeological this time, he was recalled to France by the First World War. But in 1917 he was sent back to China, in an official capacity, for a few months. This would be his last visit, and the occasion for him to make a rather bitter summary: writing to his wife, he concluded that "China, for me, is over, sucked dry. . . . I am detaching myself from it, withdrawing, going away. There are other countries in the world. Above all, there are other worlds."

A few years previously, he had witnessed the collapse of the Manchu Dynasty. He had not taken the establishment of the Republic seriously—he viewed it as a deplorable lapse of good taste. "Sun Yat-sen is a perfect cretin," he had promptly averred at the sight of the president's frock-coat and detachable collar, which he considered too ordinary. As for the Revolution, it seemed to him no more than "one of those uprisings that China absorbs, digests and eructs from time to time like wind from some great flatulent gut."

The overthrow of the Empire appalled him and filled him with despair—not that he had had any illusions about the Manchu regime, whose corruption, negligence and obscurantism were only too obvious; it was just that "the sublime fiction of the Emperor as the son of a Pure Sovereign Heaven was too admirable to be allowed to disappear. . . . I hate the rebels for their conformist attitudes, their humanitarianism, their Protestant obsession with cleanliness, and above all because they help diminish the difference between China and us; and you know how exoticism alone is truly dear to my heart."

In conclusion, Segalen said that his only hope was "soon to see a new despot arise who will spur his little yellow citizens on—I would welcome such a man with the deepest gratitude!" In the meantime, however, "the whole of the so-called modern, new and Republican China must be deliberately eliminated. . . . This is sheer apery, pitiful Bovarysm, small-mindedness, cowardice of every sort, and boredom—boredom most of all."

Well before the Revolution, however, Segalen had been disillusioned by the China of the present; as compared with his Polynesian experience, he wrote, "it is true, this country is devoid of all sensual gratification." Even Peking had only the mythical prestige of its "imperiality" with which to offset "the bleak sadness of its filthy orgies with their croaking chanteuses." As for the people, "the Chinese character is not to my liking . . . It inspires in me neither admiration nor any sense of grandeur or strength. Its every manifestation in my vicinity is tainted by infantilism or senility. [The Chinese] cry like little girls, fight like pug dogs, grimace like clowns, and are an irredeemably ugly people."

So why was Segalen over there at all? "At bottom it was not China that I came here to find, but a vision of China. That vision is now mine, and I have sunk my teeth into it." This is a key statement, and one that solves a mystery: this subtle poet had absolutely no knowledge of the sublime poetry of the Chinese; this fine connoisseur of art seems never to have looked at a single Chinese painting.[7] (In his whole correspondence he makes but one reference to that incomparable art, and then only in abstract terms, and accompanied by a foolish remark: "I am working on Chinese painting. Ancient, naturally. Contemporary does not exist.")

What is even more bewildering is that this passionate music lover was ignorant of *the very existence* of classical Chinese music—the music of scholars, a music of the soul and of silence, as played on a seven-string zither, the *guqin*. And he dared complain of living in "a country without musicality" which knew nothing but noise! He never sought to meet Chinese masters who could have initiated him into the varied disciplines of their culture; he had no social contact with either scholars or artists; indeed he seems never to have had a single conversation with any educated Chinese person.

So it was not China that was finished—"over, sucked dry"—for him, a China that he had never bitten into, but solely his "vision." And what was that vision? He described it in what he conceived as his magnum opus, *Le Fils du Ciel* (The Son of Heaven). Unfortunately, Segalen's Son of Heaven resembles the Emperor of China much as Gilbert and Sullivan's Mikado resembles the Emperor of Japan—except for the fact that the former is not very amusing.

Yet, for all that, Victor Segalen left us the miraculous accident of his *René Leys*,[8] a novel of failure and derision—and one faithful, this time, to the author's actual experience: the narrator, striving desperately to penetrate an impenetrable China, eventually succeeds only in getting himself led down the garden path by a seductive if pathetic trickster. This masterpiece escaped Segalen almost involuntarily, and in retrospect left him perplexed: a month before his death, after having his great friend Hélène Hilpert read the manuscript, he wrote her: "I find it amusing that René Leys amused you a little. But how far away it seems, how youthful…"

As a rule, conventional critics and commentators do not linger long over this book, for it makes them a little uneasy. After all, it's a kind of joke, surely? And yet it is by virtue of this "joke" that Segalen is guaranteed a passage to posterity. It is not I who make this claim, but Claudel and Rilke—hardly casual readers.

Back in France, exhausted by his prodigious efforts as physician, traveller, Sinologist, archaeologist and writer, Segalen fell into a profound depression exacerbated by a condition that medicine could not diagnose.[9] He simply felt life slipping away from him. At this juncture his wife Yvonne, frightened by the gravity of his affliction, had to call for support upon Hélène Hilpert, a very old and intimate childhood friend. Hilpert herself was in a tragic situation: she had four little children, but her husband had gone missing at the front a year earlier and she did not know whether he was dead or a prisoner. (As it turned out, his remains were found only ten years later.)

———

Right away, Segalen in his state of nervous collapse recognized another soul mate in the person of Hélène. The last year of his correspondence—from May 1918 until May 1919, just before his death—consists mostly of the eighty-nine letters that he wrote her, and as a matter of fact they constitute the most touching portion of the whole collection. These letters have nothing clandestine about them: Yvonne frequently added a personal note at the bottom of the pages written by her husband; but it pained her to see Victor, with whom she had hitherto shared everything, pursuing a dialogue with Hélène on a level to which she herself had no access.

When Yvonne had married Segalen, she had also espoused his agnosticism—and this in a quite comfortable and untroubled way. Segalen, on the other hand, was by nature a mystical soul who in a muddled way had never really come to terms with the fact of having lost his faith. Hélène was a fervent Catholic; she was also an intelligent and highly sensitive woman; she perceived Segalen's distress, and realized how very ill he was; she possessed, perhaps, ways of helping him in his present state, but she could not allow herself, or allow him, to put a foot wrong.

In a moment of particularly acute distress, Segalen exposed his difficulties to Claudel, who, with more generosity than tact, seeing the breach that was opening up in his correspondent's unbelief, charged through it like a rhinoceros, offering to come over post haste, take Segalen by the scruff of the neck and drag him into a confessional box. Segalen was touched by this heartfelt enthusiasm but chose to evade it, preferring to confide instead in his sweet friend. Who among us would not prefer to enter paradise led by the hand of a Beatrice rather than rushed there on the back of a galloping pachyderm?

How much longer would Segalen have managed to confine his tumultuous feelings to the exclusively amicable channel dictated by Hélène? We shall never know. In the spring of 1919 Segalen spent a few days of solitary rest at an inn on the edge of the legendary Huelgoat forest. The last two letters he wrote were addressed the one to Hélène and the other to his wife. They glow with a like tender feeling for his friend and for Yvonne. The next day he went walking in the forest, but did not return. Two days later his body was discovered stretched out beneath a tree. He had a wound at the ankle and had died from the resulting haemorrhage, which he had vainly sought to stanch by means of an improvised tourniquet. Those who knew Segalen called it suicide. Those who loved him called it an accident.

Today Segalen's biographers incline to the latter view, pointing out that a doctor intending to commit suicide might be expected to have less primitive means at his disposal. But what of a doctor wishing to spare his nearest and dearest the cruel discovery that he has deliberately abandoned them? His last two letters are by no means letters of farewell—and yet, ten years earlier, he had already confessed to his wife that "Truly intimate matters are never written of."

CHESTERTON
The Poet Who Dances with a Hundred Legs

IDEALLY, the title of a public lecture or a book should define or sum up the topic that is going to be treated. Therefore, allow me to explain briefly the choice of this peculiar title.

First, Chesterton the poet. Chesterton once said that he suspected Bernard Shaw of being the only man who had never written any poetry. We may well suspect that Chesterton never wrote anything else.

But what is poetry? It is not merely a literary form made of rhythmic and rhyming lines—though Chesterton also wrote (and wrote memorably) a lot of these. Poetry is something much more essential. Poetry is grasping reality, making an inventory of the visible world, giving names to all creatures, naming what *is*. Thus, for Chesterton, one of the greatest poems ever written was, in *Robinson Crusoe*, simply the list of things that Robinson salvaged from the wreck of his ship: two guns, one axe, three cutlasses, one saw, three Dutch cheeses, five pieces of dried goat flesh . . . Poetry is our vital link with the outside world—the lifeline on which our very survival depends—and therefore also, in some circumstances, it can become the ultimate safeguard of our mental sanity.

One of the many misunderstandings we often entertain on the subject of Chesterton is to picture him as a big, benign, jolly fellow, inexhaustibly possessed by innocent laughter; a man who seems to have spent all his life blissfully unaware of the nocturnal side of the human condition; a man securely and serenely anchored in sunny certainties; a man who seemingly was spared our common anguishes, and doubts and fears; a man from another age perhaps, and who could

---

Lecture to the Chesterton Society of Western Australia, Perth, September 1997.

hardly have had an inkling of the terrors and horrors that were to characterise our time. At the end of this hideous twentieth century—arguably the most savage and inhumane period in all history—we may well wonder: with his permanent and unflappable good cheer, isn't Chesterton some sort of monument from another era—if not from another civilisation? Shouldn't he appear to the modern reader as an endearing but irrelevant anachronism? For, after all, we are the children of Kafka: how could Chesterton address our anxiety?

Yet the fact is that *Kafka himself* found in Chesterton a mirror for his own anxiety. From the testimony of his young friend and admirer Gustav Janouch we know that he particularly admired *The Man Who Was Thursday* (which is indeed Chesterton's most accomplished and most haunting work of fiction). On the subject of this book, it should be noted that Chesterton himself once complained that most readers seemed never to register its full title: *The Man Who Was Thursday: A NIGHTMARE*. But this last word certainly did not escape Kafka.

When Chesterton was still an idle and dreamy young man who had half-heartedly drifted into art school, he underwent a shattering crisis. He experienced a terrifying confrontation with evil—evil not as an external menace, but as a presence in the mind, a spiritual reality generated from within himself. At that moment, he had the intuition of the central paradox which he was to explore all his life and would finally sum up near the end of his career in his masterly book on Thomas Aquinas: Christianity has reversed the old Platonic belief that matter is evil and immaterial spirits are good. In fact, the opposite is true: having created the world, God looked on all things and saw that they were good:

> There are no bad things, but only bad uses of things. If you will, there are no bad things but only bad thoughts; and especially bad intentions . . . But it is possible to have bad intentions about good things; and good things, like the world and the flesh, have been twisted by a bad intention called the devil. But the devil cannot make things bad; they remain as on the first day of creation. The work of heaven alone is material—the making of a material world. The work of hell is entirely spiritual.

As a young man, for a certain time Chesterton felt he was in danger of becoming trapped within the spiritual hell of his own hyperactive mind—and for quite a while, he literally tottered on the edge of madness. In this situation, it was poetry that finally preserved his sanity. For the gift of the poet (which is also the gift of the child) is the ability to connect with the real world, to look at things with rapt attention. Both the poet and the child are blessed with what Chesterton called "the mystical minimum": the awareness that things *are*—full stop. "If a thing is nothing else, that is good; it *is*—and *that* is good."

By the way, it is interesting to note that, at the other end of the earth, a thousand years ago, the great mystics of China and Japan (whom Chesterton never knew) developed exactly the same view. I am referring here to the masters of Zen Buddhism, who taught only through poems, paintings, paradoxes, jests and riddles. For instance, in a classic anecdote, a young disciple asks an old monk, "What is the Buddha?" The master replies, "The Buddha is a two-pound cabbage from the vegetable market in Chaozhou." The lesson is, hold on to reality: if you can fully grasp but *one* fragment of reality, however humble, in its irreducible concreteness and singularity, you hit the rock-bottom of truth, and from there, can reach salvation. Hold on to reality—just like Robinson Crusoe holds on, for dear life, to the things he salvaged from the wreck of his ship. "Two guns, one axe, three cutlasses, one saw, three Dutch cheeses..."

Secondly, I said that Chesterton is not merely a poet—I said he is *"a poet who dances with a hundred legs."* The phrase is actually borrowed from Chesterton himself. He used it in an interview to describe the most extraordinary character he ever created: Sunday, the enigmatic giant with two faces—huge, boisterous, elusive, who pulls all the strings in his sublime metaphysical fable, *The Man Who Was Thursday*. He wrote the book when he was barely thirty, but strangely enough, twenty years later, he himself in physical appearance came to look like Sunday, as various friends and visitors were to remark. (See, for instance, a letter which Valery Larbaud wrote to Paul Claudel, reporting on a visit he had made to Beaconsfield—or again, Bernard Shaw's affectionate description of his old sparring partner and friend as "A man-mountain, not only large in body and mind beyond all decency, but [who] seems to be growing larger as you look at him.")

But the practical problem for us is this: how do you sketch the portrait of a man who dances with a hundred legs? How do you keep his image in focus? This is an impossible task—and therefore don't blame me if you find that my talk is hopelessly rambling. But in the end this may not greatly matter, for I shall draw many quotes from Chesterton's writing, and these quotes alone should provide you with enough incentive to turn back to his works—what more could I wish for?

When I was invited here, I confess I felt very hesitant at first at the idea of addressing a Chesterton Society on the subject of Chesterton. I have no particular expertise on this topic. The great edition of Chesterton's *Collected Works* which is now being published in the United States will count some fifty volumes: half of them have already appeared, and of this half, my own reading has barely covered one fifth (though I am pursuing my exploration with endless delight). As you see, I am a hopeless amateur. Yet, from a Chestertonian point of view, this very lack of qualifications should constitute the best qualification. Chesterton always attached special value to this notion of the amateur, as opposed to the professional. In his *Autobiography*, he composed a loving portrait of his father, whose occupation was in real estate (in fact, the old firm is still active today, and when walking in the streets of London—or Sydney, or Perth—you can still see the name of Chesterton posted on houses for sale) but who at home, for the delight of his children, cultivated a wide range of talents and hobbies: drawing, painting, photography, magic lanterns, stained glass:

> There had been some talk of his studying art professionally in his youth; but the family business was obviously safer, and his life followed the lines of a certain contented and ungrasping prudence. He never dreamed of ever turning any of his plastic

talents to any mercenary account, or of using them for anything but his own private pleasure and ours. The old-fashioned Englishman, like my father, sold houses for his living but filled his own house with his life. To us (children) he appeared to be indeed The Man with the Golden Key, the magician opening the gates of goblin castles...but all this time he was known to the world, and even to the next door neighbours, as a very reliable and capable, though rather unambitious businessman. It was a very good lesson in what is also the last lesson in life: that in everything that matters, the inside is much larger than the outside. On the whole, I am glad that he was never a professional artist. It might have stood in his way of becoming an amateur. It might have spoilt his career—his private career. He could never have made a vulgar success of all the thousands of things he did so successfully.

The superiority of the amateur over the professional is an important and provocative notion—all the more provocative because it is not commonly held in Western culture, where a more general view usually considers that only the professional can be serious, whereas the amateur's approach is necessarily tainted with frivolity (we shall see what Chesterton had to say on the subject of seriousness versus frivolity). For me, Chesterton's position on this question has a particular appeal, since it precisely coincides with a basic tenet of Chinese classical aesthetics—a field that has occupied my interest for many years. This principle should in fact have a deep and universal relevance. Think of it: you can, and should, be fully professional insomuch as you happen to be a real estate agent, a solicitor, a grave-digger, an accountant, a dentist, etc.—but you could hardly call yourself a professional poet, for instance. If, on a passport or an immigration form, you were to write under "Occupation" the words "Human being" or "Living," the bureaucrat behind his counter would probably wonder if you were in your right mind.

None of the activities that really matter can be pursued in a merely professional capacity; for instance, the emergence of the professional politician marks the decline of democracy, since in a true democracy politics should be the privilege and duty of every citizen. When love becomes professional, it is prostitution. You need to provide evidence of professional training even to obtain the modest position of street-sweeper or dog-catcher, but no one questions your competence when you wish to become a husband or a wife, a father or a mother—and yet these are full-time occupations of supreme importance, which actually require talents bordering on genius.

Besides his description of his father, Chesterton made many other statements in praise of the amateur. These are justly famous and some have virtually become proverbs. For instance, "If a thing is worth doing, it is worth doing badly." Or again, "Just as a bad man is nevertheless a man, so a bad poet is nevertheless a poet."

He further developed the contrast between the amateur and the professional into a comparison between the universalist and the specialist, and he applied this particular insight to an issue that was always of great concern to him: the condition of women. Thus he made the point that the man must be, to a certain extent, a specialist—out of necessity, he finds himself confined in a narrow professional pursuit, since he must do one thing well enough to earn the daily bread—whereas the woman is the true universalist: she must do a hundred things for the safe-guarding and management of the home. The modern fad of denouncing the narrowness of domesticity provoked Chesterton's anger: "When domesticity is called drudgery all the difficulty arises from a double meaning of the word. If drudgery only means dreadfully hard work, I admit the woman drudges in the home, as a man might drudge building the cathedral of Amiens, or drudge behind a gun at Trafalgar." And then Chesterton goes on to survey the range of tasks within the household that require in turn, or simultaneously, the talents and initiative of a statesman, a diplomat, an economist, an educationist, a philosopher, and he concludes:

> I can understand how all this might exhaust the mind, but I cannot imagine how it could narrow it. A woman's function is laborious, but because it is gigantic, not because it is minute. I will pity Mrs. Jones for the hugeness of her task, I will never pity her for its smallness.

A first paradox which Chesterton presents for us today is the fact that he is both widely popular and relatively neglected; on the contemporary intellectual and literary scene, he appears to be simultaneously present and absent.

His presence is manifested in many ways. First, on a superficial level, just consider the number of his witticisms which have been completely absorbed into our daily speech as proverbial sayings—we find them constantly quoted in newspapers and magazines, we use them all the time; sometimes we are not even aware that they were originally coined by him.

His striking images could, in turn, deflate fallacies or vividly bring home complex principles. His jokes were irrefutable; he could invent at lightning speed surprising short-cuts to reach the truth. Thus, for instance, to those who said, "My country, right or wrong," he would reply, "My mother, drunk or sober." Or again, on democracy: "Democracy is like blowing your nose: you may not do it well, but you ought to do it yourself."

On the difficult problem of original sin and man's fall from innocence, one of his comments shed an unusual, yet illuminating light: "If you wanted to dissuade a man from drinking his tenth whisky, you would slap him on the back and say, 'Be a man.' No one who wished to dissuade a crocodile from eating his tenth explorer would slap him on the back and say, 'Be a crocodile.'"

The baroque eccentricity of such images led shallow critics to overlook the depth and seriousness of his thought, and he was constantly accused of being frivolous. But what is frivolity and what is seriousness? Chesterton explained:

> A man who deals in harmonies, who only matches stars with angels, or lambs with spring flowers, he indeed may be frivolous, for he is taking one mood at a time, and perhaps forgetting each mood as it passes. But a man who ventures to combine an angel and an octopus must have some serious view of the universe. The more widely different the topics talked of, the more

serious and universal must be the philosophy which talks of them. The mark of the light and thoughtless writer is the harmony of his subject matter. The mark of the thoughtful writer is his apparent diversity.

Reading Chesterton today, one is constantly amazed by the uncanny accuracy of so many of his analyses, by the prophetic quality of so many of his warnings—some of which were issued as early as the beginning of the twentieth century. There is a timeliness, an immediacy, an urgency in his writing, which none of his famous contemporaries can match. (How much of the social commentary of Bernard Shaw or H. G. Wells still bears scrutiny today?)

I would like to provide quickly a series of random samples, suggesting both the wide range of Chesterton's observations and the sharp relevance which so many of these still present for us now.

On politics (from a portrait he made of an important statesman of his time): "He had about the fundamentals of politics and ethics this curious quality of vagueness, which I have found so often in men holding high responsibilities. For public men all seem to become hazier as they mount higher...I think I could say with some truth that *politicians have no politics*."

The truth of this striking insight is confirmed to us every day. The other day I happened to be reading the newly published memoirs of J.-F. Revel, *Le Voleur dans la maison vide*. Revel, who held for a while the portfolio of cultural affairs in François Mitterrand's shadow cabinet (when the latter was still leader of the Opposition in France), paints a portrait of this consummate political acrobat, which appears cruelly true and verifies in its paradoxical conclusion the accuracy of Chesterton's observation.

Revel wrote, "The trouble with Mitterrand was that *he had no interest in politics*"—Mitterrand was so totally absorbed, all the time, with cunning political manoeuvres and manipulations, he was possessed with such an obsessive passion for political *means*, that he could no longer care for political *ends*. His exclusive concern was how to obtain and how to retain political power—but he never reflected on the question: political power *for what purpose*? (Paul Hasluck's *The*

Chance of Politics is another recent book which offers further illustrations of this same phenomenon.)

On the Church, in its relation to the world and its times: "The Church is the only thing that can save a man from the degrading servitude of being a child of one's own time. We do not want a Church that will move with the world. We want a Church that will move the world."

This utterance reminds me of a remarkable dialogue between Louis Massignon and Pope Pius XII. Massignon was a great Orientalist scholar (specialising in the study of ancient Islamic mysticism) and he was also a personal friend of the Pope. When the first war between Israel and the Arabs broke out, he urged the Pope to issue a solemn statement to ensure the protection of the Holy Places in Jerusalem. The Pope was hesitant: neither the Jews nor the Arabs were likely to pay attention to his words, and he objected: "Who would listen?" To which Massignon made this superb reply: "You are the Pope: you do not write in order to be read—you write in order to state the truth." (Massignon died in 1962; it is a pity he did not live to know the pontificate of John Paul II.)

On society: "It has been left to the very latest modernists to proclaim an erotic religion which at once exalts lust and forbids fertility... the next great heresy is going to be simply an attack on morality; and especially on sexual morality. And it is coming not from a few socialists... The madness of tomorrow is not in Moscow, much more in Manhattan." (He was writing this in 1926.)

And this—which is ominously apposite to our present situation (I do not believe for instance that it is a mere coincidence that we are witnessing simultaneously the development of a movement supporting euthanasia and the development of a movement in favour of homosexual marriage):

There are destructive forces in our society, that are nothing but destructive, since they are not trying to alter things, but to annihilate them, basing themselves on an inner anarchy that denies all the moral distinctions on which mere rebels base themselves. The most dangerous criminal now is the entirely lawless modern philosopher. The enemy arises not from among the people, but from the educated and well-off, those who unite intellectualism and ignorance, and who are helped on their way by a weak worship of force. More specifically it is certain that the scientific and artistic worlds are silently bound in a crusade against the family and the State.

In the early 1930s, T. E. Lawrence wrote in a letter to a friend, "I have not met Chesterton, but Bernard Shaw always tells me that he is a man of colossal genius." This small example, picked at random, is characteristic of the sort of prestige which Chesterton commanded amongst the most brilliant minds of his time.

By contrast, it is puzzling to observe that today he has become virtually invisible on our intellectual horizon. Just go into any bookshop and look for his works: most of them are unavailable and have been out of print for many years already. And when a new anthology of his wisdom came out in England a couple of months ago, the few reviews that appeared in the press were typically patronising, treating Chesterton as a sort of colourful dinosaur—mildly amusing, and utterly irrelevant. The fact is, the fashionable intelligentsia of the English-speaking world now largely ignores him. (Note, however, that among the French and the Latins, the situation is quite different; the two subtlest literary minds of our time, Paulhan and Borges, literally worshipped him—but that is another story.)[1]

It may be interesting to ponder for a moment the various reasons that have contributed to this odd neglect (which at times is even tinged with scorn and hostility). One factor may well be his Catholicism. In a way, Catholicism has done to Chesterton's reputation what the British empire did to Kipling's: in the eyes of a shallow and ignorant public, it became a liability—an occasion for both partisans and detractors to indulge in schematisations and distortions, a sectarian pretext for support or for rejection. In this reductionist perspective, Chesterton's Catholicism eventually came to obscure his catholicity. I just mentioned a newly published anthology of his writing: the unfortunate title of this book, *Prophet of Orthodoxy*, precisely illustrates the sort of simplification into which his admirers seem sometimes to fall

all too easily. To be turned into a prophet was precisely a fate of which Chesterton felt most wary. He himself identified it as a temptation that had to be resisted absolutely. He realised it was a status he could easily have achieved, had he agreed to pay the usual price—which is to isolate and emphasise only one side of the truth. This is always an easy recipe for achieving popularity and for gathering crowds of disciples; but to secure this sort of demagogic success one must mutilate a complex reality.

A second factor that may explain the relative neglect which has befallen him was shrewdly identified by Evelyn Waugh in a rather ambivalent critical assessment:

> Chesterton was a lovable and much loved man, abounding in charity and humility. But humility is not a virtue propitious to the artist. It is often pride, emulation, avarice, malice—all the odious qualities which drive a man to complete, elaborate, refine, destroy, renew his work, until he has made something that gratifies his pride, and envy and greed. And in doing so, he enriches the world more than the generous and the good, though he may lose his own soul in the process. That is the paradox of artistic achievement.

Indeed, Chesterton never attached much importance to his own writing. In this respect, he was the exact opposite of a "man of letters"—and this is one of the most endearing and admirable aspects of his personality. Generally speaking, literary people are exceedingly self-centred and vain—on the whole they are not a very attractive breed—but Chesterton did not belong to that species. For all his formidable wit, he had no urge to shine; among brilliant conversationalists, he was the strange exception: a man who truly enjoyed listening to others. He could say truthfully, "I have never taken my books seriously; but I take my opinions quite seriously." This is a very important distinction. His brother, who knew him intimately, grasped it well: "He is merely a man expressing his opinions because he enjoys expressing them. But he would express them as readily, and as well, to a man he met on a bus."

Unlike most literary men, he never endeavoured to husband carefully his ideas and intellectual resources, or to manage his career, or to plan his moves and design publishing strategies. He simply could not care less.

He wrote with the reckless generosity of genius. Mozart, who enjoyed (or suffered from?) a similar facility and composed with the same effortless flow, once said, "I write music like a cow pisses."

Chesterton's fecundity was prodigious. His secretary described how, on some occasions, he would produce two articles at the same time: he dictated one, while simultaneously writing another.

Did he write too much? It would be imprudent to discard lightly the enormous bulk of his journalistic output, for the problem is that, again, with lavish carelessness, he scattered gems everywhere, and many of these are to be found among trifling and whimsical little essays.

He had spent his secondary-school years mostly sleeping and dreaming—to the perplexity and despair of his teachers. He never entered any university; he merely attended an art school in desultory fashion. But he managed to accumulate an immense culture—literary, historical and philosophical—solely through his extensive reading. (Again, the approach of the amateur.)

Once, a woman told him with naïve admiration that he seemed to know a great many things. He replied, "Madam, I know nothing: I am a journalist."

All his life, Chesterton claimed no other title for himself but that of journalist. He gloried in being a journalist, he relished the atmosphere and romance of Fleet Street. As a perceptive critic observed, "He was a journalist because he was a democrat. Newspapers were what the ordinary people (the man on the bus!) like to read. There could therefore be no higher privilege than to write for the newspapers—whatever he might think of their proprietors."

And he had all the qualities of a superb journalist: intelligence, clarity, liveliness, speed, brevity and wit. But these are the very qualities that always damn a writer in the eyes of pretentious critics and pompous mediocrities. To impress the fools, you must be obscure. ("What I understand at once never seems true to me," confessed a female admirer to a modern French novelist). And for these people, it is inconceivable that anything expressed with imagination and humour could also have an earnest purpose. How could you possibly say something important if you are not self-important? Chesterton constantly battled against this prejudice. He explained:

> My critics think that I am not serious but only funny, because they think that "funny" is the opposite of "serious." But "funny" is the opposite of "not funny" and of nothing else. Whether a man chooses to tell the truth in long sentences or in short jokes is a problem analogous to whether he chooses to tell the truth in French or in German. The two qualities of fun and seriousness have nothing whatever to do with each other . . . If you say that two sheep added to two sheep make four sheep, your audience will accept it patiently—like sheep. But if you say it of two monkeys, or two kangaroos, or two sea-green griffins, people will refuse to believe that two and two make four. They seem to believe that you must have made up the arithmetic, just as you have made up the illustration of the arithmetic. They cannot believe that anything decorated with an incidental joke can be sensible. Perhaps it explains why so many successful men are so dull—or why so many dull men are successful.

I have talked for much too long already, and yet I have barely skimmed the surface of this huge topic. But I now realise that I could have given it another title: Chesterton: The Man Who Was In Love With Daylight. He said, "If there is one thing of which I have always been certain since my boyhood and grow more certain as I advance in age, it is that nothing is poetical, if plain daylight is not poetical; and no monster should amaze us, if the normal man does not amaze."

Most people tend to think of Chesterton as a "Catholic writer," but they do not seem to realise that his conversion occurred fairly late in life (in 1922—only fourteen years before his death; a number of his major works were written long before he actually joined the Church).

But when he finally made the move, he said that he became a Catholic in order to get rid of his sins.

But there was, I think, another motivation, equally powerful: gratitude. He once said that if he were to go to hell upon his death, he would still thank God for this life on earth. From the very beginning, the urge to thank his creator is what impelled him to write.

In Chesterton's experience, the mere fact of *being* is so miraculous in itself that no subsequent misfortune could ever exempt a man from feeling a sort of cosmic thankfulness. I wish to end here with a short prose poem which he jotted down in a notebook of his agnostic youth; it shows that this overwhelming sense of wonder and gratitude actually predated by many years his religious conversion:

EVENING
Here dies another day
During which I have had eyes, ears, hands
And the great world round me;
And with tomorrow begins another.
Why am I allowed two?

PORTRAIT OF PROTEUS
A Little ABC of André Gide

To tell the truth, I don't know what I think of him. He is never the same for long. He never gets engaged in anything, yet nothing is more engaging than his permanent evasions. You cannot judge him, for you haven't known him long enough. His very self is in a constant process of undoing and remaking. You think you have pinned him down, but he is Proteus:* he adopts the shape of whatever he happens to love. And you cannot understand him unless you love him.

—ANDRÉ GIDE, *Les Faux-monnayeurs*[1]

Gide is one of the few writers who really nauseates me, so I am naturally not an authority on him.

—FLANNERY O'CONNOR, *The Habit of Being*[2]

THE STARTING point of this (rather whimsical) little glossary of the Gidean enigma was provided to me by Alan Sheridan's work *André Gide: A Life in the Present* (Harvard University Press, 1999). Sheridan's massive *opus* (700 pages) is a model of meticulous scholarship.[3] To appreciate the biographer's achievement, one should consider how daunting was his task. Gide was a compulsive diarist; besides writing some sixty books (essays, fiction, theatre, travelogues, criticism, poetry, literary translations), he kept for more than fifty years a *Journal*[4] that fills thousands of pages. Members of his small circle of close friends were equally addicted to graphomania. First of all, Maria Van Rysselberghe—nicknamed *la Petite Dame* ("the Tiny Lady"*), who

---

*The asterisk indicates a name or a word that is the subject of an article in this glossary.

knew him for half a century and was his most intimate companion (or should we say accomplice?) during the last thirty years of his life (inasmuch as any sort of intimate companionship could be achieved with such a slippery eel)—kept an accurate and vivid record of his daily utterances and deeds, together with perceptive portraits of his literary friends and transcripts of their conversations (four volumes—nearly 2,000 pages—crammed with information). Gide's best friends were also writers: Roger Martin du Gard, Jean Schlumberger, Pierre Herbart.* After his death, they all wrote memoirs of the Gide they knew. The figure of Gide also looms large in Martin du Gard's monumental and fascinating *Journal* (three volumes—3,500 pages) as well as in Schlumberger's diaries.[5] When they were away from Paris, in their respective country residences, the friends wrote to each other at great length: the correspondence Gide–Martin du Gard and Gide–Schlumberger fills three volumes (1,400 pages). Besides, Gide also corresponded regularly with a great number of literary acquaintances, editors, writers, artists, poets, critics—his position as the co-founder and main financial backer (with Schlumberger and Gallimard) of the prestigious *Nouvelle Revue Française* (literary journal *cum* publishing house) virtually established him as the *éminence grise* of twentieth-century French literature: his voluminous published correspondence with Valéry, Claudel, Jammes, Mauriac, Jouhandeau, Romains, Suarès, Rivière, Copeau, Du Bos, Cocteau, J.-E. Blanche, Arnold Bennett, Edmund Gosse, Rilke, Verhaeren, etc., etc., amounts to some 20,000 pages.[6]

Thus, the first and main problem of Gide's biographer was not how to gather information, but how not to drown in it. Sheridan succeeded in bringing this literary flood under control, and in organising it into a lucid synthesis. Yet, just as the damming of a big river cannot be achieved without inflicting some damage on its wildlife, the discipline which Sheridan had to impose upon his rich material was perhaps not fully compatible with the lush ambiguities and contradictions of the subject. Now, in contrast with whatever certainties the reader may feel able to derive from Sheridan's authoritative study, the only purpose of my disjointed notes is to warn him against the temptation to draw conclusions—for Gide must always present an irreducible elusiveness: he was truly the great master of intellectual escape—the Houdini of modern literature.

ANTI-SEMITISM

In 1914—he was then a middle-aged, well-established writer—after a lunch with his old friend and former schoolmate Léon Blum, Gide noted in his diary[7] how he respected Blum's intelligence and culture, but resented his Jewishness. He expounded at some length on this theme:

> There is no need to enlarge here on Jewish defects; the point is: the qualities of the Jewish race are not French qualities. Even when Frenchmen are less intelligent, less resilient, less worthy in every respect than the Jews, the fact remains that only they themselves can express what they have to say. The Jewish contribution to our literature... is not so much enriching us, as it constitutes an interruption in the slow effort of our race to express itself, and this represents a severe, an intolerable distortion of its meaning.
>
> One must acknowledge that nowadays there is in France a Jewish literature that is not French literature... The Jews speak with greater ease than us, because they have fewer scruples. They speak louder than us, because they ignore the reasons that sometimes make us speak in a lower voice, the reasons that make us respect certain things.
>
> Of course, I do not deny the great merits of some Jewish works, such as the theatrical plays of Porto-Riche, for instance. But I would admire them much more willingly if they were offered to us only as translations. What would be the point for our literature to acquire new resources if it were at the expense of its meaningfulness? If, one day, the Frenchman's strength should fail, let him disappear, but do not allow his part to be played by any lout, in his name and in his place.

A few years later (August 1921), he confided to his intimate little circle his irritation and disappointment at Proust's newly published *Sodome et Gomorrhe*. He blamed Proust's method: "It betrays avarice rather than riches—the obsession never to let anything go to waste, always adding instead of saving" and ascribed this to Proust's Jewishness[8]: "The Jews have no sense of gratuitousness."[9]

In 1929, commenting to the Tiny Lady on a new novel by Henri Duvernois (an author whom he had previously praised to the skies): "Read this, it is excellent; but here, he also shows some of his limitations. Oh, he is very sensitive and subtle, but he lacks a certain…" (he searches for a word) "…a certain virginity. It would be interesting to make a history of Jewish literature" (he had just learned that Duvernois was Jewish) "…Jews often defile somehow whatever topic they touch."[10] And a few days later, on the same subject, chatting with old friends, he told them: "Of course, it always bothers me when someone happens to be Jewish. Take Duvernois, for instance; when I learned that his real name was Kahn Ascher, I suddenly understood many little things that had always bothered me in his books—my very genuine admiration notwithstanding."[11] Two years later (May 1931), at lunch with friends: "As we chat about anti-Semitism…Gide says with a laugh: 'Well, I would not like to receive a transfusion of Jewish blood.'"[12]

In 1935—German political developments were not taking place on another planet!—commenting upon a performance of the American Yiddish Art Theatre, Gide said: "I cannot get used to all these bearded faces; even when they are beautiful, they have no appeal for me…The very idea of any physical contact with them repels me, I don't know why; I feel closer to animals."[13]

After the war, at the end of his life, he was still casually making disparaging remarks on the Jewish character, in front of his secretary, Béatrix Beck, a young widow, whose dead husband was Jewish![14]

Yet would it make any sense to call Gide an anti-Semite? With equal reason, he might also be called a Stalinist Bolshevist, an anti-Stalinist and anti-communist, a Christian, an anti-Christian, a defeatist advocate of collaboration with Hitler, an anti-Nazi sympathiser, a libertarian, an authoritarian, a rebel, a conformist, a demagogue, an elitist, an educator, a corrupter of youth, a preacher, a *débauché*, a moralist, a destroyer of morality...

Literature* was the exclusive concern of Gide—it was the very purpose of his life; beside it—as he himself proclaimed[15]—"only pederasty and Christianity" could absorb his interest and fire his passion. On all other matters—which were of basic indifference to him—he had no strong opinions; his views were vague, contradictory, ill-informed, tentative, inconsistent, malleable, banal, vacillating, conventional. Herbart—who was a close confidant and companion during the last twenty years of his life—observed that he usually thought in clichés that could have come straight from Flaubert's *Dictionnaire des idées reçues*. Having quoted another of Gide's offensively stupid remarks ("I suffered yesterday: all the interlocutors I had to chat with were Jews"), Herbart added this flat comment: "This means exactly *nothing*: he 'thinks' by proxy."[16]

I do not know to what extent such an innocent explanation will satisfy most readers—but Blum himself would certainly have endorsed it, for even though he was hurt when he eventually read the passages of the *Journal* quoted above, his affection for Gide remained undiminished until his death.[17]

In conclusion: it would be very easy to compile a damning record of first-hand evidence on Gide's anti-Semitism; most probably, it would also be misleading. This example may serve as a useful methodological warning before perusing my little ABC.

BIOGRAPHICAL OUTLINE

André Gide was born in 1869. Though he died in the middle of the twentieth century, he remains in many fundamental respects a nineteenth-century writer.

He was an only child; his father was a scholar (professor of Roman law)—a frail and refined man who died too early to leave any deep imprint upon his son: André was not yet eleven at the time of his death. The mother, possessive and authoritarian, came from a very wealthy line of business people in Normandy; she gave her son a stern

Protestant education. From a very early age, Gide experienced an acute conflict between the severe demands of his mother's religiosity and the no-less-tyrannical needs of his precocious sensuality. Yet it was not until a journey to Algeria in 1895 that he discovered—under the personal guidance of Oscar Wilde—the exclusive orientation of his own sexuality.* That same year, his formidable mother died, and "having lost her, he replaced her at once with the person who most resembled her." Within two weeks, he announced his engagement with his first cousin Madeleine* (niece of his mother), who had been his beloved soul-mate since early childhood. Their marriage was never consummated, Gide having assumed from the beginning that only "loose women" can have any interest in the activities of the flesh. And, in turn, when forty-three years later Madeleine died, Gide once again felt the same sense of "love, anguish and freedom" he had experienced at the death of his mother, and "he noted 'how subtly, almost mystically' his mother had merged into his wife."[18]

With the total freedom that his inherited wealth (as well as the considerable fortune of his wife) gave him, Gide devoted the rest of his very long life to literature. He employed his time reading and writing—writing mostly about what he had read—and travelling. Simultaneously, religion continued to claim his soul, and pederasty his body. The conflict reached a climax in 1916, when, under the pressing —and sometimes clumsy—interventions of his Catholic friends (Claudel, first and foremost), Gide came close to conversion. But eventually he resisted the religious temptation and opted resolutely for the pursuit of a sexual obsession which was to assume manic proportions with the passing of the years.

From his earliest work, *Les Cahiers d'André Walter* (published in a private printing, paid for by his mother—1891), Gide's literary activity never slowed. It is difficult to summarise his production: as he said himself, "Each of my books is designed to upset those readers who enjoyed the preceding one."[19] The critic Jean Prévost described this attitude with a formula that won Gide's approval: "Gide does not confront himself, he succeeds himself."[20] His metamorphoses were not generated by dialectic contradictions, they were a succession of imaginative happenings: Proteus is constantly reinventing himself.

His most seminal work, the book which established him as the *guru* of rebellion against the bourgeois order, as the *maître à penser* for at least three successive generations of young men, is *Les Nourritures terrestres* (1901). Martin du Gard wondered if one could not apply to it what Sainte-Beuve once said of "those useful books which last only for a limited time, since the readers who benefit from them wear them down."[21] The problem is also that books such as these usually generate mediocre imitations, and eventually we cannot avoid reading them through the prism of their vulgar caricatures. Today, alas!, *Les Nourritures terrestres* reminds us of nothing so much as the kitsch of Khalil Gibran.

The quality of his short fiction is displayed in *La Porte étroite* and shines to perfection in *La Symphonie pastorale* (1919). Both novellas benefit from the inner tension of his religious *inquiétude*, still unresolved at the time; in the latter work in particular, the spiritual ambiguity is handled with diabolical cleverness, and, in spite of its stilted dialogue and cold stylistic mannerisms, the book remains deeply affecting and comes close to being a masterpiece. In his more ambitious and longer fiction, *Les Caves du Vatican* (1914) and *Les Faux-monnayeurs* (1925), he betrays the sorry fact that he is not really a novelist: he is short of breath and has little imagination. These books were hugely successful in their time but have not aged well. Mauriac was probably right when he observed that, half a century later, Gide's novels had already become mummified, whereas—in paradoxical contrast—those of Anatole France (so cruelly derided by the Surrealist generation) retained an amazing freshness.[22]

In 1924, he published *Corydon*,* a defence of homosexuality. His argumentation is clumsy and his sincerity more limited than it may appear at first, but it took considerable courage to "come out" at that time in such a public fashion.

He forcefully commented twice on public affairs—even though his notorious lack of a sense of reality* ill-prepared him for such activity. After a lengthy journey into Black Africa (French Congo and Chad, 1925–26), he wrote an eloquent denunciation of the colonial exploitation of the native populations. Then, during the 1930s, he foolishly became a fellow-traveller of Stalinist communism. His performance as "useful idiot" was short-lived, however—a brief visit to

the Soviet Union opened his eyes. It did not require exceptional per-
cipience to appreciate the plain evidence that was under his very nose,
but it certainly took exceptional courage to spell it out publicly. On
his return to Paris, he wrote at once a truthful and scathing account
of his political disenchantment. Against all expectations, natural justice rewarded his audacity: *Retour de l'URSS* (1936) was prodigiously
successful—this iconoclastic little book was reprinted eight times in
ten months and sold nearly 150,000 copies; by the end of 1937, it had
been translated into fourteen languages. None of Gide's other works
was such an immediate success.[23]

Almost until his death (in 1951), Gide continued to write, polish
and edit his *Journal*—probably his most important work. But besides
his own publications, his role in and influence upon the French literary scene were also exerted through the *Nouvelle Revue Française*,
which he had established in 1909 with a few friends. (When the Nazis
occupied France, Otto Abetz, who was in charge of German cultural
policy, observed: "There are three powers in France: communism, the
big banks and the *Nouvelle Revue Française*.")

Gide was awarded the Nobel Prize for literature in 1947. The official statement of the Nobel Committee was typically vague, but Gide
wrote a clear reply:

> If I have represented anything it is, I believe, the spirit of free
> inquiry, independence, insubordination even, protest against
> what the heart and reason refuse to approve. I firmly believe that
> the spirit of inquiry lies at the origin of our culture. It is this
> spirit that the so-called totalitarian regimes, of left and right,
> are trying to crush and gag...What matters here is the protec-
> tion of that spirit that is "the salt of the earth" and which can
> still save the world...the struggle of culture against barbarism.[24]

CHARACTER

Gide had a genius for friendship. Those who were in close and constant
contact with him all loved him. If we except the sad onset of senility

in his very last years—which, in the end, generated some strain in the harmony of his small "family" circle—for most of his life, his presence seems to have brought permanent stimulation and delight to his entourage. "Good nature is the most selfish of all virtues," Hazlitt had observed, and indeed it was Gide's colossal self-centredness that enabled him to be generally benign to all. His selfishness was quite absolute—on this account, those who knew him best and had most affection for him could entertain no illusion[25]—and thus he was also tolerant and easy-going: his unflappably pleasant disposition[26] was built upon a bedrock of indifference to whatever did not have a direct bearing on his own person.[27] His aptitude for happiness was irrepressible and disarming—as he confided to the Tiny Lady: "It is incredible how difficult I find it *not* to be happy!"[28]

Gide enlivened all that he touched; routine and stagnation were banned from his life. He was in a state of permanent "availability," vibrant anticipation of what the next moment would bring. He really never settled down anywhere: "What I need is constant change, I dislike all habits."[29] He was unable to remain in any place for long, either physically or mentally.[30] He spent more time in hotel rooms and in friends' houses than in his own apartment—which presented the forlorn, uncomfortable, gloomy, littered, impersonal and unwelcoming aspect of a temporary shelter, hardly ever lived in, with naked light bulbs dangling from the ceiling and mothballs stacked upon the seats of the armchairs. In a sense, his entire existence was but one long holiday, his leisure was unlimited, his freedom boundless, and his money plentiful. He had no family responsibilities, no professional obligations. At any time, on the spur of a fancy, he could travel to exotic places; and then, on his return, he would rest in the splendid country mansions of various acquaintances, where he enjoyed the status of guest of honour—and of shameless parasite. Most of his initiatives were taken under the impulse of a sudden inspiration, all his moves were dictated by mood and whim. Yet, for a superficial observer, these appearances of carefree and luxurious bohemia could be as misleading as the sight of a bee drifting from flower to flower on a beautiful summer afternoon: the insect may look happily intoxicated on fragrances and sunlight, whereas it is in fact relentlessly driven by the single-minded urge to deliver a load of nectar back to its honey-making factory. As Herbart perceptively remarked,[31] *gratuitousness* was utterly foreign to Gide (which is ironical, considering that he coined in his fiction the very notion of *l'acte gratuit*!): with him "impressions, readings, things and people are being sorted out and assessed in the light of one single criterion: their usefulness." In this particular respect, it is significant to note the recurrence in his diaries of expressions such as "profit" and "benefit"; whenever he records encounters with new books or visitors, instead of saying "this book is beautiful" or "this person is charming," most often he writes: "I greatly benefited from reading...," "I derived much profit from the conversation of..." Similar phrases crop up literally dozens of times in the *Journal*.

What redeemed his monstrous self-absorption and made his company so pleasant and rewarding for his intimates was his restless and ravenous appetite for discovery, his polymorphous curiosity. Béatrix Beck recalls how exhilarating it was to work as his secretary; at the time, she wrote to her sister: "Gide has become my only interest—which means that, from now on, I am interested in *everything*."[32] Gide used to end his letters with the courtesy phrase *"Attentivement vôtre"* —but, for him, this was not an empty formula; he was indeed paying attention to his interlocutor, whoever he or she might be—and therein resided the rare quality of the Gidean dialogue.* Furthermore, his attention was not directed at people only, it seems to have extended to all creatures. For instance, the Tiny Lady recorded a typical scene: "At lunchtime, in the midst of an exciting conversation, he abruptly stops and examines a fly that has a tiny parasite on one leg. In this area, nothing escapes his eye."[33] Or again, when he went to visit Herman Hesse at home in Switzerland (Gide had just been awarded the Nobel Prize for literature, and Hesse was to receive it the following year), during this first meeting between the two grand old men of letters (they had already been corresponding for some time), most of Gide's time and attention were lavished on a cat which had just had kittens.[34] Thus, the interview passed agreeably for both: Hesse was fascinated by Gide, and Gide was fascinated by Hesse's cat.

Yet, in his dealings with people, one could say of him what André Suarès said of Goethe: "He does not care for a man, however talented, if he cannot extract from him something that may be of use to his own development."[35] His curiosity was always alert, but quick to shift to another object. The instant warmth of his welcome was only matched by the abruptness with which he could drop hapless visitors once they were no longer of interest to him. Or again, he could not recognise in the street persons with whom he had enjoyed long, congenial and intimate exchanges shortly before; they had exhausted their usefulness, they were already obliterated from his memory.[36] He became easily bored not only with new acquaintances in life, but even with the creatures of his own imagination: he could not write long novels, for, after a while, he lost interest in his own characters.[37] He worked ceaselessly, however (his stern Calvinist education had instilled in him a deep aversion for laziness and waste), but he could not remain long attached to the same task, and this explains why his best writing is to be found in his slim novellas, in his short critical essays, and above all in the discontinuous jottings of his *Journal*.

CHOICES

Gide's indecisiveness, hesitations, ditherings, vacillations and contradictions were legendary among his friends. With him, no decision was ever stable or final; sometimes, in the very same breath, he managed to opt simultaneously for one course of action—and for its exact opposite. It was impossible to predict what, in the end, would be his choice, and it was wiser not even to ask.[38] He thrived on ambiguity, he relished muddle. In any debate, his interventions were so twisted and contradictory—each affirmation being cancelled by a reservation, and each reservation questioned by an afterthought—that it was impossible to know if he supported or opposed the point at stake.[39] This attitude was displayed in all matters—big and small: whether he should seek reconciliation with God, and whether he should have coffee after lunch.[40]

Living at his side, the Tiny Lady was at a vantage point to observe on a daily basis his mental pirouettes and somersaults, and, as she herself was bold and decisive by temperament, she recorded these permanent acrobatics with a mixture of amusement, amazement and exasperation. One day, as Gide was once again deliciously writhing on the hot coals of one of his religious crises, she snapped back: "If it is your wish to go to God—go! But don't fret: *soyez net*."[41] Alas, for Gide, to be driven into a corner was unspeakable agony; he always avoided the straight line (as he once said: "A direct path merely takes you to your destination"[42]) and invariably chose the oblique; his mind progressed only through meanders, or in "hooked fashion" (*en crochet*[43]); every issue had to be approached sideways. He was totally incapable of tackling problems head-on; in fact, he would rather not tackle them at all.[44] He was forever making imprudent promises, which he could not keep, and then he did not know where to escape. He was constantly torn between the spontaneous effusions of his own irresponsibility and the panic of finding himself unable to meet the obligations he had recklessly contracted. On the one hand, he never felt committed to any course of action, and on the other, he was racked with guilt every time he disappointed other people's expectations.[45]

He was essentially a bystander: "Action interests me passionately, but I prefer to watch it being performed by someone else. Otherwise I fear it would compromise me—I mean, what I actually do might limit what I could otherwise be doing. The thought that, since I have done *this*, I will not be able to do *that*—this is something I find intolerable."[46]

Gide always avoided defining his positions: "What bothers me is to have to outline my opinion, to formulate it; I hate to have anything cast in concrete; and, in the end, there is hardly any subject on which I have not changed my mind."[47] He would certainly have approved of the old Persian wisdom: "When you enter a house, always observe first where the exit is." The only domain in which he ever expressed firm views and a stable taste was literary aesthetics[48]—and even there, in old age, he lost confidence in his own judgement and became uncertain and confused.[49]

Various reasons may explain this incapacity to commit himself to any line of thought or to any definite course of action. First, he was genuinely inhibited by self-doubt and self-distrust: "I can never truly believe in the importance of what I say."[50] As various casual acquaintances noted, his great charm was that "André Gide did not know he was André Gide." (This was no longer true in later years, when he became a prisoner of his *persona*—but this is probably the inevitable fate of most great men in their old age.) More profoundly, however, his indecisiveness reflected *a refusal* to choose—for every choice entails sacrifice and loss. As he himself remarked: "Before he chooses, an individual is richer; after he chooses, he is stronger"[51]—and inner riches were more important to him than inner strength.

Yet, one day, he confessed to Martin du Gard how much he envied his firmness. Reporting this *cri du coeur*, the Tiny Lady commented: "Indeed, his own difficulty in making any decision is simply incredible. What bothers him most is not the choice itself, but the fact that, by choosing, he risks losing something unexpected and more pleasant."[52]

He could not control his intellectual greediness (in old age, this lack of restraint even found a physical expression: he would gorge himself on forbidden delicacies which, each time, made him vilely sick): "He never refuses anything. Subtraction is an operation he ignores; he is always adding up, even things that are totally contradictory. For instance, he would say in the same breath, 'Me, to enter the Academy? Never!' and then, immediately, 'To occupy Valéry's chair— why not?'"[53] He was never embarrassed by his own contradictions; to someone who objected that he could not simultaneously maintain views that were mutually exclusive, he replied by quoting a witticism of Stendhal: "I have two different ways of being: it is the best protection against error." Martin du Gard observed: "For Gide, I am afraid this was not mere jest."[54]

CORYDON

"If I had listened to other people, I would never have written any of my books," Gide once observed.[55] It was particularly true for *Corydon*; his close friends were all aghast when he expressed the intention of taking a public stand in defence of homosexuality. They strongly advised against such a project, believing it would provide his enemies with weapons, ruin his moral authority and destroy his reputation. But it was as if their apprehension worked only to spur him on his reckless course (he often confessed that recklessness appealed to him[56]). To Martin du Gard, who implored him to be prudent and not to rush things, he replied: "I cannot wait any longer...I must follow an inner necessity...I need, I NEED to dissipate this fog of lies in which I have been hiding since my youth, since my childhood...I cannot breathe in it any longer..." Martin believed that his wish to "come out" partly reflected a habit inherited from his Protestant education: the need for self-justification (which remained with him all his life) and also, perhaps, an unconscious Puritan desire for martyrdom, for atonement.[57] His wife, Madeleine, whose eye could penetrate his soul, made the same observation when she tried to warn him against publication: "I fear it is a sort of thirst for martyrdom—if I dare apply this word to such a bad cause—that pushes you to do this."[58] And to Schlumberger, who thought that *Corydon* would bring discredit on his moral authority, he replied: "You fear that I might lose my credibility on all other issues, but actually should I not regain it by acquiring a new freedom?...We were not born simply to repeat what has already been said, but in order to state what no one has expressed before us...Don't you see that, in the end, my credibility will become much greater? Once a man has no more need for compromise, how much stronger he becomes! Misunderstandings make me suffocate...I wish to silence all those who accuse me of being a mere dilettante, I wish to show them the real 'me.'"[59]

Gide eventually published, and not only was he not damned but, in the end, he was rewarded with a Nobel Prize. This conclusion, however, could not have been foreseen at the time and it must be acknowledged that, in 1924, as I have already pointed out, it required considerable courage to present a defence of homosexuality to the public. In this respect, the book retains a historical significance, even though its reasoning appears curiously flawed—and today it is hardly read at all.

Gide's argument—developed at a length that borders on the ludicrous—is that homosexuality, far from being against nature (as its traditional critics used to insist), is, in fact, to be found in nature. Here, his many examples, drawn from the natural sciences, seem to miss the real issue. Of course there may well be scientifically observed instances of homosexual cows, and homosexual whales, and homosexual ladybirds; after all, isn't nature the greatest freak show under heaven? Earthquakes and plagues, two-headed sheep and five-legged pigs... whatever *is*, is in Nature (with the exception of a few productions of the human soul, such as Chartres cathedral, the music of Bach, the calligraphy of Mi Fu, etc.). Exhaustive catalogues of natural phenomena can prove nothing, one way or another. Furthermore, not only would it be quite feasible to demonstrate that, in given circumstances, for various species of creature, homosexuality may indeed be "natural," but one could even argue (at least this was the view of Dr. Johnson[60]) that, on the contrary, it is the state of permanent, monogamous union between a man and a woman that actually goes "against nature"—since it is, in fact, a crowning achievement of *culture* (a fact acknowledged by all the great world religions, which agree that in normal circumstances such a state cannot be attained without some form of *supernatural* assistance). The point is: the issue that should be of primary concern for us is not what naked bipeds can accomplish in their original state of nature but how human beings, clad with culture, are more likely to achieve the fullness of their humanity.

A second problem of *Corydon* is that it is an apologia exclusively for *pederasty*, and, as Sheridan points out, "by claiming that the pederast, far from being effeminate, presents the zenith of maleness, Gide is justifying homosexuality in the terms of a largely heterosexual society, and therefore by implication, lining up with that society against other homosexuals."[61] Gide took pains to emphasise that the two other types of homosexual—sodomites and inverts, according to his taxonomy—inspire in pederasts "a profound disgust...accompanied by a reprobation that in no way yields to that which you [heterosexuals] fiercely show to all three."[62] Furthermore, in his description of "Greek love," Gide celebrates an ideal relation in which a caring adult initiates a youth not merely into sensual pleasure but mostly into the loftier enjoyments of knowledge and wisdom—the role of the elder partner being not so much that of a lover as that of a teacher and moral guide.[63] Here resides precisely the main flaw of the book. Inasmuch as Gide claimed to have revealed his "real self," to have cleared "the fog of lies" that had weighed upon his childhood and youth, *Corydon* is essentially fraudulent, for Gide's frenzied sexual activity—especially the monomania of his old age—was not pederastic *à la mode antique* but flatly and sordidly pedophiliac[64]—very much like today's "sex tours" which bring planeloads of wealthy Western tourists to the child brothels of South-East Asia. Now, homosexuals are usually keen to draw a line at this point; they insist—not without reason—that their sexual orientation implies no more inclination towards pedophilia than is the case for heterosexuals. If they expect, however, to find in Gide an advocate for their cause, they would be well advised to reconsider the moral (or at least tactical) wisdom of choosing such a champion.

DAUGHTER

Gide's daughter, Catherine, was born in 1923. Her mother was Elisabeth Van Rysselberghe (1890–1980), the daughter of the Tiny Lady. Elisabeth, who was briefly Rupert Brooke's lover, bitterly regretted not having been able to give birth to the poet's child. In 1920, she thought that Marc Allégret—then Gide's teenage lover—had made her pregnant. Gide was ecstatic; he said to his old lady-friend, the prospective grandmother: "Ah, *chère amie*, we are making possible a new humanity! That child must be beautiful!"[65] Once again, however, Elisabeth's hope did not come to fruition. But Gide had always thought that she deserved to have a child; a few years earlier, during a train journey, he had slipped a note to her: "I shall never love any woman, except one [thinking of his wife, Madeleine] and I have true desire only for young boys. But I cannot bear to see you without children, nor do I wish to remain childless myself."[66] Eventually, in 1922, on a secluded beach by the Mediterranean, he rediscovered with her "all the liberty that fosters amorous dispositions."[67] Catherine was born the next year.

Gide followed the growth of the child with sporadic interest; he observed her with an eye that was, by turns, fatherly and entomological. Elisabeth eventually married the writer Pierre Herbart, her junior by fifteen years (the age difference was of no real significance, Gide reassured the future mother-in-law, because, after all, Herbart was more interested in his own sex[68]), and Catherine came to live with her mother and Herbart when she was not pursuing her education in Swiss boarding schools. Occasionally, she spent brief holidays with Gide, who, one day, informed her that he was her real father. The girl was thirteen at the time, and this revelation had a mixed psychological effect on her.

Catherine is rarely mentioned in Gide's *Journal*. In 1942 (his daughter was nineteen), he noted: "Catherine might have been able to attach me to life, but she is interested only in herself, and that doesn't interest me."[69] Sheridan comments pointedly: "In other words, the daughter was behaving like the father, and the father didn't like it."[70]

She appears more frequently in the diaries of her grandmother, who remarked: "The relations between father and daughter are difficult ... This is mostly due to the fact that both are too much alike, and also because the relationship is ill-defined—which is a result of the circumstances. They do not have father–daughter exchanges; he is trying too hard to please her and is incapable of exerting any authority."[71] Meanwhile, Catherine felt more able to confide her true feelings to Martin du Gard, who recorded in his diary this conversation with her—Martin had mentioned a book by Gide and Catherine replied that she had not read it. Then, noticing Martin's surprise, she continued:

> "But you should know that I have read virtually none of his books. No ... I do not feel the slightest curiosity for his works ... I never read any of them ... Sometimes, I have picked one up, but quickly let it drop." Seeing my astonishment, she hesitates, then suddenly declares, "You know, until very recently, I detested him."
>
> "...?"
>
> "Yes."
>
> "Detested?"
>
> "As much as it is possible to detest someone!" she proceeds with determination. "His presence was horrid to me, it made me absolutely sick. For instance, whenever I had to travel with him, it was an abominable torture!"

"But . . . since when?"

"Oh, it was always like that. And certainly since I learned that he is my father."

"And before that?"

"Before, I found him dreadfully irritating and I did not enjoy seeing him. Perhaps I did not completely hate him then. Not as much as later on."

"And now?"

She is embarrassed by my inquisitive stare. She does not protest. Obviously, she does not wish to say that, now, she does not hate him. She merely says, "Now, it is no longer the same. It slightly changed this summer."

I say, "Did he ever suspect anything of this?"

"No, luckily not."[72]

A little earlier, Catherine was supposed to go abroad, but these plans had to be abandoned. Martin du Gard said to Gide:

"You must be so glad that Catherine did not leave!"

"Oh, my dear, I am more happy than I can express, especially now that our relations have become so charming," and then, after a silence, he added, "And yet, if she had gone away, after three days I would have forgotten her."[73]

At about the same time, Gide tried to make Catherine realise that she was enjoying a privileged situation: "I am afraid you may not fully appreciate how rare is the harmony that prevails in our little group. [The little group was comprised of Gide, the Tiny Lady, Elisabeth and her lover, Pierre Herbart—within that small community, Catherine was thus provided with two fathers]. Don't imagine that most families have such luck."[74]

In 1942, Gide went to North Africa, where he was to spend the remaining years of the war. On the eve of this long separation, the parting message he left for Catherine was twofold: "1. Had you wished, I could have taught you a way of reciting French verse that is now largely lost. 2. Never do anything simply out of a desire to conform, to be like the others. Do only what deeply pleases you." And he quoted the famous instruction of Madame de Lambert to her son: "My son, do nothing silly, unless it amuses you."[75]

In 1945, Catherine gave birth to a daughter, Isabelle. Gide was delighted to have a granddaughter. A year later, Catherine married Jean Lambert, a young scholar of German literature (they were to have three more children). Gide greatly enjoyed the company of his new son-in-law. In 1947, the young couple took him on a journey through Switzerland and Italy, but the old man's manic compulsion to hunt for little boys was now frightfully out of control and caused them constant worry. In France, in these innocent times, Gide's fame and his Nobel Prize were protection enough against scandal, but once abroad there was a serious risk that foreign policemen might not show a similar tolerance.

Exactly half a century earlier, Gide had thrown the bomb of his *Nourritures terrestres*, with its famous curse: "*Familles, je vous hais!*" But now, his strange little clan began increasingly to resemble a warm and cosy family. For instance, when Herbart dedicated one of his books to the Tiny Lady, Gide was greatly pleased. The Tiny Lady remarked: "It is so charming this way he has of rejoicing at one's own joys, with such warmth and sincerity. He is happy to see that those whom he loves are getting ever closer to each other."[76] At the end of 1947, she noted: "Elisabeth and I are struck by the constancy of Gide's happy mood—the joyful interest he takes in all the small things of life. Elisabeth said laughingly, 'It seems that *Families, I hate you!* is far away now. He has a way of talking about 'the children'—meaning Catherine, Jean and their two little kids—with an accent that is new; and he is completely besotted with his granddaughter, whose lively mind delights him."[77] The new year was celebrated by the whole "family"; the Tiny Lady, who was normally not inclined to sentimentality, was moved to write: "It was cheerful, tender, charming... Never before had I felt such harmony."[78]

In her memoirs, Béatrix Beck made only one mention of Catherine. One day, when she informed the young woman that, "There was a telephone call from Roger Martin du Gard," Catherine corrected her: "You must say *Monsieur* Martin du Gard." Beck still remembered

the incident half a century later: "This remonstrance hurt me indelibly. Had I not had to support my own child at the time, I would have
resigned on the spot."[79] Thus, for all her unconventional upbringing,
this fruit of a bold experiment, this beautiful specimen of a New Humanity, had come full circle and, by the age of twenty-seven, had already turned into a prim and proper *petite bourgeoise*, with a most
exacting notion of how members of the lower orders should refer to
their betters.

DEVIL

In 1920, as Gide was working on his autobiographical narrative *Si le
grain ne meurt*, he explained to Martin du Gard: "Funny to say, my
dear: if only I could borrow Christian terminology, if I dared to introduce the character of Satan into my narrative, at once everything
would become miraculously clear, easy to tell, easy to understand ...
Things have always happened to me as if the Devil existed, as if he was
constantly intervening in my life."[80]

At that time, he had already adopted a certain tongue-in-cheek approach to this subject, which, earlier on, had pressed hauntingly upon
his mind. Since childhood, his devout Protestant education had given
him a familiarity with the Holy Scriptures; more especially, well into
middle age, he remained a profound reader of the Gospels, whence he
eventually derived a clear awareness of the presence of the Evil One.
He remarked to Schlumberger: "It is strange to see the sort of reserve
which inhibits Catholics, and Protestants even more, when they
speak of the Devil. They simply conjure him away; they grant him
only a negative form of existence ... And yet, in the Gospels, the reality is totally different: the Devil has a fiercely personal existence, he is
even more sharply characterised than God ..." And then he made further comments on the theme of "the enslavement to the Devil": "The
Devil forces his slaves to recruit new subjects for him—hence the
need to pervert, to find accomplices."[81]

In 1916, an intense religious crisis brought him very close to a conversion to Catholicism; it is reflected on at great length in his *Journal*,

well summarised by Sheridan: "Gide returns obsessively to talk of God and the devil, sin and guilt, with scarcely veiled references to masturbation and his attempts to resist it." (Note that he was forty-eight at the time!):

> Yesterday evening I gave in, as one gives in to an obstinate child, to have some peace ... Since Saturday, I have been assailed again by abominable imaginings, against which I am defenceless; I find no refuge anywhere. At certain moments, I wonder if I am not going mad ... Yesterday, an abominable relapse ... I get up, my head and heart heavy and empty: full of all the weight of Hell ... Yesterday, abominable relapse that has left my body and mind in a state bordering on despair, suicide, madness ...

Throughout this period, Gide certainly addresses God as a believing (and doubting) Christian would: "Lord! You know that I have given up being in the right against anyone. What does it matter if it is to escape submission to sin that I submit to the Church! I submit! Ah! Untie the bonds that still hold me back. Deliver me from the terrible weight of this body. Ah! Let me live a little! Let me breathe! Snatch me from evil. Let me not stifle."[82]

Eventually Gide pulled out of this crisis and broke with the Catholic friends (such as Claudel) who had been trying, with more zeal than tact, to drag him into the Church. Yet the religious issue never really left his mind—to the perplexity of the Tiny Lady for whom this lingering preoccupation was utterly incomprehensible—and he could truthfully state once again: "In the end, only two things have ever interested me passionately: pederasty and Christianity."[83] But in later years, his religious concerns acquired a purely negative intensity, as Copeau noticed already in 1930: "Gide has ended up with *atheism*: he preaches it."[84] At the end of his life, his anti-Catholicism became nasty and obsessive; in 1947, Schlumberger, who admired Gide and was no altar-boy himself, was shocked by the narrow-minded hostility that coloured Gide's comments on the Church: "I am upset by the stupid anti-clericalism that reigns in his house."[85]

In the world of traditional Catholicism, it was widely—though not universally—believed that Gide was possessed by the Devil. Once, during a family dinner, Claudel declared, as he was holding a *crêpe flambée* on his fork: "This is how André Gide is going to burn in Hell!" A witness of the incident reported it to Gide, who was hugely amused.[86] Frequently confronted with this prognosis of eternal damnation, he repeated La Fontaine's reply in his own time to similar curses: "I deeply believe that the damned in Hell end up feeling like fish in water."[87]

If the Catholic side had a biased view on this matter, the testimony of Schlumberger—lifelong companion and loyal friend, who shared not only Gide's philosophy but also his sexual orientation—cannot be lightly dismissed. Schlumberger witnessed Gide's end at very close range indeed—and was appalled: "I had to stare at senility in its most perfidious aspect: old age, leaving his intelligence nearly intact, revealed all the more clearly the disorder of his behaviour . . . I could feel how his entourage was now haunted by the sordid shadows of his devils . . . His loss of control over his own erotic pulsions inspired terror in them, and could nearly have confirmed the beliefs of those who regard the flesh as the kingdom of the Prince of Darkness . . ."[88]

When Gide died, he was buried next to his wife, in the village of her country estate. The ceremony was simple and attended only by relatives, close friends and some villagers. Gide's nephew, a local notable, thought it proper to invite a Protestant pastor to say a few words. The pastor simply read a short passage from Gide's *Numquid et tu*, written forty years earlier, at the height of his religious crisis: "Lord, I come to you like a child, like the child you want me to become . . . I renounce everything that made up my pride and which, in your presence, would make up my shame. I listen and submit my heart to you."[89] Immediately after the ceremony, Martin du Gard and Schlumberger protested loudly against this religious intrusion, which they deemed to be a betrayal of Gide's intentions, a denial of his clearly stated beliefs, a violation of his final wishes. They were right, of course. And yet the intervention of the hapless pastor, however indiscreet, was nevertheless poignant; after all, these were once Gide's own true words, and they were also words of truth. Hell is not "truth seen too late" (as Hobbes said); on the contrary, it is truth seen too soon, and knowingly rejected.

DIALOGUE

"Outside my capacity for sympathy (which constitutes all my intelligence), it seems that I have no existence at all, and my moral *persona* is nothing but a number of possibilities, which, in turn, are called Ménalque, Alissa, Lafcadio." Gide wrote this to a friend: he knew himself well.[90]

His instinctive urge to sympathise was itself the reflection of a deeper need: the need to please. He had been aware of this since his youth: at the age of twenty-four, he noted in his *Journal*: "My perpetual question (it is a morbid obsession) is: Am I lovable?"[91] And fifty-five years later, at the end of his career, he concluded in that same *Journal*: "My extraordinary, my insatiable need to love and be loved: I believe this is what has dominated my life and driven me to write."[92]

"He always tried to charm people, and largely succeeded," Béatrix Beck observed.[93] The Tiny Lady had often to warn him against this excessive eagerness to make himself congenial; for instance, after he managed at last to establish pleasant relations with a person who had previously been hostile,[94] she advised him: "Beware, don't spoil it. As the situation has become fine and easy, do not exaggerate now, as often happens with you; you get carried away by some sentimental impulse of yours, and you tend to say things that are true only for a short moment—and this is a sure recipe for creating horrific disappointments later on."[95]

Gide himself was aware of the problem: "I am all too inclined to espouse other people's points of view."[96] Even in familiar exchanges, he would instinctively recoil from contradiction and ensure smoothness at any cost. Here is a typical little episode from his *Journal*:

"Valéry asks me, 'Do you know anything more boring than the *Iliad*?' I repress a spontaneous impulse to protest, but find it more friendly to reply, 'Yes, *La Chanson de Roland*.' He approves."[97]

Thus agreement had been secured—but the price of this was the suppression of his own deeply felt views on the matter, for we know how much he actually loved Homer. In the very same *Journal*, he had noted not long before: "I re-read with delight the last six books of the *Iliad*..."[98]

Similar occurrences are frequent; for instance, the Tiny Lady records (in 1937) that, chatting with the German scholar E. R. Curtius, Gide, echoing his good friend's view, expressed his "great admiration" for Thomas Mann's *Joseph*.[99] Yet from the *Journal* we learn that, two years later, he was still plodding through that very same book "with increasing boredom."[100]

He confessed: "Rather than confronting opposition, I prefer to adopt the opinion of the other party."[101] Sometimes he would rally so quickly to his interlocutor's views that it made the latter worry. Schlumberger recorded his uneasy feelings at the outcome of a discussion: "I am somewhat scared when I see him abandoning his position with so little resistance."[102] In fact Gide himself was troubled by his own instinctive reaction: "I often feel as if I were a horrible hypocrite; I have such an acute need for sympathy, I virtually *melt* into the other party. With complete sincerity, I adopt other people's opinions and thus give them a misleading impression of agreement. I would inevitably disappoint my own side—if I had one."[103]

He suffered from an inability to say "No." He wished to break with his Catholic friends, but felt hopelessly entangled in the nets of their kind concern. As the Tiny Lady reproached him for his irresolution, he finally exploded in frustration: "You must understand that I am full of weakness, I have no resistance to others, no resistance to any expression of sympathy. These people deprive me of all my resources, they rob me of my arguments, they prevent me from saying what I wish to say. I am bold and free only when I am in front of a sheet of blank paper."[104]

The written word was the last refuge of his sincerity: "I put all my integrity into my writing, whereas, when I deal with people, my only desire is that everything should go smoothly; probably it is simply that I wish to please, and this is obviously a sort of coquetry."[105]

The desire to please, the constant fear that he might disappoint other people's expectations, made him nervous: "I smoke too much, out of nervousness; there are so few people with whom I can be completely natural! I am too tense, and I smoke to give myself some poise, to overcome my agitation."[106] He was simple and unpretentious, but also very awkward. Yet dialogue remained for him the very essence of human life; he won over his interlocutors not only with his unassuming manners but, more importantly, by being an attentive listener.

Whenever he had drafted a new piece of writing, or if he had made some mistake, he amazed his friends by the meekness and humility with which he would accept their criticism, however sharp and bruising. But his critics were soon to discover that, if he had yielded to their attacks and endorsed their suggestions, it was in order to mend the flaws in his original position, which, in the end, he would re-present in a form that was now impregnable.

His receptivity and malleability were thus deceptive—and he was the first to acknowledge this fact: "By using sympathy, anyone can easily manipulate me. Previously, I warned Claudel, Beware, I am made of rubber. I agree with everything, as much as possible, and I would go to the very edge of insincerity—yet make no mistake: once alone, I revert to my original shape."[107]

The paradox is that, on the deepest level, he was perfectly blind to the point of view of others and radically unable to perceive glaring truths that had been before him all his life. The most tragic example of this incredible insensitivity can be found in the way he treated his wife, Madeleine: in the end, he managed to alienate—irreparably—the trust of the only person he truly loved.

HERBART

Gide's enemies spread many calumnies about him during his life; these should naturally be ignored—and, anyway, they pale in comparison with the truths that his friends published after his death.

The most penetrating psychological portrait of Gide was written by Pierre Herbart: *À la recherche d'André Gide* (1952). Herbart (1904–74) was the husband of the mother of Gide's daughter (readers who feel confused by this little brain-twister might refer to the entry *Daughter* above; a diagram of the relationships within the Gidean "family" would rival in its complexity the lines of descent within the chimpanzee cage at the zoo).

Herbart came from a prominent family of northern France, but carried a heavy hereditary burden. After sixteen years of apparently peaceful married life, his father had suddenly left home forever, without a cent in his pocket, become a vagrant and vanished. Some years later, the police asked the adolescent son to identify his dead body, lying in a ditch, by the side of a country road.

The Tiny Lady developed a special affection for her son-in-law, and wrote a short sketch about him.[108] Pierre was enigmatic and attractive, whimsical and unpredictable, high-strung and indolent ("divinely lazy," said the Tiny Lady—or just "plain lazy" according to Béatrix Beck, who looked at him with less indulgent eyes), violent and tender, harsh and kind, cynical and generous. Women found him irresistible—some men did too (though others, like Gallimard, who occasionally had to employ him, thought that he was "a whore").[109]

Gide first met the young man (who was twenty-three at the time) in Cocteau's country house. Herbart was then an opium addict who, later on, became an alcoholic. Gide was impressed by his natural elegance and what he discerned to be "a sort of devilish genius, a frenzied quality—all the seductions from Hell."[110] In order to help him overcome his addictions, Gide encouraged him to write and eventually persuaded Gallimard to publish his first novel. Subsequently, Gide introduced him to the mother of his daughter; they soon became lovers and married a few years later (Herbart was then twenty-eight, and Elisabeth Van Rysselberghe forty-one). In the early 1930s, Herbart became a communist sympathiser and an ardent propagandist for the Soviet Union; he was instrumental in attracting Gide into the fellow-travellers brotherhood. Together they visited the Soviet Union and shared the same disenchantment. After the war, Gide, who could not bear solitude, became more and more dependent upon Herbart, who acted as his confidant, secretary, adviser, agent, factotum and occasional driver; with him he knew he would not be bored and, in the end, he simply could not do without the young man's company.

Herbart was intuitive and had sharp psychological acumen. He was devoted to Gide, who repeatedly gave him generous financial support; he knew Gide on a familiar level of daily intimacy hardly equalled by any other friend.

The inner core of the Gidean "family" was made up of the Tiny

Lady, Herbart and Roger Martin du Gard. One day, in August 1940, as the trio were chatting together, Herbart gave his friends a first inkling of the original insight he had reached on the subject of Gide. The Tiny Lady recorded their exchange:

> I wish to reproduce in its main outline a conversation which we had one morning, Martin, Pierre and I, and during which Pierre was led to say something intriguing about Gide. We were talking about compassion—compassion as a symbol of Christianity. We were wondering if, as Hitler now seems intent on doing, it would ever be feasible to build a new world from which compassion would be excluded. Pierre said yes; Martin, no; we inquired whether compassion was already present in Antiquity, or whether it was a specific contribution of Christianity, whether it is a motivating force in art, etc., etc., when suddenly Pierre said, "I am going to make a point that runs against my own position—but it seems to me that it is this very sentiment that is missing in Gide's works; had he got it, he would be the greatest, whereas now in fact he is merely one among the great." With a somewhat mischievous smile, Martin asked, "Is he also lacking compassion in his life?" Pierre and I, we said simultaneously, "This is a much more complex question." But Pierre pursued his idea: "My explanation for this lack may seem to you very flat. I believe that, in Gide's case, it all comes down to a lack of virility." Now we were treading on very delicate ground. As I feared that Pierre might not go to the bottom of the matter, I said, "On the subject of Gide, it would be very difficult not to confront clearly the sexual issue." "Precisely," Pierre said. "I believe that Gide's sexuality has remained in an infantile state, while his sensitivity developed normally, and this imbalance had repercussions on his moral virility." Martin's eyebrows shot high up, he was agape, transfixed with attention. At this point, unfortunately, our conversation was interrupted.[111]

Twelve years later, in his *À la recherche d'André Gide* (which, by the way, was dedicated to Martin du Gard), Herbart was to pick up this broken thread. In his view, Gide's deepest compulsion was to charm people and to win their sympathy; his obsessive fear was of disappointing their expectations; he was, therefore, totally dependent on others, his own self-esteem being conditioned by their approval. In this attitude, he betrayed his lack of "virility" and his absence of "morality." Needless to say, both terms should not be understood in any narrow sense: Herbart himself was bisexual and, in his younger years, had led with cool shamelessness the life of a gigolo—unorthodox sexual practices and unconventional moral behaviour could not really shock him. What flabbergasted him, however, was Gide's monstrous insensitivity—that, for instance, he had the cheek to complain that his long-suffering and saintly wife would not co-operate in procuring local boys to alleviate his sexual needs during his stays on their country estate![112]

Gide is "emasculated," Herbart continues: one cannot trust his word, nor his loyalty, nor his discretion. He is amoral, not by a bold choice or as a challenge—but simply and literally because he is missing that particular sense. He can experience physical or aesthetic repulsion but rarely intellectual and never moral repulsion: his ignorance of morality is innate and invincible—he does not have the faintest awareness of what morality might mean.[113]

Gide's inner world is characterised by an extreme spiritual poverty: the entire realm of human passion has remained a closed book to him. He has no great genius, no imagination, no original ideas. With him, style is everything: he picks up clichés and "Gidifies" them—giving them a form that is unique.[114]

His strength resides in his tireless curiosity, his absolute freedom, his uncompromising pursuit of excellence.[115] But he is utterly devoid of the tragic sense of life; he has no experience of pathos. Hence the weird feeling which often affects sensitive readers when they plunge into his works—and on this point, Herbart quotes a passage from Julien Green that is worth pondering, for, once again, this example carries particular weight. Green, though Gide's junior by thirty years, was a friend who shared both his Protestant upbringing and his sexual orientation:

A short while ago, in a bookshop, I was browsing a reprint of Gide's *Journal*. I have never read it in its entirety, but this time, reading a few pages convinced me, once again, that I shall never be able to pursue it to the end. Why? I don't really know. Its style is exquisite, and every page is full to the brim with great intellectual riches; but in the same time as the book yields all that it can give, it also freezes the heart, and as one reads on, one feels left with less faith, with less hope, and (I say this with regret) with less love.[116]

On the subject of Gide, when reading Herbart—as well as Martin du Gard, for these two were Gide's favourite friends[117]—one wonders, on what did their unquestionable attachment rest? Not on his works: in the inner Gidean circle, there were no disciples, and both Herbart and Martin have stated that no book of Gide ever had a significant impact upon them.[118] They simply cherished the man, Herbart says, yet he could also foresee that "The particular value which his life presented will, it seems to me, become unintelligible once those who witnessed it have all disappeared."[119] Indeed.

LITERATURE

Literature was the very meaning of Gide's life, its exclusive purpose.[120] He loved literature with a devotion that was admirable and touching. Reading was as essential to him as breathing; it was both a vital need and a constant joy. Often it was also a convivial celebration, a fervour which he shared with those whom he loved most. When he was with his wife in their Normandy estate, or with his friends in Paris, entire evenings were spent reading aloud to each other.[121]

Gide was a deliberate, slow and omnivorous reader. He was never without a book in his hand, or in his pocket, or at his bedside. He read in order to write; he drew all his writing out of himself, as one draws water from a well, and only an uninterrupted stream of reading could ensure that the well would not run dry.

In his approach to literature, besides the solid foundations that traditional French schooling provided to all children of the bourgeoisie, he was equipped only with his own voracious curiosity. His enjoyment of literature was never warped by the sterile games that academics play professionally—he never attended any university. He belonged (as Sheridan accurately observes[122]) to the vanishing breed of "common readers." (E.M. Forster, who much admired him, was himself very Gidean when he wrote: "Study has a very solemn sound. *I am studying Dante* sounds much more than *I am reading Dante*. It is really much less.") At the conclusion of a symposium on his beloved Montaigne, Gide's characteristic contribution was simply to suggest with gentle irony that Montaigne would probably not have understood a word of what had just been said about him.

He was a good Latinist; from adolescence till death, Virgil's *Aeneid* remained his most constant reading.[123] He had a loving familiarity with the French classics: Montaigne first and foremost, and also Pascal, Racine, Molière, La Fontaine, Bossuet, La Bruyère, Voltaire, Stendhal, Balzac, Flaubert. On Hugo, he was ambivalent: "Sometimes execrable, always prodigious."[124] He ignored Dumas.[125]

What set him apart, however, was his openness to foreign literatures, which was exceptional for his time and in his milieu. He knew some German, a little Italian, and worked hard on his English. His command of foreign languages always remained shaky ("Honestly, as regards foreign languages, I am a hopeless case ..."[126]) but his hunger for learning and discovery was impressive. He applied himself to read Goethe (one of his greatest cultural heroes) in the original, and he devoted years of strenuous work to Shakespeare, painstakingly translating *Hamlet* into French. Strangely enough, however, he eventually became quite disenchanted with the play: "*Hamlet* lacks artistry. I wish an Englishman could explain to me in what respect it is admirable. Reading it, I never feel that I am in front of something beautiful, which I would wish to transmit to others. It is muddled and amphigoric."[127] Actually, on the subject of Shakespeare, his evolution—from admiration to prejudice—very much duplicated that of Voltaire, and he came to some curious conclusions: "I deny that there are any human teachings to be derived from his plays; his most sublime lines are in fact utterly banal, his psychology conventional. Generally speaking, theatrical plays always give me this impression, with the sole exception of Racine."[128] And again: "The English are irritating with their habit of always praising Shakespeare without reservation."[129] He found *As You Like It* "completely devoid of charm."[130] Immediately after the war he had the chance to watch *Richard III*, staged in Paris by the Old Vic; he confessed he could not understand a word of it.[131] At the very end of his life he saw *King Lear* in Laurence Olivier's interpretation. The Tiny Lady reported: "Gide was utterly disappointed by the play; he thinks it is one of Shakespeare's weakest works, without any psychological interest, quite boring in fact."[132]

He also expressed some other puzzling value judgements; for instance, he found Samuel Butler's *Erewhon* much superior to Swift's *Gulliver's Travels*, and he could not understand the popularity of the latter.[133]

He loved Browning's poetry. George Eliot's *Middlemarch* elicited his enthusiasm; as for Jane Austen, he found her novels extraordinarily well crafted, but with "a somewhat low-alcohol content." Henry James was a disappointment: "a mere socialite" (*un auteur de salon*): "his characters live only in their heads, they have nothing below the shoulders."[134] He was bored by *The Ambassadors* and could not finish it: "His manner reminds me of Proust, but, unlike Proust, it is dreary, and most of all, it lacks efficacy."[135] He read most of Thomas Hardy's novels; *The Mayor of Casterbridge* was his favourite.[136] Joyce's *Ulysses* was "needlessly long; in the end, it will remain only as a sort of monster."[137]

Claudel made him discover Conrad's novels, the reading of which gave him the desire to meet the author. He visited Conrad several times in England and developed a deep affection for him.[138] Gide loved *Lord Jim*: "One of the most beautiful books I have ever read, and also one of the saddest, and yet utterly soul-stirring,"[139] and he translated *Typhoon*. This translation was made with loving care, yet the result is odd: the style is pure Gide, with all his syntactical mannerisms and it is rife, not exactly with blunders (Gide was too conscientious and circumspect for that), but with omissions and inaccuracies that constantly betray his uncertain grasp of the language of the original.

After Conrad's death, Gide wrote a short but warm essay in his memory, concluding: "No one ever led such a wild existence; and afterwards, no one was ever able, like him, to submit life to such a patient, deliberate and sophisticated transmutation into art."[140] Still, for all the praise and friendship he lavished on Conrad, one wonders to what extent he understood either the man or the artist. He was bored by *Nostromo* and abandoned it; nor could he finish *The Secret Agent*.[141] His total lack of interest in these two prophetic works suggests an incomprehension that ran deeper than an inability to appreciate Conrad; it makes one doubt that he really understood the twentieth century. In later years, he even revised his earlier admiration and sadly came to the conclusion: "As regards Conrad, I cannot rank the writer as highly as I used to; yet, as I loved the man very much, it pains me to acknowledge this."[142]

Russian literature occupied an important place in his reading, Dostoevsky above all, and also Chekhov. He disliked Tolstoy and this was often a bone of contention with Martin du Gard, for whom Tolstoy was God. It is always interesting to explore the dislikes of an artist—sometimes they define his mind more sharply than his predilections would.[143] "I keep reading *War and Peace*, and the further I go, the more I dislike it. Of course, Tolstoy's direct observation of life is prodigious. In contrast, whenever Dostoevsky reports a conversation, one always feels that no one, anywhere, ever spoke in such a manner—whereas with Tolstoy, one's reaction is always to say: How true! But Tolstoy's dialogue, however lifelike, is nearly always devoid of interest. It is full of absurd platitudes ... For me, everything in Tolstoy is uncongenial, down to the even light that bathes with the same indifference a Napoleonic battle and Natasha's needlework."[144] "In Tolstoy, the light is implacably even, there are no shades. Compared with Dostoevsky, it is as if you were to put a painting by Detaille next to a Rembrandt."[145] (Talking to Martin du Gard:) "You are on the side of Tolstoy. As for me, I am—or at least I wish to be—on the side of Dostoevsky ... Tolstoy is a wonderful witness, but for me, this is not enough. His scrutiny always bears upon the more general aspects of man—I may say, what constitutes common humanity, what is in all of us, what we share with all other people. He shows me what I already know—more or less—what I could have found by myself with a little attention. He never offers any surprise ... Whereas Dostoevsky, ah! He always amazes me. He always reveals new things, things I had never suspected to exist: the unseen ..."[146]

He also followed, to some extent, contemporary developments in German literature. He professed public admiration for Thomas Mann, but confessed private boredom: "*Zauberberg* is an important book, quite masterly, but German novels are always such a *vide-poches*: they really pour everything into it."[147] (Here, Gide seems to be unwittingly joining Claudel, who held that the key metaphor with which to interpret the diverse manifestations of German culture was *the sausage*.[148])

Gide followed closely the French literary life of his time. Usually, writers are notoriously mean to each other; rivalries, backstabbing, jealousy are all too common among them. Gide's little circle, however, was remarkably free of these poisonous practices. The three friends—Schlumberger, Martin du Gard and Gide himself—always read out their new works to each other; they exchanged critical comments; the frankness of these could be blunt and ruthless at times, and yet they were invariably received in a spirit of unshakeable friendship.[149] And what is even more remarkable, they derived genuine delight from the successes of their friends.[150] Naturally enough, Gide did experience a mischievous pleasure when he saw his old antagonist Paul Claudel being humiliatingly rebuffed by the Académie Française (his candidacy had been defeated by a very mediocre competitor). Not without humour, he honestly acknowledged his private resentment of the overwhelming poet: "In front of Claudel, I am only aware of my own failings: he is awesome, he is overpowering, he has more breadth, more weight, more health, more money, more genius, more power, more children, more faith, etc., than I; I can only meekly listen to him."[151] Gide had watched with glee what he deemed to have been a disastrous staging of Claudel's theatrical masterpiece *Le Soulier de satin*—and yet, in the end, his own love of literature had the last word. The Tiny Lady described how, a year before his death, he came one night to the dinner table with a copy of Claudel's play in his hand: "God knows how much I normally dislike this sort of stuff, but I just opened the book at random and came upon this passage—it is truly, absolutely admirable!" For him, the Tiny Lady concluded, the literary excellence of a work always swept away all other considerations: "How I love to see this aspect of his character; it reminds me of what Flaubert said: 'Aesthetics is but a superior form of justice.'"[152]

All his life, he regretted having once—briefly, but glaringly—failed to uphold this "superior form of justice" when he overlooked Proust's manuscript of the first part of *À la recherche du temps perdu*. Although he personally took the blame for this error—and never forgave himself—it seems in fact that the decision to reject Proust's masterpiece was taken by Schlumberger (who remained largely unrepentant).[153] Eventually Gide made up for his earlier blunder by writing (in 1921) a sensitive and generous essay on Proust.[154] His private comments on Proust, as recorded over the years by the Tiny Lady, do nevertheless reflect curious contradictions—enthusiasm alternating with irritation.[155]

He paid much attention to younger writers. For instance, he felt genuine affection for Malraux; he admired his ebullient intelligence and his passion for heroic activism, but rightly judged that he was not a good writer. From the start, he perceived the exceptional brilliance of Sartre, whom he befriended—though he was disappointed (with good reason) by Sartre's later novels. He extolled the merits of Simenon ("perhaps our greatest novelist") at a time when the literati still affected to despise this all-too-successful and prolific author of commercial thrillers. More importantly, he discovered the poet Henri Michaux; he sought out both men personally and extended his friendship to them. Today, with the benefit of hindsight, one may feel that he overestimated the achievement of Simenon (in whom he appreciated all the things which he himself most cruelly lacked: a creative imagination, the sense of reality, experience of life[156]); and though he detected the deep originality of Michaux, he never really took the full measure of his genius. Nevertheless, in both cases he displayed qualities of perception and generosity that were truly admirable.

Gide believed that he and his great contemporaries, Valéry (his old friend) and Claudel (his intimate enemy) would eventually be recognised by posterity as having formed "a single team"—not simply because they belonged to the same era, but more deeply because "they had all shared the more or less secret influence of Mallarmé."[157] In fact, the literary affinities of the members of "the team" are questionable, but what is certainly worth pondering is Gide's acknowledgement of Mallarmé's influence, which, in his own case at least, was profound and long-lasting. (Actually, instead of subtitling his biography of Gide *A Life in the Present*, Sheridan could have called it more appropriately *The Last Writer of the Nineteenth Century*.)

In Gide's case, the Mallarmean inheritance found expression in the absolute primacy he gave to form and style over all other concerns. On this point, Gide's literary aesthetics never wavered: as early as 1910, in an essay on Baudelaire, he stated: "In art, where expression alone matters, ideas appear young for only a day…Today, if Baudelaire still lives on, it is thanks to his formal perfection. No artist ever relied upon anything else to reach posterity."[158] This notion acquired ever-greater importance for him with the passing of the years, and in old age, it reigned supreme in all his writings—sometimes to the dismay of his closest friends, who deplored the facility with which he would too often content himself with *lieux communs*, banal ideas, clichés and platitudes, so long as he could dress them up in exquisite Gidean garb.[159]

During his final illness, he cared little for communication; still he persisted, even on his deathbed, in correcting syntactical and grammatical improprieties in what was being said to him. The Tiny Lady observed: "He does not make allowance anymore for the slightest linguistic lapses, as if his entire capacity for attention was now exclusively focused on that single issue."[160]

Gide had invested all his resources in his style; he trusted that it alone would ensure its immortality. We are not yet in a position to assess whether this wager will ultimately pay off. Predictably enough, Claudel took a dim view of the matter: "André Gide deludes himself that he is simple, whereas he is merely flat; and he thinks he is classic, whereas he is bleak—as bleak as the moonlight over a beggars' jailhouse."[161] Yet even his loyal friends eventually came to entertain doubts about the virtues of his famed style. Schlumberger remarked that, on certain topics, Gide's unctuousness evoked "a sexton's speech"; and after re-reading *Les Caves du Vatican*, he noted: "I had forgotten the preciosity of his writing; in several chapters, Gide tries to compensate for the poverty of the contents with an accumulation of rare words, of archaic phrases and tortured syntax. At times the flavour is admirable, but it can also become tedious."[162]

MADELEINE

Two different images of Gide's wife have emerged. Recent accounts have portrayed her as a gloomy and narrow-minded bigot, who was a hindrance to her husband's human development. But it is noteworthy that none of those who expressed this view ever had the chance to meet Madeleine Gide; whereas those who actually knew her—and especially André Gide's closest friends—have given very different testimony. Shortly after Gide's death, Schlumberger was moved to write an entire book (characteristically titled *Madeleine et André Gide*: the very sequence in which the two names are printed restores a hierarchy more in accord with natural justice) to vindicate Madeleine's memory. And the Tiny Lady herself (who would have had reason to feel awkward, if not hostile, towards her) was deeply impressed by her personality. Three years before Madeleine's death, she noted: "Even though she is self-effacing, she cannot remain inconspicuous; there is a superior quality of sensitivity that radiates from her entire person."[163] She never doubted Gide's sincerity when he claimed that Madeleine was the only person he had ever really loved, and she clearly analysed what her death meant for him—a disintegration of his own life: "He has been hit in the most vulnerable part of his heart. The principal character in the play of his life is no more. He has lost his counterpart, the fixed measure with which he confronted his actions, his true tenderness, his great fidelity; in his inner dialogue, the other voice has fallen silent."[164] Her comments echoed Gide's own confession: "Since she is no more, I am merely pretending I am still alive, but I have lost interest in all things, myself included; I have no appetite, no taste, no curiosity, no desire; I am in a disenchanted world, and my only hope is to leave it soon."[165]

Madeleine's intelligence matched her sensitivity; she was highly cultured and possessed sound literary judgement. For instance, though she admired Gide's works, her admiration was never blind; whereas Gide greatly valued his own poetry, she told him with frank accuracy that it was embarrassingly mediocre. She wrote well: her letters and diary fragments (quoted at length by Schlumberger) are impressive, both for the natural elegance of their style and for the lucidity of her psychological perceptions.

Gide's personal predicament sprang from the radical divorce that, in him, separated love from sensual desire. For him, these two emotions were mutually exclusive—he could not desire whom he loved, he could not love whom he desired. Madeleine must have confusedly sensed this from the beginning (after all, in his *Cahiers d'André Walter*, Gide had confessed, "I do not desire you. Your body embarrasses me, and carnal possession appals me"[166]). She originally rejected his first offers of marriage and yielded only at long last, under the pressure of his unrelenting entreaties. She had suffered a psychological trauma in her childhood: she had witnessed the infidelity of her mother and, as a result, sex inspired in her instinctive fear and revulsion. Thus, the prospect of entering with her cousin André into that pure union of souls which had enchanted their adolescent years could appear genuinely attractive.

Gide, on his side, had started his conjugal life in a state of ignorance; later he would bring to it his inexhaustible resources of self-deception. After twenty-five years of marriage, he earnestly expounded to Martin du Gard his theory that homosexuals make the best husbands:

> The love I have for my wife is like no other; and I believe that only a homosexual can give a creature that total love, divested of all physical desire, of all trouble of the flesh: an integral love, in all its limitless purity. When I compared my marriage to the wretched, discordant marriages of those around me, I thought myself privileged: I thought I had built the very temple of love.[167]

It was only after Madeleine's death that he eventually woke up—to some extent—to what had been her grim fate:

> I am now astonished at the aberration that led me to believe that the more ethereal my love, the more worthy it was of her; and in my naïveté I never asked whether she would be content with so disembodied a love. So, the fact that my carnal desires were directed towards other objects hardly concerned me. I even arrived at the comfortable conviction that things were better thus. Desires, I thought, were peculiar to men; I found it reassuring to believe that women—except "loose women," of

course—did not have similar desires...What I fear she could not understand was that it was precisely the spiritual power of my love that inhibited any carnal desire. For I was able, elsewhere, to prove that I was not incapable of making love to a woman, providing nothing intellectual or emotional came into it...It was only later that I began to realise how cruelly I must have hurt the woman for whom I was ready to give my life...In fact, I could only develop as an individual by hurting her.[168]

When she entered into the marriage, Madeleine was innocent but not blind. Her intuition made her aware very soon of the peculiar nature of Gide's sexual compulsions. According to Gide himself, the discovery was completed for her during their honeymoon in North Africa. During a railway journey, she witnessed his furtive and frantic attempts to caress some half-naked boys who were on the train, and that same night she told him, not with reproach, but in anxious sorrow: "You looked like a criminal, or a madman."[169]

A pattern of separate lives progressively developed between husband and wife. Their intimacy was maintained through the constant flow of loving letters which Gide kept writing to her while they were apart—which was most of the time. Gide pursued his life of freedom with his friends in Paris and abroad; Madeleine withdrew alone to Cuverville, their country estate in Normandy. Gide came for occasional visits; they would again share their old enjoyment of literature and, as in the past, they would spend their evenings reading aloud to each other their favourite authors. Madeleine's only request was that Gide, while in the country, refrain from preying upon neighbouring children, so as to avoid any scandal. ("Do it elsewhere if you must, but not in Cuverville. Here at least, spare me this shame."[170]) Gide promised, but found the constraint unbearable. He often complained in his diary of the "suffocating" atmosphere of Cuverville, and "the bad sexual hygiene" from which he had to suffer there; he thought that this repression of his sensual impulses severely hindered the inspiration for his literary work. Often, he would furtively break the rules—or advance the date of his departure, and escape back to Paris.

Then came the only tragedy of Gide's entire life. He fell in love with

a sixteen-year-old adolescent, Marc Allégret. Marc's father was a Protestant pastor who, in his missionary zeal to evangelise French Africa,
neglected to look after his own family—or rather, worse than neglect-
ing it, whenever he was away and busily engaged in converting the hea-
then, the pious fool could think of nothing better than to entrust the
care of his five sons to Gide, an old friend of the family, who diligently
undertook to debauch as many of them as he could lay his hands on.
(I am not competent to adjudicate on the vexed issue of priestly celi-
bacy; I only feel that the one major objection one can make to a married clergy is that it is too cruel and unfair to their children.)

With Marc Allégret, Gide experienced for the first time—at the
age of forty-nine!—the ecstasy and the agony of being totally in love
with another human being. He discovered passion, he discovered jealousy. Desire merged with love—it had never happened to him before.
And even, many years later, after the great fires of passion had burned
themselves out, the relationship with Allégret retained a sort of warm
glow that was to last until Gide's death. Marc was not a homosexual
—Gide actually seduced him with a promise to procure him his first
mistress ("Uncle André" delivered the goods: he introduced Marc to
the daughter of the Tiny Lady, Elisabeth). He turned into a very active
womaniser and eventually made his career (financed at first by Gide
himself) in film-making. His works proved to be rather facile and
shallow; but later on, he was followed on the same path by his younger
brother, Yves Allégret, whose films have better stood the test of time.

In 1918, Gide decided, against Madeleine's most earnest entreaties
(she had guessed the entire situation, and her personal distress was
compounded by her realisation that Gide was leading the adolescent
astray, while betraying the naïve trust of the father), to take Marc with
him on a long visit to England. On his return, however, his life
changed forever—though he did not realise this immediately. One
day, some time later, he asked Madeleine to lend him his old letters,
just to check some information, and she told him that these letters—
his very best writing, their common treasure!—existed no more: she
had burned them all during his recent absence. Gide was so stunned
by the news that he thought he would die. As he was to recall later:
"Those letters were the most precious achievement of my life, the best

of me ... Suddenly there was nothing! I had been stripped of every-thing! Ah, I can imagine what a father might feel on arriving home and being told by his wife, 'Our child is dead, I have killed him!'"[171] Madeleine said: "If I were a Catholic, I'd enter a convent ... I was suf-fering too much ... I had to do something ... I re-read all those letters beforehand. They were the most precious thing I had."[172] In the mem-oir he published after his wife's death, Gide returned to this episode:

> For a whole week, I wept; I wept from morning till evening... I wept without stopping, without trying to say anything to her other than my tears, and always waiting for a word, a gesture from her ... But she continued to busy herself with petty house-hold chores, as if nothing had happened, passing to and fro, indifferent to my presence, as if she did not even notice that I was there. I hoped that the constancy of my pain would tri-umph over that apparent insensitivity, but no; and she doubt-less hoped that my despair would bring me back to God, for she admitted no other outcome ... And the more I cried, the more we became mutually estranged; I felt this bitterly; and soon it was no more on my lost letters that I was crying, but upon us, upon her, upon our love. I felt that I had lost her. Everything was crumbling within myself: past, present—our very future.[173]

Madeleine knew of Gide's pedophilia; it scared her, it hurt her—but it had not affected her feelings for him. After all, an intelligent and virtuous woman may continue to love her husband even after she discovers that he is an alcoholic, or a kleptomaniac, or a drug addict. With his passion for Marc Allégret, however, Gide had betrayed her—he had killed their love.

Eventually, the couple's old way of life resumed its original course —at least in its outward appearances. Yet Madeleine renounced all her earlier enjoyment of culture and literature, devoting herself en-tirely to numbing household chores and charitable work among the local poor. She came close to converting to Catholicism; but finally she did not make the move, as she probably feared that her husband might misinterpret this as a further break away from him.

The very heart of their union had died. Martin du Gard, who was their guest for some days, left this description:

> Their behaviour with one another is odd; it is a sort of caring politeness, a mixture of spontaneity and formality; an eager exchange of courtesies—there is tenderness in the way they look at each other and chat together, and simultaneously, at the very bottom of it all, there is an impenetrable cold—something like the low temperatures of the deep; it is not only the conjugal intimacy that is missing here, but even the simple sort of familiarity one would find between two friends, or even between two people travelling together. Their mutual love is obvious, but it is sublimated, devoid of communion. It is the love of two strangers who are never sure they really understand each other, nor really know each other, and who, deep in their secret hearts, do not have the slightest communication.[174]

A few weeks after Madeleine's death in 1938, Gide visited Martin, who wrote in his diary:

> [He told me that] this was the first real grief in his life. He spoke to me about her, at great length, of their past together, distant and recent. It is with me, he said, that he feels the freest to confide, and I believe this to be true ... But I was amazed to observe that his sorrow is not compounded with any sense of guilt. Not the slightest expression of remorse. In fact, he does not feel at all at fault, nor in the least responsible for her sacrificed existence. He merely thinks: I was such, she was such; hence, great sufferings for both of us—it could not have been otherwise.[175]

PROTEUS

In Homer's *Odyssey* (IV, 351), Proteus is a minor god who possesses vast knowledge and is able to adopt diverse forms in order to elude questions. The only way to force him to answer is to pin him down firmly until he resumes his original shape.

Gide often referred to the figure of Proteus, not without a degree of self-consciousness; one of the most characteristic passages is found in his draft for a preface to his play *Saül*: "Because of his multi-faced inconsistency, Proteus is, among all the gods, the one who has least existence. Before he chooses, an individual is richer; after he chooses, he is stronger."[176]

REALITY

In a long passage of his *Journal*, Gide developed an intriguing observation: "What is lacking in me, I think, is a certain sense of reality." He gave various illustrations of this; for instance, the difficulty he had in recognising people:

> It is not that I lack attention or interest . . . but even though I am extremely sensitive to the outside world, I can never fully believe in its reality. . . The real world always remains somewhat fantastic for me . . . I have no feeling of its reality.[177]

The material circumstances of his life certainly contributed to his abiding sense of unreality. In 1935, under the influence of his short-lived and sentimental conversion to Marxism, he had a sudden illumination and realised for the first time—at the age of sixty-seven!—that he had never known what it meant to have to work for a living. He noted in his *Journal*: "I experience today—earnestly, acutely—this *inferiority*: I have never had to earn my own bread."[178] But this belated discovery does not seem to have occupied his mind for very long: he made no further mention of it.

His attitude towards money could provide another example of his uncertain perception of the practical world. His stinginess was notorious—there are countless anecdotes that document his odd obsession with economy—but there is equally abundant evidence of his extravagant generosity. So, on balance, was he profligate or miserly? The mass of contradictory information on this subject suggests one conclusion: he simply had no concept of money—for him, money had no reality.

It is not rare for creative artists to have only a limited grasp of the trivialities of practical life; often, this very infirmity is the price they pay to be able to concentrate on their art. Yet such a disposition is certainly not conducive to shrewd political judgement, and scarcely qualifies aloof poets or imaginative authors to pronounce with authority upon all the major issues of the day. Gide not only took pride in the fact that he did not read the newspapers—hence, his famous utterance, "I call *journalism* whatever will present tomorrow less interest than it does today"[179]—but he sternly upbraided his friends for wasting their time on such a futile activity. Take this typical dialogue, as recorded by the Tiny Lady:

> *Gide*: You read too many modern things, things without any value; you should discipline yourself, and read every day some pages by a great classic: Montaigne, Goethe, La Bruyère, any one of them. It would enable you to distance yourself from daily events, from transitory facts, it would enlarge your perspective ...
>
> *Martin*: Yes, I often tried, but this ... does not provide me with material for observation and for notation, as much as modern information does.
>
> *Gide*: Yes, right, I see: you are unable to actualise the ideas of the great authors of the past; for you, their thoughts remain remote; with me, the reverse is true. If after having swallowed the prose of the daily paper, I open again my Diderot, it is the latter that I find timely."[180]

There is, of course, much value in Gide's advice; nevertheless, it should be remarked that, on all the momentous issues of their eventful times, it was Martin, simply equipped with his common sense and information drawn from the daily papers, who proved unfailingly capable of understanding the sort of world they were living in, whereas Gide allowed himself, with reckless naïveté, to be abominably deceived and manipulated by the criminal impostors of politics.

The most notorious episode was his foolish flirtation with Stalinist communism during the 1930s.[181] His political conversion was built upon the flimsiest foundations: for a while he carried Marx's *Capital* in his pocket. (He took the first four volumes on one of his sex-tours to Morocco, proclaiming: "I am plunging into them with the greatest interest"—but it seems he never finished the first volume.) When, in 1931, he began to talk about the Soviet Five-Year Plan "with great enthusiasm," Schlumberger remarked dryly: "But you seem to have suddenly discovered things that have occupied people's minds for a long time now." On homosexuality (which always remained his primary concern), he immediately assumed (without the slightest shred of evidence) that "Soviet law not only should be liberal, but even that it would probably encourage it, in order to foster virile emulation, as was done in ancient Sparta."[182] He wished the USSR would translate *Corydon*: "It seems to me to have been written for them." As late as 1936, after having been confronted with painful evidence of Soviet intolerance on this issue, "he told a half-astounded, half-amused Ilya Ehrenburg that he intended to speak to Stalin about the legal position of homosexuals in the Soviet Union." Whenever some specific misgivings would occasionally creep into his mind, Stalin soon provided the solution: "I read with the greatest interest Stalin's new speech, which exactly answers my objections and fears"; or again, "Stalin's last speech, enthralling in its lucidity and good faith, has satisfactorily addressed my very question." The problem of Trotsky, however, did slightly disturb him for a short while; and he reflected with disarming candour, "I don't really know what to think. It was so restful to fully approve of something."

From the beginning, Schlumberger marvelled that "without having had any sort of prior information on the subject, he had a sudden illumination just after reading one or two books on the Five-Year Plan. The lack of nuances, of scepticism, with which he rushes enthusiastically in this new direction confirms once again that, at heart, he is still a perpetual adolescent. Yet, for a man of sixty-one, who had previously displayed so much critical acumen, this sort of primitive fervour is rather embarrassing."[183]

Shortly after Gide's spectacular disenchantment with communism and the extraordinary success of his book *Retour de l'URSS*, Martin du Gard re-read the book. He was not favourably impressed and noted in his own *Journal*:

> In the end, what sort of contribution does this book offer? One more description of the non-existence of free speech and free thought in Russia. We already knew all that without having had to go there. And these things have already been said a hundred times, with more solid arguments and stronger documentation. Wonderful innocence! Which makes me love him even more—but this is not reason enough to extol his book...Its only value is that it provides further confirmation of his good faith. But this is a consideration that can only concern his admirers and his friends. Otherwise, this book will do him no good. Not immediately, perhaps, but later on.[184]

Gide's second great historical test came with the Nazi invasion of France. This time, luckily for him, his performance was not displayed to the public: the vigilant concern of his entourage ensured that his dismal vacillations remained strictly private. But his good friends had ample cause for concern, as indicated in the daily records of the Tiny Lady. For instance, in October 1940, having taken refuge in the South of France, he began to toy with the idea of returning to occupied Paris, to resume the activities of the *Nouvelle Revue Française*; a young German officer had written him a nice letter, leading him to believe that he would be ideally qualified to negotiate with the German authorities! The Tiny Lady had to warn him against the imprudence of such a plan.[185]

After the Pétain–Hitler meeting that paved the way for French collaboration with the Nazis, the Tiny Lady was flabbergasted by Gide's attitude: "It is strange that, on this issue, his reactions remain weak and uncertain. He spontaneously inclines towards this type of view: 'Anyway, since we have lost, why resist?'"[186]

In November 1940, Gide told her that he had "read with tremendous interest a page by Renan: 'World government, should it ever take place, would probably suit best the German genius'—and he went on:

'Naturally I wholeheartedly wish for a British victory—I cannot do otherwise—and yet, at times, I cannot help thinking that this may not be the best way out of the predicament the world is now facing. Who knows? We are perhaps not being fair to Hitler when we refuse to believe that his ultimate dream could be world harmony.'"[187]

In 1941, the indecisiveness, volatility and confusion of his political opinions caused Martin du Gard increasing concern: "Our old friend is less and less capable of steering his own boat. I have the feeling that he has lost his compass and allows the stronger winds to determine his course. There is an element of senile childishness in his attitude."[188]

In the end, his salvation came by pure accident. In 1942, he went to North Africa on a visit, but the military operations there left him stranded on the other side of the Mediterranean for the remainder of the war—safely out of political trouble. He made only one feeble attempt at commenting on current affairs, in an article published after the liberation of Paris. It did not have any impact, but Schlumberger read it with consternation: "It is full of worn-out clichés and reflects the naïveté of a man completely out of touch with the movement of ideas. He even has one unfortunate phrase on 'the immense and glorious Russia,' as if he were trying to forget his *Retour de l'URSS*."[189]

In 1950, "the senile childishness" which Martin had already detected ten years earlier grew to disturbing proportions. One day, for instance, he agreed on the telephone to sign a manifesto—without knowing what the issue was (it concerned the admission of communist China into the United Nations). He cried out to his friends: "I understand absolutely nothing, I have no idea what the matter in question was!" The Tiny Lady concluded with despair: "This small anecdote is typical of his behaviour: ever more vague, unjustifiable, changing, illogical; he was already like that in the small things of life; what would you expect him to do now regarding the fate of Europe!"[190]

His friends loved him dearly; nevertheless, when he finally died, they breathed a sigh of relief. "He was less and less able to control his own actions; we were living in permanent fear of what the next day would bring. His exemplary death (honestly prepared for, but helped by a set of favourable circumstances) provided a majestic cover-up for everything. It came not a minute too soon!"[191]

SEXUALITY

Gide repeatedly confessed his puzzlement: "I shall die without having understood anything—or so little—of the physiology of my own body." Or again: "I grow old without any hope of ever knowing my own body."[192] One day, he explained to Martin du Gard with detached objectivity the physiological details of his sexuality.[193] In his own opinion, his condition was abnormal: "a physiological paradox," "a pathological case."

Yet, another time, he also confided to Martin his indignation and sorrow at often being accused of corrupting the young: "How unfair! How could it be perverse to initiate young people into sensual pleasure?" And he explained at great length that his role was always, first and foremost, that of a patient educator: "Nothing, during the troubled years of adolescence, can replace the beneficial influence of a liaison—sensual, intellectual and moral—with an elderly guide, worthy of trust and love."[194] This is the theme he had developed in *Corydon*, but it had limited relevance to his own practices, for, in fact, what he called his "adventures" usually involved children, street kids, hotel grooms, little Arab beggars, diverse defenceless little wretches, furtively, in conditions that certainly left neither time nor space for any form of enlightened communication. The Tiny Lady observed: "One could not emphasise enough how odd his temperament is. His sensuality is so deep, so demanding, so tyrannical, ruling an entire part of his life—and yet it reaches its fulfilment so easily, so lightly, so quickly… It is bizarre to the point of defying belief. Seeing how devious he can be in order to attain the object of his desire, people naturally misjudge him, and they assume that he must be depraved in that same proportion. On the other hand, one can easily imagine what sort of fallacious pretexts he has to invent in order to justify his insinuating and hypocritical manoeuvres, when one considers how incredibly harmless are the actual activities in which they eventuate. It seems to me that these particular sexual dispositions are an important key for understanding Gide."[195]

Eventually, the way in which he became a slave to his mania distressed even the friends who had originally shared his inclinations.

Schlumberger concluded: "During his life, Gide's concern was to win respect for homosexuals; yet, because of his particular obsessions, in the end, he succeeded only in bringing discredit to their cause."[196]

Still, any person who happens to believe in the Christian faith that was originally Gide's would be ill-qualified to censure his infirmities; for the fact is that we all belong to a fallen species; to varying degrees, innocence escapes us; one way or the other, we are all cripples. In Gide's case, the contrast—extreme and tragic—between, on the one hand, the splendour of his intelligence and culture, the nobility of a mind open to all humanistic endeavours, and on the other, the grotesque and gruesome tyranny of his obsessions, is heart-breaking and should inspire compassion.

Yet, how can compassion be extended when its very need is being strenuously denied? For, after all, the real problem did not lie in Gide's sexuality but in his tortuous relation to truth.*[197]

THE TINY LADY, MARIA VAN RYSSELBERGHE (1867–1959)

As her familiar nickname indicates, "la Petite Dame" was of diminutive stature. Her various portraits—painted by her husband, Théo Van Rysselberghe (1862–1926), and by another Belgian artist, Fernand Khnopff (1851–1921)—all reflect her vivacious and bewitching grace. Born and educated in Belgium like Théo himself, she followed him to France, where they settled in 1898. Théo, who had shown great talent at the beginning of his career, working in a free and robust style very similar to that of his schoolmate, James Ensor, eventually fell under the influence of Seurat and Signac; his art turned into a dogmatic and dreary application of the Pointillist formula and, unfortunately, did not live up to its earlier promise.

Théo loved his wife, but he seems to have been somewhat bewildered by her liberated behaviour. Maria had genuine affection for her husband; she considered him a good companion, but her own sentimental life developed in tranquil breach of all conventions. She refused to conform both to bourgeois order and to Bohemian disorder.

In 1896, she fell madly in love—for one season—with the great poet

Verhaeren. This intense passion—which was reciprocated, but never consummated—was transposed by her, forty years later, into a short memoir, which is a pure and haunting masterpiece of narrative prose (*Il y a quarante ans*). Later on, she also had a liaison with the wife of a wealthy industrialist from Luxemburg; it was originally for the private enjoyment of her female friend that she began to write the chronicle of her years with Gide.

She first met Gide (who was a friend of Théo) at the end of the nineteenth century. As she was to recall: "He was then around the age of thirty...He was exceptionally attractive, his charm was overwhelming; most of all he had a deep originality: on no subject did he ever think like anyone else, not out of a taste for paradox, but simply because his vision was naturally new."[198]

Over the years, Maria and Gide developed for one another an attachment that was singularly harmonious; their personalities were utterly dissimilar, but they shared the same passion for culture, the same hunger for books and ideas. Their odd intimacy was further strengthened when Maria—through her daughter Elisabeth—became the grandmother of Gide's daughter,* to the distress of poor Théo, who had only a dim awareness of who the father of his daughter's child might actually be.

Shortly after Théo's death, Maria and Gide made arrangements that enabled them to spend the rest of their lives not exactly together, but side by side. They eventually moved into twin apartments, enjoying each other's company, while retaining their parallel freedoms. This situation was to last until Gide's death.

Their relations were a curious mixture of formality and closeness. For instance, Maria noted, seven years after they had settled into their joined existences: "Gide addressed me as 'old chap' [*mon vieux*]; it is the first time that such a thing has happened to him. He apologised at once."[199] But in the end they became very much like many old couples: indestructibly linked by a long habit, made of deep affection—and of many small irritations.

Together with Martin du Gard and Herbart, the Tiny Lady formed the triumvirate that endeavoured to steer with vigilant solicitude Gide's erratic course in his later years. As she was closest to him, she played the most important role. Her intelligence, culture and sound critical judgement had turned her into an invaluable reader and literary adviser for Gide. Besides, her feminine common sense and *sang-froid* made her indispensable in the handling and resolution of all the practical problems of everyday life—at which Gide was uniformly inept. And she even, in the final years, performed for him—with the cool detachment of a professional nurse—some services of a more intimate nature, "when no Annamite young boy could be found in the street."[200]

Her privileged position as Gide's companion put her at the very centre of the literary life of her time. Yet she always preserved her privacy. She wrote well, but she published only one small book, under the impenetrable and sexless pen-name of M. Saint-Clair, the key of which was known only to half a dozen old friends. Her great task—keeping a record of Gide's daily life and fire-side conversation—was pursued in secrecy, with only one private reader in mind, and its publication was posthumous. Her *Cahiers de la Petite Dame* is truly unique—both familiar in its perspective, and monumental in its scope. There are very few great writers about whom we possess such vivid, detailed and perceptive information. Unlike Eckermann, who was excessively in awe of Goethe and inhibited by a humourless awareness of his own humility, and unlike Boswell, who, after all, was only able to spend a rather limited time in Johnson's company, she witnessed the private life of Gide over thirty years, and although she admired him and believed in his genius, her intelligence and wit could easily match his, and being a couple of years his senior, she treated him as her equal. She observed him with inexhaustible interest—and perhaps also with a sort of detached and undemanding love; yet she always remained clear-sighted in the face of his foibles, his evasions, his manias and his self-deceptions. Her record was thorough and honest, frank yet discreet; as she explained to Schlumberger, "she never modified any of the things she knew, but there were things which she chose not to know."[201] After the death of Gide, concluding her great chronicle, she simply reflected: "How beautiful it was to live at his side! ... I am parting from us with pain, and my soul thanks his memory."[202]

But what is most remarkable for such a strong personality and articulate diarist is that she succeeded in erasing virtually all traces of her own passage through life. In this sense, in her very invisibility, she achieved a superior form of liberty. Unlike Gide, she carried no psychological traumas from childhood, no hangovers from traditional morality; she did not harbour the slightest concern for fame, she did not wish to project any image, she was indifferent to public opinion and to posterity. Béatrix Beck was right: in her very freedom, she was much more Gidean than Gide himself.[203]

TRUTH

Sheridan observed that "the heritage of Gide's Protestantism was that he hated lies ... His cult of sincerity was untypically French, undoubtedly inherited from his Huguenot forebears."[204]

Gide loved truth from his early years. He eventually abandoned the faith of his childhood (a forsaking that was not achieved without painful and dramatic turns), but he retained until death a passionate need for self-justification.

"Lying" haunted his imagination as a worthy topic for tragedy. He explained to Schlumberger: "Believe me, nothing can be as dramatic as the destruction of a mind through lying—be it self-deception or hypocrisy... If I were still in the habit of praying, I would pray without ceasing: My God, preserve me from lying!"[205] Some of the characters in his fiction were odious to him, but he knew them from the inside, and he painted them with such understanding that—to his dismay—many critics interpreted them as projections of himself. Thus Gide commented on Edouard—a character in *Les Faux-monnayeurs*, often seen as a mouthpiece for the author: "He is the archetype of the impotent, both as a writer and as a lover... He constantly lies to himself in his *Journal*, like the pastor in *La Symphonie Pastorale*. It is the same problem ... What fascinates me above all else is this self-deception."[206]

Once, his friend the philosopher Groethuysen was talking to him about the psychology of "the ambiguous person" (*l'être louche*), whom he defined as "a man who never manages to transform lies into his own truth, and who constantly shifts his stand." Gide replied: "It would be fun to create such a character, but if I were to write it, people would once again say that I was painting my own portrait."[207]

From his own direct observation, Herbart concluded: "For Gide, lies are as attractive as the truth."[208] With more subtlety, the Tiny Lady pinpointed the invisible confusion that enabled Gide to reconcile the two at the end of his life: "His commitment to sincerity is stronger than ever, but sincerity does not necessarily coincide with truth."[209]

The queasiness (so hard to describe, yet so intensely felt) that readers as different as Flannery O'Connor and Julien Green experienced when confronted with Gide is obviously related to a deeper issue (in neither case was it a question of being shocked by his sexual proclivities: Green himself was homosexual, and O'Connor was shock-proof). Saint Augustine—probably the very first modern psychologist—identified it 1,600 years ago:

> People have such a love for truth that when they happen to love something else, they want it to be the truth; and because they do not wish to be proven wrong, they refuse to be shown their mistake. And so, they end up hating the truth for the sake of the object which they have come to love instead of the truth.[210]

MALRAUX

MALRAUX IN THE PANTHEON[1]

THIS STORY is somewhat stale, I am afraid, but it still has a point. In a crowded church, the preacher ascends the pulpit and pronounces a moving sermon. Everybody is crying. One man, however, remains dry-eyed. Being asked the reason for his strange insensitivity, he explains: "I am not from this parish."

I am not French, but French is my mother language and when I am in France I always feel completely at home—with only one reservation. Whenever the issue of Malraux crops up, the evidence hits me: I am not from this parish.

I experienced it for the first time twenty years ago. In November 1976, when Malraux died, a weekly magazine in Paris invited me to write one page on the theme "What did Malraux represent for you?" I always believed that death is not an excuse for withholding judgement; I naïvely assumed that the editors expected me to express a sincere opinion—and this is precisely what I offered them. They were horrified and immediately junked my shocking contribution. And yet, in my innocence, all I had done was simply to repeat what was already obvious to many discriminating foreign critics, from Koestler to Nabokov: Malraux was essentially phony.

For instance, on the tragedy of the Chinese revolution, instead of wasting time with the artificiality of *La Condition humaine*, one should read the account of Harold Isaacs: at least he knew what he was writing about. (The first edition of *The Tragedy of the Chinese Revolution* appeared in 1938, but it took another thirty years before a French translation was finally published ...)[2]

In those early days, Malraux, who only spent a few days in China as a mere tourist in transit, pretended to the French public that he had been a people's commissar in the Chinese revolution. Later on, the epilogue of his Chinese adventures—his famous interview with Mao Zedong in 1965—proved to be an equally brazen humbug. A French sinologist recently made a comparative study of Malraux's own description of this episode (in his *Antimémoires*) and of two other contemporary accounts of the interview in question—one in Chinese (notes taken by Mao's interpreter, subsequently leaked to the Red Guards and published in China during the "Cultural Revolution"), and the other in French (compiled by the French embassy in Peking).[3] The comparison revealed that the three-hour cosmic dialogue between two philosophico-revolutionary megastars of our century had in fact been limited to a routine exchange of diplomatic platitudes that barely lasted thirty minutes. At one point in this brief and otherwise banal interview, however, Mao, who was already stewing up his forthcoming "Cultural Revolution," dropped a tantalising hint, indicating that writers and intellectuals were deeply corrupted by "revisionism," but that the youth might be mobilised against this counter-revolutionary evil. This, in a nutshell, was already a first suggestion of the gigantic explosion that was to shatter China the following year. Any interlocutor with some sense and a modicum of information would have recognised the true significance of this opportunity, jumped upon this unexpected opening and eagerly pursued the issue, but Malraux blindly ignored the cue that had just been offered him; and Mao, who by then could hardly conceal his impatience, brought the audience to an abrupt conclusion.

On the Spanish Civil War, who, after having read Orwell, could still take seriously Malraux's histrionic amphigory? Next to the stark truth of *Homage to Catalonia*, the misty and flatulent speeches of *L'Espoir* have a hollow ring of café eloquence. As to the *Musée imaginaire*—a shrewd imitation of the work of the art critic and historian Élie Faure (whose name Malraux always took great care never to mention)—Georges Duthuit demonstrated long ago in his ferocious and scholarly *Musée inimaginable* (in three volumes) that Malraux's foray into art history had probably been his boldest work of fiction.[4]

In his old age, Malraux confided to Bruce Chatwin (another seductive mythmaker—a lesser prophet perhaps, but a better writer): "In France, intellectuals are usually incapable of opening an umbrella."[5] If this observation is true, it may well explain the puzzling and enduring prestige that Malraux always commanded among these same intellectuals: people who are too clumsy to handle their own umbrellas must naturally look with awe at a man who can fire machine-guns, drive tanks and pilot aeroplanes. (In actual fact, though Malraux organised an air squadron in the Spanish war, and styled himself a colonel when he led an armoured brigade of French partisans at the end of the Second World War, his only experience of aeroplanes was that of a passenger; and he never even learned to drive a car—which I find quite endearing, actually, but then, I myself often find it difficult to open my umbrella.)

Once you discard the heroic and colourful paraphernalia of the warrior and the adventurer, and confine your scrutiny to the more austere field of literature and criticism, where stage props and other gimmicks are of little support—in the end, what remains of Malraux's self-built legend?

Nabokov, who considered Malraux "quite a third-rate writer" and was puzzled by Edmund Wilson's professed admiration for him ("I am at a loss to understand your liking Malraux's books—or are you just kidding me?") commented on *La Condition humaine*: "From childhood, I remember a golden inscription that fascinated me: *Compagnie Internationale des Wagons-lits et des Grands Express Européens*. Malraux's work belongs to the *Compagnie Internationale des Grands Clichés*." And then he pursued and produced a hilarious list of rhetorical questions, asking Wilson to tell him, for instance, "What is this 'great silence of the Chinese night'? Try and substitute 'the American night,' 'the Belgian night' etc., and see what happens..."[6]

Even in France there were a number of connoisseurs who privately expressed similar reservations. Sartre detected the trouble quite early: "Yes, Malraux has got a style—but it is not a good one." In a letter to Simone de Beauvoir, he confessed: "*La Condition humaine* is plagued, by turns, with ridiculous passages and with deadly boring pages." Exactly like Nabokov, he found Malraux's narrative technique old-fashioned and dismally reminiscent of the worst Soviet fiction. As to *Le Temps du mépris*, he simply considered it "deeply abject." (Nabokov called it "one solid mass of clichés.") Plodding through *L'Espoir*, Sartre added: "I am dragging myself through this book which may be full of ideas, but it is so boring! This chap seems to be lacking a little something, but, good God! he is lacking it badly!"[7]

The novelist and essayist Jacques Chardonne, who had questionable views in some other matters but who unquestionably knew about the subtle art of writing French prose, identified the root of the problem of Malraux's mumbo-jumbo (his "*galimatias*"): "I have attempted to read Malraux, and I became angry. I am not going to do his work for him. Let him first sort out his own ideas. Once he finds out what he is actually thinking, he will become able to express it better and quicker."[8]

An ancient Greek philosopher remarked that if horses had gods, these gods would look like horses. Every society puts in its pantheon the icons it deserves and in which it can recognise its own features. Our age has proved so far to be the age of Sham and Amnesia. But at this point you may suspect that the acrimony with which I have deplored Malraux's entry into the Pantheon in Paris conceals some grudge—well, you would have guessed right.

What irks me is this: in 1935, Boris Souvarine, a former secretary of the Third International who had escaped from Moscow back to Paris, wrote the first documented analysis of Stalin's murderous political career. This monumental and courageous work remains to this day a landmark in the unmasking of Stalinist crimes. The book was reissued in 1977, not long before Souvarine's death. In the foreword which he wrote for this new edition, Souvarine recalled the vile and sinister obstacles he had to overcome when, forty years earlier, he first attempted to publish his historical masterpiece in Paris. At the time, the leading figures of the French intelligentsia avoided him as if he had the plague. Malraux, who could have had the book published by Gallimard, flatly refused to support it; but at least he was straightforward and said: "Souvarine, I believe that you and your friends are right. However, at this stage, do not count on me to support you. I shall be on your side when you make it to the top." (*Je serai avec vous quand vous serez les plus forts.*)[9]

And yet...

Einstein (who ought to know something on this subject) once observed that good ideas are rare. It seems to me that Malraux hit upon *two* important truths—which, after all, still represents a respectable record, well above the average that can be expected from most literary men.

1. Malraux, who worshipped T. E. Lawrence and dreamed all his life of imitating him, perceived accurately what made this ambiguous hero truly inimitable. He confided to Roger Stéphane: "In reality, Lawrence desired nothing at all. *It is prodigiously hard to be a man who wants nothing.*"[10]

2. On the very first page of his *Antimémoires*, he noted one simple reflection that should stand forever as a glorious counterweight to all the heavy and endless trains of the *Compagnie Internationale des Grands Clichés*. When he asked an old priest what he had learned about human nature after having spent a lifetime hearing people's confessions, the man replied: "Fundamentally, *there are no grown-ups.*"

CURTIS CATE'S BIOGRAPHY OF MALRAUX[11]

Tristan Bernard said that he never read the books he was supposed to review: he was afraid he might become biased. He certainly had a point: the acquisition of knowledge can needlessly complicate many enterprises.

After reading Curtis Cate's biography of Malraux—a remarkable work, well-researched, perceptive and informative—I realised that, in what I had just written, I had overlooked one aspect of our subject.

The simple fact is: Malraux was obviously a genius. What exactly he was a genius at, however, is not quite clear.

Nearly all those who came in direct contact with him fell under his spell—and I am not talking here of naïve schoolboys but of famous writers, some of whom were twice his age, as well as eminent thinkers, statesmen, leaders of men, saintly monks, cunning old politicians, glamorous socialites, cynical journalists, unworldly priests. When young, he appeared to them as a prodigy; in middle age, he was their hero; old, he became a prophet. At every stage in his life, he mesmerised and dazzled a vast and diverse audience. The old Trotsky in exile was so impressed after meeting the feverish and voluble young adventurer that he wrote at once to his New York publishers, urging them to bring out an American edition of *La Condition humaine*. André Gide—whom the French literati believed to be the twentieth-century Goethe, and who was thirty years Malraux's senior—was overwhelmed by his conversation and privately complained that he could not keep up with such uninterrupted intellectual fireworks.

Malraux himself had little patience for dull minds: "I do not argue with imbeciles." (Which, by the way, might explain why he was such a bad novelist: what is life, after all, but a long dialogue with imbeciles?) The most intelligent interlocutors, subjected to his rapid-fire monologues in relentless and stupefying bursts, felt like inarticulate fools, and the sharpest wits turned speechless. His rather offensive *machismo* never discouraged bright and talented women from offering him their passionate love. His first wife was a woman of cosmopolitan culture, who supported him intellectually, spiritually and financially. (Malraux quickly managed to gamble and lose her entire fortune on the stock market—and then told her defiantly: "You really don't think I am going to work now?") When she dared to entertain literary ambitions of her own, he warned her: "It is better for you to be my wife than a second-rate writer."

With his fanciful military record, he still succeeded in inspiring the blind loyalty of authentic war heroes. Though singularly devoid of humour, he won the steadfast affection of one of the wittiest women of his time (Louise de Vilmorin). And even General de Gaulle (who appointed him as his Minister for Cultural Affairs) endured his most bizarre and ludicrous initiatives with uncharacteristic patience; his cabinet colleagues were puzzled at first, then concluded philosophically: "Malraux is mad, but he amuses the Général."

His singular magnetism was originally built on impudent lies, then further enriched by a permanent and compulsive mythomania, expressed in an unremitting verbal flow. But in the end, his theatrical performances became convincing and even respectable, for they were sustained by a gallantry that was not counterfeit. When he ventured with his young wife into the Cambodian jungle to dismantle and steal monumental Khmer sculptures, and when he had himself flown over Yemen without maps and without adequate fuel supplies in search of the mythical capital of the Queen of Sheba, he was engaging in questionable or hare-brained enterprises, but these also demanded considerable physical courage. He constantly took enormous risks; he led a restless and dramatic life in restless and dramatic times.

———

Today, Malraux's writings are hardly readable *à froid*—they are stilted, pompous, hollow, confused, verbose, obscure. But whenever we encounter the man himself—for instance, in the record of his conversations with Roger Stéphane, his faithful and lively Boswell, or in a good biography such as Cate's—something of his old magic seems to be operating again. Malraux's young and beautiful mistress (whose early death in a horrible accident was to shatter him) was once advised by a well-meaning acquaintance to give up a liaison which could hold no future for the daughter of staid bourgeois. She replied: "I prefer a liaison with a fellow like him to a marriage with a tax collector." Her quixotic choice was to entail much pain and sacrifice, but one can appreciate her wisdom. Malraux could in turns be inspiring and ridiculous, heroic and absurd—he was never mediocre. (And his adventures fired our enthusiasm when we were twenty: if we were to forget this, we would forget the better part of our own youth.)

Cate's account does not pass judgement, but conveys vividly these contradictions, which makes his book fascinating to read. At times, it can be quite funny too—witness this page describing the encounter between Malraux and Hemingway shortly after the liberation of Paris in 1944:

> During his brief visit to Paris, Malraux heard that Ernest Hemingway had arrived with the US Fourth Infantry Division and had flamboyantly "liberated" the Hôtel Ritz. This was too much for Malraux, who decided that he was not going to be upstaged in his home town by the author of *For Whom the Bell*

Tolls. Crossing the Tuileries Gardens, he headed for the Place Vendôme. In his bedroom at the Ritz, Hemingway had just removed his army boots and was busy stripping some weapons with several "bodyguards" (FFI "patriots" he had picked up on his way to the festive capital), when the tall, lean figure of André Malraux appeared in the doorway. He was in uniform, with the five distinctive silver bars of a colonel's rank on his shoulders.

"*Bonjour*, André," said Hemingway, as affably as he could.

"*Bonjour*, Ernest," replied Malraux.

It is not recorded if they shook hands, but since Hemingway's were smeared with oil, it is quite possible that they dispensed with this formality.

"How many men have you commanded?" Malraux asked.

"*Dix ou douze,*" answered Hemingway casually. "*Au plus, deux cents.*" Since he was supposed to be a war correspondent, he could not reasonably boast of having commanded more.

"*Moi, deux mille,*" announced Malraux, whose look of triumph was ruined by a facial tic.

This was an affront Hemingway was not prepared to take lying down, particularly from a Frenchman who had rushed to the support of Republican Spain months before his own tardy appearance on the scene, and whose novel *L'Espoir* had outpaced his *For Whom the Bell Tolls* by several years.

"*Quel dommage!*" said Hemingway with icy sarcasm, "that we didn't have the assistance of your force when we took this small town of Paris!"

If Malraux winced, Hemingway later did not bother to record it. Their conversation, in any case, must have been lacking in cordiality. For we have his word for it—it became one of Ernest's favourite dinner table stories—that one of his bodyguards beckoned Hemingway into the bathroom and asked, "*Papa, on peut fusiller ce con?*"

But didn't Malraux himself warn us? "There are no grown-ups . . ."

THE INTIMATE ORWELL

THE INTIMATE Orwell? For an article dealing with a volume of his diaries and a selection of his letters—*Diaries* (London: Harvill Secker, 2009); *A Life in Letters* (London: Harvill Secker, 2010)—at first such a title seemed appropriate; yet it could also be misleading inasmuch as it might suggest an artificial distinction—or even an opposition—between Eric Blair, the private man, and George Orwell, the published writer. The former, it is true, was a naturally reserved, reticent, even awkward individual, whereas Orwell, with pen (or gun) in hand, was a bold fighter. In fact—and this becomes even more evident after reading these two volumes—Blair's personal life and Orwell's public activity both reflected one powerfully single-minded personality; Blair-Orwell was made of one piece. A recurrent theme in the testimonies of all those who knew him at close hand was his "terrible simplicity"; he had "the innocence of a savage." Contrary to what some commentators had earlier assumed (myself included*), his adoption of a pen-name was a mere accident and never carried for him any particular significance. Simply, at the time of publishing his first book, *Down and Out in Paris and London* (1933), he wished to spare his parents any potential embarrassment: old Mr. and Mrs. Blair belonged to "the lower-upper-middle class" (i.e. "the upper middle class that is short of money") and were painfully concerned with social respectability. They could have been distressed to see it publicised that their only son had led the life of an out-of-work drifter and penniless

---

*See my earlier essay "Orwell, or the Horror of Politics," *Quadrant*, December 1983, reprinted in my collection of essays *The Angel and the Octopus* (Sydney: Duffy & Snellgrove, 1999).

tramp. His pen-name was thus chosen at random, as an after-thought, at the last minute before publication; but afterwards he kept using it for all his publications—journalism, essays, novels—and somehow remained stuck with it. In his private correspondence, till the very end of his life, he still signed his letters now Eric Blair (or Eric), now George Orwell (or George), simply following the form of address originally used by his various correspondents, who were either early acquaintances or later colleagues and friends. His first wife, Eileen (who died prematurely in 1945), and their adopted son, Richard, both took the name Blair; his second wife, Sonia (whom he married virtually on his deathbed), took the name Orwell. Shortly before the end of his life, he himself explained the matter very clearly to his old Eton tutor (who knew him as Blair): "About my name, I have used the name Orwell as a pen-name for a dozen years or more, and most of the people I know call me George, but I have never actually changed my name and some people still call me Blair. It is getting such a nuisance that I keep meaning to change it by deed-poll; but you have to go to a solicitor, etc., which puts me off."

All the diaries of Orwell that are extant (some were lost, and one was stolen during the Spanish Civil War in Barcelona by the Stalinist secret police—it may still lie today in some Moscow archive) were first published in 1998 by Peter Davison and included in his monumental edition of *The Complete Works of George Orwell* (20 volumes: 9,000 pages). They are now conveniently regrouped here in one volume, excellently presented and annotated by Davison. The diaries provide a wealth of information on Orwell's daily activities, concerns and interests; they present considerable documentary value for scholars, but they do not exactly live up to their editor's claim: "These diaries offer a virtual autobiography of Orwell's life and opinions for so much of his life." This assessment—as we shall see in a moment—would much better characterise the utterly fascinating companion volume (also edited by Peter Davison), *George Orwell: A Life in Letters*.

Orwell's diaries are not confessional: here he very seldom records his emotions, impressions, moods or feelings, hardly ever his ideas, judgements and opinions. What he jots down is strictly and dryly factual, events happening in the outside world or in his own little vegetable garden: his goat Muriel's slight diarrhoea may have been caused by eating wet grass; Churchill is returning to cabinet; fighting reported in Manchukuo; rhubarb growing well; Béla Kun reported shot in Moscow; the pansies and red saxifrage are coming into flower; the rat population in Britain is estimated at 4–5 million; in the slang of the East Enders the word *tart* is absolutely interchangeable with *girl* with no implications of "prostitute"—people speak of their daughter or sister as a tart; among the hop-pickers, rhyming slang is not extinct, thus for instance, *a dig in the grave* means *a shave*; (and at the end of July 1940, as the menace of a German invasion becomes very real) "constantly, as I walk down the streets, I find myself looking up at the windows to see which of them would make good machine-gun nests." The state of the weather is recorded daily as well as the count of eggs laid by his hens and the quantity of milk yielded by his goat. To some extent, the diaries could carry as their epigraph Orwell's endearing words, from his 1946 essay "Why I Write": "I am not able, and do not want, completely to abandon the world view that I acquired in childhood. So long as I remain alive and well, I shall continue ... to love the surface of the earth and to take pleasure in solid objects and scraps of useless information."

Very rarely does the diarist formulate a socio-psychological observation—but then it is always strikingly original and perceptive. Thus, for instance, on the sexual life of tramps: "they talk on sexual subjects in a revolting manner. Tramps are disgusting when on this subject because their poverty keeps them off entirely from women, and their minds consequently fester with obscenity. Merely lecherous people are all right, but people who *would like* to be lecherous but don't get the chance, are horribly degraded by it. They remind me of the dogs that hang enviously round while other dogs are copulating." In his enquiry into the condition of workers in Northern England during the Depression, he displays sensitive empathy and a remarkable capacity for *attention* to other people's predicament; thus, for instance, this subtle remark on a specific "discomfort of the working man's life:

waiting about. If you receive a salary it is paid into your bank and you draw it out when you want it. If you receive wages, you have to go and get them on somebody else's time and are probably left hanging about and probably expected to behave as though paying your wages at all was a favour." Then he describes the long wait in the cold, the hassles and expenses of journeys by tram to and from the pay office: "The result of long training in this kind of thing is that whereas the bourgeois goes through life expecting to get what he wants, within limits, the working man always feels himself the slave of a more or less mysterious authority. I was impressed by the fact that when I went to Sheffield Town Hall to ask for certain statistics, both Brown and Searle [his two local miner-friends]—both of them people of much more forcible character than myself—were nervous, would not come into the office with me, and assumed that the town clerk would refuse information. They said, 'He might give it to you, but he wouldn't to us.' Actually the town clerk was snooty and I did not get all the information that I asked for. But the point was that I assumed my question would be answered and the other two assumed the contrary." In turn, these observations develop into broader and bolder considerations:

> It is for this reason that in countries where the class hierarchy exists, people of the higher class always tend to come to the front in times of stress, though not really more gifted than the others. That they will do so is taken more or less for granted always and everywhere. Note the passage in Lissagaray's *History of the Commune* describing the shootings after the [Paris] Commune had been suppressed. They were shooting the ringleaders without trial, and as they did not know who the ringleaders were, they were picking them out on the principle that those of better class than the others would be the ringleaders. One man was shot because he was wearing a watch, another because he "had an intelligent face."

The writing in the diaries is terse, detached and impersonal. I will give just one example—it is typical, as it expresses both the drastic limitations of the form adopted by the diarist as well as some remarkable features of his personality. It is the entry of 19 August 1947, dealing with the Corryvreckan Whirlpool accident: the entire episode is disposed of in eight lines—the style is as matter-of-fact and unemotional as that of a police report. It would be all too easy for the uninformed reader to overlook the whole incident, or at least to fail to grasp its dramatic and near-fatal nature. On that day, Orwell, his three-year-old son, his nephew and niece (respectively twenty and sixteen) all escaped near-certain death by drowning in the most terrifying circumstances. Yet to gauge the gravity of the episode (which was reported at the time in the Glasgow press) one must read the full account by Orwell's nephew (in *Orwell Remembered*, eds A. Coppard and B. Crick, London: BBC Books, 1984, and quoted in large part by B. Crick in *George Orwell: A Life*, London: Secker & Warburg, 1980).

On the island of Jura (Hebrides), in the solitary Spartan and beloved Scottish hermitage where, in the final years of his life, Orwell spent most of his time—at least when he was not in hospital, for his failing health had already reduced him to semi-invalidity—he used a small rowing boat equipped with an outboard engine both for fishing (his great passion) and for short coastal excursions. Returning from one of those excursions with his little son, nephew and niece, he had to cross the notorious Corryvreckan Whirlpool—one of the most dangerous whirlpools in all British waters. Normally, the crossing can be safely negotiated only for a brief moment on the slack of the tide. Orwell miscalculated this—either he misread the tide chart or neglected to consult it—and the little boat reached the dangerous spot at exactly the worst time, just in the middle of a furiously ebbing tide. Orwell realised his mistake too late: the boat was already out of control, tossed about by waves and swirling currents; the outboard engine which was not properly secured was shaken off its sternpost and swallowed by the sea; having lost all steering the little boat overturned, spilling its occupants and all their gear into the waves. Luckily the wreck occurred near a small rocky islet; Orwell managed to grab his son who had remained trapped under the boat, and the entire party swam safely ashore. Perchance the weather was sunny; Orwell proceeded immediately to dry his lighter and collect some fuel—dry grass and peat—and soon succeeded in lighting a fire by which the castaways were then able somehow to dry and warm themselves. Having gone to inspect the islet, Orwell discovered a spring of freshwater and an abundance of nesting birds. Under his unflappably calm and thoughtful direction the little party settled down in an orderly fashion. Some hours later, by extraordinary chance in such forlorn waters, a lobsterboat that was passing by noticed their presence and rescued them.

Virtually nothing of this dramatic succession of events is conveyed in Orwell's desiccated note: half of the diary entry is devoted to naturalist's observations on the islet puffin burrows and young cormorants learning to fly. To get the full picture, as I just said, one must read the nephew's narrative. There, one is struck first by Orwell's total absence of practical competence and of simple common sense[1]—and secondly by his calm courage and absolute self-control, which prevented the little party from panicking. And yet, at the time, he entertained no illusions regarding their chances of survival: as he simply told his nephew afterwards: "I thought we were goners." And the nephew commented: "He almost seemed to enjoy it."

Conclusion: if one had to go out to sea in a small boat, one would not choose Orwell for skipper. But when meeting with shipwreck, disaster or other catastrophe, one could not dream of better company.

———

Orwell left explicit instructions that no biography be written of him, and even actively discouraged one early attempt. He felt that "every life viewed from the inside would be a series of defeats too humiliating and disgraceful to contemplate." And yet the posthumous treatment he received from his biographers and editors is truly admirable —I think in particular of the works of Bernard Crick and of Peter Davison, which are models of critical intelligence and scholarship.

John Henry Newman said: "It has ever been a hobby of mine (unless it be a truism, not a hobby) that a man's life is in his letters." This selection of Orwell's correspondence splendidly verifies Newman's observation—which otherwise may not be true for many letter-writers and especially not for "men of letters," who tend to adjust their tune to the ears of those whom they address. But Orwell is always himself and speaks with only one voice: reserved even with old friends; generous with complete strangers; and treating all with equal sincerity.

The letters illustrate all his main concerns, interests and passions; they also illuminate some striking aspects of his personality.

POLITICS

Orwell's old schoolmate and friend Cyril Connolly famously stated: "Orwell was a political animal. He reduced everything to politics ... He could not blow his nose without moralising on the conditions in the handkerchief industry." This observation has a point, yet it could also be very misleading. Eileen, his wife—probably the only person who ever understood him in depth, since she managed to love him and live with him (while being herself the very opposite of a doormat)—had a much clearer view of the matter. She said that happiness for Orwell would have been to live in the country (he hated modern urban life and detested London), cultivating his vegetable garden and writing novels. Orwell himself repeatedly said very much the same thing—and proved it during the last years of his life, when he settled in his beloved (and very inaccessible) island of Jura. He had already expressed it in an earlier poem (1935)—Orwell's poems may not be great poetry, but they always reveal his innermost feelings:

> A happy vicar I might have been
> Two hundred years ago
> To preach upon eternal doom
> And watch my walnuts grow;
> But born, alas, in an evil time
> I missed that pleasant haven ...

He once defined himself half in jest—but only half—as a "Tory Anarchist." Indeed, after his youthful experience in the colonial police in Burma, he knew only that he hated imperialism and all forms of political oppression; all authority appeared suspect to him, even "mere success seemed to me a form of bullying." Then, after his enquiry into workers' conditions in northern industrial England during the Depression, he developed a broad non-partisan commitment to "socialism": "Socialism means justice and liberty when the nonsense is stripped of it." The decisive point in his political evolution took place in Spain, where he volunteered to fight fascism: first he was nearly killed by a fascist bullet, then he narrowly escaped being murdered by Stalinist secret police: "What I saw in Spain and what I have seen of the inner-workings of left-wing political parties have given me *a horror of politics* ... I am definitely 'left,' but I believe that a writer can only remain honest if he keeps free from Party labels" (my emphasis).

From then on he considered that the first duty of a socialist is to fight totalitarianism, which means in practice, "to denounce the Soviet myth, for there is not much difference between Fascism and Stalinism." Inasmuch as they deal with politics, the *Letters* focus on the anti-totalitarian fight. In this, the three salient features of Orwell's attitude are his intuitive grasp of concrete realities, his non-doctrinaire approach to politics (accompanied with a deep distrust of left-wing intellectuals) and his sense of the absolute primacy of the human dimension. He once identified the source of his strength: "Where I feel that people like us understand the situation better than the so-called experts is not in any power to foretell specific events, but in the power to grasp what kind of world we are living in." This uncanny ability received its most eloquent confirmation when Soviet dissidents who wished to translate *Animal Farm* into Russian (for clandestine distributors behind the Curtain) wrote to him to ask for his authorisation: they wrote to him *in Russian*, assuming that a writer who had such a subtle and thorough understanding of the Soviet reality—in contrast with the dismal ignorance of most Western intellectuals—had naturally to be a fluent Russian speaker!

Non-doctrinaire approach: In a letter to an old schoolmate (1 January 1938), Eileen wrote that they called their little dog "Marx" "to remind us that we had never read Marx, and now we have read a little and taken so strong a personal dislike to the man that we can't look the dog in the face when we speak to him."

Orwell's revulsion towards all "the smelly little orthodoxies that compete for our souls" explains also his distrust of and contempt for

intellectuals. This attitude dates back a long way, as he recalls in a letter of October 1938: "What sickens me about left-wing people, especially the intellectuals, is their utter ignorance of the way things
actually happen. I was always struck by this when I was in Burma and
used to read anti-imperialist stuff." If the colonial experience had
taught Orwell to hate imperialism, it also made him respect (like the
protagonist in a Kipling story) "men who do things." "Intellectuals
depress me horribly" is another theme often encountered in the *Letters*. "Intellectuals are more totalitarian"; "the danger is that some native forms of totalitarianism will be developed here, and people like
Laski, Pratt, Zilliacus, *The News Chronicle* and the rest of them seem
to me to be simply preparing the way for this." If the situation was depressing in London, in Paris (which he visited in 1945) it was dismal:
"Sartre is a big bag of wind"; "French publishers are now commanded
by Aragon [famous writer and leading member of the Communist
Party] and others not to publish undesirable books." His own *Animal
Farm* was being translated into nine languages, but "the most difficult
to arrange was French. One publisher signed a contract and then said
it was 'impossible for political reasons.'" "In France I got the impression that hardly anyone cares a damn any longer about freedom of the
Press, etc. The Occupation seemed to me to have had a terribly crushing effect upon people or maybe a sort of intellectual decadence had
set in years before the war." (Though he adds: "The queer thing is that,
with all this moral decay, there has over the past decade or so, been
much more literary *talent* in France than in England, or than anywhere else I should say.") He unfortunately missed meeting Camus at
the time, which he regretted. These two men would have found a
common language. In a letter of May 1948, he launched a well-aimed
attack against Emmanuel Mounier and his flock of Christian fellow-
travellers: "It's funny that when I met Mounier for about ten minutes
in 1945, I thought to myself, that man's a fellow-traveller. I can smell
them." (And—if I may intrude here with a personal experience—how
I know them myself! My benighted co-religionists, cretinous clerics
and other Maoist morons who, twenty years later, were to preach the
gospel of the Chinese "Cultural Revolution"...)

One last note on the subject of Orwell's politics: in the end, he seems to have essentially reverted to his original position of "Tory Anarchist." In a letter to Malcolm Muggeridge (4 December 1948—it resurfaced very late and, unfortunately, is not included in Davison's edition of the *Complete Works*, nor in *Life in Letters*; it was reproduced in the *Times Literary Supplement* when the *Complete Works* first appeared), there is a statement that seems to me of fundamental importance: "*The real division is not between conservatives and revolutionaries, but between authoritarians and libertarians.*"

THE HUMAN FACTOR

Even in the heat of battle, and precisely because he distrusted ideology—ideology kills—Orwell always remained acutely aware of the primacy that must be given to human individuals over all "the smelly little orthodoxies." His exchange of letters (and subsequent friendship) with Stephen Spender provides a splendid example of this. Orwell had lampooned Spender ("parlour Bolshevik," "pansy poet"); then they met. The encounter was in fact pleasant, which puzzled Spender, who wrote to Orwell on this very subject. Orwell replied:

> You ask how it is that I attacked you not having met you, and on the other hand changed my mind after meeting you ... [Formerly] I was willing to use you as a symbol of the parlour Bolshie because a) your verse did not mean very much to me; b) I looked upon you as a sort of fashionable successful person, also a Communist, or Communist sympathiser, and I have been very hostile to the Communist Party since about 1935; and c) because not having met you I could regard you as a type and also as an abstraction. Even if, when I met you, I had not happened to like you, I should still have been bound to change my attitude because when you meet someone in the flesh you realise immediately that he is a human being and not a sort of caricature embodying certain ideas. It is partly for this reason

that I don't mix much in literary circles, because I know from experience that once I have met and spoken to anyone, I shall never again be able to show any intellectual brutality towards him, even when I feel that I ought to, like Labour MPs who get patted on the back by Dukes and are lost forever more.[2]

Which immediately calls to mind a remarkable passage in *Homage to Catalonia*. Orwell described how, fighting on the frontline during the Spanish Civil War, he once saw a man jumping out of the enemy trench, half-dressed and holding his trousers with both hands as he ran: "I did not shoot, partly because of that detail about the trousers. I had come here to shoot at 'Fascists,' but a man that was holding up his trousers isn't a 'Fascist,' he's visibly a fellow creature, similar to yourself, and you don't feel like shooting at him."

LITERATURE

In an otherwise stimulating essay, Irving Howe wrote: "The last thing Orwell cared about when he wrote *Nineteen Eighty-Four*, the last thing he should have cared about, was literature." This view is totally mistaken. What made the writing of *Nineteen Eighty-Four* such a gruelling struggle (of which the *Letters* provide abundant evidence) was precisely the problem of turning a political vision into "a work of art." (Remember "Why I Write": "I could not do the work of writing a book, or even a long magazine article if it were not also an aesthetic experience.") If, in the end, *Nineteen Eighty-Four* could not fully satisfy Orwell's exacting literary standards, it is only because he had to work in impossible conditions: he was pressed by time and reduced by a deadly illness to a state of invalidity. That in such a state he could finally complete such an ambitious work was in itself an amazing achievement.

From the very start, literature was always Orwell's first concern. This is constantly reflected in his correspondence. "Since early childhood I always knew I wanted to write"—this statement is repeated in various forms, all through the years, till the end. But it took him a long time (and incredibly hard work) to discover *what* to write and *how* to write it. (His very first literary attempt was a long poem, eventually discarded.) Writing *novels* became his dominant passion—and an accursed ordeal: "Writing a novel is agony." He finally concluded (accurately), "I am not a real novelist." And yet, shortly before he died he was still excitedly announcing to his friend and publisher Warburg, "I have a stunning idea for a short novel."

As the *Letters* reveal, he reached a very clear-sighted assessment of his own work. Among his four "conventional" novels, he retained a certain fondness for *Burmese Days*, which he found faithful to his memories of the place. He felt "ashamed" of *Keep the Aspidistra Flying* and, even worse, of *A Clergyman's Daughter* and would not allow them to be reprinted: "They were written for money; at that time I simply hadn't a book in me, but I was half-starved." He was rightly pleased with *Coming Up for Air*—written in one go, with relative ease, it is indeed a most remarkable book, quite prescient in the light of today's environmental concerns. Among the books worth reprinting he listed (in 1946—*Nineteen Eighty-Four* was not yet written) first of all, and in order of importance: *Homage to Catalonia*; *Animal Farm*; *Critical Essays*; *Down and Out in Paris and London*; *Burmese Days*; *Coming Up for Air*.

THE COMMON MAN

The *extraordinary* lengths to which Orwell would go in his vain attempts to turn himself into an *ordinary* man are well illustrated by the Wallington grocery episode, on which the *Letters* provide colourful information. In April 1936, Orwell started to rent and run a small village grocery in an old, dark and pokey cottage, insalubrious and devoid of all basic amenities (no inside toilet, no cooking facilities, no electricity, only oil lamps for lighting). On rainy days the kitchen floor was underwater and blocked drains turned the whole place into a smelly cesspool. Davison comments: "One may say without being facetious it suited Orwell to the ground." And it especially suited Eileen, his wonderfully Orwellian wife. She moved in the day of their marriage and the way she managed this improbable home testifies both to her heroism and to her eccentric sense of humour. The income from the shop hardly ever covered the rent of the cottage. The main customers were a small bunch of local children who used to buy a few pennies worth of lollies after school. By the end of the year, the grocery went out of business, but at that time it had already fulfilled its true purpose: Orwell was in Barcelona, volunteering to fight against fascism, and when he enlisted in the Anarchist militia, he could proudly sign: *Eric Blair, grocer.* [3]

FAIRNESS

Orwell's sense of fairness was so scrupulous that it extended even to Stalin. As *Animal Farm* was going into print, at the last minute Orwell sent a final correction—which was effected just in time. (As all readers will remember, "Napoleon" is the name of the leading pig, which, in Orwell's fable, represents Stalin):

> In chapter VIII, when the windmill is blown up, I wrote "all the animals including Napoleon flung themselves on their faces." I would like to alter it to "all the animals except Napoleon." I just thought the alteration would be fair to Stalin as he did stay in Moscow during the German advance.

POVERTY AND ILL-HEALTH

Orwell was utterly stoic and never complained about his material and physical circumstances, however distressing they were most of the time. But from the factual information provided by the *Letters*, one realises that his extreme poverty ceased only three years before his death (first royalties windfall from *Animal Farm*), whereas his health became a severe and constant problem (undiagnosed tuberculosis) virtually from his return from Burma (age twenty-five). In later years it required frequent, prolonged and often painful treatment in various hospitals. For the last twelve years of his short existence (he died, aged forty-six, in 1950) he was in fact an invalid—but he insisted most of the time on carrying on with normal activity.

His entire writing career lasted for only sixteen years; the quantity and quality of work produced during this relatively brief span of time would be remarkable even for a healthy man of leisure; that it was achieved in his appalling state of permanent ill-health and poverty is simply stupendous.

WOMEN

In his relations with women, Orwell seems to have been generally awkward and clumsy. He was easily attracted to them, whereas they seldom found him attractive. Still, by miraculous luck, he found in Eileen O'Shaughnessy a wife who was able not only to understand him in depth, but also to love him truly and bear with his eccentricities without giving up any of her own originality—an originality that shines through all her letters. If Orwell was a failed poet, Eileen, for her part, was pure poetry.

Her premature death left Orwell stunned and lost for a long time. A year later he abruptly approached a talented young woman he hardly knew (they lived in the same building); with a self-pity that was utterly and painfully out of character for such a proud man, he wrote to her telling her how sick he was and inviting her "to become the widow of a literary man." "I fully realise that I'm not suited to someone like you who is young and pretty... it is only that I feel so desperately alone... I have no woman who takes an interest in me and can encourage me... of course it's absurd a person like me wanting to make love to someone of your age. I do want to, but I wouldn't be offended or even hurt if you say no..." The woman was flabbergasted and politely discouraged him.

Some years earlier he had made an unfortunate and unwelcome pass at another woman. This episode is documented by the editor with embarrassing precision—at which point readers might remember Orwell's hostility to the very concept of biography ("every life viewed from the inside would be a series of defeats too humiliating and disgraceful to contemplate"). Do biographers, however serious and scrupulous, really need or have the right to explore and disclose such intimate details? Yet we still read them. Is it right for us to do so? These questions are not rhetorical: I honestly do not know the answer.

SOLID OBJECTS AND SCRAPS OF USELESS INFORMATION— TREES, FISHES, BUTTERFLIES AND TOADS

Just as in "Why I Write," Orwell evoked the simple pleasure he took "in solid objects and scraps of useless information," in his famous "Thoughts on the Common Toad" he added: "If a man cannot enjoy the return of spring, why should he be happy in a labour-saving Utopia? ... I think that by retaining one's childhood love of such things as trees, fishes, butterflies and—to return to my first instance—toads, one makes a peaceful and decent future a little more probable." His endearing and quirky tastes, his inexhaustible and loving attention to all aspects of the natural world crop up constantly in his correspondence. The *Letters* are full of disarming *non sequiturs*: for instance, he interrupts some reflections on the Spanish Inquisition to note the daily visit a hedgehog pays to his bathroom. While away from home in 1939, he writes to the friend who looks after his cottage: his apprehension regarding the looming war gives way without transition to concerns for the growth of his vegetables and for the mating of his goat: "I hope Muriel's mating went through. It is a most unedifying spectacle by the way, if you happened to watch it. Did my rhubarb come up, I wonder? I had a lot and then last year the frost buggered it up." To an anarchist friend (later a professor of English in a Canadian university) he writes an entire page from his Scottish retreat, describing in minute detail all aspects of the life and work of local crofters: again the constant and inexhaustible interest in "men who do things" in the real world.

THE END

While already lying in hospital, he married Sonia Brownell[4] three months before his death. At the time he entertained the illusion that he might still have a couple of years to live and he was planning for the following year a book of essays that would have included "a long essay on Joseph Conrad" (if it was ever written, it is now lost). He also said that he still had "two books on his mind"—alongside "the stunning idea for a short novel" mentioned earlier.

He began drawing up plans to keep a pig, or preferably a sow, at his hermitage in the Hebrides. As he wrote to his sister, who was in charge of the place, "the only difficulty is about getting her to a hog once a year. I suppose one could buy a gravid sow in autumn, to litter about March, but one would have to make very sure that she really was in pig the first time."

In his hospital room, at the time of his death, he kept in front of him, against the wall, a fine new fishing rod, a luxury in which he had indulged himself on receiving the first royalties from *Nineteen Eighty-Four*. He never had the chance to use it.

His first love—dating back to his adolescence and youth—who was now a middle-aged woman, wrote to him in hospital out of the blue, after an estrangement and silence of some twenty-seven years. He was surprised and overjoyed and resumed correspondence with her. In his last letter to her, he concluded that, though he could only entertain a vague belief in some sort of after-life, he had one certainty: "Nothing ever dies."

TERROR OF BABEL
Evelyn Waugh

There is but one sorrow, which is not to be a Saint.

—LÉON BLOY

ON READING Stephen Spender's autobiography, Evelyn Waugh commented: "To see him fumbling with our rich and delicate language is to experience all the horror of seeing a Sèvres vase in the hands of a chimpanzee." One would have to devise a statement to the exact opposite effect to describe accurately the delight which Waugh's grace and dexterity with words never fails to arouse in his readers.

Waugh exemplifies the primordial importance of *style*. He infuriated a great many fools in his time, not only because he took a mischievous pleasure in taunting them (let us admit it, to irritate idiots actually is enjoyable), but, more essentially, because he stubbornly held onto a timeless (and therefore untimely) truth. The arbiters of public opinion do not forgive those who openly mock intellectual fashions or transgress political and aesthetic taboos. Social conformity has its dungeons where the irreverent are to be confined behind thick walls of silence until complete oblivion. With Waugh, however, the trouble was that, while alive, his flamboyant and formidable personality could not easily be ignored or dismissed. On his death, the intelligentsia at last breathed a sigh of relief, and, from the grudging homages that were paid to the deceased, one could see that the dour undertakers of the literary establishment had firmly set their minds

---

Review of Martin Stannard: *Evelyn Waugh: No Abiding City 1939–1966* (London: J. M. Dent & Sons, 1992).

on burying him for good. Actually, this task proved quite impracticable and Waugh's wit continued to shine more brightly than ever, however much the stern guardians of political correctness would have wished to turn it off. The fact is, in order to get rid of Waugh, one would probably first have to get rid of the English language.

In his time, the splendour of his style as well as his hilarious inventions ensured that all his works remained in print. Twenty-five years later, a new generation of readers now discovers that Waugh is not merely fun, he is also wise—and his wisdom addresses our present anguish at a depth that none of his contemporaries seem to reach. Which of them indeed could promise us what he was already offering his readers nearly half a century ago—"A hope, not indeed that anything but disaster lies ahead, but that the human spirit, redeemed, can survive all disasters"?

Waugh dropped out of university without completing a degree. He never considered himself an "intellectual"—in fact he found this very notion utterly outlandish. At first he wanted to become a painter, and then thought of taking up carpentry or printing. When he finally came to literature he approached it like a *craft*, and retained this unconventional attitude all his life. Quite late in his career, to a literary journalist who had asked if his fiction was supposed to convey some "message," he gave this characteristic answer: "No, I wish to make a pleasant object. I think any work of art is something exterior to oneself, it is the making of something, whether it's a bed table or a book."

Such a conception, which would naturally occur to a painter, sculptor, an engraver or a cabinet-maker, does not normally come to a writer, and we can perhaps find here a clue to the strikingly *concrete* quality of his writing. (It should be noted, by the way, that terms such as "abstract" and "abstraction" are used by him in an invariably pejorative sense.) Without a solid ground from which to rebound, imagination cannot soar; fantasy peters out in a vacuum; humour, waywardness, whimsicality quickly become tedious if developed in arbitrary isolation from the objective world. If Waugh's invention is permanently throwing off sparks, it is because it always operates within the hard-edged frame of reality, and his wildest fantasies are always subjected to the discipline of a most rigorous structure. When *A Handful of Dust* was first published, old Belloc immediately detected this exceptional quality of craftsmanship. He wrote to Waugh: "I could not let it go . . . It is really a remarkable thing, and it owes this quality to *construction*, which today is in prose as rare as virtue. Every word is right and in its right place, so that the effect is a maximum for the material employed."

Actually, the way in which Waugh manipulates language is akin to the *poetic* mode of literary creation: his is first of all *an art of words*. This is the reason why poetry, by its very nature, is essentially untranslatable—or to put it in a different form, any piece of literature is translatable only inasmuch as what it says can be dissociated from the way in which it is being said. In a poem, these two aspects are indivisible: if the poem is really good, displace one word and the entire piece collapses. A poem cannot exist outside the words in which it originally became incarnate, any more than a person could survive outside his own skin. In this respect, Waugh once made a very revealing criticism of Graham Greene's use of language: "[Greene's] is not a specifically literary style at all. The words are functional, devoid of sensuous attraction, of ancestry and of independent life. Literary stylists regard language as intrinsically precious, and its proper use as a worthy and pleasant task. A polyglot could read Mr. Greene, lay him aside, retain a sharp memory of all he said and yet, I think, entirely forget what tongue he was using. The words are simply mathematical signs for his thought." Indeed, it would not be impossible to impart the gist of *The Power and The Glory* to someone who had not read the book, simply by re-telling it in other words, whereas it would be absurd and pointless to attempt the same exercise with *Decline and Fall*.

"The written word obsessed Waugh," Martin Stannard notes in his biography, "and in this he lived entirely. Words on paper were to him almost tactile, malleable, subject to control. He thought in words, in perfect sentences." A young American scholar who visited him in his country residence retained a vivid memory of an inscription which he found in the bathroom affixed upon the cistern of the toilet; handwritten and initialled E. W., the notice provided instructions on how to operate the toilet's faulty flush:

The handle should return to the horizontal when the flow of water ceases. Should it fail to do so, agitate gently until it succeeds.

One feels as if the exquisite precision of the wording was designed to overcome the chaos and the rebelliousness of brute things. Waugh would have fully appreciated the famous anecdote from the life of a great Chinese calligrapher: as a ferocious tiger was terrorising a certain corner of the country, at the request of the local population, the calligrapher wrote a large inscription: *TIGERS NOT WELCOME*. The sheer magnificence of his calligraphy had such *authority* that the beast relented and left the district.

"Literature is simply the appropriate use of language"—Waugh made this striking and characteristic statement in a letter to Ann Fleming at the very end of his career. It sums up neatly his aesthetic principles, but should not be misconstrued as some sort of formalist manifesto. On the contrary, for him "the appropriate use of language both implied and guaranteed the proper functioning of a right mind." Aesthetics is a form of ethics, as he made clear in his rebuke of John Mortimer's views: "'Many writers [Mortimer says] are not very good at anything except writing, and the value of their work is often not to be judged by the quality of their thoughts.' But writing is the expression of thought. There is no abstract writing. All literature implies moral standards and criticisms."

On a superficial level, Waugh's views may seem contradictory: on the one hand, he multiplies statements such as "I have no psychological interest ... I regard writing not as an investigation of character, but as an exercise in the use of language, and with this I am obsessed"— and, on the other hand, he emphatically rejects the possibility of a form of "abstract writing." Stannard finely analyses the deeper coherence of his attitude: "At the root of Waugh's pronouncements, there is something much simpler and, at the same time, infinitely more complex: the terror of Babel. One thing alone, in Waugh's view, kept men sane: the sense of unified, agreed meaning. Ultimately this 'meaning' was God. In temporal terms, it was language. The post-structuralist notions of the (almost) infinite plurality of meaning would have been anathema to him: that way lay Picasso and *Finnegans Wake* ... Waugh looked on his books as independent systems of order in a nightmare existence." In this sense, the order of words established by the writer's pen would keep madness at bay, as the Chinese calligrapher's brush could chase tigers away.

Waugh would certainly have subscribed to Samuel Johnson's moving utterance: "Of the uncertainties of our present state, the most dreadful and alarming is the uncertain continuance of reason." The fear of incipient lunacy seems to have haunted him recurrently. On a creative level, a more benign form of his "madness" expressed itself as an ability to turn all reality into private fantasy. As a protective device against the bruising contact of life, he was determined to see events and people as a fiction from which he was separate. (In this sense, of course, there may be an element of mild schizophrenia at the source of all creative writing—after all, art is a desperate attempt to make a cruel reality a little less intolerable.) Without detracting in the least from Waugh's well-known courage, one may even wonder to what extent his fearlessness in front of all sorts of dangers (during the war, for instance, he constantly displayed a bravery that bordered at times on downright recklessness) was not also rooted in his imaginative powers and in his capability to cut himself off from reality in order to become a detached spectator of his own predicament. The same mechanisms of imagination which produce feelings of panic, can also—if guided by a forceful will—generate courage.

In everyday life, Waugh was constantly casting acquaintances and friends into fantastic roles, and generally turning the people he met into characters in a private charade; often he would use this myth-making talent to hilarious effect. A good illustration is provided, for instance, by his visit to the great poet Paul Claudel. The majestic patriarch of Catholic letters—a genius of immense authority—had invited Waugh and Christopher Sykes to have lunch in his Paris apartment. This is how Waugh related the meeting in his diary:

> The old man was deaf and dumb. All his family—wife, sons and daughters-in-law—sat round the table. He greeted me by putting into my hands a newly printed *édition de luxe* of some

verses of his. A present? I began to thank him. He took it away and put it on a table. I had the impression it was to be my prize if I behaved well. Lively conversation mostly in English. Every now and then the old man's lips were seen to move and there would be a cry: "Papa is speaking!" and a hush broken only by unintelligible animal noises. Some of these were addressed to me, and I thought he said: "How would you put into English *potage de midi*?" I replied: "Soup at luncheon." It transpired that he was the author of a work named *Partage de midi*. His tortoise eyes glistened with hostility. After luncheon there was a great deal of fuss among the womenfolk as to whether or not Papa was to have cognac. He got it, brightened a little, called for an album and made me sit by him, as his arthritic fingers turned the pages... Anything that caught his fancy had been pasted [in the album]. Some were humorous, some not. There was a group of the Goebbels family. "That's funny," I said, feeling on safe ground. "I think it very sad," he mumbled... When we left, he came to the drawing room door and laid his hand on the *édition de luxe*, gave me another look of reptilian hate, and left it on its table. Next day, he told a daughter-in-law that both Christopher [Sykes] and I were "*très* gentlemen."

Christopher Sykes, however, gave a completely different account. Not only had Claudel been perfectly hospitable, genial and lively, but virtually none of the grotesque incidents mentioned in Waugh's narrative did actually take place. In particular, Waugh's horrible *gaffe* was pure fiction. One would have guessed as much: it is very difficult to believe that Waugh, who admired Claudel, would not have known even the title of one of his masterpieces: "It *transpired* that he was the author of a work named *Partage de midi*..." It transpired indeed! (One is reminded of Philip Larkin's tranquil impudence: "Deep down, I think foreign languages irrelevant.") Shortly after the encounter with Claudel, Sykes was astonished to hear Waugh describing for the first time this fictitious incident to a common friend; he stuck to his invention after that, as he obviously had come to believe it sincerely. Perhaps it was not simply one more instance of the novelist's instinct at work; more exactly, "the novelist's instinct" was itself an expression of a deeper defence against the threats which reality was directing at his self-esteem: from Sykes' testimony, we know that, immediately before the visit, Waugh was virtually paralysed with nervousness—a most uncharacteristic and humiliating condition for a man whose powerful personality usually inspired fear in all those who approached him. (On their way to Claudel's apartment, Waugh insisted that they first stop in a church to pray for success; and then during the entire visit, he feigned total ignorance of the French language, for fear of making mistakes and bringing ridicule upon himself.) Obviously, meeting Claudel had momentous meaning for him, and he was desperately eager to make a favourable impression on the grand old man. Yet, things did not work out the way he would have wished; as Sykes observed, "he somehow detected that Claudel, for all his geniality, did not like him." In Waugh's version, however, the *mot de la fin* was provided by Claudel commenting the next day to his daughter-in-law: "Waugh is *très* gentleman." Actually this is probably a clue for the deep wound which may have triggered the entire fiction: according to Sykes, Claudel's impression was precisely the opposite: "Later, Claudel told a friend of mine that he had been very interested to meet Evelyn Waugh, '*Mais*,' he added, '*il lui manque l'allure du vrai gentleman*' ('he does not look like a real gentleman')!"

Similar examples of bizarre incidents abound in Waugh's life and make his biography remarkably colourful. (Stannard's work, which is masterful and seems definitive, should not make us neglect the earlier study by Sykes, with its wealth of anecdotes; and more recently, in his autobiography, Auberon Waugh has produced a portrait of his father which, in its utterly unsentimental truthfulness, is deeply affecting.[1]) There was, however, a dark side to his imaginative power: he had suffered from recurrent bouts of persecution mania since his early twenties, and after his first wife's traumatic desertion he exhibited symptoms of schizophrenia. In late middle age, his most frightening slide into hallucinations and lunacy was faithfully chronicled in *The Ordeal of Gilbert Pinfold*. Eventually this latter breakdown was diagnosed as having resulted from a progressive poisoning induced by his protracted abuse of strong sleeping drugs; yet it is interesting to note that at first he consulted a priest, as he wondered if he was not pos-sessed by the Devil. (Some twenty-five years earlier, when Belloc first met the brilliant young novelist, Waugh's future mother-in-law asked the old sage's opinion of Waugh, and Belloc made the startling reply: "He has a devil in him.")

While in the army during the war he had been forced to submit to a psychological examination, because of his erratic and impossible be-haviour: "The doctor appears to have been told that Waugh was a drunkard and tried to impute to him (with some good reason) unhap-piness and frustration through adolescence. Waugh suffered ninety minutes of this and managed at last to turn the tables: 'You have been asking me a great many questions. Do you mind if I now ask you one?' The psychiatrist offered no objection. 'Why then,' Waugh asked, 'have you not questioned me about the most important thing in a man's life—his religion?'"

There is no doubt that religion was indeed the most important thing in Waugh's life. Any biographer who failed to recognise this would be wasting their time—and ours. Such a reproach was directed at Stannard by one critic, but seems to me unwarranted. Stannard not only provides a wealth of inspiring quotes from Waugh's writings, but has also unearthed impressive evidence of charitable deeds which Waugh secretly performed as a form of spiritual cultivation, and which bear eloquent testimony to the absolute seriousness of his com-mitment. If he sometimes brought to the everyday practice of his Catholic faith some of the eccentricity which also characterised most other aspects of his life (for instance, as an acquaintance recalled, dur-ing Lent, when having lunch in a restaurant, he would produce min-iature scales at the table to weigh out precisely the quantities of allowable food!), his faith was not a matter for posturing; it cost him too dearly, in every respect, for its sincerity to be questioned. In his remarkable correspondence, whenever the subject of religion is being discussed, he relinquishes his usual whimsicality and writes with sim-plicity, depth, gravity and a most touching sense of urgency. For all his gluttony and drunkenness, his passionate attachment to all things of beauty, his selfishness, his impatience, his unkindness and anger (a close friend once asked how he could reconcile his generally beastly behaviour and his Christianity; Waugh replied: "You have no idea how much nastier I would be if I was not a Catholic. Without supernatural aid, I would hardly be a human being"), what he derived from his Catholicism was a fundamental ability not to take this world too seriously. Stannard shows a sound grasp of this central issue in his choice of a subtitle for the second and final volume of his biographical study, *No Abiding City*—a reference to St. Paul (Hebrews XIII, 14): *non enim habemus hic manentem civitatem, sed futuram inquirimus* ("For we have here no abiding city, but we seek one that is to come"), which Waugh was particularly fond of quoting. Chesterton had already observed: "The Church is the only thing that can save a man from the degrading servitude of being a child of one's own time," but for Waugh, the Church not only secured liberation from the world, it also provided a force and an inspiration to go *against* the world—*contra mundum*.

Among Waugh's works, *The Life of the Right Reverend Ronald Knox*—a biography of the scholarly priest who translated the Vulgate into English—is probably one of the less read; the author had intended it essentially as an act of *pietas* to the memory of a deceased friend. Yet nothing written by Waugh is indifferent; at the very beginning of this book there is an episode of haunting power, which although bearing little relation to the main topic, must obviously have affected Waugh in a very personal way. In a few memorable pages, he describes the death of Knox's maternal grandfather, an Anglican clergyman who ended his missionary life in Zanzibar in a state of total poverty, loneliness and dereliction, under the indifferent and uncomprehending eyes of the natives. This seems to have been a theme that presented special meaning for Waugh. Earlier on, for instance, he once summed up the subject of *A Handful of Dust* as "the civilised man's helpless plight among savages." The interesting twist in the latter description is that, if indeed the main character of the novel ends up as a captive in the Amazonian jungle, this final mishap occurs merely as a sort of epilogue—actually the true savages who destroyed his life with mindless cruelty were smart members of fashionable London society.

Those who bear witness, staunchly and faithfully, to a spiritual tradition are reduced by the modern world to a condition of "aborigines, vermin by right of law, to be shot at leisure, so that things may be safe for the travelling salesmen." Modern man, who moves with the times and seeks power without grace, is finally a much greater menace to human integrity than tattooed cannibals. Thus, in *Brideshead Revisited*, we are told that Rex Mottram, politico and tycoon, epitome of worldly success (he is still very much alive among us today, forever aspiring to become our leader), "wasn't a complete human being at all. He was a tiny bit of one, unnaturally developed; something in a bottle, an organ kept alive in a laboratory. I thought he was a sort of primitive savage, but he was something absolutely modern and up-to-date that only this ghastly age could produce: a tiny bit of a man pretending he was the whole."

What is wrong with "the age of the common man" is not that it might endanger elitist privilege but the fact that it is built upon a false premise—for there is no such creature. In a memorable BBC interview, a journalist who thought he would cleverly expose Waugh's social prejudices merely revealed his own incapacity to shed trendy stereotypes:

> *Journalist*: You have not much sympathy with the man in the street, have you, Mr. Waugh?
>
> *Waugh*: You must understand that the man in the street does not exist. He is a modern myth. There are individual men and women, each one of whom has an individual and immortal soul, and such beings need to use streets from time to time.

But there are also more insidious forms of intellectual perversion—those which borrow a religious disguise to subvert religious values. The phenomenon is not limited to progressive-minded Christians who do not believe in Christ, or to enlightened theologians who preach atheism; it consists more broadly—as Desmond MacCarthy described in his perceptive comments on *The Loved One*—in the entire "silly optimistic trend in modern civilisation which takes for granted that the consolations of religion can be enjoyed without belief in them, and seeks to persuade us that there is nothing really tragic in the predicament of man."

At the end of his life, with an anguish that came close to despair, Waugh witnessed the dreadful invasion of shallowness and puerility which began to undermine and destroy some of the most precious and venerable traditions of the Church. He confessed to a friend: "The buggering up of the Church is a deep sorrow to me," and in the privacy of his diary he went further: "Pray God I will never apostatise but I can only now go to Church as an act of duty and obedience—just as a sentry at Buck[ingham Palace] is posted with no possibility of his being employed to defend the sovereign's life."

As he sank even further into a pathological state of melancholy, he reviewed the bleak landscape of his soul—his spiritual dryness, his emotional loneliness, the dreariness and boredom of his family life, the wretchedness of his own foul temper, the general aridity of his soul[2] and at the end of a desolate litany of failings, doubts and despondency, he pondered that even the saints did not seem much better off, and yet concluded: "But to aim at anything less than sanctity is not to aim at all."

He did not derive much comfort or consolation from his faith: he simply knew it to be true, and that was that. As he explained in a letter to a friend: "Praying is not asking but giving. Giving our love to God, asking for nothing in return... Do you believe in the Incarnation and Redemption in the full historical sense in which you believe in the battle of El Alamein? That's important. Faith is not a mood."

Only his religion could—quite ruthlessly—put this proud man in his humble place; he realistically accepted that, in a theological perspective, his unique talents in the end did not amount to much: "I cannot think of a single Saint who attached much importance to art... The Church and the world need monks and nuns more than they need writers... A youth who is inarticulate in conversation may well be eloquent in prayer... The Church does not exist in order to produce elegant preachers, or artists, or philosophers. It exists to produce Saints."

After reading *Helena*, John Betjeman confessed to him a certain puzzlement: "Helena did not seem to me like a saint." Waugh replied: "Saints are simply souls in Heaven... and each individual has his own peculiar form of sanctity which he must achieve or perish. It is no good my saying 'I wish I were like Joan of Arc or St. John of the Cross,' I can only be St. Evelyn Waugh—after God knows what experiences in Purgatory."

On the question of purgatory, it should merely be observed that the meanest judges in this world were not even able to keep him for one single day in their *literary* purgatory; as to the other one, God's sweet mercy will have taken good care of that.

THE TRUTH OF SIMENON

All writers are monsters.

—Henry de Montherlant

Cioran wondered how the perspective of having a biographer never discouraged anyone from having a life. We should at least ask ourselves how the perspective of having to provide posthumously the topic of an academic eulogy does not discourage more people from becoming academicians. In Simenon's case, perhaps, he believed that he had sufficiently succeeded in concealing his tracks, and thought that the false candour of his many confessions would always be protection enough against our indiscreet admiration.

Samuel Johnson said: "Nobody can write the life of a man but those who have eat and drunk and lived in social intercourse with him." I am not sure if this sort of experience would have been of much use to Simenon's biographer—or to any other great writer's, for that matter. Isaac Bashevis Singer once observed (forgive this abundance of quotations, it is not pedantry—simply, the fact is that, for the last fifteen years, I have been frequenting books more than people; furthermore, why should we attempt clumsily to reinvent what good writers have better said before us?) that, even if Tolstoy were living next door, instead of paying him a visit, he would rather stay home and read *Anna Karenina* again. This is elementary wisdom. The encounter of geniuses is not always an occasion for sublime exchanges. The only meeting between James Joyce and Marcel Proust is a good

---

Speech to the Académie Royale de Littérature Française of Belgium on the occasion of my election to the Chair of Georges Simenon (1992).

example: these two giants of modern literature once shared a taxi, but they spent the entire time arguing whether to open or shut the window. (This anecdote must be true, since it was invented by Nabokov.)

People are often surprised when they realise that, in life, great writers do not bear much resemblance to the image they had formed of them while reading their works. For instance, with naïve astonishment they may discover that a fierce polemicist, whose fire and violence had filled them with awe, actually is a quiet, shy and retiring man; or again, the orgiastic prophet of burning passion, who had stirred their sensual imagination, proves in fact to be a eunuch; or the famous adventurer, who set their minds dreaming of exotic horizons, wears slippers and never leaves his cosy fireside; or the aesthete from whose exquisite visions they drew so much inspiration eats from plastic plates and wears hideous neckties. They should have known better. Quite frequently, an artist creates in order to compensate for a deficiency; his creation is not the joyous and exuberant outpouring of an overflow—it is more often a pathetic attempt to answer a want, to bridge a gap, to hide a wound.

Hilaire Belloc admirably described this divorce between the writer and his writing:

> I never knew a man yet who was consonant to his work. Either he was clearly much greater and better than his work, or clearly much less and worse ... In point of fact it is not the mere man who does the thing: it is the man inspired. And the reason we are shocked by the vanity of artists is that, more or less consciously, we consider the contrast between what God has done through them, and their own disgusting selves ... When the work is of genius, he is far below it: he is on a different plane. No man is himself a genius. His genius is lent him from outside.

Simenon granted countless journalistic interviews. In his free time (that is, when he was not writing novels) he would entertain journalists sometimes as often as twice or three times a week. The media found him to be a golden topic. With apparent good will, but not without shrewdness, he complied with their many requests; in front of television cameras, he performed his old routine with well-oiled smoothness; he deftly fed his numerous visitors all the humbug they wished to swallow, in the same fashion as, at the zoo, one throws peanuts to the monkeys.

He enjoyed worldwide celebrity. His fame can be conveniently encapsulated in a series of figures which, though often quoted, never cease to amaze: his books have been translated into fifty-seven languages and published in forty countries; he wrote some 450 novels—the exact figure, which may possibly constitute a world record of fecundity in the history of literature, still escapes the investigations of the most diligent researchers, as in his youth he produced countless pot-boilers (adventure stories, soft pornography watered down with sentimental romance) that were issued in cheap, obscure and short-lived serial publications, under twenty-seven different pen-names. In his early period, he would sometimes turn out one or two novels in the course of a single day. As success came, he began to travel restlessly; at the same time, he became a compulsive landlord, setting up for himself thirty-two successive residences. And also, naturally, let us not forget the 10,000 women with whom, according to his own computations, he managed over the years to have sexual intercourse.

However, Mauriac warned us: the true life of a writer can only be told by the children of his imagination. Do Simenon and his creatures tell the same story? We might, for instance, subject them to a single elementary test, such as the one Malraux suggested when he said that, in order to know a man, one should examine his attitudes towards God, towards sex and towards money.

On God, Simenon's characters remain generally silent, which is fairly normal. Their creator's silence, however, was positively shrill, which is rather odd: "I would rather walk stark naked in the streets than confess my true views regarding the existence of God."

On the subject of sex, Simenon was fond of portraying himself as a man liberated from all taboos: "I enjoy perusing beautiful female bodies...Quite often, prostitutes give me more pleasure than non-professionals...I have sex straightforwardly, healthily, as often as I feel the need to." He cultivates sexual pleasure "without afterthoughts and without fuss." If we are to believe him, it would seem that, for him, regular participation in orgies was some sort of exercise akin to bicycle riding or calisthenics.

For his creatures, however, things are not so easy or pleasant. Unremitting loneliness crushes the entire world of his fiction, where loveless passions are leading inexorably to disaster, and sex is nearly always a grim, shameful, hasty and furtive experience. Thus, for instance, the protagonist of the most autobiographical of all his novels imagines:

> ...dingy beds, wallpaper in tatters, a broken-down and stained sofa; he sees, he wants to see the face of a woman, with dark rings under her eyes, a weary mouth and a sickly body, slowly stripping her clothes in a grey twilight, with a mixture of boredom and disgust...Everything is so ugly! It is dirty—that is the word: dirty—and he wished it to be even more dirty, dirty to a point which would make you cry from disgust or pity, which would make you crawl on the floor and moan.

Finally, one cannot leave this subject without mentioning the contrast—rather striking, you will admit—between, on the one hand, Simenon's jolly polygamist binges and, on the other, Maigret's austere monogamy (and there is no need to be Freud or Jung to be able to identify Maigret as Simenon's "mythical ego").

On the subject of money, it would be all too easy to juxtapose the spectacular success of the creator with the sordid end of nearly all his creatures. Paradoxically, as the former became a prisoner of his own wealth and fame, we see the latter dropping their worldly moorings and drifting away in a sort of desolate freedom. At the peak of his career, Simenon was living in a pseudo-castle which he designed himself—a mixture of palace, factory, health resort and fortress where he was waited on by an army of secretaries, butlers, chauffeurs, cooks and gardeners. Whereas Simenon's novels resemble life, his life increasingly resembled a novel—one of those cheap romances which, in his early years, he would sign with phony aristocratic pseudonyms such as Jean du Perry or Germain d'Antibes, and entitle suggestively *Voluptuous Embraces*, *Frivolous Perversities* or *Alone Among Gorillas*.

In contrast with this literary businessman, beaming and prosperous,

Simenon's characters break your heart: they are small people, humble and lonely; rebels and misfits; failures, losers, victims. Look at Maigret (even him!): "When Maigret has to enter a wealthy household, he feels unwelcome and embarrassed, he is uneasy, he knows he does not fit into these splendid surroundings . . ."; "Maigret is not comfortable when he must deal with important people . . . He is both in awe of, and shocked by, the upper class." His father was the intendant of an aristocrat, and he himself remained indelibly marked by his servile origin: "There is a certain type of human relations, of social habits, for which there is no cure. One can recover from many diseases, but never from that—a certain humility in front of certain people." In fact Simenon told the same story a hundred times; his major novels have only one theme: the fall of a man. Fate, an outside incident, an inner impulse, suddenly triggers an implacable process of disintegration. A man wakes up and finds himself a stranger amidst his own people; he tries to break free from his familiar chains, and he perishes.

Since Simenon gave so many interviews and published lengthy tape-recorded confessions, some people might believe that he was inclined to self-exposure. This is not the case at all. He merely endeavoured obstinately to project a certain image of himself—the image of "an ordinary man," a man without problems, at peace with himself.

A judge, handed the Simenon file, would certainly be puzzled by the flagrant discrepancies between the cheeky self-confidence of the accused and the harrowing evidence of his characters. But didn't Maigret himself warn us never to trust judges? Judges understand nothing. If they understood, how could they still judge?

Once, however, as if by inadvertence, Simenon made a genuine confession. A writer may sometimes speak most truthfully about himself when he thinks he is merely commenting on another writer whom he particularly likes. In 1960, in a radio broadcast devoted to Balzac, Simenon said things far more revealing than the lengthy, embarrassing and superfluous memoirs he dictated at the end of his life. In this portrait of Balzac, some statements carry a singular weight: "The need to create other men, to draw out of oneself a crowd of different characters, could hardly arise in a man who finds himself harmoniously adjusted to his own little world. Why should anyone obstinately endeavour to live out other people's lives, if he is himself self-confident and without revolt?"

It can hardly be doubted that Simenon was utterly and irretrievably "ill-at-ease in his own skin," that he never recovered from having been deprived of his mother's affection, that his whole life was a long and impossible attempt to get even for all the humiliations of his mean and narrow childhood; yet, in the end, these matters should only concern professional psychologists. Let us return to literature.

The urge to create characters, to invent other beings, reaches in Simenon the proportions of an obsession so exclusive and devouring that one could use his case to make a clinical analysis of the physiology and pathology of literary creation. Indeed, it is this very compulsion that injects his novels with a sense of inescapable necessity. Reading his works, one verifies the truth of Julien Green's observation: "The only books that matter are those of which it could be said that their author would have suffocated had he not written them." Few writers were ever so purely and totally *novelists*; good connoisseurs such as Gide and Mauriac noticed this very soon—and their admiration for Simenon's phenomenal ability was tinged with a shade of envy: how did he manage—this uncouth and commonplace Belgian shopkeeper—to outclass them so bedazzlingly on their own home ground?

Conversely, as soon as Simenon stopped writing novels, it was as if he ceased to exist. He had nothing to say, or when he insisted on speaking he would utter platitudes, or display an embarrassing caddishness with cold insensitivity. Never mind! To an acrobat who had just walked across the Niagara Falls on a wire, who would think to ask what he can do *besides*? Even though Simenon at rest could sometimes provoke the perplexity of his admirers, these unfortunate impressions never detracted from the superior powers of his art. Open any of his major novels: at once, a magic takes effect. From the first paragraph, you are gripped as if by the jaws of a steel trap that will not release its hold until the final full stop of the last page; and, even then, after you have shut the book, you remain stunned, and it takes quite a while to re-enter your own familiar little world, having glimpsed while you were reading its dark and vertiginous reverse side.

Reading Simenon makes us realise how tenuous the boundary is between life experience and the imaginary experience. Some twenty or thirty years later, the memories we retain of certain episodes from his novels persist in haunting us more obsessively than do memories of actual events that happened to ourselves. In fact, these readings were themselves events in our lives.

The strength of Simenon is to achieve unforgettable effects by ordinary means. His language is poor and bare (like the language of the unconscious), making him the most translatable of all writers: his writing loses nothing by being turned into Eskimo or Japanese. It would be difficult to make an anthology of his best pages: he does not have best pages, he only has better novels, in which everything hangs together without a single seam.

"One always writes too much," Chardonne used to say. Had he published ten times less, Simenon would have enjoyed a literary position a hundred times more important. Detective stories (an utterly boring genre, by its very definition)—which, actually, he himself did not take very seriously and produced industrially as a form of relaxation from his authentic literary creation—ensured his wealth and popularity; yet, at the same time for millions of readers they obscured his true genius, which he invested nearly exclusively in what he called his "tough novels" (*romans durs*). The latter exacted from him such an intense, nervous effort that sometimes, before starting to write, he would suffer fits of vomiting. Each time, he had to assume imaginatively the persona of his main protagonist—to become him—and then to see with the mind's eye the world his pen was conjuring as it followed an inner dictation. This psychic metamorphosis is common to all "visionary" writers—Julien Green (once more!) described it well in various passages of his *Journal*. This phenomenon reached such an intensity that there were times when it scared Simenon, times when he felt drawn towards an uncertain border where his very sanity might founder.

The mental tension required by this type of writing cannot be sustained long, as it tolerated no interruption and no relaxation; the first draft of Simenon's novels was generally completed in eight or ten days. His masterpieces are therefore always brief: written in one breath, and designed to be read at one sitting.

The first draft was nearly a definitive version—subsequent corrections concerned only details. Simenon's original manuscripts are amazingly neat; in their swift tidiness they remind us of Mozart's autographic musical scores. To bring these two names together here may appear incongruous—and it is, in every respect, except one which is essential: the workings of the creative mind. For both artists, the starting point was of crucial importance: a musical phrase, an initial vision, was *given them*; this first phrase once being set, the rest followed quickly, in one impetus, without hesitation, in a continuous flow—what Mozart called *il filo*. The speed of this process, its triumphant decisiveness, self-confidence and certainty can make shallow observers speak of "facility"; this is a very misleading impression, as, in order to sustain the rhythm of the inner dictation without breaking its thread, the artist must mobilise powers of concentration that are nearly superhuman.

This type of creation, however, confronts us with an enigma (which Shaffer grasped well in his *Amadeus*—musicologists and historians who criticised him missed the point): the created work possesses a splendour and a depth that far exceed the calibre of its creator. The work is not only greater than its author, it is different in nature: it comes from somewhere else. The author shocks those who admire his work; in contrast with it, he seems vacuous. And yet—was it not precisely this very emptiness that enabled him to provide a free channel for his works to be born?

An artist can take full responsibility only for those of his works that are mediocre or aborted—in these, alas! he can recognise himself entirely—whereas his masterpieces ought always to cause him surprise. Georges Bernanos, who was certainly not inclined to literary daintiness, commented on his *Diary of a Country Priest*: "I love this book as if it had not been written by me." And actually, in a sense—the sense suggested by Belloc in the observation which I quoted at the beginning—it was not by him. Indeed, could any clear-sighted writer ever believe that the source of his inspiration lies within himself? He might as well believe that he owns the rainbow or the moonlight which transfigures for one moment his little garden!

In the end, the gift of writing novels is not unlike God's grace: it is arbitrary, incomprehensible and sublimely unjust. It is not a scandal if novelists of genius prove to be wretched fellows; it is a comforting miracle that wretched fellows prove to be novelists of genius.

I have still not told you when Simenon was born, when he died, or how he lived. I have said nothing of the triumphs of his public life or of the dramas of his private life; I did not dwell on his parents, his origins, his career, his travels, his adventures, his pipes, his women, and all the Maigret folklore ... And you begin to see—I trust—why I shall not raise these matters. They are all false tracks, red herrings, dead-ends; they lead nowhere. What a zealous researcher might finally catch in his net—after dragging bleak expanses of mud—would hardly repay his efforts. Every life leaves behind an accumulation of broken odds and ends—bizarre and sometimes smelly. Rummaging there, one can always unearth enough evidence to establish that the deceased was both monstrous and mediocre. Such a combination is quite common—whoever doubts it needs only look at himself in a mirror.

Why should anyone work so hard to portray a Simenon who, in the end, looks like anybody else? The only Simenon who interests us resembles nobody, and this is what enabled him to write *Letter to My Judge*, *Widow Couderc*, *The Escapee*, *The Man Who Watched Trains Go By*, and so many other novels where, strangely, again and again, we return to draw the courage to contemplate our own misery without flinching. The truth that inhabited Simenon lies in his works, and there only. Whoever still insists to look elsewhere for it ought to reflect upon T. S. Eliot's lines:

> By this, and only this, we have existed
> Which is not to be found in our obituaries,
> Or in memories draped by the beneficent spider,
> Or under seals broken by the lean solicitor
> In our empty rooms.

THE BELGIANNESS OF
HENRI MICHAUX

Georges Perros, who was a marvellously sensitive reader ... had told me that "Even if one knows nothing of his background, reading Henri Michaux carefully leaves one in no doubt that he is Belgian."

—MICHEL BUTOR

This need [of Michaux's] to dig deep, this persistence of his, is not French. It is the advantage and the drawback of having been born in Brussels.[1]

—CIORAN

IN BELGIUM

Je plie / Je coule / Je m'appuie sur les coups que l'on me porte / ... / Et toi, qui en misère as abondance / Et toi, / Par ta soif, du moins tu es soleil / Épervier de la faiblesse, domine!

I fold / I sink / I lean into the blows I am dealt / ... / And you, who find abundance in poverty / And you, / who by your thirst, at least, are sunshine / Hawk of your weakness, dominate!

—HENRI MICHAUX, *Épreuves, Exorcismes*

ARTISTS who are content merely to hone their gifts eventually come to little. The ones who truly leave their mark have the strength and the courage to explore and exploit their shortcomings. Michaux sensed this from the outset: "I was born with holes in me." And he knew in an inspired way how to take advantage of it. "I have seven or eight senses. One of them is the sense of lack.... There are sicknesses which leave nothing at all of a man who is cured of them." Precautions were thus in order: "Always keep a reserve stock of maladaptation." In this area, however, Michaux was well provisioned from birth.

For in the first place he was Belgian. And not just Belgian, but a native of Namur—the province of a province. (The French tell Belgian jokes; the Belgians tell Namur jokes.) Speaking of Michaux, Jorge Luis Borges—rather well placed to appreciate such things, since Buenos Aires is not exactly the centre of the earth—stressed how great an advantage might be drawn from culturally marginal origins: "A writer born in a great nation is in danger of assuming that the culture of his native country suffices. In this, paradoxically, he is the one who tends to be provincial."[2]

At bottom, Belgianness is a diffuse awareness of a lack. The lack, first and foremost, of a language. In their use of French, Belgians are plagued by insecurities. Some stagger along in Walloon ruts; the rest flounder in a bog of Flemish expressions. Disturbed and anxious, they limp first on one leg and then on the other. For Michaux, however, the infirmity was even more radical: born in a Walloon town, then incarcerated while still a child in a strictly Flemish boarding school, he pulled off the remarkable feat of starting out in life hampered by *both* handicaps at once.[3]

Of course, Michaux soon sloughed off his "Walloon," and completely forgot the Flemish of his childhood, but something remained, something essential that imparts a unique flavour to his voice: "I do not always think directly in French." What is more, this circumstance made him especially sensitive to his compatriots' mistrustful, clumsy and hesitant attitude to language. In one of his very earliest writings, he observed that in Belgium "the commonest of insults is *stoeffer*, which means a pretentious person, a poseur. Belgians are afraid of pretentiousness ... especially the pretentiousness of the spoken or written word. Hence their accent—their notorious way of speaking French. The key here is this: Belgians believe that words are pretentious in themselves. They cloak and muffle them as much as they can, so much so that they become inoffensive and well-behaved. Speaking should be done, they think, rather as you might open your wallet, making sure to hide the large bills, or as if raising the alarm in the case of an accident—and even then gesturing broadly with the hands to help ease the word's passage."

After the lack of language comes a lack of space. "This sad, over-peopled land...muddy countryside squelching underfoot, terrain for frogs...no wildness. What is wild in this country? Wherever you thrust your hand you come upon beets or potatoes, or a turnip, or a rutabaga—stomach stuffing for the livestock as for this entire race of eaters of as much starch and stodge as possible. A few dirty, sluggish, devastated rivers with no place to go. Caskets, ho!... A landscape of little hills fit for motor-coach tourists; endless files go up, come down, looping, spiralling; ants, worker ants of a toiling country, toiling more that any other...."

Europe has a good many small countries, but this is the only one, seemingly, to take pride in its exiguity. It proclaims its smallness, boasts of it with satisfaction, basks in it, drapes itself in it like a flag. Have you ever heard the Dutch, the Danish, the Portuguese or the Swiss referring to themselves as "little Dutchmen," "little Danes," etc.? What is more, Belgium feels uncomfortable, uneasy, with its present form, and considers itself still *too big*! It would like to become even smaller, and it will no doubt do so. New plans are afoot to fragment the country even further, to split it up into ever smaller sections that can wriggle in complete autonomy like a worm severed by a gardener's spade.

———

But from the beginning the worst thing for Michaux was people: "The Belgians were the first human beings that I had the chance to be ashamed of."

"A race of shiny noses! A disgusting race that dangles, loiters, trickles—such was the race in the midst of which he was born. Masses of poor people, or rather of petty-rich ones. Rich people.... A people bloated, but bursting with inner strength, not noble, but proliferating." This original sin was very intimate for Michaux: "Have always felt estranged from my family.... The farther back I go into my childhood, the stronger my feeling of being a stranger in my parents' house."

For someone guilty of being a stranger at home, it was absolutely essential to find an elsewhere to offset this alarming state of affairs. But where to run to? "That Flemish countryside! You cannot contemplate it without putting everything in doubt. Those low houses that have not dared to risk another story upward, then all of a sudden a tall church steeple shoots into the air, as if this was the only thing in man capable of ascending, the only thing with a chance in the heights." Michaux too had sought that "chance in the heights": his earliest wish was to become a saint. In time, alas, you abandon such a wish, but you never get over it, never find consolation for its loss: "My father refused to let me join the Benedictines. The dream of my adolescence had been sainthood. I fell from a great height—very disorientated—when I lost my faith around twenty years of age.... I got into literature for lack of any better alternative.... Too impressed by the saints to take other people and their writings seriously.... What I am and what I do seemed to me then, and still seem to me—quite objectively, and by no means out of modesty—to be wretched. The achievements of almost all others seem likewise wretched, if not worse. The saints, even if their starting-point—at least as I see it—is mistaken ... are a magnificent fullfillment of man." (Much later on, moreover, during Michaux's visit to India, this never-forgotten aspiration of his adolescence gave him a particularly acute insight into a certain kind of professional holiness: "Nothing is sadder than failure. Rarely do the religious Hindus bear the mark of divinity. They have it as the critic of the *Times* and professors of literature have the stamp of literary genius.")

ELSEWHERE

> The author has often lived elsewhere.... He has found himself more at ease than in Europe. That is already something. At times he was very nearly domesticated. But not truly. One cannot be too wary about countries.
>
> —HENRI MICHAUX, Preface to *Ailleurs*

From the start travel emerged as Michaux's essential activity. It has been said that illnesses are the journeys of the poor; how much truer still to say that illnesses are the first and most prodigious journeys of children. Michaux had his full ration very early on, and throughout his life, and what is more he continually drew inspiration from those journeys. In parallel with this experience of sickness, he began botanical and entomological explorations in the family garden that foreshadowed the great expeditions of his youth and maturity. He observed the battles of ants and made friends with plants ("at the age of eight I was still dreaming of being classified as a plant"). Insects, mollusks and invertebrates never lost their fascination for him: "At the age of 34, and only then, I discovered cuttlefish. I adopted them, and came to believe, after hours and hours of watching them, that they likewise adopted me."

The most fundamental form of respect for others is the attention one pays them. Michaux saw no good reason why such attention should be confined to human beings: "For animals we tend to apply crowd psychology. Sparrows. Mice. But this particular sparrow, this particular mouse, what are their names?" To his relationship to trees, Michaux brought all the psychological insight and courtesy that he showed to his own kind (though what was his own kind?): just re-read his account of his encounters with bamboo, banyan or baobab. In the most natural way, without strain or affectation, he could adopt the point of view of a sheep or a tiger—even get inside the skin of a flea: "There is no evidence to show that the flea living on a mouse fears the cat." Michaux's bestiary is not anthropomorphic—rather, it is his insects that offer us an entomology of man: "Civilised insects do not understand that man does not secrete his pants. The others find nothing extraordinary about that fact." *Ecuador* (1929)—a work still experimental in some respects, but already masterly—provided a first demonstration of the poet's method, as perfectly summed up in the book's odd blurb: "The Author says not a word about the Panama Canal, but he does happen to speak about a fly."

Michaux's *Plume* affords a revealing glimpse of his experience of travel. Plume travels incessantly, but he has no talent for this activity: he knows only its disappointments, forever running into frustrations, having accidents, and falling prey to misunderstandings, misadventures, humiliations and ordeals that are sometimes ridiculous and sometimes sinister. "Plume could not say that he was excessively well treated when traveling. Some people pushed past him without warning; others wiped their hands nonchalantly on his jacket. In the end he got used to this. He preferred to travel modestly.... He said nothing, made no complaint. He thought of those unfortunates who could not travel at all, whereas for his part he could travel, and traveled all the time."

Why did Michaux travel? It was an essentially painful experience for him, as suggested by the disturbing metaphor of his expedition to the centre of the "opaque and slow life" of an apple: "I placed an apple on my table. Then I put myself inside the apple.... There was some groping about, various experiences. A whole long tale.... Leaving was not at all easy, and nor is explaining it. But I can tell you in one word—and that word is *suffering*. When I arrived inside the apple, I was freezing." As for Michaux's expeditions to South America, to Asia, they tried him in ways that were by no means metaphorical. As he confessed to a confidant, "I treated myself brutally, I forced myself to walk, but my body responded badly to these adventures." And elsewhere, in an interview: "I am not physically designed for adventure; my wounds do not heal; eight times they almost had to cut my leg off, and I have heart attacks."

In a laconic but highly significant autobiographical sketch that Michaux wrote for one of his commentators, he explained (speaking of himself in the third person) what he expected from travel: "He travels *against*. To rid himself of his native land, his attachments of every kind and everything that clings to him, despite himself, of Greek or Roman or Germanic culture, or of Belgian habits. Voyages of expatriation." He travels in a sense to purge himself: "Not to acquire anything. To impoverish yourself. That is what you need."

Michaux was not at ease traveling, yet the journey brought him relief—for he was even less at ease at home. Disquiet, which is abnormal for the settled, is at least natural in the traveler: being abroad offers existential angst a reassuring justification. This puts one in mind of a poem by Philip Larkin, "The Importance of Elsewhere" (although Larkin, be it said, has absolutely nothing in common with Michaux except for poetic genius and the challenge of being): "Lonely in Ireland since it was not home / Strangeness made sense.... / Living in England has no such excuse: / These are my customs and establishments / It would be much more serious to refuse. / Here no elsewhere underwrites my existence."

The reader who wishes to know more about Michaux's travels may usefully consult Jean-Pierre Martin's biographical study *Henri Michaux* (Paris: Gallimard, 2003). Unfortunately, on a matter of particular interest to me, namely the maritime interlude in the poet's life, this otherwise remarkable work failed to satisfy my curiosity. Granted, information is scant. But did the biographer follow up all possible avenues? And have the logical conclusions been fully drawn?

After completing his secondary education at a Jesuit school in Brussels, when Michaux was prevented by his father from becoming a monk, he eventually enrolled at the Université Libre de Bruxelles for first-year science in preparation for medicine. But he dropped out after a few months and resolved to go to sea. Breaking off with his parents, he left for France and for three months wandered from port to port (Dunkirk, Malo-les-Bains, Boulogne-sur-Mer) in a desperate search for a chance to put out to sea. His mood swung continually from extreme exaltation to deep depression. The mirage of embarkation formed again and again, only to dissipate each time. In late July 1920 he announced to Herman Closson, the close friend and former schoolmate with whom he had maintained a continuous correspondence since leaving Belgium, that "A week from today I shall certainly have left." After which he sent no news. The following year he surfaced in Marseilles, returned to his parents' house in Brussels, and then began his military service, from which he would be discharged a few months later on the grounds of a weak heart.

The first time that Michaux ever evoked his seaman's career was a quarter-century later, in 1946, in a letter-cum-memorandum to René Bertelé, who had asked him for biographical details: "I left Belgium at twenty-one and signed on as a seaman." Later still, in 1957, in "Quelques renseignements sur cinquante-neuf années d'existence" (Some Particulars on Fifty-Nine Years of Existence), written at the request of another commentator and biographer, Robert Bréchon, he supplied a little more information about his seagoing ventures:

> 1920. Boulogne-sur-Mer. Took ship as a seaman on a five-mast schooner.
>
> Rotterdam: second embarkation. Aboard *Le Victorieux*, ten thousand tons, a good-looking vessel which the Germans had just delivered to France. There were fourteen of us in cramped crew's quarters in the bow. Remarkable, unexpected and invigorating camaraderie. Bremen, Savannah, Norfolk, Newport News, Rio de Janeiro, Buenos Aires. Back in Rio, the crew, complaining of bad food, refused to go on and reported sick en bloc. In solidarity, he left the fine ship with them … thus avoiding the wreck of the vessel twenty days later south of New York.
>
> 1921. Marseilles. The worldwide laying-up of ships (former troop and supply transports) was at its height. No chance of signing on. The great window had closed. He had to turn his back on the sea.

Finally, at the age of eighty, in 1979, in answer to a query from an editor of the reference periodical *Contemporary Authors*, Michaux supplied the following additional information: "I never sailed under the Belgian flag. Twice I managed to sign on as a seaman on French ships, even though I had no qualifications at all. I was twenty-one."

The oddly belated and fragmentary nature of these details puzzles me. The first boat on which Michaux was hired was a sailing ship. And a strange one indeed: a "*cinq-mâts schooner*," he tells us. But the term does not exist.[4] Michaux was sailing on a French vessel; as occasional a sailor as he was, it is scarcely conceivable that after several months of life on board he had never learnt or retained the French name for the type of boat he was on. It is worth noting too that five-masted sailing vessels (rigged as schooners) were hardly to be found in Europe: they made their appearance early and soon disappeared, and were used for the most part in the United States, on both coasts, for transporting lumber or for offshore fishing. Such a boat, sailing under the French flag, would have been a rare bird indeed!

As for the second boat, Michaux did not trouble to say whether it was a sailing or a motor vessel; on the other hand, he gave its name, *Le Victorieux*, and its provenance as war reparation from Germany to France. On the basis of these two pieces of information it should be possible to trace this vessel in maritime archives, notably those of Lloyd's. Furthermore, if *Le Victorieux* foundered in 1921 off New York, the press must have reported the event at the time. Most of the ships on which Joseph Conrad sailed, for example, have been quite precisely identified by his biographers (name of vessel, tonnage, rigging, crew lists, etc.). Michaux's two boats would call for much less research, but it has not been done.

Another enigma too surrounds Michaux's seafaring. During his feverish search for employment as a seaman, he sent an unending flow of letters, as we have seen, to Herman Closson, the only friend to whom he opened up, keeping him abreast of the ups and downs of his quest and confiding in him about his alternating hopes and disappointments. Sometimes, if we are to believe him—although it becomes harder and harder to do so—he was within a hair's breadth of casting off. Finally (as mentioned above), Michaux bragged that "A week from today I shall certainly have left." Michaux was without vanity, but he had a diabolical pride; after such a declaration there would have been no backing down. But then what happened next? He disappeared. Complete silence. If he really did go to sea, and put in at all those exotic ports, whose very names would have fired the imaginations of the two adolescents, why did he never send so much as a triumphant postcard to his old chum whom he so loved to impress (not to mention the fact that he was an inveterate sender of postcards his whole life long)? But this time there was no word, no card—NOTHING! The correspondence with Closson did not resume until the very end of 1921—by which time Michaux was just beginning his national service in a Belgian barracks.

Let me mention one last reason—but not the least—for us to be mystified. For any sensitive and imaginative young man, and *a fortiori* for a young poet of genius, the very first sea voyage aboard an oceango-ing sailing ship must be a rough, overwhelming and unforgettable adventure. In Michaux's case, however, the experience left strictly *no trace* in his poetic output with the exception of a couple of short sibyl-line sentences in a prose piece on a completely different subject: "Poor A., what are you doing aboard that boat? Months pass; suffering, suf-fering. Sailor, what are you doing? Months pass; suffering, suffering." By contrast, when Michaux sailed to Ecuador some seven years later, the three-week crossing from Amsterdam to Guayaquil inspired the superb opening of his *Ecuador*—some twenty pages. In other words, his modest, indeed banal and routine experience as a simple passenger on a semi-cargo ship was enough to sharpen his capacity to observe and stir his imagination far more thoroughly than his supposed two years as a seaman!

In their chronology at the beginning of the first volume of the Pléi-ade edition of Michaux's complete works, the editors Raymond Bel-lour and Ysé Tran conclude, apropos of the years 1919–1921, that "No document exists offering details of Michaux's voyages as a sailor be-sides those particulars that he himself shared or made public." And Jean-Pierre Martin confirms this: "Of these crossings there is no trace. All we have is Michaux's own brief and retrospective testimony. Only a biographical note written by him over thirty years later." Yet Martin draws no inference from this.

For my own part, so long as we have no proof of the reality of this maritime chapter, I shall continue to think that it belongs to the sphere of the imagination. Which is not by any means to call Michaux a liar. He is a poet. And I take the word in the first two meanings as-signed it in Samuel Johnson's great dictionary: "Poet: an inventor; an author of fiction."

MICHAUX'S TOMB

I am afraid—afraid that, once dead, I shall have in some sense to live even longer.

—HENRI MICHAUX, "Note sur le suicide"

In these bibles [the Pléiade editions] errors become definitive.
　　　　—ARAGON, as reported by Matthieu Galey, *Journal I*

One day, a good twenty years ago, because in my writings on China I had several times expressed my admiration for Michaux, I received a letter from an unknown reader who wanted to know how it was possible for me to give so much consideration to an author who had so stupidly truckled to Maoism. When you publish books you are bound to receive a quantity of eccentric or bizarre letters, but this one seemed to break all bounds. The qualities that make Michaux especially dear to us are precisely his tonic disrespect, his honed intelligence and his absolute originality: all his ideas were arrived at independently, thanks to a sort of wild naïveté, and he never allowed himself to follow any kind of fashion. It should be added that when he was traveling in China (1932) the very name of Mao was still largely unknown. Clearly my correspondent must be a crazy compulsive letter-writer. I tossed the letter away, but the memory of it continued to nag vaguely at me, for, as absurd as its content had been, its form and style in no way suggested that the writer was a lunatic. But what could the letter possibly refer to?

The answer to the puzzle was revealed to me only many years later, when the first volume of Michaux's complete works came out in a Pléiade edition. There I learnt that from 1963 to 1972 Michaux had worked on a reissue of all the works he had published with Gallimard; and that with this in mind he had undertaken to revise, correct and rewrite a number of his old texts. This vast revision was disastrous overall (we shall see why in a moment)—but, alas, this was the version that the Pléiade editors chose to follow blindly[5]—forgetting, apparently, that the first duty of a literary editor is to exercise critical judgement, and that the first duty of a critic is sometimes (as D. H. Lawrence said) to keep a work out of the hands of its creator.[6]

The phenomenon of writers of genius who, late in life, cease to understand their own greatest achievements, who disavow and distort their own work, or set about recasting and mutilating it, is certainly alarming, but it is by no means unusual. Had his death not supervened, Gogol would have utterly ruined his *Dead Souls* by adding a frightful second part in the shape of a moral sermon. Tolstoy in his old age judged that he had been guilty of wasting his time writing a frivolous novel such as *Anna Karenina*, and that he would have been better employed producing religious propaganda. At the end his life, Henry James undertook to rewrite a number of his novels for a new edition of his complete works; a certain tortured verbosity which is often thought to typify his style is in reality the result of this late and unfortunate revision, which at the time elicited a horrified reaction from the New York critics: "One wishes Mr. James would demonstrate more respect for the classics, not least those that came from his own pen." And Conrad, suffering in the twilight of his days from a veritable paralysis of the imagination, renounced the rich ambiguity of the great novels of his maturity. Even the creators of comic books may fall victim to this deplorable revisionitis: Hergé redrew all the *Tintin*s of the early part of his career, and in so doing killed all the verve and spice that had infused the graphics of the original plates.[7]

The greater a work's originality and perfection, the greater its vulnerability to the risk of later ill treatment at the hands its creator. An inspired work is one which has by its very definition *escaped* its author; this creates the danger that the author will want to recapture it and strive maladroitly to regain control over it. No artist dwells on a par with his finest creations, and this gap can become a source of perplexity and hostility in him. It is not surprising, therefore, that in Michaux's case it was *A Barbarian in Asia*—his masterpiece—that was the most cruelly manhandled by his revisions.

Michaux's struggles with his rebellious child prodigy were initiated rather early. Discomfort was already apparent in the author's new preface of 1945: "Twelve years now separate me from this voyage. It is there. I am here. . . . It cannot be developed. Nor can it be corrected."

In point of fact, however, Michaux was itching to correct it! His preface to the American edition (New York: New Directions, 1949) did not bode well. Although stupidity was never his strong suit, he was led to say stupid things. He bleated edifying platitudes quite beside the point: "Man needs a vast far-sighted aim, extending beyond his lifetime. A training rather than a hindrance for the coming planetary civilisation. To avoid war—construct peace." Blah, blah, blah.

(One is reminded of Chaplin, who, having had the genius to make *The Great Dictator*, felt the need to attach to it a long schmaltzy sermon addressed to every *belle âme* on the planet.) Finally, in the new edition of 1967, thirty-five years after *Barbarian* was written, Michaux could restrain himself no longer: this time he would take on the text itself and fix it once and for all. He began by writing a new preface in which he apologised for ever perpetrating such a work, one that "embarrassed and offended" him, that made him ashamed.

He would have liked, he went on, as a "counterweight," to introduce elements that were "more serious, more thoughtful, more profound, more experienced, more educated." But (thank the Lord!) the book put up a resistance. So what could be done? First of all, cut—cut more or less everywhere, removing all those disrespectful passages that Michaux now found shocking and intolerable. Later, in the wake of a last visit to Japan, Michaux edulcorated *Barbarian* even further for the new edition of 1989. For want of space, let me cite just a few samples of this self-censorship—instances chosen completely at random (I have signalled deleted matter by means of italics)[8]:

> ...*Hindu religion* [is] *double-faced, one for the initiated, the other for fools. Humility is certainly a quality of the highest order; but not degradation.*

> *The Hindu is often ugly, with an ugliness that is vicious and poor.*

> *In France you tell dirty jokes and you laugh at them. Here* [in India] *you tell them, you absorb them without laughing. You follow them dreamily. You visualise the interplay of organs.*

> [The literature of] the Chinese which is almost devoid of heartbreak poetry, of complaint, has no charm whatsoever for the European, *excepting a hundred or so librarians, who by dint of reading know nothing whatsoever about anything.*

> *A Chinese general who does his business in his trousers, who begs the colonel to take his place in the battle, surprises no one. No one*

calls for his trousers to be displayed. Everyone thinks this quite natural. One day I saw five officers who were swearing to exterminate I don't remember whom. They looked like rabbits.

[The Chinese:] *An old, old childish people that does not want to know what is at the bottom of anything, that has no principles, but "cases"; no law, but "cases"; no morals, but "cases."*

A Chinese prostitute is less obviously sensual than a European mother of a family. She immediately shows affection. She seeks to attach herself.

[In Japan] The men are *ugly,* without sparkle—they are sad, wasted and dry... *The look of very little men, petty clerks without a future, of corporals, subordinates,* servants of Baron X or of Mr. Z or of the papaland... *little pig eyes and decayed teeth.* The women... are *stocky, short, for the most part* solid, *and all flank from leg to shoulder. The face is sometimes pleasant,* but the pleasantness lacks *purpose and* emotion; *the head is always so big, big with what? With emptiness? Why such a big head, for such a small face and still less expressiveness?*...The same in character as in appearance: a great indifferent, insensitive blanket, but a trifle touchy and sentimental *(like soldiers),* laughing in little wild bursts *like a servant girl....*

A religion of insects, *exactly the religion of ants, Shintoism with its famous* cult of the anthill, *an ant people.*

[Japan is] *a country... where a young girl who is not very rich is normally sold to a brothel keeper, to serve the multitude (as far as they have individuality!) Service, always service!*

In the censored and rewritten version of 1989, Michaux felt it necessary to add a special note of apology at the beginning of the chapter on Japan, asking that he be forgiven for certain pages that he read "with embarrassment, even stupefaction in places. Half a century has elapsed, and the portrait is unrecognisable." (In point of fact they were droll and glaringly true to life!) Michaux ends this preliminary note on a tone that is soothing and sycophantic, not to say insufferably priggish and patronising: "The Japan of that time, with its cramped, suspicious and tense feel, has been surpassed. It is clear that, at the far end of the earth, Europe has now found a neighbour."

———

Michaux's excisions are frequently combined with rewriting. The new version of *A Barbarian in Asia* sets out to file down all sharp points, smooth all angles, and dull the tone overall. So much effort expended to humour everyone, to offend no sensitive ear! No indecency, no familiarity! Respect all taboos! Tread on no one's toes! Consideration for the old and the crippled, compassion for every widow and orphan! Thus the Brahmins, originally described as "jealous as hunchbacks, but always ignorant as carp," are now taxed soberly with being merely "jealous, often ignorant."

Or again: "The priest is a pimp and his temple is full of women" is demurely reduced to "the temple has women."

In the original, as compared with the natural nobility of Arabs and Hindus, "the Europeans here all look like plain workmen or errand-boys." Revised version: "the Europeans seem fragile, secondary, transitory."

In the original, as opposed to the exquisite modesty of Bengali women, "European women seem like whores." The newer text, after likewise evoking the modesty of Bengali women, is content to interject a chaste "How different from European women!"

The idiom becomes academic and starchy. Where the original has "a poor blind man in Europe automatically arouses a distinct compassion. In India, if he thinks he can count on his blindness to move people, *just let him try*," the revised version reads: "In India, let him not count on his blindness to move people."

The delightful sideswipes vanish. For instance, "The poetry of a people is more deceptive than its dress; it is manufactured by aesthetes, *who are bored and who are only understood among themselves*" is prudently neutralised: "The poetry of a people, which at any period is manufactured by aesthetes, is more deceptive than its dress."

Vigorous expression gives way to reverences (along with gratuitous cultural parentheses as guarantors of the author's good breeding). For example, consider this original text: "While many countries that one has liked become, as the distance from them increases, *almost ridiculous* or insubstantial, Japan, which I *frankly detested*, grows almost dear to me."—and compare it with the revision: "While many countries that one has liked tend, as the distance from them increases, to fade away, Japan, which I rejected, now takes on greater importance (the memory of an admirable Noh play has made its way into my mind and is extending its sway over me)."

Strong words are replaced by feeble ones. "Who will gauge the weight of the *imbeciles* in a civilisation?" becomes "Who will gauge the weight of the *mediocre* in a civilisation?"

With the passage of thirty-five years, the poet is a convert to the use of soap. Originally, he had noted approvingly that the Chinese "*detests water (dirt, moreover, is excellent for the personality)*"—words that disappear completely in the revised version. Elsewhere in *Barbarian,* he had written: "*In the opinion of a relatively dirty man like myself,* washing, like a war, is a trifle puerile, because it has to be done all over again after a while." In the corrected version, the general idea is retained, but the touching personal allusion goes by the board.

A scatological tendency had long been spontaneous and natural for Michaux, but the revision meant purging his prose of any reference, even the most figurative, to alimentary functions. The Indians, he had written, "are all constipated....This constipation is the most irritating of all, a constipation of the breath and the soul." This is turned in the corrected version into "The Indians are all rigid, set in concrete....This constriction, the most irritating of all, that of the breath and the soul...." The same obsession with decency led him, in the case of *Ailleurs*, to suppress "La Diarrhée des Ourgouilles"—a whole section of earthy Bruegelian imagining describing "diarrhea accompanied by autophagy: man is digested and evacuated little by little by his own gut."[9]

By cutting and rewriting so many passages, Michaux certainly damaged *A Barbarian in Asia*, but what put the finishing touches to the destruction were his *additions*. I have shown how he disavowed his critical vision of Japan—a distinctly perverse disavowal when one considers that in 1932 he had very accurately grasped the nature of a society suffocating under a sinister military-fascist regime. (By analogy, intelligent and sensitive visitors to Berlin in the late 1930s who testified in all honesty to their revulsion would scarcely need to apologise today!) But on the subject of China, things are even worse: Michaux unquestioningly accepts the image of China put about by Maoist propaganda in France during the "Cultural Revolution." He denies a reality he so clearly perceived in the past on the basis of crass lies being fed him in the present. From the start, in the new preface, he strives to invalidate his masterpiece: "In China, the [Maoist] revolution, by sweeping away habits and ways of being, acting and feeling unchanged for centuries, even for millennia, has also swept away a great many opinions, including not a few of mine. *Mea culpa*—not only for not *seeing* well enough, but even more for failing to *feel* what was gestating, what was about to undo the seemingly permanent. Did I really see nothing? Why? Ignorance?..." This is enough to make one weep. And then, throughout the book, Michaux inserts new notes intended to rectify, in the light of the sacred revelations of Maoism, everything heretical in his earlier thoughts.

"In a single generation," he writes, "politics, economics and the transformation of the social classes have created a new 'man in the street' in China. The man I once described and the one that I and other visitors once observed is no longer recognisable.... China has returned to life. We should be happy no longer to recognise it, to perceive it differently: as ever startling, ever extraordinary." Michaux comments as follows on a passage in which he had evoked the fear that restrained the Chinese from making connections with foreign visitors: "How extraordinary it must feel for anyone returning there now—in the very towns where people once shrank away from them—to encounter self-confident faces, no longer evasive but smiling, friendly, open." By a grim irony, Michaux added this note while the "Cultural Revolution" was in full spate, at a time when passers-by in the street dared not give you directions, because the mere act of exchanging a couple of words with a foreigner could immediately be treated as a crime. Similarly, whereas the first edition of *Barbarian* simply stated that "No city has gates as massive as Peking," the revised version embellishes: "No city in the world has gates as massive, as beautiful, or as reassuring as those of Peking." How true! But how in the world could Michaux have made these additions at the very moment when the "Cultural Revolution" was completing the demolition of those very gates?

The poet who fifteen years earlier had so very well understood that "One who sings in a group will, when asked, put his brother in prison," now joined the vast chorus of "useful idiots" singing the praises of Chairman Mao—that "man of boldness, author of the Little Red Book, so simple, so reasonable.... Mao Zedong who turned China around, utterly transforming a thousand-year-old society in a few years, who conceived the boldest of projects, some of which were unrealisable, but were realised [*sic*], others almost harebrained in their audacity, as for example the setting up of small village blast-furnaces to produce steel, an idea that bucked the advice of all the technicians, or the creation of new villages with collective dormitories...."

———

There is no need to continue with this inventory of nonsense. Even coming, as they do, from eminent writers, such claims are inane; coming from Michaux they are terrifying. How could this irreducibly free spirit have calmly swallowed propaganda addressed by criminals to idiots? How could this utterly original poet have changed into a yes-man thinking in clichés and writing in slogans? How could such a master of insolence fall to his knees and fill the air with fake incense?

What happened?

What happened, quite simply, is that *Michaux turned into a Frenchman!*

But whoa! Don't let me be misunderstood. I am not silly enough to think that the nation that produced Rabelais and Hugo, Montaigne and Pascal, Stendhal and Baudelaire is in any way lacking in literary intelligence (even if, when it comes to Maoism, some members of the

French intellectual elite have easily beaten the world record for stupidity). No, what I am saying is something quite different.

If there is one thing that Belgians are absolutely convinced of it is their own insignificance. Paradoxically, this vouchsafes them an incomparable kind of freedom—a salutary disrespect, a blithe impertinence bordering on the ingenuous. The ant has no qualms about walking across an elephant's foot; and there are little birds that go pecking inside the crocodile's gaping mouth (the crocodile does not mind—after all, it saves him brushing his teeth). To put it another way, the Belgian is a sort of court jester: since nothing he says can be taken seriously, *he can say whatever he likes.* Throughout the first half of his long existence, this was how Michaux spontaneously saw himself. A reader largely unacquainted with Michaux, or one whose knowledge of *A Barbarian in Asia* was confined to the samples of self-censorship that I provided above, might even suppose that Michaux's work must amount to an odious racist tract produced by the colonial-imperial era. Michaux must have fallen victim himself to this misapprehension of the uninformed reader when, later, after he had turned into a Frenchman, he re-read his writings; indeed he acknowledged this when he said that he felt "embarrassed" and "ashamed" and undertook to cut all the passages that offended his newfound sense of the proprieties.

The truth is that Michaux's most ferocious barbs were aimed at his compatriots, which is quite natural inasmuch as he knew the Belgians full well, and did not like them. But when, amidst his Asiatic travels, he published a journal article, a funny and pitilessly accurate short essay on Argentina and the Argentines, the splenetic reaction of the Buenos Aires press staggered and dismayed him. He immediately vented his confusion in a vehement and telling letter to a South American woman friend. Clearly, he did not understand how these Argentines, whom he liked very much, could take umbrage at his statements, for as a Belgian he was quite used to hearing far worse things said about his own country.

Michaux settled down in Paris at twenty-five. He had fled Belgium; in the early days he returned as little as possible, and eventually not at all. But—and this is significant—in order to write *Ailleurs* (1928), one of his major works, he felt the need to spend six months at a hotel in Antwerp. In Paris, indiscernibly and gradually, his life became more livable; he began to enjoy an intelligent, sociable and agreeable type of existence. Solitary and withdrawn as he was, there was nothing wild about Michaux. His circle of acquaintances, though hardly fashionable, was by no means narrow. Cioran, who had friendly feelings for Michaux, and who knew him well (though affection never blunted the acuity of Cioran's judgement), gently applied to him Jean-Louis Forain's cruel description of "a hermit who knows the railway timetable."

When I say that Michaux became French, I am not, of course, talking about a change of passports, which is inconsequential, but rather about adopting a different attitude: he was now entitled to bestow certificates of good conduct and medals for meritorious contributions, be it to Mao's China or to post-war Japan (something that would never have occurred to him while he was still Belgian). But at the same time he was obliged to mind his language. An arrogant Belgian is a contradiction in terms—a notion whose very evocation is laughable. But arrogance is something the suspicion of which the French must continually beware. In foreign parts, among disinherited indigenous people, the French are often led willy-nilly to parade their national identity like some kind of holy sacrament that must never be dishonoured.[10] Thus Michaux, being a decent man, felt a moral obligation to censor *A Barbarian in Asia*.

In the end Michaux forgot his own principles—"Always keep a reserve stock of maladaptation" and "There are sicknesses which leave nothing at all of a man who is cured of them."

Delivered from his Belgianness, he cut himself off from the central inspiration of his genius, but he now lived with less difficulty. Perhaps, indeed, he eventually succeeded in finding a kind of happiness. Even if his readers were thereby the losers, who can blame him?

POSTSCRIPT

A reliable source, whose information comes from someone close to Michaux, tells me that, at the very end of his life, for a foreign edition of *A Barbarian in Asia*, Michaux urged his translator to use not the revised but the original version of his book. If this information is correct—and I have no reason to doubt it—then we must conclude that Michaux eventually became aware of the error he had made in rewriting his masterpiece. And, further, that the choice of the Pléiade editors, which served to ratify and consecrate this error, is all the more deplorable for it.

THE SINS OF THE SON
The Posthumous Publication of Nabokov's Unfinished Novel

> The bitterness of an interrupted life is nothing compared to the bitterness of an interrupted work: the probability of a continuation of the first beyond the grave seems infinite by comparison with the hopeless incompleteness of the second. *There* perhaps it will seem nonsense, but *here* all the same it remains unwritten.
>
> —VLADIMIR NABOKOV, 1965
> unpublished, unfinished Russian continuation of *The Gift*

WHEN WRITING novels, Vladimir Nabokov proceeded in a very peculiar fashion: he used first to form in his mind a complete vision of the entire work, and then would start to jot down, on filing cards, a first draft of disconnected fragments without logical or chronological order. These cards—of a size slightly smaller than a standard postcard—carried each, on the recto side only, a short passage (from one line to one or two paragraphs) couched in his large and fairly legible handwriting. Some cards stood in isolation, presenting one detached sentence—an idea, a descriptive touch; others formed numbered sequences of sustained narrative (twenty-odd cards in two instances). In a second stage, he would shift and assemble the cards, elaborating a tentative structure, sketching links and connections, weaving together the various threads of the plot. The composition would progressively take shape, till a continuous, final, clean draft could be established, welding together all the earlier elements into a seamless whole.

Nabokov began work on his last novel in 1975, but he was soon interrupted by a series of accidents and deteriorating health. At the time of his death (1977), the first stage of the process was not even half complete; what remains is only a set of 138 filing cards—which, if printed continuously in standard book-format, would scarcely fill thirty pages.

What should have been done with these 138 filing cards? As his son, Dmitri, recalls, during his final illness on his hospital bed Nabokov instructed his wife, the admirable Vera, that should the book "remain unfinished at his death, it was to be burned."

The devoted widow could not bear to execute this instruction to the letter—it would have entailed the destruction of what was for her a most precious memento—but she respected her husband's will in its essential aspect: she never disclosed these uncorrected fragments to the reading public. After her death in 1991, Dmitri Nabokov, only son of the extraordinary couple, became sole custodian of the Nabokov literary estate. Eighteen years later, after having done "a great deal of thinking" (described in a convoluted and obscure paragraph in his introduction), he finally decided to have them published in the present form as *The Original of Laura: A Novel in Fragments*: a large, luxurious volume presenting, on 138 cardboard pages printed on only one side, detachable facsimile reproductions of the 138 filing cards; each card occupies the upper half of a page, with its contents reproduced in printed form on the lower half.

If the reader so wishes, he can detach any card (or all of them) by simply pressing along the frame. Then, having the cards in hand, he becomes free to shuffle or re-arrange them in whatever order he deems to be closer to Nabokov's original design (or finds more pleasing to his own personal taste). Without its cards, the book, now hollowed out, can be shelved back in your library: its outer aspect remains unchanged, yet it now conceals a cavity in which you can conveniently store your last will, your house keys, a small flask of old Calvados or your wife's favourite earrings.

———

But what of Nabokov's original design? Laura is the main character of a novel-within-the-novel; she is based on Flora, mistress of the author of the novel-within-the-novel. Flora also has a husband, an elderly neurologist who is conducting an experiment upon himself involving a new method of mental suicide by progressive self-obliteration from consciousness, starting at the tips of his toes. Flora had a Lolita-type experience in her childhood with a lodger of her mother's, a middle-aged pervert called this time not Humbert Humbert, but Hubert Hubert. Yet it would be utterly unfair and unwise to reduce a literary experience to the mere unravelling of some incomplete plot lines—one might as well watch on a screen the performance of a great violinist with the sound switched off.

What, then, of the literary experience? The 138 filing cards can easily be read in a sitting. The dominant impression is one of confusion and frustration—actually it brought irresistibly to my mind Balzac's description of "the unknown masterpiece" in his philosophical short story of the same title. An old painter, called Frenhofer, has been working for ten years on what he believes will be his ultimate masterpiece. Young artists are in awe of his genius and worship the bedazzling skill of his brush; they are burning with desire to contemplate his latest work, but Frenhofer keeps his studio tightly locked at all times. One day, however, two disciples are finally admitted inside. They are flabbergasted. The unknown masterpiece is standing on its easel, but at first they can see nothing. "The old man is playing a practical joke on us!" said one. "I can only see a chaos of colours, a jumble of bizarre lines—the whole thing is but an incoherent wall of paint!" Coming closer, they discover in one corner of the canvas the extremity of a bare foot still untouched by the surrounding anarchy—but what a foot! Delicate, feminine, alive! With a mixture of admiration and consternation they stare at this tiny fragment of pure perfection afloat in the midst of an unspeakable disaster.

The 138 Nabokovian filing cards present a similarly puzzling assemblage. There are, here and there, a few echoes of his sharp wit, flashes of the familiar fireworks. In these spots one recognises the master's hand, but too often these faint traces are a reminder not so much of his old magic as of his less endearing mannerisms. For instance, one card attempts a pointless debunking of a series of major modern French writers, lumped together simply because, apart from sharing an alleged "mediocrity," their patronyms start with the letter

M. Thus, on this asinine basis, Michaux finds himself gratuitously paired with Montherlant (misspelt by Nabokov as "Montherland"!)—whereas, in actual fact, these two writers have *nothing* in common but their literary genius. This sort of petulant self-importance was detected long ago by Hannah Arendt, who wrote to Mary McCarthy:

> There is something in [Nabokov] which I greatly dislike, as though he wanted to show you all the time how intelligent he is. And as though he thinks of himself in terms of "more intelligent than." There is something vulgar in his refinement, and I am a bit allergic to this kind of vulgarity because I know it so well, know so many people cursed with it.

Arendt adds that the book of Nabokov which she admires above all is his "long essay on Gogol" (*Nikolai Gogol*, Norfolk, Conn.: New Directions, 1944), a slim volume that is in fact a flamboyant manifesto of Nabokovian literary aesthetics. However much I love *Pnin* and admire *Lolita*, I confess I am in full accord with Arendt's preference.

Why publish now (against Nabokov's clear and clear-sighted instructions!) these fragmented, tentative, unfinished, uncorrected and largely uninspired drafts?

After Nabokov's death, his widow was first in charge of the administration of his literary estate, until her own death fourteen years later. Vera's own attitude concerning this particular issue deserves all our attention, for no other human being could have been more qualified, both on moral and on aesthetic grounds, to take the right decision in such a matter.

When Vera first met Vladimir (in 1923) they were both young Russian exiles, wandering through Europe—she was twenty-one, he twenty-four. Both were highly educated and exceptionally gifted. They had experienced similar tragedies, and they shared the same precarious existence in a time of great turmoil. They fell in love, married and, for more than half a century, they virtually never parted, however briefly, from each other's company: they were inseparable. Witnesses who had the privilege to observe them at close range during their very last years marvelled at the evident freshness and intensity of their mutual love. From the outset Vera had recognised Vladimir's genius; her faith never wavered. When critical acclaim and huge international success finally crowned Nabokov's literary art (it came fairly late in life, with the publication of *Lolita* in 1955), it was no surprise to Vera—it merely confirmed what she had always known. With her intelligence and her cosmopolitan culture, she could have had a career of her own; yet, from the start, she decided to put herself completely and exclusively at the service of Nabokov's creative activity. She became not only his first reader and literary adviser, but also his secretary, typist, agent, driver, assistant, translator, public relations manager, telephonist, editor—and muse. Though she deliberately made herself invisible to the eyes of the public (inasmuch as this was feasible for such a radiant beauty), her relationship with her husband was anything but subservient; Nabokov admired her and relied upon her judgement. Without doubt, some theorists with an agenda will sooner or later conclude that Nabokov's books were actually written by Vera (in fact, she wrote part of his correspondence); yet such stupidity may unwittingly contain a subtle truth: he wrote his books, but she made him. Without Vera, what sort of books would he have written? No one can tell, though surely they would have been the work of a different man.

Vera had her own opinions, which Nabokov greatly valued. Twice she prevented him from burning the manuscript of *Lolita*, and she succeeded in persuading him to pursue a work of which he had despaired. Her respect for his writing was scrupulous and uncompromising; during Nabokov's academic career, for example, when some illness prevented him from giving a lecture, Vera would act as substitute teacher, reading to the class the lecture he had drafted, without allowing herself to modify a single comma.

———

Regarding *The Original of Laura*, however, Vera followed only half of Nabokov's instructions. Love prevented her from destroying drafts handwritten by her husband; but taste and literary judgement prevented her from publishing them.

Eighteen years after his mother's death, Dmitri finally decided to publish these posthumous fragments. It would be impertinent for us to speculate on his motivations. He was close to his parents; his affection and admiration for his father are evident, as is his devotion to his father's works; he spent much time preparing editions and translations of Nabokov's writings. Anyway, Dmitri's love and dedication are not the issue here. The question is: what about his taste and judgement?

In this field, he once had a notorious lapse. At the time of the international triumph of *Lolita*—as a film adaptation was being prepared —young Dmitri (he was twenty-six at the time) had the idea to stage in Italy (where he was pursuing his opera-singing career) a fake casting contest for the part of Lolita. In *Vladimir Nabokov: The American Years*, Brian Boyd writes (drawing on Dmitri's own words, as quoted in Vladimir's selected letters and Dmitri's published memoirs):

> For two days his Milan apartment was invaded by "decidedly postpubescent aspiring nymphets, some with provincial mothers in tow." When his father saw a magazine photograph of the "finalists" surrounding Dmitri on his oversized satin-covered bed, he cabled his son at once to stop "the Lolita publicity" immediately. And he sent a stern letter, warning Dmitri that such a puerile stunt could only harm his own career.

Of course, Dmitri was duly contrite afterwards. This youthful indiscretion took place nearly fifty years ago; it would be far-fetched to invoke it today against the old man who recently took the initiative to publish *The Original of Laura*. Still, one may regret that on this occasion, no stern fatherly cable could have come in time to put a quick stop to this enterprise.

CUNNING LIKE A HEDGEHOG

In memory of Jean-François Revel (1924–2006), man of letters, man of integrity, friend

G.K. CHESTERTON, whose formidable mind drew inspiration from a vast culture—literary, political, poetical, historical and philosophical—once received the naïve praise of a lady: "Oh, Mr. Chesterton, you know so many things!" He suavely replied: "Madam, I know nothing: I am a journalist."

The many enemies of French philosopher Jean-François Revel often attempted to dismiss him as a mere journalist which, of course, he was among many other things, and very much in the Chestertonian fashion.

At first it may seem odd to associate these two names: what could there be in common between the great Christian apologist and the staunch atheist, between the mystical poet and the strict rationalist, between the huge, benevolent man-mountain and the short, fiery, nimble and pugnacious intellectual athlete (and, should we also add, between the devoted husband and the irrepressible ladies' man)? One could multiply the contrasts, yet, on a deeper level, the essence of their genius was very much alike.

Revel was an extrovert who took daily delight in the company of his friends:

Various lines in this essay repeat things I have said elsewhere in different contexts; on purely literary-aesthetic grounds I should therefore have omitted it altogether. The problem is, these are things I do believe in, and which are relevant to my arguments. Revel's presence is irreplaceable—it should not disappear from my book.

> I am the most sociable creature; other people's society is my joy. Though, for me, a happy day should have a part of solitude, it must also afford a few hours of the most intense of all the pleasures of the mind: conversation. Friendship has always occupied a central place in my life, as well as the keen desire to make new acquaintances, to hear them, to question them, to test their reactions to my own views.

Always sparring with his interlocutors, he was passionately committed to his ideas, but if he took his own beliefs with utter seriousness, he did not take his own person seriously. Again, one could apply to him what Chesterton's brother said of his famous sibling: "He had a passionate need to express his opinions, but he would express them as readily and well to a man he met on a bus."

Revel's capacity for self-irony is the crowning grace of his memoirs, *The Thief in an Empty House*. Personal records can be a dangerous exercise, but in his case it eventuated in a triumphant masterpiece.

His humour enchanted his readers but kept disconcerting the more pompous pundits. The French greatly value wit, which they display in profusion, but humour often makes them uneasy, especially when it is applied to important subjects; they do not have a word for it, they do not know the thing.

Whereas wit is a form of duelling—it aims to wound or to kill—the essence of humour is self-deprecatory. Once again, a Chestertonian saying could be apposite:

> My critics think that I am not serious, but only funny, because they think that "funny" is the opposite of "serious." But "funny" is the opposite of "not funny" and nothing else. Whether a man chooses to tell the truth in long sentences or in short jokes is analogous to whether he chooses to tell the truth in French or German.

What compounded the dismay of Revel's pretentious critics was his implacable clarity. One of his close friends and collaborators said he doubted if Revel, in his entire career, had written a single sentence that was obscure. In the Parisian intellectual world such a habit can easily ruin a writer's credit, for simple souls and solemn mediocrities are impressed only by what is couched in opaque jargon. And, in their eyes, how could one possibly say something important if one is not self-important?

With the accuracy of his information and the sharpness of his irony, Revel deflated the huge balloons of cant that elevate the chattering classes. They felt utterly threatened, for he was exposing the puffery of the latest intellectual fashions upon which their livelihood depended. At times they could not hide their panic; for instance, the great guru of the intelligentsia, Jacques Lacan, during one of his psychoanalytical seminars at the Sorbonne, performed in front of his devotees a voodoo-like exorcism. He frantically trampled underfoot and destroyed a copy of Revel's book *Why Philosophers?*, in which Lacan's charlatanism was analysed.

Yet such outbursts were mere circus acts; far more vicious was the invisible conspiracy that surrounded Revel with a wall of silence, well documented in Pierre Boncenne's *Pour Jean-François Revel: Un esprit libre* (Paris: Plon, 2006), a timely and perceptive book that takes the full measure of Revel's intellectual, literary and human stature.

A paradoxical situation developed: Revel's weekly newspaper columns were avidly read, nearly every one of his thirty-odd books was an instant bestseller, and yet the most influential "progressive" critics studiously ignored his existence. His books were not reviewed, his ideas were not discussed, if his name was mentioned at all it was with a patronising sneer, if not downright slander.

Revel was quintessentially French in his literary tastes and sensitivity (his pages on Michel de Montaigne, François Rabelais and Marcel Proust marry intelligence with love; his anthology of French poetry mirrors his original appreciation of the poetic language), in his art of living (his great book on gastronomy is truly "a feast in words") and in his conviviality (he truly cared for his friends).

And yet what strikingly set him apart from most other intellectuals of his generation was his genuinely cosmopolitan outlook. He spent the best part of his formative and early creative years abroad, mostly in Mexico and Italy. In addition to English (spoken by few educated French of his time) he was fluent in Italian, Spanish and German; until the end of his life he retained the healthy habit of starting every day (he rose at 5 a.m.) by listening to the BBC news and reading six foreign newspapers.

On international affairs, on literature, art and ideas, he had universal perspectives that broke completely from the suffocating provincialism of the contemporary Parisian elites. In the eighteenth century, French was the common language of the leading minds of continental Europe; twentieth-century French intellectuals hardly noticed that times had changed in this respect; they retained the dangerous belief that whatever was not expressed in French could hardly matter.

Revel never had enough sarcasm to denounce this sort of self-indulgence; on the bogus notion of *le rayonnement français*, he was scathing: "French culture has radiated for so long, it's a wonder mankind has not died from sunstroke." He fiercely fought against chauvinist cultural blindness, and especially against its most cretinous expression: irrational anti-Americanism. At the root of this attitude he detected a subconscious resentment: the French feel that when Americans are playing a leading role in the political-cultural world they are usurping what is by birthright a French prerogative.

By vocation and academic training Revel was originally a philosopher (he entered at an exceptionally early age the École Normale Supérieure, the apex of the French higher education system). He taught philosophy and eventually wrote a history of Western philosophy (eschewing all technical jargon, it is a model of lucid synthesis).

However, he became disenchanted with the contemporary philosophers who, he felt, had betrayed their calling by turning philosophy into a professional career and a mere literary genre. "Philosophy," he wrote, "ought to return to its original and fundamental question: How should I live?" He preferred simply to call himself "a man of letters."

Ancient Greek poet Archilochus famously said, "The fox knows many things but the hedgehog knows one big thing." Revel was the archetypal fox, but at the same time he held with all the determination of a hedgehog to one central idea that inspires, pervades and motivates all his endeavours: the belief that each individual destiny, as well as the destiny of mankind, depends upon the accuracy—or the falsity—of the information at their disposal, and upon the way in which they put this information to use. He devoted one of his books specifically to this issue, *La Connaissance inutile* (Useless Knowledge), but this theme runs through nearly all his writings.

Politics naturally absorbed a great amount of his attention. From the outset he showed his willingness to commit himself personally and at great risk: as a young man in occupied France he joined the Resistance against the Nazis. After the war, his basic political allegiance was, and always remained, to the Left and the principles of liberal democracy. He was sharply critical of Charles de Gaulle and of all saviours and providential leaders in military uniforms.

Yet, like George Orwell before him, he always believed that only an uncompromising denunciation of all forms of Stalinist totalitarianism can ensure the ultimate victory of socialism. Thus—again, like Orwell—he earned for himself the hostility of his starry-eyed comrades.

Revel's attempt at entering into active politics was short-lived, but the experience gave him an invaluable insight into the essential intellectual dishonesty that is unavoidably attached to partisan politicking. He was briefly a Socialist Party candidate at the 1967 national elections, which put him in close contact with François Mitterrand (then leader of the Opposition). The portrait he paints of Mitterrand in his memoirs is hilarious and horrifying.

Mitterrand was the purest type of political animal: he had no politics at all. He had a brilliant intelligence, but for him ideas were neither right nor wrong, they were only useful or useless in the pursuit of power. The object of power was not a possibility to enact certain policies; the object of all policies was simply to attain and retain power.

Revel, having drafted a speech for his own electoral campaign, was invited by Mitterrand to read it to him. The speech started, "Although I cannot deny some of my opponent's achievements..." Mitterrand interrupted him at once, screaming, "No! Never, never! In politics never acknowledge that your opponent has *any* merit. This is the basic rule of the game."

Revel understood once and for all that this game was not for him and it was the end of his political ambition. Which proved to be a blessing: had politics swallowed him at that early stage in his life, how much poorer the world of ideas and letters would have been. (And one could have said exactly the same about his close friend Mario Vargas Llosa, who—luckily for literature—was defeated in presidential elections in Peru.)

Dead writers who were also friends never leave us: whenever we open their books, we hear again their very personal voices and our old exchanges are suddenly revived. I had many conversations (and discussions: different opinions are the memorable spices of friendship) with Revel; yet what I wish to record here is not something he said, but a silence that had slightly puzzled me at the time. The matter is trifling and frivolous (for which I apologise), but what touches me is that I found the answer many years later, in his writing.

A long time ago, as we were walking along a street in Paris, chatting as we went, he asked me about a film I had seen the night before, Federico Fellini's *Casanova* (which he had not seen). I told him that one scene had impressed me by its acute psychological insight into the truth that love-making without love is but a very grim sort of gymnastics. He stopped abruptly and gave me a long quizzical look, as if he was trying to find out whether I really believed that, or was merely pulling his leg. Unable to decide, he said, "Hmmm," and we resumed our walk, chatting of other things.

Many years later, reading his autobiography, I suddenly understood. When he was a precocious adolescent of fifteen, at school in Marseilles, he was quite brilliant in all humanities subjects but hopeless in mathematics. Every Thursday, pretending to his mother that he was receiving extra tuition in maths, he used to go to a little brothel. He would first do his schoolwork in the common lounge and, after that, go upstairs with one of the girls. The madam granted him a "beginner's rebate," and the tuition fee generously advanced by his mother covered the rest.

One Thursday, however, as he was walking up the stairs his maths teacher came down. The young man froze, but the teacher passed impassively, merely muttering between clenched teeth, "You will always get passing marks in maths." The schoolboy kept their secret and the teacher honoured his part of the bargain; Revel's mother was delighted by the sudden improvement in his school results.

I belatedly realised that, from a rather early age, Revel had acquired a fairly different perspective on the subject of our chat.

At the time of Revel's death in April 2006, Vargas Llosa concluded the eloquent and deeply felt obituary he wrote for our friend in the Spanish newspaper *El País*: "Jean-François Revel, we are going to miss you so much." How true.

THE EXPERIENCE OF LITERARY TRANSLATION

MONOLINGUALISM OR POLYGLOTISM?

CERTAIN writers display an indifference, indeed even a hostility, towards anything not written in their own language. In a conversation, Roland Barthes declared: "I have little knowledge of foreign literature; I only really love what's written in French." In an interview published in the *Paris Review*, Philip Larkin expressed similar views, but much more vigorously:

> Q: In one early interview you stated that you were not interested in any period but the present, or in any poetry but that written in English. Did you mean that quite literally? Has your view changed?
> A: It has not. I don't see how one could ever know a foreign language well enough to make reading poems in it worthwhile. Foreigners' ideas of good English poems are dreadfully crude: Byron and Poe and so on. The Russians liking Burns. But deep down I think foreign languages irrelevant. A writer can have only one language, if language is going to mean anything to him.

By contrast, there are many writers who are inspired, stimulated and fascinated by foreign languages; either they produce literary translations (from Baudelaire to Pasternak, examples abound) or they themselves try to create in the borrowed language (as in the French poems of T. S. Eliot and Rilke, or the English poems of Pessoa). There also exists the phenomenon of bilingual writers: Beckett and Julien Green (even if the latter wrote nothing in his mother tongue and left to others the task of translating his novels into English). Finally and most notably, there is the particularly interesting case of writers who adopt a new language, or who shift languages (Conrad, Nabokov, Cioran, to name but a few).

But the opposition between those who are monolingual and those who are polyglot is perhaps artificial. Deep down, it may be worth asking if the two camps are not in the end motivated by an identical concern. Is it not the selfsame passion which locks Larkin into his language and chases Cioran out of his? For the one and for the other, precisely, "language really matters."

On this subject, Cioran unwittingly cast a curious light. In the course of a rare interview granted to a Greek journal, he set about excoriating the Romanian language and celebrating French: according to him, Romanian was a soft, oily, sloppy, unkempt language, whereas French possessed stature, rigour, discipline. Whatever the objective characteristics of the two languages may be, it is clear that Cioran, unbeknownst to himself, was simply opposing the distance and marmoreal majesty of a foreign tongue to the damp and creepy intimacy of a tongue familiar to him. A writer can draw his strength from the very resistance offered him by language: Anthony Burgess remarked that Conrad's English went slack as it became more familiar to him—paradoxically, it was when Conrad knew English less well that he wrote it better. Henri Michaux possesses a unique way of manipulating French: one might think that words were so many foreign bodies to him, which he turns, turns over, sniffs, and which he never ceases to distance himself from. To the amazement of one of his interlocutors, he once confessed the extent of the difficulty he experienced writing in what he said he could never take to be his mother tongue! Before the English language Nabokov stands like a wonder-struck child before a toyshop window: he juggles and plays with words as if with a prodigious parti-coloured spinning top. If, for a writer, losing his or her language is a desperate nightmare, acquiring another can also amount to the most miraculous of gifts.

TRANSLATION: LABOURS OF LOVE AND LUXURY GOODS

To be fair, I should point out that it is not always a lack of culture which lets down modern translations. Many translators work in material conditions which condemn them to producing poor drudge-work, however competent and gifted they may in fact be. It is very hard to produce satisfactory literary translations while trying to live from them. However talented the translator, if he is translating as a means of earning his living, he must constantly be choosing between botching the work and dying of hunger. A good translation is at one and the same time a labour of love and a luxury good. To translate is to pursue a passion (at times a costly one!); it rarely becomes a profit-able activity.

Let me cite a personal experience: of all the translations I have done, the one dearest to my heart, in that it cost me the most trouble and gave me the greatest joy, was that of the classic of American litera-ture *Two Years Before the Mast* by R. H. Dana (1840).

I rewrote my manuscript three times and was eighteen years on the job. Even though my French version—*Deux années sur le gaillard d'avant*—in the end was well received by critics and public alike, I had fun with a little calculation, placing my royalties alongside the num-ber of hours spent on this work: it's as clear as day that any street sweeper or night watchman is paid a hundred times better. Arthur Waley, a genius of translation whose renditions of the Chinese ex-erted a considerable influence over English letters during the first half of the twentieth century, described well the vicissitudes of our task: "Hundreds of times have I sat, for hours on end, before passages *whose meaning I understood perfectly*, without seeing how to render them into English." All translators are constantly confronted by this cruel situation, but those among them who are obliged to produce a certain number of lines and pages per day in order to live can barely permit themselves the luxury of pursuing the obsessive search for the single natural and perfect solution; time is pressing, and they may need to cut short and—sick to the soul—fall back on lame compro-mises.

INVISIBLE MAN

The paradox which the translator encounters while obstinately pursuing his harrowing task inheres in the fact that he is not setting about erecting a monument to commemorate his talent, but on the contrary is endeavouring to efface all trace of his own existence. The translator is spotted only when he has failed; his success lies in ensuring he be forgotten. The search for the natural and proper expression is the search for that which *no longer feels like a translation*. What is required is to give to the reader the illusion that he has direct access to the original. The ideal translator is an invisible man. His aesthetic is that of the pane of glass. If the glass is perfect, you cease to see it, viewing only the landscape beyond it; it is only in so far as the glass contains flaws that you become conscious of the thickness of the glass which hangs between you and the landscape.

TRANSLATION AS A SUBSTITUTE FOR CREATION (I)

Somewhere, Roland Barthes remarked: "A creative writer is one for whom language is a problem." As is often the case with Barthes, the brio of the formulation conceals a lack of intellectual rigour.

Barthes's phrase is both too narrow and too broad. Too narrow in that there exist creative writers for whom, in fact, language is not a problem—from Tolstoy to Simenon, the list is a long one, of inventors of worlds and characters who write in a functional, neutral, lack-lustre language. (Nabokov could not forgive Dostoevsky his flat, loose prose, which he judged suited to serialised romance. Evelyn Waugh reproached his fellow novelist and friend Graham Greene with using words without regard to their specific weight and autonomous life, wielding them as indifferent tools.) One might even claim that, frequently, the capacity for invention and creation is accompanied by a certain indifference to language, whereas an extreme attention to language can inhibit creation. Barthes's phrase is too broad, however, in that for literary translators language always constitutes the central problem, and this in spite of the fact that translators are *not* creative per se. Translation is often a substitute for creation, whose procedures it imitates. As Maurice-Edgar Coindreau, the great translator and introducer to France of modern American literature, put it, "The translator is the novelist's ape. He must make the same grimaces, whether these please him or not." Translation can mimic creation as much as it likes, but it can never claim the same status; "creative translation" could only ever be a pejorative term, rather as it is said of a corrupt accountant that he practises "creative accounting."

A SUBSTITUTE FOR CREATION (II)

There is a passage in Jules Renard's correspondence which should be of interest to any writer, where he accurately describes the permanent and inexhaustible anguish of creativity: "However much I should be used to it, every time I am asked for something, anything, I'm troubled as if I were writing my first line. This has to do with the fact that I do not progress, that I write when it comes to me, and that *I'm always afraid it won't come*." When this anxiety is confirmed and freezes into a block, the work of translation, which is a sort of pseudo-creation, can become a writer's refuge. Literary history offers numerous examples, from Baudelaire to Valery Larbaud: not only translation, but several other alternative activities can fill the same role—theatrical adaptations, for example, as when Camus adapted Faulkner. Equivalents present themselves from the other arts: Shostakovich talks in his memoirs of this stabbing terror of sterility, and gives various recipes for preventing inspiration from drying up: he underlines the usefulness of the work of orchestral transcription, for example— the goal being to preserve at all costs a form of artistic activity, an imitation of creative activity in order to "prime the pump" or to cross the desert in search of a new spring. As a temporary or permanent substitute for creation, translation is closely allied to creation, and yet it is of a different nature, for it offers an *artificial inspiration*. In place of the "I write when it comes to me, and I'm always afraid it won't come," what we now have is the comforting certainty of "It's arrived, here it is!" One can sit down at one's table every morning at the same hour, assured of giving birth to something. Of course, the quality and the quantity of daily production can vary, but the nightmare of the blank page is, for its part, definitively exorcised. It is, moreover, this very reassuring guarantee which fundamentally places translation in the domain of the artisan rather than in that of the artist. However difficult translation may sometimes be, as distinct from creation it is fundamentally *risk-free*.

A SUBSTITUTE FOR CREATION (III)

One can only really translate successfully those books which one would have liked to write oneself. For a literary translation to be inspired and lively, the translator must achieve identification with the author, by whose spirit he becomes inhabited. It would seem to me impossible to translate well a writer for whom I had neither sympathy nor respect, or whose values I did not share, or whose intellectual, moral, artistic and psychological universe was indifferent or hostile to me. This is so commonplace that it is repeated by every master-translator. So Coindreau: "A translator must know his own limitations and not take on works which he himself could not, or more exactly would not, have wished to write. Translating is an act of loving collaboration." And Valery Larbaud: "I'll never be shaken from the idea that a translation whose author begins by telling us in his preface that he chose it because he liked the original has every chance of being good." But then Larbaud goes much further, as he develops the idea that translation is a sort of sublime plagiarism. According to him, the writer's first gesture is that of plagiarism. (Malraux underlined the same phenomenon in the plastic arts, commenting for example on the way in which the young Rembrandt used to imitate Lastman: "Genius begins with pastiche.") Larbaud continues: "It is only later, when we have noticed that as a general rule we don't like our own works, that it is enough for us to like a poem or a book to feel that it is not our own; it is only then that we note the difference between yours and mine, and that plagiarism becomes not merely odious to us, but impossible. And yet there remains in us something of this primitive instinct for appropriation. It dwells deep within us as one of the instinctive vices of childhood, which the full development of our character refuses to permit to be reawakened."

Contact with a masterpiece communicates a sort of electrical charge: remember the famous cry of the young Correggio discovering a masterpiece by Raphael: *"Anch'io son pittore!"* ("I too am a painter!"). In the literary field, according to Larbaud, there exists a "profound instinct to which translation responds, and which turns individuals, depending on their moral worth, or perhaps on their degree of intellectual strength, into plagiarists or translators." Translation is, then, a sublimation of our spontaneous propensity for theft or plagiarism: "Translating a work which we like means penetrating into it more deeply than we can do by a simple reading; it means possessing it more completely, in some ways appropriating it to ourselves. That is always the goal for us, plagiarists as we all are at origin."

A SUBSTITUTE FOR CREATION (IV)

The fact that translation is a substitute for creation has its corollary: translations have a rightful place in a writer's *oeuvre*, alongside his original works. It is legitimate and appropriate to include, for example, in an edition of the complete works of Baudelaire, of Proust, of Larbaud, or of Lu Xun, the translations they did. The great modern Chinese writer Zhou Zuoren, whose essays are interspersed with a vast range of translations (Greek classics, classical and modern Japanese literature, English literature), developed this idea: a writer can translate various texts in order to give form to things he had within himself but which he could not find other means of expressing. This is why it is appropriate to include these translations in any collection of his own works. The same goes for the quotations and the notes on reading that certain writers accumulate, and that the English sometimes call a commonplace book (see for example that of E. M. Forster, published recently, or Montesquieu's *Spicilège*). String together all the pages that you have copied out over the course of your readings and, without there being a single line by you, the ensemble may turn out to be the most accurate portrait of your mind and your heart. Such mosaics of quotations resemble pictorial "collages": all the elements are borrowed, but together they form original pictures.

SOME TECHNICAL PROBLEMS

When the translation is into English (for instance), the question is less that of knowing the foreign language than that of knowing English. This could be turned into an axiom: *It is desirable to understand the language of the original, but it is indispensable to master the target language.* This formula may look like both a joke and a truism, but it is a fact that there are translations which are literary masterpieces, which have exerted considerable influence, and which have been composed by translators who barely knew the language of the original, if they knew it at all; their sole qualification was that of being great stylists in their mother tongue. The most singular and illustrious case of this is without doubt that of Lin Shu (1852–1924), a capital figure in the literary history of modern China. Without knowing a single word of any foreign language, Lin Shu translated nearly 200 European novels, and this vast constituency of foreign fiction contributed powerfully to the transformation of the intellectual horizon of China at the end of the empire. Convalescent after a serious illness, towards 1890, Lin Shu was visited by a friend who had recently returned from France. The friend spoke to him of a novel very popular in Europe at the time, *La Dame aux camélias*, and suggested to him that he undertake its translation. The two collaborated in the following manner: the friend recounted the plot, while Lin Shu transcribed it into classical Chinese. This Chinese *Dame aux camélias* was a prodigious success. It needs to be said that it is vastly superior to the original: even while it is scrupulously faithful to the narrative of Dumas *fils*, reproducing it paragraph by paragraph, sentence by sentence, its style is admirable for its nobility and force of concision—imagine what a serialised novel would become if rewritten in the Latin of Tacitus! (Mao Zedong, receiving a delegation of French senators, lauded *La Dame aux camélias* as the finest example of French literary genius, much to the perplexity of his visitors: like all intellectuals of his generation, he had read Lin Shu's translation, a half a century previously, and had retained an indelible memory of it.) Encouraged by this initial success, Lin Shu stuck to his course and undertook translations with various collaborators; entirely at the mercy of their variable knowledge and tastes, he built an enormous and heteroclite *oeuvre*, translating pell-mell the giants of world literature—Hugo, Shakespeare, Tolstoy, Goethe, Dickens—as well as good second-tier authors such as Walter Scott and R.L. Stevenson, and popular writers such as Anthony Hope and H. Rider Haggard (for whom he developed a particular predilection); and then also the spokesmen of oppressed nations—of the Poles, the Hungarians, the Serbs, the Bosnians…and even Hendrik Conscience, with his *Leeuw van Vlaanderen* (Lion of Flanders)!

As to what concerns us here, what the fascinating case of Lin Shu illustrates is the importance of style: the literary art of the translator can even compensate for profound linguistic incompetence—though this is, of course, an extreme example. As a general rule it would be fair to say that if the translator is truly a writer, even the occasional mistaken meaning cannot spoil his work. By contrast, all the resources of philology will be of no use to him if he writes without literary ear. From which it emerges also that the best translators are normally those who translate from a foreign language into their mother tongue, and not vice versa. One example will serve: in English, the two most authoritative translations of Confucius's *Analects* were for a long time those of Arthur Waley and D.C. Lau. The relatively old translation by Waley contains some rather flagrant mistakes and several debatable interpretations, but it is written in an admirable English. The more recent translation by Lau is more reliable philologically, but from a literary point of view it seems to have been composed on a computer, by a computer. An English-speaker who knows nothing of Confucius would do better to start by passing through Waley: even if he is led astray on certain points of detail, at least he will discover that Confucius's *Analects* constitute a beautiful book, whereas there is a risk that this essential aspect will escape readers of Lau's more accurate translation. Equally, French scholars of German have severely criticised the translations of Kafka by Alexandre Vialatte.

While accepting that Vialatte did make numerous errors, when I read the new, rigorously correct versions which are now replacing the old ones, it seems to me that what Vialatte still offers, and which is more fundamental than philological exactitude, is literary truth. Even if his knowledge of German can often be found wanting, his understanding of the genius of Kafka—of the essentially *comic* nature of this genius—is in the end the yardstick of a truer sense of the text; a sense which, in turn, is served in French by Vialatte's incomparable artistic abilities. What we encounter here is an illustration of the primordial axiom established by St. Jerome, the patron saint of our fellowship: "*non verbum e verbo, sed sensum exprimere de senso*"—render the sense rather than the words of the text.

VERBUM E VERBO

When rendering the words of the text, it happens to all translators to go astray here and there, but such accidents are remediable, as are basic spelling errors and typos. The recipe for success is simply to use good dictionaries, preferably of the monolingual variety. The easiest to render are difficult expressions; the hardest are easy expressions. By this I mean that abstruse expressions and rare terms declare themselves, can be spotted from afar; they are hazards clearly marked that can be negotiated with prudence, dictionary in hand. The danger arises with words of simple and everyday appearance that one believes one grasps perfectly, whereas in their context they may in fact be drawing on quite different technical or specialised vocabulary, or on a non-codified use of spoken language. I had intended to offer some examples of surprising blunders committed by excellent translators in order to demonstrate how profoundly knowledgeable translators, expert at unravelling the most complex linguistic puzzles from within the enclave of their libraries, far from the street and its life, managed to fall into very basic traps. But what's the use in nitpicking? I am sure my meaning is clear, being at root nothing but an illustration of the old principle of navigation: it is dangerous not to know one's position, but *not to know that one does not know* is much worse.

Let me mention again the particular problem posed by obscure or corrupt passages in ancient texts. Certain translators err here by an excess of ingenuity: they create meaning in passages which no longer possess any; and where the original is hermetic and bumpy, their translation gives a deceptive impression of lucidity and fluidity. Jean Paulhan highlighted this phenomenon (*à propos* of a translation of *Lao Zi*): "The best translators are in this case the stupidest ones, who respect obscurity and don't seek to make sense of the matter to hand."

SENSUM EXPRIMERE DE SENSO

The errors committed of the order of "*verbum e verbo*" are venial and easily spotted. But in the domain of "*sensum exprimere de senso*," all errors are fatal. Mistakes of meaning can be made, and inevitably are, but what are unpardonable are mistakes of judgement and tone. The way in which a translator chooses to convey the *title* of a work he is translating clearly indicates this, with Coindreau again supplying interesting examples. The title of William Styron's novel, *Set This House on Fire* (which, with its biblical resonance, offers a challenge which Coindreau rises to magnificently with *La Proie des flammes*), were it to be translated by *Fous le feu à la baraque*, would instantly become the title of a cheap thriller. Steinbeck's title *The Grapes of Wrath* is awkwardly rendered by *Les Raisins de la colère*, a title belonging to a pirate Belgian edition of the novel which gained notoriety during the Second World War, obliging Coindreau to let go of the brilliant solution he had envisaged: *Le Ciel en sa fureur*. In English, *grapes* possesses a solemn biblical ring, where the classic allusion to La Fontaine's verse gives in the end the best possible equivalent, whereas the French connotation of "grapes" (think of "*vignes du Seigneur*") evokes rather a Bacchic and Rabelaisian universe. *Wuthering Heights* by Emily Brontë became, in the translation by F. Delebecque, *Les Hauts de Hurle-vent*—a masterstroke. Coindreau explains why he translated *God's Little Acre* (by E. Caldwell) as *Le Petit arpent du bon Dieu*: "*Le Petit arpent de Dieu*" sounded bad, he says, like some sort of Canadian swearword! "*Bon* Dieu" corresponds to the way in which one imagines the protagonist, an old peasant, smutty and sly, might naturally express himself. As for me, when it came to the narrative by Dana, *Two Years Before the Mast*, the expression "before the mast" would literally turn into "*devant le mât*" or "*en avant du mât*," neither of which means much in French. In English, sailing "before the mast" means sailing as an ordinary seaman, since on tall ships the crew's quarters were in the forecastle, and the sailors, unless on duty, were strictly confined to the space "before the fore mast" (the aft section of the ship being reserved for the exclusive use of officers and passengers). To translate the title as "*Deux ans de la vie d'un matelot*" would have been too explicit, where what was required was an echo of the nautical jargon which Dana employs to such superb effect. As what was required was, moreover, avoidance of the infelicitous assonance of "deux ans"—"gaillard *d'avant*," what I finally opted for was *Deux années sur le gaillard d'avant*.

THE TEST OF THE TRANSLATION

It is possible to be creative in a language that one knows only imperfectly: Conrad was still far from mastering English at the time he wrote *Almayer's Folly*. It is *impossible* to translate into a language which one knows only imperfectly. No other literary activity demands so total a mastery of the language in which one is working; one must possess every register, one must be capable of playing in every key and on every scale. When one is composing, if one comes up against an obstacle, one has at one's disposal numerous sidesteps: one can always tackle the subject from another angle, or if it comes to it one can even invent something else. When translating, by contrast, problems are immutable, and there is no question of avoiding or sidestepping them; they must all be confronted and resolved, one by one, wherever they present themselves. Translation not only deploys every resource of writing, it is also *the supreme form of reading*. In order to appreciate a text, re-reading is better than reading, learning by heart is better than re-reading; but one *possesses* only what one translates. First, translating implies total comprehension. When we've read a text with interest, with pleasure, with emotion, we naturally presume that we've entirely understood it . . . until the moment comes when we try to translate it. Then, what we usually discover is that rather than understanding, what we've been left with is the imprint of the text's movement on our imagination and sensibility; sufficient to sustain a reader's attention—but the translator, for his part, requires firmer foundations on which to base his work. Certainly, vague passages must be rendered in a vague manner; obscure passages must be rendered obscurely. But in order to produce an adequate obscurity and vagueness, the translator must previously have penetrated the fog to capture whatever is hiding behind it.

Paradoxically, the translator must know more about the work than the author knows himself, for the author, carried by inspiration, can sometimes yield to the intoxication of words. Such transports are forbidden to the translator, who must forever remain sober and lucid. A cunning writer may bluff his readers, but he can never deceive his translator. The work of translation reveals pitilessly: it turns the work inside out, unpicks its lining, exposes its stitching. Translation is the severest test to which a book can be submitted. In discursive prose, nothing that has a meaning is untranslatable; the corollary being that untranslatable passages generally are found to be meaningless. Translation is an implacable detective of pretentious nonsense, a sonar for measuring false depths. A work may have pleased us on a first read, but if its seduction is not wholesome, it will not withstand the test of translation. To translate a book means living in intimacy with it for months and years, and this when frequenting books can turn out to be much like frequenting people: intimacy is capable of increasing love and respect, just as it is capable of producing disaffection and contempt.

TRANSLATABLE AND UNTRANSLATABLE

Some writers are easy to translate: Simenon, Graham Greene, and in general all novelists whose plots can be disentangled from their language. Some are hard to translate: Chardonne, Evelyn Waugh, and in general any novelist whose narrative is indissociable from its language.

It so happens that I read Simenon in English and Greene in French. Some of their novels stay with me after even twenty-five or thirty years, and yet I am curiously unable to tell which I read in the original and which in translation. In the first case, language is a mere instrument of creation; in the second, it constitutes the very stuff of the work. The closer a work approaches the poetic mode, the less it is translatable. The "idea" of a poem is present only as it takes form in words; a poem doesn't exist outside its verbal incarnation, any more than an individual exists outside his skin. Degas said to Mallarmé that he had heaps of ideas for poems and was dismayed not to be able to write them. Mallarmé responded: "But Degas, it's not with ideas that we make poetry, it's with words." While it isn't entirely absurd to recount a Tolstoy novel, it would be inconceivable to recount a Baudelaire poem. Hence poetry is by definition untranslatable (whence derives Goethe's recommendation that verse be translated in prose, to forestall any readerly illusions). However, it does happen that a poem in one language can inspire *another poem* in another language. Such miracles do happen! But the existence of miracles does not cancel the existence of natural laws; rather it confirms it.

TRANSLATIONS WHICH ARE SUPERIOR TO THEIR ORIGINALS

I believe it was Gide who remarked of a writer he did not care for, "He is much improved by translation." This happy gibe raises the curious issue of translators who improve on their originals. Examples abound here. Gabriel García Márquez has said that Gregory Rabassa's translation of *One Hundred Years of Solitude* is much superior to its original Spanish version. I have spoken above of Lin Shu; not only does *La Dame aux camélias* gain from being read in Chinese, but—if Arthur Waley is to be believed—the same might be said of Dickens's novels. But the most noteworthy case is probably that of Baudelaire as translator of Edgar Allan Poe. Anglo-Saxon connoisseurs who read French are practically unanimous in preferring Baudelaire's translations to Poe's originals, generally judging Poe to be "boring, vulgar and lacking a good ear"; while the way in which, following Baudelaire, great French poets such as Mallarmé, Claudel and Valéry could worship him and take seriously his indigestible mishmash of pseudoscience and metaphysical fantasy remains for English and American critics a source of infinite perplexity. The fact is that it is often mediocre writers who lend themselves best to the glorious misunderstandings of translation and exportation, whereas writers of genius resist the efforts of translators. Du Fu, the greatest and most perfect of all the Chinese classic poets, becomes grey and arid in translation, whereas his contemporary Hanshan, whose work is flat and vulgar and was, quite rightly, largely ignored in China, enjoyed a huge success in colourful poetic reincarnations in Japan, in America and in France... Translation may serve as a perverse screen serving to occlude instances of true beauty, while conferring a sudden freshness upon worn-out clichés. The poetry of Mao Zedong, for example, owed its fortune not only to the pounding of propaganda and the political myths of a certain era, but also to the fact that it clearly belongs to that category of works which are "improved by translation," the translation succeeding in concealing their original vulgarity. In that ferociously funny novel *Pictures from an Institution*, Randall Jarrell says of one of his characters: "He would not like German half so well if he should learn it. *There is no such happiness as not to know an idiom from a masterstroke.*" And in *The Catcher in the Rye* the young hero completely muddles up the meaning of a line of Robert Burns (which gives Salinger the title of his novel): this marvellous mistake becoming the source for him of a much purer and deeper poetic delight than would have been drawn from a correct reading of the poem in question... A "homage to the mistake" remains to be written.

ON READERS' REWARDS AND WRITERS' AWARDS

AS YOU may perhaps remember, some time ago the English actor Hugh Grant was arrested by the police in Los Angeles: he was performing a rather private activity in a public place with a lady of the night. For less famous mortals, such a mishap would have been merely embarrassing; but for such a famous film star, the incident proved quite shattering. For a while, it looked as if his professional career might sink—not to mention the damage inflicted upon his personal life. In this distressing circumstance, he was interviewed by an American journalist, who asked him a very American question: "Are you receiving any therapy or counselling?" Grant replied, "No. In England, we read novels."

Half a century earlier, the great psychologist Carl Gustav Jung developed the other side of this same observation. He phrased it in more technical terms: "Man's estrangement from the mythical realm and the subsequent shrinking of his existence to the mere factual—that is the major cause of mental illness." In other words, people who do not read fiction or poetry are in permanent danger of crashing against facts and being crushed by reality. And then, in turn, it is left to Dr. Jung and his colleagues to rush to the rescue and attempt to mend the broken pieces.

Do psychotherapists multiply when novelists and poets become scarce? There may well be a connection between the development of clinical psychology on the one hand and the withering of the inspired imagination on the other—at least, this was the belief of some eminent practitioners. Rainer Maria Rilke once begged Lou Andreas-

Address to the New South Wales Premier's Literary Awards, 2002.

Salomé to psychoanalyse him. She refused; she explained to him, "If the analysis is successful, you may never write poetry again." (And just imagine: had a skilful shrink cured Kafka of his existential anxieties, our age—and modern man's condition—could have been deprived of its most perceptive interpreter.)

Many strong and well-adjusted people seem to experience little need for the imaginative life. Thus, for instance, saints do not write novels, as Cardinal Newman observed (and he ought to have known, since he came quite close to being a saint, and he wrote a couple of novels*).

Especially, practical-minded people and men of action are often inclined to disapprove of literary fiction. They consider reading creative literature as a frivolous and debilitating activity. In this respect, it is quite revealing that, for example (as I have already pointed out in an earlier essay), the great polar explorer Mawson—one of our national heroes—gave to his children the stern advice not to waste their time reading novels; instead, he instructed them to read only works of history and biography in order to grow into healthy individuals.

Allow me to dwell a short moment on this particular advice, for it reflects two very common fallacies. The first fallacy consists in failing to see that, by its very definition, all literature is in fact imaginative literature. Distinctions between genres—novels and history, poetry and prose, fiction and essay, etc.—are essentially artificial; these conventional classifications are of practical use mostly for booksellers and librarians who have to compile catalogues or arrange books on crowded shelves; otherwise, above a certain level of literary quality, they present little relevance. For the perceptive reader, indeed, Proust's great novel is in fact a philosophical essay; Montaigne's essays are more diverse and surprising than any novel; Gibbon's and Michelet's histories remain alive first and foremost as great literature; and, of course it would be ludicrous to reduce a polymorphous giant such as Shakespeare to the absurdly minor and narrow craft of playwrighting. As to the art of fiction, we have already learned that its aim is nothing less than "to render the highest kind of justice to the visible universe,"[1]

---

*I hope this will not now hinder the smooth progress of his canonisation.

whereas the mission of the historian is to imagine the past—since history is believed only when a talented writer has invented it well. Novelists are the historians of the present; historians are the novelists of the past.*

The second Mawsonian fallacy results from a mistaken notion of what "health" is. On this subject, I think that Laurence Sterne provided the correct perspective in his description of a visit he made to his doctor:

> —Sir, the doctor told me, your health is perfectly normal.—On hearing this, I began to rejoice, when the doctor pursued:— Such a condition is exceedingly rare: it is a cause for concern and calls for extreme caution.

Since Mawson just took us to Antarctica, before leaving this particular field I might also add that I have always preferred the example of Shackleton—a much greater man. In the darkest depth of disaster, when all members of his expedition had to discard every piece of superfluous luggage, he refused to abandon his beloved copy of Browning's collected poems. One day, some scholar should write a doctoral thesis on "The Role of Poetry in Polar Exploration"—but right now, I had better not wander too far away from my subject. My point was simply this: whatever fragile harmony we may have been able to achieve within ourselves is exposed every day to dangerous challenges and to ferocious batterings, and the outcome of our struggle remains forever uncertain. A character in a novel by Mario Vargas Llosa gave (what seems to me) the best image for this common predicament of ours: "Life is a shitstorm, in which Art is our only umbrella."

This observation, in turn, brings us to the very meaning of tonight's function—the NSW Premier's Literary Awards. Any well-ordered state must naturally provide for public education, public health, public transport, public order, the administration of justice, the collection of garbage, etc. Beyond these essential services and responsibilities, a truly civilised state also ensures that, in the pungent squalls of their

---

*These notions are developed further in an earlier essay, "Lies That Tell the Truth."

daily lives, citizens are not left without umbrellas—and therefore it encourages and supports the arts. The Premier's Literary Awards are one important aspect of this enlightened policy.

The beauty of all literary awards is that they produce only winners—there can be no losers here. For this is not a competition, and in this respect it resembles more a lottery. When we buy a lottery ticket in support of some charity, we expect nothing in return. Yet, if one day we were to receive a phone call informing us that our number had just won a sports car or a holiday in Tahiti, we would be surprised—and delighted. We would be delighted precisely because of our surprise. Though it may be pleasant to obtain something after a long and hard struggle, to be given it without even having had to ask—this is pure bliss.

Without doubting the quality of his own work, a writer who receives a literary award is perfectly aware that he is very lucky indeed. Not only does he know that this honour could have gone to any other writer on the short-list, but he also knows that there are many equally deserving writers not on the short-list; and furthermore, it is quite conceivable that the most deserving writer of all did not even succeed in having his manuscript accepted for publication—it was rejected by twelve different publishers, and may have to wait another twenty years before having its true worth duly recognised.

Yet these considerations should not tarnish in the least the happiness of the winners. Ultimately lotteries are designed to benefit not their winners, but handicapped children, or guide dogs for the blind, or whatever good cause is sponsoring them. And it is the same with the literary awards: year after year, they have only one true and permanent winner, always the same—and it is literature itself, our common love, which we have all gathered here tonight to support and celebrate.

WRITERS AND MONEY

THERE is no sublunary topic on which Samuel Johnson did not, at some time, issue a pithy and definitive statement; this particular subject is no exception, and although the Johnsonian quote is well known, it should still provide an apt starting point for our own little survey: "No man but a blockhead ever wrote except for money." Boswell faithfully recorded this utterance of the master, but he was shocked. Surely Johnson said this in jest? Did his own noble and tireless activity in the service of literature not give the lie to such a cynical paradox?

Yes and no. We know, for instance, how Johnson dashed off *Rasselas* at stupendous speed in order to pay for his mother's funeral. Under the pressure of financial necessity, he could display a prodigious capacity for work, but his natural inclination towards indolence was no less colossal. Later in life, when his material circumstances finally became more secure, he wrote rather little. To Boswell, who had expressed respectful puzzlement at this relative idleness, he retorted tartly: "No, sir, I am not obliged to do any more. No man is obliged to do as much as he can do. A man is to have part of his life for himself."

Yet Johnson's attitude was not shared by all the great writers of his time. Voltaire, for instance, instead of writing in order to make money, made money in order to write. Through shrewd investments and clever financial operations, he accumulated an enormous wealth (bringing him a yearly income of £140,000) which, in turn, enabled him to acquire a splendid estate located strategically on the border between the kingdom of France and the republic of Geneva. This gave him the liberty to write and to publish as he pleased: whenever he offended censors on the one side of the border, he could find instant refuge on the other side.

Rousseau, who, for all his personal frailties, had a much nobler soul, also aimed at intellectual freedom but, unlike Voltaire, he never coveted riches. Although his books triumphed throughout Europe, in an age that ignored copyright they brought him fame but earned him hardly any royalties. In the last part of his life, he declined generous offers of patronage from the great and the powerful and opted instead for independent poverty: he made a meagre living by copying musical scores. He carefully calculated how many pages he needed to copy every day to keep his modest household afloat, and once he had done his daily quota, the rest of the time was entirely his own. In this way, he could secure both self-sufficiency and inner peace. He said: "I always considered that the condition of author is not, and cannot be, glorious and honourable, if it were also to become a paid craft. You cannot think lofty thoughts when you think for a living."

In the eighteenth century, the livelihood of most writers depended either upon the patronage of the court and the aristocracy or upon the commercial activities of printers and booksellers. Modern publishing with its personal—yet also delicate and sometimes antagonistic—relations between authors and publishers was born in the nineteenth century. In our time, writers' views on the subject were bitterly summarised by Edmund Wilson: "All publishers are dogs." (It would be interesting to know what the publishers thought of this notoriously unpleasant customer.)

Authors' complaints about publishers have been voiced on many different tunes, but their concert generally amounts to endless variations on the same theme: money. Either they moan piteously, like Henry James writing to his publisher: "The delicious ring of the sovereign is conspicuous in our intercourse by its absence." Or they thunder with foaming fury and throw colourful abuse like L.-F. Céline: "If you were not robbing me, you would not be conforming to my views of human nature." And, as his publisher had refused to increase an advance on royalties and advised "more patience," he retorted: "Patience is a virtue for donkeys and cuckolds! If only you could kindly wipe your arse with my contract and let me free to leave your filthy brothel!" Yet screams merely betray powerlessness. Georges Simenon, wanting to rescind an agreement that had proved disadvantageous to him, resorted to different tactics: he achieved his aim by putting to good use his intuitive knowledge of the human heart. The novelist assessed how much it would be worth for him to redeem his original contract; then filled a briefcase with banknotes and won his negotiation simply by emptying the briefcase over the publisher's desk.

Yet few writers ever find themselves in a position to perform such coups. Although some of the great and famous—Balzac, Dumas, Hugo, Walter Scott, Dickens, Maupassant—made (and sometimes lost) huge fortunes, for most of the others, literary genius amounted to a curse, at least as far as their material well-being was concerned. Literary history abounds with heartbreaking episodes of utter destitution. Dostoevsky, for instance, finding himself stranded abroad, penniless and starving, wrote *The Eternal Husband* in a last attempt to obtain emergency relief from his publishers. But as he was about to dispatch the manuscript on which his last hope rested, he discovered that he did not even have money for the postage. The despair and despondency experienced by Baudelaire were, in a sense, even more cruel: at the end of his life, the poet undertook to calculate the earnings of his entire literary career; he arrived at a grand total of 15,892 francs and 50 centimes—and the friend who recorded this grim exercise concluded: "Thus, this great poet, this perfect artist, who had worked so hard and without respite for the last twenty-six years, had earned on average *one franc and 70 centimes* per day."

What hurt Baudelaire most was not poverty itself (his mother, who loved him dearly, was wealthy and would not have allowed him to starve), but what poverty meant: the cold indifference of the reading public. Leaving aside the problem of naïve authors who are cheated by dishonest publishers, there is no doubt that, when writers whine and curse about money matters (as they seem to be doing most of the time in their correspondence with publishers), it is not because they are needy or greedy; actually, what they are craving is not royalties but attention and appreciation. In this sense, money is for them a mere symbol, and if they were suddenly to win $10 million in a lottery, such a bonanza would hardly assuage their deeper anguish. On this issue, the interesting suggestion made by Cyril Connolly some seventy-five years ago still retains all of its relevance, and it might be well worth reviving it: "I should like to see the custom introduced of readers who are pleased with a book sending the author some small cash token: anything between half-a-crown and £100. Authors would then receive what their publishers give them as a flat rate, and their 'tips' from grateful readers in addition, in the same way that waiters receive a wage from their employers and also get what the customer leaves on the plate. No more than £100—that would be bad for my character—not less than half-a-crown—that would do no good to yours."

Steinbeck remarked: "The profession of book writing makes horse racing seem like a solid, stable business." Still, book writing at least need not be a profession—it can be a compulsion, an art, an illness, a therapy, a joy, a mania, a blessing, a madness, a curse, a passion, and many other things besides, whereas book publishing must always confront first and foremost the ruthless uncertainty that characterises all business ventures. Could this explain the apparent meanness with which some publishers seem to treat their innocent authors? When Richard Henry Dana completed his immortal *Two Years Before the Mast* (1840), he was only twenty-five, he had no publishing experience, but he needed money urgently. He considered himself lucky to find a New York publisher willing to pay a lump sum of $250 for all the rights on the book for the next thirty years. Out of this deal, the publisher was eventually to earn $50,000—a colossal sum at the time—not a cent of which ever went to the hapless author. (When a British edition came out in London, the English publisher felt moved to give $500 to Dana, even though he was under no legal obligation to do so; in the entire history of publishing, this must be the only instance of a publisher paying an author money not owed to him. Conversely, there are also equally surprising and admirable examples of writers declining royalties which they deemed excessive. Before setting sail on a cruise across the Pacific, R. L. Stevenson was offered by the editor of *Scribner's* magazine $3,500 for a series of twelve monthly articles; he replied, "I feel sure you all pay too much here in America, and I beg you not to spoil me any more. For I am getting spoiled; I do not want wealth and I feel these big sums demoralise me.")

Returning to Dana's unfortunate experience, one may feel that his New York publisher took unfair advantage of his ignorance; actually, this businessman may have been ruthless, but he was not devious and, at the start, he took a considerable risk in publishing the manuscript of an unknown young writer. The fact is that no one could ever have foreseen the huge and long-lasting success of such an unusual work.

Jacques Chardonne, before he became a distinguished novelist, worked as the assistant of a great publisher. His observations on the publishing business are particularly perceptive since he developed a career on both sides of the literary fence. His old boss (who was a notorious gambler) formulated an original philosophy of his trade: "On every book you publish, you are bound to lose money; therefore, the secret of a good publisher is to publish as few books as possible—ideally, none at all." From his own experiences, Chardonne himself concluded: "Any truly good book will always find 3,000 readers, no more, no less.* We used to publish every year translations of some forty foreign novels. Invariably, one of these would suddenly sell 100,000 copies (which would pay for all our other publications)—and *we never knew why*."

The truthfulness of this admission is especially noteworthy. Quite often, publishers, however shrewd and experienced, can hardly know what they are doing. With good reason, they could invoke the famous phrase (coined by Cocteau in another context), "Since we do not understand these mysteries, we might as well pretend that we are organising them."

It is all too easy to laugh at the naïveté of the American publisher who rejected Orwell's *Animal Farm* on the grounds that "animal stories do not sell anymore." The original manuscript did not have much more luck at home with such a sophisticated connoisseur as T. S. Eliot, who advised Faber and Faber against publication. And, as everyone remembers, the greatest novel of the twentieth century, Proust's *A la Recherche du temps perdu*, was at first pronounced unreadable and unpublishable by the most authoritative judges of the time, Gide and Schlumberger—and Proust had to print the first volume of his monumental work at his own expense. Publishers may argue that they are businessmen and cannot afford to play the part of patrons of the arts,

---

*This figure does not seem to have varied significantly over the past 400 years.

but the problem, of course, is that in this field, lapses of aesthetic judgement make in the end little commercial sense.

From being a craft, publishing has progressively turned into an industry; one consequence of this transformation is that it has become increasingly geared towards the production of "best-sellers." Yet, by their very nature, best-sellers are elusive: they *happen*, they cannot be willed, as writers themselves know all too well, however skilful as artisans some of them may be. "No one can write a best-seller by trying to," Somerset Maugham observed and, at the end of a long and hugely successful career, he ought to have known. He recalled in his *Writer's Notebook* how he once attempted with a friend to accomplish deliberately this very feat; they had much fun writing it—and therefore failed. "The persons to whom we submitted our manuscript one and all said the same thing: 'It looks as though you had written it with your tongue in your cheek.'" The conclusion is obvious: "You cannot write anything that will convince, unless you are yourself convinced. The best-selling writer sells because he writes with his heart's blood . . . He gives the great mass of the public what they want, because that is what he wants himself."

When a book is successful, the prejudice that it *cannot* be good is as silly as the belief that it *must* be good. As experience constantly confirms, the commercial triumph of a book—or its dismal failure—means simply nothing as far as its literary value is concerned. Hilaire Belloc had the final word on this subject—do not complain that I am quoting him at too great a length; actually my little paper has had no other purpose but to bring this remarkable page back to your attention:

> To those who have had to pursue letters as a trade (and to this I have been condemned all my life since my twenty-fifth year), it certainly is the hardest and the most capricious and, indeed, the most abominable of trades, for the simple reason that it was never meant to be a trade.
>
> A man is no more meant to live by writing than he is meant to live by conversations, or by dressing, or by walking about and seeing the world. For there is no relation between the function

of letters and the economic effect of letters, there is no relation between the goodness and the badness of the work, or the magnitude of the work, and the sums paid for the work. It would not be natural that there should be such a relation, and in fact, there is none.

The truth is missed by people who say that good writing has no market. That is not the point. Good writing sometimes has a market, and very bad writing sometimes has a market ... Writing important truths sometimes has a market; writing the most ridiculous errors and false judgements sometimes has a market. The point is that the market has nothing to do with the qualities attached to writing. It never has and never will ... The relationship between the excellence or the usefulness of a piece of literature, and the number of those who will buy it in a particular form, is not a causal relationship, it is a purely capricious one.

OVERTURES

THE IDEA for this little essay first came to me many years ago, as I was browsing in a bookshop. I saw a copy of Chesterton's *The Napoleon of Notting Hill*; I knew the book only by its title; out of curiosity, I picked it up, opened it at the first page and read the beginning of the first sentence of Chapter One: "The human race to which so many of my readers belong…"

I bought the book on the spot and left the shop in a hurry. The sight of an old man laughing loudly all by himself in a public place can be somewhat disconcerting, and I did not wish to disturb the other customers.

I cannot say that the rest of the book fully lived up to its glorious opening but, having pitched its key so high from the start, what novel could maintain itself at that level over 200 pages? Still, *The Napoleon of Notting Hill* is a delight; it contains a great many pearls of wisdom ("Just as a bad man is nevertheless a man, so a bad poet is nevertheless a poet") and offers enlightening observations on the essentially *democratic* nature of the monarchic system—actually the most democratic of all, provided the king be chosen once every year by lottery, a notion that could be useful in our republic debate.

Yet, for me, the most memorable aspect of my little experience in the bookshop was the discovery that sometimes a really inspired line in a book can compel you to buy it at once. Naturally, shrewd writers have not been slow to notice that it should be possible to trigger such an irresistible urge in their potential customers. In consequence, some of them manipulate their openings the way a fly fisherman dangles his lure in the hope of hooking a trout. See, for instance, how Anthony Burgess started his *Earthly Powers*:

It was in the afternoon of my eighty-first birthday and I was in bed with my catamite when Ali announced that the archbishop had come to see me.

In this case, the fisherman scored a bite—for I bought the book—but he did not actually land the fish—since this weighty volume has been majestically gathering dust on my shelves, still unread after nineteen years. In a way, I wonder if Burgess's clever opening is not to genuine literature what an artificial fly is to natural insects: a little too shiny, and ultimately indigestible. The search for effect comes, here, dangerously close to one of those tongue-in-cheek entries in the competition named after Edward Bulwer-Lytton, the once popular author of *The Last Days of Pompeii*, and his now notorious opening of *Paul Clifford*: "It was a dark and stormy night ..." An example of a winning entry:

Stanislaus Smedley, a man always on the cutting edge of narcissism, was about to give his body and soul to a back alley sex-change surgeon to become the woman he loved.

For *Earthly Powers*, Burgess contrived an opening that was striking indeed; the only problem was precisely that it was contrived, and this is probably why, in the end, it could not provoke, in this reader at least, a real urge to persist.

The danger with talented artists is that too often it is their very eagerness to impress that ruins their more ambitious efforts. This willingness to resort to gimmicks reflects the domination of advertising over every facet of contemporary culture.

Hemingway was an early and influential exponent of this trend, often apparent in his stylistic mannerisms. See, for instance, the self-conscious wit displayed at the start of his story "In Another Country":

In the fall, the war was still there, but we did not go to it anymore ...

How smart indeed! If only the author's cleverness had been better concealed. In some writers this fatal desire to show off their ability betrays a competitive streak, which taints their writing with vulgarity and ultimately kills their art.

The disease was accurately diagnosed by Arthur Koestler half a century ago, in an interview he gave to the *New York Times* shortly after he settled in the United States. His comments remain so pertinent that they deserve to be quoted at length:

> The longer I live here the more I get the feeling that there is something radically wrong with the literary life in America... If you were to ask me what a writer's ambition in life should be, I would answer with a formula.
>
> A writer's ambition should be to trade a hundred contemporary readers for ten readers in ten years, and for one reader in a hundred years. But the general atmosphere in this country directs the writer's ambition into different channels... on immediate success here and now. Religion and art are the two completely non-competitive spheres of human striving and they both derive from the same source. But the social climate in this country has made the creation of art into an essentially competitive business. On the best-seller charts—this curse of American literary life—authors are rated like shares on the Stock Exchange... Can you fathom the whole horror of what this implies? And can you fathom the grotesqueness of Hemingway, America's greatest living novelist, talking of his books in terms of "defending the title of champ"? I know he meant to be funny, but it just isn't. It is a give-away; it betrays the basic assumption that writing is a competitive business like prize-fighting.

What appeared in 1950 to a European writer as a weird and barbaric American practice has become a common feature of international literary life. Yet do not misunderstand me; in principle I have no objection to first lines that generate instant excitement. Effective openings are first and foremost *inspired* openings.

Inspiration is most enchanting and free when the writer is on the threshold of a new creation. Victor Hugo—a compulsive creator—

jotted down dozens of dazzling openings for novels he never completed, nor seriously contemplated writing; he was simply indulging in the pure magic of beginnings.

Inspired openings in literature have much in common with the overtures of great operas. A literary equivalent of the feverish expectation the orchestra can foster before the curtain rises is in the first paragraph of *Moby-Dick*, which opens with a breathtaking *allegro con brio*:

> Call me Ishmael. Some years ago—never mind how long precisely—having little or no money in my purse and nothing particular to interest me on shore, I thought I would sail about a little and see the watery part of the world. It is a way I have of driving off the spleen and regulating the circulation. Whenever I find myself growing grim about the mouth, whenever there is a damp, drizzly November in my soul; whenever I find myself involuntarily pausing before coffin warehouses, and bringing up the rear of every funeral I meet...then I account it high time to get to sea as soon as I can.

Melville brusquely grabs you by the lapels and his grip never relaxes until, some 600 turbulent, bewildering pages later, he finally lets go of you. At that point, at long last, as the drama is finally over, there is a sudden change of pace: the narrator's voice turns into *largo maestoso*, then softly fades away. Ishmael's ship is lost with all hands, Ishmael alone survives, the coffin of his mate Queequeg becomes his lifebuoy, until another ship, searching for some of her own missing crew, rescues him:

> The great shroud of the sea rolled on as it rolled five thousand years ago...Buoyed up by the coffin for almost one whole day and night, I floated on a soft and dirge-like main. The unharming sharks, they glided by, as if with padlocks on their mouths; the savage seahawks sailed with sheathed beaks. On the second day, a sail drew near, nearer, and picked me up at last. It was the devious-cruising Rachel, that in her retracing search after her missing children, only found another orphan.

Coffins had been evoked on the first page, and a coffin bobs on the surface on the last: the ending is linked to the beginning with an invisible thread that crosses the oceanic immensity of the narrative. But it is too early to raise the issue of endings—I shall return to it.

The trumpet-blast overture is a feature of political essays. Jean-Jacques Rousseau made brilliant use of it in his *Contrat Social*:

Man was born free; yet he is everywhere in chains.

Nearly a century later, Karl Marx injected similar impetus into the first words of the *Communist Manifesto*:

A spectre is haunting Europe—the spectre of communism.

Its 150th anniversary was celebrated last year. The criminal bankruptcy of all the states that used to call themselves "communist" has given a bad name to Marxism, which is perhaps unfair; after all, where has it ever really been tried? I am not competent to assess whether Marxism might still have a political future; one thing, however, is certain: whatever is well written is bound to last. On literary grounds alone, the future of Marx's *Manifesto* is secure.

Rousseau's philosophical treatise heralded the French Revolution, and in the private realm his impact was as momentous: his *Confessions* opened the floodgates for the effusions of Romanticism.

From the start, Rousseau's autobiography presents a heady cocktail of naïve simplicity and stunning megalomania:

I have resolved on an enterprise which has no precedent and which, once complete, will have no imitator. I propose to display before my fellow-mortals a man in the full truth of nature; and this man shall be myself.

Half a century later, however, Stendhal introduced a cool distrust of all cant in exploring the self. With its swift and casual elegance, the opening of his *Mémoires d'un touriste* offers the best antidote to Rousseau's egomania:

> It is not out of egotism that I say "I"; it is simply the quickest way to tell the story.

Accusations of complacency directed at the authors of autobiographies and memoirs were deftly deflected once and for all by Alexander Herzen in *The Pole Star*, with:

> Who is entitled to write his reminiscences?
> Everyone.
> Because no one is obliged to read them.

———

The overtures of some novels have become virtual proverbs. Think, for instance, of the first words of *A Tale of Two Cities*: "It was the best of times, it was the worst of times"; and I suppose even those who have never read *Anna Karenina* would recognise its opening sentence:

> All happy families are alike; each unhappy family is unhappy in its own way.

Sometimes, lesser writers are also capable of a stroke of genius. The first words of *The Go-Between* are in all memories—even in the memories of those who have never heard the name L. P. Hartley:

> The past is a foreign country: they do things differently there.

Conversely, there are masterpieces that begin in a most inconspicuous manner, and it is only in hindsight that their low-keyed openings have come to acquire the magical resonance they have for us today. When Proust wrote, "For a long time I used to go to bed early..." his first readers could hardly have foreseen where this deceptively bland and modest statement would take them. Some 4,000 pages later, however, they found themselves in the position of a swimmer who, having slipped quietly into the waters of a lazy river, is soon overwhelmed by an invisible current and carried away to the middle of the ocean.

In philosophical fables, however, the usual aim is to puzzle readers and catch their attention from the outset. In *Metamorphosis*, for example, Kafka entraps us at once in an inexorable nightmare:

> As Gregor Samsa awoke one morning from uneasy dreams, he found himself transformed in his bed into a gigantic insect.

Grown-up fairytales observe the same method. When you read the first sentence of a story by Marcel Aymé, you immediately react like a child—you *must* find out what happens next. *The Dwarf* begins:

> As he reached the age of thirty-five, the dwarf of the Barnaboum Circus started to grow.

Some writers find the initial spark in words, others in ideas, and others again in an image—an inner vision. The latter are perhaps the quintessential fiction writers. For them, very often, writing is an obsessive activity, sometimes performed as if in a trance, and generally conducted under the blind dictation of their subconscious. Writing is the safety valve that preserves their very sanity; if they did not write, they would hardly survive: Graham Greene, Georges Simenon, Julien Green—however different as individuals—are typical of this remarkable breed. Their novels—and particularly their opening scenes—linger hauntingly in the memory. Yet what we remember is not words or phrases; it is the visual impact of cinematic frames on the screen of our imagination. When Greene was still an obscure journalist and met the film producer Alexander Korda, he was abruptly asked if he had any story in mind that might be turned into a film. Greene immediately improvised the opening scene of a thriller: "Early morning on Platform 1 at Paddington; the platform is empty—except for one man who is waiting for the last train from Wales. From below his raincoat a trickle of blood forms a pool on the platform." "Yes, and then?" asked Korda. "It would take too long to tell you the whole plot," Greene replied, not having a clue how he would go on: "It still needs some more working out." But a friendship was struck that eventuated in the making of *The Third Man*. We will never know what the bleeding man on the platform was up to, but his image remains with us, as it did with Korda.

The impeccable wordsmith and original thinker Paul Valéry's preamble for his philosophical essay "Monsieur Teste" stays etched in the mind when the essay itself is a blurry impression:

> Stupidity is not my strong point. I have seen many people; I have visited a few countries; I have taken part in various undertakings without liking them; I have eaten nearly every day; I have caressed a few women. Today I can still recall a good hundred faces, two or three great shows, and perhaps the gist of some twenty books. What I remember is neither the best nor the worst of these things: simply what has managed to remain, remains. This arithmetic relieves me of any surprise that I am growing old.

But the hyper-rationality of Valéry's intelligence produced in him a strong prejudice against the art of fiction. To his mind, a novelist's invention was deplorably devoid of intellectual necessity. He toyed with the idea of compiling an anthology of first lines from famous novels, to demonstrate the asinine triviality of a literary genre in which a book may begin with a statement as vacuous as: "The marchioness went out at five o'clock," a phrase that became a shorthand indictment for a certain type of fiction. The surrealist movement appropriated Valéry's gibe in its ferocious literary crusade against all novels and novelists—but these inquisitorial outbursts had no noticeable impact upon the general health of European and American fiction, which continued to flourish. Here are two brilliantly effective novel openings from the 1930s (one could think of many dozens more). First, Evelyn Waugh's *Vile Bodies*:

> It was clearly going to be a bad crossing.
>
> With Asiatic resignation, Father Rothschild S.J. put down his suitcase in the corner of the bar and went on deck. (It was a small suitcase of imitation crocodile hide. The initials stamped on it in Gothic characters were not Father Rothschild's for he had borrowed it that morning from the *valet-de-chambre* of his hotel. It contained some rudimentary underclothes, six important new books in six languages, a false beard and a school atlas and gazetteer heavily annotated.)

We sense that the book will contain resources just as surprising and diverse. Or again, George Orwell's *Coming Up for Air*:

> The idea really came to me the day I got my new false teeth.

One could not suggest with greater economy the mood of gloom and despair that is going to pervade this prophetic indictment of a modern world poisoned by synthetic food, cretinised by commercial advertisements and ransacked by real-estate developers.

———

Chekhov remarked that writers would often benefit by cutting off the beginnings and the endings of their stories—for these are usually the weakest parts in their work. It would not only be inconceivable but simply impracticable to effect such surgical interventions on Chekhov's own stories; their beginnings and endings are all the more effective for being virtually invisible—and there lies one of the secrets of his art.

Lopping off the introductory sentences of a narrative is a conceit often used to startling effect in eighteenth-century literature. We don't really begin to read Sterne's *Sentimental Journey*: we are casually and unexpectedly dumped into it:

"They order," said I, "this matter better in France."

This sort of abrupt opening produces the youthful and exhilarating feeling one experiences when jumping into a train already in motion. We are carried away with similar speed and whimsicality by Diderot at the beginning of *Jacques le fataliste*—and, quite significantly, here again it is travel that provides the leading metaphor:

> How did they meet? Perchance, like everybody. What were their names? What does it matter to you? Where did they come from? From the nearest place. Where did they go? Who knows where he is going? What were they saying? The master said nothing; and Jacques said, that his Captain used to say, that whatever happens to us on earth, good and bad, was already written in heaven.

As we just saw, Chekhov used to put the difficulty of the ending on a par with that of the beginning. Yet it is impossible to present here any exemplary selection of endings: the emotional impact, the artistic excellence of a great ending is totally dependent upon the entire book that precedes it. To my mind, the ending of Flaubert's *Sentimental Education* is sublime; but either you have read the book, and naturally agree with me—or you have not read it, and my pronouncement will merely amount to a fatuous exercise in name-dropping. I must simply limit myself to a few marginal observations on some unusual forms of ending.

First is the delayed-release ending in which the real ending does not occur with the last sentence on the last page of the book but takes place a few seconds later, in the imagination of the reader. This technique somehow operates on the model of a very nasty type of bomb, whose truly devastating explosion is not the one that is produced on impact, but the second one that is delayed by a few minutes. Example: in Greene's *Brighton Rock*, Rose, a naïve and kind girl, hopelessly in love with a young gangster, receives for the first time a present from her callous lover: a six-penny gramophone record on which he has recorded what she assumes to be a personal message of love. But the reader has already been told that what the little punk recorded was a dirty flow of savage abuse aimed at the innocent girl. The young man is killed, Rose returns to her sordid lodgings in a state of utter despair, her only comfort the thought that she still has the record of his voice—her only treasure—which, now at last, she will listen to; the book ends on this sentence describing her journey home:

> She walked rapidly in the thin June sunlight towards the worst horror of all.

Alternative endings are a trick famously performed by John Fowles in *The French Lieutenant's Woman*. He proposes two options: gloomy or happy; the reader can take his pick. It is a cheeky display of *savoir faire* by a virtuoso of story-telling, but it is precisely the sort of artifice that helped give a bad name to the art of the novel. Perhaps Valéry had a point after all when he complained that fiction writing was essentially frivolous, since one can imagine different endings to the same novel—whereas the closure of a good poem has an immutable necessity.

Weird endings are a third category. In the exceptionally rich field of modern Japanese fiction, Tanizaki Jun'ichiro occupies a towering position and *The Makioka Sisters* (1948) is generally considered to be his masterpiece. Yukiko, the third of the four sisters, is in danger of becoming an old maid, when finally a suitable fiancé is found for her. The book ends as she prepares to go to Tokyo for her marriage:

> [Yukiko's] stomach had for some time been upset, and even after repeated doses of wakamatsu and arsilin, she was troubled by diarrhoea on the twenty-sixth [the day of her departure]. The wedding kimonos arrived on the same day. Yukiko looked at them and sighed—if only they were not for her wedding.
>
> Yukiko's diarrhoea persisted through the twenty-sixth and was a problem on the train to Tokyo.

Finally, there are missing endings. Two great novels that endeavour to tackle the ultimate questions of the human condition have remained without an ending—which, in retrospect, may be a most fitting conclusion.

Kafka, in his final masterpiece *The Castle*, tells the story of a young man who repeatedly attempts—always in vain—to overcome arcane hurdles to gain access to a mysterious castle. Will his persistence succeed? We shall never know, for Kafka died before he could complete his manuscript.

In *Bouvard et Pécuchet*, Flaubert describes how two old bachelors living in retirement, after a dreary career as menial clerks, launch themselves into an encyclopaedic survey of all human knowledge. Their naïve venture soon becomes a circumnavigation of the immense, uncharted continent of human idiocy. At the start of his mad and desperate enterprise, Flaubert's intention had been to portray his characters as two despicable fools—but the creatures soon rebel against their creator and reclaim their individual dignity. This momentous change occurs halfway through the book, when we are told that "a pitiful ability began to develop in their minds—the ability to detect stupidity, and not to tolerate it." From that moment, Bouvard and Pécuchet become Flaubert himself, whose task, gigantic and hopeless, turned into mental—and physical—agony. He died at work, collapsing under the strain like a donkey crushed by its burden.

In his last work, Kafka described the search for salvation; Flaubert, the quest for meaning. But these pursuits take us into mysteries no mortal can fathom. It seems strangely appropriate that death should have intervened, ensuring these heroic explorations remain open—forever.

Part III
CHINA

THE CHINESE ATTITUDE TOWARDS THE PAST

Le Tibre seul, qui vers la mer s'enfuit,
Reste de Rome. O mondaine inconstance!
Ce qui est ferme, est par le temps détruit,
Et ce qui fuit, au temps fait résistance.
—JOACHIM DU BELLAY, *Les Antiquités de Rome* (1558)

CHINA is the oldest living civilisation on Earth.[1] Such a unique continuity naturally implies a very complex relation between a people and their past. It seems that there is a paradox at the heart of this remarkable cultural longevity: cultivation of the moral and spiritual values of the ancients appears to have most often combined with a curious neglect of, or indifference (even at times downright iconoclasm) towards, the material heritage of the past. (Whether the spiritual continuity was achieved in spite of, or *thanks to*, a partial destruction of the material expressions of tradition is itself another issue, which will only be briefly evoked later on.)

This essay attempts a preliminary exploration of the parallel phenomena of spiritual preservation and material destruction that can be observed in the history of Chinese culture. The topic being vast, I shall merely outline here some of the directions and themes which a fuller inquiry ought to pursue. At this stage, my intention is not to provide any answers, but simply to define the question.

SPIRITUAL PRESENCE AND PHYSICAL ABSENCE OF THE PAST IN CHINA

In his autobiography, Carl Gustav Jung described how, in his old age, he wished to go to Rome, which he had never visited before. He had always postponed this project, fearing that he might not be able to withstand the emotional impact of such an encounter with the living heart of Europe's ancient culture. Eventually, as he entered a travel agency in Zurich to buy his ticket, he fainted and remained unconscious for a short interval. After this experience, he wisely decided to abandon his plans—and he never saw Rome.[2] Most sinologists are not endowed with antennae as subtle as Jung's—and yet, even without being possessed of such sensitivity, it would be difficult for whoever studied classical China to approach the China of today and not to feel constantly touched, moved, overwhelmed by the extraordinary aura that seems to emanate everywhere from a land so suffused with history.

The presence of the past is constantly felt in China. Sometimes it is found in the most unexpected places, where it hits the visitor with added intensity: movie-theatre posters, advertisements for washing machines, televisions or toothpaste displayed along the streets are expressed in a written language that has remained practically unchanged for the last 2,000 years. In kindergarten, toddlers chant Tang poems that were written some 1,200 years ago. In railway stations, the mere consultation of a train timetable can be an intoxicating experience for any cultural historian: the imagination is stirred by these long lists of city names to which are still attached the vivid glories of past dynasties. Or again, in a typical and recent occurrence, archaeologists discovered in a 2,000-year-old tomb, among the foodstuff that had been buried with the deceased, *ravioli* which were in every respect identical to those that can be bought today in any street-corner shop. Similar examples could be multiplied endlessly.

Yet, at the same time, the paradox is that the very past which seems to penetrate everything, and to manifest itself with such surprising vigour, is also strangely evading our *physical* grasp. This same China which is loaded with so much history and so many memories is also oddly deprived of ancient monuments. In the Chinese landscape, there is a *material* absence of the past that can be most disconcerting for cultivated Western travellers—especially if they approach China with the criteria and standards that are naturally developed in a European environment. In Europe, in spite of countless wars and destruction, every age has left a considerable amount of monumental landmarks: the ruins of classical Greece and Rome, and all the great medieval cathedrals, the churches and palaces of the Renaissance period, the monuments of the Baroque era—all these form an unbroken chain of architectural witnesses that perpetuate the memory of the past, right into the heart of our modern cities. In China, on the contrary, if we except a very small number of famous *ensembles* (the antiquity of which is quite relative), what strikes the educated visitor is the monumental absence of the past. Most Chinese cities—including and especially those which were ancient capital cities or prestigious cultural centres—present today an aspect that may not look exactly new or modern (for, if modernisation is a target which China has now set for itself, there is still a long way to go before it can be reached), yet they still appear strangely devoid of all traditional character. On the whole, they seem to be a product of late-nineteenth-century industrialisation. Thus, the past which continues to animate Chinese life in so many striking, unexpected or subtle ways seems to inhabit *the people* rather than the bricks and stones. The Chinese past is both spiritually active and physically invisible.

It should be noted that, when I mention this physical elimination of the past, I am not trying to refer once more to the widespread and systematic destruction perpetrated by the "Cultural Revolution." During the last years of the Maoist era, this destruction, it is true, literally resulted in a cultural desert—in some cities 95 to 100 per cent of historic and cultural relics were indeed lost forever. However, we must immediately point out that, if in so many cities it was possible for mere gangs of schoolchildren to loot, burn and raze to the ground the near totality of the local antiquities, it was because in the first instance there had not been much left for them to destroy. Actually, very few monuments had survived earlier historical disasters and, in consequence, the Maoist vandals found only rare targets on which to expend their energy. In this perspective, it might even be a mistake to look at the "Cultural Revolution" as if it was an accidental aberration. If we place it in a broader historical context, it may appear in fact as the latest expression of a very ancient phenomenon of massive iconoclasm, which was recurrent all through the ages. Without having to go very far back in time, the Taiping insurrection in the mid-nineteenth century produced a devastation that was far more radical than the "Cultural Revolution"—I shall come back later to this question of the periodic destruction of the material heritage of the past, which seems to have characterised Chinese history.

Thus, the disconcerting barrenness of the Chinese monumental landscape cannot be read simply as a consequence of the chaotic years of the Maoist period. It is a feature much more permanent and deep— and it had already struck Western travellers in the nineteenth and at the beginning of the twentieth century.

In this particular respect, I think it would be difficult to find a witness better qualified and more articulate than Victor Segalen (1878– 1919), a remarkable poet who was also a sinologist and archaeologist of considerable achievement; he spent several years in China at the end of the empire, and led two long archaeological expeditions into the more remote provinces of the interior. In one prose poem, "Aux dix mille années"[3] (1912), he memorably summarised the paradox which is, I think, at the root of the Chinese attitude towards the past. (My entire essay was originally triggered by this piece, and what I am trying to do here is merely to provide a comment to it.)

Segalen's poem is a meditation on the relation between Chinese culture and time. It starts from a comparative evocation of the architectural principles of the great civilisations of the past, and opposes them to the Chinese conception. The non-Chinese attitude—from ancient Egypt to the modern West—is essentially an active, aggressive attempt to challenge and overcome the erosion of time. Its ambition is to build for all eternity by adopting the strongest possible materials and using techniques that will ensure maximum resilience. Yet, by doing this, the builders are merely postponing their ineluctable defeat. The Chinese, on the contrary, have realised that—in Segalen's words—"nothing immobile can escape the hungry teeth of the ages." Thus, the Chinese constructors yielded to the onrush of time, the better to deflect it.

Segalen's reflection developed from technically accurate information: Chinese architecture is essentially made of perishable and fragile materials; it embodies a sort of "in-built obsolescence"; it decays rapidly and requires frequent rebuilding. From these practical observations, he drew a philosophical conclusion: the Chinese actually transferred the problem—eternity should not inhabit the building, it should inhabit the builder. The transient nature of the construction is like an offering to the voracity of time; for the price of such sacrifices, the constructors ensure the everlastingness of their spiritual designs.

LIMITS OF CHINESE ANTIQUARIANISM

Although, on the whole, it would not be wrong to say that the Chinese largely neglected to maintain and preserve the material expressions of their culture, such a statement would obviously require qualification.

Antiquarianism[4] did develop in China and constitutes in itself a topic that would deserve a thorough study. Here I wish merely to emphasise its two major limitations: first, antiquarianism appeared very late in Chinese cultural history; secondly, it remained essentially restricted to a narrow category of objects.

On the first point: although some aspects of antiquarianism (mostly literary) had already appeared in late Tang (after the crisis of An Lushan's rebellion in 756), it essentially developed from the beginning of the Song (eleventh century)—in Western terms, this may seem quite ancient, but in Chinese history it is in fact rather late, as it represents the beginning of modern times. The Song displayed a passionate curiosity in antiquity, and this interest found many expressions: the first manifestations of scholarly archaeology, the study and collection of antique bronzes, the great systematic compilations of ancient epigraphs. More generally, Song tastes and fashions all began to reflect this new cult for the artistic forms of the past.

What is remarkable is that in China the development of antiquarianism actually reflected a highly abnormal situation. It resulted from a spiritual crisis and represented a new desire to define and affirm a Chinese cultural identity. The Song empire was a menaced world, a mutilated empire. Not only had the Chinese territory dangerously shrunk, but for the first time the Chinese emperors had to deal not with mere nomadic raiders but with alien leaders ruling in their own right. China's aggressive neighbours now possessed set institutions and a fairly sophisticated culture; they directly challenged the Chinese traditional conception whereby China was the centre of the world. From the eleventh century, the Chinese faith in the universality of their world order seems to have been deeply shaken by the permanent politico-military crisis resulting from the foreign menace, and it is in this particular context that, for the first time in Chinese history, a massive cultural escape took place backwards in time: Chinese intellectuals effected a retreat into their glorious antiquity and undertook a systematic investigation of the splendours of their past. (Modern scholars have called this phenomenon "Chinese culturalism" and see in it a forerunner of the nationalism that was to develop many centuries later in reaction against the Manchu rule and Western aggressions.)

In this perspective, antiquarianism appears essentially as a search for spiritual shelter and moral comfort. Antiquarian pursuits were to provide Chinese intellectuals with much-needed reassurance at a time when they felt threatened in their cultural identity.

On the second point (the limited object of antiquarianism), traditionally Chinese aesthetes, connoisseurs and collectors were exclusively interested in calligraphy and painting; later on, their interest also extended to bronzes and to a few other categories of antiques. However, we must immediately observe that painting is in fact an extension of calligraphy—or at least, that it had first to adopt the instruments and techniques of calligraphy before it could attract the attention of the aesthetes. As to the bronzes, their value was directly dependent upon whether they carried epigraphs.[5] In conclusion, it would not be an excessive simplification to state that, in China, the taste for antiques has always remained closely—if not exclusively—related to the prestige of the *written word*.

ART COLLECTIONS

A study of Chinese antiquarianism should naturally include a chapter on art collecting in China. On this important topic we must limit ourselves here to a few basic remarks.[6]

The earliest collections recorded in history were the imperial collections. The early collections of the archaic rulers were composed of symbolic objects, with magic and cosmological properties, the possession of which entailed possession of political power. Progressively, the magico-cosmological collections of "maps and documents" (*tuji* or *tushu*) evolved into art collections of "calligraphy and painting"—the transition took place around the end of the Han period. (Note the ambiguity of the word "tu" which means both *map* and *image*. Originally, to possess the map-image of a territory was to have control over that territory. In international relations in pre-imperial China, when a state yielded territory to another state, the transaction was effected by surrendering the map-image of that territory.)

It is interesting to observe that, even after the magico-cosmological collections turned into aesthetic collections, the memory of their original function never disappeared completely. For instance, a Tang emperor, who was a connoisseur and avid collector, having learned that one of his high officials had some very rare ancient paintings, "invited" him to present them to the imperial collections. Needless to say, this kind of "invitation" could not be declined, and the minister, heartbroken, complied immediately. The emperor personally acknowledged the gift, and in his letter took pains to emphasise that, in taking possession of these paintings, he was not pursuing an idle and frivolous private aesthetic curiosity but actually meant to assume fully his public responsibility as a ruler.[7]

In fact, the imperial collections never entirely lost their archaic role of legitimising political authority. It is remarkable to see how this function has actually survived until today. Chiang Kai-shek, who was never particularly noted for his artistic inclinations, diverted considerable resources and energy in a time of acute emergency in order to have the former imperial collections removed to Taiwan just before he had to evacuate the mainland. By doing this, it was generally considered that he had secured a fairly substantial support for his claim that he still was the legitimate ruler of all China. At the time, Peking experienced this move as a bitter political setback, and the presence of the imperial collections in Taiwan has always remained a very sore point for the People's Republic. The Communist leaders too can hardly be suspected of much aesthetic indulgence—and yet, as soon as they assumed power, they immediately attempted to rebuild an "imperial" collection in Peking—partly by "inviting" private collectors to contribute their paintings (in a fashion quite similar to the Tang episode evoked earlier), and partly by buying back, at great cost, some ancient masterpieces of Chinese art on the international art market.[8]

All through history, imperial collections achieved an extraordinary concentration of ancient masterpieces, amounting at times to a virtual monopoly over the artistic heritage of the past. Two important consequences resulted from this situation.

1. Without access to the imperial collections—and only a very small number of high-ranking officials enjoyed such a privilege—it was practically impossible for most artists, aesthetes, connoisseurs and critics to acquire a full, first-hand knowledge of ancient art. On this subject, even historians were dealing mostly with abstract concepts, unverified stereotypes and literary information.[9] Sifting through the vast literature of connoisseurs' notes, one is constantly struck by the fact that, when the writers refer to ancient paintings which they personally had the chance to examine, these works are seldom more than 200 years old. Moreover, it is not uncommon to come across influential critics and collectors who confess that they hardly ever saw any works by famous artists who lived barely one century before them.[10] (This situation provided ideal conditions for a thriving industry of art forgery—another important topic that unfortunately cannot be covered here.[11])

2. It is mostly because each dynasty achieved a huge concentration of art treasures that China's heritage repeatedly suffered such massive losses. The fall of practically every dynasty entailed the looting and burning of the imperial palace, and each time, with one stroke, the cream of the artistic production of the preceding centuries would

vanish in smoke. The stunning extent of these recurrent disasters is documented in great detail by the historical records.[12]

Here, a side comment could be made. We must lament the grievous losses that were inflicted upon the cultural heritage of China—and of mankind—and yet, we may wonder if there was perhaps not *some* relation between the inexhaustible creativity displayed by Chinese culture through the ages and the periodic *tabula rasa* that prevented this culture from becoming clogged up, inhibited and crushed under the weight of the treasures accumulated by earlier ages. Like individuals, civilisations do need a certain amount of *creative forgetfulness*. Too many memories can hinder intellectual and spiritual activity, as it is suggested in a well-known tale by Jorge Luis Borges, describing the ordeal of a man who cannot forget anything. A total, perfect, infallible memory is a curse: the mind of Borges's character is turned into a huge garbage heap from which nothing can be subtracted, and where, as a result, no imaginative or thinking process can take place any more—for to think is to discard.

IDEOLOGICAL BACKGROUND: THE CULT OF THE PAST IN CHINESE THOUGHT

As we have just noted, Chinese antiquarianism remained limited both in time (it appeared late) and in scope (it was mostly concerned with the diverse manifestations of the written word).

These limitations may seem paradoxical when we consider that two important cultural factors ought apparently to have produced an environment particularly conducive to antiquarian pursuits. These factors are:

1. that China's dominant ideology—Confucianism—extolled the values of the past; and

2. that China from a very early age developed an extraordinary sense of history—it actually possesses the longest uninterrupted historiographical tradition.

On the question of the Confucian cult of the past,[13] two significant qualifications should be made. First, in ancient Chinese thought, the cult of the past was far from being a universal dogma. The quarrel between the "ancients" and the "moderns" occupied a considerable part of the philosophical debates in pre-imperial China—the most creative period in the history of Chinese thought. At the end of that period, the modern school gained the upper hand, thus providing the ideological framework for the establishment of the first Chinese empire. (In fact, the notorious initiative of the first emperor, who decided "to burn the books and bury the scholars alive," marked the gruesome climax of this movement to obliterate the past.) Shortly before, the last (and most agile) of the great exponents of Confucianism, Xun Zi, had come to terms with "modernism" and accommodated the Confucian tradition to the prevalent trends of the time.[14]

Secondly, it is true that Confucius considered antiquity as the repository of all human values. Therefore, according to him, the sage's mission was not to *create* anything anew but merely to *transmit* the heritage of the ancients. In actual fact, such a program was far less conservative than might first appear (Confucius himself played a revolutionary role in his time): the antiquity to which he referred was a *lost* antiquity, which the sage had to seek and practically to *reinvent*. Its actual contents were thus highly fluid and not susceptible to objective definition or circumscription by a specific historical tradition. Similarly, in later periods, nearly all the great Confucian reformers in Chinese history used to invoke the authority of the ancients to condemn modern practices—but what was meant by these semantic conventions practically amounted to the exact opposite: their so-called antiquity referred to a mythical Golden Age—actually their utopian vision of the *future*—whereas the so-called modern practices referred to the inheritance of the recent past; that is, in fact, the *real past*.

On the question of the great historiographical tradition of China and the unique awareness of history developed by Chinese culture, only one basic observation should be made here, in direct connection with our topic. It is true that China produced from a very early period a magnificent historiography. Two thousand years ago, Chinese historians already displayed methods that were remarkably modern and scientific; this, however, should not lead us to misunderstand their objective, which remained essentially philosophic and moral.

From a very early stage—well before Confucius—the Chinese evolved the notion that there could only be one form of immortality: the immortality conferred by history. In other words, life-after-life was not to be found in a supernature, nor could it rely upon artefacts: man only survives in man—which means, in practical terms, in the memory of posterity, through the medium of the written word.[15]

This brings us back to our starting point, Segalen's poetical intuition that Chinese everlastingness does not inhabit monuments, but people. Permanence does not negate change, it informs change. Continuity is not ensured by the immobility of inanimate objects, it is achieved through the fluidity of the successive generations.[16]

A CASE STUDY: THE "PREFACE TO THE ORCHID PAVILION"

After having dealt with theoretical notions, let us now conclude by examining one exemplary case—a concrete instance that illustrates the actual mechanisms of the relationship between a "spiritual" tradition and its material expression.

My example is taken from calligraphy, which—as I already pointed out—is considered in China as the supreme art. The particular piece I am going to present is itself traditionally considered as the absolute masterpiece of this supreme art. In the entire history of Chinese art there is probably no other individual work that could claim a similar prestige, or could have exerted as wide and lasting an influence. It became a cornerstone in the development of calligraphy. Practically all the major calligraphers of later centuries defined themselves in relation to this particular work.

This arch-famous work is called the *Lan ting xu*, or *Preface to the Orchid Pavilion*, by Wang Xizhi (307–365), the greatest calligrapher of all ages.[17]

First, a few words need to be said on the work itself and the circumstances of its creation. In 353, on the occasion of a spring ritual, a group of scholars went on an excursion to a beautiful spot called the Orchid Pavilion. It was a merry and refined gathering, dedicated to the enjoyment of friendship, poetry and wine. At the end of the day, all the poems that had been improvised by the participants were collected, and Wang Xizhi wrote a preface to the collection. The preface itself is a short prose-essay in 320 words. On that day, Wang Xizhi was particularly inspired, and when he calligraphed his preface, he really surpassed himself. Later on, he repeatedly tried to recapture the unique quality of his original creation, and literally made hundreds of attempts to reduplicate his own masterpiece, but never succeeded in equalling the miraculous beauty of the *premier jet*.

How was this calligraphy handed down in history? Here the plot thickens and even acquires the bizarre and murky twists of a detective story.

After Wang Xizhi's death, the *Orchid Pavilion* was kept by his descendants and remained within the family. However, during the first 200 years of its existence, no mention was ever made of it; seemingly, no one had a chance to see it.

Two hundred and fifty years later, it came into the hands of a monk who made copies of it, had these distributed and thus laid the ground for Wang's subsequent artistic reputation.

Three hundred years later, Wang's calligraphic style aroused the enthusiasm of Emperor Tang Taizong. Taizong avidly hunted for his calligraphies and gathered the most exhaustive collection of his autographs (2,290 items—all to be eventually scattered). However, the crowning jewel, the *Orchid Pavilion*, was still missing from this collection. After devious manoeuvres, combining deception and violence, the emperor finally succeeded in securing possession of the masterpiece—at the cost of a human life.[18] Taizong treasured the *Orchid Pavilion* and ordered copies to be made from it (both tracing copies and free-hand copies); these copies were then carved on stone and rubbings were taken from the stone tablets. Eventually the original stones were lost or destroyed, but new tablets were carved from the original rubbings. As the original rubbings themselves disappeared, new rubbings were taken from later engravings—and with the passing of time, the study of the pedigree of these copies of copies of copies, and the establishment of their genealogical tree, became a specialised discipline of mind-boggling complexity.

Meanwhile, Wang Xizhi's original manuscript had long ceased to be available for reference. Tang Taizong, who died in 649, had demanded that the *Orchid Pavilion* be buried with him in his grave at Zhaoling—some 30 kilometres north of what is now Xi'an, where it should still be lying today (if the imperial records told us the truth).

Remarkable paradox: it was only *after* it finally disappeared forever in the imperial grave that this particular work (which very few calligraphers ever saw in its original form) began to exert its strongest influence, through various indirect and questionable copies. It eventually had its greatest impact at the beginning of the Song period (eleventh century)—700 years after Wang Xizhi's time. It was then popularised by a calligrapher of genius, Mi Fu, who, under the guise of propounding Wang's calligraphic style, displayed in fact his own personal creations. The educated public was unable to distinguish the Mi product from the Wang label, as, by this time, practically nothing remained of Wang Xizhi's original works, with the exception of a few very small, uncertain fragments. From then on, the prestige and influence of the *Orchid Pavilion* continued to grow steadily. As L. Ledderose neatly summarised it: "It seems somehow uncomfortably symptomatic that it was the lost *Orchid Pavilion* that was to emerge as the most celebrated work in the history of Chinese calligraphy...What is even more astonishing is that the *Orchid Pavilion* in addition to being glorified also became a stylistic model: it has been studied by calligraphers for centuries although nobody has ever seen the original!"[19]

Furthermore, there was a final, ironic twist to the story. In 1965, the famous scholar and archaeologist Guo Moruo ignited a bomb that threw the Chinese academic world into turmoil and initiated a heated and still unresolved debate. According to Guo's findings, not only is the calligraphy of the *Orchid Pavilion*, as we know it through its Tang and Song copies, from a much later date than Wang Xizhi, but even the text itself could not have been composed by him: in other words, Wang Xizhi neither wrote it nor calligraphed it. The sublime model which inspired the entire development of Chinese calligraphy, the aesthetic and technical cornerstone of this art, *may in fact never have existed*!

Whether or not this conclusion is accurate (there are some flaws in Guo's argumentation, but let us leave that aside), it can still provide us with an important clue to the broader issue we have attempted to address: *the vital strength, the creativity, the seemingly unlimited capacity for metamorphosis and adaptation which the Chinese tradition displayed for 3,500 years may well derive from the fact that this tradition never let itself be trapped into set forms, static objects and things, where it would have run the risk of paralysis and death.*[20]

In a sense, one of the best metaphors for this tradition could be provided by the description of a Chinese garden which a Ming scholar wrote in the sixteenth century. It was a fashion among intellectuals and artists to write records of beautiful gardens, but in the case of our writer, there was a new dimension added to the genre. The garden he described was called the Wuyou Garden—which means "The Garden-that-does-not-exist." In his essay, the author observed that many famous gardens of the past have entirely disappeared and survive only on paper in literary descriptions. Hence, he wondered why it should be necessary for a garden to have first existed in reality. Why not skip the preliminary stage of actual existence and jump directly into the final state of literary existence which, after all, is the common end of all gardens? What difference is there between a famous garden which exists no more, and this particular garden which never existed at all, since in the end both the former and the latter are known only through the same medium of the written word?[21]

Western visitors in China seem to have been irritated to the point of obsession with what came to be called "Chinese lies" or the "Chinese art of stage-setting and make-believe." Even intelligent and perceptive observers did not completely escape this trap; in a clever piece written a few years ago by a good scholar,[22] I came across an anecdote which, I think, has a much deeper bearing than the author himself may have realised. A great Buddhist monastery near Nanking was famous for its purity and orthodoxy. The monks were following a rule that conformed strictly to the original tradition of the Indian monasteries: whereas, in other Chinese monasteries, an evening meal is served, in this particular monastery every evening the monks received only a bowl of tea. Foreign scholars who visited the monastery at the beginning of this century much admired the austerity of this custom. These visitors, however, were quite naïve. If they had had the curiosity actually to look into the bowls of the monks, they would have found that what was served under the name of "tea" was in fact a fairly nourishing rice congee, similar in every respect to the food which is being provided at night in all other Chinese monasteries. Only in this particular monastery, out of respect for an ancient tradition, the rice congee was conventionally called "the bowl of tea."

I wonder if, to some extent, Chinese tradition is not such a "bowl of tea," which under a most ancient, venerable and constant name can in fact contain all sorts of things, and ultimately anything but tea. Its permanence is first and foremost a *permanence of names*, covering the endlessly changing and fluid nature of its actual contents.

If this observation is correct, it could also have interesting implications in other areas, and you would naturally be free, for instance, to read in it a forecast regarding the eventual fate of Marxism-Leninism and Mao Zedong Thought. This essay, however, was only concerned with China's past.

POSTSCRIPT

As this essay was going to the printers, I belatedly obtained a remarkable article by F. W. Mote, "A Millennium of Chinese Urban History: Form, Time and Space Concepts in Soochow."[23] Reading some of the conclusions which Professor Mote drew fifteen years ago from a case study in Chinese urban history, one will realise that the ideas I ventured here are both less original and more sound than might have first appeared!

Having quoted a Western writer who observed at the beginning of the twentieth century that there were no ancient ruins in Suzhou, Mote comments:

His observation is largely correct. Is Soochow then a city of ancient monuments, or a city in which the awareness of antiquity comes from something else? In our tradition we tend to equate the antique presence with authentically ancient physical objects. China has no ruins comparable to the Roman Forum, or even to Angkor Wat, which is a thousand years younger. It has no ancient buildings kept continually in use such as Rome's Pantheon and Istanbul's Hagia Sophia. It does not have those, not because of incapacity to build with "hewn stone, as in Athens and Rome" as du Bose suggests. It does not have those because of differences in attitude—a different attitude toward the way of making the monumental achievement, and a different attitude toward the ways of achieving the enduring monument.

Mote then illustrates his point by sketching the history of Suzhou's Great Pagoda—with a history going back to the third century AD, it was modified, destroyed and rebuilt many times during the ages, ending up as a twentieth-century construction:

This history is typical of China's ancient monuments. No building with such a pedigree would count for much as an authentic antiquity even in the United States, much less in Rome. It certainly would not count for much among Ruskin's Stones of Venice.

Mote concludes:

The point most emphatically is not that China was not obsessed with its past. It studied its past, and drew upon it, using it to design and to maintain its present as has no other civilization. But its ancient cities such as Soochow were "time free" as purely physical objects. They were repositories of the past in a very special way—they embodied or suggested associations whose value lay elsewhere. The past was a past of words not of stones. China kept the largest and longest-enduring of all mankind's documentations of the past. It constantly scrutinized that past as recorded in words, and caused it to function in the life of its present. But it built no Acropolis, it preserved no Roman Forum, and not because it lacked the materials or the techniques. Its enduring structures of cut stone in antiquity were most characteristically burial vaults secreted underground, and, in the later imperial era, were bridges. Those vaults and bridges were called upon to serve a different level of utility; enduring public monuments to man's achievements did not call forth those means.

Chinese civilization did not lodge its history in buildings. Even its most grandiose palace and city complexes stressed grand layout, the employment of space, and not buildings, which were added as a relatively impermanent superstructure. Chinese civilization seems not to have regarded its history as violated or abused when the historic monuments collapsed or burned, as long as those could be replaced or restored, and their functions regained. *In short we can say that the real past of Soochow is a past of the mind*, its imperishable elements are moments of human experience. *The only truly enduring embodiments of the eternal human moments are the literary ones.* [My emphasis throughout.]

This final point is then illustrated by the concrete example of Soochow's Maple Bridge which became a poetical topic in literary history:

In all that psycho-historical material associated with the Maple Bridge, the bridge as an object is of little importance ... No single poem refers to its physical presence. The bridge as idea was an item in the consciousness of all Chinese ... yet, its reality to them was not the stones forming its span so much as the imperishable associations with it; those eternal moments realized in words. The physical object is entirely secondary. Anyone planning to achieve immortality in the minds of his fellow men might well give a lower priority to building some great stone monument than to cultivating his human capacities so that he might express himself imperishably in words, or at least be alluded to in some enduring line by a poet or essayist of immortal achievement.

1986

ONE MORE ART
Chinese Calligraphy

THE DISCOVERY of a new major art should have more momentous implications for mankind than the exploration of an unknown continent or the sighting of a new planet.

Since the dawn of its civilisation, China has cultivated a particular branch of the visual arts that has no equivalent anywhere else in the world. On first encounter, Westerners misnamed it "calligraphy" by false analogy with a mere decorative craft that was more familiar to them. Although it was always one of the most sublime achievements of the Chinese genius, only today are art lovers outside China progressively beginning to prospect the riches of this artistic El Dorado that has finally opened up to them.

Like painting (which, being born of the same brush, is its younger brother rather than its twin), Chinese calligraphy addresses the eye and is an art of space; like music, it unfolds in time; like dance, it develops a dynamic sequence of movements, pulsating in rhythm. It is an art that radiates such physical presence and sensuous power that it virtually defies photographic reproduction—at times even, its execution can verge on an athletic performance; yet its abstract and erudite character also has special appeal for intellectuals and scholars who adopted it as their favourite pursuit. It is the most elite of all arts—it was practised by emperors, aesthetes, monks and poets—but it is also one of the most popular. Its tools—brush, ink and paper—can be simple and cheap and are within the reach of nearly anybody—schoolchildren, women, modest townsfolk, bohemian drunks, hermits. Its

Review of Jean François Billeter: *The Chinese Art of Writing* (New York: Skira Rizzoli, 1990).

manifestations are ubiquitous and diverse—from the refined studio of the aristocratic connoisseur to the gaudy signs of the marketplace. In China, the written word lives and reigns everywhere—on the walls of palaces and temples, as well as on those of wine shops and teahouses, and at new-year time, its inspiring and sacred presence graces the doors of even the poorest farmhouses in the most remote hamlets.

The practice of the art of writing is not the exclusive preserve of specialists. The calligraphic brush can yield rewards that are as multiform as the human quest itself. To the unworldly, it affords a path of spiritual cultivation, and for the ambitious it is a prerequisite to climbing the ladder of a political career. Until recently, no Chinese statesman could truly command respect without being also master of the brush; social prestige as well as intellectual and artistic reputations could not be secured without a skilful handwriting. Thus, for centuries, literally millions of Chinese have devoted themselves to the exercise of calligraphy; in the practice of this art, they have sought self-expression or social promotion, self-oblivion or inner concentration; they practised calligraphy out of necessity or out of passion—as a solace, as a convention, as an escape, as an obsession, as a liberation; for many, it was a drug, an *ascesis*, a private madness, an austere discipline, a way of life; the best of them found in it the perfect paradigm of *efficient activity*, a method for achieving the harmonious integration of mind and body, the key to supreme enlightenment.

The very centrality of the place calligraphy occupies in Chinese life and culture paradoxically explains why the West took such a long time to appreciate it as an art. When two great civilisations, utterly foreign to each other, come into direct contact, it seems that, at first, they cannot exchange anything but blows and trinkets. Mutual access to the core of their respective cultures necessitates a lengthy and complex process. It demands patience and humility, for outsiders are normally not allowed beyond a certain point: they will not be admitted to the inner chambers of the spirit, unless they are willing to shed some of their original baggage. Cultural initiation entails metamorphosis, and we cannot learn any foreign values if we do not accept the risk of being transformed by what we learn.

In the case of Chinese calligraphy, the difficulty is further compounded by two more obstacles. First, by its very nature, calligraphy is intimately linked with Chinese language; its full appreciation may at times require a certain familiarity with a rich and intricate network of historical, philological and cultural references. To what extent is it necessary to be able to read Chinese in order fully to enjoy Chinese calligraphy? A preliminary (and crude) answer may be provided in the form of another question: To what extent is it necessary to be able to read music in order to enjoy a musical performance? Such knowledge would naturally help, without being strictly indispensable; the degree of sensitivity of the spectator (or the listener) can, to some degree, make up for what he may be lacking in intellectual information.

In the appreciation of calligraphy, the main advantage that can be derived from the ability to read Chinese is not so much that the viewer has access to the content of the calligraphic inscription (this content can be quite indifferent, as we shall see immediately). It is rather that, knowing the rules and graphic mechanisms of the Chinese script, he is able to follow and to reconstruct in his mind the successive movements of the calligrapher's brush.

The relation between calligraphic form and literary content (i.e. between the calligraphy itself and the text it conveys) might in a way be compared to the relation between painters and their models in Western portrait painting. There are exceptional encounters where the genius of the sitter may add an extra sparkle to the genius of the painter—think, for instance, of the portrait of Thomas More by Holbein, or of Chopin by Delacroix. Most of the time, however, the very identity of the model is largely irrelevant. (Who was Mona Lisa? Who cares?) Similarly, there are some instances of great calligraphies inspired by admirable texts; usually, however, the nature of the text which provided a base—or a mere pretext—for the calligraphic performance has no significant bearing upon the artist's achievement, and there are many examples of sublime calligraphies that took flight from dull and trite dissertations.

Furthermore, there is even a style of calligraphy—a particularly exciting and creative one—which renders the original text practically *illegible* for most viewers: the so-called grass-script (*cao shu*) in its "crazy" form (*kuang*) is a sort of frenzied stenography, dashed in a wild outburst of intoxicated inspiration. Only practitioners and specialists can decipher it—and yet, even for the common viewer, it is one of the most spectacular and appealing styles. Its illegibility poses no obstacle to the enjoyment of the ordinary public, since—as we have just said—this enjoyment does not reside in a literary appreciation of the contents but in an imaginative communion with the dynamics of the brushwork. What the viewer needs is not to read a text but to retrace in his mind the original dance of the brush and to relive its rhythmic progress.

A second, even more fundamental, obstacle to appreciating calligraphy derives from a fact I have already mentioned: with their writing the Chinese actually possess *one more art*—calligraphy has no parallel in any other of the great literate civilisations. As a result, the very existence of this art could not immediately register in the consciousness of early Western travellers. The reason is that, usually, people do not see, they only recognise. And what they do not recognise remains invisible to them. For centuries, foreign visitors to China, even if they were highly educated, remained simply blind to the Chinese art of calligraphy—or when they took notice of it, they betrayed a staggering incomprehension. Thus, for instance, in the mid-nineteenth century, a French missionary who, otherwise, was a fluent linguist and an exceptionally perceptive observer, with a long and intimate experience of China, could still express this typical comment: "Chinese writing is displayed everywhere for decoration, but it is unpleasant at first sight and shocks by its oddity." In the long run, however, he admitted that one could progressively "become used to" this weird sight.

To call it "calligraphy" was a way of conceding to it some sort of artistic merit. Still, the choice of this name was unfortunate and generated a deeper sort of misunderstanding. By its very etymology, "calligraphy" means "beautiful writing"; i.e. writing that is made beautiful by the addition of various ornaments or by application of a decorative treatment—a definition which suits diverse decorative arts or minor arts that are more familiar to us, such as—let us say—Gothic calligraphy or Arabic calligraphy. What the Chinese call *shu*, however, simply means "handwriting"; the word is often paired with *hua*, "painting" —and in this context, to speak of "beautiful writing" would be as preposterous as to speak of "beautiful painting." As J. F. Billeter points out in *The Chinese Art of Writing*, it is the writing itself that is the art, and it needs no adventitious or optional "artistic" complement to reach that status.

———

Clichés can unwittingly reflect deeper truths. Many years ago, a facetious colleague sent me a copy of an old cartoon from Ripley's famous series *Believe It or Not!* This particular item dealt with China and presented an assortment of fanciful or semi-factual distortions and common beliefs about Chinese language, culture, history and customs. The interest of this cartoon was that it offered a fairly representative summing up of the popular perception of China in the Western consciousness. The gist of this perception was not so much that China was enigmatic, complicated and bizarre, as more specifically that it was a topsy-turvy world: the Chinese do everything exactly in reverse of our "normal" usages and procedures. For instance, "When the Chinese build a house, they start from the roof"; "When in mourning, they wear white"; "They write upside down, and right to left"; "When greeting someone, they shake their own hand," etc. None of these observations is actually wrong. And the general conclusion is basically valid. Here lies, in fact, the secret of the inexhaustible attraction which China and the West have always exerted upon each other: within the human experiment, they stand at each other's antipodes. It might even be tempting to compare their mutual fascination to the magnetism that draws the two sexes together, but this erotic metaphor should probably be resisted here, since its inspiration is too narrowly Western.[1]

China poses a permanent challenge to various notions which we naïvely assume to have universal validity—but which prove in fact to find application only within the limits of our own cultural world. In linguistics, for instance, there is a basic axiom according to which writing is necessarily preceded by speech—and this principle actually seems to tally with common sense and common experience. If you go to China, however, your cosy certainty begins to evaporate: the primacy of speech, which has commanded all our culture since antiquity, may well have been a mere Indo-European idiosyncrasy.

When Saint Augustine first met Saint Ambrose, he was amazed by the exceptional ability the latter had to read silently: when reading, his lips did not move and the written message would pass directly from the book to his mind, without the intermediary of sound. This talent was still so rare at the time that Augustine felt moved later on to make a special note of it, betraying his own puzzlement:[2] such was the empire of the spoken word in Western culture at the dawn of the Christian era. The first sentence of Saint John's Gospel, "In the beginning was the Word," summed up the inheritance of antiquity and defined a continuing reality at the heart of our cultural world. One could neatly propose a parallel definition for the civilisation of China by formulating the reverse statement: *In the beginning was the Script*.

The earliest examples of the Chinese script—which mark the beginning of known historical records in China—date back to some 3,700 years ago. (As the graphic style of this writing appears sophisticated and mature, one must assume that it already had a long history; in the future, archaeology might well unearth evidence of earlier writing.) Even though written characters evolved considerably through the ages, modern Chinese writing can still be traced back, without interruption, to these early models: there is a direct continuity. This archaic script ("oracle bones inscriptions," found on tortoise shells and shoulder blades of oxen, where they had been carved for divination procedures) was used to forecast the outcome of all major decisions of the state: harvest and hunting, war and peace. Hence, from the very beginning, script was intimately associated with the spirits and with political authority. These inscriptions did not record language, but meanings—directly, and speechlessly; they transcended language. One might compare them, in a way, to the symbolic or pictographic indications (increasingly complex and nuanced) that are now being used in international airports, where they provide directions without language, which every traveller understands at once, not within his own idiom, but beyond all idioms.

This Chinese emblematic meta-language developed independently from contemporary speech. For convenience, however, the written characters were progressively given conventional sounds; thus, eventually the inscriptions did not merely convey silent meanings, they could also be read aloud. In the end, they themselves generated a language—monosyllabic and non-inflected (features that remain as the special marks of its artificial origin)—and since this language carried all the prestige of magic and power, it gradually supplanted the vernacular originally spoken. Needless to say, this schematic description of the birth of the Chinese language as we know it today is simplistic and partly hypothetical; what seems certain, nevertheless—and of essential importance—is that, in Chinese, there was a unique anteriority of script over speech.

Boswell once suggested to Dr. Johnson that the Chinese were not barbarians and he invoked as evidence "the written characters of their language":

Johnson: Sir, they have not an alphabet. They have not been able to form what all other nations have formed.

Boswell: There is more learning in their language than in any other, from the immense number of their characters.

Johnson: It is only more difficult from its rudeness; as there is more labour in hewing down a tree with a stone than with an axe.[3]

It would be all too facile to dismiss Johnson's observation on account of the prejudice it reflected. The unfortunate reality of the prejudice does not invalidate the accuracy of the observation, once we divest it from its unnecessary value judgement. Whereas Boswell was admiring the shimmering sophistication of the surface manifestations of Chinese culture, Johnson correctly perceived the essential primitiveness that lay at its core: this combination of a *donné* of elementary and primeval simplicity with stupendous complexity and refinement in the actual applications and modalities at the superstructure level is a constant character of the Chinese genius.

Western technology, with its high efficiency but narrow specialisation and rigidity of function, is the product of a rupture: in order to conquer nature, Western man chose to cut himself off from it. Chinese civilisation, on the contrary, endeavoured to maintain the primordial unity; but the price of its uninterrupted communion with the world was a reduced capacity to control it; this, in turn, was compensated for with increased ingenuity, subtlety and elegance in the practical solutions devised to solve the various problems of human adaptation to material reality. In the Judeo-Christian culture, the original myth of conquest and disunion is Babel; the bold attempt at mastering the world ended in the accursed confusion of tongues—and from that point on, language was to separate people instead of bringing them together. China, on the contrary, continued to live in a pre-Babelian condition; as Billeter suggests, its script, which conveys meaning beyond language and transcends all differences of speech, links mankind to its earliest origins and proposes the very emblem of an essential unity.

In China, the original function of the written word—which possessed the demiurgic power of ordering the cosmos and of generating reality—never disappeared entirely, but it was progressively eclipsed by its aesthetic virtues. Calligraphy in the narrow sense of the word—i.e. writing considered as an artistic pursuit, as a means of self-expression, and an outlet for the calligrapher's individual sensitivity—began to develop at the end of the Han period (third century AD). From that time on, it progressively turned into a specialised discipline, with its masters, theoreticians, critics, collectors and connoisseurs, and came to occupy the leading position among all the visual arts (with painting as its close second).

Calligraphy is executed in ink, on silk or paper, with a brush. (Even when carved into stone or wood, the carving endeavours to convey an illusion of brushwork.) The calligraphic brush is a typical product of Chinese ingenuity; once again, it marries deceptive simplicity of a structural principle with utter subtlety and versatility of its actual applications. The extreme sensitivity of this instrument has, for a corollary, its diabolic difficulty of handling. In order to master the brush (and not be led by it), the calligrapher has to achieve a high degree of mental concentration, physical balance and muscular control; long years of intensive training are required to reach a minimum level of competence. (The famous painter Chang Ta-ch'ien once paid a visit to Picasso and presented him with a superb Chinese brush. Picasso toyed with his new tool for the next few days; the awkward graphic mess he made of it is quite instructive.) The ink, far from being stable and monochrome, offers a wide range of nuances: its shine, its depth, its blackness, its pallor, its thickness, its fluidity, its dryness, its wetness echo every mood and inflection of the brush itself, the work of which can be slow or fast, rough or smooth, impetuous or subdued, naïve or cultured, violent or delicate. As a result, the textural quality of a work of Chinese calligraphy, its "fleshiness" or its "boniness," has a sensual dimension which no reproduction can adequately convey.

The silk or paper used for calligraphy has an absorbent quality; the lightest touch of the brush, the slightest drop of ink, registers at once—irretrievably and indelibly. This is a medium that tolerates no error, no correction, no hesitation. The brush acts like a seismograph of the mind, answering every pressure, every turn of the wrist; the record of its course on the blank page is instantaneous, complete and final. The written characters are the only materials at the disposal of the calligrapher. Not only is he not allowed to create new graphic structures, but this limited material is itself strictly predetermined: each character must be written with a specific number of brushstrokes that are arranged in a precise pattern, and follow each other in preordained sequence. (In Billeter's felicitous phrase, "Ultimately it is the fixed order of the strokes that makes calligraphy a visible music.") There is therefore no latitude for initiative; or, rather, all the resources of invention and creation are exclusively channelled into expression.

Calligraphy is *par excellence* an art of interpretation. (To some extent the same could be said of the main artistic disciplines of China: poetry, painting, music. In each, expression matters more than invention, but it is in calligraphy that this particular aesthetic feature finds its most perfect illustration.) This does not lessen the creativity of the calligrapher, but rather intensifies it; his is a creation of the second degree. A musical comparison may be of some help here: Glenn Gould or Sviatoslav Richter are no less artists for not having themselves composed *The Well-Tempered Clavier*. Great interpreters efface themselves the better to serve their models; but the more successful they are at this task, the more deeply their individual temperaments and sensitivities are being revealed in their interpretations. Every touch from a great pianist, every stroke from a great calligrapher, becomes a mirror of the interpreter's mind.

In calligraphy, the supreme aesthetic category is naturalness. Naturalness is reached when the calligrapher can forget all rules. But it is only after he has achieved full mastery of all rules that he becomes able to forget them. Calligraphy was a favourite exercise for monks and hermits, for its aesthetic paradox echoes the paradox of ascetic discipline. Through the ages, in the East as in the West, the great mystics who achieved complete obliteration of the self were also the most forceful and original personalities. In the art of calligraphy, as in spiritual life itself, when self-denial is complete, self-expression reaches its plenitude.

———

Jean François Billeter is a distinguished Swiss scholar who brings to Chinese studies a remarkably broad philosophical, literary and artistic culture. Having read and admired a number of his shorter essays, as well as his doctoral thesis on a fascinating "heretic" thinker of the Ming period, Li Zhi, I had awaited his magnum opus on Chinese calligraphy with eager anticipation. The book, which is superbly produced—the illustrations are magnificent and, sometimes, also provocative and surprising—kept me enthralled in its first half and, as my earlier references to it may suggest, I have drawn abundant inspiration from it in writing this essay. At a certain point, however, the book veered into what appeared to me as a rather idiosyncratic philosophy—and I must confess that I simply lost my footing (which certainly disqualifies me from writing a fair, comprehensive review). I wonder if Thoreau's famous warning "Beware of all enterprises that require new clothes" should not also be applied to discursive essays: Beware of all thoughts that require new concepts. Those which Billeter is using here baffle me all the more since, while they are probably not familiar to the Western reader, neither have they any equivalent in the rich theoretical and critical literature which the Chinese themselves have developed on the subject. In particular, his chapters on

"Body Sense" and "The Active Body"—which, in the author's per-spective, are obviously of central importance—develop notions that remain opaque to me. For instance, he concludes:

> Let me sum up the results of this inquiry [into the "Body Sense"], the better to apply them to the art of writing. Underly-ing all our relations to the visible and even to the real is projec-tion, a complex and variable phenomenon emanating from the body proper, in other words, from our bodily subjectivity. It is by the body proper that inside and outside communicate, that our exchanges with the world take place. The body proper is the source of all spatiality, of all organization of space ... and, on this background, of every image, whether perceived or pro-duced. The process of projection ... "merges with the very stuff of the visible."

Having spent some time trying to understand these reflections, I wonder now if I did not waste my effort, for I see that in a more recent article Billeter writes: "I must point out that the notion of 'projection' which I previously used in my *Chinese Art of Writing* does not appear to me defensible any longer: it should be revised."[4]

As I was working my way with some perplexity through the central chapters of the book, I was frivolously reminded of an anecdote told by Elie Wiesel.[5] A rabbi had to attend a ceremony in a nearby town. He hired a coachman to drive him there. But once on the road, at the first hill, the coachman asked him to come down and help push the coach, for the horse was old and weak. The rabbi had to push for most of the way. When they finally arrived at their destination, the rabbi said to the coachman: "I can understand why you came: you needed to earn your payment. I can understand why I came: I needed to attend a ceremony. But I cannot understand why we brought a horse along." The question that nagged me through the exposé of Billeter's philoso-phy was similar: What need was there to drag calligraphy into this?

I have little doubt that, with the passing of time, Billeter's book will prove to be a work of major significance—but I must also admit that I am incapable of doing it justice. Before writing this article, I read it for the second time; I felt all my old bafflement and frustrations being revived, but simultaneously I was struck once again by the wealth of original and stimulating views it contains, as well as by the illuminating quotations it draws from a wide literary spectrum—Western and Chinese.

To take only one example, on a question which has particularly far-reaching implications: Billeter rightly observes that Chinese traditional aesthetics dispenses altogether with the concept of beauty. On this theme, he presents a mutually illuminating series of references to both Chinese and European writers. Fu Shan, a great calligrapher of the seventeenth century, declared: "Rather than clever, gracious, deft and proper, I prefer being awkward, unpleasing, disconnected but true to myself." Such a view, Billeter suggests, would have met with the approval of Stendhal, who always put authenticity above all other values: "I think that to be great in anything at all, *one has to be oneself.*" For Billeter, a similar idea of true originality was evoked by Nietzsche: "Each of us carries within himself a productive originality which is the very core of his being; and if he becomes aware of this originality, a strange aura, the aura of the extraordinary, shapes itself around him."

In the quest for originality, the first requirement is to eschew vulgarity. Billeter quotes the nineteenth-century calligrapher Liu Xizai, who said: "The difficult thing about calligraphy is not how to please, but how to avoid trying to please. The desire to please makes the writing trite, its absence makes it ingenuous and true." At this point, I feel tempted to mention Braque's remark to a visitor who was showing him a fake Braque and insisted that it looked genuine. The painter replied: "How could I possibly have ever painted a thing like this—it is the exact opposite of a Braque: it is *beautiful!*"

I also found much of interest in the abundant and remarkable footnotes of Billeter's book. To the common reader, this may sound (I am afraid) like some sort of veiled irony, but no sinologist will ever mistake the sincerity and weight of this particular praise. Which one of us would not dream that it might be said of his work of a lifetime: "He wrote a few good footnotes"?

AN INTRODUCTION TO CONFUCIUS

Lu Xun (who is rightly considered to be the greatest writer of modern China; he died in 1936, and—by the way—strongly disliked Confucius for reasons that will be noted in a moment) observed that whenever a truly original genius appears in this world, people immediately endeavour to get rid of him. To this end, they have two methods. The first one is *suppression*: they isolate him, they starve him, they surround him with silence, they bury him alive. If this does not work, they adopt the second method (which is much more radical and dreadful): *exaltation*—they put him on a pedestal and they turn him into a god. (The irony, of course, is that Lu Xun himself was subjected to both treatments: when he was alive, the Communist commissars bullied him; once he was dead, they worshipped him as their holiest cultural icon—but this is another story.)

For more than two thousand years, Chinese emperors have set and promoted the official cult of Confucius. It became a sort of state religion. Now the emperors have gone (or have they?), but the cult seems very much alive: as recently as October 1994, the Communist authorities in Peking sponsored a huge symposium to celebrate the 2,545th anniversary of Confucius's birth. The main guest speaker was the former prime minister of Singapore, Lee Kuan-yew. He was invited apparently because his hosts wished to learn from him the magic recipe (supposedly found in Confucius) for marrying authoritarian politics with capitalist prosperity.

Karl Marx once warned overenthusiastic followers that he was not a Marxist. With better reason, one should say that Confucius was certainly not a Confucianist. Imperial Confucianism only extolled those statements from the Master that prescribed submission to the established authorities, whereas more essential notions were conveniently ignored—such as the precepts of social justice, political dissent and the moral duty of intellectuals to criticise the ruler (even at the risk of their lives) when he was abusing his power, or when he oppressed the people.

As a result of these ideological manipulations, in modern times many enlightened and progressive-minded Chinese came spontaneously to associate the very name of Confucius with feudal tyranny; his doctrines became synonymous with obscurantism and oppression. All the great revolutionary movements in twentieth-century China were staunchly anti-Confucian—and it is easy enough to sympathise with them. Moreover—if I may invoke here a personal experience—I still remember the dismay expressed by various Chinese friends on learning that I was translating the *Analects* of Confucius*: they wondered how I could suddenly sink into that sort of intellectual and political regression.

I certainly feel no need to justify the orientation taken by my work. Yet such a justification would be all too easy to provide, for an obvious reason: no book in the entire history of the world has exerted, over a longer period of time, a greater influence on a larger number of people than this slim volume. With its affirmation of humanist ethics and of the universal brotherhood of man, it inspired all the nations of Eastern Asia and became the spiritual cornerstone of the most populous and oldest living civilisation on earth. If we do not read this book, if we do not appreciate how it was understood through the ages (and also how it was misunderstood)—how it was used (and how it was misused)—in one word, if we ignore this book, we are missing the single most important key that can give us access to the Chinese world. And whoever remains ignorant of this civilisation, in the end, can only reach a limited understanding of the human experience.

This consideration alone would more than justify our interest in Confucius, even if he should have been every bit as distasteful a character as so many leading Chinese intellectuals portrayed him as being

---

The Analects of Confucius: translation and notes by Simon Leys (New York: Norton, 1997).

earlier in this century. Whether he was such is not for me to say. Confucius can speak for himself—and the marvellous fact is precisely that, across twenty-five centuries, it seems at times he is directly addressing the very problems of our age and of our society.

But this *modernity* of Confucius is an aspect which, paradoxically, non-Chinese readers may be in a better position to appreciate. The only advantage that can be derived from our status as ignorant foreigners is precisely the possibility of looking with a kind of unbiased innocence at this book—as if it were all fresh and new. Such innocence is denied to native readers. For them, the *Analects* is *the* classic *par excellence*. And before proceeding further, we should first briefly consider what is implied by the notion of a "classic."

THE NATURE OF A CLASSIC

A classic is essentially a text that is open-ended—in the sense that it lends itself constantly to new developments, new commentaries, different interpretations. With the passing of time, these commentaries, interpretations and glosses form a series of layers, deposits, accretions, alluvions, which accumulate, accrue, superimpose on one another, like the sands and sediments of a silting river. A classic allows for countless uses and misuses, understandings and misunderstandings; it is a text that keeps growing—it can be deformed, it can be enriched—and yet it retains its core identity, even if its original shape cannot be fully retrieved anymore. In an interview, Jorge Luis Borges once said:

> Readers create anew the books they read. Shakespeare is more rich today than when he wrote. Cervantes too. Cervantes was enriched by Unamuno; Shakespeare was enriched by Coleridge, by Bradley. That's how a writer grows. After his death, he continues to develop in the minds of his readers. And the Bible, for instance, today is richer than when its various parts were first written. A book benefits from the passing of time. Everything can be of benefit to it. Even misunderstandings may help an au-

thor. Everything helps—even readers' ignorance or carelessness. After you have read a book, you may retain an inaccurate
impression of it—but this means that it is being amended by
your memory. That happens often to me. Caramba! I don't
know whether I dare to confess this—but whenever I quote
Shakespeare, I realise that I have improved on him!

In a sense (if I may use such a trivial image) the way in which every
statement in a classic can gather the comments of posterity may be
compared to a hook, or a peg on the wall of a cloakroom. Successive
users of the cloakroom come one after the other and hang on the peg
hats, coats, umbrellas, bags and whatnot; the load swells up, heavy,
colourful, diversified, and eventually the hook disappears entirely under it. For the native reader the classic is intricate and crowded, it is a
place filled with people, and voices, and things and memories—vi-
brating with echoes. For the foreign reader, on the contrary, the classic often presents the forlorn aspect of the cloakroom after hours—an
empty room with mere rows of bare hooks on a blank wall, and this
extreme austerity, this stark and disconcerting simplicity, accounts in
part for the paradoxical impression of *modernity* which he is more
likely to experience.

THE ANALECTS AND THE GOSPELS

The *Analects* are the only place where we can actually encounter the
real, living Confucius. In this sense, the *Analects* are to Confucius
what the Gospels are to Jesus. The text, which consists of a discontinuous series of brief statements, short dialogues and anecdotes, was
compiled by two successive generations of disciples (disciples and disciples of disciples), over some seventy-five years after Confucius's
death—which means that the compilation was probably completed a
little before, or around, 400 BC. The text is a patchwork: fragments
from different hands have been stitched together, with uneven skill—
there are some repetitions, interpolations and contradictions; there
are some puzzles and countless loopholes. But on the whole there are

very few stylistic anachronisms: the language and syntax of most of the fragments is coherent and pertains to the same period.[1]

On one essential point the comparison with the Gospels proves particularly enlightening. Textual problems have led some modern scholars to question the credibility of the Gospels and even to doubt the historical existence of Christ. These studies provoked an intriguing reaction from an unlikely source: Julien Gracq—an old and prestigious novelist, who was close to the Surrealist movement—made a comment which is all the more arresting for coming from an agnostic. In a recent volume of essays,[2] Gracq first acknowledged the impressive learning of one of these scholars (whose lectures he had attended in his youth), as well as the devastating logic of his reasoning; but he confessed that, in the end, he still found himself left with one fundamental objection: for all his formidable erudition, the scholar in question had simply no *ear*—he could not *hear* what should be so obvious to any sensitive reader—that, underlying the text of the Gospels, there is a masterly and powerful unity of style, which derives from one unique and inimitable voice; there is the presence of one singular and exceptional personality whose expression is so original, so bold that one could positively call it *impudent*. Now, if you deny the existence of Jesus, you must transfer all these attributes to some obscure, anonymous writer, who should have had the improbable genius of inventing such a character—or, even more implausibly, you must transfer this prodigious capacity for invention to an entire committee of writers. And Gracq concluded: in the end, if modern scholars, progressive-minded clerics and the docile public all surrender to this critical erosion of the Scriptures, the last group of defenders who will obstinately maintain that there *is* a living Jesus at the central core of the Gospels will be made up of artists and creative writers, for whom the psychological evidence of *style* carries much more weight than mere philological arguments.

WHO WAS CONFUCIUS?

Having noted why and how a novelist could perceive an essential aspect of the Gospels which a scholar had failed to grasp, it is time now to return to Confucius. There is naturally no need to defend his historical existence—it was never put into question—but any reader of the *Analects* ought certainly to develop the sort of sensitivity that Gracq displayed in his reading of the Gospels and become similarly attuned to Confucius's unique voice. The strong and complex individuality of the Master is the very backbone of the book and defines its unity. Elias Canetti (to whom I shall return later) summed it up neatly: "The *Analects* of Confucius are the oldest complete intellectual and spiritual portrait of a man. It strikes one as a modern book."

Traditional historiography tells us that Confucius was born in 551 and died in 479 BC. (These dates may not be accurate, but modern scholarship has nothing better to offer.)

Over the centuries, the official Confucian cult has created a conventional image of the Master and, as a result, many people have tended to imagine him as a solemn old preacher, always proper, a bit pompous, slightly boring—one of these men who "push moderation too far." In refreshing contrast with these common stereotypes, the *Analects* reveals a living Confucius who constantly surprises. In one passage, for instance, the Master provides an intriguing self-portrait: the governor of a certain town had asked one of the disciples what sort of man Confucius was, and the disciple did not know how to reply, which provoked Confucius's reaction: "Why did you not simply tell him that Confucius is a man driven by so much passion that, in his enthusiasm, he often forgets to eat and remains unaware of the onset of old age?"

That Confucius should have chosen *enthusiasm* as the main defining aspect of his character is revealing, and is further confirmed by other episodes and statements in the *Analects*. For example, after Confucius listened to a rare piece of ancient music, we are told, the emotion took him by surprise; "for three months, he forgot the taste of meat." Elsewhere again, he stated that love and ecstasy were superior forms of knowledge. On various occasions he could also upset and shock his entourage. When his beloved disciple Yan Hui died prematurely, Confucius was devastated; his grief was wild, he cried with a violence that stunned people around him; they objected that such an excessive reaction did not befit a sage—a criticism which Confucius rejected indignantly.

In contrast with the idealised image of the traditional scholar, frail and delicate, living among books, the *Analects* shows that Confucius was adept at outdoor activities: he was an accomplished sportsman, he was expert at handling horses, he practised archery, he was fond of hunting and fishing. He was a bold and tireless traveller in a time when travel was a difficult and hazardous adventure; he was constantly moving from country to country (pre-imperial China was a mosaic of autonomous states, speaking different dialects but sharing a common culture—a situation somewhat comparable with that of modern Europe). At times, he was in great physical danger and narrowly escaped ambushes set by his political enemies. Once, in despair at his lack of success in trying to convert the civilised world to his ways, he contemplated going abroad and settling among the barbarians. On another occasion, he toyed with the idea of sailing away on a seagoing raft, such as were used in his time for ocean voyages (this daring plan was to puzzle to no end the less adventurous scholars of later ages).

Confucius was a man of action—audacious and heroic—but ultimately he was also a tragic figure. This has perhaps not been sufficiently perceived.

The fundamental misconception that developed regarding Confucius is summed up by the label under which imperial China undertook to worship him—and, at the same time, to neutralise the subversive potential originally contained in his political message. For 2,000 years, Confucius was canonised as China's First and Supreme *Teacher* (his birthday—28 September—is still celebrated as Teachers' Day in China). This is a cruel irony. Of course, Confucius devoted much attention to education but he never considered teaching his first and real calling. His true vocation was politics. He had a mystical faith in his political mission.

Confucius lived in a period of historical transition, in an age of acute cultural crisis. In one fundamental respect, there was a certain similarity between his time and ours: *he was witnessing the collapse of civilisation*—he saw his world sinking into violence and barbarity. Five hundred years before him, a universal feudal order had been established, unifying the entire civilised world: this was the achievement of one of China's greatest cultural heroes, the Duke of Zhou.

But now the Zhou tradition was no longer operative, the Zhou world was falling apart. Confucius believed that Heaven had chosen him to become the spiritual heir to the Duke of Zhou and that he should revive his grand design, restore the world order on a new ethical basis, and salvage the entire civilisation.

The *Analects* is suffused with the unshakable belief Confucius had in his heavenly mission. He constantly prepared for it; in fact, the recruitment and training of his disciples was part of his political plan. He spent virtually his entire life wandering from state to state in the hope of finding an enlightened ruler who would at last give him a chance and employ him and his team—who would entrust him with a territory, however small, where he might establish a model government. All his efforts were in vain. The problem was not that he was politically ineffectual or impractical—on the contrary. The elite of his disciples had superior competences and talents, and they formed around him a sort of shadow cabinet: there was a specialist in foreign affairs and diplomacy, there were experts in finance, administration and defence. With such a team, Confucius presented a formidable challenge to the established authorities: dukes and princes felt incapable of performing up to his standards, and their respective ministers knew that, should Confucius and his disciples ever get a foothold at court, they themselves would quickly be without employment. Wherever he went, Confucius was usually received with much respect and formal courtesy at first; in practice, however, not only did he find no political opening, but cabals eventually forced him to leave. Sometimes, even, local hostility swiftly developed and, quite literally, he had to run for his life. Early in his career, Confucius had once, briefly, been in office at a fairly low level; after that, never again in his life was he to occupy any official position.

From this point of view, one may truly say that Confucius's career was a total and colossal failure. An admiring posterity of disciples were reluctant to contemplate this stark reality: the humiliating failure of a spiritual leader is always a most disturbing paradox which the ordinary faithful cannot easily come to terms with. (Consider again the case of Jesus: it took 300 years before Christians became able to confront the *image* of the cross.[3])

Thus, the tragic reality of Confucius as failed politician was replaced by the glorious myth of Confucius the Supreme Teacher.

THE POLITICS OF CONFUCIUS

Politics—as I have just indicated—was Confucius's first and foremost concern; but, more generally, this is also true of ancient Chinese philosophy. On the whole (with the only *sublime* exception of the Daoist, Zhuang Zi), early Chinese thought essentially revolved around two questions: the harmony of the universe and the harmony of society—in other words, cosmology and politics.

The eremitic life may be tempting for a sage, but since we are neither birds nor beasts, we cannot escape among them; we must associate with our fellow men. And when the world loses the Way, the sage has a moral duty to reform society and to set it back on track.

Politics is an extension of ethics: "Government is synonymous with righteousness. If the king is righteous, how could anyone dare to be crooked?" The government is of men, not of laws (to this very day, this remains one of the most dangerous flaws in the Chinese political tradition). Confucius had a deep distrust of laws: laws invite people to become tricky and bring out the worst in them. The true cohesion of a society is secured not through legal rules but through ritual observances. The central importance of *rites* in the Confucian order may at first appear disconcerting to some Western readers (conjuring up in their minds quaint images of smiling Oriental gentlemen, bowing endlessly to each other), but the oddity is merely semantic; one needs only to substitute for the word "rites" concepts such as "*mœurs*," "civilised usages," "moral conventions" or even "common decency" and one immediately realises that the Confucian values are remarkably close to the principles of political philosophy that the Western world inherited from the Enlightenment. Montesquieu in particular (who, paradoxically, did not share in the Chinese euphoria of his time, as he detected a ruthless despotism at work in the political practice of eighteenth-century China) developed notions that unwittingly recapitulated Confucius's views that a government of rites is to be preferred to a government of laws; Montesquieu considered that an increase in law-making activity was not a sign of civilisation—it indicated on the contrary a breakdown of social morality, and his famous statement, "*Quand un peuple a de bonnes mœurs, les lois deviennent simples*," could have been lifted straight from the *Analects*.

According to Confucius, a king leads by his moral power. If he cannot set a moral example—if he cannot maintain and promote rituals and music (the two hallmarks of civilisation)—he forfeits the loyalty of his ministers and the trust of the people. The ultimate asset of the state is the trust of the people in their rulers: if that trust is lost, the country is doomed.

Confucius often said that if only a ruler could employ him, in one year he would achieve a lot, and in three years he would succeed. One day a disciple asked him, "If a king were to entrust you with a territory which you could govern according to your ideas, what would you do first?" Confucius replied, "My first task would certainly be *to rectify the names*." On hearing this, the disciple was puzzled. "Rectify the names? And that would be your first priority? Is this a joke?" (Chesterton or Orwell, however, would have immediately understood and approved the idea.) Confucius had to explain: "If the names are not correct, if they do not match realities, language has no object. If language is without an object, action becomes impossible—and therefore, all human affairs disintegrate and their management becomes pointless and impossible. Hence, the very first task of a true statesman is to rectify the names."

And this is, in fact, what Confucius himself endeavoured to do. One can read the *Analects* as an attempt to redefine the true sense of a series of key concepts. Under the guise of restoring their full meaning, Confucius actually injected a new content into the old "names." Here I shall give only one example, but it is of momentous importance: the notion of "gentleman" (*junzi*, Confucius's ideal man). Originally it meant an aristocrat, a member of the *social* elite: one did not become a gentleman, one could only be *born* a gentleman. For Confucius, on the contrary, the "gentleman" is a member of the *moral* elite. It is an ethical quality, achieved by the practice of virtue, and secured through education. Every man should strive for it, even though few may reach it. An aristocrat who is immoral and uneducated (the two notions of morality and learning are synonymous) is not a gentleman, whereas any commoner can attain the status of gentleman if he proves morally qualified. As only gentlemen are fit to rule, political authority should be devolved purely on the criteria of moral achievement and intellectual competence. Therefore, in a proper state of affairs, neither birth nor money should secure power. Political authority should pertain exclusively to those who can demonstrate moral and intellectual qualifications.

This view was to have revolutionary consequences: it was the single most devastating ideological blow that furthered the destruction of the feudal system and sapped the power of the hereditary aristocracy, and it led eventually to the establishment of the bureaucratic empire—the government of the scholars. For more than 2,000 years, the empire was to be ruled by the intellectual elite; to gain access to political power, one had to compete successfully in the civil service examinations, which were open to all. Until modern times, this was certainly the most open, flexible, fair and sophisticated system of government known to history (it was the very system that impressed and inspired the European *philosophes* of the eighteenth century).

CONFUCIUS ON EDUCATION

It is often remarked that the most successful and dynamic societies of East and South-East Asia (Japan, Korea, Taiwan, Hong Kong and Singapore) share a common Confucian culture. Should one therefore conclude that the *Analects* might actually yield a secret formula that would make it possible elsewhere to inject energy into flagging economies and to mobilise and motivate a slovenly citizenry?

The prosperity of a modern state is a complex phenomenon that can hardly be ascribed to one single factor. Yet there is indeed one common feature that characterises the various "Confucian" societies—but it should be observed that this same feature can also be found in other social or ethnic groups (for instance, certain Jewish communities of the Western world) which are equally creative and prosperous and yet do not present any connection with the Confucian tradition—and it is the extraordinary importance which these societies all attach to *education*. Any government, any community or any family willing to invest a considerable proportion of its energy and resources in education is bound to reap cultural, social and economic benefits comparable to those currently being achieved by the thriving "Confucian" states of Asia, or by some dynamic and wealthy migrant minorities of the Western world.

In affirming that the government and administration of the state should be exclusively entrusted to a moral and intellectual elite of "gentlemen," Confucius established an enduring and decisive link between education and political power: only the former could provide access to the latter. In modern times, even after the abrogation of the civil service examination system and the fall of the empire, although education ceased to be the key to political authority—which, in this new situation, was more likely to come out of the barrel of a gun—the prestige traditionally attached to culture continued to survive in the mentality of the Confucian societies: the educated man, however poor and powerless, still commanded more respect than the wealthy or the powerful.

Confucian education was open to all—rich and poor, noble and plebeian. Its purpose was primarily *moral*: intellectual achievement was only a means towards the end of ethical self-cultivation. There was an optimistic belief in the all-pervasive power of education. It was assumed that errant behaviour came from a faulty understanding, a lack of knowledge: if only the delinquent could be taught and be made to perceive the mistaken nature of his actions, he would naturally amend his ways. (The Maoist concept of "re-education" that was to generate such dreadful excesses at the time of the "Cultural Revolution" was in fact one of the many unconscious resurgences of the Confucian mentality, which paradoxically permeated the psychological substructure of Maoism.)

Most importantly, Confucian education was humanistic and universalist. As the Master said, "A gentleman is not a pot" (or also, "A gentleman is not a tool")—meaning that his capacity should not have a specific limit, nor his usefulness a narrow application. What matters is not to accumulate technical information and specialised expertise, but to develop one's humanity. Education is not about *having*, it is about *being*.

Confucius once rebuffed quite rudely a disciple who asked him about agronomy: "Better ask any old peasant!" For this reason, it is often alleged now that Confucianism inhibited the development of science and technology in China. But there are no real grounds for such an accusation. Simply, in these matters Confucius's concerns centred on education and culture—not on training and technique, which are separate issues altogether—and it is difficult to see how one could address these topics any differently, whether in Confucius's time or in ours. (C. P. Snow's famous notion of the "Two Cultures" rested on a basic fallacy: it ignored the fact that, like humanity itself, culture can only be one, by its very definition. I have no doubt that a scientist can be—and probably should be—better cultivated than a philosopher, a Latinist or a historian, but if he is, it is because he reads philosophy, Latin and history in his leisure time.)

THE SILENCES OF CONFUCIUS

In the short essay he wrote on Confucius, Elias Canetti (whom I quoted earlier) made a point that had escaped most scholars.[4] He observed that the *Analects* is a book which is important not only for what it says but also for what it does *not* say. This remark is illuminating. Indeed, the *Analects* make a most significant use of the unsaid—which is also a characteristic resource of the Chinese mind; it was eventually to find some of its most expressive applications in the field of aesthetics: the use of silence in music, the use of void in painting, the use of empty spaces in architecture.

Confucius distrusted eloquence; he despised glib talkers, he hated clever word games. For him, it would seem that an agile tongue must reflect a shallow mind; as reflection runs deeper, silence develops. Confucius observed that his favourite disciple used to say so little that, at times, one could have wondered if he was not an idiot. To another disciple who had asked him about the supreme virtue of humanity, Confucius replied characteristically, "He who possesses the supreme virtue of humanity is reluctant to speak."

The essential is beyond words: all that can be said is superfluous. Therefore a disciple remarked, "We can hear and gather our Master's teachings in matters of knowledge and culture, but it is impossible to make him speak on the ultimate nature of things, or on the will of Heaven." This silence reflected no indifference or scepticism regarding the will of Heaven—we know from many passages in the *Analects* that Confucius regarded it as *the* supreme guide of his life. But Confucius would have subscribed to Wittgenstein's famous conclusion: "Whereof one cannot speak, thereof one must be silent." He did not deny the reality of what is beyond words, he merely warned against the foolishness of attempting to reach it with words. His silence was an affirmation: there *is* a realm about which one can say nothing.

Confucius's silences occurred essentially when his interlocutors tried to draw him into the question of the afterlife. This attitude has often led commentators to conclude that Confucius was an agnostic. Such a conclusion seems to me very shallow. Consider this famous passage: "Zilu asked about death. The Master said, 'You do not know life; how could you know death?'" Canetti added this comment: "I know of no sages who took death as seriously as Confucius." Refusal to answer is not a way of evading the issue but, on the contrary, it is its most forceful affirmation, for questions about death, in fact, always "refer to a time *after* death. Any answer leaps past death, conjuring away both death and its incomprehensibility. If there is something *afterwards* as there was something *before*, then death loses some of its weight. Confucius refuses to play along with this most unworthy legerdemain."

Like the empty space in a painting—which concentrates and radiates all the inner energy of the painting—Confucius's silence is not a withdrawal or an escape; it leads to a deeper and closer engagement with life and reality. Near the end of his career, Confucius said one day to his disciples: "I wish to speak no more." The disciples were perplexed. "But, Master, if you do not speak, how will little ones like us still be able to hand down any teachings?" Confucius replied, "Does Heaven speak? Yet the four seasons follow their course and the hundred creatures continue to be born. Does Heaven speak?"

I have certainly spoken too much.

1997

POETRY AND PAINTING
Aspects of Chinese Classical Aesthetics

CHASING bits of truth is like catching butterflies: pin them down and they die. "As soon as one has finished saying something, it is no longer true." This observation by Thomas Merton[1] could serve as a warning for the reader and should indicate the proper way of perusing this little essay.

In Chinese classical studies, it is necessary to specialise. It is also impossible.

Specialisation is necessary. The wealth, scope and diversity of Chinese culture wildly exceed the assimilating capacities and intellectual resources of any individual—and more particularly, they should drive to despair the wretched Western sinologists who, unlike their Chinese colleagues, did not have the chance to start their training in early childhood and thus approach their discipline at least fifteen years late.

Specialisation is impossible. China is an organic entity, in which every element can be understood only when put under the light of other elements; these other elements can be fairly remote from the one that is under consideration—sometimes they do not even present any apparent connection with it. If he is not guided by a global intuition, the specialist remains forever condemned to the fate of the blind men in the well-known Buddhist parable: as they wanted to figure out what an elephant actually looked like, they groped, one for the trunk, one for the foot, one for the tail, and respectively concluded that an elephant was a kind of snake, was a kind of pillar, was a kind of broom.

Conversely, the global intuition that alone can grasp the essential

Gauss Seminars in Criticism, Princeton University, 1980.

nature of the subject (we shall have much need for it here) is invariably accompanied by a shocking neglect—if not downright ignorance—of surface details. This problem should not worry us too much, if we remember Lie Zi's story about the connoisseur of horses.[2] This parable was quoted earlier in this volume*: it should be used as an introductory warning whenever we attempt to make general statements, not only on Chinese culture but also on any rich and complex issue in the field of the humanities.

In the course of this inquiry, I may well become guilty of simplifications verging on distortion that could at times induce the reader to suspect that here too the colour and the sex of the beast have been mistaken... Anyway, I shall seek no further excuses; after all, what is an enterprise like this but an attempt to prolong or to echo, however clumsily, those moments of bliss that we sometimes experience in our encounters with poems and paintings? (Can artistic and literary criticism have any other justification?)

China is a world. Any tourist who has just spent two weeks there will tell you that much. (Though, in this case, I wonder if it is not a misunderstanding, as I doubt that the People's Republic has actually succeeded in preserving the *universality* that defined Chinese culture for some 3,000 years. Of course, it is obviously too early now to attempt an evaluation of thirty years of illiterates' rule. But this is another story.)

Still, when it is applied to traditional China, this old cliché—as is often the case with commonplace statements—covers a truth that runs much deeper than one usually suspects while uttering it.

More exactly, one should say that China is a certain world view, a way of conceiving the relations between man and the universe—a recipe for cosmic order.

The key concept of Chinese civilisation is *harmony*; whether it is a matter of organising human affairs within society or of attuning individuals to universal rhythms, this same search for harmony equally motivates Confucian wisdom and Daoist mysticism. In this respect, both schools appear complementary rather than antagonistic, and

---

*See "Lies That Tell the Truth."

their main difference pertains to their area of application—social, exterior and official for the former; spiritual, interior and popular for the latter.

The various currents of Chinese thought all spring from one common cosmological source. This cosmology (its system is schematically summarised in the most ancient, precious and obscure of all Chinese canonical treatises, *The Book of Changes*) describes all phenomena as being in a ceaseless state of flux. Permanent creation itself results from the marriage of two forces that oppose and complement each other. These two forces—or poles—represent a diversification of "having." "Having," in turn, is a product of "non-having" (*wu*),[3] a concept that is constantly mistranslated as "nothingness," whereas it rather corresponds to what Western philosophy would call "being." The Chinese thinkers have wisely considered that "being" can only be grasped *negatively*: the Absolute that could be defined and named, that could *have* qualifications, properties and characteristics, or that could lend itself to all the limitations of a positive description, obviously cannot be the true Absolute—it merely belongs to the realm of "having," with its ephemeral and kaleidoscopic flow of phenomena. The process that we just sketched here does not form a mechanical chain, nor is it the outcome of a causal sequence. It could be better described as an organic circle within which various stages can simultaneously co-exist. In the earliest texts, "non-having" seems sometimes to precede "having," but in later commentaries their relation is described in the form of an exchange, a dialectical union of complementary opposites, giving birth to one another.[4] "Being" is the fecund substratum, the field where "having" germinates—or, to put it in other words, emptiness is the space where all phenomena are nurtured. Thus, "being" can only be grasped in its hollowness; it is only its absence that can be delineated, in the same fashion as an intaglio seal shows its pattern through a blank: it is the *absence* of matter that reveals the design. The notion that the Absolute can be suggested only through emptiness presents momentous implications for Chinese aesthetics, as we shall see later.

It is by cultivating the arts that a gentleman can actually realise the universal harmony that Chinese wisdom ascribes as his vocation: the supreme mission of a civilised man is to grasp the unifying principle of things, to set the world in order, to put himself in step with the dynamic rhythm of Creation.

The arts are essentially poetry, painting and calligraphy; music should also be included here (for the Chinese scholar, music means only the zither *qin*); however, my incompetence in the latter field shall unfortunately prevent me from making more than passing reference to it.

A gentleman practises the arts in order to realise his own humanity. For this very reason, unlike all crafts (sculpture, carving, architecture, music played on vulgar instruments and so forth), no art could constitute a professional, specialised activity. One should naturally be competent in all matters pertaining to poetry, calligraphy and painting inasmuch as one is a gentleman, and no one, *unless* he is a gentleman, can achieve this competence. By definition, such fundamental activities can only be pursued by non-professionals; when it comes to living, aren't we all amateurs?

PAINTING AND POETRY

One exemplary figure embodied the union of painting and poetry: Wang Wei (699–761). He was one of China's greatest poets, and as a painter he has been credited with the invention of a new style that was eventually to constitute what is conventionally described today as "Chinese painting"—monochrome ink landscape executed with a calligraphic brush.

Su Dongpo (1036–1101), himself a very versatile literary and artistic genius of no lesser stature, commented on this subject: "In every poem by Wang Wei there is a painting, and in every one of his paintings there is a poem." This observation was subsequently quoted so often that it became a cliché. We must attempt to rediscover its original meaning and restore its full impact.[5]

First, this famous statement can be taken as a factual description. Consider, for instance, the following verses:

River waves flow beyond the world
Mountain mass hangs in half-emptiness...

When we read these words, they immediately conjure a vision that countless paintings have made familiar to us: a river flows towards a destination that lies beyond the page, carrying away a lonely little boat or a couple of drifting ducks, whereas in the empty expanse of the silk, a few faint touches of ink hint that, somewhere above the invisible riverbank, a mountain must be hiding in the mist.

However pertinent such a visual association may appear, we should keep in mind that this type of pictorial parallel is based on an anachronism: what the Tang poem just suggested is in fact a Song painting, which came into existence only some 300 years later! As for Wang Wei's own paintings, although no original survives, the kind of image that various indirect witnesses enable us to reconstruct seems oddly out of place with the type of vision suggested by his poems. In contrast with the fluid and subtle economy of the poems, most probably his pictorial style was still painstakingly detailed and not yet free from archaic linear stiffness.

Moreover, if it is not wrong to say that painting and poetry express two sides of the same inspiration, it should be observed that it was only in the Yuan period—six centuries after Wang Wei—that scholars began to inscribe poems on their paintings, or to trace paintings under their poems, with the same brush and under the same impulsion. Wang Wei, painter and poet, may provide a convenient symbol of the union of these two arts; yet, in fact, his historical activity has very little relevance for our topic. The real meaning of Su Dongpo's statement lies elsewhere—and it could be summarised in a double axiom, which we shall try to analyse: *The aesthetic principles and expressive techniques of poetry have a pictorial character. The aesthetic principles and expressive techniques of painting have a poetical character.*

Whereas any poem, by its very nature, is normally expressed in the form of a sequence unfolding *in time*, Chinese poetry attempts, in a way, to fit words *in space*.[6] The spatial potential of the Chinese poem can be grasped first on a superficial level, if we simply consider the fact that the poem can, and should, be calligraphed; in this calligraphic form it can be exhibited and contemplated just like a painting. However, the spatial quality of the poem is not merely an outcome of Chinese writing; it has a much more essential origin, which is to be found in the very structure of the language. This could be well illustrated, for instance, by the use and technique of the "parallel verses," which constitute a basic device of Chinese poetry.

Parallel couplets not only form the central core of all "regular poems" (*lü shi*), they are also constantly used in all other prosodic forms and can even be produced as independent units. Schematically they are comprised of two symmetrical verses; in each verse, every word possesses the same morphological status and performs the same grammatical function as its symmetric word in the other verse; whereas, in meaning, they are either similar or, better, antithetical—which fully achieves their mirror effect. Hence, a full enjoyment of a perfect couplet supposes a double reading—both vertical and horizontal. For instance, in a classic example from Du Fu (712–770),

Cicadas' voices gather in the old monastery
Birds' shadows fly over the cold pond

morphological and syntactical correspondences are rigorously observed between the two lines, so as to turn each verse into a perfect match for the other. Moreover, the interplay of the parallelisms enables us not only to read the lines vertically but also to read them *across*: in this way, the "cicadas' voices" echo the "birds' shadows," "cold" prolongs "old," and the "monastery" is reflected in the "pond." From the first line to the second there is no logical sequence nor rational progression; what we observe here is not the linear unfolding of a discursive exposé but the circular coiling up of two contrasting images—non-successive, simultaneous, closely imbricated into one another. Unlike the discursive mode of expression that forges ahead and develops in time, the parallel mode suspends the time flow and winds upon itself. There is no anteriority or posteriority between the two images: they are both autonomous *and* tightly welded together, like the two sides of the same coin. In a formally perfect couplet, it should even be possible to read the second sentence before the first without affecting the meaning (this possibility is well illustrated by the habit, in Chinese interiors, of hanging parallel sentences on both sides of a painting or of any other central ornament). They do not develop a discourse—together they organise a space.

The use of parallel sentences is not the only means by which the Chinese poetic language is brought close to pictorial expression. In a more general and fundamental fashion, the entire poem can turn into a pure juxtaposition of images. It is precisely this aspect of the Chinese art of poetry which, at the beginning of the twentieth century, fascinated Western poets, Ezra Pound in particular, and was to exert a significant influence on modern English poetry.

Some sinologists who know much and understand little have laughed at Pound's translations from classical Chinese. It is true that Pound knew very little Chinese and his translations are full of absurd mistakes. And yet, the fact that several excellent Chinese scholars have come to his defence should make us ponder: Pound's transpositions may be philologically preposterous, but they often achieve a structure and rhythm that are much closer to the original Chinese than are most scholarly attempts.[7]

Pound had a mistaken idea of the Chinese language, but his mistake was remarkably stimulating and fecund, as it was based on one important and accurate intuition. Pound correctly observed that a Chinese poem is not articulated upon a continuous, discursive thread, but that it flashes a discontinuous series of images (not unlike the successive frames of a film). Where he went astray was in seeking to explain the imagist properties of the Chinese poetical language by the alleged pictographic nature of Chinese writing. Actually, as any beginner learns after a couple of lessons, most Chinese characters are not "tiny pictures"—*stricto sensu* pictographs represent barely 1 per cent of the Chinese lexicon—and yet the strange thing is that Pound never shed this mistaken notion; it inspired some of his most bizarre and unfortunate interpretations.

Actually, the real reasons that explain the imagist character of Chinese poetry, the factors that enable Chinese poets to deliver directly a series of perceptions without having to pass through the channels of grammatically organised discourse, pertain to two specific features of classical Chinese: morphological fluidity (the same word can be a noun or a verb or an adjective, according to the context) and, more importantly, syntactic flexibility (rules governing word order are reduced to a bare minimum; sentences can be without a verb; verbs can be without a subject; particles and grammatical trappings are practically non-existent).

Without venturing into the quicksands of linguistics, let us merely look at one or two examples. Wen Tingyun (818–872?) describes travellers departing before dawn in two famous verses that, translated word for word, read like this:

Roosters-sounds; thatch-inn; moon.
Man-footprint; plank-bridge; frost.

This collection of discontinuous and simultaneous perceptions, this series of scattered brushstrokes, can be reconstructed and interpreted in discursive language. We could say: "As one can still see the setting moon hanging over the thatched roof of the country inn, one hears roosters crowing everywhere. The travellers must have already left: their footprints are marked in the frost on the planks of the bridge." The pictorial resources of classical Chinese free the poet from all such verbose detours and from the need to express logical connections; he does not explain, he does not narrate—he makes us see and feel directly. What he presents the reader with is not a statement but an actual experience.

The same phenomenon is also nicely illustrated by the much-admired beginning of a poem attributed to Ma Zhiyuan (end of the thirteenth century).

Dead ivy; old tree; dusk crows.
Little bridge; running creek; cottage.
Ancient path; west wind; lean horse . . .

(It should be observed, however, that the imagist approach is not the exclusive mode of Chinese poetry; discursive language also has a part to play. In fact, Chinese prosody is based upon a dialectical combination of these two modes, and this combination finds its most systematic and sophisticated expression in the form of the "regular poem" (*lü shi*). Nevertheless, it is true to say that the imagist language constitutes the *major* mode of Chinese poetry.[8])

We have just seen how Chinese poetry attempts to borrow channels that normally belong to pictorial expression. We shall now examine how painting adopts the status and methods of poetry.

———

At first contact, the physical outlook of a Chinese painting already betrays its literary nature. Western painting, crafted by artisans, has the heavy, stiff, massive and dumb presence of a piece of furniture: it hangs forever on its wall, gathering dust and fly droppings, awaiting a new coat of varnish every fifty years. Chinese painting, on the contrary, is mounted in the form of a scroll—which, historically, is related to the family of books. It genuinely belongs to the realm of the written word, as various expressions show: "to paint a painting" (*hua hua*) is a rather vulgar way of talking; the literate prefer to say: "to write a painting" (*xie hua*). The tools the writer needs—paper, ink and brush—are sufficient for a painter. The mounting of the painting—fragile, quivering at the faintest breeze—forbids permanent exhibition and only allows one to display the painting for the time of an active and conscious *reading*.

The highest type of pictorial style is called *xie yi*, which means the style that *writes* the *meaning* of things (instead of describing their appearances or shapes). The guiding principle for this form of painting is "to express the idea without the brush having to run its full course" (*yi da bi bu dao*). The ideal painting is achieved not on paper but in the mind of the spectator; for the painter, the whole skill consists in selecting those minimal visual clues that will allow the painting to reach its full and invisible blossoming in the viewer's imagination. This point leads us into another theme: the active function of emptiness—the role played by "blanks" in painting, by silence in music, the poems that lie beyond words. We shall come back to this question later on.

Finally, in parallel with the observations made earlier on the spatial dimension of the poetical language, we should also note the time dimension that is expressed in a supremely sophisticated form of Chinese painting, the horizontal scroll (*shoujuan* or *changjuan*). The horizontal scroll has a physical structure that is identical to that of an archaic book; it cannot be hung, it can only be viewed on a table, through a progressive "reading" process—one hand unrolling one end of the scroll as the other hand rolls up the other end (in this way the viewer can himself select an infinite number of compositions, depending on which segments of the scroll he chooses to isolate as he pursues this scanning process). The eye is being led along the scroll, following an imaginary journey. Pictorial composition unfolds *in time*, like a poem or a piece of music; it starts with an overture, develops in a succession of movements, now slow, now quick, provides restful intervals, builds up tensions, reaches a climax, concludes with a finale.

COMMUNION WITH THE WORLD

Painters and poets are associated with the cosmic creation. Artistic creation participates in the dynamism of the universe. Through his artistic activity a gentleman becomes both imitator of, and collaborator with, the Creator.[9] Hence, the poet Li He (790–816) could say:

> The poet's brush completes the universal creation:
> It is not Heaven's achievement.

Painters and art theoreticians expressed a similar idea, using practically the same words. Zhang Yanyuan (810?–880?) wrote: "Painting brings the finishing touch to the work of the universal Creator." It should be noted that in the West many artists reached similar conclusions. For them, however, these were empirical or intuitive observations; unlike their Chinese counterparts, they did not have the possibility to link such reflections to a cosmological system. To borrow an example close to home, I quote A. D. Hope's definition of poetry:

I have very little faith, as a professional critic of literature, in most of the descriptions or definitions of poetry on which the various schools depend. "The imitation of Nature," "the over-flow of powerful emotions," a "criticism of life"—well, yes and no: none of them seem to me a satisfactory basis of criticism.

As a poet, I find them exasperating. I know of no definition of the nature and function of poetry that satisfied me better than … the view of poetry as a celebration, the celebration of the world by the creation of something that adds to and completes the order of Nature.[10]

It would be extremely easy to translate this last sentence into Chinese; in China, poets, painters and aesthetes have never stopped making this same statement for the last 1,500 years!

In Chinese poetry, communion with the universe is expressed by various means. We should first mention the unique resources the Chinese language affords poets (we already have alluded to it): the blurry fluidity of syntax and morphology that allows a permanent confusion between subject and object and establishes a sort of porosity, or permeability, between the poet and the surrounding world. A classical example can be found in the first two verses of Meng Haoran's (689–740) "Spring Morning":

Spring-time sleep is not aware of dawn;
Singing birds are heard everywhere …

Who is the sleeper? His person is nowhere described or defined— is it I or he or she? The poem suggests a depth of slumber in which the conscious self drifts and dissolves amid confused perceptions of dawn; singing birds vaguely heard in this sleep become the objects of a perception without subject.

A similar effect can be found in one of Wang Wei's most often quoted poems; here, moreover, the world is being personified—the natural surroundings become an active partner. These verses are often rendered in a way that, without being flatly wrong, considerably weakens the flavour of the poem:

> In the empty mountains, no one is seen;
> Yet, voices are being heard...

Actually, the poem literally says:

> Empty mountain sees no one,
> Only hears voices...

Quite naturally, it is with a poet such as Li Bai, deeply imbued with Daoist mysticism, that this personification of all things, this dialogue with the universe acquires full intensity and exuberance. As the poet identifies himself with the thing he contemplates, the subject eventually vanishes, totally absorbed into the object: perfect communion is achieved. We see this in the short poem "On Contemplating Mount Jingting":

> All birds have flown away high in the sky;
> One lazy cloud drifts alone.
> Without tiring, I look at Mount Jingting, Mount Jingting
>   looks at me;
> Finally, there remains only Mount Jingting.

(Li Bai is a poet who can associate with mountains and rivers; he converses with the sun and the stars, as you and I chat with our old friends; he drinks at the banquet of the planets, he rides on the tails of comets. For instance, if one night there is no one with whom to share his bottle of wine, he improvises at once a little party with three guests—himself, the moon and his own shadow—and this lively drinking bout ends with an appointment for another gathering next spring, in the Milky Way...)

For the painters, the identification of the subject with the object assumes an even greater importance: nothing should come between the painter and the thing he observes. Su Dongpo expressed this most eloquently as he was praising the bamboos painted by his friend Wen Tong: if the latter could achieve natural perfection in his art, it was because he had no more need to look at bamboos when painting them, as *he himself had become a bamboo*.

In order better to appreciate all the implications of such an attitude, it might be useful, by contrast, to refer back for a moment to our own familiar world. In Sartre's *Nausea*—a good example of Western consciousness pushed to its paroxysm—there are two objects whose sight provokes in Roquentin a feeling of existential absurdity so acute that it results in actual retching: a pebble polished by the sea, and an oddly twisted tree root. It is interesting to note that, for Chinese aesthetes, it was precisely such types of objects that could actually induce *ecstasy*—in fact, they were sought by connoisseurs and collectors even more avidly than the masterpieces of artists.

In order to dominate the natural world, Western man cut himself off from it. His aggressive, heroic and conquering attitude towards the environment can be seen, for instance, in the art of classical gardens (every civilisation always reveals its vision of the world in its gardens). Look at Versailles, where we see nature being distorted, bound, raped, cut and remoulded to conform to a purely human design; geometric plans are forced upon it, in complete disregard of its original essence. In such a rigorously anthropocentric perspective, any natural form, any spontaneous pattern that is not man-made and whose enigmatic complexity owes nothing to the human mind appears immediately threatening. Its irreducible and perplexing autonomy limits and challenges man's empire.

The Chinese, on the contrary, renounced domination of nature to remain in a state of communion with it (today, of course, is another story: the West, having reached the end of the road, belatedly discovers ecology and makes frantic attempts to negotiate some form of reconciliation with the natural environment, whereas China adopts with uncritical enthusiasm some of the most disastrous of our earlier attitudes). In complete contrast with Roquentin, *Homo occidentalis extremus*, who vomits in front of a stone whose grain and shape would have provoked utter bliss in a Chinese connoisseur, one thinks at once of the exemplary gesture of Mi Fu (1051–1107), one of the most admirable and typical exponents of Chinese aestheticism at its climax. Mi, having reached the seat of his new posting in the provincial administration, put on his court attire, but instead of first paying a courtesy call to the local prefect, he went to present his respects to a rock that was famous for its fantastic shape (even today, *Mi Fu Bowing to the Stone* remains a subject very popular with painters). Needless to say, this spectacular initiative proved costly for his official career. Yet, by this very gesture, he made it clear for generations to come that, beyond all social hierarchies and conventions, there exists another set of priorities that cannot suffer any compromise. The strangely shaped rock, whose forms had not been carved by human hands, presented in its profile and its patina a direct imprint of the cosmic Creator; for this reason, it also constituted a supreme model and criterion in any creative undertaking. Painters are the privileged interpreters who can decipher and translate the universal consciousness that is written on rocks and clouds, in the twists of branches and roots, in the veins of the wood, in the billowing of mists and waves.

Probably the best way to examine this theme of "communion with the universe" in Chinese art is still to study the central role played by the concept of *qi* in the aesthetic theories.

Qi is sometimes translated as "spirit," which could be misleading, unless one remains aware that the Chinese have a materialistic notion of spirit and a spiritualistic notion of matter. Far from being antithetical, the two elements indissolubly permeate each other. A good example of this conception can be found, for instance, in the well-known "Hymn of the Righteous *Qi*," written in the thirteenth century by Wen Tianxiang (this piece appears in every anthology, and when Chinese schools were still dispensing a literary education, all schoolchildren could recite it by heart). After having conquered China, the Mongol invaders wished to secure the co-operation of Wen, who had been a prestigious minister under the last Song emperor. Wen rejected their offers and was thrown into jail. There, waiting to be executed, he composed his famous "Hymn." In the introduction he wrote for his poem, he described the conditions in his prison: for many weeks, he says, he was surrounded by all kinds of pestilential *qi*—dampness, cold, filth, hunger, disease—and yet he observed that, alone among the other captives, he continuously enjoyed excellent health. His explanation was very simple: he was inhabited by a *qi* of righteousness—his unwavering loyalty towards the defeated dynasty—which naturally enabled him to repel the influences of all the nefarious *qi*. Whereas a Western mind would wish to distinguish between different realms, for the Chinese classical mentality, one single concept of *qi* can simultaneously cover physiological realities and abstract principles, material elements and spiritual forces. In Wen Tianxiang's world, it is quite normal that the fire of patriotism should melt ice, and that morality should overcome illness. (Would it be irrelevant to note in this connection that modern developments of psychosomatic medicine seem to confirm to some extent these traditional conceptions? Chinese yoga—which is called "discipline of the *qi*" and which is essentially based on meditation and breathing techniques—is now being used with some measure of success to cure various illnesses, and more particularly to treat certain forms of cancer.)

The literal meaning of *qi* is "breath" or "energy" (etymologically, the written character designates the steam produced by rice being cooked). In a broader and deeper sense, it describes the vital impulse, the inner dynamism of cosmic creation. For an artist, the most important task is to collect this energy within the macrocosmos that surrounds him, and to inject it into the microcosmos of his own work. To the extent that he succeeds in animating his painting with this universal breath, his very endeavour echoes the endeavours of the cosmic Creator.

Painting is thus, in a literal sense, an activity of *creation* and not of *imitation*; this is precisely the reason why it possesses a unique prestige, a sacred character. This notion is important and deserves to be carefully examined. In the West, both classical antiquity and Renaissance culture considered that art possessed an essentially *illusionist* nature. Thus, for instance, according the well-known Greek anecdote, the competition between Parrhasios and Zeuxis ended in a double deceit: the birds that wanted to peck the grapes, and the spectators who wished to lift up the veil, eventually met with a mere painted board. Many legendary anecdotes about Renaissance artists reflect a similar mentality. Thus, Michelangelo is described as angrily hitting his *Moses*, because the statue would not talk or move: the lifeless marble infuriated him all the more for being so intensely lifelike. But in China the earliest anecdotes about famous artists all suggest a diametrically opposite conception; while Western artists applied their ingenuity to deceive the perceptions of the spectator, presenting him with skilful fictions, for a Chinese painter, the measure of success was not determined by his ability to fake reality but by his capacity to *summon* reality. The supreme quality of a painting did not depend on its illusionist power but on its efficient power; ultimately, painting achieved an actual grasp over reality, exerting a kind of "operative" power. A horse from the imperial stables began to limp after Han Gan had painted its portrait; it was subsequently found that the artist had forgotten to paint one of its hooves. Or again, the emperor who had commissioned Wu Daozi to paint a waterfall on a wall of the palace, a little later asked the painter to erase his painting; at night the noise of the water prevented him from sleeping.

In an archaic stage, painting was thus invested with magic powers. When magic matures, it becomes religion; in a sense, one might say that painting—more specifically *landscape painting*—constitutes the visible manifestation and the highest incarnation of China's true religion, which is a quest for cosmic harmony, an attempt to achieve communion with the world. Eventually the function of painting was redefined in aesthetic terms; still, in order to appreciate fully all the implications of the aesthetic concepts, one must keep in mind the archaic notions (well illustrated by the magic anecdotes) from which they are derived. The relation between the painted landscape and the natural landscape is not based on imitation or representation; painting is not a symbol of the world, but proof of its *actual presence*. As a painter and theoretician of the eleventh century neatly summarised it, the purpose of painting is not to describe the *appearances* of reality, but to manifest its truth. The painted landscape should be invested with all the efficient powers of mountains and rivers; and if this can be achieved, it is because the creator of the painting operates in union with the universal Creator; his performance follows the same principles and develops along the same rhythms. Artistic creation and cosmic creation are parallel; they differ only in scale, not in nature.

Here again, it is striking to see how Western artists often arrived at similar conclusions by purely intuitive and empirical means. Flaubert, for instance: "What seems to me the highest (and the most difficult) thing in Art, is not the ability to provoke laughter, or tears, or to make people horny or angry, but *to act like Nature does*."[11] Or again, Claudel: "Art imitates Nature not in its effects as such, but in its causes, in its 'manner,' in its process, which are nothing but a participation in and a derivation of actual objects, of the Art of God himself: *ars imitatur Naturam in sua operatione*."[12] Picasso put it more concisely but no less explicitly: "The question is not to imitate nature, but to work like it."[13]

It is in the theories of *qi* and of its action that we can find the best descriptions of the relation between artistic creation and cosmic creation. These theories occupy a central position in Chinese aesthetics. At first the concept of *qi* might easily appear rather esoteric and abstruse to Western readers; in fact, it must be emphasised that it is also a concrete, practical and technical notion that can be effectively demonstrated and experienced. Thus, for instance, successful transmission and expression of *qi* can be directly conditioned by technical factors, such as correct handling of the brush, movements of the wrist, angle of contact between the tip of the brush and the paper, and so forth. *Qi* in itself is invisible, but its effects and action are as evident and measurable as, for instance, the effects and action of electrical energy. Like electricity, it is without body or form, and yet its reality is physical: it can be stored or discharged; it pervades, informs and animates all phenomena. Although to fully grasp this concept would require us to refer to Chinese philosophy and cosmology, its aesthetic applications present universal relevance. Once more, the Chinese have analysed more systematically and more deeply a phenomenon of which Western painters did not remain unaware: a painting must be invested with an inner cohesion that underlies forms and innervates the intervals between forms. In a mediocre painting, forms are separated by dead intervals and blanks are negative spaces. But when a painting is charged with *qi*, there are exchanges of current that pass between the forms; their interaction makes the void vibrate. A painter should aim to turn his painting into a sort of energy field where forms constitute as many poles between which tensions are created; these tensions—invisible, yet active—ensure the unity and vital dynamism of the composition. All these basic notions have been experimented with and explored by Paul Klee, for instance. What is perhaps one of the best descriptions of the role of *qi* was provided by André Masson without any reference to Chinese painting: "A great painting is a painting where intervals are charged with as much energy as the figures which circumscribe them."[14]

It is in the art of painting that the concept of *qi* found some of its most obvious applications; yet in literature it plays a role that is no less important. Han Yu (768–824) described its operation with a striking image: "*Qi* is like water, and words are like objects floating on the water. When the water reaches a sufficient level, the objects, small and big, can freely move; such is the relation between *qi* and words. When *qi* is at its fullness, both the amplitude and the sound of the sentences reach a perfect pitch."[15] As we can see, the *qi* of literature is essentially the same as the *qi* of painting: in both arts, it is an energy that underlies the work, endowing it with articulation, texture, rhythm and movement. (Flaubert, labouring on *Madame Bovary*, was precisely seeking to let this invisible yet active current pass through his book, as it was only this inner circulation that could bring breath and life to the words, sentences and paragraphs and make them cohere; as he himself wrote, one must feel in a book "a long energy that runs from beginning to end without slackening."[16])

It should be noted, incidentally, that the action of *qi* can be observed nowhere more clearly than in these purely imagist verses (two examples of which were given above), where syntax completely disappears and grammatical connections dissolve. There we see the fleet of words, all moorings having been cast loose, which is set unanimously in motion; the swell, rocking them on a common rhythm, alone ensures their cohesion.

For any artist, whether a painter or a poet, it is thus imperative that he be able first and foremost to grasp and nurture *qi*, and to impart its energy to his own creation. If his works are not vested with this vital inspiration, if they "lack breath," all the other technical qualities they may present will remain useless. Conversely, if they are possessed of such inner circulation, they may even afford to be technically clumsy; no formal defect can affect their essential quality. Hence, also, the first task of a critic will be to gauge the intensity of *qi* expressed in any given work of art.

The unique emphasis put on the expression of *qi* has important consequences: originality and formal invention are not valued *per se*. So long as the artist is able to transmit *qi*, it is quite irrelevant whether the formal pretext of his work is original or borrowed. Theoretically, one can conceive of a copy that may be superior to its model, to the extent that it succeeds in injecting more *qi* into its borrowed composition.

Primacy of expression over invention is thus a fundamental aspect of Chinese aesthetics. The best example can be found in calligraphy,[17] which—as everyone knows—is considered in China as *the* supreme art of the brush. No other art is more narrowly governed by formal and technical conventions, leaving less room to the artist's imagination and initiative: not only are calligraphers not allowed to invent the form of any written character, but the number of brushstrokes and the very order in which the brushstrokes must follow each other are rigorously predetermined. On the other hand, paradoxically, calligraphy is also the art that can afford an individual with the greatest scope to display in a direct and lyrical way his unique personality, mood and temper, and all the subtle, intimate nuances of his sensibility.

A similar phenomenon is to be found in painting and in poetry. For a layman, at first sight, Chinese painting may appear rather limited and monotonous; landscapes, for instance, are invariably built on a combination of mountains and rivers, organised on the basis of a few set recipes. These stereotyped formulas are themselves filled with conventional elements—trees, rocks, clouds, buildings, figures—whose treatment is standardised in painting handbooks that are straightforward catalogues of forms. The range of poetry is equally narrow: it uses a rigidly codified symbolic language, a set of ready-made images (the song of the cuckoo that makes the traveller feel homesick; the wild geese that fail to bring news from the absent lover; the east wind with its springtime connotations; the west wind and the funereal feelings of autumn; mandarin ducks suggesting shared love; ruins of ancient monuments witnessing the impermanence of human endeavours; willow twigs exchanged by friends as a farewell present; moon and wine; falling flowers; the melancholy of the abandoned woman leaning on her balcony). In a sense, one could say that Chinese poetry is made of a narrow series of clichés embroidered upon a limited number of conventional canvases. And yet such a definition, although it would be literally accurate, would nevertheless miss the point; a deaf man could as well describe a Bach sonata for cello as a sequence of rubbings and scratching effected upon four gut-strings stretched over an empty box.

Poetry is, of course, untranslatable by its very nature; in the case of Chinese poetry, however, this impossibility is further compounded with a basic misunderstanding. Here, indeed, translation operates like a perverse screen that saves the chaff in order to eliminate the grain. What the translator offers to the reader's admiration is precisely the least admirable part of the poem: its subject matter (generally trite) and its images (borrowed, nine times out of ten, from a conventional catalogue and hence utterly devoid of originality). The specific quality of the poem necessarily escapes the translator, since (as is also the case with painting and calligraphy) *it does not reside in a creation of new signs, but in a new way of using conventional signs*. For a poet, the supreme art is to position, adjust and fit together these well-worn images in such a way that, from their unexpected encounter, a new life might spark.

In this sense, one should say that in Chinese art, the emphasis is always on *interpretation* rather than on *invention*. "Interpretation" should be understood here in the musical sense of the word. Ivan Moravec, let us say, is not a lesser artist for not having himself composed the Chopin nocturnes that he interprets. And yet, it is through the very fidelity of his interpretation that he manages to express his own individuality and sensibility. It is his *creative* genius that is different from the one of Claudio Arrau, or of any other musician interpreting this same piece. *By narrowing the field of its invention, an art intensifies the quality of its expression*—or rather, it shifts creation from the first arena to the second. (Actually, this axiom has a validity that goes beyond Chinese aesthetics: see, for instance, in modern European art the beginnings of Cubism. For Braque, Picasso and Gris, the world suddenly seemed to shrink to the mere dimensions of a guitar, a newspaper and a fruit dish—the very conventions that freed these artists from the need to define a new subject matter allowed them to concentrate entirely on the problem of elaborating a new language. Earlier, one mountain and twelve apples had already fulfilled the same function for Cézanne.)

For a painter or a poet, the question is not how to eliminate stereotypes, but how to handle them in such a way that, through the stereotypes, the "current" may flow. Under the efficient power of *qi*, a conventional mountain-and-water combination can then become a microcosmic creation, the worn-out image of falling flowers can turn into a poignant and universal metaphor of fate, and the old cliché of the abandoned woman on her balcony becomes an effective summing-up of the entire human condition.

THE POWER OF EMPTINESS

Earlier, we pointed out that in Chinese philosophy the Absolute only manifests itself "in hollow": only its absence can be circumscribed. We met a first important application of this conception in the precept that recommends the painter always reveal only half of his subject in order to better suggest its totality. Not only can the message reach its destination without having to be fully spelled out, but it is precisely because it is not fully spelled out that it can reach its destination. In this sense, the "blanks" in painting, the silences in poetry and music are active elements that bring a work to life.

There is something more important than a finished work of art: it is the spiritual process that preceded it and guided its execution. The poet Tao Yuanming (372–427) used to carry everywhere with him a zither without strings, on which he played mute music: "I only seek the meaning that lies at the heart of the zither. Why strain myself to produce sounds on the strings?"

The finished work is to the spiritual experience of the artist as the graph recorded by the seismograph is to an earthquake. What matters is the experience; the work itself is a mere accidental consequence, a secondary result, a visible (or audible) leftover—it is nothing but "the imprint left perchance in the snow by a wild swan." This is the reason why sometimes the ink of the brushstroke, the sound of the musical note are divested of part of their material substance; they are thinned out in order better to reveal the actual gesture that originates and underlies them. (To achieve this result in painting and calligraphy, the brushstroke is applied with an ink load that is deliberately insufficient; in this way, the ink mark is striated with "blanks" that show the inner dynamics of the stroke; this technique is called *fei bai*, which means "flying white." A similar effect is found in music, when the sound of the fingernail modulating the vibrato on the string becomes louder than the original sound of the note.)

Literature, too, has its "blanks." Sometimes they function as hinges for the composition; sometimes they enable the poem to suggest the existence of another poem that lies beyond words. To a degree, Western literature also knows these two uses of emptiness. A good illustration of the latter one was provided by Virginia Woolf when she presented Vita Sackville-West with what she called her best work—a splendidly bound volume, made purely of blank pages. As to emptiness used as a compositional device, Proust very subtly describes how Flaubert handled this technique: "To my mind, the most beautiful thing in *Sentimental Education* is not a sentence, it is a blank . . . [by which Flaubert finally] rids the narrative of all the deadwood of storytelling. He was thus the first writer who succeeded in giving it a musical quality."[18]

In turn, Proust's observation was well commented upon by Maurice Nadeau: "Proust noticed it: the 'blanks' in the narrative of *Sentimental Education* as well as in *Madame Bovary* are their supreme achievement . . . At every subtle turn of Emma's fate, whenever a secondary narrative accompanies the main story, we encounter this 'unsaid.' The same current pervades objects and consciousness, the material world and the psychological world exchange their respective qualities; reality and the expression of reality merge into one single totality that rests upon 'the inner dynamics of style.'"[19] The Flaubertian notion of "inner dynamics of style" irresistibly calls to mind the Chinese concept of *qi*; it should be observed that it is precisely *emptiness* that provides the best conductor for this "current."

Void is the space where the poem-beyond-the-poem can develop;
Chinese poetry has various devices to create it. Thus, for instance, at
the beginning of the famous four-line poem by Wang Zhihuan describing the immense scenery that can be seen from a tower at the
mouth of the Yellow River, the first two verses outline the widest possible horizon:

> The sun sinks beyond the mountains
> The Yellow River flows into the ocean...

At this point the reader feels that the poet has reached the utter limit
of his vision; actually, the real function of these two verses is merely to
tighten a spring whose sudden release, at the end of the poem, is going
to launch the reader's imagination into the infinitely vaster spaces of
the unseen:

> However, if you wish to see an even greater scene
> Climb one more story!

The last verse is not a point of arrival, but a point of departure. This
"trampoline effect" is often used by poets, especially in the four-line
poems whose extreme compactness (the entire poem may have twenty
syllables only) is thus prolonged with an infinite echo.

Another method consists in building the poem around a central
core of emptiness, where a truth resides that cannot be approached
or expressed. The traditional metaphor used for this purpose is that
of the unsuccessful attempt to meet a hermit-sage who possesses the
ultimate answer. The hermit's presence is real and near—it is attested
by various clues, even by his direct messengers—and yet he himself
remains invisible and unreachable. A good thousand years before
Kafka's *Castle*, Jia Dao summarised this myth in a well-known four-
line poem:

> Under a pine tree, the boy-servant, having been asked where his
>   master was,
> Answers: "He went to collect medicinal herbs;

I only know that he is somewhere in this mountain.
Where? Mist hides everything."

Since the essential point is beyond words, a poem can only talk *beside* the subject—it describes a desire. Thus, in Tao Yuanming:

I built my hut among people
And yet their noise does not disturb me.
How is this possible, I ask you?
Solitude can be created by the mind, it is not a matter of
  distance.
Plucking chrysanthemums at the foot of the hedge,
I gaze toward the faraway mountains.
At dusk the mountain air is beautiful,
When birds are returning.
Truth is at the heart of all this:
I wish to express it, yet find no words.

The same theme found a new expression with Wang Wei:

In the evening of life, I am only fond of silence;
I do not care anymore for the business of the world.
Having measured my own limits,
I merely wish to return to my old forest.
The wind that blows in the pine trees plays with my belt.
In the mountain, I play the zither under the moon.
You ask what is the ultimate answer?
It is the song of a fisherman sailing back to shore.

Any work of art—poem, painting, piece of music—plays the part of a "fisherman's song": beyond the words, forms and sounds that it borrows, it is a direct, intuitive experience of a reality that no discursive approach can embody.

In our time, the subtlest of all modern critics, Zhou Zuoren (1885–1968), summarised in one pithy sentence this living tradition of which he himself was a product: "All that can be spelled out is without importance."

This axiom—needless to say—is also valid for essays that deal with Chinese aesthetics.

1983

ETHICS AND AESTHETICS
The Chinese Lesson

In the catalogue of an individual retrospective held a year and a half ago at the Stedelijk Museum in Amsterdam, there is a striking statement by the painter to whose memory the exhibition was devoted. At a crucial turning point in his career, the artist in question sent a batch of recent paintings to a friend and explained to him: "The next lot has to be better and I just don't feel capable of being better yet ... I have the awful problem now of being a better person before I can paint better."

No, it wasn't a Chinese scholar-painter from another century who wrote these lines. It was in fact Colin McCahon (1919–87), an important New Zealand painter of our age. The author of the catalogue, Murray Bail—a true connoisseur of Western art—in quoting this statement could not hide his puzzlement: can one imagine Michelangelo or Rubens, Ingres or Delacroix, Matisse or Picasso making such an extraordinary statement?

For traditional Chinese aesthetes, on the other hand, such a notion goes without saying, and McCahon was doing little more than repeating a truth which, in their eyes, should be obvious to any serious artist. How the self-taught New Zealand painter, locked away in the isolation of his far-off land, had come to develop, without realising it, such a "Chinese" view remains an enigma which we will not try to elucidate here. We will simply note that he read a great deal and that since the middle of the twentieth century, numerous philosophical and aesthetic elements of Chinese and Japanese thought have been filtering into Western consciousness via countless works of vulgarisation, indeed even best-selling novels. Remember, for example, Robert Pirsig and his famous *Zen and the Art of Motorcycle Maintenance* (an astonishing best-seller in the '70s, the book, even today, retains its freshness and originality; it bears re-reading): "You want to know how to paint a perfect painting? It's easy. Make yourself perfect, and then just paint naturally."

As they are the products of our common human nature, it is quite normal that all the great civilisations should cultivate values that are basically similar, but they go about it in different ways and without necessarily attaching to them the same importance. What one may consider a basic axiom, regard as fundamental and embrace as a tenet may appear in the other only as a brilliant intuition, grasped by a few exceptional individuals.

This idea that the aesthetic quality of the work of art reflects the ethical quality of its author is so essential to Chinese thought that it sometimes runs the risk of becoming an oft-repeated cliché whose meaning can end up being distorted through mechanical and simplistic application. In the West, on the other hand, though not entirely unheard of, this same notion rarely undergoes methodical development. Thus Vasari, for example, can quite naturally point to a link between the spiritual beauty of Fra Angelico's painting and the saintliness that characterised his monastic existence, but, by the same token, it would hardly occur to him to attribute the artistic shortcomings of other works to the moral failings of their authors.

China's four major arts—poetry, calligraphy, painting (in ink, by means of a calligraphic brush) and music for *qin* (seven-stringed zither)—are practised not by professionals but by amateurs belonging to the scholarly class. Traditionally, these various disciplines could not be performed as a profession: an artist who would accept payment for his art would disqualify himself and see himself immediately reduced to the inferior condition of artisan. Although the poet, musician, calligrapher and painter (and quite often the same man is all of these at once) may let connoisseurs or a few chosen friends enjoy gratis the products of their art (sometimes, also, it is this limited but talented public that fires their inspiration), the fact remains that the prime aim of their activity is the cultivation and development of their own inner life. One writes, one paints, one plays the zither in order to perfect one's character, to attain moral fulfilment by ensuring that one's individual humanity is in harmony with the rhythms of universal creation.

The Chinese aesthetic, which, in the field of literary, calligraphic, pictorial and musical theories has produced a wealth of philosophical, critical and technical literature, developed without making any reference to the concept of "beauty" (*mei*; the term *meixue*, "study of beauty," is a modern one, especially coined to translate the Western notion of aesthetics). When this concept crops up it is often in a pejorative sense, since to strive for beauty is, for an artist, a vulgar temptation, a trap, a dishonest attempt at seduction. Aesthetic criteria are functional: does the work do what it does efficiently, does it nourish the vital energy of the artist, does it succeed in capturing the spirit that informs mountains and rivers, does it establish harmony between the metamorphoses of forms and the metamorphoses of the world?

But even as he is creating his work, it is always and essentially on himself that the artist is working. If one realises this, one can understand the meaning and *raison d'être* behind the numerous statements and precepts which, through the ages, constantly associate the artistic quality of the painting with the moral quality of the painter. One could give any number of examples: "If the man is of high moral quality, this will inevitably be reflected in the rhythm and spirit of his painting"; "the qualities and flaws of the painting reflect the moral superiority or mediocrity of the man"; "he who is of inferior moral worth would not be able to paint"; "those who learn painting put the development of their moral self above all else"; "the painting of those who have succeeded in building this moral self breathes with a deep and dazzling sense of rectitude, transcending all formal aspects. But if the painter lacks this quality, his paintings, charming as they may superficially appear, will give out a kind of unwholesome breath which will be obvious in the merest brushstroke. The work reflects the man: it is true in literature and it is just as true in painting."

But some critics have gone even further and have tried to identify in the works of famous artists either the expression of particular virtues they have shown in their lives or a reflection of their moral failings. For instance, the eighteenth-century scholar-poet Zhang Geng wrote:

What a man writes presents a reflection of his heart, allowing one to perceive his vices and virtues. Painting, which comes from the same source as writing, also holds up a mirror to the heart. In the beginning, whenever I looked at the paintings of the Ancients, I still doubted the soundness of this opinion, but after studying the lives of the painters, I venture to say that it is correct. Indeed, if we look at the different artists of the Yuan period (that is to say a period of national humiliation, under the Mongol occupation) we see Ni Zan had broken all ties with the ordinary, everyday world, and his painting is also characterised by a severe austerity and a detached elegance stripped of all ornamentation. Zhao Mengfu, on the other hand, could not resist temptation (he collaborated with the invaders) and his calligraphy, like his painting, is tainted with prettiness and a vulgar desire to please . . .

This last passage, contrasting two emblematic figures—Ni Zan and Zhao Mengfu—opens a dangerous trend in criticism: the deep meaning of an ethical reading of the work of art is lost only to be replaced by a sort of narrow and dogmatic "political correctness." There is no doubt that the art of Ni Zan is sublime—a limpid and distant vision of pale, empty landscapes, cleansed of all worldly blemishes—but very little is known about the historical person Ni Zan himself, and the anecdotes attesting to his purity and his detachment could well be no more, on the whole, than an imaginary projection of the virtues suggested by his paintings. The case of Zhao Mengfu is even more curious: an aristocrat who agreed to put himself at the service of the Mongol invaders, he was traditionally regarded by posterity as a vile traitor, but the problem is that, in his painting and especially in his calligraphy, he also proves himself a prodigiously talented artist. In order to resolve this embarrassing contradiction, it is conventional for critics generally to choose to condemn, despite the evidence before their eyes, the "vulgarity" of his overly splendid calligraphy (a judgement that tends to bring to mind the famous condemnation pronounced by the Surrealists against Paul Claudel: "One cannot be

French ambassador and poet"—as if Claudel hadn't been both one and the other!).

But even such naïve and simplistic rantings have failed to affect the deep understanding the great Chinese artists have always retained regarding this ethical dimension of their work. And the calligraphers, in particular, are all the more conscious of it, since the practice of their art constitutes for them a daily asceticism, a genuine hygiene of their whole physical, psychic and moral being, whose efficacy they themselves can measure in an immediate and concrete fashion. Moreover, in this sense calligraphy is not just the product of their character —their character itself becomes a product of their calligraphy. This reversal of the "graphological causality" has been noted by Jean-Francois Billeter in his *Art chinois de l'écriture*, and he has supported his observation with aptly chosen quotations. The supreme beauty of a piece of calligraphy indeed does not depend on beauty. It results from its natural appropriateness to the "truth" that the calligrapher nurtures within himself—authenticity, original purity, absolute naturalness (what the Germans call *Echtheit*): "In calligraphy, it is not pleasing that is difficult; what is difficult is not seeking to please. The desire to please makes the writing trite, its absence renders it ingenuous and true," wrote the calligrapher Liu Xizai, quoted by Billeter, who further illustrates these words with a statement by Stendhal: "I believe that to be great in anything at all, you must be yourself."

In fact to invoke Stendhal in this context strikes me as particularly interesting. The perfection of the work of art depends entirely on the true human worth of the artist; this moral notion at the basis of all Chinese aesthetics is found also in the West, but here it is more the mark of a few exceptional minds, of which Stendhal is a perfect example. His whole aesthetic sense is passionately and furiously moral— remember for example his condemnation of Chateaubriand: "I have never been able to read twenty pages of Chateaubriand... At seventeen I almost had a duel because I made fun of *la cime indéterminée des forêts* which had many admirers in the 6th Dragoons... M. de Chateaubriand's fine style seems to me to tell a lot of little fibs. My whole belief in style lies in this word." In this same spiritual family of geniuses both sublime and "eccentric" (in the Chinese sense of the word), we must also include Simone Weil (a whole aesthetic could be constructed from the rich mine of her *Cahiers*)—or again Wittgenstein, one of whose statements seems to me particularly appropriate as a conclusion to this little article, for indeed it proposes a criterion for literary criticism that is as original as it is effective (speaking of Tolstoy): "There is a real man, who has a *right* to write."

2004

ORIENTALISM AND SINOLOGY

EDWARD Said's main contention is that "no production of knowledge in the human sciences can ever ignore or disclaim the author's involvement as a human subject in his own circumstances." Translated into plain English, this would seem to mean simply that no scholar can escape his original condition: his own national, cultural, political and social prejudices are bound to be reflected in his work. Such a common-sense statement hardly warrants debate. Actually, Said's own book is an excellent case in point; *Orientalism* could obviously have been written by no one but a Palestinian scholar with a huge chip on his shoulder and a very dim understanding of the European academic tradition (here perceived through the distorted prism of a certain type of American university, with its brutish hyper-specialisation, non-humanistic approach, and close, unhealthy links with government).[1]

My task here is not to write a review of *Orientalism* (thank God!), but merely to see whether Said's arguments present any relevance for Chinese studies.

Said seems to include "sinology" implicitly in his concept of "orientalism." (I insist on the word *seems*; the point remains obscure, like a great many other points in his book.) Said's contention is that whenever an orientalist makes a statement in his own specialised area, this statement accrues automatically to the broader picture of a mythical

---

Reply to an inquiry launched by the Asian Studies Association of Australia: scholars involved in different areas of Asian studies were invited to comment on the relevance of Edward Said's *Orientalism* (New York: Pantheon, 1979) to the problems entailed in the approaches and methods of their respective fields.

"East." I do not know whether this is true for scholars involved with Near and Middle East studies, but it certainly does not apply to sinologists. The intellectual and physical boundaries of the Chinese world are sharply defined; they encompass a reality that is so autonomous and singular that no sinologist in his right mind would ever dream of extending any sinological statement to the non-Chinese world. For a serious sinologist (or for any thinking person, for that matter) concepts such as "Asia" or "the East" have never contained any useful meaning. No sinologist would ever consider himself an orientalist. (Some sinologists, it is true, may occasionally be seen participating in one of those huge fairs that are periodically held under the name of "International Orientalist Congress," but this is simply because similar junkets undertaken under the mere auspices of the Club Méditerranée would not be tax-deductible.)

Orientalism is a colonialist-imperialist conspiracy.[2] Quite possibly. To some extent, it may also be true for sinology. Who knows? One day it will perhaps be discovered that the best studies on Tang poetry and on Song painting have all been financed by the CIA—a fact that should somehow improve the public image of this much-maligned organisation.

Orientalists hate and despise the Orient; they deny its intellectual existence and try to turn it into a vacuum. Whether most sinologists love China or hate it is largely irrelevant. One important fact is absolutely evident: Western sinology in its entirety is a mere footnote appended to the huge sinological corpus that Chinese intellectuals have been building for centuries to this day. The Chinese are our first guides and teachers in the exploration of their culture and history; fools who ignore this evidence do so at their own risk and pay dearly for it. Further, it should be noted that today a significant proportion of the leading sinologists in the Western academic world *are* Chinese; through their teaching and research, they play a decisive role in Western sinology.

The notion of an "other" culture is of questionable use, as it seems to end inevitably in self-congratulation, or hostility and aggression. Why could it not equally end in admiration, wonderment, increased self-knowledge, relativisation and readjustment of one's own values, awareness of the limits of one's own civilisation? Actually, most of the time, all of these seem to be the natural outcome of our study of China (and it is also the reason why Chinese should be taught in Western countries as a fundamental discipline of the humanities at the secondary-school level, in conjunction with, or as an alternative to, Latin and Greek). Joseph Needham summed up neatly what is the common feeling of most sinologists: "Chinese civilisation presents the irresistible fascination of what is totally 'other,' and only what is totally 'other' can inspire the deepest love, together with a strong desire to know it." From the great Jesuit scholars of the sixteenth century down to the best sinologists of today, we can see that there was never a more powerful antidote to the temptation of Western ethnocentrism than the study of Chinese civilisation. (It is not a coincidence that Said, in his denunciation of "illiberal ethnocentrism," found further ammunition for his good fight in the writings of a *sinologist* who was attacking the naïve and arrogant statement of a French philosopher describing Thomistic philosophy as "gathering up the whole of human tradition." Indignant rejection of such crass provincialism will always come most spontaneously to any sinologist.)

"Interesting work is more likely to be produced by scholars whose allegiance is to a discipline defined intellectually and not to a field like Orientalism, [which is] defined either canonically, imperially, or geographically." The sinological field is defined linguistically; for this very reason, the concept of sinology is now being increasingly questioned (in fact, in the John King Fairbank Center for Chinese Studies at Harvard, I recently heard it used as a term of abuse). Perhaps we ought to rejoice now as we see more historians, philosophers, students of literature, legal scholars, economists, political scientists and others venturing into the Chinese field, equipped with all the intellectual tools of their original disciplines. Still, this new trend is encountering one stubborn and major obstacle that is not likely ever to disappear: no specialist, whatever his area of expertise, can expect to contribute significantly to our knowledge of China without first mastering the Chinese literary language. To be able to read classical and modern Chinese it is necessary to undergo a fairly long and demanding training that can seldom be combined with the acquisition and cultivation

of another discipline. For this reason, sinology is bound to survive, in fact, if not necessarily in name, as one global, multidisciplinary, humanistic undertaking, based solely upon a specific language prerequisite. Actually, this situation, imposed by the nature of things, does have its advantages. Chinese civilisation has an essentially *holistic* character that condemns all narrowly specialised approaches to grope in the dark and miss their target—as was well illustrated a few years ago by the spectacular blunders of *nearly all* the "contemporary China" specialists. (In this respect, it is ironic to note that it was precisely the so-called Concerned Asian Scholars—on whom Said set so much store in his book, as he saw in them the only chance of redemption for the orientalist establishment—that failed most scandalously in their moral responsibilities toward China and the Chinese people during the Maoist era.)

"We should question the advisability of too close a relationship between the scholar and the state." You bet we should! On this point I could not agree more with Said—yet it is hardly an original conclusion. The very concept of the "university" has rested for some 700 years on the absolute autonomy and freedom of all academic and scholarly activities from any interference and influence of the political authorities. It is nice to see that Said is now rediscovering such a basic notion; I only deplore that it took him 300 pages of twisted, obscure, incoherent, ill-informed and badly written diatribe to reach at last one sound and fundamental truism.

1984

THE CHINA EXPERTS

PARIS taxi drivers are notoriously sophisticated in their use of invective. "*Hé, va donc, structuraliste!*" is one of their recent apostrophes—which makes one wonder when they will start calling their victims "China Experts"!

Perhaps we should not be too harsh on these experts; the fraternity recently suffered a traumatic experience and is still in a state of shock. Should fish suddenly start to talk, I suppose that ichthyology would also have to undergo a dramatic revision of its basic approach. A certain type of "instant sinology" was indeed based on the assumption that the Chinese people were as different from us in their fundamental aspirations, and as unable to communicate with us, as the inhabitants of the oceanic depths; and when they eventually rose to the surface and began to cry out sufficiently loudly and clearly for their message to get through to the general public, there was much consternation among the China pundits.

Professor Edward Friedman, a teacher of Chinese politics at an American university, recently wrote a piece in the *New York Times* that informed its readers that various atrocities had taken place in China during the Maoist era. That a professor of Chinese politics should appear to have discovered these facts nearly ten years after even lazy undergraduates were aware of them may have made them news only for the *New York Times*; nevertheless, there was something genuinely touching in his implied confession of ignorance.

Madam Han Suyin, who knows China inside out, seldom lets her intelligence, experience and information interfere with her writing. One rainy Sunday I amused myself by compiling a small anthology of her pronouncements on China and learned that the "Cultural Revolution" was a "Great Leap Forward" for mankind, and that it was an abysmal disaster for the Chinese; that the Red Guards were well-behaved, helpful and democratic-minded, and that they were savage and terrifying fascist bullies; that the "Cultural Revolution" was a tremendous spur for China's economy, and that it utterly ruined China's economy; that Lin Biao was the bulwark of the revolution, and that Lin Biao was a murderous warlord and traitor; that Jiang Qing tried hard to prevent violence, and that Jiang Qing did her best to foster violence.

Professor Friedman and Madam Han Suyin represent the two extremes of a spectrum—the first one apparently in a state of blissful ignorance, the other knowing everything—yet the way in which both eventually stumbled suggests that, in this matter at least, the knowledge factor is, after all, quite irrelevant. What a successful China Expert needs, first and foremost, is not so much China expertise as expertise at being an Expert. Does this mean that accidental competence in Chinese affairs could be a liability for a China Expert? Not necessarily—at least not as long as he can hide it as well as his basic ignorance. The Expert should in all circumstances say nothing, but he should say it at great length, in four or five volumes, thoughtfully and from a prestigious vantage point. The Expert cultivates Objectivity, Balance and Fair-Mindedness; in any conflict between your subjectivity and his subjectivity, these qualities enable him, at the crucial juncture, to lift himself by his bootstraps high up into the realm of objectivity, whence he will arbitrate in all serenity and deliver the final conclusion. The Expert is not emotional; he always remembers that there are two sides to a coin. I think that even if you were to confront him with Auschwitz, for example, he would still be able to say that one should not have the arrogance to measure by one's own subjective standards Nazi values, which were, after all, quite *different*. After every statement, the Expert cautiously points to the theoretical possibility of also stating the opposite; however, when presenting opinions or facts that run counter to his own private prejudices, he will be careful not to lend them any real significance—though, at the same time, he will let them discreetly stand as emergency exits, should his own views eventually be proved wrong.

Ross Terrill, an Australian writer now settled in the United States, has been acclaimed there as the ultimate China Expert. I think he fully qualifies for the title.

Between the Charybdis of Professor Friedman and the Scylla of Madam Han Suyin, Mr. Terrill has been able to steer a skilful middle course. I would not go so far as to say that he has never imparted to his readers much useful insight on China (actually, I am afraid he has misled them rather seriously on several occasions); nevertheless, unlike his less subtle colleagues, he has managed to navigate safely through treacherous and turbulent waters and to keep his Expertise afloat against tremendous odds. By this sign you can recognise a genuine Expert: once an Expert, always an Expert.

When I was invited to review Terrill's biography of Mao (New York: Harper and Row, 1980), I initially declined the suggestion; it seemed to me that the book in itself hardly warranted any comment. However, its significance lies more in what it omits than in what it commits. If I eventually accepted the task, it was not merely to offer a few observations on the "*physiologie de l'Expert*" but rather to take the opportunity to correct a bias of which I may have been guilty in the past when reviewing some of Terrill's earlier works. (These works include *800,000,000: The Real China* (1972), *Flowers on an Iron Tree* (1975), *The Future of China* (1978), and *The China Difference* (1979), which, like *China and Ourselves* (1970), is a collection of essays by various authors, edited and with an introduction by Terrill.)

My first encounter with his writings was inauspicious. Opening at random his *Flowers on an Iron Tree*, I came upon a passage in which he described, as if he had visited it, a monument in China that had been razed to the ground years before. After that, it was hard for me to conjure away a vision of Terrill at work on his travelogue, busying himself with the study of outdated guidebooks without actually leaving his hotel room. For a long time this unfortunate *fausse note* was to colour (unfairly, no doubt) the impression I had formed of Terrill's endeavours. Now, not only do I feel that my indignation was somewhat excessive, but I begin to see that in all the liberties Terrill takes with reality, there is always a principle and a method, both of which I completely overlooked at the time: when he sees things which are not there, at least he recognises that these are things that *should be* there. This gives a kind of Platonic quality to his vision—it may be of little practical value, but it certainly testifies to the essential goodness and idealistic nature of his intentions.

All too often his statements are likely to provoke strong reactions in any informed reader; but these reactions, in their very violence, appear at once so totally out of tune with the style of this gentle and amiable man that one feels immediately ashamed of them. To attack Mr. Terrill seems as indecent as to kick a blind man's dog.

His basic approach is that of the perfect social hostess guiding the dinner-table conversation: be entertaining, but never controversial; avoid all topics that might disturb, give offence or create unpleasantness; have something nice to say to everybody. (His *Mao*, for instance, is dedicated "To the flair for leadership which is craved in some countries today, and equally to the impulse of ordinary people to be free from the mystifications of leadership." His next work will probably be dedicated "To the Hare—and to the Hounds.")

Most of Terrill's utterances come across as bland and irresistible truisms. (For which he seems to share a taste with some famous statesmen. Remember de Gaulle: "China is a big country, inhabited by many Chinese"; or Nixon's comment on the Great Wall: "This is a great wall.") Here is a sampling from his books: "A billion people live in China, and we don't"; "Chopsticks are a badge of eternal China, yet it seems that eternal China might now be changing into another China"; "It is not very startling to say that China needs peace; so does every other country. But not every country gets peace." "Change will not make China like the United States. But it will make post-Mao China different from Mao's China" (change generally does make things different from what they used to be, while different things are seldom similar); "Mao rules them, Nixon rules us, yet the systems of government have almost nothing in common"; "Could the Congo produce a Mao? Could New Zealand?" (One is tempted to add: Could Luxembourg produce a Mao? Could Greenland? Or Papua New Guinea? The possibilities of variation on this theme are rich indeed.)

Under this relentless *tir de barrage* of tautologies the reader feels progressively benumbed. Sometimes, however, he is jerked out of his slumber by one of Terrill's original discoveries: "Superstitions are gone that used to make rural people of China see themselves as a mere stick or bird rather than an aware individual." If he genuinely believes that in pre-Communist China people saw themselves as "a stick or bird," we can more easily understand why he deems Maoist society to have achieved such a "prodigious social progress."

Terrill claimed that he was not a proponent of Maoism, but he made no secret of his admiration and sympathy for the regime ("[it is] somewhat absurd for non-Chinese to think of themselves as 'Maoists.' To be Maoist—when far from China—is hardly helpful to China, one's own society, or the relationship between the two. The editors of this book [*China and Ourselves*] are certainly not Maoists. They admire the Chinese revolution")—this very regime which, as we now learn from the *People's Daily* and from Deng Xiaoping himself (and even, to some extent, from Terrill's latest writings!) went off the track as early as 1957 and ended up in a decade of near civil war and of "feudal-fascist terror."

Terrill visited China several times; his most extensive investigations, resulting in his influential *800,000,000: The Real China*, were conducted during the early 1970s—a time that was, by the reckoning of the Chinese themselves, one of the bleakest and darkest periods in their recent history. The country that had been bled white by the violence of the "Cultural Revolution" was frozen with fear, sunk into misery; it could hardly breathe under the cruel and cretinous tyranny of the Maoist gang. Though it is only now that the Chinese press can describe that sinister era in full and harrowing detail, its horror was so pervasive that even foreigners, however insensitive to and well insulated against the Chinese reality, could not fail to perceive it (though it is true, sadly, that too few of them dared at the time to say so publicly). Yet what did Terrill see? "To be frank, my weeks in China exceeded expectations...The 1971 visit deepened my admiration for China and its people..." In that hour of ferocious oppression, suffering and despair, of humiliation and anguish, he enjoyed "the peace of the brightly coloured hills and valleys of China...the excellence of Chinese cuisine..."

Do not think, however, that his enjoyment was merely that of a tourist: "I happen, too, to be moved by the social gains of the Chinese revolution. In a magnificent way, it has healed the sick, fed the hungry and given security to the ordinary man of China." Maoism was "change with a purpose...the purposive change bespeaks strength, independence, leadership that was political power in the service of values." "China is a world which is sterner in its political imperatives but which in human terms may be a simpler and more relaxed world." How much more relaxed? Even though the country is tightly run, "this near total control is not by police terror. The techniques of Stalinist terror—armed police everywhere, mass killings, murder of political opponents, knocks on the door at 3 a.m., then a shot—are not evident in China today...Control is more psychological than by physical coercion...the method of control is amazingly light-handed by Communist standards..." "The lack of a single execution by the state of a top Communist leader is striking...even imprisonment of a purgee is rare...Far more common has been the milder fate of Liu Shaoqi and Deng Xiaoping in 1966...They lived for many months in their own homes. No doubt they lounged in armchairs and read in the *People's Daily* the record of their misdeeds...Liu was sent to a village, his health declined and in 1973 he died of a cancer..." (Actually, if one did not know of Terrill's essential decency, one might suspect him of making here a very sick joke indeed; Liu, who was very ill, was left by his tormentors lying in his own excrement, completely naked on the freezing concrete floor of his jail, till he died. As for Deng, though it is true that he was less roughly treated, he confessed in a recent interview that he spent all those years in constant fear of being assassinated.)

According to Terrill, Maoism has worked miracles in all areas: it "feeds a quarter of the world population and raises industrial output by 10 per cent per year"; it has achieved "thirty years of social progress"; thanks to it, even the blind can now see and the paralytic can walk, as Terrill himself observed when visiting a hospital: "The myth of Mao is functional to medicine and to much endeavour in China... it seemed to give [the patient] a mental picture of a world he could rejoin, and his doctors a vital extra ounce of resourcefulness..." In conclusion, "there are things to be learned [from Maoism]: a public health system that serves all the people, a system of education that combines theory and practice, and economic growth that does not ravage the environment."

The impossibility of substantiating these fanciful claims never discouraged Terrill; for him, it was enough to conjure up those mythical achievements by a method of repetitive incantation, reminiscent of the Bellman's in Lewis Carroll:

> Just the place for a Snark! I have said it twice:
> That alone should encourage the crew.
> Just the place for a Snark! I have said it thrice:
> What I tell you three times is true.

Alas! After he had said it three times, there came the turn of the Chinese to talk, and they told the world quite a different story. Not only the dissenters writing on the Democracy Wall in Peking, but even the Communist leadership itself was to expose in gruesome detail the dark reality of Maoism: the bloody purges, the random arrests, tortures and executions; the famines; the industrial mismanagement; the endemic problems of unemployment, hunger, delinquency; the stagnation and regression of living standards in the countryside; the corruption of the cadres; the ruin of the educational system; the paralysis and death of cultural life; the large-scale destruction of the natural environment; the sham of the agricultural models, of Maoist medicine.

As a result of these official disclosures, Terrill has now to a large extent already effected his own *aggiornamento*: his latest book, *Mao*, as well as some of his recent articles, reflects this new candour. Sometimes it does not square too well with the picture presented by his earlier writings—but who cares? Readers' amnesia will always remain the cornerstone of an Expert's authority.

The *People's Daily* has already apologised to its readers for "all the lies and distortions" it carried in the past, and has even warned its readers against "the false, boastful and untrue reports" that it "still often carries." The China Experts used to echo it so faithfully—will they, this time again, follow suit and offer similar apologies to their own readers?

Or perhaps they were living in a state of pure and blessed ignorance. It is a fact that *official* admissions of Maoist bankruptcy are a very recent phenomenon; nevertheless, for more than twenty years, voices of popular dissent have been heard constantly in China, turning sometimes into thunderous outcry. These voices were largely ignored in Terrill's works; having first carefully stuffed his ears with Maoist cotton, he then wonders why he can hear so little, and concludes, "To be sure, it is very hard for us to measure the feelings of the Chinese people on any issue"!

Terrill's approach ignores the very existence of Maoist atrocities. Whenever this is not feasible, two tactics are simultaneously applied.

Tactic number one: similar things also happen in the so-called democracies—"The Chinese had their own Watergate, and worse." (Note the use of "worse"; compare with "Smith cut himself while shaving, Jones had his head cut off with the guillotine; Jones's cut was worse.") Or again, "Red Guards smash the fingers of a pianist because he has been playing Beethoven's music. To a Westerner who expects to be able to do his own thing, such action suggests a tyranny without equal in history. In New York City, two old folk die of cold because the gas company turned off the heat in the face of an unpaid bill of twenty dollars. To a Chinese who honours the elderly, it seems callous beyond belief." Terrill has curious ideas about the Chinese; his statement logically means that in China, smashing the fingers of a pianist is a practice that provokes no revulsion because Chinese do not cultivate individual taste in music; moreover, he would have us believe that, for the Chinese, it is perfectly acceptable to smash a pianist's fingers so long as the pianist is reasonably young... As regards the elderly New York couple, it would not be true to say that their tragedy met only with indifference in the West: actually, it created a feeling of scandal to the point that it was reported in the press and hence could come to Mr. Terrill's attention; I do not believe that the kind of thing that happened to the elderly New York couple would attract much attention in China. Not because the Chinese are particularly callous, but for the simple reason that they have already used up all their tears, mourning for *hundreds and thousands* of elderly people—cadres, teachers, etc.—who died not as a result of neglect and administrative indifference, but because they were tortured to death by Red Guards on the rampage. Moreover, if a moral equivalence can be drawn between accidental death and wilful murder, I suppose that the next step for Terrill would be to write off political executions in totalitarian regimes by putting them on a par with traffic casualties in democracies.

The second tactic develops directly out of the notion according to which the smashing of pianists' fingers should be somewhat more acceptable in countries that have no individualistic tradition: we should endeavour "to perceive China on her own terms." Once more, the idea is not to hear what the Chinese have to say on the subject of Maoism—an initiative that Terrill never takes ("it is very hard for us to measure the feelings of the Chinese people on any issue"), but merely to see the People's Republic through orthodox official Maoist eyes. A logical extension of this principle would be to say that Nazi Germany should be perceived in a Hitlerian perspective, or that, to understand the Soviet system, one should adopt a Stalinist point of view (so sadly missing in, for example, the works of Solzhenitsyn or Nadezhda Mandelstam). Here we come to Terrill's fundamental philosophy: it is indeed (in the words of one of his titles), "the China difference."

Things happened in Maoist China that were ghastly by any standard of common decency. Even the Communist authorities in Peking admit this much today. Terrill maintains, however, that, China being "different," such standards should not apply. Look at the cult of Mao, for instance—it was grotesque and demeaning, and the hapless Chinese experienced it exactly as such. Not so, says Terrill, who knows better; being Chinese and thus different, they ought to have thoroughly enjoyed the whole exercise: "To see these pictures of Mao in China is to be less shocked than to see them on the printed page far from China. This is not our country or a country we can easily understand, but the country of Mao...The cult of Mao is not *incredible* as it seems outside China. It becomes odd only when it encounters our world...It is odd for us because we have no consciousness of Chinese social modes..." (Meanwhile, Mr. Terrill has changed his mind on this question; in his latest book, he now qualifies the cult of Mao as "grotesque." Such a shift should not surprise—earlier on, he told us that we always "evaluate China from shifting grounds"; he recalls, for instance, that when he first visited China in 1964, he was still a churchgoer and, as such, felt critical of the fact that the Maoists closed churches; but a decade later, as he was no longer going to church, the closed churches did not bother him anymore: "I saw the issue under a fresh lens. I did not put the matter in the forefront of my view of China, and as a result, I saw a different China." One should pass on this recipe to the *Chinese* churchgoers; it might help them to take a lighter view of their present condition.)

Following the fall of Madam Mao, the Chinese expressed eloquently the revulsion they felt for her "model operas" (and indeed, it seems that mere common sense should have enabled anyone to imagine how sophisticated audiences normally react to inferior plays); yet Terrill prefers to consider the issue from the angle of "the China difference" and thus produces this original comment: "When Mao's last wife rode high in the arts, there were only nine approved items performed on China's national stage. Such a straitjacket over the mental life of hundreds of millions of people seems amazing to a Westerner. Why did the theatre-loving Chinese people put up with it? Again, we can glimpse the size of the gulf between Chinese values and our own by considering one of their questions: How can a people with the traditions of the American Revolution tolerate the cruelty and inefficiency of having some 7 per cent unemployed?" I wonder if the thought of the 7 per cent unemployed in America ever helped frustrated theatregoers in China to put up with idiotic plays; I even doubt that this same thought ever helped the *millions* of unemployed Chinese to put up with their own condition, which is much worse than the Americans' since the Chinese state does not grant them any unemployment benefits.

Having analysed at length Terrill's method and philosophy, I have very little to add concerning his latest effort. Up to the time of the "Cultural Revolution," the life of Mao had already been studied by a number of serious and competent scholars. In this area, Terrill does not shed new light; he produces rather an anecdotal adaptation of his predecessors' works, with plenty of dialogue, local colour and exotic scenery.

It is only on the subject of Mao's last years that Terrill might have provided an original contribution. Unfortunately, the diplomatic constraints that he imposed upon himself when dealing with topics that are still taboo for the Peking bureaucracy prevented him from tackling seriously the two central crises of Mao's twilight: on the one hand his attempts at destroying Zhou Enlai, and on the other the emergence of a popular anti-Mao movement that culminated in the historic Tian'anmen demonstration of 5 April 1976. On the first point, though he has already noticeably shifted his views, Terrill remains unable to confront the issue squarely—as this would entail the admission that the "Gang of Four," which persecuted Zhou until his death, was actually a "Gang of Five" led, inspired and protected by Mao himself. On the second point, he entirely ignores the vast, spontaneous and articulate movement of anti-Maoist dissent (the famous "Li Yizhe" manifesto of 1974 is not even mentioned) and curtly dismisses its climax—the April Fifth Movement, whose importance in Chinese contemporary history already ranks on a par with the May Fourth Movement—terming it a mere "riot," a "mêlée" barely worth one page of sketchy and misleading description.

If these failures tend to disqualify *Mao* as historiography, the book still presents in its form and style a quaint charm that will certainly enchant readers of the old *Kai Lung Unrolls His Mat* series: chronological indications are mostly provided in terms of "Year of the Rat" or "Year of the Snake"; Terrill's disarming weakness for zoomorphic similes finds new outlets: since Mao once described his own character as half tiger and half monkey, we are kept informed, at every turn of his career, of what the tiger does, and what the monkey thinks ("It irritated the monkey in him that Lin Biao spoke of absolute authority," and so forth). These touches will delight Terrill's younger readers, while adolescents may find more enjoyment in passages such as this description of Mao's accession to full power: "Jiangxi had been mere masturbation, alongside this full intercourse with the radiant bride of China."

1981

ROLAND BARTHES IN CHINA

Sed perseverare...

IN APRIL and May of 1974, Roland Barthes made a trip to China with a small group of his friends from the review *Tel Quel*. This visit coincided with a colossal, bloody purge launched nation-wide by the Maoist regime. This was the famous and sinister "campaign of denunciation of Lin Biao and Confucius" (*pi Lin pi Kong*). Upon his return, Barthes published an article in *Le Monde* which offered a strangely jolly view of this totalitarian violence: "Its very name—*Pilin-Pikong* in Chinese—has the joyful tinkle of a sleigh-bell, and the campaign comprises made-up games: a caricature, a poem, a children's sketch during which, suddenly, a little girl in make-up assails the ghost of Lin Biao between two ballet dances: the political Text (and it alone) gives rise to these little 'happenings.'"

At the time, reading this immediately put me in mind of a passage from Lu Xun, the most inspired Chinese pamphleteer of the twentieth century: "Our Chinese civilisation, so highly vaunted, is nothing but a feast of human flesh prepared for the rich and powerful, and what we call China is merely the kitchen where this stew is concocted. Those who praise us are to be excused only inasmuch as they do not know what they are talking about, like those foreigners whose high positions and pampered lives have rendered them completely blind and obtuse."

Two years later, Barthes's article was republished as a luxurious slim volume intended for collectors.[1] The author had added a postface, which prompted me to make the following remarks:

Mr. Barthes explains what made his report so original (an originality that vulgar fanatics so badly misapprehended at the time): his objective, he tells us, was to attempt a new kind of commentary, a "commentary in the register of 'no comment'" which would be a way of "suspending an utterance without thereby nullifying it." Mr. Barthes, who already has many claims on the esteem of scholars, now seems to have acquired another one, which should earn him immortality, by inventing the unheard-of category of a "discourse neither affirmative, nor negative, nor yet neutral"—"the desire for silence as a special form of discourse." By virtue of this discovery, all of whose implications are not immediately discernible, he has contrived—amazingly—to bestow an entirely new dignity upon the age-old activity, so long unjustly disparaged, of saying nothing at great length. It surely behooves us, in the name of all those old biddies who chatter away every afternoon between five and six in their tea shoppes, to offer Mr. Barthes a resounding thank you. Finally, in the same postface—and there must be many people for whom this is the strongest reason of all to be grateful to Mr. Barthes—he defines the intellectual's proper role in the world of today, his true function, his honour and his dignity, as the valiant maintenance—in face of and in opposition to "the never-ending parading of the Phallus" by the politically committed and other unpleasant proponents of "brute meaning"—of an exquisite trickle of lukewarm water from a tiny spigot.

And now the same publisher has offered us the text of notes that Barthes made daily about various events and experiences on that famous trip.[2] I wondered whether reading this journal might perhaps alter my opinion.

In his notebooks, Barthes scrupulously records, one after the other, the endless servings of propaganda dished up during visits to agricultural communes, factories, schools, zoos, hospitals, and so forth. For example: "Vegetables: last year, 230 million pounds + apples, pears, grapes, rice, maize, wheat; 22,000 pigs + ducks.... irrigation works:

550 electric pumps; mechanisation: tractors + 140 monocultural-ists.... Transport: 110 trucks, 770 teams of draught animals; 11,000 families = 47,000 people ... = 21 production brigades, 146 produc-tion teams. ..." And precious information of this kind is supplied over some two hundred pages, punctuated by brief, very elliptical personal notes, e.g.: "Lunch: look, it's French fries!"; "Forgot to wash my ears"; "*Pissotières*"; "What I'm deprived of: no coffee, no salad, no flirting"; "Migraines"; "Nausea." Only the rarest rays of sunshine interrupt the fatigue, greyness, and ever-worsening boredom—as for instance a long and tender squeeze of the hand from a "charming worker."

Could the spectacle of an immense country terrorised and stupe-fied by the rhinoceritis of Maoism have entirely anaesthetised Barthes's capacity for outrage? The only trace of indignation seems to have been reserved by him for the atrocious food served on the flight home: "The Air France lunch is so vile (pear-shaped rolls, exhausted chicken in a greasy sauce, dyed salad, floury cabbage tasting of choco-late—and no more champagne!) *that I'm on the verge of writing a let-ter of complaint.*" [My emphasis.]

But let us not be unfair: anyone may write down a mass of non-sense for private use; we can reasonably be judged only on our public pronouncements. Whatever one might think of Barthes, no one can deny that he had intelligence and good taste. No wonder, therefore, that he carefully refrained from publishing these jottings. But then who in God's name decided to proceed with this dismaying exhuma-tion? If this strange initiative originated with his friends, we should probably recall Vigny's warning that "A friend is no more malicious than the next man."

In the January 2009 issue of *Magazine Littéraire*, Philippe Sollers claimed that these notebooks exemplify the virtue of "common de-cency," as lauded by George Orwell. It seems to me, to the contrary, that by virtue of what he fails to say Barthes manifests an *uncommon indecency*. In any case Sollers's comparison is incongruous: Orwell's "common decency" is grounded in simplicity, honesty and courage; Barthes certainly had qualities, but not those particular ones. The only words of George Orwell that spring readily to mind apropos of the "Chinese" writings of Barthes (and of his friends at *Tel Quel)* are these: "One has to belong to the intelligentsia to believe things like that: no ordinary man could be such a fool."

2009

THE WAKE OF AN EMPTY BOAT
Zhou Enlai

ALONE among the Maoist leaders, Zhou Enlai had cosmopolitan sophistication, charm, wit and style. He certainly was one of the greatest and most successful comedians of our century. He had a talent for
telling blatant lies with angelic suavity. He was the kind of man who
could stick a knife in your back and do it with such disarming grace
that you would still feel compelled to thank him for the deed. He gave
a human face (and a very good-looking one) to Chinese communism.
Everyone loved him. He repeatedly and literally got away with murder. No wonder politicians from all over the world unanimously worshipped him. That intellectuals should also share in this cult is more
disturbing—although there are some extenuating circumstances.

Zhou was a compulsive seducer. I am of course not referring to his
behaviour with women, which was always said to be exemplary and
anyway should not concern us. What I mean is simply that, for him, it
seems no interlocutors ever appeared too small, too dim or too irrelevant not to warrant a special effort on his part to charm them, to wow
them, and to win their sympathy and support. I can state this from
direct and personal experience, an experience that was shared over the
years by hundreds and thousands of enraptured visitors—primary-
school teachers from Zanzibar, trade unionists from Tasmania, Progressive Women from Lapland—not even the Pope had to cope with
such time-consuming, bizarre and endless processions of pilgrims. He
was also the ultimate Zelig of politics, showing tolerance, urbanity
and a spirit of compromise to urbane Western liberals; eating fire and
spitting hatred to suit the taste of embittered Third World leaders;
displaying culture and refinement with artists; being pragmatic with

pragmatists, philosophical with philosophers, and Kissingerian with Kissinger.

It should not be forgotten that besides these strange and absorbing social activities, he was also directing the entire administration of the most populous nation on earth. He personally solved a thousand problems a day, having to substitute in practically every matter for a timorous bureaucracy that was forever reluctant to make any decision or bear any responsibility. He dispatched the affairs of the state with the supreme efficiency of an old Daoist ruler who knows that one should govern a large empire the way one cooks a little fish. He seemingly never slept and still looked always relaxed. He could simultaneously display an exacting attention for minute details that was worthy of a fussy housewife, and a breadth of vision that awed the greatest statesmen of our time. Although he permanently occupied the centre of the stage, his public activity was still a mere sinecure compared with the other show—far more intense, absorbing and momentous—that was running non-stop offstage in the dark recesses of inner-party politics. There he had to perform incredible acrobatics in order to remain on top of the greased pole—eliminating rivals in a relentless power struggle, dodging ambushes, surviving murderous plots hatched by old comrades, and so on. His task became more and more superhuman as he had to lend single-handedly, for the benefit of a bemused international audience, an impressive façade of humanity, intelligence and sanity to a regime whose increasing cruelty, ineptitude and madness were finally to come out in the open during the last ten years of the Maoist era.

Zhou's reputation may eventually suffer from the posthumous debunking of Mao (which is a paradox, as, in the end, Mao ruthlessly attempted to get rid of him). Still, some Chinese intellectuals are now probably being unfair when they describe him as having merely played Albert Speer to Mao's Hitler. Zhou's relation to his master did not reflect a straightforward subordination; the actual situation was far more complex. For many years before Mao reached supreme power, Zhou had actually been running the Chinese Communist Party behind the screen of a series of ineffectual or unlucky nominal leaders who were purged one after another. Zhou weathered these successive crises practically unscathed; from these early days onward, he displayed an uncanny ability for political survival that was to become the hallmark of his long career. He developed methods that made him unsinkable: always exert power by proxy; never occupy the front seat; whenever the opposition is stronger, immediately yield.

His unique skills made him forever indispensable, while simultaneously he cultivated a quality of utter elusiveness; no one could pin him down to a specific political line, nor could one associate him with any particular faction. He never expressed personal ideas or indulged in penning his own theoretical views. Where did he really stand? What did he actually believe? Apparently he had no other policies but those of the leader of the moment, and nourished no other ambitions but to serve him with total dedication. Yet the brilliance of his mind, the sharpness of his intelligence, the electrifying quality of his personal magnetism, eloquence and authority constantly belied the kind of bland selflessness that he so studiously displayed in the performance of his public duties; Zhou's enigma lay in the paradox that, with all his exceptional talents, he should also present a sort of disconcerting and essential *hollowness*.

Twenty-three hundred years ago, Zhuang Zi, in giving advice to a king, made him observe that when a small boat drifts in the way of a huge barge, the crew of the barge will immediately shout abuse at the stray craft; however, coming closer, if they discover that the little boat is empty, they will simply shut up and quietly steer clear of it. He concluded that a ruler who has to sail the turbulent waters of politics should first and foremost learn how to become *an empty boat*.

History provides few examples of statesmen who were as successful as Zhou Enlai in mastering this subtle discipline. It enabled him to become the ultimate survivor. There was no limit to his willingness to compromise. Once, when the communists had to co-operate again with the nationalists, a local party cadre rebelled against this shameless fraternisation with fascist butchers and indignantly asked Zhou, "Should we become mere concubines?" Zhou replied coolly, "If necessary, we should become prostitutes." Yet he was not seeking survival for survival's sake; he survived in order to win. He combined utter fluidity with absolute resilience, like water, which takes instantaneously the shape of whatever container it happens to fill and simultaneously never surrenders one single atom of its own nature—in the end it always prevails. The contrast between the posthumous fates of Mao and Zhou is quite illuminating in this respect. Mao's mummy was left to rot in a huge and grotesque mausoleum in the heart of Peking, as if better to witness from this vantage point the dismantling of all his policies. As for Zhou, once more, he vanished into thin air—quite literally this time, since he wisely requested that his ashes be scattered over the country—and beyond his death it is still he who is ruling today over China, through his own hand-picked successors.

Zhou made history for half a century and wielded enormous power over one-quarter of mankind; yet he apparently never succumbed to the temptation of self-aggrandisement and the lust for supremacy to which none of the other Chinese leaders remained immune. He withstood countless trials, crises, humiliations and dangers; he repeatedly served, with stoic loyalty, leaders who did not have his ability or his experience; and yet he never wavered in his commitment to Chinese communism. From where did he derive his spiritual strength? What motivated him? Like many bourgeois intellectuals of his generation, in his youth he was fired by intense patriotism. In his early twenties, while in Europe, he seems to have identified once and for all the salvation of China with the victory of communism. We know nothing more of his spiritual evolution. Zhou's conundrum was thus compounded with a tragic irony: this man who generously dedicated himself, soul and body, to the service of China, ended up as the staunchest pillar of a regime that managed to kill more innocent Chinese citizens in twenty-five years of peace than had the combined forces of all foreign imperialists in one hundred years of endemic aggression.

1984

ASPECTS OF MAO ZEDONG

SOME MISUNDERSTANDINGS acquire historical dimensions. In the celebrated interview he granted Edgar Snow, Mao Zedong allegedly described himself as "a lonely monk walking in the rain under a leaking umbrella." With its mixture of humorous humility and exoticism, this utterance had a tremendous impact on the Western imagination, already so well attuned to the oriental glamour of the *Kung Fu* television series. Snow's command of the Chinese language, even at its best, was never very fluent; some thirty-odd years spent away from China had done little to improve it, and it is no wonder that he failed to recognise in this "monk under an umbrella" (*heshang da san*) evoked by the chairman a most popular Chinese joke. The expression, in the form of a riddle, calls for the conventional answer "no hair" (since monks keep their heads shaven), "no sky" (it being hidden by the umbrella)—which in turn means by homophony (*wu-fa wu-tian*) "I know no law, I hold nothing sacred." The blunt cynicism shown by Mao in referring to such a saying to define his basic attitude was as typical of his bold disregard for diplomatic niceties as its mistaken and sentimental English adaptation by Snow is revealing of the compulsion for myth-making, of the demand for politico-religious kitsch among certain types of Western intellectual.

In fact, the crude riddle so naïvely misunderstood by Snow provides us with one of the keys for understanding Mao's complex and contradictory personality. There is little doubt that Mao's spontaneous inclinations generally favoured radical policies, and yet, looking at the countless twists and turns of his entire career, leafing through many of his earlier writings, it would be easy to put together a file on the subject of his "revisionist capitulationism" and "rightist opportunism" thick enough to hang three dozen Liu Shaoqis and Deng Xiaopings. And for that matter, his record as "leftist adventurist" could without difficulty eclipse even Lin Biao's. Actually, in order to discourage such an exercise, the Peking authorities wisely refrain from publishing Mao's complete works: the authorised version of the *Selected Works* is a carefully censored one. Although Mao was genuinely impatient with bureaucratic practices, he nevertheless became both the architect and the cornerstone of the most gigantic totalitarian bureaucracy this planet has ever known.

To reconcile such paradoxes, one must either learn the mental acrobatics of a very sophisticated game played by the enlightened vanguard and called "dialectics," or, more vulgarly, face the fact that rather than being the prophet-philosopher as described by his worshippers, Mao was essentially always and foremost a practical politician for whom what mattered above everything was *power*—how to obtain it, how to retain it, how to regain it. In order to secure power, no sacrifice was ever too big—and least of all the sacrifice of principles. It is only in this light that it becomes possible to understand his alternations between compromise and ruthlessness, benevolence and ferocity, suppleness and brutality, and all his abrupt volte-faces: none of these were ever arbitrary.

Although political power was the ultimate yardstick of all his actions, it would of course be foolish to assume that a man of such stature was merely pursuing power for power's sake. He had an acute awareness of his place in history; this intense historical consciousness—which in our age he shared perhaps only with de Gaulle—also made him profess an unabashed admiration for the great tyrants of the past: Napoleon, Qin Shihuang...If the fluctuating tactical imperatives make it very difficult at times to distinguish his actual policies from those of his successive rivals and scapegoats, his *style* remained unique. We can grasp it most clearly in some of his artistic creations. His calligraphy (one of the major arts of China) is strikingly original, betraying a flamboyant egotism, to the point of arrogance, if not extravagance; at the same time it shows a total disregard for the formal discipline of the brush, and this contempt for technical requirements condemns his work, however powerful, to remain essentially inarticulate. His poetry, so aptly described by Arthur Waley as "not as bad as Hitler's painting, but not as good as Churchill's," was rather pedantic and pedestrian, managing to combine obscurity with vulgarity; and yet, within the framework of an obsolete form, it remains, in its very awkwardness, remarkably unfettered by conventions. Moreover, the fact that he devoted some part of his energy to the uncertain pursuit of the aesthetic hobbies of a traditional gentleman and scholar is in itself quite revealing. As Erica Jong has observed: "There is nothing fiercer than a failed artist. The energy remains, but having no outlet, it implodes in a great black fart of rage which smokes up all the inner windows of the soul." And sometimes it drives a man into politics.

This phenomenon of the failed artist as a statesman, of political leadership as self-expression, ought some day to be properly analysed; in the course of such a study, Mao could provide one of the most exemplary cases. The kind of idealism, subjectivism and voluntarism that inspired his most daring initiatives betrays the aesthete's typical approach. Even some of his basic political utterances rest on artistic metaphors—like his famous observation about China's "poverty and blankness," which make her more easily available, like a blank page for the free improvisation of a great artist's brush ... Like a sculptor who submits the yielding clay to his inspiration, shapes it in accordance with an inner vision, the artist-statesman, using history and nations for his material, attempts to project in them the images from his mind. This visionary quality accounts for most of the unexpected, dazzling victories of Mao's maturity; unfortunately, it was also at the root of the increasingly erratic, capricious and catastrophic initiatives of his late years when, increasingly divorced from reality, ever more absorbed in his lonely dream, he repeatedly brought the very regime he himself had created to the brink of chaos and destruction.

Strangely enough for a leader of such stature, Mao had very little personal charisma. He was a poor speaker, with a high-pitched, unpleasant and monotonous voice. His thick Hunanese accent, of which he never could rid himself, did little to improve this. The masses could easily relate to leaders like Zhu De and Peng Dehuai because of their simplicity and human warmth; they liked Zhou Enlai for his patrician charm and selfless dedication to the service of the nation. But with

Mao it was a different story; well-orchestrated propaganda imposed his image upon the people as that of a Sun-God. More than 2,000 years of imperial tradition have created in the collective consciousness the constant need for a unique, supreme, quasi-mystical head; the shaky and brief republican interlude did not succeed in providing any convincing substitute for this, and Mao knew shrewdly how to manipulate this traditional legacy to his own advantage.

That he was in fact the main organiser of his own cult cannot be doubted; he justified the necessity of it to Edgar Snow by observing cynically, "Khrushchev did not build his own cult, look what happened to him!" But if he became a god for the masses, those who were in direct contact with him were somewhat put off by his aloofness, his secretive and devious ways, his utter lack of personal loyalty, the ruthlessness with which he could get rid of lifetime companions-in-arms and faithful assistants once they had become a hindrance or dared to voice criticism. One of his early admirers, the American journalist Agnes Smedley—a dedicated revolutionary who had the courage, during the war, to break through the Kuomintang blockade and join the communists in Yan'an—gave in 1943 a remarkably frank account of her first encounter with him:

> His hands were as long and sensitive as a woman's...Whatever else he might be he was an aesthete. I was in fact repelled by the feminine in him. An instinctive hostility sprang up inside me, and I became so occupied with trying to master it, that I heard hardly a word of what followed...The following months of precious friendship both confirmed and contradicted his inscrutability. The sinister quality I had at first felt so strongly in him proved to be a spiritual isolation...In him was none of the humility of Zhu De. Despite that feminine quality in him, he was as stubborn as a mule, and a steel rod of pride and determination ran through his nature.

In complete contrast with the intellectual revolutionary elite of his time, which was sophisticated, urban and cosmopolitan, Mao belonged to the old inward-looking peasant world. His intellectual landscape was furnished not so much with Western Marxist writings—which he read belatedly, in a haphazard and superficial way—as with Chinese classical literature, historiography and fiction, with which he developed a lively if patchy and unsystematic familiarity, typical of a self-taught provincial genius.

When already the master of China, he had himself photographed at his desk for an official portrait: it was not by accident that the collection of books stacked in front of him was not one of Marxist classics, but a famous series of eleventh-century Chinese manuals on imperial bureaucratic government. His attacks against Confucius sprang from a pathetically Confucian frame of mind; he still lived in a world—utterly foreign to younger Chinese generations—where Confucius occupied the place and fulfilled the function he envisaged for himself, that of Supreme Teacher of an all-encompassing orthodoxy. The anti-Confucius campaign was but one more expression of the living anachronism he himself had become. His world was still a ritual world, ruled by ideology rather than laws, by dogmatic scriptures—yesterday the Confucian classics, today the Little Red Book—rather than popular debate.

When he pronounced "the primacy of the red over the expert," he was merely rephrasing a 2,400-year-old axiom from the Confucian *Book of Rites*: "What is achieved by technique is inferior, what is achieved by virtue is superior." Such deep roots in the Chinese traditional universe accounted for his most brilliant achievements in the past: when waging guerrilla war in the remote peasant heartland of old China, he had no rival. But when it came to confronting a new world and a new age, when he had to guide China into the modern era, his very strength turned into his worst limitation. He always tried to reduce new problems and issues to terms more familiar to him, those of the backward peasant hinterland, the nostalgic arena of his early victories.

He attempted to move the fight back to his own battlefield, away from the disquieting areas of contemporary ideas and technology that were the preserve of people of whose language he had only an uncertain grasp—those odious intellectuals, academics, specialists and experts for whom he demonstrated a relentless and obsessive hatred.

Here lies his tragedy: he outlived himself by some twenty years. If he had died a few years after the liberation, he would have gone down in history as one of China's most momentous leaders. Unfortunately, during the last part of his life, by stubbornly clinging to an outdated utopia, by becoming frozen in his own idiosyncrasies and private visions, less and less attuned to the objective realities and needs of a new era, he became in fact a major obstacle to the development of the Chinese revolution. The ultra-conservative faction (mistakenly labelled "Left" by some Western observers), bent on keeping China in tight isolation in order to preserve her ideological purity, used him as a buttress in their last, most desperate stand against the long-overdue movement towards a true modernisation and opening of the country.

China has lost her "Great Leader." This should allow her at last to start forging ahead again, after an all too long and abnormal interlude of chaotic rule and cultural stagnation. For a nation such as the Chinese, the loss should not be crippling: do truly great peoples ever need a "Great Leader"?

1976

THE ART OF INTERPRETING NON-EXISTENT INSCRIPTIONS WRITTEN IN INVISIBLE INK ON A BLANK PAGE

IN ANY debate, you really know that you have won when you find your opponents beginning to appropriate your ideas in the sincere belief that they themselves just invented them. This situation can afford a subtle satisfaction; I think the feeling must be quite familiar to Father Ladany, the Jesuit priest and scholar based in Hong Kong who for many years published the weekly *China News Analysis*. Far away from the crude limelight of the media circus, he has enjoyed three decades of illustrious anonymity. All "China watchers" used to read his newsletter with avidity; many stole from it—but generally they took great pains never to acknowledge their indebtedness or to mention his name. Father Ladany watched this charade with sardonic detachment. He would probably agree that what Ezra Pound said regarding the writing of poetry should also apply to the recording of history: it is extremely important that it be written, but it is a matter of indifference who writes it.

China News Analysis was compulsory reading for all those who wished to be informed of Chinese political developments: scholars, journalists, diplomats. In academe, however, its perusal among many political scientists was akin to what a drinking habit might be for an ayatollah, or an addiction to pornography for a bishop: it was a compulsive need that had to be indulged in secrecy. China experts gnashed their teeth as they read Ladany's incisive comments; they hated his clear-sightedness and cynicism; still, they could not afford to miss one single issue of his newsletter, for, however disturbing and scandalous

---

Review of Laszlo Ladany: *The Communist Party of China and Marxism 1921–1985: A Self-Portrait* (Stanford: Hoover Institution Press, 1988).

his conclusions, the factual information he supplied was invaluable and irreplaceable. What made *China News Analysis* so infuriatingly indispensable was the very simple and original principle on which it was run (true originality is usually simple): all the information selected and examined in *China News Analysis* was drawn exclusively from official Chinese sources (press and radio). This austere rule sometimes deprived Ladany's newsletter of the life and colour that could have been provided by less orthodox sources, but it enabled him to build his devastating conclusions on unimpeachable grounds.

What inspired his method was the observation that even the most mendacious propaganda must necessarily entertain some sort of relation with the truth; even as it manipulates and distorts the truth, it still needs originally to feed on it. Therefore, the untwisting of official lies, if skilfully effected, should yield a certain amount of straight facts. Needless to say, such an operation requires a *doigté* hardly less sophisticated than the chemistry which, in *Gulliver's Travels*, enabled the Grand Academicians of Lagado to extract sunbeams from cucumbers and food from excreta. The analyst who wishes to gather information through such a process must negotiate three hurdles of thickening thorniness. First, he needs to have a fluent command of the Chinese language. To the man in the street, such a prerequisite may appear like elementary common sense, but once you leave the street level and enter the loftier spheres of academe, common sense is not so common any longer, and it remains an interesting fact that, during the Maoist era, a majority of leading "China experts" hardly knew any Chinese. (I hasten to add that this is largely a phenomenon of the past; nowadays, fortunately, young scholars are much better educated.)

Secondly, in the course of his exhaustive surveys of Chinese official documentation, the analyst must absorb industrial quantities of the most indigestible stuff; reading Communist literature is akin to munching rhinoceros sausage, or to swallowing sawdust by the bucketful. Furthermore, while subjecting himself to this punishment, the analyst cannot allow his attention to wander, or his mind to become numb; he must keep his wits sharp and keen; with the eye of an eagle that can spot a lone rabbit in the middle of a desert, he must scan the arid wastes of the small print in the pages of the *People's Daily* and pounce upon those rare items of significance that lie buried under mountains of clichés. He must know how to milk substance and meaning out of flaccid speeches, hollow slogans and fanciful statistics; he must scavenge for needles in Himalayan-size haystacks; he must combine the nose of a hunting hound, the concentration and patience of an angler and the intuition and encyclopaedic knowledge of a Sherlock Holmes.

Thirdly—and this is his greatest challenge—he must crack the code of the Communist political jargon and translate into ordinary speech this secret language full of symbols, riddles, cryptograms, hints, traps, dark allusions and red herrings. Like wise old peasants who can forecast tomorrow's weather by noting how deep the moles dig and how high the swallows fly, he must be able to decipher the premonitory signs of political storms and thaws, and know how to interpret a wide range of quaint warnings—sometimes the Supreme Leader takes a swim in the Yangtze River, or suddenly writes a new poem, or sponsors a ping-pong game: such events all have momentous implications. He must carefully watch the celebration of anniversaries, the non-celebration of anniversaries, and the celebration of non-anniversaries; he must check the lists of guests at official functions and note the order in which their names appear. In the press, the size, type and colour of headlines, as well as the position and composition of photos and illustrations, are all matters of considerable import; actually they obey complex laws, as precise and strict as the iconographic rules that govern the location, garb, colour and symbolic attributes of the figures of angels, archangels, saints and patriarchs in the decoration of a Byzantine basilica.

To find one's way in this maze, ingenuity and astuteness are not enough; one also needs a vast amount of experience. Communist Chinese politics are a lugubrious merry-go-round (as I have pointed out many times already), and in order to appreciate fully the déjà-vu quality of its latest convolutions, you would need to have watched it revolve for half a century. The main problem with many of our politicians and pundits is that their memories are too short, thus forever preventing them from putting events and personalities in a true historical perspective. For instance, when, in 1979, the "People's Republic" began to revise its criminal law, there were good souls in the West who applauded this initiative, as they thought that it heralded China's move toward a genuine rule of law. What they failed to note, however—and which should have provided a crucial hint regarding the actual nature and meaning of the move in question—was that the new law was being introduced by Peng Zhen, one of the most notorious butchers of the regime, a man who, thirty years earlier, had organised the ferocious mass accusations, lynchings and public executions of the land-reform programs.

Or again, after the death of Mao, Western politicians and commentators were prompt to hail Deng Xiaoping as a sort of champion of liberalisation. The *Selected Works* of Deng published at that time should have enlightened them—not so much by what it included, as by what it excluded; had they been able to read it as any Communist document should be read, i.e. by concentrating first on its gaps, they would have rediscovered Deng's Stalinist-Maoist statements, and then, perhaps, they might have been less surprised by the massacres of 4 June 1989.

More than half a century ago, the writer Lu Xun (1881–1936), whose prophetic genius never ceases to amaze, described accurately the conundrum of China-watching:

> Once upon a time, there was a country whose rulers completely succeeded in crushing the people; and yet they still believed that the people were their most dangerous enemy. The rulers issued huge collections of statutes, but none of these volumes could actually be used, because in order to interpret them, one had to refer to a set of instructions that had never been made public. These instructions contained many original definitions. Thus, for instance, "liberation" meant in fact "capital execution"; "government official" meant "friend, relative or servant of an influential politician," and so on. The rulers also issued codes of laws that were marvellously modern, complex and complete; however, at the beginning of the first volume, there was one blank page; this blank page could be deciphered only by those who knew the instructions—which did not exist. The

first three invisible articles of these non-existent instructions read as follows: "Art. 1: Some cases must be treated with special leniency. Art. 2: Some cases must be treated with special severity. Art. 3: This does not apply in all cases."

Without an ability to decipher non-existent inscriptions written in invisible ink on blank pages, no one should ever dream of analysing the nature and reality of Chinese communism. Very few people have mastered this demanding discipline, and, with good reason, they generally acknowledge Father Ladany as their doyen.

———

After thirty-six years of China-watching, Father Ladany finally retired and summed up his exceptional experience in *The Communist Party of China and Marxism, 1921–1985: A Self-Portrait*. In the scope of this article it would naturally not be possible to do full justice to a volume which analyses in painstaking detail sixty-five years of turbulent history; still, it may be useful to outline here some of Ladany's main conclusions.

The Communist Party is in essence a secret society. In its methods and mentality it presents a striking resemblance to an underworld mob.[1] It fears daylight, feeds on deception and conspiracy, and rules by intimidation and terror. "Communist legality" is a contradiction in terms, since the party is above the law—for example, party members are immune from legal prosecution: they must be divested of their party membership before they can be indicted by a criminal court. (That a judge may acquit an accused person is inconceivable: since the accused was sent to court, it means that he is guilty.) Whereas even Mussolini and Hitler originally reached power through elections, no communist party ever received an electorate's mandate to govern.

In China, the path that led the communists to victory still remains partly shrouded in mystery. Even today, for party historians, many archives remain closed and there are entire chapters that continue to present insoluble riddles; minutes of decisive meetings are nowhere to be found, important dates remain uncertain; for some momentous episodes it is still impossible to identify the participants and to reconstruct accurately the sequence of events; for some periods one cannot even determine who were the party leaders!

As Ladany points out, a communist regime is built on a triple foundation: dialectics, the power of the party, and a secret police—but, as to its ideological equipment, Marxism is merely an optional feature; the regime can do without it most of the time. Dialectics is the jolly art that enables the Supreme Leader never to make mistakes—for even if he did the wrong thing, he did it at the right time, which makes it right for him to have been wrong, whereas the Enemy, even if he did the right thing, did it at the wrong time, which makes it wrong for him to have been right.

Before securing power, the party thrives on political chaos. If confronted with a deliquescent government, it can succeed through organisation and propaganda, even when it operates from a minuscule base. In 1945, the communists controlled only one town, Yan'an, and some remote tracts of countryside; four years later, the whole of China was theirs. At the time of the communist takeover, the party members in Peking numbered a mere 3,000, and Shanghai, a city of 9 million people, had only 8,000 party members. In a time of social and economic collapse, it takes very few people—less than 0.01 per cent of the population in the Chinese case—to launch emotional appeals, to stir the indignation of the populace against corrupt and brutal authorities, to mobilise the generosity and idealism of the young, to enlist the support of thousands of students, and eventually to present their tiny communist movement as the incarnation of the entire nation's will.

What is even more remarkable is that, before 1949, wherever the population had been directly exposed to their rule the communists were utterly unpopular. They had introduced radical land reform in parts of North China during the civil war, and, as Ladany recalls:

Not only landowners but all suspected enemies were treated brutally; one could walk about in the North Chinese plains and see hands sticking out from the ground, the hands of people buried alive ... Luckily for the communists, government propaganda was so poorly organised that people living in regions not occupied by the communists knew nothing of such atrocities.

Once the whole country fell under their control, it did not take long for the communists to extend to the rest of the nation the sort of treatment which, until then, had been reserved for inner use—purging the party and disciplining the population of the so-called liberated areas. Systematic terror was applied on a national scale as early as 1950, to match first the land reform and then the campaign to suppress "counter-revolutionaries." By the fall of 1951, 80 per cent of all Chinese had had to take part in mass accusation meetings, or to watch organised lynchings and public executions. These grim liturgies followed set patterns that once more were reminiscent of gangland practices: during these proceedings, rhetorical questions were addressed to the crowd, which, in turn, had to roar its approval in unison—the purpose of the exercise being to ensure collective participation in the murder of innocent victims; the latter were selected not on the basis of what they had done, but of who they were, or sometimes for no better reason than the need to meet the quota of capital executions which had been arbitrarily set beforehand by the party authorities.

From that time on, every two or three years, a new "campaign" would be launched, with its usual accompaniment of mass accusations, "struggle meetings," self-accusations and public executions. At the beginning of each "campaign" there were waves of suicides: many of the people who during a previous "campaign" had suffered public humiliation, psychological and physical torture at the hands of their own relatives, colleagues and neighbours found it easier to jump from a window or under a train than to face a repeat of the same ordeal.

What is puzzling is that in organising these recurrent waves of terror the communists betrayed a strange incapacity to understand their own people. As history has amply demonstrated, the Chinese possess extraordinary patience; they can stoically endure the rule of a ruthless and rapacious government provided that it does not interfere too much with their family affairs and private pursuits, and as long as it can provide basic stability. On both accounts, the communists broke this tacit covenant between ruler and ruled. They invaded the lives of the people in a way that was far more radical and devastating than in the Soviet Union. Remoulding the minds, "brainwashing" as it is usually called, is a chief instrument of Chinese communism, and the technique goes as far back as the early consolidation of Mao's rule in Yan'an.

To appreciate the characteristics of the Maoist approach one need simply to compare the Chinese "labour rectification" camps with the Soviet Gulag. Life in the concentration camps in Siberia was physically more terrifying than life in many Chinese camps, but the mental pressure was less severe on the Soviet side. In the Siberian camps the inmates could still, in a way, feel spiritually free and retain some sort of inner life, whereas the daily control of words and thoughts, the actual transformation and conditioning of individual consciousness, made the Maoist camps much more inhuman.

Besides its cruelty, the Maoist practice of launching political "campaigns" in relentless succession generated permanent instability, which eventually ruined the moral credit of the party, destroyed much of society, paralysed the economy, provoked large-scale famines, and nearly developed into civil war. In 1949, most of the population had been merely hoping for a modicum of order and peace, which the communists could easily have granted. Had they governed with some moderation and abstained from the needless upheavals of the campaigns, they could have won long-lasting popular support and ensured steady economic development—but Mao had a groundless fear of inner opposition and revolt; this psychological flaw led him to adopt methods that proved fatally self-destructive.

History might have been very different if the original leaders of the Chinese Communist Party had not been decimated by Chiang Kaishek's White Terror of 1927, or expelled by their own comrades in subsequent party purges. They were civilised and sophisticated urban intellectuals, upholding humanistic values, with cosmopolitan and open minds, attuned to the modern world. While their sun was still high in the political firmament, Mao's star never had a chance to shine; however bright and ambitious, the young self-taught peasant was unable to compete with these charismatic figures. Their sudden elimination marked an abrupt turn in the Chinese revolution—one may say that it actually put an end to it—but it also presented Mao with an unexpected opening. At first, his ascent was not exactly smooth; yet, by 1940 in Yan'an, he was finally able to neutralise all his rivals and to remould the entire party according to his own conception. It is this Maoist brigade of country bumpkins and uneducated soldiers, trained and drilled in a remote corner of one of China's poorest and most backward provinces, that was finally to impose its rule over the entire nation—and, as Ladany adds, "This is why there are spittoons everywhere in the People's Republic."

Mao's anti-intellectualism was deeply rooted in his personal experiences. He never forgot how, as a young man, intellectuals had made him feel insignificant and inadequate. Later on, he came to despise them for their perpetual doubts and waverings; the competence and expertise of scholarly authorities irritated him; he distrusted the independence of their judgements and resented their critical ability. In the barracks-like atmosphere of Yan'an, a small town without culture, far removed from intellectual centres, with no easy access to books, amid illiterate peasants and brutish soldiers, intellectuals were easily singled out for humiliating sessions of self-criticism and were turned into exemplary targets during the terrifying purges of 1942–44. Thus the pattern was set for what was to remain the most characteristic feature of Chinese communism: the persecution and ostracism of intellectuals. The Yan'an brigade had an innate dislike of people who thought too much; this moronic tradition received a powerful boost in 1957, when, in the aftermath of the Hundred Flowers campaign, China's cultural elite was pilloried; nine years later, finally, the "Cultural Revolution" marked the climax of Mao's war against intelligence: savage blows were dealt to all intellectuals inside and outside the party; all education was virtually suspended for ten years, producing an entire generation of illiterates.

Educated persons were considered unfit by nature to join the party; especially at the local level, resistance to accepting them was always greatest, as the old leadership felt threatened by all expressions of intellectual superiority. Official figures released in 1985 provide a telling picture of the level of education within the Communist Party, which makes up the privileged elite of the nation: 4 per cent of party members had received *some* university education—they did not necessarily graduate—(against 30 per cent in the Soviet Union); 42 per cent of party members only attended primary school; 10 per cent are illiterate ...

The first casualty of Mao's anti-intellectualism was to be found, interestingly enough, in the field of Marxist studies. When, after fifteen years of revolutionary activity, the party finally felt the need to acquire some rudiments of Marxist knowledge (at that time virtually no work of Marx had yet been translated into Chinese!), Mao, who himself was still a beginner in this discipline, undertook to keep all doctrinal development under his personal control. In Yan'an, like an inexperienced teacher who has gotten hold of the only available textbook and struggles to keep one lesson ahead of his pupils, he simply plagiarised a couple of Soviet booklets and gave a folksy Chinese version of some elementary Stalinist-Zhdanovian notions. How these crude, banal and derivative works ever came to acquire in the eyes of the entire world the prestige and authority of an original philosophy remains a mystery; it must be one of the most remarkable instances of mass auto-suggestion in the twentieth century.

In one respect, however, Mao Zedong Thought did present genuine originality and dared to tread ground where Stalin himself had not ventured. Mao explicitly denounced the concept of a universal humanity; whereas the Soviet tyrant merely *practised* inhumanity, Mao gave it a theoretical foundation, expounding the notion—without parallel in the other communist countries of the world—that the proletariat alone is fully endowed with human nature. To deny the humanity of other people is the very essence of terrorism; millions of Chinese were soon to measure the actual implications of this philosophy.

At first, after the establishment of the People's Republic the regime was simply content to translate and reproduce elementary Soviet introductions to Marxism. The Chinese Academy of Sciences had a department of philosophy and social sciences but produced nothing during the 1950s, not even textbooks on Marxism. Only one university in the entire country—Peking University—had a department of philosophy; only Mao's works were studied there.

When the Soviet Union denounced Stalin and rejected his *History of the Communist Party—Short Course*, the Chinese were stunned: this little book contained virtually all they knew about Marxism. Then, the Sino–Soviet split ended the intellectual importations from the USSR, and it was conveniently decided that Mao Zedong Thought represented the highest development of Marxist-Leninist philosophy; therefore, in order to fill the ideological vacuum, Mao's Thought suddenly expanded and acquired polyvalent functions; its study became a reward for the meritorious, a punishment for the criminal, a medicine for the sick; it could answer all questions and solve all problems; it even performed miracles that were duly recorded; its presence was felt everywhere; it was broadcast in the streets and in the fields, it was put to music, it was turned into song and dance, it was inscribed everywhere—on mountain cliffs and on chopsticks, on badges, on bridges, on ashtrays, on dams, on teapots, on locomotives; it was printed on every page of all newspapers. (This, in turn, created some practical problems: in a poor country, where all paper is recycled for a variety of purposes, one had always to be very careful, when wrapping groceries or when wiping one's bottom, not to do it with Mao's ubiquitous Thought—which would have been a capital offence.) In a way, Mao is to Marx what Voodoo is to Christianity; therefore, it is not surprising that the inflation of Mao's Thought precluded the growth of serious Marxist studies in China.[2]

No tyrant can forsake humanity and persecute intelligence with impunity; in the end, he reaps imbecility and madness. When he visited Moscow in 1957, Mao declared that an atomic war was not to be feared since, in such an eventuality, only half of the human race would perish. This remarkable statement provided a good sample of the mind that was to conceive the "Great Leap Forward" and the "Cultural Revolution." The human cost of these ventures was staggering: the famines that resulted from the "Great Leap" produced a demographic black hole into which it now appears that as many as 50 million victims may have been sucked. The violence of the "Cultural Revolution" affected 100 million people. If, on the whole, the Maoist horrors are well known, what has not been sufficiently underlined is their asinine lunacy. In a recent issue of the *New York Review*, Jonathan Mirsky quoted an anecdote (from Liu Binyan, Ruan Ming and

Xu Gang's *Tell the World*) that is so exemplary and apposite here that it bears telling once more. One day, Bo Yibo was swimming with Mao. Mao asked him what the production of iron and steel would be for the next year. Instead of replying, Bo Yibo told Mao that he was going to effect a turn in the water; Mao misunderstood him and thought that he had said "double." A little later, at a party meeting, Bo Yibo heard Mao announce that the national production of iron and steel would double the next year.[3]

The anecdote is perfectly credible in the light of all the documentary evidence we have concerning Mao's attitude at the time of the "Great Leap": we know that he swallowed the gigantic and grotesque deceptions fabricated by his own propaganda, and accepted without discussion the pleasing suggestion that miracles were taking place in the Chinese countryside; he genuinely believed that the yield of cotton and grain could be increased by 300–500 per cent. And Liu Shaoqi himself was no wiser: inspecting Shandong in 1958, and having been told that miraculous increases had been effected in agricultural output, he said: "This is because the scientists have been kicked out, and people now dare to do things!" The output of steel, which was 5.3 million tons in 1957, allegedly reached 11 million tons in 1958, and it was planned that it would reach 18 million in 1959. The grain output which was 175 million tons in 1957, allegedly reached 375 million tons in 1958, and was planned to reach 500 million in 1959. The Central Committee solemnly endorsed this farce (Wuchang, Sixth Plenum, December 1958)—and planned for more. Zhou Enlai—who never passed for a fool—repeated and supported these fantastic figures and announced that the targets laid in the Second Five Year Plan (1958–1962) had all been reached in the plan's first year! All the top leaders applauded this nonsense. Li Fuchun and Li Xiannian poured out "Great Leap" statistics that were simply lies. What happened to their common sense? Only Chen Yun had the courage to remain silent.

Graphic details of the subsequent famine were provided in the official press only a few years ago, confirming what was already known through the testimonies of countless eye-witnesses.

As early as 1961, Ladany published in *China News Analysis* some of these reports by Chinese travellers from all parts of China:

All spoke of food shortage and hunger; swollen bellies, lack of protein and liver diseases were common. Many babies were stillborn because of their mothers' deficient nutrition. Few babies were being born. As some workers put it, their food barely sufficed to keep them standing on their feet, let alone allowing them to have thoughts of sex. Peasants lacked the strength to work, and some collapsed in the fields and died. City government organisations and schools sent people to the villages by night to buy food, bartering clothes and furniture for it. In Shenyang the newspaper reported cannibalism. Desperate mothers strangled children who cried for food. Many reported that villagers were flocking into the cities in search of food; many villages were left empty... It was also said that peasants were digging underground pits to hide their food. Others spoke of places where the population had been decimated by starvation.

According to the *Guang Ming Daily* (27 April 1980), in the northwest the famine generated an ecological disaster: in their struggle to grow some food, the peasants destroyed grasslands and forests. Half of the grasslands and one-third of the forests vanished between 1959 and 1962: the region was damaged permanently. The *People's Daily* (14 May 1980) said that the disaster of the "Great Leap" had affected the lives of 100 million people who were physically devastated by the prolonged shortage of food. (Note that, at the time, China experts throughout the world refused to believe that there was famine in China. A BBC commentator, for instance, declared typically that a widespread famine in such a well-organised country was unthinkable.)

Today, in order to stem the tide of popular discontent which threatens to engulf his rule, Deng Xiaoping is invoking again the authority of Mao. That he should be willing to call *that* ghost to the rescue provides a measure of his desperation. Considering the history of the last sixty years, one can easily imagine what sort of response the Chinese are now giving to such an appeal.

Deng's attempts to revive and promote Marxist studies are no less unpopular. Marxism has acquired a very bad name in China—which is quite understandable, though somewhat unfair: after all, it was never really tried.

1990

THE CURSE OF THE MAN WHO COULD SEE THE LITTLE FISH AT THE BOTTOM OF THE OCEAN

SINCE the Peking massacres,* the question has already been put bluntly to me several times: Why were most of our pundits so constantly wrong on the subject of China? What enabled you and a tiny minority of critics to see things as they really were, and why did hardly anyone ever listen to you?

At first I declined the invitations to write on this theme. The idea of sitting atop a heap of dead Chinese bodies to cackle triumphantly "I told you so! I told you so!" like a hen that has just laid an egg is not particularly appealing. Furthermore, for the first time in many decades, there is a remarkable and truly moving unanimity on the issue of China. This should be a cause for some comfort—actually it is the only heartening aspect that can be found in the present nightmare. With such unanimity, it should even become possible to exert some useful influence on public opinion, and then also on our politicians. Thus, this is certainly not the time to settle old accounts or to revive ancient polemics. In fact, there never should be a time for such a mean and destructive exercise; when it is a matter of finally arriving at the truth, there can be no latecomers, and we know from the Gospel that the workers who come only at the end of the afternoon are entitled to the same reward as those who have been labouring in the vineyard since daybreak.

If we consider it from a more universal and philosophical angle, however, one question might be of real interest: How and why do we usually endeavour to protect ourselves against the truth?

It would be grossly unfair to ask, for instance: Why did Shirley

---

*Tian'anmen, 4 June 1989.

MacLaine or Professor Fairbank make their notorious statements about China? (One will remember, for example, that at a time when China had sunk into an abyss of misery, oppression and terror, the distinguished historian from Harvard wrote: "The Maoist revolution is, on the whole, the best thing that has happened to the Chinese people in many centuries.") A more pertinent question would be: Why are we forever willing to vest Shirley MacLaine and Professor Fairbank with so much intellectual and moral authority? For, in the end, the only authority they can ever possess is the one we are giving them.

What people believe is essentially what they *wish* to believe. They cultivate illusions out of idealism—and also out of cynicism. They follow their own visions because doing so satisfies their religious cravings, and also because it is expedient. They seek beliefs that can exalt their souls, and that can fill their bellies. They believe out of generosity, and also because it serves their interests. They believe because they are stupid, and also because they are clever. Simply, they believe in order to survive. And because they need to survive, sometimes they could gladly kill whoever has the insensitivity, cruelty and inhumanity to deny them their life-supporting lies.

When I am told that I was dead right all along on the subject of communist China, such a compliment (for it is generally intended as a compliment) can hardly flatter my vanity; indeed, forcing me as it does to re-examine the reasons for which I had to adopt my rather lonely stand, the results of such an examination give me little cause for self-satisfaction, and even less reason to be sanguine about the future. As far as I am concerned, I could already foresee my fate many years ago; the writing is on the wall (and ironically, it may not be in Chinese).

Let us not kid ourselves. The facts which I have been describing during these last twenty years may have been distasteful and unpalatable—they were also public knowledge. They were all too easy to collect—there was no need to search for them, they kept coming at you; their evidence was as plain and direct as a punch on the nose. My first encounter with communist political practice was in 1967 in Hong Kong, when I found on my doorstep the dying body of a courageous

Chinese journalist—seconds after he had been horribly mutilated by communist thugs. After that first elementary introduction to communist politics, the rest was clear sailing. For the next few years, I merely listened to the conversations of a few Chinese friends and every day I read a couple of Chinese newspapers over breakfast. This modest intellectual equipment eventually enabled me to write four books on Chinese current affairs, which apparently were quite sound and reliable, since their contents have been confirmed by the subsequent developments of history and by countless testimonies of unimpeachable Chinese witnesses.

Yet I dare affirm that, in these four books—even though they passed for a while as shocking, scandalous and heretical—it would be impossible to find a single revelation, a single original view or personal idea. From beginning to end, I merely translated and transcribed what would have appeared at the time, to any reasonably informed Chinese intellectual, as mere common sense and common knowledge—tragic, yes, but also utterly banal. The only technical competence required for this task—an expertise that could hardly be deemed exceptional, since it is shared by more than 1 billion people on earth—was a good knowledge of the Chinese language. In a way, with my modest transcriptions, I was turned into the ultimate Bouvard and Pécuchet of Chinese politics.

It seems rather apposite to evoke here the image of Flaubert's diligent and earnest *imbéciles*. If indeed a man of middling intelligence (whose courage is, alas, well below average) could perform a task which most of his equally well-informed and much brighter colleagues would never have contemplated touching, it is quite obvious that, in order to do this, besides the basic prerequisite of language which I have just mentioned, only one qualification was necessary: an uncommon degree of foolishness.

Among primitive tribes, idiots and madmen are the objects of particular respect and enjoy certain privileges; since their condition frees them from the normal constraints of prudence and wisdom, they alone can be forgiven for speaking the truth—an activity that would naturally not be tolerated from any sane person. For Truth, by its very nature, is ugly, savage and cruel; it disturbs, it frightens, it hurts and it kills. If, in some extreme situations, it is to be used at all, it must be taken only in small doses, in strict isolation, and with the most rigorous prophylactic precautions. Whoever would be willing to spread it wildly, or to unload it in large quantities, just as it comes, is a dangerous and irresponsible person who should be restrained in the interest of his own safety, as well as for the protection of social harmony.

Ancient Chinese wisdom already expounded this notion; there is in the book of Lie Zi (third century BC) a parable about a man whose particular talent enabled him to identify thieves at first sight: he only needed to look at a certain spot between the eye and the brow, and he could recognise instantly whether a person was a thief. The king naturally decided to give him a position in the Ministry of Justice, but before the man could take up his appointment, the thieves of the kingdom banded together and had him assassinated. For this reason, clear-sighted people were generally considered cripples, bound to come to a bad end; this was also known proverbially in Chinese as "the curse of the man who can see the little fish at the bottom of the ocean."

Yet sometimes—as we have just witnessed in Peking—truth breaks free. Like a river that ruptures its dams, it overwhelms all our defences, violently erupts into our lives, floods our cosy homes, and leaves high and dry in the middle of the street, for all to see, the fish that used to dwell in the deep.

Such tidal waves can be very frightening; fortunately, they are relatively rare and do not last long. Sooner or later, the waters recede. Usually, brave engineers set to work at once and start rebuilding the dykes. The latest attempts by the communist propaganda organs to explain that "no one actually died in Tian'anmen Square" may betray a slightly excessive zeal (one is reminded of the good souls who, probably wishing to restore our faith in human nature, insisted that, in Auschwitz, gas was used only to kill lice), but if we give them enough time, in due course their ministrations will certainly succeed in healing the wounds that the brutal dumping of raw and untreated truth inflicted upon our sensitivities.

Whenever a minute of silence is being observed in a ceremony, don't we all soon begin to throw discreet glances at our watches? Exactly how long should a "decent interval" last before we can resume business-as-usual with the butchers of Peking? The senile and ferocious despots who decided to slaughter the youth, the hope and the intelligence of China may have made many miscalculations—still, on one count, they were not mistaken: they shrewdly assessed that our capacity to sustain our indignation would be very limited indeed.

The businessmen, the politicians, the academic tourists who are already packing their suitcases for their next trip to Peking are not necessarily cynical—though some of them have just announced that, this time, the main purpose of their visit will be to go to Tian'anmen Square to mourn for the martyrs!—and they may even have a point when they insist that, in agreeing once more to sit at the banquet of the murderers, they are actively strengthening the reformist trends in China. I only wish they had weaker stomachs.

Ah humanity!—the pity of us all!...

1989

THE CAMBODIAN GENOCIDE

It is a mark of fundamental human decency to feel ashamed of living in the twentieth century.

—Elias Canetti

One remembers the last lines of Kafka's *Trial*: Josef K., an innocent citizen who fell into an incomprehensible and endless web of judicial proceedings for reasons that will never be revealed to him, is in the end taken by two official-looking gentlemen to a deserted quarry; there, with a sort of stupid bureaucratic formality, without violence, without anger and without a single word, they undertake to execute him. As one of the two gentlemen turns a knife twice in his heart, K. has one last conscious feeling: "It was as if the shame would outlive him."

Many readers have experienced perplexity on encountering this last sentence. Yet Primo Levi, who wrote a short essay on Kafka, was puzzled by their puzzlement. He explained:

This last page takes my breath away. I, who survived Auschwitz, would never have written it, or not in this way: out of inability, or insufficient imagination, certainly, but also out of a sense of decency in the face of death (which Kafka either ignored or rejected); or perhaps simply out of lack of courage. The famous phrase—source of so much discussion—which closes the book like a gravestone ("It was as if the shame would outlive him") presents no enigma to me at all. What should Josef K. be ashamed of? He is ashamed of many contradictory things... Still, I feel there is, in his shame, another element which I know well. At the end of his harrowing journey, the fact that such a corrupt tribunal does exist and spreads its infection to all its surroundings causes him shame... After all, this tribunal was made by man, not by God, and K. with the knife already stuck in his heart experiences the shame of being a man.

The horrors of the twentieth century were to confirm Kafka's prophetic intuition. At the end of that same century, the Cambodian genocide stands as a most extreme and most grotesque epilogue: it was not only a monstrous event, it was also the *caricature* of a monstrosity.

By simplifying forms and amplifying lines, a caricature can reveal the inner essence of its subject. In this sense, Khmer Rouge propaganda, in its primitive crudity, grasped a central reality:

The whole world keeps its eyes on Democratic Kampuchea, for Khmer Revolution is the most beautiful and the most pure.

Khmer Revolution is without a precedent in world history. It resolved the eternal contradiction between city and country. *It develops Lenin and goes beyond Mao Zedong.*

This is quite true, in fact; in the light of the Khmer Rouge experiment, one can see more clearly the fundamental dynamics that informed the great Hitlero–Lenino–Stalino–Maoist tradition. Twentieth-century totalitarianism wore a variety of cultural garbs, with different degrees of sophistication, yet its basic elements remained fairly simple and never greatly varied. A quarter of a century ago, Kazimierz Brandys summed it up neatly (with the clear-sightedness that characterises so many Polish intellectuals, who on this subject have acquired a bitter expertise): "Contemporary history teaches us that all you need is one mentally sick individual, two ideologues and three hundred murderous thugs in order to take power and gag millions of people."

The Cambodian terror offers a perfect illustration of this outline, as shown in Francis Deron's monumental work *Le Procès des Khmers rouges: trente ans d'enquête sur le génocide du Cambodge* (The Trial of the Khmer Rouge: A Thirty-year Investigation of the Cambodian

Genocide, Paris: Gallimard, 2009), which analyses the ascent of the Khmer Rouge movement, its victory, its brief and bloody reign, its downfall, its lengthy artificial survival (thanks, among others, to the culpable collusion of the West!)—and, at long last, its approaching punishment, as justice is finally catching up with a handful of still-surviving, semi-senile criminals.

It is a cliché to say that journalists are the historians of the present time—but it is true. For his entire journalistic career, Deron was an influential and respected correspondent, covering China at first, and then South-East Asia. In his latest book he tackles thirty years of the Cambodian tragedy; he unravels its complex threads, outlines the biographies of the main protagonists, clarifies and interprets the sequence of events; now and then he intersperses his historical narrative with vivid vignettes drawn from his old reporter's notebooks. The architecture of the book is composite, but it is organised with method and clarity.

Deron benefited from his in-depth experience of Maoist China; his two earlier books on the "Cultural Revolution" and its aftermath superbly prepared him to grasp the nature and significance of the Khmer Rouge phenomenon. What Maoism took twenty years to achieve in China—the great purges of intellectuals ("The Hundred Flowers" movement), the enforced lowering of the entire nation to the primitive level of the countryside (the "Great Leap" backward, with its makeshift village blast-furnaces, peasants confined to "People's Communes" dormitories—and the gigantic famine which ensued), and finally the "Cultural Revolution" and the murderous savagery of the Red Guards—all these initiatives were to be found again in the brief experiment of "Democratic Kampuchea," but they were recycled and compressed within a period of only three years and ten months. The imitation was therefore grossly simplified and exaggerated; the objectives were the same, but they were pursued by means even more ferocious—and more dreadfully *stupid*.

The Khmer Rouge achieved complete control over all of Cambodia from 17 April 1975 (conquest of Phnom Penh by Pol Pot) until 7 January 1979 (fall of Phnom Penh, arrival of the Vietnamese army). During such a relatively short period, the regime succeeded in its grandiose project: the total destruction of society. From the outset, it had only modest means (which confirms Brandys's formula, quoted above): the Cambodian Communist Party numbered a mere 18,000 members, who were leading an army of 85,000 men. With these cadres, the regime was able to mobilise the bulk of its forces: a huge and fearsome mass of illiterate and savage youngsters and children, fanatically indoctrinated and heavily armed, and vested with discretionary powers over the whole population. As a result, at the fall of the regime, *Cambodia had lost between one-quarter and one-third of its population*: a self-genocide the magnitude of which is without precedent in the history of humankind.

This program of National Communism took form from the very moment Phnom Penh was overtaken. On Pol Pot's orders, the capital city was emptied of all its inhabitants, within three weeks. The entire urban population—including even sick patients in the hospitals—was forcibly deported on foot and thrown on the highways of the country and the tracks of the bush. Those who survived this exodus ended up reduced to the condition of slaves in crowded agricultural camps. (When the Vietnamese army eventually entered Phnom Penh three years later, they found there only seventy civilians wandering in a ghost city amidst the stench of rotting bodies.)

Having thus lobotomised the country (Phnom Penh was its very brains), the regime could more easily eliminate in the provinces all forms of administrative institution, education, public health, established religion and all other expressions of civilised life.

Symbolic gesture: in deserted and lifeless Phnom Penh, the army that had come out of the forest undertook to throw into the river all the electrical and mechanical appliances they could grab from the city shops, offices and private residences—in a word, all the equipment of modern life. (Note that, outside the capital city, nine-tenths of Cambodia was without electricity.) This anti-modern frenzy did not even spare the motorbikes of the local Harley-Davidson club: the fact that these machines were in perfect working condition and the bush cruelly lacked motorised transportation could not save them from this watery ending. Another thing that attracted the virulent hostility of the Khmer Rouge: people wearing glasses. Spectacles were to be confiscated and destroyed on the spot, and their owners arrested and sent to labour camps to await eventual execution, on the suspicion that they were educated and therefore belonged to the oppressor class. (By the way, Son Sen—the chief enforcer of the regime—himself wore glasses; he was eventually murdered by his own comrades in 1997, but not for that reason.)

This wild delirium originated from the top; Pol Pot's rare declarations betrayed his complete divorce from reality. He was praising the splendid progress of the country, the development of industrial and agricultural production, of economy, of education and culture, at the very moment when that part of the population which had temporarily escaped massacre was tottering on the edge of starvation in a state of primeval deprivation—schools had been destroyed, commerce had vanished, money had been abolished and, in the bush, some executioners practised cannibalism.

The total inversion of reality that was expressed in the leader's speeches was not part of a propaganda effort—it reflected Pol Pot's actual and sincere beliefs; and these beliefs, in turn, proved contagious, since neither his Chinese allies nor his Vietnamese enemies were ever able to perceive the imminence of his downfall. Having laid the country to waste and turned the population into deaf and mute beasts of burden, the ruling clique started to self-destruct by indulging in demented purges. And then, in this situation of instability and weakness, Pol Pot chose to launch border attacks against the Vietnamese enemy. Reacting to these insane provocations, the Vietnamese army, five times superior in strength, entered Phnom Penh after a *Blitzkrieg* whose swiftness and ease took everyone by surprise, including the invaders themselves.

Yet, after this complete and final collapse of their actual power, the Khmer Rouge did not vanish entirely. In order to counter an imaginary Soviet–Vietnamese menace (allegedly bent on subverting all South-East Asia), an improbable Sino–American alliance enabled the Khmer Rouge to survive artificially under two forms: in a few pockets of jungle on the Thai border, as smugglers and traffickers of rubies and precious timber; and in New York, as official representatives to the United Nations of a non-existent "Democratic Kampuchea." Thus, for another dozen years, the votes of the murderers carried in the General Assembly as much weight as the votes of—let us say—Germany and Japan, and more weight than the Vatican. (After the fall of Saigon in 1975, Kissinger asked the foreign affairs minister of Thailand to convey to Pol Pot the friendly wishes of the American people, adding for his interlocutor's benefit: "Of course, these people are murderous thugs, but this should not affect our good relations." The administration of Jimmy Carter—under the influence of Brzezinski, and notwithstanding the rhetorical emphasis which the president himself placed on human rights—pursued essentially the same line.)

If, in the long run, the extreme irrationality of the Pol Pot regime condemned it to disintegration, the recipe which ensured its absolute authority in the short term can be described in a single word: terror.

Regarding the system of terror established by the Khmer Rouge, we are rather well informed. At the highest level, the main centre for organised torture and death in Phnom Penh, the prison of Tuol Sleng, kept voluminous, detailed and meticulous archives. Its director, the chief torturer Duch, is also well known: on this subject, we already have the invaluable testimony of the French orientalist scholar François Bizot, who, before the Khmer Rouge came to power, was Duch's prisoner in the forest for several months in 1971. To Bizot's earlier report, first published in French in 2000 and later in English as *The Gate*, should now be added the statements and confessions which Duch himself has made since his arrest in 1999.

All the prisoners sent to Tuol Sleng were destined to be executed (of the 15,000 inmates that were successively processed in the prison during its three years of activity, there were only fourteen survivors). The task of the centre was to extract from these people confessions that would retrospectively justify their arrest and provide evidence and names for further arrests. They were not arrested because they were guilty: they were guilty because they were arrested. Guilty of what? Their confessions would tell. Quite often, their transfer was accompanied with instructions regarding the sort of crime to which they should confess, and then torture ensured that an adequate confession was obtained. For the accused person, the final outcome was already decided; only one thing still depended upon his own choice:

the length of his suffering under torture. The only way of shortening this was to produce a confession with names of accomplices, as suggested by the interrogator. All this senseless rubbish was minutely collected and stored in files—with some confessions being 100 pages long!

At the very beginning, Tuol Sleng still dealt with genuine enemies: former collaborators of the inept pro-American regime of Lon Nol. Very soon, however, such customers became scarce and, by the second year (1976), inner purges of the Khmer Rouge movement began to occupy all the attention and energy of interrogators and executioners. Eventually, during its last months of activity, the prison began to devour its own jailers!

When Phnom Penh fell into the hands of the Vietnamese, Duch, who had organised and supervised with tireless and scrupulous zeal the whole enterprise of interrogation, torture and death, vanished in the chaos of the rout. Twenty years later, someone recognised him by accident: he was employed in a remote town by a Christian association for humanitarian relief—he himself (he said) had converted to Christianity. Right now, he is being tried by the tribunal of Phnom Penh, a court jointly appointed by Cambodia and the United Nations to judge the crimes of the Khmer Rouge. He has already confessed: "I am profoundly sorry for all the murders, for the past. *My only desire was to be a good Communist.*"

Tuol Sleng was merely the highest organ of a vast repressive system whose tentacles embraced the entire country. In the south-west area *alone*, thirty-eight small Tuol Sleng centres for interrogation and torture have been counted, at a level immediately subordinate to that of Phnom Penh; furthermore, seventy-eight "killing fields" have been identified, as well as 6,000 charnel-houses. The slaughtering of condemned people was a dreary task, done by hand: the victims had their skulls smashed with a heavy club (their children were disposed of with less effort: they were thrown from the upper floors of buildings). In the conclusion of his book, Deron quotes the testimony of an American officer, Rick Arrant, who, attached to an information service, had to collect reports from Cambodian refugees at the Thai border; he remained haunted by what a woman had told him of the *sound* of those clubs smashing the skulls of prisoners kneeling on the edge of a freshly dug pit: "just like the sound of fallen coconuts hitting the ground." In 2003, this same officer was to take part in the American invasion of Iraq, where he was sent to…the prison of Abu Ghraib! (He has since changed his occupation: back in the Far East, he is pursuing field research for a work on the martyrdom of Cambodia.)

One mistake must be avoided. Descriptions of the Cambodian genocide strike our imaginations and shock our feelings—the horror is unbearable, and precisely because it is unbearable, we instinctively attempt to dismiss it from consciousness by supposing that these events, in their exotic remoteness, are so foreign to us that they might as well belong to another planet.

In fact, they concern us directly.

When the Khmer Rouge entered Phnom Penh, several Cambodians took refuge in the French embassy. The Khmer Rouge soon came to the embassy and demanded that these people be handed back to them, with the only exception being those who were carrying French passports. They threatened the *chargé d'affaires*: if their demand was not met within twenty-four hours, the embassy would be invaded and *all* its occupants would be arrested. In order to protect at least the 200-odd French and other foreign nationals who were sheltering in the embassy, the *chargé d'affaires* surrendered all his Cambodian guests into the hands of the Khmer Rouge—thus sending them to their deaths. He made a dreadful decision; but what was the alternative? Who would dare to judge him? A French journalist, however, in order to save one Cambodian woman (whom he did not know; he merely saw her despair) suggested that he marry the woman on the spot. The *chargé d'affaires* still had some 200 blank passports in his office—but he refused to proceed; he knew the journalist was already married, therefore this would be bigamy—which the law prohibits.

The Khmer Rouge perpetrated some two million murders. However, one of these at least should be put on the account of a Western diplomat, a man unable to perceive that, under a criminal authority, respect for the rules also becomes a crime. This conscientious bureaucrat was truly one of us.

———

Coincidence: as I was finishing my reading of Deron's book, I received a letter from an old Parisian friend—a faithful correspondent who, from time to time, keeps me informed of the latest happenings on the French literary and intellectual scene. He was commenting upon the return to fashion of a certain form of trendy Maoism:

> I cannot repress a feeling of apprehension when I consider how criminal Maoist lies manage to endure and to revive with complete impunity... Look for instance at the popular success now enjoyed by the "radical" thinker Alain Badiou, who prides himself on being an emeritus defender of the "Cultural Revolution." Badiou now writes, for example: "Regarding figures such as Robespierre, Saint-Just, Bakunin, Marx, Engels, Lenin, Trotsky, Stalin, Mao Zedong, Chou En-lai, Tito, Enver Hoxha, Guevara and a few others, it is of essential importance that we do not allow reactionary critics to neutralise and negate them, by means of outlandish anecdotes aiming at creating a context of criminalisation."

It is probably wrong of me to quote here this illustrious philosopher, whose works I never read (and I do not forget the old Chinese proverb—in fact, invented by Jacques Maritain—"Never take stupidity too seriously"). Yet I am shocked: what an injustice! *The name of Pol Pot has been omitted from Badiou's little pantheon.* He fully deserves a place there, especially at this precise moment: the "outlandish anecdotes" collected in Deron's book and "the context of criminalisation" now created by the Phnom Penh trial might otherwise "neutralise and negate" his glorious memory.

2009

ANATOMY OF A "POST-TOTALITARIAN" DICTATORSHIP

The Essays of Liu Xiaobo on China Today

> Better than the assent of the crowd: The dissent of one brave man!
>
> —SIMA QIAN (145–90 BC)
> *Records of the Grand Historian*

> Truth will set you free.
>
> —*Gospel according to John*

THE ECONOMIC rise of China now dominates the entire landscape of international affairs. In the eyes of political analysts and statesmen, China is seen as potentially "the world's largest economic power by 2019." Experts from financial institutions suggest an even earlier date for such a prognosis: "China," one has said, "will become the largest economy in the world by 2016." This fast transformation is rightly called "the Chinese miracle." The general consensus, in China as well as abroad, is that the twenty-first century will be "China's century." International statesmen fly to Peking, while businessmen from all parts of the developed world are rushing to Shanghai and other provincial metropolises in the hope of securing deals. Europe is begging China to come to the rescue of its ailing currency.

All thinking people wish now to obtain at least some basic understanding of the deeper dynamics that underlie this sudden and stupendous metamorphosis: What are its true nature and significance? To

Review of Liu Xiaobo: *No Enemies, No Hatred: Selected Essays and Poems*, edited by Perry Link, Tienchi Martin-Liao, and Liu Xia, foreword by Václav Havel (Cambridge: Belknap Press/Harvard University Press, 2012).

what extent is it viable and real? Where is it heading? Bookshops are now submerged by a tidal wave of new publications attempting to provide information about China, and yet there is (it seems to me) one new book whose reading should be of urgent and essential importance, both for the specialist and for the general reader alike—the new collection of essays by Liu Xiaobo, judiciously selected, translated, and presented by very competent scholars, whose work greatly benefited from their personal acquaintance with the author.[1]

The award of the Nobel Peace Prize in 2010 brought the name of Liu Xiaobo to the attention of the entire world. Yet well before that, he had already achieved considerable fame within China, as a fearless and clearsighted public intellectual and the author of some seventeen books, including collections of poetry and literary criticism as well as political essays. The Communist authorities unwittingly vouched for the uncompromising accuracy of his comments. They kept arresting him for his views—four times since the Tiananmen massacre in June 1989. Now he is again in jail, since December 2008; though in poor health, he is subjected to an especially severe regime. As Pascal said, "Trust witnesses willing to sacrifice their lives," and this particular witness happens to be exceptionally well qualified in other ways as well, both by the depth of his information and experience, and by his qualities of intelligence and moral fortitude.

———

Born in 1955 in northeastern China, Liu truly belongs to the generation of "Mao's children," which, by an interesting paradox, eventually produced the boldest dissenters and most articulate activists in favour of democracy—for example, Wei Jingsheng, hero of the Democracy Wall episode in Peking between 1978 and 1979, who spent eighteen harsh years in prison before being exiled to the West. Liu Xiaobo pays frequent homage to these early pioneers. He was too young to participate in the Cultural Revolution, but this movement—ironically—had a positive impact upon his life.

Like most intellectuals, his parents, who were teachers, were deported to a collective farm in the countryside; having followed them there, Liu was mercifully deprived for several years of all conventional schooling. He was to appreciate it in retrospect: these years of lost schooling "allowed me freedom." Escaping the indoctrination of Maoist pedagogy, he read at random a huge variety of books—all the printed matter he could lay his hands on—and thus discovered the principle that was to guide him from then on: one must think for oneself.

After Mao's death, universities were at long last allowed to reopen; in 1977 Liu joined the first group of students admitted again into higher education, first in his home province, later on at Peking Normal University. He pursued studies in Chinese literature with great success; finally, eleven years later, after obtaining his doctorate, he was appointed to a teaching post in the same university. His original mind, vast intellectual curiosity, and gifts for expression ensured a brilliant academic career; quite early, he reached a large audience extending far beyond the classroom, and acquired the reputation of an enfant terrible in the Chinese cultural world.

In the debates over literature and ideas, his views were refreshingly free from dogmatic convention; yet at this early stage, he did not get involved in political issues. The turning point of his development took place in 1989, with the Tiananmen massacre on June 4 and its aftermath. Shortly before, Liu's reputation as an original critic of ideas had brought him invitations abroad. Meanwhile, in Peking, the movement of political protest and demands for democratic reform were gathering momentum: a huge crowd of students together with their enthusiastic supporters and sympathizers had gathered and camped on Tiananmen Square, the very heart of the capital.

At that moment, Liu Xiaobo was in New York, having accepted an invitation to teach political science at Columbia's Barnard College. Like many Chinese intellectuals before him, Liu had first idealized the West; however, his experiences, first in Europe and then in the United States, soon shattered his illusions. During a visit to the Metropolitan Museum in New York, he experienced a sort of epiphany that crystallized the turmoil of his latest self-questioning: he realized the shallowness of his own learning in the light of the fabulous riches of the diverse civilizations of the past, and simultaneously perceived the inadequacy of contemporary Western answers to mankind's modern predicament. His own dream that Westernization could be used to reform China suddenly appeared to him as pathetic as the attitude of "a paraplegic laughing at a quadriplegic," he confessed at the time:

> My tendency to idealize Western civilization arises from my nationalistic desire to use the West in order to reform China. But this has led me to overlook the flaws of Western culture.... I have been obsequious toward Western civilization, exaggerating its merits, and at the same time exaggerating my own merits. I have viewed the West as if it were not only the salvation of China but also the natural and ultimate destination of all humanity. Moreover I have used this delusional idealism to assign myself the role of saviour....
>
> I now realize that Western civilization, while it can be useful in reforming China in its present stage, cannot save humanity in an overall sense.
>
> If we stand back from Western civilization for a moment, we can see that it possesses all the flaws of humanity in general....
>
> If I, as a person who has lived under China's autocratic system for more than thirty years, want to reflect on the fate of humanity or how to be an authentic person, I have no choice but to carry out two critiques simultaneously. I must:
>
> 1. Use Western civilization as a tool to critique China.
> 2. Use my own creativity to critique the West.

While Liu was still in New York, the student movement in Peking continued to develop, not realizing that it was now set on a collision course with the hard-line faction of the Communist leadership—the faction to which Deng Xiaoping was finally to give free rein. But Liu sensed that a crisis would soon be reached, and he made a grave and generous decision: he gave up the safety and comfort of his New York academic appointment and rushed back to Peking. He did not leave the square during the last dramatic days of the students' demonstration; he desperately tried to persuade them that democratic politics must be "politics without hatred and without enemies," and simultaneously, after martial law was imposed, he negotiated with the army in the hope of obtaining a peaceful evacuation of the square.

Thanks to his intervention, countless lives were saved, though in the end he could not prevent wider carnage—we still don't know how many students, innocent bystanders, and even volunteer rescuers disappeared during the bloodbath of that final night. Liu himself was arrested in the street three days after the massacre and imprisoned without trial for the next two years. He came out of jail a changed man. He was dismissed from the university and banned from publishing and from giving any public lectures within China.

Owing to the Internet, however ("the Internet is truly God's gift to the Chinese people," as he was to say later on), he was able to develop a new career as a freelance commentator on Chinese society and culture. His articles and essays were published overseas in various Chinese-language periodicals (mostly in Hong Kong and Taiwan); and within China itself, he reached a wide readership through the Web, which still frustrates official censorship. His influence and prestige among Chinese dissidents culminated in December 2008 with his sponsorship of Charter 08—a collective document inspired by the example set thirty years earlier in Communist Czechoslovakia by Václav Havel and his friends, Charter 77.

Charter 08 is a model of moderation and cool reason: it spells out the basic principles and fundamental rights that should inspire China's long-overdue political reform: an ideal of democracy, humanism, and nonviolence, institutionally guaranteed by separation of powers, freedom of opinion, "free and fair competition among political parties," and the establishment of a federal republic (which, in fact, had already been envisioned a century ago, when the first Chinese republic was established).

There is nothing in such a program that should appear radical or inflammatory. Zhao Ziyang—former Chinese prime minister (1980–1987), former general secretary of the Communist Party (1987–1989), and the main architect of the first movement of reform and opening to the outside world in the post-Mao era—came in his final years to express views that are remarkably similar to those of Charter 08. At the end of his life, during his enforced internal exile, Zhao came to the conclusion—clearly expressed in his political testament—that the Chinese political system needed to be reformed:

> "Dictatorship of the proletariat" has become a rigid, purely formal structure, protecting the tyranny of a minority—or of a single person; the way of the future, towards true modernization, is parliamentary democracy—on the Western model. This transformation would probably require a fairly long period of transition; yet it is feasible, as it is already shown by the examples of Taiwan and South Korea....

All the essays of Liu Xiaobo included in the present volume deal with a period of twenty years—from Tiananmen to Charter 08. During this period, though several times arrested and detained without trial, Liu was active in freelance political journalism. Having no regular employment, he managed to make a precarious living with his pen.

Some of the essays focus on specific events, from which the author draws deeper lessons; others address broader sociopolitical and cultural issues, which are then illustrated with examples drawn from current incidents.

A good example of the first type is provided by an important article exposing the horrendous case of the "Black Kilns." (Later on, at Liu's last trial, this was one of the six essays adduced as evidence of his criminal attempt at "subversion of state power.") In May 2007, parents of children who had gone missing in Henan province reported their disappearance to courageous local television journalists. It turned out that operators of the brick kilns in Shanxi province had organized large kidnapping networks to supply their kilns with slave labour, and local authorities in two provinces had apparently been complicit in these criminal rackets.

The police proved singularly inept in their attempt to dismantle these abominable networks: only a small number of children were found and rescued—10 percent of the more than one thousand missing. Penal sanctions, which are usually ruthless in dealing with dissent from Party authority, were glaringly perfunctory and superficial: ninety-five Party members and public officials were involved, but they were merely subjected to "Party discipline," and not to criminal charges. Higher officials only received "serious warning from the Party." Liu concludes: "The mighty government, with all of its advantages and vast resources, is not ready to do battle with the Chinese underworld." The main concern of the Communist Party, he writes, is to maintain its tight monopoly over all public power. Officials at every level are appointed, promoted, or dismissed at the exclusive will of a private group: the Party itself.

> The first priority of officials is always to serve the higher-ups (because, in effect, this serves oneself) and not to serve the people below.

As for the judicial system—also used by the Party to protect its monopoly of power—it is utterly reluctant to tackle issues involving the alliance between the Party and the underworld:

> In China the underworld and officialdom have interpenetrated and become one. Criminal elements have become officialized as officials have become criminalized. Underworld chiefs carry titles in the National People's Congress and the People's Political Consultative Conference, while civil officials rely on the underworld to keep the lid on local society.

Another essay deals with the "Land Problem." In the Mao era, farmers lost their land and were reduced to virtual serfdom in the "communes." They were bound to work on land that was no longer theirs. During the catastrophic madness of the Great Leap Forward the poverty of the farmers reached the point where they did not have food to eat or clothes to wear. In some places people were driven to cannibalism. More than forty million people starved to death during the great Mao-made famine of 1958–1962. Not long after Mao died in 1976, a "half-baked liberation" of the serfs took place: farmers were given the right not to own land but to use it, unless farmland needed to be "developed" and it then reverted to state property.

> Officials wielding the power of the state and invoking "government-ownership of land" have colluded with businessmen all across our country.... The biggest beneficiaries of the resultant land deals, at all levels, have been the Communist regime and the power elite.... Farmers are the weakest among the weak. Without a free press and an independent judiciary, they have no public voice, no right to organize farmers' associations, and no means of legal redress.... And that is why, when all recourse within the system...is stifled, people are naturally drawn to collective action *outside* the system....
>
> Most of the major clashes that have broken out in China in recent years have pitted commoners against officials. Most have occurred at the grassroots in the countryside, and most have been about land. Local officials, protecting the vested interests of the power elite, have been willing to use a range of savage means, drawing on government violence as well as on the violence of the criminal underworld, to repress the uprisings.

Apart from Liu's essays dealing with injustices and various forms of criminal abuses of power, other articles address more general questions: for instance, the meaning and implications of the rise of China as a great power, still a matter of great uncertainty. The very rapid growth of a market economy and people's increased awareness of private property rights have generated enormous popular demand for more freedom, and this ultimately might have an effect on China's international position. On the other hand, the Communist government's

> jealous defense of its dictatorial system and of the special privileges of the power elite has become the biggest obstacle to movement in the direction of freedom.... As long as China remains a dictatorial one-party state, it will never "rise" to become a mature civilized country....

The Chinese Communists ... are concentrating on economics, seeking to make themselves part of globalization, and are courting friends internationally precisely by discarding their erstwhile ideology.

At home, they defend their dictatorial system any way they can, [whereas abroad] they have become a blood-transfusion machine for a host of other dictatorships. ... When the "rise" of a large dictatorial state that commands rapidly increasing economic strength meets with no effective deterrence from outside, but only an attitude of appeasement from the international mainstream, and if the Communists succeed in once again leading China down a disastrously mistaken historical road, the results will not only be another catastrophe for the Chinese people, but likely also a disaster for the spread of liberal democracy in the world. If the international community hopes to avoid these costs, free countries must do what they can to help the world's largest dictatorship transform itself as quickly as possible into a free and democratic country.

Yet what hope is there for such a transformation to take place? The regime itself is rigid. After more than twenty years of "reform," the only feature of Maoist ideology that is being unconditionally retained by the Communist Party is the principle of its absolute monopoly over political power. There is no prospect that any organization will be able to muster the political force sufficient to bring regime change anytime soon. Liu writes: "There is ... no sign, within the ruling elite of an enlightened figure like Mikhail Gorbachev or Chiang Ching-kuo, who ... helped turn the USSR and Taiwan toward democracy." Civil society is unable to produce in the near term a political organization that might replace the Communist regime.

In an essay titled "To Change a Regime by Changing a Society" (also cited as evidence in his criminal trial), Liu spells out his hopes: political tyranny would remain, but the people would no longer be ignorant or atomized; there would be a new awareness of solidarity in the face of injustice, and a common indignation provoked by the blatant corruption and the various abuses of power committed by local authorities. There would be new advances in civic courage, greater awareness of people's rights. Also greater economic independence fosters more freedom on the part of citizens to move, to acquire, and to share information.

The Internet in particular enables exchanges and diffusion of ideas in ways that largely escape government censorship; government control of thought and speech grows less and less effective. To become a free society, the only road for China can be that of a gradual improvement from the bottom up. This gradual transformation of society will eventually force a transformation of the regime.

However, in direct contradiction to such hopes, Liu also bleakly describes the spiritual desert of the urban culture in "post-totalitarian China." The authorities, he writes, are enforcing a rigorous amnesia of the recent past. The Tiananmen massacre has been entirely erased from the minds of a new generation—while crude nationalism is being whipped up from time to time to distract attention from more disturbing issues. Literature, magazines, films, and videos all overflow with sex and violence reflecting "the moral squalor of our society."

China has entered an Age of Cynicism in which people no longer believe in anything.... Even high officials and other Communist Party members no longer believe Party verbiage. Fidelity to cherished beliefs has been replaced by loyalty to anything that brings material benefit. Unrelenting inculcation of Chinese Communist Party ideology has...produced generations of people whose memories are blank....

The post-Tiananmen urban generation, raised with prospects of moderately good living conditions, [have now as their main goals] to become an official, get rich, or go abroad.... They have no patience at all for people who talk about suffering in history.... A huge Great Leap famine? A devastating Cultural Revolution? A Tiananmen massacre? All of this criticizing of the government and exposing of the society's "dark side" is, in their view, completely unnecessary. They prefer to use their own indulgent lifestyles plus the stories that officialdom feeds them as proof that China has made tremendous progress.

I know of Western liberals who, confronted with the extreme puritanism of the Maoist era, naïvely assumed that, after long repression, sexual liberation was bound to explode sooner or later and would act like dynamite and open the way toward a freer society. Now an "erotic carnival" (Liu's words) of sex, violence, and greed is indeed sweeping through the entire country, but—as Liu describes it—this wave merely reflects the moral collapse of a society that has been emptied of all values during the long years of its totalitarian brutalization: "The craze for political revolution in decades past has now turned into a craze for money and sex."

Some on the left attribute the present spiritual and moral emptiness of Chinese society to the spread of the market and to globalization, which are also blamed for China's enormous corruption. On the contrary, Liu shows that the deep roots of today's cynicism, hedonism, and moral bankruptcy must be traced back to the Mao era. It was then, at a time that leftist nostalgia now paints as one of moral purity, that the nation's spirit suffered its worst devastation; the regime was

> antihumane and antimoral.... The cruel "struggle" that Mao's tyranny infused throughout society caused people to scramble to sell their souls: hate your spouse, denounce your father, betray your friend, pile on a helpless victim, say anything to remain "correct." The blunt, unreasoning bludgeons of Mao's political campaigns, which arrived in an unending parade, eventually demolished even the most commonplace of ethical notions in Chinese life.

This pattern has abated in the post-Mao years, but it has far from disappeared. After the Tiananmen massacre, the campaign of compulsory amnesia once again forced people to betray their consciences in public shows of loyalty. "If China has turned into a nation of people who lie to their own consciences, how can we possibly build healthy public values?" And Liu concludes:

> The inhumanity of the Mao era, which left China in moral shambles, is the most important cause of the widespread and

oft-noted "values vacuum" that we observe today. In this situation sexual indulgence becomes a handy partner for a dictatorship that is trying to stay on top of a society of rising prosperity.... The idea of sexual freedom did not support political democracy so much as it harked back to traditions of sexual abandon in China's imperial times.... This has been just fine with today's dictators. It fits with the moral rot and political gangsterism that years of hypocrisy have generated, and it diverts the thirst for freedom into a politically innocuous direction.

In a last short piece written in November 2008, Liu looked "Behind the 'China Miracle.'" Following the Tiananmen massacre, Deng Xiaoping attempted to restore his authority and to reassert his regime's legitimacy after both had melted away because of the massacre. He set out to build his power through economic growth. As the economy began to flourish, many officials saw an opportunity to make sudden and enormous profits; their unscrupulous pursuit of private gain became the engine of the ensuing economic boom. The most highly profitable of the state monopolies have fallen into the hands of small groups of powerful officials. The Communist Party has only one principle left: any action can be justified if it upholds the dictatorship or results in greater spoils. Liu concludes:

In sum, China's economic transformation, which from the outside can appear so vast and deep, in fact is frail and superficial.... The combination of spiritual and material factors that spurred political reform in the 1980s—free-thinking intellectuals, passionate young people, private enterprise that attended to ethics, dissidents in society, and a liberal faction within the Communist Party—have all but vanished. In their place we have a single-barreled economic program that is driven only by lust for profit.

One month after writing this, on December 8, 2008, Liu was arrested and eventually charged with "inciting subversion of state power"—whereas his only activity was, and has always been, simply to express his opinions. After a parody of a trial—which the public was not allowed to attend—he was sentenced to eleven years in jail on December 25, 2009.[2] When, one year later, he was awarded the Nobel Peace Prize, Chinese authorities acted hysterically: his wife, his friends, and his acquaintances were all subjected to various forms of arbitrary detention to ensure that none of them would be able to go to Oslo to collect the prize on his behalf. Today his wife, Liu Xia, is in her second year of house arrest without charges. These dramatic measures had one clear historical precedent: in 1935, the Nazi authorities gave the same treatment to the jailed political dissenter Carl von Ossietsky.

At the Oslo ceremony, an empty chair was substituted for the absent laureate. Within hours, the words "empty chair" were banned from the Internet in China—wherever they occurred, the entire machinery of censorship was automatically set in motion.

Foreign experts in various intelligence organizations are trying to assess the growing strength of China, politically, economically, and militarily. The Chinese leaders are most likely to have a clear view of their own power. If so, why are they so scared of a frail and powerless poet and essayist, locked away in jail, cut off from all human contacts? Why did the mere sight of his empty chair at the other end of the Eurasian continent plunge them into such a panic?

POSTSCRIPT

More than half a century ago, Czesław Miłosz (who was particularly well placed to comment on such matters) warned us that, contrary to what we tend to assume, our traditions, our social and legal institutions, cannot ensure us any real or permanent protection against gross abuses of state authority:

The man of the East cannot take Americans seriously because they have never undergone the experiences that teach men how relative their judgments and thinking habits are. Their resultant lack of imagination is appalling.... *If something exists in one place, it will exist everywhere.*

This phrase has a particular resonance for me. For the last five years, I have been engaged in a long, gruesome battle with Belgian officialdom (Belgium—the "Stateless State," as the regretted Tony Judt aptly called it—is my country of origin). The blunder of a consular official had illegally deprived two Belgian citizens by birth of their sole nationality—reducing them to statelessness. It would have been easy enough to correct the original mistake, but (as Liu Xiaobo remarked in different circumstances) the main concern and industry of bureaucrats is not to rectify their mistakes, but to conceal them. The fate of these two young men, suddenly turned stateless by sheer administrative stupidity, is of particular concern to me: they happen to be my twin sons.

A Chinese friend who knows of my predicament remarked that, since over the years I have spent much time denouncing Chinese abuses of power, it would be sensible for me now to look closer to home. He has a point; yet reading Liu Xiaobo has not been a diversion from my duty toward my family: it gave me added awareness that, in the defense of human rights, our fight is universal and indivisible.

One interesting twist in the unfolding of the Belgian government's denial of my sons' rights: the diplomat who was the main architect of a cover-up (which still delays the judicial resolution of the affair) recently obtained the posting he long coveted, as a reward for his zeal—he is now ambassador in Peking, where he ought to feel like a fish in the water. Our present Belgian ambassador in Australia, also knowing the truth, came to apologize *privately*. Unfortunately, he cannot do so publicly; as he said, this would be the end of his career. Why?

February 2012

Part IV
THE SEA

FOREWORD TO *THE SEA IN FRENCH LITERATURE*

OBJECTS AND LIMITS OF THIS ANTHOLOGY

JOSEPH Conrad remarked that the love of literature does not make a writer, any more than the love of the sea makes a sailor. This is cruelly true: poor frustrated lovers—failed writers and armchair sailors—may this anthology at least bring you some consolation!

In my undertaking, I set myself three rules, while allowing myself two infractions, which I ought to mention at the outset.

First rule: in principle, all the selections in this anthology deal with *the sea*. In practice, however, I did not narrowly limit myself to salt water; here and there, my readers will also encounter lakes, rivers and canals. Strictly speaking, the title of my anthology should thus be modified—putting *Water* instead of *The Sea*—but such a title would lose in flavour what it could gain in accuracy.

Second rule: this is not an anthology of *sea* literature, it is a *literary* anthology of the sea. One could very well compile a collection of documentary writings, narratives and accounts by navigators, adventurers, seamen, sportsmen, oceanographers, yachtsmen, castaways, etc.; such a collection could provide diverse and fascinating information, but it would constitute an altogether different enterprise. As a rule, my selection draws exclusively from the works of *writers*. On this point, I am afraid you might quarrel with me here and there: "Why," you might say, "do you grant Marteilhe, Duguay-Trouin, Garneray[1] the qualification of 'writer' which you deny Gerbault, Bombard,

---

La Mer dans la littérature française, Vol. 1 de François Rabelais à Alexandre Dumas, Vol. 2 de Victor Hugo à Pierre Loti (Paris: Plon, 2003).

Moitessier or Tabarly?"[2] Of course, I could attempt to justify myself, invoking the fact that, in the past, amateur memorialists often wrote with more verve and style than many modern writers, but I ought better honestly admit that, in some cases, I broke my own rule: some pages should perhaps have been omitted. If I retained them, it is simply because they pertain to books that I admire and love, but which I feel have been unfairly ignored or forgotten and deserve to be revived.

Third rule: all the pieces selected (even when written by foreigners) were originally written in French.[3] This rule has suffered no exception.

My very first intention had been to make a universal anthology of the sea in literature—the Bible, Homer, Virgil, Li Bai, Su Dongpo, Camoens, Defoe, Hugo, Dana, Melville, Conrad... but I soon realised the huge naïveté and incoherence of such a project; furthermore, as regards the Anglo-American domain, it has already been covered by a number of excellent anthologies.[4] Last but not least, from a first random survey, I began to perceive that French sources would provide rich and original material, which alone would easily justify being gathered in one volume (actually I ended up with two, totalling more than 1,500 pages).

In contrast with Great Britain, where, for obvious geographical and historical reasons, language and culture have always been closely related to the sea,[5] France, whose maritime ventures were hardly less impressive, never succeeded in integrating these into the national consciousness. The problem was that French seafaring activities were essentially confined to the provinces—Flanders, Normandy, Brittany, Gascogne, Basque country, Provence—whereas from the point of view of Paris, which, alas, commands everything, the sea remained generally invisible. And yet it never ceased to inspire writers, including some of the greatest: Rabelais, Chateaubriand, Hugo, Baudelaire, Michelet, Valéry... The sea is truly present in French literature, though its actual importance is still not sufficiently appreciated, and I hope that my anthology may be a first step towards remedying this ignorance.

MAN AND THE SEA

The fascination that the sea exerts upon even the most insensitive landlubbers is a universal phenomenon which can be observed on all the shores of the world. Robert Frost captured this everyday mystery in a poem of mesmerising simplicity (by the way, do not be surprised to find an abundance of English and American quotes in this introduction to a *French* anthology: since they were eventually excluded from the main body of my work, this is a way for me to salvage at least some of the material I had originally selected):

> The people along the sand
> All turn and look one way;
> They turn their back on the land,
> They look at the sea all day.
>
> As long as it takes to pass
> A ship keeps raising its hull;
> The wetter ground like glass
> Reflects a standing gull.
>
> The land may vary more,
> But wherever the truth may be
> The water comes ashore
> And the people look at the sea.
>
> They cannot look out far
> They cannot look in deep,
> But when was that ever a bar
> To any watch they keep?[6]

Should we therefore conclude that the love of the sea is a common feature of all mankind? Edmund Wilson denied this with a strange sort of angry passion in a short essay on "Things I Consider Overrated":

I believe that a genuine love for the sea is one of the rarest things in the world; it is a special and bizarre taste, very seldom acquired. Of course, everybody loves the sea as it appears from the shore:...here the sea is romantic and beautiful because one does not have to see too much of it. But what can be said for it in its absolute state, with no beach to civilize it? How can one enjoy its colossal stupidity, its monotony, its flatness?...It is as sterile as the Sahara; its lifelessness is overpowering. On a sea voyage one finds oneself shut in and oppressed by the presence of a great nothingness. It is really not picturesque: it is too empty for that...all the waves resemble one another perfectly and there are millions of them in sight; it makes one uncomfortable to see them all behave in precisely the same manner. The human soul is appalled and ashamed by the primal stupidity of Nature. On board ship, the spirit of man, baffled and repelled by the ocean, feels its life swept uncomfortably bare by the disappearance of its proper setting. It is a prisoner, a slave,—with an unassailable jailor, a jailor who is incorruptible because it cannot feel or understand, because it is not sufficiently intelligent to accept a bribe...[7]

Yet this idea that the sea is a jail—or, more precisely, that a sailor's condition is the condition of a convict—is not a new one. Samuel Johnson had already expressed it in most memorable fashion: "No man will be a sailor who has contrivance enough to get himself into a jail; for being in a ship is being in a jail, with the chance of being drowned....A man in a jail has more room, better food and commonly better company."[8] But it must be said that, in Johnson's time—and until not so long ago—life at sea was barbarous indeed. The catalogue of its miseries makes one shudder: stinking discomfort, inhumane crowdedness, permanent humidity, the heat and the cold, rats, vermin, mouldy and rotting food, brackish water, brutishness of the company, sadistic ferocity of the ship's discipline, constant risk of breaking one's neck or drowning when falling from a yard in heavy weather, danger of shipwreck, permanent menace of scurvy on long voyages, death after slow, hideous agony...

Johnson's utterances on this subject do not merely reflect the prejudices of an eccentric genius who had no experience of the sea;[9] they were constantly confirmed by countless reliable witnesses, and it is quite impressive to note that, more than a century later, a writer as superbly qualified as Robert Louis Stevenson could state it again: life at sea is not liveable. After having explored the Pacific for six months on board a superb schooner he had chartered for this very purpose, he confessed in a letter to a friend: "And yet the sea is a horrible place, stupefying to the mind and poisonous to the temper; the sea, the motion, the lack of space, the cruel publicity, the villainous tinned foods, the sailors, the captain, the passengers—but you are amply repaid when you sight an island, and drop anchor in a new world."[10]

Still, whenever Stevenson evokes the sea in his writings, he does it with convincing expressive power. Is it not precisely because his personal experience had freed him from the illusions and stereotypes that too often mar or adulterate the images of the sea offered by even some of the greatest writers? Think of Baudelaire, for instance. Baudelaire's youthful seafaring adventure was less serious than is often assumed; he later drew some magnificent metaphors from the sea, but he also made bombastic statements, the hollowness of which make true seamen laugh. On his famous and grandiloquent apostrophe "*Homme libre, toujours tu chériras la mer!*" one is tempted to pour cold water, such as this description of a nasty squall by the great sailor Éric Tabarly: "...down below [on board *Pen Duick II*] the drenched sails spill water everywhere: it is a fucking mess, but now is not the time for housekeeping. All through the night, in turns, I lie down, taking off my wet-weather gear, then putting it on again and climbing back on deck to reset the tension of the sheets to match the ceaseless wind-shifts. To the naïve dreamers who believe they will find freedom on the high seas, I have only this advice: look for it elsewhere!"[11]

Quite often, when sea lyricism flows on the written page, it is completely at odds with the author's actual experiences on the water. One of the best examples of this divorce is provided by John Masefield's *Sea Fever* (1902)—perhaps the most popular sea poem in the English language: "I must go down to the seas again, to the lonely sea and the sky, / And all I ask is a tall ship and a star to steer her by..." etc.[12]

On each re-reading, this poem unfailingly delivers its impact with the humiliating efficiency of a punch to the stomach. But why is its wizardry of such dubious quality? When adolescent, Masefield had been sent to join a sail training ship. As he suffered from sea-sickness, he hated the experience, which lasted for a year or so, and it was to remain for him the most wretched period of his life. Once the ordeal was over, he swore never again to set foot on a boat and settled down as far inland as possible for the remainder of his days. Simultaneously, however, he shrewdly undertook a lyrical exploitation of his aborted maritime career, without disclosing its nauseous reality. This innocent trickery cost him a high price in aesthetic terms: his clever verses stand for all time as the ultimate example of nautical kitsch.

To the glib chatter of phony mariners, true sailors answer only with silence. It is as if the very gifts of imagination and expression that characterise writers, and the stolid virtues of self-control and sound judgement indispensable to seamen, were mutually exclusive. In his famous *Typhoon*, Joseph Conrad shows that it is Captain McWhirr's very lack of imagination that enabled him to face unflinchingly the fury of wind and waves—and to save his ship. Yet, the danger once overcome, he could not even manage to communicate his experience: he wrote to his wife, but the letter was so long and boring that Mrs. McWhirr did not even bother to read it to the end.

Should we conclude that sea adventure is essentially an invention of landlubbers? One would be inclined to invoke here the ancient Daoist wisdom: "Those who know don't speak; those who speak don't know." And the fact is, most sailors don't have much to tell about the sea. It is simply their natural element; when at sea, they feel at home. One of the most colourful sea adventurers, Sir Francis Drake, summed it up with disarming and terse sincerity: "It is not that life ashore is distasteful to me. But life at sea is better."[13] What can one add to that? On this topic, seamen always repeat the same thing. Thus, in one of his last essays, Conrad confessed: "The monotony of the sea is easier to bear than the boredom of the shore."[14] And earlier on, in a short story (which, paradoxically, is a masterpiece of disturbing and suspenseful ambiguity), he described the feeling of peace and relief experienced by a sea captain who, after a long stay ashore, finds himself again with a good ship under his feet: "And suddenly I rejoiced in the great security of the sea, as compared with the unrest of the land, in my choice of that untempted life presenting no disquieting problems, invested with an elementary moral beauty by the absolute straightforwardness of its appeal and by the singleness of its purpose."[15]

Between the eloquence of literary men (who talk about what they do not know) and the silence of sailors (who know but do not talk), there are fortunately a few sailors who decided to write—such as Conrad—and a few writers who learned to sail—such as Hilaire Belloc, whom I have not quoted yet but to whom I wish to leave the last word. The final page of his *Cruise of the "Nona"* expresses exactly the feelings that sustained me through the long years I spent working on this anthology:

The sea is the consolation of this our day, as it has been the consolation of the centuries. It is the companion and the receiver of men. It has moods for them to fill the storehouse of the mind, perils for trial, or even for an ending, and calms for the good emblem of death. There, on the sea, is a man nearest to his own making, and in communion with that from which he came, and to which he shall return. For the wise men of very long ago have said, and it is true, that out of salt water all things came. The sea is the matrix of creation, and we have the memory of it in our blood.

But far more than this is there in the sea. It presents, upon the greatest scale we mortals can bear, those not mortal powers that brought us into being. It is not only the symbol or the mirror, but especially it is the messenger of the Divine.

There, sailing the sea, we play every part of life: control, direction, effort, fate; and there can we test ourselves and know our state. All that which concerns the sea is profound and final. The sea provides visions, darknesses, revelations. The sea puts ever before us those twin faces of reality: greatness and certitude; greatness stretched almost to the edge of infinity (greatness in extent, greatness in changes not to be numbered), and the certitude of a level remaining for ever and standing upon the deeps. The sea has taken me to itself whenever I sought it and has given me relief from men. It has rendered remote the cares and the wastes of the land; for of all creatures that move and breathe upon the earth we of mankind are the fullest of sorrow. But the sea shall comfort us, and perpetually show us new things and assure us. It is the common sacrament of this world. May it be to others what it has been to me.[16]

IN THE WAKE OF MAGELLAN

WHAT DO you know about Magellan?

Ask this question of any educated person—a person (according to John Cowper Powys) whose culture is made of what remains after one has forgotten all one set out to learn—and you will probably receive the answer: Portuguese navigator who demonstrated that the earth is round when he achieved the first circumnavigation of the globe, in the early sixteenth century.

This answer is incomplete and partly mistaken.

First, though Magellan was indeed Portuguese, he sailed for Spain—personally commissioned by Charles V. His foreign origin provoked suspicion and resentment among his Castilian officers; some of them detested him, and their hostility was to climax in a mutiny that nearly brought the entire expedition to a premature end.

Secondly, Magellan died halfway through the voyage, killed in an absurd fight with Filipino natives whom he was recklessly attempting to teach a lesson. The circumnavigation was not achieved by him but by his lieutenant Elcano (one of his earlier enemies).

Thirdly, it had been known since the time of ancient Greece that the earth is round. A classical mathematician had even calculated—quite accurately—its circumference. A majority of the Fathers of the Church inherited this knowledge and shared it with many medieval scholars. What the expedition actually demonstrated—turning Magellan into the unwitting forefather of globalisation—was the circumnavigability of the globe: oceans all communicate; contrary to what early cartographers imagined, they are not inland seas surrounded by impassable continental walls.

Finally, the circumnavigation was improvised under the pressure of circumstances; it never was the purpose of the expedition. The original objective was quite different: it was, in fact, an attempt to find an alternative route to the spices of the East. And indeed, the royal instruction had clearly prescribed that the expedition should return by the very same way they came.

At the beginning of the Renaissance, the first great voyages of discovery were accomplished by Portuguese navigators; their daring and seamanship remained for a long time unequalled in the Western world. First, they succeeded in sailing round Africa; then they pushed further east to India, and finally they reached the Malay Peninsula. The initial impulse of these prodigious voyages had been religious and strategic: the idea was to establish a direct link between Western Christianity and the mythical Prester John, who (it was first believed) would be found in Ethiopia, and then was supposed to have settled in India. In this way, it might become possible eventually to encircle Islam. However, in the course of this elusive quest, it was very quickly realised that the venture could also generate fabulous commercial profits through the importation of spices.

Together with gold, spices constituted for several centuries the main value standard in the economic life of Europe. Pepper was sold by the grain (and it was the same in China: during the Ming dynasty, imperial civil servants were paid partly in money and partly in measures of pepper). Besides pepper, there were also cloves and nutmeg: their sole production centre was in the Moluccas; Westerners merely knew the names of these islands, but had not yet reached their shores. For a long time, Eastern spices were brought westwards by Arab traders, up to Egypt; then, from Alexandria, their distribution throughout Europe belonged to the monopoly of Venice.

Yet, once the Portuguese settled on the Malabar Coast, and then, more importantly, in Malacca, they began to deal directly with Malay coastal traders who were bringing spices from the Moluccas straight to their factories. Thus bypassing the old Arabo-Venetian monopoly, Portugal suddenly found itself in control of an inexhaustible source of riches. Spain soon wished to imitate its example. To prevent their commercial competition turning into armed conflict—which would dangerously weaken the Christian world—the two kingdoms adopted a solution originally proposed by the Pope: by treaties, the world would be divided into two halves: the eastern one belonging to Portugal and the western one to Spain. Since this agreement forbade Spanish ships using the traditional eastern sea route to the Spice Islands, the idea of trying to reach them by a westward route became increasingly attractive. In fact, this had already been the dream of Christopher Columbus: until his death (in 1506) Columbus remained convinced that he had landed in the Far East—and he believed that, had he sailed a few hundred leagues further north, he would have reached Hangzhou, the former capital of the Chinese empire!

However, by the early years of the sixteenth century, an awareness grew that between Western Europe and Eastern Asia there stood a continental barrier. The breadth of this "Terra Firma" was grossly underestimated, and its length was still unknown; also, it was soon realised that an unknown sea, the "South Sea" (Pacific Ocean), did lie on its other side: Balboa saw it after crossing on foot the Isthmus of Panama (in 1513). But how could this sea be reached by boat?

Two years after Balboa's discovery, a Portuguese navigator followed the Brazilian coast southwards and eventually reached the vast estuary of Río de la Plata. He sailed into it, believing it was the entrance of a passage leading to the South Sea. He realised the mistake too late: local Indians killed and ate him (in 1516).

The division of the world into two hemispheres was largely theoretical: in practice, the boundary could not be drawn with precision. Unlike parallels of latitude (running horizontally) which refer to astronomical data—they can be calculated by observing the position of the sun and other celestial bodies—the meridians of longitude (running vertically) are an abstract convention: before the invention of the marine chronometer, in the second half of the eighteenth century, it was impossible for a ship to determine accurately its position.

Therefore, this global division merely translated into one vague general practice: expeditions that set sail eastwards belonged legally to the Portuguese, whereas those that sailed westwards pertained to the Spaniards. Besides this broad principle, there was also another rule: all unknown lands should belong to the country of the discoverer. In the first half of the sixteenth century, the theologians of Salamanca started to question the ethical validity of a division of the world that made no reference to natural law nor to the rights of natives. A more irrefutable objection arose in the second half of the century with the irresistible ascent of two new sea powers: England and Holland. When a Spanish ambassador demanded that England compensate the damages caused by the raids and lootings of Sir Francis Drake, Queen Elizabeth replied:

> The South Sea like all other oceans is common property of all mankind. The awarding by the Bishop of Rome of a country that does not belong to him is a fantasy. Spaniards have no more rights than any others over what they themselves usurped, and no one owns a country simply because he erected some huts there, or gave the name of some saint to a cape or to a river.

Still, let us not anticipate. In Magellan's time, things had not yet reached this point, and when the navigator presented to Charles V his idea that there must be somewhere in the southern parts of Terra Firma a passage leading directly to the Spice Islands, the great monarch grasped at once the extraordinary benefit which Spain might draw from such a discovery: the possibility of securing a legitimate short-cut to the source of Portugal's prosperity. Earlier on, Magellan had vainly tried to get the Portuguese court interested in his project. Now this same court realised too late that such an expedition, under the Castilian flag, was going to endanger its own eastern trade. Eventually, the Portuguese navy attempted to obstruct the progress of Magellan's ships, with only limited success.

———

Charles V entrusted Magellan with the supreme command of a flotilla of five ships, with a total crew of 237 men. Of Magellan himself, we know very little. His original name was Fernão de Magalhaes; he was probably born around 1480 in northern Portugal. It seems that he was a soldier much more than a seaman. He served for seven years in the Portuguese possessions in India and on the Malay Peninsula; there, he acquired his knowledge of the East and his experience of the sea; he distinguished himself for his bravery in battle. His officers and crew were in the main subjects of the Kingdom of Castile (mostly Andalusians and Basques); there was also a strong cosmopolitan component: some thirty Portuguese, twenty Italians (mostly Genoese), a few Frenchmen, some Greeks, a few Flemish. The ships were fairly small, three-masted, twenty-odd metres in length—barely the size of a modern super-yacht. On board, the men were crowded into a minuscule space.

Provisions comprised wine, oil, vinegar, sea biscuit, anchovies in barrels, smoked fish, smoked bacon, beans, lentils, flour, garlic, onions, casks of cheese rubbed in oil. These provisions were to prove insufficient during the crossing of the Pacific, the immensity of which no one could have foreseen. What is worse, they did not include any food that could have prevented scurvy, a dreadful illness whose actual cause was still not understood, though in fact it is fairly simple: it results from a vitamin deficiency that can easily be remedied by drinking lime juice and eating sauerkraut (as Captain Cook successfully instructed his sailors to do some 250 years later). Scurvy was to kill half the crew—more than military engagements, accidents and all other diseases combined.

Detailed inventories of the supplies and equipment have been preserved; for instance, there were "eight chamber pots and three rat traps for each ship; five large drums and twenty small drums for entertainment." There were also various presents and goods for barter: "200 red caps, 200 red handkerchiefs; 20,000 small bells of three different sorts; 400 dozen German knives of very inferior quality; 50 dozen scissors; 1,000 mirrors; 1,000 combs."

Sea charts and navigation instruments were wretchedly inadequate; longitude could not be calculated; speed and distance covered were assessed through crude and grossly inaccurate estimation. And even if the navigators had been able to determine the exact co-ordinates of their position, most of the time this could hardly have amounted to more than a tiny point in the middle of a huge blank.

Finally, it should be noted that two chaplains, with all their equipment (sacred vases, liturgical vestments, altars), were attached to the expedition, which had a significant religious and apostolic character—as we shall see later on.

The flotilla left Spain in September 1519. In December, it reached Brazil, where it dropped anchor. The crew proceeded ashore for the execution of a ship's master (each ship was under the command of a captain, seconded by a master and a pilot or navigator): on the way, Magellan had sentenced him to death for sodomising a ship's boy.

Then the flotilla sailed south, for as long as the season allowed. Days became shorter; the weather turned cold and rough. Discontent developed among the Spanish captains, as Magellan refused fully to disclose his plans to them.

Magellan decided that the ships should lie up for winter in a desolate cove of the Patagonian coast. A mutiny broke out; one captain involved in the rebellion was killed on the spot; another was captured, sentenced, beheaded and quartered ashore. As to the true leader of the rebellion and his main accomplice—one of the priests—they were both marooned on a deserted beach, having been provided with, in total, one sword and a bottle of wine. They were never heard of again. This false clemency—more cruel, in fact, than death—was probably due to the fact that the first was related to a Spanish grandee (he was the illegitimate son of an archbishop) and the other was a man of God.

After a grim wintering of five months (in that latitude, winter days have only four or five hours of light), from early April to the end of August, the flotilla—which, by then, had lost one ship, when a sudden gale drove it ashore and destroyed it—pursued its southward course. In October 1520, one year and one month after leaving Spain, Magellan finally discovered the entrance of the passage for which he had searched with such obstinate passion, and which was to carry his name. The Magellan Strait is some 600 kilometres long; for the most part, it is wide and deep, but also scattered with reefs; it follows a meandering course at the foot of tall snowy mountains from which blasts of icy winds blow down with sudden violence. Near the end of the strait, when the crew of the longboat that had been sent to reconnoitre returned and reported they had seen the open sea, "Magellan in his joy began to cry." It is the only display of emotion that was ever recorded of him.

Magellan had taken thirty-four days to sail the length of the strait. A good half-century later, Drake made the same crossing in sixteen days—in winter!—with the help of a favourable wind. However, after this time it was seldom used, as the strait is so hazardous and difficult to negotiate. For sailing ships, the best way is further south; it was discovered in 1616 by a Dutch navigator, the first ever to go round Cape Horn—which he named after his native town, Hoorn.

The flotilla—which by now was reduced to three units (one ship had deserted at the entrance of the strait and returned to Spain, where, on arrival, its crew was thrown in jail)—entered the Pacific Ocean, which it took nearly three months to cross, following a diagonal course, south-east to west-north-west, from the exit of the strait to the island of Guam. The crossing was horrendous. Having exhausted their food supplies, the men were in their hunger gnawing the baggy-wrinkle of the rigging. Pigafetta, the Italian secretary who kept a record of the voyage, described their wretched condition:

> Wednesday, 23 November 1520. We came out of the Strait and entered the Pacific Sea, on which we remained three months and ten days without having any fresh supplies. We were eating old biscuit that had turned into dust, all full of worms and the urine stench of rats which had eaten the better part of it; for drink, we only had a stinking yellowish water. We also ate the oxen hides that serve as chafe-guard on the mizzen antenna; having been long exposed to the sun and the weather, they had become very tough; we marinated them in sea water for four– five days and grilled them before eating. We also ate sawdust and rats . . .

The worst horror was the rottening scurvy, which turned its victims into walking corpses before killing them: "their gums became so swollen, they could not absorb any food and starved; those who survived washed their mouths with urine and sea water."

Blindly missing the Polynesian archipelagos, the ships crossed the vastness of the Pacific Ocean without seeing land, with the sole exception of two tiny islands—uninhabited and unapproachable. Modern commentators have attempted to identify them as various atolls; but their original descriptions suggest forbidding cliffs of volcanic origin. I wonder if they could have been the islands of Pitcairn and Henderson?

After a short stop in Guam, where fresh supplies revived the crew, the ships sailed to the Philippines. There, on the island of Cebu, Magellan established friendly relations with the local king. After one week, the king expressed his desire to become a Christian. He was thus baptised, together with the queen and 2,000 of their subjects. A makeshift church was promptly built; big crosses were erected on top of hills nearby. Magellan then suggested imposing the authority of the "Christian king" over all of his neighbours. When one of them rebuffed his interference, Magellan decided to punish him—and to use the opportunity to show the Christian king the invincible military superiority of his new friends and protectors. Taking only forty men with him in the longboat, he landed on the island of the recalcitrants; there, ambushed by a large army, he was killed with six of his companions after a brief and desperate fight.

The remnants of his little troop re-embarked in disarray. This unexpected rout gave the Christian king food for thought: these strangers were, after all, only temporary visitors, whereas he had to live permanently with his neighbours—it would therefore be wiser to accommodate the latter. He invited to a feast some twenty-six officers and sailors and, in a surprise move, massacred them all. He failed, however, to overtake the three ships; in panic, they lifted anchor and set sail at once, abandoning ashore their dead and dying. Thus ended the stay in Cebu; it had lasted only twenty-three days.

The expedition had not only lost its leader, it did not have enough crew now to man the three ships. It was decided to burn one of them; her crew and equipment were divided between the two remaining units, *Trinidad* and *Victoria*.

For the following eight months, from May to December 1521, the search for cloves resumed; the ships wandered through the Indonesian archipelago, now trading, now indulging in occasional piracy. At long last they reached the Moluccas, where they spent six weeks on the island of Tidore, the main producer of cloves. Loaded with this precious cargo, the *Victoria* set sail for Europe under the command of Elcano. It was out of the question that her crew—so reduced and exhausted—could face again a crossing of the Pacific, followed by the hazards and rigours of the Magellan Strait; therefore, Elcano had no choice but to follow the traditional Portuguese route. The *Trinidad* could not set sail immediately: its hull, eaten up by shipworms, had turned into a sieve. After various mishaps, the *Trinidad* was eventually to fall into the hands of the Portuguese. Her crew spent a long time in the Portuguese jails of Malaya, India and Africa; a few last survivors eventually returned to Spain many years later.

The *Victoria* took seven months to cross the Indian Ocean, to go round the Cape of Good Hope and finally reach the islands of Cape Verde, on the west coast of Africa. Another thirteen men died on the way, of illness and exhaustion. The hull leaked badly; pumps had to be manned all the time. At Cape Verde, Elcano wished to buy some African slaves to work the pumps, which the crew was now too weak to operate. Twelve men were sent ashore to negotiate this purchase; as they were offering cloves in payment, Portuguese authorities immediately suspected that the *Victoria* had trespassed into the trading preserve of Portugal. They arrested the twelve and prepared to take possession of the ship and confiscate her priceless cargo. Elcano had barely time to lift anchor and escape; his crew, further depleted, scarcely managed to hoist at half-mast a mainsail that was now too heavy for them.

On 6 September 1522, the *Victoria* returned to that same port of Sanlúcar de Barrameda she had left three years earlier. Of the original crew only eighteen men remained. On Tuesday, 9 September, "they all entered Sevilla, barefoot, each only in his shirt, with lit candle in hand, to thank God for having brought them back alive into port." And just as Phileas Fogg was to observe at the end of his journey around the

world in eighty days, they discovered with amazement that their calculation of the date was mistaken by one day—"and therefore they
had eaten flesh on Fridays and celebrated Easter on a Monday."

———

The above narrative should not lead you to believe that I am very
knowledgeable on this particular subject. Actually, regarding Magellan, I knew hardly more than the hypothetical educated person
quizzed at the outset. However, I have just finished reading a monumental work, *Voyage de Magellan (1519–1522): La relation d'Antonio
Pigafetta & autres témoignages*, edited by Xavier de Castro, Jocelyne
Hamon and Luis Filipe Thomaz, and published in Paris last year. It
gathers in two volumes (1,000 pages) all the documents pertaining to
this extraordinary expedition, as well as contemporary records of participants and witnesses (with the addition of notes on various questions of history, geography, linguistics and anthropology). It is a
model of lucid, rigorous and exhaustive scholarship. In what I have
written here, I have barely touched on what makes the reading of this
book such a disturbing experience. The feeling of absolute outland-
ishness, of extreme exoticism, does not result from the evocation of
remote tribes in far-away lands speaking incomprehensible tongues
and practising bizarre religious rituals or weird sexual customs—no,
it is in fact the way in which Magellan and his companions appear to
us utterly unknowable. In a letter addressed to a woman who wrote
historical novels, Henry James pointed out (very courteously) what
appeared to him the essential impossibility of her activity:

> You may multiply the little facts that can be got from pictures
> and documents, relics and prints as much as you like—the real
> thing is almost impossible to do, and in its essence the whole
> effect is as nought: I mean the invention, the representation of
> the old CONSCIOUSNESS, the soul, the sense, the horizon, the
> vision of individuals in whose minds half the things that make
> ours, that make the modern world, were non-existent. You have
> to think with your modern apparatus a man, a woman—or

rather fifty—whose own thinking was intensely otherwise conditioned, you have to simplify back by an amazing tour de force—and even then it's all humbug.

What gives such an overwhelming power to this book is precisely the fact that it is the "real thing," in all its mystery.

———

One last word, regarding the Christian king (and his subjects, all converted in one week and baptised en masse): the Western navigators had vested much hope in him, yet did not seem particularly surprised by his eventual betrayal—after all, Christian kings in Europe did not behave differently. There are still in Indonesia—precisely in the Moluccas area—some old Christian communities whose fidelity is all the more heroic that it is maintained against a tide of Islamist persecution. It is remarkable to learn that the Jesuits welcome more novices there than they do in their neighbouring Australian province. One can almost foresee the day when Indonesian missionaries might be sent to preach the Gospel in a largely de-Christianised Australia...

As the Portuguese say: God writes straight with crooked strokes.[1]

RICHARD HENRY DANA AND HIS
TWO YEARS BEFORE THE MAST

After all, most of what we write remains sterile. The small part
of our writing which ought to survive is, without doubt, that
part which was touched by an inspiration from our youth, one
of those strong visions, nourished in secret, and unforgettably
coloured by the first storms of virility.

—Georges Bernanos

It is often said that Richard Henry Dana's *Two Years Before the
Mast* is the most beautiful of all books of the sea, but this seems to me
a somewhat poisoned compliment, as if one were to praise *Madame
Bovary* for being the best account of adultery in Normandy or to celebrate *The Diary of A. O. Barnabooth* as a masterpiece of hotel and
railway sleeping-car literature.

Without doubt, Dana's book successfully conveys the experience
of rounding Cape Horn under sail, as well as countless other aspects
of seamen's life and work on the square-riggers of the nineteenth century, with a vividness and intensity that has few equals. Herman Melville vouched for it: "but if you want the best idea of Cape Horn, get
my friend Dana's unmatchable *Two Years Before the Mast*. But you can
read, and so you must have read it. His chapters describing Cape
Horn must have been written with an icicle."

However, the reason it succeeds in suggesting these realities, better
than any other book of the sea, is precisely the fact it is much more
than a book of the sea. It is something different altogether: under the
appearances of a sober autobiographical narrative it hides a singularly
rich and complex work of art.

Of course, its significance was recognised long ago: it stands among the great classics of nineteenth-century American literature, yielding in importance only to Dana's junior and admirer, Melville, whose beginnings were inspired by his example. Nevertheless, even though connoisseurs and scholars, literary historians, writers and critics have fully acknowledged Dana's literary accomplishment, and though for more than 100 years studies have multiplied on his subject, one must forgive ordinary readers who simply love this book as a gripping sea adventure: after all, there are no bad reasons for loving a good book. And, anyhow, the author began to take the full measure of his achievement only fairly late in life—too late, in fact, for at that time he also realised that he had missed his true calling.

Dana was born in 1815 into an old patrician family of Cambridge, Massachusetts. He was a pure product of the Puritan society of New England, an elite that, armed with Protestant faith, British culture, American democracy and Yankee patriotism, was possessed with an unshakeable belief that it constituted the salt of the earth.

The members of this closed society had a haughty awareness of the privileges they had inherited at birth, but these in turn were matched by a demanding notion of their duties and responsibilities. Always under the eye of a stern God, they were permanently subject to the scrutiny of their individual conscience. This austere high bourgeoisie knew how to marry mysticism with realism and audacity with common sense. Their prosperity and their power, fruits of their courage and industry, were to them signs of God's favour.

Soon after the start of his law studies at Harvard University, Dana was struck by a mysterious illness, the symptoms of which were migraines and failing eyesight (these were thought to be the sequels to measles; in fact they may well have had a nervous origin). As the doctors could suggest no remedy, he decided to cure himself by adopting a completely different way of life: he enlisted as an ordinary seaman on a ship bound for California—at that time still a remote and half-wild province of Mexico—for a voyage of at least two years around Cape Horn. He was nineteen.

The hard life of a seaman—and he took pride in mastering all its technical aspects as a thorough professional—soon achieved its original purpose: Dana's health was restored. But, more important, it allowed him to discover not only new skies, but also an entirely new side of the human condition: to enter the sailor's world, with its language, ways and customs that are utterly foreign to landlubbers. Ashore, he observed a Spanish and Catholic America with its exotic society of Mexicans, Native Americans and kanakas (as the indentured labourers from the Sandwich Islands, now Hawaii, were called).

Two years later, on his return to Boston, he resumed his earlier university studies. Simultaneously he wrote in six months a first draft of his seafaring experiences.

The year 1840 marked for him a decisive turning point: after graduation, he opened a law office in Boston, married the daughter of a respected local family and finally found a publisher for *Two Years Before the Mast*. These three events were to determine the orientation of the rest of his life.

He was successful in his professional activity and in his personal life: his law office kept him intensely busy, his wife gave him six children (five daughters and one son) and rock-solid support until the end of his life. Thus he found himself permanently anchored in the position of respected citizen, *pater familias*, warden of the Episcopalian Church and patron of the arts and letters.

His father was himself a writer of some distinction; his uncle, Washington Allston, was a famous painter and poet who introduced him to the cultured circles of Boston; his own son was to marry the daughter of Henry Wadsworth Longfellow; he patronised the same club as Ralph Waldo Emerson.

He became an influential scholar, specialised in international law and admiralty law. (Incidentally, it was he who formulated the still universally accepted principle that sailing vessels have right of way over those under power.)

Soon, also, he made himself quite famous by his political activity: with courage and eloquence, he joined the movement against slavery, and for a while it appeared as if even the highest office of the land might be within his reach.

Meanwhile, the publication of *Two Years Before the Mast* earned him at once, if not royalties (a disastrous contract deprived him of the fortune that was exclusively to enrich his publishers*), then at least extraordinary fame; at that time only a new novel by Charles Dickens, then at the high point of his immense popularity, could enjoy similar attention. The success of his book was immediate, universal (loved by the public and praised by the sophisticated critics) and long-lasting: since its first publication 170 years ago, it has never been out of print.

This tremendous (and unexpected) success further strengthened Dana's social position, but instead of taking advantage of such a triumphant beginning to pursue his literary career, Dana not only became increasingly busy with his activity at the Bar, he launched himself more fully into politics; in this field, however, his ambitions were finally derailed by the vile intrigues of some rivals.

He had in him the makings of a great writer, but he chose instead to become a distinguished lawyer and a failed politician. Like other people of his caste, constant exercise of self-examination enabled him to draw a clear-sighted assessment of his achievements. At fifty-seven, he wrote in a letter to his son: "My life has been a failure compared to what I might and ought to have done. My great success—my book—was a boy's work, done before I came to the Bar."

After having exhausted himself all his life in an activity that was intensely absorbing but not really creative, it seems that Dana, in his final years, eventually found a certain form of inner peace: he abandoned his law office to his son and together with his wife went into self-imposed exile from the United States. The old couple first spent two years in Paris, then moved to Rome. Paradoxically, it was in Rome, the Latin and papist Babylon, that our New England Puritan finally felt as if he had reached port. He confessed, "At last I found my life's dream." Yet he was not able to enjoy it long: three years later, in 1882, he died of pneumonia. As one of his biographers recalls, "The ghost of his former strength took hold of him at the very end, and during his last days he suffered from hallucinations, struggling to leave his bed as if he wished, once again, to launch himself into some

*See above, p. 267.

long and hazardous journey." He was buried in that same Protestant cemetery that had contained the graves of Keats and Shelley.

The personality of Dana was deeply divided. First among all his critics, D. H. Lawrence perceived this inner conflict. This insight was all the more remarkable in that Lawrence had virtually no biographical information on Dana: his brilliant 1924 essay, published in *Studies in Classic American Literature*, was simply based on a reading of *Two Years Before the Mast*.

In a way, Dana's decision to go to sea had been a challenge thrown at his conventional society, at the establishment that had produced and nourished him. Then, on his return, the writing of his book was a continuation and a memorial of this youthful rebellion. Dana's return to Boston was like the return of the prodigal son and for this reason his literary achievement could have no further development. The transparent simplicity of *Two Years Before the Mast* is misleading: the power and inner tension of his narrative are largely the products of all that Dana chose to hide. One single incident can provide a good example of this.

In the middle of his journey, Dana went through a crisis of which he gives us only a truncated picture. In California, just before starting the return journey, the captain ordered Dana to move to another ship, one that would remain there for another two years. This instruction plunged Dana into panic and in his desperation he went to extraordinary lengths to secure his early return home. The methods he adopted then did, in fact, alienate him from the other sailors. They were suddenly reminded of what Dana had tried so hard to make them forget: he was not one of them, he belonged to the privileged class.

But why did the prospect of another two years in California provoke such terror in Dana's mind? The explanations he provided are not very convincing. Such a delay, he said, would virtually have prevented him from resuming his studies at Harvard and therefore would have condemned him to remain a sailor for the rest of his life. This argument does not hold water.

From the testimony of one of his seafaring companions, another young bourgeois from Boston who had enrolled on the same ship, we learn something of Dana's life ashore. He was sharing a hut with a friendly young Indian woman. It seems our Puritan did enjoy for quite a while the brutish bliss of being simply young, carefree and healthy on a sunny Californian beach: he had discovered the animal innocence of life before the Fall.

However, as soon as the captain's new instructions managed to turn this happy interlude into a more permanent way of life, Dana became terrified. As in R. L. Stevenson's disturbing tale, where past a certain point Mr. Hyde can no longer revert to his Dr. Jekyll identity—since the chemistry of his organism had been irretrievably altered—Dana realised that should he pursue his Californian life any longer, he would reach a point of no return. This would indeed condemn him to remain a sailor for the rest of his life; there would be no more possibility to reintegrate his original self.

In a short and illuminating autobiographical sketch he wrote for himself in 1842 (this remarkable page was discovered and published more than a century later), Dana described how, after his return to Boston, he went through a dramatic mystical crisis, at the end of which he received confirmation within the Episcopalian Church. Regarding his Californian experience, he summed it up in only one phrase: "Not a man in my ship was more guilty in God's sight than myself."

During the remaining years of his life he numbed himself with a constant overload of work, plunging himself into frenzied activity close to neurosis and repeatedly provoking severe depression, which in turn required prolonged rest. At times, also, he suffered bouts of his old illness: migraines, failing eyesight, fainting fits.

At other times he retained a furious lust for adventure and physical effort in open air; he would go hunting and camping with trappers, whose simple and primitive way of life delighted him, and he amazed them with his exceptional physical resilience.

His need for escape sometimes took other forms: far from Boston, he would take advantage of his travels to explore the lower depths of big cities such as New York and London. In a way somehow similar to George Orwell's exploration in the next century of the marginal worlds of tramps and hoboes, he would disguise himself in sailor's clothing and descend into "dark, filthy, violent and degrading regions of saloons and brothels in the harbour districts" or he would spend an evening there chatting with prostitutes.

We know of these episodes only because he wrote them down in private diaries not meant for publication. He was never discovered or identified during these dangerous dives—imagine the scandal that would have resulted—but one wonders to what extent he was not unconsciously looking for such a liberating accident.

Meanwhile, he applied all his energy to discharge with stoic nobility the obligations of a model husband, model father, model parishioner and model citizen. It seems as if the institutions of marriage, family, church and law, as well as his dedication to serving the common good, were so many defences against the "madness of art" that was so obviously his original calling. As for literature, he never wrote anything again.

Part V
UNIVERSITY

THE IDEA OF THE UNIVERSITY

THE TITLE of my little talk is *An Idea of the University*. This is, of course, a humble homage to Cardinal Newman's great book *The Idea of a University*—a classic work published a little more than 150 years ago, which has lost nothing of its relevance for us today and should remain the basic reference for any reflection on the problems of the university.

This topic is huge—but I shall not be long, for I shall approach it only from the very limited perspective of my own modest personal experience. In doing this, I may repeat things which I have already said or published before. I apologise for this repetitiveness—it cannot be helped, I am afraid: a simple desire to remain truthful to one's experiences and beliefs is often the enemy of eloquence and novelty.

I have spent all my active life in universities: first, as a student, of course (but, in a sense, every academic always remains a student till his death). For nearly forty years, I have pursued research and carried on teaching in various universities, first in the Far East, then mostly in Australia, with some periods in Europe and in the United States. My career was happy; I have been lucky: all my life, I had the rare opportunity to do work which I loved in congenial and stimulating environments. Only, near the end, deep modifications began to affect the university—I am not talking here of any specifically *Australian* problems, but of a much more broad and universal malaise. As these transformations were progressively taking the university further away from the model to which I had originally devoted my life, I finally decided to quit—six years before reaching retirement age. Considering the

Address to the Campion Foundation Inaugural Dinner, Sydney, 23 March 2006.

way things have evolved since then, it is a decision that I have never regretted. Nevertheless, the fact remains that I was a deserter. I am not proud of that. Yet today my heart is with the brave people who are starting Campion College and will continue to fight the good fight—and it is to show them my support that I have come here tonight.

Near the end of his life, Gustave Flaubert wrote in one of his remarkable letters to his dear friend Ivan Turgenev a little phrase that could beautifully summarise my topic: "I have always tried to live in an ivory tower; but a tide of shit is beating at its walls, threatening to undermine it." These are indeed the two poles of our predicament: on one side, the need for an "ivory tower," and on the other side, the threat of the "tide of shit."

Let us consider first the ivory tower. C. S. Lewis observed that, to assess the value of anything—be it a cathedral or a corkscrew—one should first know its purpose. Intellectual impostures always require convoluted jargon, whereas fundamental values can normally be defined in clear and simple language. Thus, the commonly accepted definition of the university is fairly straightforward: *a university is a place where scholars seek truth, pursue and transmit knowledge for knowledge's sake—irrespective of the consequences, implications and utility of the endeavour.*

In order to function, a university requires basically four things—two of these are absolutely essential and necessary; the other two are important, but not always indispensable.

First, a community of scholars. Sir Zelman Cowen told this anecdote: some years ago in England, a bright and smart politician gave a speech to the dons at Oxford. He addressed them as "employees of the university." One don immediately stood up and corrected him: "We are not employees of the university, *we are the university.*" And one could not have put it better: the only employees of the university are the professional managers and administrators—and they do not direct or control the scholars, they are at the service of the scholars.

The second essential thing, a good library for the humanities and well-equipped laboratories for the scientists. This is self-evident and requires no further comment.

Third, the students. The students constitute, of course, an important part of the university. It is good and fruitful to educate students; but students should not be recruited at any cost, by all means, or without discrimination. (Note: in this country, foreign students who pay fees bring every year nearly $2 billion to our universities. In the university where I last taught, in a written communication addressed to all staff, the vice-chancellor once instructed us to consider our students not as students but as *customers*. On that day, I knew that it was time for me to go.)

I dream of an ideal university that would deliver no degrees, nor give access to any specific occupation, nor award any professional qualifications. The students would be motivated by one thing only: a strong personal desire for knowledge—the acquisition of knowledge would be their only reward. In fact, this is no mere utopian dream of mine. Examples of this model actually operate; the most illustrious one was established in the sixteenth century and is still the highest seat of learning in Paris: the Collège de France.

The fourth requirement for operating a university: money. It would be foolish to deny the importance of money, and yet remember that one has seen great universities performing their task in conditions of extreme deprivation. But this is certainly not the time or place to pursue this particular line of thought.

Having thus sketched out the "ivory tower," let us examine now the "tide of shit" that is beating at its walls.

Two points are particularly under attack. First, the *elitist character* of the ivory tower (which results from its very nature) is denounced in the name of equality and democracy. The demand for equality is noble and must be fully supported, but only within its own sphere, which is that of social justice. It has no place anywhere else. Democracy is the only acceptable political system; yet it pertains to politics exclusively, and has no application in any other domain. When applied anywhere else, it is death—for truth is not democratic, intelligence and talent are not democratic, nor is beauty, nor love—nor God's grace. A truly democratic education is an education that equips people intellectually to defend and promote democracy within the political world; but in its own field, education must be ruthlessly aristocratic and high-brow, shamelessly geared towards excellence.

The second aspect of the ivory tower that is constantly under attack is its *non-utilitarian character*. The heart of the problem is memorably expressed in the paradox of Zhuang Zi, a Daoist philosopher of the third century BC and one of the most profound minds of all time: "People all know the usefulness of what is useful, but they do not know the usefulness of the useless." The superior utility of the university—what enables it to perform its function—rests entirely upon what the world deems to be its uselessness.

Vocational schools and technical colleges are very useful—people all understand that. As they cannot see the usefulness of the useless universities, they have decided to turn the universities into bad imitations of technical colleges. Thus the fundamental distinction between liberal education and vocational training has become blurred, and the very survival of the university is put in question.

The university is now under increasing pressure to justify its existence in utilitarian and quantitative terms. Such pressure is deeply corrupting. I have no time now to examine all aspects of this corruption; let me give you just one example—only one, but it has ominous significance. In Europe, not long ago, a respected university hit hard by funding cuts felt compelled to wind up some of its courses. An entire department had to be closed down—the most vulnerable, the least economically viable, a department which had more lecturers than students, which offered no future to its graduates, which performed no visible service to society and the state. The department that was abolished was the Department of Pure Philosophy—ivory tower within the ivory tower, historical heart and origin of the university itself.

When a university yields to the utilitarian temptation, it betrays its vocation and sells its soul. Five centuries ago, the great Renaissance scholar Erasmus defined with one phrase the essence of the humanist endeavour: *Homo fit, non nascitur*—One is not born a man, one becomes it. A university is not a factory producing graduates, as a sausage factory produces sausages. It is a place where a chance is given to men to become what they truly are.

A FABLE FROM ACADEME

*This piece, written nearly half a century ago, was never published,
but it circulated privately among friends, and friends of friends.
Eventually, I received quite a few letters from academics in far-
away places—complete strangers—assuring me that they had personally witnessed the very incident evoked in my little fable: they
even recognised the protagonists! This confirmed for me what I
had always suspected: reality imitates fiction.*

THERE was in Timbuctoo a great university that was the cultural
pride of the entire country. A very old scholar called Hutudan was
lecturing in the Department of Applied Pataphysics of that university. Pataphysics (as you surely know) is the science by which movements of the tails of cows are observed in the morning in order to
forecast whether it will rain in the afternoon. It is a very subtle discipline that requires exceptionally sharp eyesight, as the slightest
twitching of the tails must be individually recorded and interpreted.
Hutudan was blessed with good eyes and even though he was quite a
fool in many other respects, his unique pataphysical expertise had
won him great international fame; he was professionally sought out
and consulted from all over the world, and the post office had to use
two camels to bring his incoming mail every day. Disciples flocked to
him. His days were busy and happy.

In the Department of Applied Pataphysics there was another
scholar called Galosh. No one could remember exactly when, how or
why Galosh had become a member of the department. The poor man
was born blind, and his infirmity naturally prevented him from taking part in regular pataphysical work. However, it was eventually

found that Galosh had a few *talents de société*—for instance, he could juggle three telephones while simultaneously typewriting with his toes. Hence, he was entrusted with some secretarial duties, which enabled him to feel useful in spite of his physical handicap. This greatly raised his morale. His three telephones were constantly ringing, his typewriter was rattling and clinking. His days were busy and happy.

Unfortunately, after many years of this life, Galosh became bored with his telephones and began to nourish the dream of becoming a leading pataphysician. Since the various duties within the department had to be detailed in typewritten form, and since he was the only person who knew how to type, he hit upon a brilliant idea: he would invite other blind men to come and train Hutudan's disciples; as for Hutudan himself and all the colleagues who could see, they would be exclusively employed in the cleaning and maintenance of the departmental toilets.

As I have said, Hutudan was rather obtuse in all matters that did not pertain to pataphysics. This time, however, it did not take him too long to realise that something untoward was afoot. So, one day, he waxed his moustache, brushed his teeth, polished his shoes and went to knock at the door of the vice-chancellor, the wise and prudent Professor Krokodil. When I say that he knocked at the vice-chancellor's door, this is merely a manner of speaking, for there was no door to knock at. Professor Krokodil had undertaken to break the world record of wise and prudent academic administration: he had already managed to run the university for thirty years without making a single decision or taking a single initiative. In order to preserve his record in its immaculate state, he stayed in permanent hiding and transformed the chancellery into a fortress surrounded by a moat; its only access was over a drawbridge manned by an army of drunken dwarfs. On that day, however, Professor Krokodil happened to be fishing in the moat, and thus Hutudan was able to shout his story from across the water, in spite of all the interference from the drunken dwarfs. Professor Krokodil listened to him attentively before shouting back to him: "Don't you worry, sir! I shall look into this matter. I'll be in touch with you very soon."

Actually, when he heard the story, the wise and prudent Professor

Krokodil felt utterly indignant: Hutudan was really reacting in a most irresponsible manner—even if his complaint was groundless, it could potentially damage the reputation of the university; but if it proved to be *true*, then the consequences would naturally be far worse. This could obviously not be tolerated. He immediately instructed his most trusted assistant, the dean (whose name I forget), to launch an inquiry into the matter. The dean was a very insignificant man; so insignificant, in fact, that everyone constantly forgot his name—he had to carry it written on a filing card which was attached to the lapel of his coat with a clothes-peg.

As soon as he received his brief, the dean set to work. First, he conducted a long interview with the tea-lady of the faculty, during which they discussed the weather. He faithfully recorded these meteorological considerations. Then, he tore some twenty pages from an outdated telephone directory. Finally, he picked up an old issue of *The Timbuctoo Times*, destined for use as wrapping paper in a nearby fish-and-chip shop. Back in his office, he stapled together the minutes of his conversation with the tea-lady, the pages torn from the telephone directory, and the fish-and-chip wrapping. He put everything in a folder; with the colour pencils that Santa Claus had given him at Christmas, he wrote on the cover: *REPORT PRESENTED TO THE VICE-CHANCELLOR ON THE TEACHING OF PATAPHYSICS AND OTHER MATTERS RELATED AND UNRELATED.*

The vice-chancellor devoured the report from cover to cover, and felt immensely relieved. He immediately wrote to Hutudan: "As promised, I consulted with the dean on the matter you raised. You will be pleased to learn that the dean's report does not contain the *slightest* shred of evidence supporting the misgivings and fears you voiced." Upon reading this, Hutudan was greatly relieved too; he went back to scrubbing the departmental toilets with a lighter heart.

From time to time, Hutudan still experiences brief pangs of nostalgia; he misses the autumn mornings in the meadows with their smell of mist and mushroom, when he would guide eager young pataphysicians in their first attempts at observing cows swinging their tails—but then he remembers what Professor Krokodil told him: to employ a world-famous pataphysician to clean the toilets is to adopt a "multi-disciplinary approach"—that is what they do in all modern universities nowadays.

Galosh is still blind as a bat, but it does not matter really; he received a diploma of clear-sightedness *honoris causa* and was recently made pataphysician extraordinary. It is rumoured that even greater things are in store for him—but this I cannot ascertain, for I do not live in Timbuctoo.

Part VI
MARGINALIA

I PREFER READING

People say that life is the thing, but I prefer reading.
—Logan Pearsall Smith

SOME PEOPLE seem to know everything and understand nothing: usually this is a reproach one would be tempted to throw at *academic* critics, but it came irrepressibly to mind as I was reading the last volume (posthumously published) of Edmund Wilson's notebooks, *The Sixties*. Actually, long ago, oblique hints in Anaïs Nin's diaries, as well as the fascinating Wilson–Nabokov correspondence (I hope to come back to it on a later occasion) should have warned us of a central hollowness inside the old giant of American letters.

For the most part, *The Sixties* is made up of endless name-dropping and a dreary record of attendance at social and literary functions—the climax being an official dinner at the Kennedy White House. The book is not altogether uninteresting, though; there are occasional flashes of sharp perception (for instance, Cartier-Bresson "is so little provincial that one should not take him for a modern Frenchman"); there are also provocative observations from illustrious interlocutors—for example, Malraux told him that the New York Metropolitan Museum was "*un musée de province*," whereas the National Gallery in Washington should be considered the real thing (this judgement may seem unfair at first, and yet when you think of it, it has an intriguing pertinence).

There are also distasteful and grossly indiscreet passages. Could any form of sexual exhibitionism ever be redeemed by youth and beauty? I very much doubt it, but what is sure is that old people who expose themselves are always painfully obscene. Wilson records love-making sessions with his wife in the same way as a zoologist would describe the laborious coition of elephants; one episode appears at the end of a paragraph that had started with the mention of an appointment at the dentist—the unconscious association seems lugubriously appropriate.

Still, these are mere trifles. What dumbfounded me is the following confession: "(I had dinner with Mike Nichols); he had just read Tolstoy's *Death Of Ivan Ilyich*, which had made a great impression on him. *I do not care for this story as much as many people do. I do not believe that a man like Ivan Ilyich could ever look back on his life and find it so empty and futile*; I don't believe that Tolstoy, in the period where he was writing his great novels would ever have invented such a character."

Gore Vidal, in a review of *The Sixties*, specially extolled this very passage: "This is simply true. Ivan Ilyich would not have regarded his past life as empty and futile any more than Edmund Wilson could ever have found his life anything but fascinating and full." In this extraordinary comment, Vidal unwittingly hit the nail on the head: the corollary of his observation is indeed that, if an eminent and influential Supreme Court magistrate such as Ivan Ilyich can, in the light of his approaching death, suddenly discover that his apparently successful life was in fact dreadfully wanting in some essential human aspects, this would also mean that eminent and influential men of letters such as Wilson and Vidal ought perhaps to re-examine whether their sense of importance and achievement was warranted. But this is probably an exercise which no successful man would willingly contemplate. Yet whoever feels in the end that he had a successful life must not have been aiming very high in the first instance.

Late last year, Cynthia Blanche concluded her review of Dorothy Hewett's *The Toucher*: "Surely age without wisdom must be the worst fate to befall anyone: the sure sign of an empty life." In a lifetime, Wilson and Vidal devoured entire libraries; that, in the end, so much reading seems to have generated so little understanding is sad and puzzling.

———

And yet, are books really so useless? I still believe that at least political leaders and statesmen should try to read more literature. This might enable them to acquire an elementary self-knowledge that, in turn, could prevent them from making disgraceful fools of themselves when they are forced into retirement. This thought occurred to me as I came across a comment by Orson Welles on *King Lear*: "Lear becomes senile by giving power away. The thing that keeps people alive in their old age is power... But take power away from any of these old men who run the world—in this world that belongs only to young people—and you'll see a 'babbling, slippered pantaloon.'"

Talking of Orson Welles, I wonder if many people still remember how, soon after the Second World War, his artistic reputation in Europe was nearly wrecked for a while by a blistering attack which Sartre launched against *Citizen Kane*. The profound silliness of this diatribe is startling half a century later:

> Although *Kane* might have been interesting for the Americans, it is completely *démodé* for us, because the whole film is based on a misconception of what cinema is all about. The film is in the past tense, whereas we all know that cinema has to be in the present tense. "I *am* the man who is kissing, I *am* the girl who is being kissed, I *am* the Indian who is being pursued, I *am* the man pursuing the Indian." Any film in the past tense is the antithesis of cinema. Therefore *Citizen Kane* is not cinema.

The impact of this condemnation was devastating. *The Magnificent Ambersons* was shown soon afterwards in Paris but failed miserably. The cultivated public always follows the directives of a few propaganda commissars: there is much more conformity among intellectuals than among plumbers or car mechanics.

A few years earlier, Jorge Luis Borges (who wrote superb film reviews) had also expressed a critical opinion of *Citizen Kane*, but whereas Sartre's censure now appears odious and ridiculous in its self-importance and dogmatism (it was actually dictated by a "politically correct" anti-American prejudice), Borges made a point that should retain its validity—even for the admirers of *Citizen Kane*:

We all know that a feast, a palace, a huge enterprise, a lunch of writers or of journalists, a cordial atmosphere of frank and spontaneous comradeship are all particularly hideous. *Citizen Kane* is the first film that made conscious use of this reality… It is not an intelligent film, but it is the work of a *genius*—in the most nocturnal and Germanic sense of this ugly word.

Sartre had an unquestionable genius (and we just learned what this means)—which may not be enough to reach posterity; in this respect, Borges was perhaps better equipped: he had a sense of humour—which is also the other side of a genuine humility.

———

Trans-cultural literary comparisons are sometimes risky. The basic problem was aptly summed up in a fable by Randall Jarrell: "The Patagonians have two great writers; the name of the most famous one is Gomez. The Patagonians call Shakespeare 'the English Gomez.'"

Only once did I have a chance to attend a public lecture given by Manning Clark; it was in many respects a memorable experience. The topic of the talk was Henry Lawson, and it took place in one of Canberra's largest lecture halls. The vast auditorium was jam-packed with a respectful and enthusiastic public, young and old, all communing in fervour and anticipation. When Manning Clark climbed onto the stage, there remained not one empty seat in the hall; people were standing against the walls and sitting on the stairs. At once, the small and frail old man commanded effortlessly a silence that had a monumental quality. He spoke with eloquence and passion, without notes. The ultimate test for a lecturer is always the ability to think on his feet and to talk empty-handed: then you know what he has to say—and if he has something to say. Manning Clark captured and retained the total attention of his huge audience for the full hour of the lecture.

As I came to Australia relatively late in life, I had never read anything by Lawson. The gist of Manning Clark's lecture was that Lawson was "Australia's Chekhov," and the point was made with such convincing force that as soon as the lecture was over, I rushed to the nearest bookshop and bought a copy of the *Portable Lawson*. I started reading at once—but this was an anti-climax. The stories were readable, for sure, interesting, even touching—but in what one might call a Patagonian fashion: this was more Gomez than Shakespeare, if you see what I mean.

Retrospectively, the brilliant lecture suddenly appeared to have been built around a hollow core of myth and fantasy. And yet I felt not so much disappointment or cynicism as a genuine gratitude: after all, my mind had been stirred and my curiosity aroused; I had felt a compelling urge to look for the original sources and to read them; as a result, I had been able to form my own opinion on an interesting subject. Could any teacher aim for more?

———

Should I buy Patrick White's *Letters*? I am still hesitating. The truth is, I was never able to finish any of his novels—I confess this with shame. I always watch with envy and frustration the true connoisseurs who derive from his impenetrable prose an enjoyment that remains obstinately denied to me. Although I am perhaps not alone in suffering from this singular disability (actually I know a number of people who share it, and not all of them are illiterate), it is always stupid to flaunt one's infirmities as if they were a badge of originality; thus, Roger Stéphane, having once foolishly declared to Gide that he found Goethe unreadable, was coolly put back in his place by the Master: "*Tant pis pour vous.*" And whenever I re-read "The Screaming Potato" (this prose-poem is scarcely a page long but it ranks on an equal footing with the masterpieces of the genre, from Baudelaire to Lu Xun), I feel that I should—and I know that I will—attempt once more to find an access point to his fiction. Meanwhile *Flaws in the Glass* had moved me—but in the way one is affected by the groaning of a man in pain. And now all the extracts and quotations from the *Letters* which have been published in the newspapers have further stimulated my desire to read this volume. Yet $50—which should be no obstacle for a true *aficionado*, however penniless—seems a steep price for someone who merely wishes to satisfy an idle taste for literary gossip. The traditional method which enables writers to obtain new books is to secure a free copy for reviewing, but this entails a double pitfall:

1. You have to write the review;

2. You have to read the book (even if you discover that, after all, it was not really your cup of tea).

And the obligation to finish a book when you do not enjoy it is a ghastly prospect. I would sooner sip, spoonful by spoonful, an entire bottle of cod-liver oil. Since the reviewing formula appears fraught with too great a risk, only one solution remains: wait for the paperback edition to appear. Meanwhile, I keep browsing the hard-cover volume in bookshops.

The other day, in the course of this exercise, I came across his letter to Dorothy Green. I am not absolutely sure of this attribution: one can hardly take notes when browsing. (Oh, for a civilised bookshop that would provide deep sofas where one could read and write at leisure, under a cloud of tobacco smoke, with good coffee at hand!) In that letter, White was vilely berating his correspondent for the disgraceful lack of self-respect she had displayed in accepting a perfectly respectable Australian honour; and then, practically in the same breath, he expressed his own desire to visit the Soviet Union—on the condition that the Communist authorities invite him, and pay for all his expenses. Obviously he had not perceived any contradiction between the two halves of his letter. I found this hilarious. I cannot wait for the paperback edition.

A WAY OF LIVING

There are many ways of living, and reading is one of them...
When you are reading you are living, and when you are dreaming you are living also.

> —J.L. Borges, answering an interviewer who asked if he did not regret having spent more time reading than living

IN PRAISE OF LAZINESS

We have just visited old neighbours who recently retired and settled on the coast. As I was congratulating them on what appeared to me a blissful state of unlimited leisure they replied rather defensively that, actually, in their new situation they found themselves much more busy than they ever were during their professional lives. Now, they proudly explained, there were so many activities and commitments that they had to draw up a tightly organised timetable which was posted on the door of the fridge: yoga classes, bowling club, bushwalking, reading group, bingo, lectures, cooking classes, arts and crafts (in the latter field, the hand-painted plates that covered the walls made one regret that the lady of the house had not opted instead for judicious Doing Nothing).

Chesterton has already confessed his puzzlement at this sort of attitude: "There are some who complain of a man doing nothing; there are some, still more mysterious and amazing, who complain of having nothing to do. When actually presented with some beautiful blank hours or days, they will grumble at their blankness. When given the gift of loneliness, which is the gift of liberty, they will cast it away;

they will destroy it deliberately with some dreadful game with cards, or a little ball . . . I cannot repress a shudder when I see them throwing away their hard-won holidays by doing something. For my own part, I can never get enough Nothing to do."

The poet Reverdy said: "I need so much time to do nothing that I have none left for work." This is a good definition of the poetical activity, which itself is the supreme fruit of the contemplative life. However much we should value the contribution of Martha attending to the household chores, we must always remember that it was Mary, by simply sitting at the feet of the Lord, who chose the better part. What the vulgar call laziness can in fact reflect better judgement and demand greater inner strength and spiritual resources than the facile escape into activism. La Bruyère put it beautifully (but I despair to convey in translation the rhythm of the most perfect classical French prose): "In France you need great inner strength and vast learning to do without official position or employment, and simply stay home, doing nothing; almost no one has sufficient character to do this with dignity, or to fill their days without what is commonly called 'business.' And yet the only thing that the wise man's leisure lacks is a better name: meditation, conversation, reading and inner peace should be called 'work.'"

From the earliest antiquity, leisure was always regarded as the condition of all civilised endeavours. Confucius said: "The leisure from learning should be devoted to politics and the leisure from politics should be devoted to learning." Government responsibilities and scholarly wisdom were the twin prerogatives of a gentleman and *both were rooted in leisure.* The Greeks developed a similar concept—they called it *scholê*; this word literally means the state of a person who belongs to himself, who has free disposition of himself and therefore: rest, leisure; and therefore, also, the way in which leisure is used: study, learning; or the place where study and learning are conducted: study-room, school (actually *scholê* is the etymological root of "school"). In ancient Greece, politics and wisdom were the exclusive province of the free men, who alone enjoyed leisure. Leisure was not only the indispensable attribute of "the good life," it was also the defining mark of a free man. In one of Plato's dialogues, Socrates asks rhetorically, "Are we slaves, or do we have leisure?"—for there was a well-known proverb that said "Slaves have no leisure."

From Greece, the notion passed to Rome; the very concept of *artes liberales* again embodies the association between cultural pursuits and the condition of a free man (*liber*), as opposed to that of a slave, whose skills pertain to the lower sphere of practical and technical activity.

These views were maintained in European culture. Samuel Johnson was merely stating the evidence of common sense when he observed that "all intellectual improvement arises from leisure." But a century later, Nietzsche was to note the erosion of civilised leisure under what he considered to be a deleterious American influence: "There is something barbarous, characteristic of 'Red-skin' blood, in the American thirst for gold. Their restless urge for work—which is the typical vice of the New World—is now barbarising old Europe by contamination, and is fostering here a sterility of the mind that is most extraordinary. Already we are ashamed of leisure; lengthy meditation becomes practically a cause for remorse ... 'Do anything rather than do nothing': this principle is the rope with which all superior forms of culture and taste are going to be strangled ... It may come to a point where no one will yield to an inclination for *vita contemplativa* without having an uneasy conscience and feeling full of self-contempt. And yet, in the past, the opposite was true: a man of noble origin, when necessity compelled him to work, would hide this shameful fact, and the slave worked with the feeling that his activity was essentially despicable."

Now the ironical paradox of our age, of course, is that the wretched *lumpenproletariat* is cursed with the enforced leisure of demoralising and permanent unemployment, whereas the educated elite, whose *liberal* professions have been turned into senseless money-making machines, are condemning themselves to the slavery of endless working hours—till they collapse like overloaded beasts of burden.

THE PARADOX OF PROVINCIALISM

In a homage to Henri Michaux (arguably the greatest poet in the French language this century), Borges made an interesting point: "A writer who was born in a big country is always in danger of believing that the culture of his native country encompasses all his needs. Paradoxically, he therefore runs the risk of becoming provincial." Naturally, the poet from Buenos Aires was in a good position to detect the secret strength of the poet from Namur (Michaux loathed his birthplace—the province of a province).

In the time of Goethe, Weimar was a town somewhat smaller than Queanbeyan today. I wonder if there was not a direct relation between the universal reach of Goethe's antennae (not only did he keep abreast of the latest developments on the English and French literary scenes, but he even displayed an enthusiastic interest in newly translated Chinese novels!) and the narrow horizon of his provincial abode. My point is *not* that Queanbeyan is shortly going to produce a Goethe—though this remains of course entirely possible; the emergence of genius is always arbitrary and its manifestation presents no necessity. I merely wish to underline Borges's paradox: cosmopolitanism is more easily achieved in a provincial setting, whereas life in a metropolis can insidiously result in a form of provincialism.

People who live in Paris, London or New York have a thousand convincing reasons to feel that they are "where the action is," and therefore they tend to become oblivious to the fact that rich developments are also taking place elsewhere. This is something which educated people who live in a village are unlikely ever to forget. (Still, needless to say, there is one thing worse than ignoring the outside world when in New York, and that is ignoring the outside world when in Queanbeyan.)

Culture is born out of exchanges and thrives on differences. In this sense, "national culture" is a self-contradiction, and "multiculturalism" a pleonasm. The death of culture lies in self-centredness, self-sufficiency and isolation. (Here, for example, the first concern—it seems—should not be to create an Australian culture, but a cultured Australia.)

When modern navigators reached Easter Island, they were confronted with an enigma: What was the meaning of the colossal stone monuments that stood on top of the cliffs? Who had carved these monoliths? By what feats of sophisticated engineering were they erected? Since the local population could not offer the slightest clue to answer these questions, it was assumed that they were late-comers and that the original nation of monument-builders had vanished with their entire civilisation. Archaeological and anthropological research eventually solved the riddle: the early settlers had reached the island by accident; at first they maintained their culture and technology, but then, marooned for centuries in complete isolation, deprived of out-side contacts, challenges and stimulations, their descendants progres-sively could no longer muster the energy to cultivate their burdensome heritage; eventually they ceased to understand it, and in the end its very memory was lost. In its lonely and perfectly sterile purity, Easter Island is the ultimate paradigm of a "national culture."

CIGARETTES ARE SUBLIME

After a long wait, I finally obtained a copy of Richard Klein's book in praise of smoking, *Cigarettes Are Sublime*—but I put it on a shelf and have not opened it yet. Why? I suspect that I may unconsciously fear that this book achieves something I have vaguely dreamed of doing myself. (Whenever you have a good idea, do not put it into practice, there is no need for that—sooner or later, someone else is bound to hit upon the same concept, and will do a better job of it.)

What I had in mind actually was a sort of anthology—pictorial and literary—celebrating tobacco. For the pictures, I would have started with seventeenth-century *Tabagies* by the old masters from the Low Countries—Brouwer, Van Ostade, Teniers, etc. Then, for the modern times, there would have been Baudelaire with his pipe, as seen by Courbet; Manet's portrait of Mallarmé, showing the poet wrapped in the blue smoke of his cigar; Van Gogh's *Pipe on a Chair*, Cézanne and Degas's various portraits of smokers. Even musicians could have been mobilised for my purpose: Bach, for instance, once professed in the same breath his serene faith in God and the trust he put in his pipe—the only pity is that, having already made a cantata praising coffee, he did not go one step further and compose a Tobacco Cantata.* What a magnificent anthem this would have constituted for today's embattled smokers!

On the literary side, my anthology would have been faced with an embarrassment of riches. Balzac could have contributed many quotable passages on cigars. (For instance, there is a memorable episode in *La Fille aux yeux d'or*, after young de Marsay finally succeeds in winning the favours of the mysterious and elusive Girl With the Golden Eyes and spends a wild night of passion with her. As he walks out of her house in the early dawn, he lights up a cigar and, drawing a long puff, says to himself: "This at least is something no man will ever tire of!") Yet the opening quote should naturally belong to Samuel Johnson; it is no surprise that this inexhaustible font of wisdom on all sublunary topics should have repeatedly celebrated the virtues of tobacco; for example, he attributed the admirable placidity of the Dutch to their habit of smoking (and of playing draughts). For Johnson, who was haunted by a neurotic fear of madness, tobacco appeared as a powerfully soothing influence, and Hawkins heard him say: "As smoking is going out of fashion, insanity is growing more frequent." Today, the manic fanaticism of the anti-smoking lobby eloquently confirms the accuracy of this observation.

Actually, the current antics of the anti-tobacco activists would have provided rich material for an entire section of my anthology. Some time ago, it was reported in an English magazine that in a fairly crowded railway compartment, a couple who had been engaged in passionate kissing for some time eventually came to perform full sexual intercourse under the impassive eyes of the other passengers; it was only when, *post coitum*, the lovers attempted to light a cigarette that their co-travellers abandoned their reserve and reminded them indignantly that it was most improper to smoke in a public place.

This revealing anecdote finds an odd corollary in another railway episode, which the father of C. S. Lewis was fond of recounting; A. N. Wilson reproduced this story in his biography of Lewis. The scene is in Ulster at the beginning of the century; Albert Lewis (the father of

---

*Actually, it seems he did.

C. S.) "was travelling in an old-fashioned train of the kind which has no corridor, so that the passengers were imprisoned in their compartments for as long as the train was moving. He was not alone in the compartment. He found himself opposite one other character, a respectable-looking farmer in a tweed suit, whose agitated manner was to be explained by the demands of nature. When the train had rattled on for a further few miles and showed no signs of stopping at a station where a lavatory might have been available, the gentleman pulled down his trousers, squatted on the floor and defecated. When this operation was completed, and the gentleman, fully clothed, was once more seated opposite Albert Lewis, the smell in the compartment was so powerful as to be almost nauseating. To vary, if not drown the odour, Albert Lewis got a pipe from his pocket and began to light it. But at that point, the stranger opposite, who had not spoken one word during the entire journey, leaned forward and censoriously tapped a sign on the window, which read *NO SMOKING*. For C. S. Lewis, this anecdote of his father's always enshrined in some insane way a truth about Northern Ireland and what it was like to live there."

There is no doubt that, if the Anti-Smoking Brigade had its way, the whole world would soon be turned into one grim and lunatic Ulster. This, I think, must be the reason why, even though I hardly smoke anymore, whenever I am offered the choice I always instinctively opt for the smoking section in coffee shops, waiting rooms, restaurants and other public places: *the company is better*. In one respect, smokers do enjoy a spiritual superiority over non-smokers—or, at least, they possess one significant advantage: they are more immediately aware of our common mortality. On this particular point, they certainly owe the anti-smoking lobby a debt of gratitude. The warnings that, by law, must now be printed on all tobacco products unwittingly echo a beautiful ancient ritual of the Catholic Church: on Ash Wednesday, as every faithful is marked on the forehead with the blessed ashes, the priest reminds him, "Remember that you are dust, and to dust you will return." Most of the time, modern life endeavours to blunt or to obliterate this awareness of mortality. It should not be confused with a morbid cult of death—which is abhorrent to Christian humanism. (*¡Viva la muerte!* was an obscene fascist slogan:

when one of Franco's generals launched it at the beginning of the Spanish Civil War, Unamuno—who was then at the end of his life—denounced it in a speech of sublime passion); on the contrary, this awareness is a celebration of life. Mozart confessed in a letter that the thought of death accompanied him every day, and that it was the deep source from which all his creation sprang. It certainly explains the inexhaustible joy of his music.

I do not mean that the inspiration which can be drawn from the ominous warnings issued by the official Health and Correct Thinking agencies will turn all smokers into new Mozarts, but they will certainly endow smoking with a new seduction—if not with metaphysical meaning. I confess when I look at them, I am seriously tempted to buy cigarettes again.

TELL THEM I SAID SOMETHING

SOME TIME ago, newspapers reported the results of an inquiry conducted among the general public to determine "the hundred most beautiful words in the English language." Predictably enough, motherhood, peace, love, liberty, spring, etc. duly appeared on the list. Yet from the outset this rather silly exercise was doomed to insignificance, for the simple reason that it was predicated upon the illusory notion that words can have a value by themselves. Actually, words are to some extent like colours, of which Delacroix could say, "Give me mud, I shall turn it into the most luminous female flesh—as long as I am free to choose which colours to put by its side."

By their very nature, words are neutral and indifferent. It is only from their context that they draw their most pungent emotional charge. Racism and sexism are a form of leprosy of the mind and should be mercilessly fought; yet for the most part the fight against racist and sexist *language* aims at the wrong target. I know of a righteous American journal that censored a contributor who referred to *The Nigger of the "Narcissus."* And some equally righteous French publications endeavour to feminise words such as *auteur* (author) and *écrivain* (writer) into the hideous monsters *auteure* and *écrivaine*... Yet words are innocent. No perversions are to be found in dictionaries; they lie solely in people's minds—and that's the battlefield where the good fight ought to be fought.

It is not the words themselves, but the circumstance and manner in which they are uttered that give them meaning and impact. Stendhal (who served in Napoleon's army) liked to recall that when General Murat was charging the enemy at the head of his cavalry, he used to stir the spirits of his horsemen by shouting to them: 'My bum is round,

round as a plum.' Under enemy fire, in the heat of battle, these idiotic words became simply sublime—and the men were all willing to get themselves killed, just for the privilege of following such a hero.

In his first theatrical triumph, *La Cantatrice chauve* (The Bald Soprano), Ionesco exploited with great originality—and to splendid effect—the dichotomy that can exist between, on the one hand, the original meaning of words and, on the other, the meanings suggested by the tone, intention and gestures of the speaker. A good half a century earlier, Anatole France made use of the same conceit. In *Le Livre de mon ami*, the narrator recalls an episode from his adolescence: he had developed a passionate admiration for a beautiful female pianist who gave private recitals in his parents' house. One night, at the end of a piece, the pianist suddenly turned towards her young admirer and asked him: "Did you like that?" "Oh yes, *sir*!" the hapless boy stuttered, overcome with emotion. His blunder plunged him into such a distress that he swore never to appear again in the beautiful musician's presence. Forty years later, however, he met her perchance at a social gathering. Chatting about the successes of her long and brilliant career, the pianist confessed that eventually one became blasé about applause; yet once, in her earlier days, she received a compliment that she never forgot: a young man was so moved by her music, he called her "sir."

The circumstance that lends words their greatest weight is the proximity of death. The "swan song" image does not pertain to the Western tradition alone. It is there already in *The Analects of Confucius*: "When a bird is about to die, his song is sad; when a man is about to die, his words are true." Shakespeare seems to echo it: "The tongues of dying men / Enforce attention like deep harmony." Besides, in Anglo-Saxon common law a statement made by a dying man possesses a special evidentiary status, since "a dying man is presumed not to lie."

No wonder the last words of the great are piously collected. The famous *"Mehr Licht"* ("More light") of Goethe—assuming that he actually said it, and that he did not merely mean to ask that the shutters be opened—seems to suggest a lofty aspiration towards enlightenment and wisdom. By comparison, Thomas Mann's ultimate query, "Where are my glasses?" sounds rather flat. At the moment of giving up the ghost on a hospital bed, the colourful Irish playwright Brendan Behan still had the wit to thank the nun who was wiping his brow: "Thank you, Sister! May all your sons become bishops."

I am especially moved by the way old Countess de Vercellis died. Jean-Jacques Rousseau, who witnessed it, describes the episode in his *Confessions*: "With her serene mind and pleasant mood, she made the Catholic religion attractive to me. In the very end, she stopped chatting with us; but as she entered the final struggles of agony, she let off a big fart. 'Well,' she said, turning over in her bed, 'a woman that farts is not dead.' These were her last words."

The most heartbreaking last words are those of Pancho Villa. As the Mexican revolutionary was about to be shot, he found himself suddenly lost for words. He begged some journalists who stood nearby: "Don't let it end like this! *Tell them I said something.*" Yet this time the journalists, instead of making something up, as is their usual practice, soberly reported the failure of inspiration in all its naked truth. Trust journalists!

DETOURS

A direct path merely takes you to your destination.

—André Gide

SIDEWAYS

Alan Bennett describes in one of his journals how, during a visit
to Egypt, he found himself trapped among cohorts of tourists trudg-
ing wearily through dusty wastes of sand and rocks under a merciless
sun: the famous site he had come to admire looked merely like a stone
quarry full of sweaty crowds. He wondered if tourism was not like
pornography: a desperate search for lost sensation. The fact is, the only
impressions that truly register on our sensibilities are accidental—we
did not seek them out (let alone book an organised tour!).

As E. M. Forster observed, "Only what is seen sideways sinks deep."
There are also Egypts of the mind; in the end, it is perhaps chance
encounters with books and random jottings, however shallow, that
can best escape dreariness.

CREATIVE MISUNDERSTANDINGS

In the arts, there are works that benefit from being misunderstood.
Many years ago, a journalist who was interviewing Julien Green discovered to his surprise that this austere writer was a great fan of the
James Bond movies. But according to a friend who often accompanied
the old man to the cinema, it appeared that he was always getting the
plot-lines hopelessly mixed up.

This of course explains everything: the silliest scenario must acquire a disturbing depth after it has percolated through the filters and alembics of the author of a novel such as *Moira*.

On the subject of these creative misunderstandings, I still recall some African audiences with imaginations that bordered on sheer genius. In my youth, I once had the chance to make a fairly long journey on foot through the country of the Bayakas in a poor and remote corner of the Kwango region in the Congo. There, in the villages of the bush, an enterprising Greek merchant, who had a four-wheel-drive jeep and an electric generator, would come from time to time and organise a film session. (I am of course referring to the time before independence; for today, even if there should still be any enterprising Greek merchants around, I doubt very much that they would find passable tracks to reach these distant hamlets.)

The films that were shown on these rare and festive occasions were old Hollywood productions from the '30s and '40s—with *femmes fatales* holding white telephones and cigar-chomping gangsters in pinstripe suits. Did they come with a soundtrack? I do not remember now, but in any case it would have been of limited use, since the spectators understood only Kiyaka. Nevertheless they managed to invent for themselves, on the sole basis of these bleary black-and-white images flickering on a makeshift screen under the stars, in the warm night full of screeching insects, prodigious stories that no screenwriter could have conceived, even had he let his imagination run wild.

In these ancient American productions, black actors were rare and they were invariably confined to minor parts: doormen, shoe-shiners, cooks, railway porters. Yet it was on them that the passionate interest of the public entirely focused. To their eyes, these fleeting walk-ons were the true protagonists of the film. The very scarcity of their visible interventions would only confirm the occult and central importance of the roles that the collective inspiration of the audience was bestowing on them. Whenever they unexpectedly reappeared on screen for a few seconds, a roar of enthusiasm greeted their return, which had been awaited with intense expectation. Sometimes the black supernumerary would make only one appearance, and never come back. But it did not matter: he became all the more free to pursue his adventures in that other film, invisible and fabulous, of which the screen could only show the feeble negative image.

HAWAII STOPOVER

The most depressing thing is to watch these crowds of tourists, who paid a not inconsiderable amount to come here and secure for themselves eight days of happiness. In the motley uniforms of holiday convicts, they patrol lugubriously this huge Luna Park while trying hard to persuade themselves that they are getting their money's worth of fun.

Léon Bloy commented on the famous passage of St. Paul—"In this life we perceive things obscurely, as if in a mirror"—wondering whether the main point of the apostle's observation was that our world presented an *inverted* image of the other world. This would suggest, for instance, that the pleasures of the living are merely a reflection of the torments of the damned.

And when you come to think of it, it is easy to see how the delights of Hawaii, a cruise ship or a holiday resort could provide a fairly convincing image of hell.

COINCIDENCE

I was working on my translation of *The Analects of Confucius* and I had just reached the passage (12.18) "Lord Ji Kang was troubled by burglars. He consulted with Confucius. Confucius replied, 'If you yourself were not covetous, they would not rob you even if you paid them to.'" On that same day, my little boat was broken into, and I lost a few small things to which I had the weakness to be attached.

I should have drawn some comfort from this coincidence. Indeed, I cannot help but feel that, at times, the supreme teacher is merely addressing one side of my psychology, which resembles to a deplorable extent that of Ah Q, the famous satirical character (created by Lu Xun) who invented a way to transform all the defeats of his wretched existence into as many "moral victories."

Nevertheless, it remains true that one should own only those things one can possess casually.

SHADES OF SALAZAR

I just found in an old notebook a press clipping that I must have cut from a news magazine about thirty-five years ago. At the time I thought it might provide one day an interesting argument for a play or philosophical tale. Here it is:

> ### SHADES OF SALAZAR
> Though the 36-year rule of Portugal's Antonio de Oliveira Sala-zar ended last year, the old man is not yet aware of it. Still im-mobilised after a stroke and a coma 13 months ago, Salazar calls cabinet meetings, and his old ministers faithfully attend—even though some of them are no longer in the cabinet. No one has found the courage to tell the 80-year-old dictator that he has been replaced.

But I never managed to do anything with it. There are realities upon which no fiction can improve.

DEADLY PERFECTION

The Pazzi Chapel is probably one of the purest expressions of the Flo-rentine Renaissance; the austere clarity of its lines, the balance of its forms, the refinement of its proportions, the rigorous unity of its com-position organise all the various decorative elements and subordinate them to a leading concept. Nothing has been left to chance, and therein may lie its only flaw. Such perfection stands like a no-entry sign, barring the way to any interference from life, to any improvised initiative that could disrupt this serene harmony.

The problem is even more evident in the admirable church of San Spirito (another Brunelleschi masterpiece, on the other side of the

Arno), because this monument happens also to be an active parish church. There is therefore no possibility of turning it into a museum insulated from the vulgar contaminations of everyday life. And one can immediately gauge the extent to which its very perfection makes it vulnerable to the slightest aggressions from common reality. An exuberant and florid baroque altar in a side chapel, an ugly modern plaster saint daubed in garish colours in a corner, an original window that has been walled in for some trivial reason of convenience, another window that has been arbitrarily enlarged—all these clumsy additions and transformations make a cacophony of jarring notes; they amount to as many outrages. To borrow a boxing term, the monument cannot absorb any punches; every minute alteration is a savage blow that stuns and disfigures.

In contrast, the great medieval cathedrals, which were not designed as individual solutions to aesthetic problems but presented a collective attempt at embracing a cosmic totality, were usually left unfinished. By definition, it should not be possible ever to finish them. They remain in a state of openness; they have a limitless capacity to welcome and integrate the contributions of successive generations; they have strong stomachs; they happily swallow and digest the alluvia of the centuries, the styles of diverse ages.

In this sense, the great cathedrals—disparate and alive—are truly transpositions into stone of St. Augustine's vision: "I no longer wished for things to be better, because I began to consider the totality. And in this sounder perspective, I came to see that, though the higher things are obviously better than the lower ones, the sum of all creation is better than the higher things alone."

LIVING IMPERFECTION

Perfection demands it be preserved in a sterile glass case, sheltered from the weather, untouched by time, abstracted from life, mummified in a museum. By its very nature, it is rigid, brittle and unadaptable. But if perfection can be deadly, the corollary is that it is imperfection that ensures the survival of an artistic creation. For only what is imperfect, incomplete, unfinished, remains susceptible to modification and adaptation. It affords a margin for compromise and transformation.

Instead of being fatally dented by the various accidents of life, imperfection can be harmoniously completed by them. Michelangelo said that a statue was not really finished unless it had rolled down from a mountain. In different places, at different times, great artists have always remained aware of this. In classical Japan, a famous master of the art of gardens instructed one of his disciples to clean the garden. The zealous disciple executed his task to perfection. The master came to inspect his work and frowned. Without a word, he walked to a young tree and gave its trunk a vigorous kick. Three dead leaves fell upon the immaculately manicured grass. The master smiled at last: "Now it looks a little better."

Degas used to curse the deadly pervasiveness of impeccable taste: "They will eventually design artistic piss-pots that will make their users suffer from retention of urine." And Auden, visiting I Tatti, the Italian mansion of the great aesthete and art collector Bernard Berenson, suggested one improvement for the exquisitely decorated sitting room: "One should just add on the sofa a purple satin cushion embroidered with *Souvenir from Atlantic City*."

We rightly deplore the degradation of so many admirable monuments of the past, but we should also derive some comfort from the thought that many hideous modern structures will make quite attractive ruins one or two hundred years from now.

The beauty of Angkor is truly beyond words. Neither descriptions nor photographs can capture it, for Angkor is also made of all the scents and sounds of the forest, the drumming of a sudden downpour on the leaves, the buffaloes bathing in the moats at sunset, the sound of water dripping from the stone vaults after the late afternoon storm, the millions of insects whose concert turns the evening air into a massive block of deafening noise, with stunning breaks of pure silence. That said, one must also acknowledge that Khmer art is not always of supreme quality. The miracle of Angkor is the product of a fortuitous encounter between the work of man and the work of nature. The

French curators who formerly looked after the site understood this. What they were preserving with so much skill and sensitivity was not the original Angkor built by the sometimes pedestrian Khmer sculptors and architects, but the inspired and fragile ghost of Angkor, which was created by the erosion of eight centuries and the invasion of the jungle.

To an extent, one could say the same thing about Venice. Venice is so much more than the sum of its parts, or rather it is quite different from that sum. I am not being sacrilegious when I venture to state what is, after all, historical evidence: 500 years ago, Venice was very much the equivalent of what are today Chicago or Dallas. This dream world, this exquisite shimmering mirage of water and marble cupolas, was once a brutal display of entrepreneurial wealth, a nouveau-riche show of arrogant opulence, a flashy triumph of parvenu bad taste.

LITERARY PRESENCE

In Taiwan, some time ago, a historical literary magazine published an article analysing a little-known aspect of the life of Han Yu, a great writer of the ninth century (Tang dynasty). The author of this study said that Han Yu had contracted venereal disease while frequenting prostitutes during his stay in southern China, and that the drugs (derived from sulphur) which he took in the hope of curing himself eventually caused his death.

A descendant of Han Yu, from the thirty-ninth generation, considered that the reputation of his ancestor had been defamed by the magazine. Acting in the name of the illustrious victim, he took the magazine to court and won the case. The editor was sentenced to a fine of $300, or a month in jail. The editor appealed, but the appeal was rejected.

In this particular case, one may naturally deplore the restriction that was imposed upon freedom of expression. But one should also admire a society in which historical awareness is so keen that it makes it possible to treat the memory of a writer who has been dead for nearly 1,200 years as if he were our contemporary.

SONATA FOR PIANO AND VACUUM CLEANER

One day, as he was practising at his piano, the young Glenn Gould—
he was fourteen at the time—had a revelation. The maid who was
cleaning the room suddenly switched on her vacuum cleaner quite
close to the piano. At once the dreadful mechanical noise drowned
out Gould's music but, to his surprise, the experience was far from
unpleasant. Instead of listening to his own performance, he suddenly
discovered that he could follow it from within his body through a
heightened awareness of his music-making movements. His entire musical experience acquired another dimension that was both more physical and more abstract: bypassing his sense of hearing, the fugue he
was playing soundlessly transmitted itself from his fingers to his mind.

Analysing this episode afterwards, he said, "I could feel, of
course—I could sense the tactile relation with the keyboard, which is
replete with its own kind of acoustical associations, and I could imagine what I was doing, but I couldn't actually hear it. The strange thing
was that all of it suddenly sounded better than it had without the
vacuum cleaner, and those parts which I couldn't actually hear
sounded best of all." (Mark Twain once said that the music of Wagner
was better than it sounded; I agree with Twain but fear this is not
quite the point Gould was trying to make.)

Gould's sudden discovery of the difference between music heard in
the abstraction of the inner mind and music produced concretely by
playing an instrument, though it was enjoyable in his particular case,
was not unlike the tragic predicament of Beethoven, whom deafness
compelled to explore this other dimension of the musical experience.
Or, to take a pictorial comparison, one thinks of the great paintings
of water lilies that Monet executed at the end of his life, with his vision severely impaired by cataracts. There are also the superbly forbidding landscapes in dark ink which the twentieth-century Chinese
master Huang Binhong created in complete blindness in his early
eighties. Surgery eventually restored part of his vision, but even before
this intervention, he never stopped painting; though he could not
see the actual effect of his brushstrokes, he relied on the rhythmic

sequence of the calligraphic brushwork, which he had mastered through the daily exercise of a lifetime. For him, painting had disappeared as a visual experience, but it remained as a vital breathing of his whole being. In their fierce blackness, these late landscapes of Huang Binhong are to the eye what the harsh complexity of Beethoven's last quartets are to the ear.

The silent music that Beethoven and Gould had discovered through very different accidents has been known for ages among Chinese musicians. Perhaps it came more naturally to them because the scores of Chinese classical music do not indicate notes: they are fingering charts. Today, masters of the zither (*guqin*), in their daily practice, occasionally play the "silent zither": they go soundlessly through the various moves of an entire piece, letting hands and fingers fly above the instrument without ever touching the strings.

In the early fifth century, one great eccentric, Tao Yuanming, who is also China's most beloved poet, went one step further: he became famous for the stringless zither which he used to carry everywhere with him. When people asked what such an instrument could be good for, he replied: "I seek only the inspiration that lies within the zither. Why should I strain myself on its strings?"

FAITH

People who go to church to pray for rain seldom bring their umbrellas along.

INDIGENEITY

On the thorny issue of indigeneity and its painful and poisoned sequels of nationalistic fever, flag crazes, racism and hatreds, the old surrealist writer Scutenaire said something which, if it is not the final word, remains at least worth pondering: "Let everyone stay home: Maoris in Greenland, Basques in Ethiopia, Redskins in New Guinea, Eskimos in Slovakia and Celts in Siberia."

HOW TO READ?

It is very frustrating to watch someone who, being *nearly* right, proves nevertheless to be *totally* wrong. To borrow Chesterton's image, the feeling is as irritating as the sight of somebody's hat being perpetually washed up by the sea and never touching the shore. I experienced it the other day in a bookshop, as I was browsing Harold Bloom's latest book, *How to Read and Why*. The book contains many robust and salubrious observations that deserve to be heartily applauded, such as, "I would fear in the long run for the survival of democracy if people stopped reading" or "watching a screen is not reading." And at first I was delighted to note that, in his selection of the world's greatest literary masterpieces, Bloom rightly ranked Chekhov's short story "The Student." But when he proceeded to explain the reasons for his choice, he immediately gave such an obtuse reading of the story he professed to admire that, at once, it cancelled all the credit one might have been tempted to grant his literary perception.

As is often the case with Chekhov's best works, "The Student" is very short—barely three pages—and virtually devoid of events. A young student in theology has returned to his village for Easter: on Good Friday, having spent the afternoon hunting in the woods, he walks back home at dusk. The weather is still bitterly cold and he stops briefly to warm himself by a bonfire which a widow and her grown-up daughter have lit in their courtyard. Standing by the fire and chatting with the two women, he is suddenly reminded of the Passion Gospel which was read in church the day before, and he retells it to them: on the night Jesus was arrested, Peter had also stood by such a fire in the courtyard of the High Priest's palace. As he was warming himself among the guards and servants, they started asking him questions: he took fright and denied three times having ever had any acquaintance with Jesus. At that moment, a cock crowed, and realising what he had done, "he went out and wept bitterly."

As the student takes leave of the women, he is surprised to see that the widow is quietly sobbing and her daughter looks distressed, "as if holding back a terrible pain." Walking into the incoming darkness, he ponders the women's emotion:

Their weeping meant that all that happened to Peter on that terrible night had a particular meaning for them ... Obviously what he had just told them about happenings nineteen centuries ago had a meaning for the present, for both women and also probably for this God-forsaken village, for himself, for all people. It had not been his gift for poignant narrative that had made the women weep. It was because Peter was near to them ... Joy suddenly stirred within him ... Crossing the river by ferry, and then climbing the hill, he looked at his home village and the narrow strip of cold crimson sunset shining in the west. And he brooded on truth and beauty—how they had guided human life there in the garden, and in the High Priest's palace, how they had continued without a break till the present day ... A sensation of youth, health, strength—he was only twenty-two years old—together with an anticipation, ineffably sweet, of happiness, strange, mysterious happiness gradually came over him. And life seemed enchanting, miraculous, imbued with exalted significance.

Chekhov wrote some 250 short stories; among all of them, he singled out "The Student" as his favourite. Harold Bloom finds his choice surprising: "Why did Chekhov prefer this story to scores of what seem to many of his admirers far more consequential and vital tales? I have no clear answer ... Nothing in 'The Student,' except what happens in the protagonist's mind, is anything but dreadfully dismal. It is the irrational rise of impersonal joy and personal hope out of cold and misery, and the tears of betrayal, that appear to have moved Chekhov himself ..." Yet Bloom remains puzzled: "The rejoicing has no trace of authentic piety or of salvation."

If the story seems mysterious, it is because the simplicity of the soul is the greatest mystery under heaven. Otherwise, it presents only one genuine enigma: Chekhov, who was a confirmed agnostic, displays here an intuitive grasp of the religious experience, reaching to its very essence—which usually escapes the learned speculations of theologians. We may naturally assume that the student in the story was pious and learned; he sincerely believed that the events surrounding

Peter's denial took place 1,900 years ago in the courtyard of the High Priest's palace; his faith had already taught him that the Gospel narrative is *true*; then, suddenly, the tears of the women showed him that this story is *real*: it is happening to all of us, now. The tears of the women enable the young theologian to effect a giant leap: from abstract knowledge to actual experience, from truth to reality—which is the ground of all truths. (As C. S. Lewis put it: "Truth is always about something, but reality is what truth is about.") Instead of pondering dogmas and doctrines, the student suddenly faced evidence. Hence his joy, which was overwhelming and mysterious indeed, but which presented nothing "irrational" (contrary to Bloom's strange assessment).

Yet Chekhov—with his scrupulous intellectual honesty—did not altogether discount other elements in the student's ecstatic happiness: "youth, health, strength"—for, after all, "he was only twenty-two years old."

URINALS AND EDITORIAL PRACTICES

At the end of the nineteenth century, as France was swept by a wave of fanatical anticlericalism, many town councils and municipalities adopted the policy of erecting *urinoirs* along the walls of local cathedrals and churches; under the pretext of ensuring hygiene and public decency, the brilliant idea was to have the entire male population of the town pissing day and night against the most venerable monuments that the religious had built.

It seems to me that many modern editors of classic works of literature—and also many film-makers adapting literary masterpieces to the screen—are impelled by a somewhat similar desire for desecration. They append impertinent and preposterous introductions, they impose cover designs and presentations in complete contradiction with the expressed intention of the authors, they write film scripts that negate the meaning of the book they are supposed to adapt, they coolly chop off the epigraphs that the authors had lovingly selected—they generally display patronising arrogance and crass ignorance; they behave as if they were the proprietors of the works they should serve and preserve. Here are some examples (in no particular order). In the cinema, we recently saw what became of Graham Greene's masterpiece *The End of the Affair*—no need here for further comment. With books, it is in the paperback reprints of classics that most sins are committed. Just a glance at my humble shelves brings at random *Lady Chatterley's Lover*, with a lurid cover on which is printed in characters larger than the title, "Now a sensuous film starring Sylvia Kristel." Poor Lawrence; you really did not deserve such an indignity. A new reprint of *Lolita* carries on its cover a reproduction of one of Balthus's most patently paedophiliac paintings: a little girl caressing herself with an ambiguous smile—yet Nabokov, in his correspondence with his publishers, had taken pains to discuss at great length the question of the dust-jacket of this book, and he stipulated with utter firmness and clarity: "There is one subject which I am emphatically opposed to: any kind of representation of a little girl" (letter, 1 March 1958).

As if later editors would bother to follow authors' instructions—they do not even read their writing. Conrad is particularly ill-treated, it seems; without any warning or justification, in a Penguin reprint of *Almayer's Folly*, the editor took the liberty of simply dropping the famous epigraph that Conrad had borrowed from Henri-Frédéric Amiel: *Qui de nous n'a eu sa Terre promise, son jour d'extase et sa fin en exil?* (Who among us did not have his Promised Land, his day of ecstasy and his end in exile?) Not only is the sentence magnificent and provides the key to the entire novel, but it also supplies an important biographical clue to Conrad's literary creation (Amiel, whose diaries Conrad first read during an early stay in Geneva, reappears, in a metamorphosed shape, as the placid Swiss narrator who witnessed the ravings of Slavic terrorists in *Under Western Eyes*). The paperback reprint of *Heart of Darkness* (Oxford Classics) carries a scholarly introduction that is grotesque and delirious: it proposes an elaborate phallic reading of the novel. I paraphrase: "Look at the Congo River on the map; don't you see? It is obviously a huge, creeping phallus!" and so on. Literary scholars are particularly adept at cultivating this sort of nonsense: they seem permanently drunk on the psychedelic milk they keep sucking from the twin *mammelles* of Freud and Marx. Amazing examples of this merry art are too numerous to be quoted here.

The resolute and invincible blindness of some editors can also be quite impressive. Stendhal's treatise *On Love (De l'Amour*, 1822) is invariably presented under this title; yet, when Stendhal published *La Chartreuse de Parme* (1839), he printed at the beginning of his novel a list of his other works in which he indicated the full and final title under which he intended his essay on love to be known thereafter: *De l'Amour et des diverses phases de cette maladie*. It was studiously ignored by all subsequent editors—though it should certainly not be irrelevant for us to know that Stendhal viewed love as a sort of illness.

THE PHILOSOPHER AND THE POET

Sometimes it takes a poet to deflate effectively the windy pronouncements of a philosopher. To Theodor Adorno, who declared that, after Auschwitz, no art was possible, Joseph Brodsky replied: "Indeed, not only art, but breakfast as well."

OLYMPICS

I recently had a chance to see again the notorious (yet remarkable) documentary film that Leni Riefenstahl made of the 1936 Olympic Games in Berlin. I was struck by one tiny detail, which certainly was not deliberate and could not have attracted anyone's attention at the time. In a passage devoted to the sailing competition, the camera caught for an instant the face of a crew member on a boat, at the height of a race. He was hauling in the jib sheet with all his might, and a cigarette was dangling from his lips.

This image lasted for little more than two seconds, but for us it is stunning. At the time, it was so spontaneous, familiar and natural; today, it seems to come from another era.

In the Olympic Games nowadays, it is commonly accepted that many competitors show up stuffed to the gills with all sorts of drugs (which the relevant authorities are careful *not* to control, unless it is by methods whose ineffectualness has been duly guaranteed beforehand).

Yet should any sportsman enter the stadium with a cigarette or a pipe in his mouth, one dares not contemplate the fate that would befall him.

Surely, at the least he would be locked in a madhouse, if not stoned to death on the spot by righteously angry crowds.

But why does this simple image from an old documentary fill us with so much nostalgia? Is it not because it suddenly brings back memories from a bygone age, when it was still possible to engage in a sporting competition *just for the sheer fun of it*?

AUTOCRATS

One characteristic of autocrats which is inimitable is their naïveté. After all, despots are perhaps less cynical than credulous. An example is the anecdote told by Shostakovich in his memoirs: a general of Tsar Nicholas I had a daughter who married a Hussar against her father's will. The father begged the tsar to intervene, and Nicholas immediately issued two edicts: the first one, to cancel the marriage; the second, *to restore the daughter's virginity*.

BUSHFIRE

By mid-afternoon, our entire street—a dead end, climbing halfway up a wooded hill—is shrouded in acrid smoke, as opaque as a thick fog, creating an eerie twilight. By five o'clock, this grey fog turns red—a diffuse colour of fire, though no flames are visible yet. Electricity and telephone have been cut. We load the car with some essential belongings; documents and papers fill our suitcase; in my briefcase, stacked with letters and manuscripts, there is room left for only one book. There are some ten thousand books in the house—old and new, read or unread, all equally loved, needed, irreplaceable; which one should I save? There is no time now to ponder this question; in a hurry, I grab a thick volume (1,000 pages)—recently arrived, as yet unread: Cioran's *Cahiers 1957–1972* (his posthumous masterpiece, as it turns out)...

Unlike the neighbouring suburb, our area was ultimately spared. The next day we unloaded the car, unpacking at leisure our emergency luggage. As I was going to put the Cioran volume back in its original place on the shelf, propelled by a sudden impulse I opened it at random and came across the following entry (p. 410, top of the page):

> Henri Thomas told me, a long time ago, that he saw in a cemetery in Normandy a grave bearing this inscription: X***, born on ——, deceased on —— and underneath: MAN OF PROPERTY.

I burst out laughing. In my haste, I had picked up exactly the right book. I don't remember who said this, but it is absolutely true: "Past a certain age, we read nothing perchance."

MEMENTO MORI

DO YOU grieve at the thought that your life must come to an end? The alternative could be worse—Swift showed it convincingly in *Gulliver's Travels*. Arriving in Luggnagg, Gulliver heard of the existence of "Immortals" among the local population. From time to time a child is born with a large round mark on his forehead, a sure sign that he is a "Struldbrugg": he will never die. This phenomenon is not hereditary; it is purely accidental—and extremely rare. Gulliver is transported with wonderment: so, there are some humans that are spared the anguish normally attached to our condition. These Struldbruggs must be able to store a prodigious wealth of moral and material resources through the ages—a treasure of knowledge, experience and wisdom!

In the face of Gulliver's enthusiasm, his hosts can scarcely hide their smiles. Though the Struldbruggs are indeed immortal, they do age: after a few centuries they have lost their teeth, their hair, their memory; they can barely move; they are deaf and blind; they are hideously shrunken with age (the appearance of women is especially ghastly). The natural transformation of language deprives them of all means of communication with the new generations; they become strangers in their own society; burdened with all the miseries of old age, they survive endlessly in a state of desolate stupor. The progress of medicine provides us today with good illustrations of Swift's vision.

Recently, browsing again through Albert Speer's *Spandau Diaries*, I came across an intriguing passage. In the seventeenth year of his imprisonment, Speer noted: "Today I read in Turgenev's *Fathers and Sons* a sentence that strangely paraphrases my recent bout of calculations [to fight his crushing boredom, Speer devised elaborate mathematical variations on the remaining time of his sentence]: 'In prison, time is said to flow even more quickly than in Russia.' How time must have slowed down in Russia these days!"

Perchance, I had just been re-reading *Fathers and Sons*, and the passage in question actually says the exact opposite. Turgenev describes a middle-aged man who was abandoned by his mistress; broken-hearted, he returned to Russia, where "he no longer expected anything much of himself or of others, and he undertook nothing new"; he aged in loneliness, boredom and bitterness. "Ten years passed in this way—drab, fruitless years, but they sped by terribly quickly. Nowhere does time *fly* as it does in Russia; in prison, they say, it *flies* even faster." Turgenev states clearly that, in the emptiness of the days, time passes at lightning speed. For Speer, however, who was still young and possessed of a fierce vitality, the enforced inaction of prison life was a torture; instinctively he misread Turgenev's statement as an ironic way of saying: time passes slowly in Russia, nearly as slowly as it does in jail.

Alexis Carrel, in his classic *L'Homme, cet inconnu* (Man the Unknown), analysed the difference between chronological time (the solar time measured by chronometers and calendars), which is immutable and exterior to man, and *interior* time, which differs with each individual, and within every individual from one age to the other. For instance, in early childhood a year is of seemingly endless duration, for it overflows with physiological events (growth) and psychological events (the uninterrupted absorption of new information and impressions). As one grows older these stimulations become fewer—Evelyn Waugh, lamenting the increasing difficulty of inventing new plots for novels, noted, "Nothing that happens to one after the age of forty makes any impression"—and it results in an acceleration of time, which rushes through this yawning emptiness.

At the age of seventy-nine, Tolstoy observed in his diary that only children and old people live the true life, as the former are not yet subject to the illusion of time and the latter are finally freeing themselves from it. Indeed, at the end of our lives we are like the window-cleaner who falls from the hundredth floor of a skyscraper: the speed of his fall accelerates wildly; yet, until he hits the pavement, he remains suspended in a timeless void.

We never cease to be astonished at the passing of time: "Look at him! Only yesterday, it seems, he was still a tiny kid, and now he is bald, with a big moustache; a married man and a father!" This shows clearly that time is not our natural element: would a fish ever be surprised by the wetness of water? For our true motherland is eternity; we are the mere passing guests of time. Nevertheless, it is within the bonds of time that man builds the cathedral of Chartres, paints the Sistine Chapel and plays the seven-string zither—which inspired William Blake's luminous intuition: "Eternity is in love with the productions of time."

ACKNOWLEDGEMENT

Putting together the disparate essays of this book entailed some delicate editing, which Chris Feik effected (once again!) with tact and skill. All my gratitude goes to him.

S.L.

PUBLICATION DETAILS

QUIXOTISM

"The Imitation of Our Lord Don Quixote" first appeared in *The New York Review of Books* (11 June 1998); it was reprinted in *The Angel & the Octopus* (Sydney: Duffy & Snellgrove, 1999).

"An Empire of Ugliness" first appeared in the *Australian Review of Books* (March 1997); it was reprinted in *The Angel & the Octopus* (Sydney: Duffy & Snellgrove, 1999).

"Lies That Tell the Truth" was published in the *Monthly* (November 2007).

LITERATURE

"The Prince de Ligne, or the Eighteenth Century Incarnate" first appeared as the preface to Sophie Deroisin, *Le Prince de Ligne* (Brussels: Académie Royale de Langue et de Littérature Française de Belgique/Le Cri, 2006); it has been translated from the French for the present volume by Donald Nicholson-Smith.

"Balzac" first appeared in the *New York Review of Books* (12 January 1995); it was reprinted in *The Angel & the Octopus* (Sydney: Duffy & Snellgrove, 1999).

"Victor Hugo" first appeared in the *New York Review of Books* (17 December 1998); it was reprinted in *The Angel & the Octopus* (Sydney: Duffy & Snellgrove, 1999).

"Victor Segalen Revisited Through His Complete Correspondence" was originally published as "Victor Segalen revu à travers sa correspondance complète" in *Le Figaro littéraire* (3 February 2005); it has been translated from the French for the present volume by Donald Nicholson-Smith.

"Chesterton: The Poet Who Dances with a Hundred Legs" is the text of a lecture delivered to the Chesterton Society of Western Australia, Perth, September 1997.

An abridged version of "Portrait of Proteus: A Little ABC of André Gide" was published in *Best Australian Essays 2000* (Melbourne: Black Inc., 2000).

"Malraux" first appeared in the *New York Review of Books* (29 May 1997); it was reprinted in *The Angel & the Octopus* (Sydney: Duffy & Snellgrove, 1999).

"The Intimate Orwell" first appeared in the *New York Review of Books* (26 May 2011).

"Terror of Babel: Evelyn Waugh" first appeared in the *Independent Monthly* (March 1993); it was reprinted in *The Angel & the Octopus* (Sydney: Duffy & Snellgrove, 1999).

"The Truth of Simenon" is the text of a speech delivered to Académie Royale de Littérature Française of Belgium on the occasion of Leys's election to the Chair of Georges Simenon (1992); it was reprinted in *The Angel & the Octopus* (Sydney: Duffy & Snellgrove, 1999).

"The Belgianness of Henri Michaux" first appeared as "Belgitude de Michaux" in *Le Magazine littéraire* (January 2007); it has been translated from the French for the present volume by Donald Nicholson-Smith.

"The Sins of the Son" first appeared in the *Monthly* (February 2010).

"Cunning Like a Hedgehog" first appeared in the *Australian Literary Review* (1 August 2007).

"The Experience of Literary Translation" has been adapted by the author from "L'Expérience de la traduction litteraire," published in *L'Ange et le cachalot* (Editions du Seuil, 1998), translated by Dan Gunn. It was published in *Notes from the Hall of Uselessness* (Lewes: Sylph Editions, 2008) and in *Best Australian Essays 2009* (Melbourne: Black Inc., 2009).

"On Readers' Rewards and Writers' Awards" is the text of an address to the 2002 New South Wales Premier's Literary Awards.

"Writers and Money" first appeared in the *Bulletin* (17 December–24 January 2003).

"Overtures" first appeared in the *Australian Review of Books* (May 1999).

CHINA

"The Chinese Attitude Towards the Past" is the text of the Morrison Lecture at the Australian National University (1986); it was first published in *The Angel & the Octopus* (Sydney: Duffy & Snellgrove, 1999).

"One More Art: Chinese Calligraphy" first appeared in the *New York Review of Books* (18 April 1996); it was reprinted in *The Angel & the Octopus* (Sydney: Duffy & Snellgrove, 1999).

"An Introduction to Confucius" first appeared in Simon Leys's translation of *The Analects of Confucius* (New York: Norton, 1997).

"Poetry and Painting: Aspects of Chinese Classical Aesthetics" first appeared in *The Burning Forest* (New York: Holt, 1986).

"Ethics and Aesthetics: The Chinese Lesson" was first published in *Le Magazine Littéraire*. It was translated from the French by Mary Coupe and published in the *Diplomat* (August–September 2004) and *Best Australian Essays 2004* (Melbourne: Black Inc., 2004).

"Orientalism and Sinology" first appeared in the *Asian Studies of Australia Review* (April 1984); it was reprinted in *The Burning Forest* (New York: Holt, 1986).

"The China Experts" first appeared as "All Change Among the China-watchers" in the *Times Literary Supplement* (6 March 1981); it was reprinted in *The Burning Forest* (New York: Holt, 1986).

"Roland Barthes in China" was first published as "Roland Barthes en Chine" in *La Croix* (4 February 2009); it has been translated from the French for the present volume by Donald Nicholson-Smith.

"The Wake of an Empty Boat: Zhou Enlai" first appeared in the *Times Literary Supplement* (26 October 1984); it was reprinted in *The Burning Forest* (New York: Holt, 1986).

"Aspects of Mao Zedong" was first published in the *Australian* (13 September 1976); it was reprinted in *Broken Images* (London: Allison & Busby Limited, 1979).

"The Art of Interpreting Non-Existent Inscriptions Written in Invisible Ink on a Blank Page" first appeared in the *New York Review of Books* (18 April 1996); it was reprinted in *The Angel & the Octopus* (Sydney: Duffy & Snellgrove, 1999).

"The Curse of the Man Who Could See the Little Fish at the Bottom of the Ocean" first appeared in the *New York Review of Books* (22 June 1989); it was reprinted in *The Angel & the Octopus* (Sydney: Duffy & Snellgrove, 1999).

"The Cambodian Genocide" first appeared in the *Monthly* (September 2009).

"Anatomy of a 'Post-Totalitarian' Dictatorship: The Essays of Liu Xiaobo on China Today" first appeared in the *New York Review of Books* as "He Told the Truth About China's Tyranny" (9 February 2012).

THE SEA

"Foreword to *The Sea in French Literature*" is adapted and translated by the author from Simon Leys, *La Mer dans la littérature française*, Vol. 1, "De François Rabelais à Alexandre Dumas"; Vol. 2, "De Victor Hugo à Pierre Loti" (Paris: Plon, 2003).

"In the Wake of Magellan" first appeared in the *Monthly* (August 2008).

"Richard Henry Dana and His *Two Years Before the Mast*" first appeared in English in the *Australian Literary Review* (3 November 2010).

UNIVERSITY

"The Idea of the University" is the text of Simon Leys's address to the Campion Foundation Inaugural Dinner, Sydney, 23 March 2006.

MARGINALIA

"I Prefer Reading" first appeared in the *Independent Monthly* (1994); it was reprinted in *The Angel & the Octopus* (Sydney: Duffy & Snellgrove, 1999).

"A Way of Living," first appeared in the *Independent Monthly* (1995); it was reprinted in *The Angel & the Octopus* (Sydney: Duffy & Snellgrove, 1999).

"Tell Them I Said Something" first appeared in the *Monthly* (February 2006).

An earlier version of "Detours" first appeared in *Notes from the Hall of Uselessness* (Lewes: Sylph Editions, 2008).

"Memento Mori" first appeared in the *Monthly* (June 2006).

NOTES

THE IMITATION OF OUR LORD DON QUIXOTE

1. For this episode of Nabokov's career, I am drawing most of my information from Brian Boyd, *Vladimir Nabokov: The American Years* (Princeton University Press, 1991), pp. 213–14. The lectures were published posthumously as *Lectures on Don Quixote* (San Diego: Harcourt Brace Jovanovich, 1983).

2. Random observations on Cervantes and Don Quixote are scattered through several volumes of Montherlant's notebooks. He also wrote an introduction to a paperback reprint of *Don Quichotte* (Paris: Livre de Poche, 1961), which in turn was reproduced in the posthumous collection of his critical essays (*Essais critiques*, Paris: Gallimard, 1995).

3. *La Vida de Don Quixote y Sancho* was first published in 1905. An English translation was issued by Princeton University Press as Vol. 3 of *Selected Works of Miguel de Unamuno* (Bollingen Series, 1967). Here, I have used the French translation by J. Babelon, *La Vie de Don Quichotte et de Sancho Pança* (Paris: Albin Michel, 1959).

4. ... *Sufro yo a tu costa,*
    Dios no existente, pues si Tú existieras
    Existiría yo también de veras.
    (from *Rosario de sonetos líricos*)

5. *Don Quixote's Profession*, originally a series of three lectures, was first published as a monograph by Columbia University Press in 1958. It was subsequently reproduced in a collection of Van Doren's essays, *The Happy Critic* (New York: Hill and Wang, 1961). This volume, like most of Van Doren's other writings, has now become extremely rare.

THE PRINCE DE LIGNE

1.   The letter is a very fine one. The Prince is tactful enough to cloak his
     generosity with a jocular tone. Since Sophie Deroisin quotes only one
     sentence of it, let me give the text in its entirety:

     I am, Sir, the person who came to see you the other day. I shall
     not return, though I am longing to do so; but you dislike both
     devotees and their devotion.

     Consider my proposals. No one reads in my country; you will be
     neither admired nor persecuted. You will have the key to my li-
     brary and gardens; you will see me there or not, as you please. You
     will have a little country-house a quarter of a league from mine.
     You can plant, sow, do what you like.

     Jean-Baptiste [Rousseau] and his wit came to die in Flanders,
     but he was merely a writer of verse; let Jean-Jacques and his genius
     come and live there. Let it be in my house, or as it were in his, that
     you continue to live *vitam impendere vero*. If you want still greater
     freedom, I have a tiny plot of detached land, where the air is good,
     the sky fair; and it is only eighty leagues from here, I have neither
     archbishop nor Parliament, but the finest sheep in the world.

     There are honey-bees at the other house I offer you. If you like
     them, I will leave them; if you do not, I will remove them else-
     where: their republic will treat you better than that of Geneva,
     which you have honoured so greatly and to which you will have
     done so much good.

     Like you, I hate thrones and dominations; you will reign over
     no one, but no one will reign over you. If you accept my offer, I will
     come to fetch you and will conduct you myself to the Temple of
     Virtue, which will be the name of your abode. But we shall not call
     it by that name; I will spare your modesty all the triumphs you
     deserve.

     If all this displeases you, Monsieur, consider that it has never
     been suggested. I shall not see you again, but I shall continue to
     read you and to admire you, though I shall not tell you so.

                                    (translation by Sir Leigh Ashton, modified)

2.   Let it be said *en passant* that this observation actually reveals what is
     wrong with Wagner himself.

3.   It is worth noting that Ligne himself, though he considered Mozart "an
     excellent and charming composer," gave higher marks to Gluck.

4. In a recent work, *Het Belgisch Laberint* (Utrecht: De Arbeiderspers, 1989), Geert van Istendael has drawn the interesting corollary that "Europe will be Belgian or will not exist."

5. In Belgium, up until the end of the eighteenth century, the aristocracy and the various elites (e.g., painters) were conventionally looked upon as "Flemings." Soldiers and multifarious other down-and-outs were deemed "Walloons."

6. Ligne would write to Casanova:
    > I used to believe like you that the sum of the good was greater than the sum of the bad.
    >
    > But two years ago today, on the unhappiest day of my own life, I learnt that my poor Charles had lost his, and since then I feel that all my blessings combined (and I have received a prodigious quantity of them) have not brought me, either in general or in particular, one thousandth part in pleasure of all the pain with which this frightful loss afflicted, and will continue to afflict me....Can I even compare the life of my poor Charles with his death? I adored him for his valour, his character, his simple, jesting and sociable gaiety; but he never gave me as much pleasure alive as he hurt me in ceasing to live....

BALZAC

1. Quoted by Haydn Mason, "Voltaire et Shakespeare," in *Visages de Voltaire* (Brussels: Académie Royale de Langue et de Littérature Françaises, 1994), p. 23.

2. José Cabanis gathered a collection of these purple patches in his succulent *Plaisir et lectures* (Paris: Gallimard, 1982), Vols. 1 and 2.

3. This "Portrait de Balzac" was made for French radio and was broadcast in 1960. It is reproduced in Alain Bertrand, *Georges Simenon* (Lyon: La Manufacture, 1988), pp. 215–40.

4. These views may appear odd to Western minds, but they were commonly held in China, where they received special development in Daoist sexual theory and practice—and I wonder if Balzac did not draw from that very source. Robb points out that, in his youth, Balzac "profited from his father's multifarious interests, which, at a time, included all things Chinese." Balzac himself declared: "At the age of fifteen, I knew everything it was possible to know about China."

5. This is exactly the definition of what psychologists call "eidetic memory." Eidetic memory is similar in some of its effects to hallucination, but, unlike hallucination, it is not a morbid phenomenon. Many children are naturally endowed with this ability to store and recall at will accurate and vivid images from the past, but they lose it as they grow up. Some novelists and some painters maintain and develop this gift through the very practice of their craft. It was systematically cultivated by Chinese painters (the prevalence of eidetic memory among the Chinese may have resulted from their early learning, and constant use, of an ideographic script).

    Sartre (in his treatise *L'Imaginaire*) took for granted the validity of Alain's view that there is an essential difference between what is perceived and what is imagined; Alain used to illustrate the distinction by putting the question: If you pretend that you can *see* the Pantheon without standing in front of it, then please tell us how many columns you see on its façade. Yet a well-trained Chinese painter—or, in Europe, Leonardo da Vinci or Daumier—would have been able to meet that very challenge and, shutting his eyes, could have counted the columns from the image in his mind.

6. Following this, Balzac then singled out the two most pernicious practices that can sap the willpower of a writer: an excessive *consommation* of cigars and the frequent writing of book reviews. (For Balzac, the proper approach to literary journalism consisted simply in writing under a pen-name effusive praise of his own novels.)

VICTOR HUGO

1. *Oeuvres complètes de Victor Hugo* (Paris: Bouquins Laffont, 1989), *Océan*, p. 290. This detached fragment from the huge mass of Hugo's posthumously published papers bears a small heading: "The Revilers." What Hugo had in mind therefore was not the flaws of the great but the fact that greatness, by its very nature, presents an open field for base vermin. Taken in the first meaning, however, this observation could also be applied to Hugo, even in the most literal sense: the heroic Juliette Drouet—his loving, long-suffering mistress—noted that the great poet had filthy underwear, his personal hygiene was deplorable (he kept using her toothbrush) and, on occasion, he even gave her fleas.

2.   Eighty years after their original publication as newspaper columns, these *Letters from Paris* were eventually collected in a volume, excellently edited and presented by Leon Edel. (*Henry James: Letters from Paris*, New York University Press, 1957.)

3.   It would be inaccurate to ascribe these Hugolian flourishes to the onset of senility: thirty-five years earlier, he had already made similar pronouncements: "Vienna, Berlin, Saint Petersburg and London are only cities; Paris is a brain ... At the present time, the French spirit comes to replace the old soul of every nation. The greatest intelligences of today, representing for the whole universe politics, literature, science and art, all belong to France, and France offers them to civilisation." (*Oeuvres complètes, Le Rhin*, p. 425.) Or again: "French literature is not only the best, but the only literature there is." (Quoted in Robb, p. 228.) But didn't Hugo himself warn us? "All men of genius, however great, are inhabited by a beast which parodies their intelligence." (*Ibid*, p. 137.)

4.   *Time*, 27 April 1998.

5.   If one day one were to compile an anthology of all the great books that *were never written*, this one should certainly enjoy pride of place. We only know how Baudelaire intended to conclude it: "In my novel, which will show a scoundrel, a genuine scoundrel, assassin, thief, incendiary and pirate, the story will end with this sentence: 'Under the trees which I planted myself, surrounded by my family which worships me, by my children who cherish me, by my wife who adores me, I am now enjoying in peace the recompense of my crimes.'" (Recorded by Baudelaire's first biographer, Charles Asselineau, and quoted in Henri Troyat, *Baudelaire*, Paris: Flammarion, 1994, p. 324.)

6.   Solomon Volkov, *Conversations with Joseph Brodsky: A Poet's Journey Through the Twentieth Century* (New York: Free Press, 1998), p. 87.

7.   Edmond et Jules de Goncourt, *Journal: Mémoires de la vie littéraire* (Paris: Bouquins/Laffont, 1989), Vol. 2, pp. 1, 162.
     Edmond de Goncourt, who, in his notorious diary, turned himself into the peeping *concierge* of the French literary world, was always salivating on the latest piece of scabrous gossip. Hugo, with his ravenous sexual appetite (far from decreasing with old age, his carnal cravings developed into a compulsive mania that never relented, virtually until

his death at age eighty-three), provided a constant aliment for Goncourt's prurient notes. With his wife Adèle, his permanent mistress, Juliette Drouet, and his numerous casual mistresses (actresses, *basbleus*, fashionable beauties, revolutionary heroines), Hugo was never short of female company; nevertheless, he also experienced a quasi-pathological need for furtive sexual encounters with all the successive maidservants of his own household, countless prostitutes and other humble and anonymous partners—volunteer or professional. He kept a personal record of these activities, usually including mention of the modest expenses they entailed (he was notoriously thrifty) and a brief description each time of the type of transaction involved; all this was written in a coded language (a macaronic mixture of Latin, broken Spanish and private hieroglyphs) in order to ward off the prying eyes of his principal mistress, who was fiercely jealous. Even in times of crisis and personal tragedy, his sexual urge seems to have escaped his control. When his beloved daughter Adèle became mentally unbalanced and eloped to the West Indies, she was eventually brought back to Europe under the care of a black nurse called Madame Baa. Adèle was incoherent (she never recovered her sanity) and could not recognise the members of her family. Hugo's distress showed in his diary: "I saw Adèle. My heart is broken...Another door closed, darker than that of the tomb." But a few days after this dramatic reunion, he could not resist the exotic curiosity which Madame Baa had aroused in him, and he was soon able to record in the same diary the success of this new experiment: "The first Negress in my life."

8.   Paul Valéry, *Degas, danse, dessin*, in *Oeuvres* (Paris: Pléiade-Gallimard, 1993), Vol. 2, p. 1208.

9.   Volkov, *op. cit.*, p. 218. A fortuitous circumstance (fortuitous? Past a certain age, nothing we read can be fortuitous!) made me read simultaneously Brodsky's *Conversations* and Robb's *Hugo*. I found this totally unplanned *rapprochement* most inspiring. On the subject of "the linguistic impulse" in which Brodsky had a quasi-mystical faith (according to Volkov, he felt it was not only possible but inevitable that any crucial life decision would be reached first in a poem dictated by the inner demands of language), I find Brodsky's testimony of particular value, for, in his case, these views could certainly not be lightly dismissed as some sort of formalistic cant: he had vouched for them with his freedom and his life.

10. For Hugo, words had a physiognomy, a physical reality, akin to what ideographs represent for the Chinese: "Words have each their own figure. Bossuet wrote 'thrône' [*Note*: the regular French spelling is "trône'] in accordance with the splendid seventeenth-century spelling, which was so stupidly mutilated, simplified and castrated in the eighteenth century. If you take the 'h' out of 'thrône,' you take the seat away. Capital 'H' is the chair seen from the front, small 'h' is the chair seen in profile." (*Océan*, p.153.) Paul Claudel (who did not like Hugo very much, yet shared essential traits with him—both were poets with a cosmic inspiration, who wrote their best work in prose) has made similar observations on the ideographic nature of alphabet writing. (But Claudel had a relatively long and deep experience of China.)

11. Quoted in Robb, p. 337.

12. It is not sufficiently recognised yet that Hugo is one of the greatest writers of the sea in any language—in my anthology *La Mer dans la littérature française*, he occupies 300 pages, which I hope may begin to set the record straight in this respect. (And, by the way, he exerted a direct influence upon the double vocation—nautical and literary—of Joseph Conrad, who mentioned in *A Personal Record* the works of Victor Hugo as among the most memorable readings of his childhood; note that Conrad's father, Apollo Korzeniowski, had translated *Les Travailleurs de la mer* into Polish, as well as other works by Hugo—novels and dramas.)

13. He adopted "Ego Hugo" as his crest. "Hu(e)! Go!" is a Frenglish pun he coined after his expulsion from Jersey, where his political activities had upset the local authorities (he subsequently settled in nearby Guernsey, where he was to spend the remaining—and longer—part of his exile):

J'entends en tous lieux sur la terre
Un bon tutoiement compagnon,
Et du Hu de la France au Go de l'Angleterre,
Les deux syllabes de mon nom.

(Everywhere on earth / I hear a familiar address / Calling with a French Hu [*Hue* = "Gee up," to a horse] and an English Go / The two syllables of my name.)

His own name was an inspiring leitmotif for Hugo not only in his writings but, more especially, in his paintings.

14. "I consider Baudelaire as the greatest poet of the nineteenth century...
But I do not mean that, if one had to choose the most beautiful poem of
the nineteenth century, one should look for it in Baudelaire. I do not
believe that among all the *Fleurs du mal*...one could find one poem
that equals 'Booz endormi.'" He follows with two pages of subtle and
perceptive analysis of the poem. See "À Propos de Baudelaire," in Marcel Proust, *Contre Sainte-Beuve, Pastiches et mélanges, essais et articles*
(Paris: Pléiade/Gallimard, 1971), pp. 618–20.

15. "Tout reposait dans Ur et dans Jérimadeth" (All were asleep in Ur and
in Jerimadeth). Jerimadeth (the word rhymes with *demandait*, three
lines down) sounds like the biblical name of a place, but in fact there is
no such place—it is a phonetic equivalent of "J'ai rime à *dait*" (I've got a
rhyme for *dait*).

16. In this perspective, one can better appreciate why the Surrealist movement and the practitioners of *écriture automatique* recognised Hugo as
their ancestor. André Breton himself—the Pope of Surrealism—acknowledged it (such generosity was not usual for him): "Hugo is a Surrealist when he isn't stupid."

17. Quoted in Claude Roy, *Victor Hugo témoin de son siècle* (Paris: Editions
J'ai Lu, 1962), pp. 13, 14.

18. Quoted in Jean-Marc Hovasse, *Victor Hugo chez les Belges* (Brussels: Le
Cri, 1994), p. 27.

19. *Océan*, pp. 273, 276, 286.

20. Adèle Foucher (1803–1868) and Victor Hugo were teenage sweethearts;
when they married, he was only twenty and she nineteen; both were
virgins and passionately in love. Soon, however, their union did cool
down. Adèle had no great interest in poetry and was quite bewildered
by the frightful physical frenzy of Victor's passion. Marriage gave the
latter a first revelation of the ecstasies of the flesh, which from then on
he was to explore relentlessly with other, more responsive partners.
Nevertheless, Adèle dutifully bore him five children; after one early
lapse, for the rest of her life she discharged with dignity her role of wife
and mother; she became the loyal servant of Hugo's glory, and until her
own death gave him her unstinting support.

21. Just a few months ago, I was struck to find in an influential Chinese magazine (published in Hong Kong) a dialogue between Jin Yong and Ikeda Daisaku on the subject of Victor Hugo. (Jin Yong—pen name of Cha Liang-yong [Louis Cha]—is a prolific, talented and hugely successful author of historical novels, who has rightly been called "the Chinese Alexandre Dumas." The first volume of his most famous series, *The Deer and the Cauldron*, masterfully translated into English by John Minford, was published in 1997 by Oxford University Press. Ikeda is a religious leader, former president of Soka Gakkai.) Both read *Les Misérables* when they were adolescents, and they comment on the indelible impression this left upon them. The remarkable impact of Hugo on at least two successive generations of intellectuals and writers in China and Japan is a topic that deserves a special study. (See Jin Yong and Ikeda Daisaku: "Da wenhao Yuguo: yi renxing zhi guang zhaohui shijie," in *Ming Bao* monthly, January 1998, pp. 82–8.)

22. In Brussels alone, within two weeks of the first printing of Volume One, *eleven* pirated editions came out. See Hovasse, *op. cit.*, p. 98.

23. Tolstoy worked on *War and Peace* from 1863 till 1868. *Les Misérables*, which he read in February 1863 as he was in the decisive gestation stage of his most ambitious project, revealed to him what could be achieved by combining the epic sweep of history with the particular incidents of individual destinies—by mixing fictional characters and historic figures. See *Tolstoy's Diaries*, edited and translated by R. F. Christian (London: Flamingo, 1994), pp. 154, 158 and 508.

24. Hugo's involvement with China had two aspects: in public affairs, he showed active human concern and denounced vigorously Western imperialist aggressions in China. (To this day, the Chinese remember his generous interventions.) On the cultural side, however, his awareness of China never went beyond the superficial *chinoiserie* that was in fashion at the time. One can freely speculate on what his response would have been had he ever seen real Chinese paintings—especially the wild splashed-ink improvisations of the monk-painters of the Song, or the works of the great eccentric scholarly painters of the Ming and the Qing—but the fact is that he had no inkling of their existence. Hugo's *chinoiseries*, however, have a grotesque exuberance that is mesmerising, humorous and delightfully crazy; during his exile, he designed an entire *salon chinois* for his mistress—complete with carved wood panelling,

carved and painted screens and furniture. This amazing ensemble has been moved to Paris and reconstructed in the Maison de Victor Hugo in the Place des Vosges.

25. See *Journal de Eugène Delacroix*, A. Joubin ed. (Paris: Plon, 1950), Vol. 2, p. 88.

26. See André Malraux, *Les Voix du silence*, (Paris: Gallimard, 1952), pp. 416–18.

27. Pushkin was commenting in a letter on the indecent curiosity with which people were trying to obtain information about the private life of Byron. (Quoted in S. Volkov, *Conversations with Joseph Brodsky, op. cit.*, p. 141.)

VICTOR SEGALEN REVISITED

1. English translations are, respectively: *A Lapse of Memory*, tr. Rosemary Arnoux (Mount Nebo, Queensland: Boombana, 1995); *Steles*, tr. Andrew Harvey and Iain Watson (Middletown, Connecticut: Wesleyan University Press, 2007); and *Paintings*, tr. Andrew Harvey and Iain Watson (London: Quartet, 1991).

2. *Les Habits neufs du président Mao: Chronique de la "Révolution culturelle"* (Paris: Éditions Champ Libre, Collection Bibliothéque Asiatique, 1971). English-language translation by Carol Appleyard and Patrick Goode: *The Chairman's New Clothes: Mao and the Cultural Revolution* (London: Allison and Busby, 1977, revised 1981).

3. Victor Segalen, *Correspondance*, presented by Henri Bouillier, edited by Annie Joly-Segalen, Dominique Lelong and Philippe Postel. 2 vols. (Paris: Fayard, 2004).

4. At this university, if we are to believe Marianne Bourgeois's congenial *Monsieur Sié* (Paris: La Différence, 2003), the poet's name continues to be pronounced, Paris-fashion, as "Segalein," although he himself always insisted on the Breton "Segalène" (see *Correspondance* 1, p. 1,273).

5. It was at this time that Segalen paid a visit to Jules Renard, then recently elected to membership of the Académie Goncourt. In a letter to his wife, Segalen announced that he was going to see Renard, but thereafter he made no further mention of it. Renard, for his part, devoted a few lines in his *Journal* (14 November 1907) to the occasion: "Had a visit

from [Segalen], author of *Les Immémoriaux*. Under thirty, I think. Navy doctor. Has already made his trip around the world. Seems young, sickly, pale, ravaged, too curly-haired, a mouth full of gold presumably brought back from over there along with tuberculosis. Situation middling but adequate. Would like the Prix Goncourt not for the money but in order to write another book." And that was that. In all likelihood neither ever read a word the other wrote. Indeed it would be hard to picture two writers, two men even, more profoundly dissimilar: life experience, interests, style, aesthetic—not one thing in common. This was a non-meeting of two asteroids each whirling around on its own orbit. Ultimately the only real meeting point would be in the mind of any reader who happened to nourish a like passion for the work of each writer.

6. Morrison was the London *Times*'s correspondent in Peking from 1895 to 1912, then an adviser to the President of the Chinese Republic until his death. An *éminence grise* of the British government's foreign policy, then of the Chinese government's foreign policy, he exercised an exceptionally acute and superbly well-informed judgement on Far Eastern matters. (Until the advent of the Communist regime, the main artery of Peking, Wangfujing Street, was known to the foreign community as Morrison Street.)

7. Its title notwithstanding, the small work *Peintures* has nothing to do with Chinese painting.

8. The best French editions are those produced by Sophie Labatut (Paris: Châtelain-Julien, 1999; Paris: Folio-Gallimard, 2000). English-language translation by J. A. Underwood: *René Leys* (Woodstock, New York: Overlook, 1988; New York: NYRB, 2003).

9. He had just given up opium, which he had smoked for twenty-odd years. Although he denied the impact of this, the absence of the drug must surely have worsened his state.

CHESTERTON

1. If the Chesterbelloc was in half part a French animal, the French half—paradoxically enough—was not on the Belloc side. Chesterton's sensibility may have been quintessentially English, but his intellectual attitude was oddly continental (and this in turn may account for the fact that he found some of his most perceptive readers *outside* the English-speaking

world). Contrary to the pragmatic approach which is so characteristic of the English, Chesterton always held that no fruitful practical initiative can ever be taken without first being set within a clear conceptual framework.

He illustrated this point in a remarkable parable: "Suppose that a great commotion arises in the street about something, let us say a lamp-post, which many influential persons desire to pull down. A grey-clad monk, who is the spirit of the Middle Ages, is approached upon the matter, and begins to say, in the arid manner of the Schoolmen, 'Let us first of all consider, my brethren, the value of light. If the light be in itself good . . .' At this point he is somewhat excusably knocked down. All the people make a rush for the lamp-post, the lamp-post is down in ten minutes and they go about congratulating each other on their unmedieval practicality. But as things go on they do not work out so easily.

"Some people have pulled the lamp-post down because they wanted the electric light; some because they wanted old iron; some because they wanted darkness, because their deeds were evil. Some thought it not enough of a lamp-post, some too much; some acted because they wanted to smash municipal machinery; some because they wanted to smash something. And there is war in the night, no man knowing whom he strikes. So gradually and inevitably, today, tomorrow or the next day, there comes back the conviction that the monk was right after all, and all depends on what is the philosophy of light. Only what we might have discussed under the gas-lamp, we now must discuss in the dark."

PORTRAIT OF PROTEUS

1.   Charles Du Bos used this passage from Gide's most ambitious novel as an epigraph to his *Dialogue with André Gide* (1928), a critical essay which considerably strained the relationship between the two old friends.

2.   Letter of 17 March 1956 to Shirley Abbott.

3.   I found very few errors. Page 235, Maria Van Rysselberghe's love for Émile Verhaeren was not "unreciprocated" (far from it!) but unconsummated (as Sheridan himself qualifies it accurately further down the same page). Page 574, the name of the film director who adapted *La Symphonie pastorale* to the screen is not "Jean Delaunay" but Jean Delannoy. Page 619, Roger Martin du Gard did not die "aged sixty-seven"

but seventy-seven. Page 432, it is not altogether accurate to state that Martin du Gard's apprehensions regarding his daughter's marriage with Marcel de Coppet were unfounded; though, indeed, the couple did produce healthy children and (alcoholism and tuberculosis notwithstanding) Coppet lived a long life, the marriage itself did not last and collapsed in great bitterness. In the index, the names of the Marx Brothers and of Stalin are missing. (In the text, mention of a pleasant evening at the movies, watching *A Night at the Opera*, could convey the misleading impression that Gide appreciated the genius of the Marx Brothers. This was unfortunately not the case, as is evidenced in other passages of the *Cahiers de la petite dame*.) Larbaud's Christian name is not "Valéry" but Valery. Page 20, "*classe de premier*" should read *class de première*; page 229, "*désbabille*" should be *déshabillé*; page 578, "*problèmes actuelles*" is a mistake for *problèmes actuels*; page 663, "André Suarez" is a misspelling of André Suarès. But I am nitpicking here. These errors are all minor, and the very fact that so few of them are to be found in a work of such magnitude gives a measure of Sheridan's care and reliability.

4. Gide's *Journal* (two volumes) was issued in Pléiade, in two different editions. When I quote from Vol. 1, I refer to the earlier (1949) edition, whereas Vol. 2 refers to the latest (1997) edition. (The two editions do not share the same pagination.)

5. Sheridan's bibliography is remarkably comprehensive. Yet a few interesting books have come out since the publication of his work: Jean Schlumberger, *Notes sur la vie littéraire, 1902–1968* (Paris: Gallimard, 1999, abridged hereafter as *Schlum.*), and also Béatrix Beck, *Confidences de Gargouille* (Paris: Grasset, 1998), in which one chapter deals with the author's experiences as Gide's last secretary (hereafter abbreviated as *Beck*). Besides, I must also mention the first volume of an important biography, Claude Martin, *André Gide, ou La Vocation du bonheur, 1869–1911* (Paris: Fayard, 1999); Vol. 2, 1911–1951, is being prepared. Finally, another Pléiade volume, André Gide, *Essais critiques* (Paris: Gallimard, 1999); this monumental collection encompasses the near-totality of Gide's critical endeavour—which may well prove to be his most lasting achievement.

6. Besides these individual correspondences, there is also a general correspondence, the inventory of which was established by Claude Martin—25,000 letters!

7.   *Journal* I, pp. 396–8, entry of 24 January 1914.

8.   Proust's mother was Jewish—like Montaigne's. Without mentioning this particular fact, Gide made a perceptive comparison of the two writers in the fine essay he wrote on Proust (originally collected in *Incidences*, now reproduced in *Essais critiques, op. cit.*, pp. 289–93.)

9.   Maria Van Rysselberghe: *Les Cahiers de la Petite Dame* (Paris: Gallimard, 1973), hereafter abridged as *PD*, Vol. 1, p. 99.

10. *PD* 2, p. 22.

11. *PD* 2, p. 30.

12. *PD* 2, p. 146.

13. *PD* 2, p. 439.

14. *Beck*, p. 91.

15. *PD* 3, p. 303. See also art. *Devil* and note 79, infra.

16. Pierre Herbart: *À la Recherché d'André Gide* (Paris: Gallimard, 1952), hereafter abridged as *Herbart*, p. 36.

17. Blum wrote to Gide in January 1948, expressing his deep friendship, but he confessed that these passages from the *Journal* did hurt him. (See *Journal* 2, pp. 1,054, 1,502, note 4.) After Blum's death in 1950, his widow came to see Gide and told him: "He loved you more than you loved him. Not only were you his best friend, but you were his only friend." Gide was touched—and somewhat puzzled. (See *Schlum.*, p. 330.)

18. Sheridan, p. 127.

19. *Journal* I, p. 787 (24 June 1924).

20. Jean Prévost, *Caractères*, quoted in *PD* 4, p. 121.

21. Quoted by R. Martin du Gard, *Notes sur André Gide* (Paris: Gallimard, 1951), abridged hereafter as *Martin*, p. 90.

22. Francois Mauriac, *Bloc-notes* (Paris: Seuil, 1993), Vol. 3, p. 449, entry of 28 February 1964.

23. Sheridan, p. 510.

24. Sheridan, p. 593.

25. Gide grieved at the death of his wife Madeleine. The Tiny Lady commented: "When Gide says that he never loved anybody more than his wife, I believe him and I am sure that he is telling the truth. But when he pretends that he loved her more than himself, he is wrong—he lies. He was incapable of that—he loved nothing more than himself." See *Schlum.*, p. 346. On Gide's selfishness—shocking, spontaneous, absolute—see also *Herbart*, pp. 49–55.

26. In old age (he was seventy-three at the time), he once confided to the Tiny Lady that "anger had always been a very rare experience for him—but he found it to be a *delightful* feeling: a sort of release." (*PD* 3, p. 293.)

27. His oldest and best friend, Roger Martin du Gard, eventually took a dimmer view of the ethical cost of the Gidean attitude. In a letter to his daughter (20 April 1936), Martin issued this earnest warning: "Gide's example is baneful. His happiness is built upon ruins. His joy is made of other people's sufferings. I do not condemn him. Yet, though I sometimes envy his happiness, his joy, his freedom, my envy is only superficial; it hits me accidentally, in the weak spot of my own selfishness; at the very bottom, however, I would not wish to be happy in such a way—by trampling upon other people. Gide never felt genuinely involved with anything; he never committed himself to any form of action; all that counts for him is a temporary mood, the seductiveness of the moment. It is a way of life—it can never be mine. I am not fooled by the false boldness of those who 'break free.' It is only a form of attractive sophistry. The limits of freedom are marked by our neighbour's presence. To breach these boundaries is only a gesture of phoney courage. I have other rules of life—rightly or wrongly—and I am too far into my own journey to change them." (R. Martin du Gard, *Journal* [Paris: Gallimard, 1993], Vol. 2, p. 1,177.)

28. *PD* 1, p. 31. He said this in 1919—scarcely a year after having experienced the only tragedy of his life. Again, in 1934: "The effort it takes to put myself in a bad mood is quite extraordinary. When I am in front of some serious trouble, sometimes I try very hard to be gloomy but I never succeed." (*PD* 2, p. 416.) And finally, in 1949—two years before the end of his long life: "Even though the future inspires me a black and opaque pessimism, which I do not wish to acknowledge, and even though I am now physically diminished, I still find myself incapable of being unhappy." (*PD* 4, p. 146.) Even domestic catastrophes could not distress

him—for instance, as his rich library was being ruined by a leaking roof during a violent rainstorm (lying sick in bed, he directed the rescue operations, shouting instructions from a distance: "Leave Meredith, save Conrad!"), he pretended to be upset, but could hardly hide his excitement at the event. He said the next day to the Tiny Lady: "Shall I tell you the main result of yesterday's disaster? I have never worked better." (*PD* 3, p. 124; 4, p. 54.)

29. *PD* 2, p. 417.

30. Sheridan, p. 196.

31. *Herbart*, p. 54.

32. *Beck*, p. 152.

33. *PD* 2, p. 40.

34. Sheridan, p. 587.

35. *Martin*, p. 94.

36. His inability to recognise people's faces was notorious and often gave rise to embarrassing or ludicrous incidents. See for instance *PD* 1, p. 196.

37. This was noted by several critics and connoisseurs. For instance: "André lacks a gift that is essential for any genuine novelist: he is unable to tolerate boredom. As soon as some acquaintance turns stale, he loses all curiosity in him. It is the same with the characters in his novels: generally speaking, somewhere around page 150, his creatures cease to interest him—and then he quickly rushes a slap-dash ending." (Jacques Copeau, quoted in *Martin*, p. 30.)

38. *PD* 1, p. 371.

39. *PD* 2, p. 425.

40. On the coffee issue (choice between regular or decaffeinated), once, as orders were to be taken to the kitchen ahead of serving, Gide finding himself suddenly confronted with a decision in *advance* cried out in despair: 'You are robbing me of my possibilities of hesitation!' (*PD* 4, p. 98.)

41. B. Beck, Preface to M. Saint-Clair: *Il y a quarante ans* (Paris: Gallimard, 1968), p. iv. ("M. Saint-Clair" was the pen-name of Maria Van Rysselberghe.)

42. "Le chemin droit, dit Gide, ne mène jamais qu'au but." (M. Saint-Clair, *op. cit.*, "Galerie privée," p. 171.)

43. *Martin*, p. 119; *PD* 3, p. 18: "Je ne m'habitue pas à ce que Pierre (Herbart) appelle si justement la marche en crochet de son esprit, à ses reactions à retardement qui laissent toujours les autres s'engager avec le sentiment de son approbation."

44. "[Gide said:] 'I always found it more beneficial to refuse problems in my life.' As if this were possible!, I thought . . . But it is true, he always refuses to face problems in any clear-cut fashion, and that is how he is able to reach several solutions that are in contradiction with each other." (*PD* 4, p. 132.)

45. *PD* 4, p. 103.

46. *Martin*, p. 113–14.

47. *PD* 4, p. 149.

48. *PD* 1, p. 205.

49. Gide asked the Tiny Lady *what he should think* of Faulkner's *Light in August* (a French translation of which had just appeared). (*PD* 4, p. 202). Gide had just finished reading the new novel of Sartre, *La Mort dans l'âme*; the Tiny Lady asks: "What do you think of it?—I am waiting for you to read it, in order to know!" She reflected for herself: "I don't like this kind of responsibility." (*PD* 4, p. 187.)

50. *PD* 4, p. 41.

51. Gide, draft preface to a translation of *Nourritures terrestres*. This text was discarded by Gide, but the Tiny Lady preserved some fragments— see *PD* 2, p. 70. See also here below, art. *Proteus*.

52. *PD* 4, pp. 20, 37.

53. *Schlum.*, p. 316.

54. *Martin*, pp. 32–3.

55. *Herbart*, p. 67.

56. *PD* 2, p. 534.

57. *Martin*, pp. 45, 46.

58. *PD* 1, p. 12.

59. *Schlum.*, p. 132.

60. Boswell, *Life of Johnson* (entry of 31 March 1772): "A question started, whether the state of marriage was natural to man. JOHNSON: Sir, it is so far from being natural for a man and woman to live in a state of marriage, that we find all the motives which they have for remaining in that connection, and the restraints which civilized society imposes to prevent separation, are hardly sufficient to keep them together."

61. Sheridan, pp. 377–8.

62. *Ibid*. Also Gide, *Journal* 1, p. 671. It should be remarked that Gide himself had, to some extent, such an attitude towards Proust. Both met only on very few occasions—each time talking for hours about homosexuality. In this particular area, Gide seems to have been both fascinated and repelled by Proust's idiosyncrasies.

63. Even in the eyes of righteous men of Antiquity, did pederasty ever present such a lofty moral character? One may wonder. Otherwise, what sense should be made (for example) of the passage where Marcus Aurelius, praising the many virtues of his adoptive father, Emperor Antoninus Pius, especially mentions "the efforts he made to suppress pederasty"? (*Meditations* [Harmondsworth: Penguin Classics], Book I, 16, p. 40).

64. Sheridan largely evades this issue, which he dispatches in one mere paragraph, p. 377.

65. Sheridan, p. 335; *PD* 1, p. 44.

66. Sheridan, p. 294; *PD* 1, p. 150.

67. Sheridan, p. 356; *PD* 1, p. 151.

68. *PD* 2, p. 156.

69. *Journal* 2, p. 796 (1 January 1942).

70. Sheridan, p. 551.

71. *PD* 3, p. 269.

72. R. Martin du Gard, *Journal* 3, pp. 403–4.

73. *PD* 3, p. 250.

74. *PD* 3, p. 267.

75. *PD* 3, p. 307.

76. *PD* 3, p. 24.

77. *PD* 4, p. 79.

78. *PD* 4, p. 53.

79. *Beck*, p. 51.

80. *Martin*, pp. 18–19.

81. *Schlum.*, p. 75.

82. Sheridan, p. 288; quotes from *Journal* 1, pp. 530, 531, 560, 572, 573.

83. *PD* 3, p. 303. Also quoted by Malraux (with a slight variant: "... religion et pédérastie") in his preface to *PD* 1, p. xx. In 1950, barely one year before Gide's death, the Tiny Lady noted once again: "As Gide told me nearly fifty years ago, what interests him most is Christianity and pederasty." This had not changed. (*PD* 4, p. 190.)

84. Sheridan, p. 438.

85. *Schlum.*, p. 289, also p. 192.

86. *PD* 2, p. 437; Sheridan, p. 606. Note that, on the Catholic side, there was no unanimity on this subject. For instance, Georges Bernanos, whose genius was inspired by a profound spirituality, dissociated himself from these anathemas: "I cannot share the rather crude views of Claudel and Massis who believe that Gide is possessed by the devil." And he proclaimed publicly his admiration for Gide: "a great writer, one of the greatest in our literature"—while reserving his most ferocious barbs for his co-religionist Claudel: "*J'avouerais volontiers que la disproportion de l'homme à l'oeuvre, de l'héritier spiritual de Rimbaud à ce Champenois roublard qui ajoute chaque année un galon de plus à sa casquette, donne l'idée de je ne sais quelle truculente imposture.*" (See J. Bothorel: *Bernanos, le mal-pensant* [Paris: Grasset, 1998], pp. 118, 161.) On this issue, Francois Mauriac's numerous comments are of particular interest. His position was more complex: unlike Bernanos, he knew Gide personally, and unlike Claudel, he retained affection and sympathy

for Gide. (Mauriac was a repressed homosexual.) His assessment of the
question, however, it is disturbing: "During my life, I had, if not the
evidence, at least the feeling that Evil is really and substantially *a person*.
Some individuals who I knew were great sinners did not at all convey to
me the impression that they might be possessed, whereas in some others
whose life was apparently less dissolute, I felt that sort of presence. Certain lives which I was able to observe over a fairly long period of time,
appeared to me as if bathed in a weird and murky light...There are
people who had to struggle all their lives against a presence which they
themselves unhesitatingly identified. I shall only mention one of
them—since he himself mentioned it publicly and repeatedly: André
Gide, whose example is all the more striking in that, towards the end of
his life, it seemed that he could no more speak of the devil without
turning it into a joke. And yet, it would appear that, earlier on, he never
doubted, not that he was possessed by the devil, but at least that he had
to deal with him directly..." Mauriac quotes two passages from Gide;
the first one, from *Si le grain ne meurt*: "I recently realised that an important actor in this drama might well have been the devil. At first I
will tell it without taking into account the participation of this protagonist, whom I came to identify only long afterwards." The second
passage is from *Journal des Faux-monnayeurs*: "Certain days, I discover
in me such an invasion of evil, that it feels as if the Prince of Darkness
had already established Hell within myself." (F. Mauriac: *Oeuvres auto-
biographiques*, Pléiade [Paris: Gallimard, 1990], "Ce que je crois," chap.
VII, pp. 608–9.)

87. *PD* 2, p. 432. Gide learned this witticism from his German friend Curtius, who once quoted it to him in 1935, when describing his life in Nazi
Germany.

88. *Schlum.*, pp. 15–16.

89. "Numquid et tu," *Journal* 1, p. 588. The incident at the funeral is described in *Schlum.*, p. 345 and Sheridan, pp. 617–18.

90. Letter to F.-P. Alibert, quoted by Schlumberger: *Madeleine et André
Gide* (Paris: Gallimard, 1956), p. 171. Ménalque, Alissa and Lafcadio are
characters in his books—respectively: *Les Nourritures terrestres, La
Porte étroite* and *Les Caves du Vatican*.

91. *Journal* 1, p. 37 (3 June 1893).

92. *Journal* 2, p. 1,066 (3 September 1948).

93. *Beck*, p. 167.

94. Hélène, the neurotic and aggressive wife of R. Martin du Gard. She felt an acute revulsion towards Gide: sometimes, his mere presence made her physically ill.

95. *PD* 3, pp. 49–50, 58.

96. *PD* 4, p. 119.

97. *Journal* 1, p. 1,325.

98. *Journal* 1, p. 1,271.

99. *PD* 3, p. 38.

100. *Journal* 2, p. 663.

101. *PD* 4, p. 17.

102. *Schlum.*, pp. 187, 188.

103. *PD* 1, p. 31.

104. *PD* 1, p. 408.

105. *PD* 3, p. 111.

106. *PD* 2, p. 17.

107. *Journal* 2, p. 825.

108. See M. Saint-Clair: "Galerie privée," in *Il y a quarante ans*, pp. 169–71.

109. *Schlum.*, p. 369.

110. *PD* 2, pp. 150, 152–3, 156.

111. *PD* 3, p. 187.

112. "He said to an intimate acquaintance: 'What a wonderful role my wife could have played for me, if only she had agreed to!—Which role?—Well, she could have helped me to attract children into our house.'" (*Herbart*, pp. 38–9).

113. *Herbart*, pp. 35, 40.

114. *Herbart*, pp. 52–3. The last point is also made by R. Martin du Gard (*Martin*, p. 121).

115. *Herbart*, p. 75.

116. Julien Green: *Journal—1946–1950* (entry of 15 June 1948), quoted in *Herbart*, p. 52.

117. "I am sure these two are the friends whom Gide likes most." (*PD* 4, p. 145).

118. *Herbart*, pp. 9–10; "I belong to a generation for whom *Les Nourritures terrestres* was indifferent…I felt that Gide was merely charging through open doors." And *Martin*, p. 139: "It is a fact: not one book of Gide ever became for me one of these *livres de chevet* which mould unconsciously one's personality through long and constant acquaintance. Tolstoy, yes. Chekhov, Ibsen, George Eliot, yes. And some others too. But Gide, no. Not even his *Nourritures*, not even his *Journal*."

119. *Herbart*, pp. 69–70.

120. Music also occupied a significant place in his life; over prolonged periods of time, he would spend many hours a day at his piano—and even, during his various stays abroad, in Italy or in North Africa, securing the daily use of a good piano was always an important concern of his. But he confessed to the Tiny Lady that he was not naturally a musician: "I make do with intelligence and culture, as a substitute for innate talent." (*PD* 1, p. 262.) Bach and Chopin seem to have inspired him most. Regarding Chopin, in particular, he was deeply dissatisfied with most of the great interpretations of his time, and he developed his own theories on the subject. His *Notes sur Chopin*, published in 1939 and 1948, were unfortunately not included in the 1999 Pléiade volume of *Essais critiques*. (The *Notes* were at last reissued by Gallimard in 2010.)

   He had no original taste in painting: "Painting did not interest me naturally; my interest for painting is a mere consequence of culture" (*PD* 2, p. 427). Once, on learning that an important retrospective exhibition of Degas had already concluded, Gide exclaimed with spontaneous relief: "Good! We won't need to visit it!" (*PD* 3, p. 14.) This *cri du coeur* is revealing: looking at painting seems to have been for him more a sort of cultural obligation than a natural enjoyment. Still, he wrote an essay on Poussin (also missing from the otherwise excellent edition of *Essais critiques*). In his *Journal*, references to painters are rare, but some are quite shrewd—like this one, for example, on Delacroix: "Neither in his writing nor in his painting does he succeed in getting really close to his inner self—as Baudelaire, Stendhal or Chopin could all do; and yet he knew how to appreciate these artists." (*Journal* 2, p. 311.) Other entries are downright frustrating: for instance, he noted having met Vuillard and Vallotton in the Louvre (*Journal* 1, p. 119)—but he did not record what they said and what they saw. (Then why bother mentioning such a meeting? This is pointless name-dropping!)

121. They read classics, poetry, essays, novels, in French and sometimes in English—the range and diversity of these readings were formidable. For instance, Gide wrote (in a letter to Dorothy Bussy, 19 November 1918): "On the advice of Mme. (Edith) Wharton, my wife and I are reading aloud *Two Years Before the Mast* by Dana . . . Do you know it? Rather special, but fascinating." (I would confidently bet that no other member of the French literary elite of the time would even have known the name of this great American classic.)

122. Sheridan, p. 411.

123. As a young man, he wrote down various resolutions for self-improvement (one is reminded of Great Gatsby!), and these already included "devout reading of Virgil" (see *Journal* 1, p. 48). At the end of his life, his love for Virgil (and also for Ovid's *Metamorphoses*) had intensified (see *PD* 3, pp. 324, 328). In 1947, visiting Germany, he found himself—for the first time in four years—without his copy of *Aeneid*: he immediately purchased a new one. At about the same time, Martin du Gard described him "walking in the streets at night, and stopping under lamp-posts to pursue the reading of his pocket edition of Virgil." (See Martin du Gard, *Journal* 3, p. 810.)

124. *PD* 1, p. 50.

125. *PD* 2, p. 561; *PD* 3, p. 166.

126. *PD* 3, p. 364.

127. *PD* 1, p. 137.

128. *PD* 2, p. 43.

129. *PD* 1, p. 143.

130. *PD* 2, p. 416.

131. *PD* 3, p. 364.

132. *PD* 4, p. 52.

133. *PD* 1, p. 202.

134. *PD* 1, p. 169; *ibid*. p. 45.

135. *PD* 4, p. 215.

136. *Journal* 2, pp. 912–13.

137. *PD* 2, p. 51.

138. After his 1913 visit, Gide told Schlumberger: "I wish I could do something for Joseph Conrad. It is revolting to see him in his present situation. I just spent three days with him, and I have a very great affection for him. His books are not obtaining the attention they deserve: he can hardly live from his pen ... When I see the sort of success enjoyed by a man like [Arnold] Bennett, in comparison with Conrad's poverty, I am overcome with indignation. And on top of all that, Conrad feels tired, worn out. 'Sometimes,' he told me, 'I pace up and down in my study-room without being able to extract one single idea out of myself. I have nothing to say anymore.' I would like to send a present to his children. Have you any suggestion?" (*Schlum*., p. 51.)

    In the course of his otherwise very congenial conversations with Conrad, Gide encountered only one point of friction: the mere mention of the name Dostoevsky made Conrad seethe with disgust and indignation; Gide was rightly puzzled (after all, the first chapter of *Under Western Eyes* is pure Dostoevsky!) and would have wished to pursue the discussion in a more rational manner, but, on this particular subject, all he could draw out of his highly emotional host were a few more confused imprecations. (See *Essais critiques*, p. 876.)

139. *Essais critiques*, p. 877.

140. *Ibid*.

141. *Journal* 2, p. 923; *Journal* 1, p. 803.

142. *PD* 2, p. 107.

143. Gide himself made this observation; remarking that Du Bos disliked Balzac, Daumier and Mozart, he added: "It makes sense. It should be very interesting to delineate in this way ... not exactly the limits (for

this would imply passing judgements), but the *impossibilities* of each one. It would be very revealing." (*PD* 1, pp. 347–8.)

144. *Schlum.*, pp. 142–3.

145. *PD* 3, p. 369.

146. *Martin*, pp. 38–9.

147. *PD* 2, p. 51.

148. "Tout est saucisse en Allemagne, une enveloppe bourrée de choses disparates: la phrase allemande est une saucisse, l'Allemagne politique est une saucisse, les livres de philologie et de science avec leurs notes et références, saucisses; Goethe, saucisse!" (Paul Claudel: *Journal*, Pléiade [Paris: Gallimard, 1968], Vol. 1, p. 223.)

149. For instance, the Tiny Lady described how Schlumberger read aloud his new novel to Gide continuously over two days; these sessions were followed by Gide's very frank criticisms ("The book does not succeed in catching our interest," etc. . . .). The Tiny Lady commented: "The entire discussion was carried out in a completely fraternal spirit, without any artifice, without any touch of vanity—the whole feeling was so pure." (*PD* 2, p. 429.) On another occasion, it was Martin du Gard's turn: he read *Les Thibault* for ten days—sometimes at the rate of nine hours per day! Once again, criticisms, however severe, were proffered and taken in a spirit of mutual emulation, with literary perfection as common aim. (*PD* 2, pp. 537–8.) Both Schlumberger and Martin du Gard wrote very harsh letters to Gide at the time of his communist infatuation. Gide immediately telephoned Schlumberger to thank him, and he showed Martin's letter to the Tiny Lady, adding: "Isn't this an admirable letter? . . . Such force, such breath! . . . And I feel that he is right on many points." (*PD* 2, p. 299.)

150. Martin du Gard was very much Gide's junior, both in years and in literary achievements; yet he received the Nobel Prize for literature ten years ahead of Gide. On learning the news, both Gide and the Tiny Lady were positively delirious with joy: "Martin, our Martin has got the Nobel Prize! . . . What happens to us is really fantastic!" (*PD* 3, p. 48.)

151. *Journal* 1, p. 805.

152. *PD* 4, p. 213.

153. See Pascal Mercier, introduction to *Schlum.*, p. 22.

154. "Billet à Angèle," in *Essais critiques*, pp. 289–93.

155. Reading *Le Côté de Guermantes*, Gide said: "It is done so well, that it makes me feel a little depressed. In comparison, my own work seems so crude!" (*PD* 1, p. 71.) *Sodome et Gomorrhe*, however, greatly upset him: he felt that Proust had slandered homosexuality by reducing it to its effeminate manifestations. (*PD* 1, pp. 98–9.) He found *La Prisonnière* exasperating: "It looks as if Proust were parodying Proust and the substance of the book is totally devoid of interest." Still, he had to acknowledge: "It is of considerable importance for literature. After having read Proust, one can no longer be completely the same person again." (*PD* 3, p. 155.)

156. And yet was he really blind to Simenon's limitations? One may doubt it. One day, Simenon, who had lunch with Gide, told him: "The main temptation I should guard myself against is…" He searched for a phrase, and Gide immediately suggested: "The temptation to fart above your arse." "Exactly," said Simenon. (*PD* 3, p. 359.)

157. *Journal* 2, pp. 1,057–8.

158. "Baudelaire et Monsieur Faguet," in *Essais critiques*, pp. 248–9.

159. Criticising some pages by Duhamel, Martin du Gard was induced to extend his observations to the style of Gide himself: "The danger of being able to write well is also the ability to lend a pleasant form to thin or mediocre ideas, to ghosts of ideas … It generates the fatal temptation to give a veneer of consistency, density, weight and character to whatever comes to mind and should not deserve to be written down. Through this mechanical operation of style, one can present at little cost an appearance of thought without any effort … The shine of the varnish hides the low quality of the wood that was used." (Martin du Gard: *Journal* 3, pp. 527–8.)

Gide had shown Martin a draft of the address he was going to deliver in Oxford, on being awarded a Doctorate *honoris causa*. Martin found that its form was very polished, but the elegance of the style could not redeem the vacuity of the content: "I told it to him very bluntly. He agreed, and for once, I regretted my frankness, for he immediately decided: 'You are absolutely right! Tomorrow I will send them a telegram, and cancel everything!' But I believe he will once again change his mind. As soon as I leave, it will seem to him that his speech was not so bad after all, he will read it again to himself, let his prose sing, and take delight in its subtle phrasing." Martin guessed right: in the end, Gide went to Oxford and delivered his elegantly hollow speech. (*Ibid.*, pp. 810–11.)

Schlumberger once pointed out to Gide a mistake he had made in a translation from Goethe, but he was shocked by Gide's reply: "I know, I have tried to put it differently, but all my other versions lacked in rhythm." Schlumberger commented: "I have noted this reaction, as, once again, it shows his constant willingness to sacrifice meaning to form." (*Schlum.*, p. 236.)

The Tiny Lady summed up: "I believe that he attaches so much importance to the question of form, that the question of content ceases somehow to interest him." (*PD* 4, p. 16.) Earlier on, after reading his *Journal*, she put the question to him: "I confess I do not always understand why you select certain things for recording in your diary, whereas you omit other things that should have been equally, or more, interesting. Could it be that your choice is simply determined by the possibility of finding at once a form that is pleasing?" Gide confirmed the accuracy of her guess. (*PD* 3, p. 361.)

160. *PD* 4, p. 233.

161. Paul Claudel: *Journal* 1, p. 969.

162. *Schlum.*, pp. 176, 246–7.

163. *PD* 2, p. 376.

164. *PD* 3, p. 78; Sheridan, p. 525.

165. *Et nunc manet in te* and *Journal* 1, p. 1,310; also Sheridan, p. 524.

166. This was addressed to Madeleine, and she had read it before marrying André. See *Martin*, p. 84.

167. Account of Martin du Gard (1920), quoted by J. Schlumberger: *Madeleine et André Gide*, p. 186.

168. *Et nunc manet in te*, pp. 1,128–9; and Sheridan, p. 525.

169. *Et nunc manet in te* (in the 1960 Pléiade edition of *Journal 1939–1949*), p. 1,134.

170. *Schlum.*, pp. 178–9, 220.

171. Account of Martin du Gard, quoted in Schlumberger: *Madeleine et André Gide*, p. 191–2.

172. Account of the Tiny Lady, quoted in Schlumberger, *op. cit.*, pp. 196–7.

173. *Et nunc manet in te, op. cit.*, p. 1,148.

174. *Martin*, pp. 61–2.

175. *Martin*, pp. 131–2.

176. *PD* 2, p. 70.

177. *Journal* 1, pp. 798–801.

178. *Journal* 2, pp. 487–8.

179. *Journal* 1, p. 720.

180. *PD* 2, p. 531.

181. Well described by Sheridan, pp. 445–90. Quotes not otherwise identified here are drawn from Sheridan's account.

182. *PD* 2, p. 204.

183. *Schlum.*, p. 167.

184. Martin du Gard, *Journal* 2 (27 November 1936), pp. 1,208–9.

185. *PD* 3, p. 198.

186. *PD* 3, p. 201.

187. *PD* 3, p. 205.

188. Martin du Gard, *Journal* 3, p. 404.

189. *Schlum.*, p. 266.

190. *PD* 4, p. 190.

191. *Schlum.*, p. 16. (Quoted from *La Porte est ouverte* in Paul Mercier's preface.)

192. *Si le grain ne meurt*, quoted in *PD* 2, p. 128; *Journal* 1, p. 573.

193. Martin du Gard, *Journal* 2, pp. 232–3.

194. *Martin*, pp. 96–8.

195. *PD* 2, p. 114.

196. *Schlum.*, p. 368. On that same page, Schlumberger had just noted that Mauriac told him after reading the memoir of Jean Lambert (Gide's son-in-law), which alluded to the old man's monomania: "We must face the fact: Gide was truly a sick person, one of those madmen who need to be locked away." (Once again, it should be recalled that Mauriac was himself a repressed homosexual, and that he had a genuine friendship with Gide.)

197. Gide's moral blindness and capacity for self-deception staggered even his closest friends. Martin du Gard tells how Gide's daughter, who was seventeen at the time, had become the object of the timid sentimental attentions of one of her former teachers. Gide was indignant and wanted to write to the man: "Sir, stop bothering this child. I forbid you to meet her again." The situation, he said, was "odious." This reaction bemused Martin: "Our good old Gide has in fact spent all his life committing breaches of trust that were far more severe! How many times did he worm his way into a friendly family, multiplying warm approaches to the parents, with the sole purpose of getting closer to their son—sometimes a thirteen-year-old schoolboy—and of joining him in his room, arousing his sexual curiosity, teaching him sensual pleasure! He was more clever than Catherine's teacher, more diabolic with his temptations, more daring also. How many times did he succeed in hoodwinking the parents, in securing the complicity of the child, in indulging with him in sweet and perverse games? But then, to his mind, there was nothing 'odious' in this premeditated debauching of a young boy, whom his parents had entrusted to his friendly care!" (Martin du Gard, *Journal* 3, pp. 361–2.)

198. *PD* 4, pp. 253–4.

199. *PD* 2, p. 406.

200. Béatrix Beck tells in her memoirs: "Some time after the death of Gide, Dominique Drouin (his nephew) told me that the Tiny Lady had confided to him: 'I have to fetch a little Annamite for him, and when I cannot find any, I act as a substitute.' And Drouin added: 'When you think of these two bags of bones.'... I have a strong visual imagination and I somatise easily: I had to vomit on the spot." (*Beck*, p. 161.)

201. *Schlum.*, p. 346.

202. *PD* 4, p. 252.

203. Béatrix Beck, Preface to M. Saint-Clair, *Il y a quarante ans*, p. iv.

204. Sheridan, pp. 370 and 633.

205. *Schlum.*, p. 96.

206. *Schlum.*, p. 150.

207. *PD* 2, p. 58.

208. Quoted in *PD* 3, p. 16.

209. *PD* 4, p. 204.

210. Saint Augustine: *Confessions*, X, (xxiii) 34: "Sic amatur veritas, ut qui-cumque aliud amant, hoc quod amant velint esse veritatem, et quia falli nolent, nolunt convinci quod falli sint. Itaque propter eam rem oderunt veritatem, quam pro veritate amant."

MALRAUX

1.   In November 1996, on the twentieth anniversary of his death, Malraux was awarded the form of immortality which the French nation bestows upon its most illustrious cultural heroes: his mortal remains were moved with great pomp into the Pantheon in Paris.

2.   *La Tragédie de la révolution chinoise*, translation by R. Viénet (Paris: Gallimard, 1967).

3.   J. Andrieu, "Mais que se sont dit Mao et Malraux?" in *Perspectives Chinoises*, No. 37, October 1996. (An abridged version of this article was published in *Le Nouveau quotidien*, Lausanne, 3 December 1996.)

4.   G. Duthuit, *Le Musée inimaginable* (Paris: José Corti, 1956). Duthuit pointed out, with great scholarly accuracy, the countless historical howlers in Malraux's *Musée imaginaire: les voix du silence*. He also exposed his hollowness, obscurity, logical non sequiturs, and other factual mistakes. His demonstration (in two volumes of text and one volume of illustrations) was brilliant, rigorous and devastating—but it reached only a small circle of specialised scholars.

5.   B. Chatwin, *What Am I Doing Here?* (London: Picador, 1990), p. 133.

6.   *The Nabokov–Wilson Letters 1940–1971*, ed. Simon Karlinsky (London: Weidenfeld & Nicholson, 1979), p. 175.

7.   J.-P. Sartre, *Lettres au Castor* (Paris: Gallimard, 1983), Vol. 2, pp. 159, 167, 163, 192.

8.   Letter to Roger Nimier, 8 January 1953 (in Jacques Chardonne–Roger Nimier, *Correspondance*, Paris: Gallimard, 1984, p. 91.) Two samples of Malraux's *galimatias* (out of possible hundreds) are provided by Curtis Cate (p. 372): "The language of Phidias' forms or of those of the pediment of Olympia, humanistic though it is, is also as specific as that of the masters of Chartres and Babylon or of abstract sculptures, because like that of the great Italians of the fourteenth to the sixteenth centuries, it simultaneously modifies the representation and its style." Or again: "Between Cézanne's *Still Life with Clock*, which strives only to be a painting, and his canvases which have become a style, there resurfaces the call which raises up Bach over and against negro music, and Piero della Francesca over and against barbarian arts—the art of mastery, as opposed to that of the miracle."

9.   B. Souvarine, *Staline* (Paris: Champ Libre, 1977), pp. 11–12.

10. R. Stéphane, *André Malraux: entretiens et précisions* (Paris: Gallimard, 1984), p. 91.

11. C. Cate, *André Malraux: A Biography* (New York: Fromm, 1997).

THE INTIMATE ORWELL

1.   On this subject, Orwell's wife, writing to his sister (from Marrakech in 1938) observed with wry amusement: "He did construct one dugout in Spain [during the Civil War] and it fell down on him and his companions' heads two days later, not under any kind of bombardment, but just from the force of gravity. But the dugout has generally been by way of light relief; his specialities are concentration camps and famine. He buried some potatoes against the famine, and they might have been very useful if they hadn't gone mouldy at once. To my surprise he does intend to stay here [in Marrakech] whatever happens. In theory this seems too reasonable and even comfortable to be in character."

2. Orwell and Spender became friends—but on the subject of Spender's poetry, Orwell's literary judgement never wavered; he simply chose not to comment.

3. This reminds me of Georges Bernanos (the two writers have much in common besides their fight against Franco). The great French novelist and pamphleteer exiled himself to Brazil shortly before the Second World War—he was disgusted by France's political and moral decline. He sank all his meagre savings in the purchase of a cattle farm (which was soon to go bankrupt) and at the time wrote to a friend: "I have just bought 200 cows and thus acquired the right to call myself no longer 'man of letters' but cattleman, which I much prefer. As a cattleman I shall be able to write what I think."

4. A young and beautiful woman—though somewhat hare-brained, she managed to edit (with the collaboration of I. Angus) the excellent *Collected Essays, Journalism and Letters of George Orwell* (London: Secker & Warburg, 1969). These four volumes remain invaluable; not every reader can afford the twenty volumes of Davison's editions of the *Complete Works*.

TERROR OF BABEL: EVELYN WAUGH

1. Christopher Sykes, *Evelyn Waugh: A Biography* (London: Collins, 1975); Auberon Waugh, *Will This Do?* (London: Arrow, 1991). Postscript of 1998: one more title should be added now to this small bibliography—Selena Hastings, *Evelyn Waugh: A Biography* (London: Sinclair-Stevenson, 1994).

2. Once more, one is reminded of Belloc and of the remarkable letter he wrote to Chesterton on the occasion of the latter's conversion to Catholicism: "The Catholic Church is the exponent of *Reality*. It is true. Its doctrines in matters large and small are statements of what is. This it is which the ultimate act of the intelligence accepts. This it is which the will deliberately confirms . . . I am by all my nature of mind sceptical . . . And as to the doubt of the soul, I discover it to be false: a mood, not a conclusion . . . To you, who have the blessing of profound religious emotion, this statement may seem too desiccate. It is indeed not enthusiastic. It lacks meat. It is my misfortune. In my youth I had it: even till lately. Grief has drawn the juices from it. I am alone and unfed, the more do I affirm the Sanctity, Unity, the Infallibility of the Catholic

Church. By my very isolation do I affirm it, as a man in a desert knows that water is right for man; or as a wounded dog, not able to walk, yet knows the way home."

THE BELGIANNESS OF HENRI MICHAUX

1. As a matter of fact Michaux was born not in Brussels but in Namur (which only reinforces the point).

2. In the light of his own experience, Cioran, who was profoundly sympathetic to both Michaux and Borges, has this to say about the latter: "By the time I reached twenty, things Balkan had nothing further to offer me. Such is the tragedy—and also the benefit—of being born in a minor or indifferent cultural environment. I worshipped what was foreign. Whence my hunger to venture abroad into literature and philosophy, falling upon them with an unhealthy passion. What happens in Eastern Europe must necessarily occur too in the Latin American countries, and I have noticed that their representatives are infinitely better informed and more cultured than Westerners, who are incurably provincial. Neither in France nor in England have I encountered anyone with a curiosity to rival that of Borges, which is almost maniacal, almost a vice—and I say "vice" advisedly, for when it comes to art and thought anything that does not tend towards a slightly perverse fervour is superficial, and therefore illusory.... Borges was condemned to universality, forced into it, obliged to direct his mind in every direction if only to escape the asphyxiating atmosphere of Argentina. It is the South American void that makes the writers of the whole continent more lively and varied than West Europeans paralysed by tradition and incapable of breaking out of their prestigious atrophy."

3. When Jacques Brosse told him how he had written an account of a psychological experience with the greatest of ease, Michaux responded enviously: "Ah, but it's obviously not the same for you: you write in your mother tongue!"

    "Surely," Brosse replied, "you're not telling me that they don't speak French in Namur?"

    "It's not French they speak—it's Walloon!"

    Michaux added that, at the boarding school where he was locked up at the age of seven, "surrounded by stinking little peasants" who were brutal and spoke only in their own dialect, "Flemish became my second language, which I spoke as well, if not better, than French." "Did you know," the poet once asked an interviewer, "that as an adolescent I briefly contemplated writing in Flemish?" His very first revelation of poetry came from reading Guido Gezelle: "Gezelle was the great man. But I quickly realised that I could never equal him." It must indeed be said that this West-Flemish priest-poet succeeded in making sublime verbal music in his obscure patois; his verses are forever engraved in the memory of anyone exposed to them on a school bench.

4.   It is a strange French and English hybrid. The French equivalent of "schooner" is *goélette*. Michaux's term might refer either to a *cinq-mâts goélette* or a *goélette à cinq mâts*. The difference between the two types of rigging is substantial: the first carries square sails on the foremast, whereas the five masts of the second are all fore-and-aft rigged. Late in his life, probably embarrassed by the juvenile bragging and exaggerations of his letters to Closson, Michaux prevailed upon his correspondent to return them to him, and no sooner did he get them back than he destroyed them—to the consternation of his old friend. But even though the originals thus perished, the content of the letters survived, unbeknownst to the two correspondents, in the shape of photocopies made fifteen years earlier by a third party who had access to Closson's papers. This eventually made posthumous publication possible—something which Michaux would doubtless have opposed. One might well wonder, moreover, what caused the vehemence with which he sought to erase all traces of this unique phase of his life.

5.   And let it not be objected that the original versions and variants are supplied in the endnotes! In the first place, only some of them are; but the most important thing is that average readers can hardly be expected to enjoy reading a text when, for every page, they have to flip back a dozen times to notes in microscopic print a thousand pages further on. The dismal truth is that Michaux's greatest writings are now unavailable in their incomparable original versions. We can but dream of a sort of anti-Pléiade edition that brought them together in a single volume.

6.   Needless to say, I have no desire lightly to pass a negative judgement upon editors who have accomplished a gigantic task, successfully assembling a mass of materials, texts and information otherwise inaccessible to general readers. (Without this indispensable reference tool, for instance, I should never have been able to write the present essay.) But

still, from an aesthetic and literary standpoint, the great monument that they have erected seems very much like a tomb containing not a few eviscerated mummies.

7. *L'Île noire* in its successive revisions is a particularly sad illustration of this process.

8. [The English translation by Sylvia Beach (New York: New Directions, 1949; reprint, 1986) is of the original version. Beach's translation is used here throughout, with occasional modifications—*Translator*.]

9. The reference to Bruegel here is more than a mere analogy. Michaux may very well have derived the idea of the diarrhoea of the Ourgouilles from Bruegel's painting *The Fall of the Rebel Angels* (in the Musées Royaux des Beaux-Arts de Belgique, which the poet knew well): this work shows (among other figures) a hideous big-bellied demon who, as he plunges head-first down into hell, is devouring his own foot while firing off great fuliginous farts. Michaux acknowledged to François Cheng that, although he had scant interest in oil painting (he preferred ink washes, and most of all Chinese painting), Flemish art was well known to him, and he had a very special liking for Bruegel and his mastery of the art of combining the real and the imaginary. (See Cheng Baoyi, *Ye Dong* [*La Nuit remue*], introduction, p. x.)

10. Chateaubriand (who was no fool) gives us an eloquent sample of this national consciousness. During the retreat of the Armée des Princes (in whose ranks he had enlisted as a volunteer), wounded and sick, Chateaubriand collapsed by the side of the road near Namur; goodhearted Walloon peasant women took him up and cared for him. The Vicomte described this in the following terms: "I noticed that these women treated me with a kind of respect or deference: there is in the nature of the French something elevated and sensitive that other peoples recognise" (*Mémoires d'outre-tombe*, X, 2). It is hard to picture Plume abroad being led to voice a thought of that kind.

ON READERS' REWARDS AND WRITERS' AWARDS

1. These are the words of Joseph Conrad, in what remains the classic manifesto of the art of the novel—his famous preface to *The Nigger of the "Narcissus."* The first sentence reads in full: "Art itself may be defined as a single-minded attempt to render the highest kind of justice to the

visible universe, by bringing to light the truth, manifold and one, underlying its every aspect."

THE CHINESE ATTITUDE TOWARDS THE PAST

1. The civilisations of Egypt, the Middle East, Persia and ancient India are no less ancient, but their continuity has been broken. Only the Jewish tradition may present a significant parallel to the phenomenon of spiritual continuity which I am trying to study here.

2. "I have travelled a great deal in my life, and I should very much have liked to go to Rome, but I felt that I was not really up to the impression the city would have made upon me. Pompeii alone was more than enough; the impressions very nearly exceeded my powers of receptivity... In 1921 I was on a ship sailing from Genoa to Naples. As the vessel neared the latitude of Rome, I stood at the railing. Out there lay Rome, the still smoking and fiery hearth from which ancient cultures had spread, enclosed in the tangled root-work of the Christian and Occidental Middle Ages. There classical antiquity still lived in all its splendour and ruthlessness.

   "I always wonder about people who go to Rome as they might go, for example, to Paris or to London. Certainly Rome as well as these other cities can be enjoyed aesthetically but if you are affected to the depths of your being at every step by the spirit that broods there, if a remnant of a wall here and a column there gaze upon you with a face instantly recognised, then it becomes another matter entirely. Even in Pompeii, unforeseen vistas opened, unexpected things became conscious, and questions were posed which were beyond my power to handle.

   "In my old age—in 1949—I wished to repair this omission, but was stricken with a faint while I was buying tickets. After that, the plans for a trip to Rome were once and for all laid aside." C. G. Jung, *Memories, Dreams, Reflections* (London: Collins, 1973), pp. 318–19.

3. AUX DIX MILLE ANNÉES
   Ces barbares écartant le bois, et la brique et la terre, bâtissent dans le roc afin de bâtir éternel!

   Ils vénèrent des tombeaux dont la gloire est d'exister encore; des ponts renommés d'être vieux et des temples de pierre trop dure dont pas une assise ne joue.

   Ils vantent que leur ciment durcit avec les soleils; les lunes meurent en polissant leurs dalles; rien ne disjoint la durée dont ils s'affublent, ces ignorants, ces barbares!

Vous! fils de Han, dont la sagesse atteint dix mille années et dix mille dix milliers d'années, gardez-vous de cette méprise.

Rien d'immobile n'échappe aux dents affamées des âges. La durée n'est point le sort du solide. L'immuable n'habite pas vos murs, mais en vous, hommes lents, hommes continuels.

Si le temps ne s'attaque à l'oeuvre, c'est l'ouvrier qu'il mord. Qu'on le rassasie: ces troncs pleins de sève, ces couleurs vivantes, ces ors que la pluie lave et que le soleil éteint.

Fondez sur le sable. Mouillez copieusement votre argile. Montez les bois pour le sacrifice; bientôt le sable cèdera, l'argile gonflera, le double toit criblera le sol de ses écailles:

Toute l'offrande est agréée!

Or, si vous devez subir la pierre insolente et le bronze orgueilleux, que la pierre et que le bronze subissent les contours du bois périssable et simulent son effort caduc:

Point de révolte: honorons les âges dans leurs chutes successives et le temps dans sa voracité.

V. Segalen, *Stèles* (Paris: Crès, 1922), pp. 29–31.

4. By "antiquarianism" I mean not only the taste and passion for all things antique but also their various corollaries: the development of archaeology, the activities of art collectors, dealers and forgers, the aesthetics of archaism ("ancient is beautiful," the poetry of the past, meditation over ancient ruins as a literary theme, etc. etc.).

5. A telling illustration of this point can be found in Li Qingzhao's moving memoir, *Jin shi lu houxu* (1132). After the fall of the Northern Song, as Li was fleeing south, she had to carry with her the precious collections of her husband. The latter, who was prevented by his official duties from accompanying her, gave her precise instructions concerning those parts of the collections that could be discarded, and those that should be retained at all costs, should the situation force her to reduce her luggage. The most dispensable possessions were the *printed* books (as opposed to handwritten copies); then the pictorial albums (as opposed to individual paintings); then the bronzes that *carried no epigraphs*; then the printed books published by the Imperial College; then the paintings of average quality... The most treasured items—besides the vessels and relics pertaining to the ancestors cult (under no conditions were

these ever to be discarded)—were the antique bronzes with epigraphs, precious paintings and calligraphies and rare manuscripts. *Li Qingzhao ji jiaozhu* (Peking: Renmin wenxue chubanshe, 1979), pp. 179–81.

6. The classic study on art collecting in China is R. van Gulik, *Chinese Pictorial Art as Viewed by the Connoisseur* (Rome, 1958). (Reissued by Hacker Art Books: New York, 1981.) On the particular subject of the imperial collections, see L. Ledderose, "Some observations on the imperial art collection in China," in *Transactions of the Oriental Ceramic Society* 43 (1978–1979): pp. 33–46.

7. The episode, which occurred in 818, involved Emperor Xianzong and the grandfather of the great art historian Zhang Yanyuan; the latter told it in his *Lidai ming hua ji*. See Zhang Yanyuan, *Lidai ming hua ji* (Peking: Renmin meishu chubanshe, 1963), Vol. 1, Chap. 2, pp. 10–11. See also W. Acker, *Some T'ang and pre-T'ang texts on Chinese painting* (Leiden: Brill, 1954), pp. 138–41.

8. It is at this time, for example, that *The Night Revels of Han Xizai* by Gu Hongzhong (tenth century) and *Qingming Festival along the River* by Zhang Zeduan (twelfth century) returned to China. (Both paintings are kept in the Ancient Palace Museum, Peking.)

9. The fact that an author describes in vivid terms the pictorial style of a given artist never implies that he actually saw any works by that artist; sometimes, in another passage of the same text, he may even explicitly acknowledge that he never had such an opportunity.

10. For example, Mi Fu (1051–1107), who was one of the most learned connoisseurs of his time, with privileged access to the best collections, confessed that, in his entire life, he only saw *two* authentic paintings by Li Cheng, the greatest and most influential landscape painter of the tenth century (Li Cheng died in 967, less than a century before Mi Fu's birth). Mi Fu, *Hua shi*, in *Meishu congkan* (Taipei, 1956), Vol. 1, p. 88. See also N. Vandier-Nicolas, *Le Houa-che de Mi Fou* (Paris: Presses universitaires de France, 1964), pp. 32–33. Similar evidence can be found in abundance, it only remains to be systematically compiled.

11. Besides being an important business, art forgery also fulfilled very significant artistic and socio-cultural functions. Every scholarly family *had* to possess a collection of paintings and calligraphy; needless to say, not every scholarly family had the financial means to acquire ancient works

of art, the supply of which was necessarily limited. Hence, forgers provided "imaginary" collections, which conformed to stylistic stereotypes and simultaneously popularised those stereotypes. In this respect, forgeries played a role not entirely dissimilar to the one which is taken now by cheap, popular prints and reproductions. This situation largely persists till today: I have seen eminent Chinese intellectuals living in narrow circumstances, who derived immense enjoyment and spiritual solace from an assortment of ludicrous fakes. (One is reminded of Balzac's notorious collections of phony Titians and ridiculous Raphaels—these bizarre *croûtes* acted as a powerful stimulant on his visionary imagination.)

Finally, it should also be observed that Chinese forgeries could achieve very high standards of aesthetic and technical quality. In every period, including our own time, some of the greatest artists had no qualms about indulging in this activity.

12. Jorge Luis Borges, "Funes the Memorious," *Labyrinths* (Harmondsworth: Penguin, 1981), pp. 87–95.

13. On this subject see also Wang Gungwu, "Loving the Ancient in China," in I. McBryde, ed., *Who Owns the Past?* (Melbourne: Oxford University Press, 1985).

14. Xun Zi's journey to the totalitarian state of Qin, as its power was on the rise, calls irresistibly to mind the political pilgrimages that Western intellectuals undertook in the 1930s to the Soviet Union of Stalin. Xun Zi's account of his visit (*Xun Zi* 16: "Qiang guo") could in a way be summarised by Lincoln Steffens's notorious utterance: "I have seen the future and it works."

15. I am referring here to a famous passage of the *Zuo zhuan* (twenty-fourth year of Duke Xiang) which relates a dialogue that took place between Shusun Bao and Fan Xuanzi. Fan asked: "What is immortality? Could it be the continuous transmission of certain titles within a same family?" and he invoked the example of his own ancestors who had occupied high positions since the Xia dynasty. "No," replied Shusun, "that is merely a case of hereditary privilege, which can be found everywhere and merely rests upon a continuity of the family clan. The true immortality consists in establishing virtue, in establishing deeds and in establishing words [that can continue to live in posterity], whereas the mere preservation of the greatest dignity cannot be called freedom from decay." The philosophical interpretation which I present

here comes from Qian Mu, *Zhongguo lishi jingshen* (Taipei: Guomin chubanshe, 1954), pp. 94–5.

16. The ancestors cult, which was the cornerstone of Chinese culture and society, should be studied in this connection.

17. On this subject, I am drawing heavily from L. Ledderose's masterful study, *Mi Fu and the Classical Tradition of Chinese Calligraphy* (Princeton University Press, 1979).

18. It was suspected that the *Orchid Pavilion* was in the hands of a monk called Biancai, but the monk denied possessing it. Emperor Taizong then dispatched the censor Xiao Yi, disguised as an itinerant scholar, to visit Biancai. Xiao Yi gained the confidence of the monk and showed him various autographs of Wang Xizhi from the imperial collection, which he had brought along to be used as bait. Excited by this sight, Biancai told his visitor that he could show him even better stuff—and he picked from among the rafters of the roof where it was hidden the original scroll of the *Orchid Pavilion*. In front of this masterpiece, Xiao Yi pretended to be unmoved and even questioned its authenticity. Biancai, suffocating with indignation, stormed out of his hut. Xiao Yi grabbed the calligraphy, put on his court attire, and when Biancai returned, the visitor informed the monk that, from now on, the *Orchid Pavilion* would belong to the imperial collection. Struck with horror and grief, Biancai fainted. When he recovered, it was found that he could not swallow anymore—the emotional shock having resulted in a constriction of his gullet. Unable to absorb any solid food, he died a few months later. This arch-famous anecdote has provided the subject of many paintings.

19. L. Ledderose, *op. cit.*, p. 20.

20. This is the positive aspect of the phenomenon—but it also has a negative side. Modern Chinese intellectuals, progressives and revolutionaries have increasingly felt strangled by the seeming invincibility and deadly pervasiveness of tradition. The outstanding exponent of the struggle to get rid of the past was of course Lu Xun, who analysed with unique clear-sightedness the desperate nature of the modernisers' predicament: they can never pin the enemy down, for the enemy is a formless, invisible ghost, an indestructible shadow.

21. Liu Shilong, "Wuyou yuan ji," in *Wan Ming bai jia xiao pin*, pp. 104–7. This delightful (and very Borgesian!) little essay was brought to my at-

tention some years ago in a seminar given at the Australian National University by Dr. Tu Lien-che.

22. Holmes Welch, "The Chinese Art of Make-Believe," *Encounter* (May, 1968).

23. *Rice University Studies* 59.4 (1973).

ONE MORE ART: CHINESE CALLIGRAPHY

1. The view that human beings, as sexual creatures, are essentially incomplete belongs to Western culture; the Chinese view is that every individual contains in himself both yin and yang elements, and therefore should be able to achieve his own perfection in isolation.

2. *Confessions*, Vol. 1, 3: "When Ambrose was reading, his eyes ran over the page and his heart perceived the sense, but his voice and tongue were silent. He did not restrict access to anyone coming in, nor was it customary even for a visitor to be announced. Very often, when we were there, we saw him silently reading and never otherwise...We wondered if he read silently perhaps to protect himself in case he had a hearer interested and intent on the matter, to whom he might have to expound the text being read if it contained difficulties...If his time were used up in that way, he would get through fewer books than he wished. Besides, the need to preserve his voice, which used easily to become hoarse, could have been a very fair reason for silent reading. Whatever motive he had for his habit, this man had a good reason for what he did." (I am quoting here the beautiful translation by Henry Chadwick, Oxford University Press, 1991.)

3. Boswell, *Life of Samuel Johnson*, entry of 8 May 1778.

4. See "Arrêt, vision et language," in *Philosophies*, No. 44 (December 1994).

5. In a book recording a series of dialogues with François Mitterrand, *Mémoire à deux voix* (Paris: Odile Jacob, 1995), which, for the rest, is unfortunately without interest.

AN INTRODUCTION TO CONFUCIUS

1. On these problems of chronology and textual analysis, see E. Bruce Brooks, *The Original Analects* (Columbia University Press, 1998).

2. Julien Gracq, *Les carnets du grand chemin* (Paris: José Corti, 1992), pp. 190–91.

3. The earliest images of the cross discovered by archaeology were *anti-Christian* graffiti, whereas the art of the Catacombs only used abstract symbols to represent Christ. The cross was a hideous instrument of torture, a reminder of abject humiliation and death; it is only in the time of Constantine that it began to be displayed as a triumphant symbol of victory over evil; and yet it still took nearly another thousand years before medieval artists dared to represent *the dead Christ hanging on it*.

4. Elias Canetti, *The Conscience of Words* (New York: Seabury Press, 1979), pp. 171–5.

POETRY AND PAINTING

1. Quoted by Monica Furlong, *Merton: A Biography* (London: Collins, 1980), p. 266.

2. *Lie Zi* (Peking: Wenxue guji kanxingshe, 1956), Book 8, pp. 10–11.

3. It may be amusing to note in passing that the latest discoveries of modern physics seem to verify the oldest notions of Chinese cosmology. Discarding the theory according to which the universe was the product of an explosion, some scientists are now propounding the theory of an original "bubble"; according to these views, as a cosmologist from MIT put it, "it is very tempting to assume that the universe emerged from nothing…Possibly the most far-reaching recent development…in cosmology is [the] realisation…that the universe is a free lunch." (*Newsweek*, 7 June 1982, p. 83.)

4. On this question, one should read the masterful essay by A. C. Graham, "Being in Western Philosophy Compared with *Shih/fei* and *Yu/wu*," *Asia Major*, VII (1959): pp. 79–112.

5. The best study on this subject is still Qian Zhongshu's "Zhongguo shi yu Zhongguo hua" in *Kaiming shudian ershi zhou nian jinian wenji* (Shanghai: Kaiming Shudian, 1947). I have briefly outlined Qian's theory in *Les Propos sur la peinture de Shitao* (Brussels: Institut belge des hautes études chinoises, 1970), pp. 98–9 (new edition: *Les Propos sur la peinture du Moine Citrouille-amère*, Paris: Plon, 2007). A new version

of Qian's essay can be found in *Jiu wen si pian* (Shanghai: Shanghai guji chubanshe, 1979).

6.   This phenomenon was analysed with great perception and subtlety by François Cheng in his book *Chinese Poetic Writing* (Indiana University Press, 1982)—an admirable work to which I shall never adequately acknowledge all my debts. Later on in this essay, I also borrow freely from James J. Y. Liu, *The Art of Chinese Poetry* (University of Chicago Press, 1962).

7.   See Wai-lim Yip, *Ezra Pound's Cathay* (Princeton University Press, 1969), and more specifically, the very important article by Y. K. Kao and T. L. Mei, "Syntax, Diction and Imagery in T'ang Poetry," *Harvard Journal of Asiatic Studies*, 31 (1971): pp. 51–136. Like François Cheng (mentioned earlier), Y. K. Kao provides us with fundamental insights on the nature of Chinese poetry. Without such guides, I would never have ventured to write this little essay. On the merits of Pound's translations, see also some interesting examples in S. W. Durrant, "On Translating *Lun Yü*," *Chinese Literature: Essays, Articles, Reviews*, 3, No. 1 (January 1981): pp. 109–19.

8.   On the combination of discursive and imagist modes in Chinese poetry, see the article by Kao and Mei (cited above) and also the beautiful book by Kang-i Sun Chang, *The Evolution of Chinese Tz'u Poetry from the late T'ang to the Northern Sung* (Princeton University Press, 1980).

9.   The expression "Creator" with a capital *C* is used here as a convenient shorthand for what would otherwise require a lengthy paraphrase: "The inner driving force that moves the entire process of cosmic creation." The notion of a personal God, exterior to His creation, is utterly foreign to Chinese cosmology. (Classical Chinese treatises do sometimes speak of the Creator in a personified way, but this is a mere literary device—similar to our metaphors the "smiles" of Spring, the "anger" of the ocean, and so on.) *Natura naturans* would probably be a more appropriate term, but since I am trying to express myself in English, I am reluctant to use it.

10.   A. D. Hope, *The Pack of Autolycus* (Canberra: Australian National University Press, 1978).

11.   Quoted by Maurice Nadeau in his introduction to the new edition of *Madame Bovary* (Paris: Folio, 1981), p. 6.

12. P. Claudel, *Journal* I (Paris: Pléiade, 1968), p. 473.

13. F. Gilot, *Vivre avec Picasso* (Paris: Calmann-Levy, 1965), p. 69.

14. Quoted by D. Kahnweiler, *Juan Gris* (Paris: Gallimard, 1946), p. 188.

15. On this question, see D. Pollard, "Ch'i in Chinese Literary Theory," in A. A. Rickett, ed., *Chinese Approaches to Literature from Confucius to Liang Ch'i-ch'ao* (Princeton University Press, 1978), p. 56.

16. Quoted by Nadeau in his introduction to *Madame Bovary*, p. 8.

17. Or in music. A good introduction to this topic can be found in R. H. van Gulik, *The Lore of the Chinese Lute* (Tokyo: Tuttle, 1968). The melodic repertory of the zither is limited, although it presents extraordinarily rich variations and nuances of timbre: "The [zither] is not easy to appreciate, chiefly because its music is not primarily melodical. Its beauty lies not so much in the succession of notes as in each separate note in itself. 'Painting with sounds' might be a way to describe its essential quality. The timbre being thus of the utmost importance, there are very great possibilities of modifying the colouring of one and the same tone. In order to understand and appreciate this music, the ear must learn to distinguish subtle nuances: the same note, produced on a different string, has a different colour; the same string when pulled by the forefinger or the middle finger of the right hand, has a different timbre. The technique by which these variations in timbre are effected is extremely complicated: of the vibrato alone, there exist no less than twenty-six varieties." (van Gulik, *The Lore of the Chinese Lute*, pp. 1–2.)

18. M. Proust, "A propos du style de Flaubert," in *Contre Sainte-Beuve* (Paris: Pléiade, 1971), p. 595: "To my mind, the most beautiful thing in *Sentimental Education* is not a sentence, it is a blank. Flaubert has just described in many pages the minutest moves of Frédéric Moreau. Then he tells us that Frédéric sees a policeman charging with his sword against a rebel who falls dead: 'And Frédéric, open-mouthed, recognised Sénécal.' Then, a 'blank,' a huge 'blank,' and without the slightest transition, suddenly time is no longer measured in quarters of an hour but in years, in dozens of years; I repeat the last words I just quoted in order to show this extraordinary shift of speed for which there was no preparation: 'And Frédéric, open-mouthed, recognised Sénécal. He travelled. He came to know the melancholy of the steamboat, the cold awakening in the tent, etc. . . .'"

19. Maurice Nadeau in Introduction to *Madame Bovary*, pp. 15–16. Claude Roy made similar observations on Stendhal (*Stendhal par lui-même* [Paris: Seuil, 1971], p. 47): "A novel by Stendhal is written in a way that is the exact opposite of nine out of ten of the great novelists who came before him. The narrative progresses as much through what is said as through what is omitted. There are two novels within *Red and Black*—the novel of the events that are printed, and the novel of the events that are eluded: the latter are no less important. One could write another version of Julien's story, simply by filling in all the blanks of the narrative. Just imagine another writer describing the first night which Julien spent with Mathilde: all the things he would have to write, Stendhal puts in a semicolon: 'Julien's prowess was equal to his happiness; "I cannot go down the ladder," he said to Mathilde when he saw the dawn appear...' A semicolon alone accounts for a whole night, two lovers in each other's arms, their ecstasy, their mutual love-confessions, their pleasure, etc. In *Vanina Vanini*, the entire story ends with a two-minute scene that occupies three pages of dialogue. Then, two lines only: 'Vanina stood dumbfounded. She returned to Rome; and the newspaper is reporting that she just married Prince Savelli.'" Stendhal's latter quote is remarkably similar to the Flaubert passage that Proust admired so much (see previous note). Strange power of litotes! Because it relies on the reader's imagination, it is more effective than an explicit description. Claude Roy pursues: "What seems to us discretion on Stendhal's part appeared in his time as impudence. He shocked his readers, who felt that he was telling too much." Splendid illustration of the aesthetic principle "less is more." If literature has its litotes, and painting its blanks, music also has its silences: it may be apposite to quote here Daniel Barenboim's warning to the musicians of his orchestra that they should carefully observe the pauses of a score: "Silence is the paper on which all music is written."

ORIENTALISM AND SINOLOGY

1. The words "European" and "American" are to be understood here as abstract categories, not as geographical notions. Actually, I wonder to what extent the European academic tradition can still be found in Europe. Quite recently, the dean of the Asian Studies Faculty of one of the oldest and most prestigious European universities sent me a warm and generous invitation to come and lecture on Chinese classical culture. In

his innocence, he added, "As our university has now established with the People's Republic of China an important exchange program, which should not be put in jeopardy, it would be best if your lectures would not touch on contemporary issues." What shocked me most was that he obviously felt this was a perfectly sensible and decent proposition.

2. The passages in italics summarise various points made by Said (when quotation marks are used, they reproduce his own words). Some readers may rightly feel that my approach to this serious topic is selective, arbitrary, incoherent and flippant. I could not agree more with such criticism—I merely tried to imitate Said's method.

ROLAND BARTHES IN CHINA

1. Roland Barthes, *Alors, la Chine?* (Paris: Christian Bourgois, 1975).

2. Roland Barthes, *Carnets du voyage en Chine,* ed. Anne Herschberg Pierrot (Paris: Christian Bourgois, 2009). English translation by Andrew Brown: *Travels in China* (Cambridge, England, and Malden, MA: Polity, 2012).

THE ART OF INTERPRETING NON-EXISTENT INSCRIPTIONS WRITTEN IN INVISIBLE INK ON A BLANK PAGE

1. Looking at this phenomenon from an East European angle, Kazimierz Brandys made similar observations in his admirable *Carnets* (Paris: Gallimard, 1987).

2. Epilogue: in 1982, a *People's Daily* survey revealed that over 90 per cent of Chinese youth do not have an inkling of what Marxism is.

3. *New York Review of Books*, 26 April 1990.

ANATOMY OF A "POST-TOTALITARIAN" DICTATORSHIP

1. *Two* books, actually; a similar (yet not identical) collection, in French, appeared earlier in 2011: Liu Xiaobo, *La philosophie du porc et autres essais*, selected, translated, and introduced by Jean-Philippe Béja (Paris: Gallimard). Since the contents of both volumes do not completely overlap, one would wish for a third collection that could combine both. For more information on Liu himself—his life, activities, arrest, and trial, see Perry Link, *Liu Xiaobo's Empty Chair* (New York Review Books, 2011).

2. On December 23, 2011, the writer Chen Wei, who had been arrested in February after posting essays online calling for freedom of speech and other political reforms, was convicted of the same crime of "inciting of subversion of state power" and sentenced, following a two-hour trial, to nine years in prison.

FOREWORD TO *THE SEA IN FRENCH LITERATURE*

1. Jean Marteilhe (1684–1777), a young Protestant who, trying to escape religious persecution in France, was arrested at the border and sentenced to serve on the galleys. Faithful to his religion, he rowed as a slave-convict for twelve years; eventually freed, he exiled himself to Holland, where he published a most remarkable narrative of his ordeal, well described in his long title, *Mémoires d'un Protestant, condamné aux galères de France pour cause de religion, écrits par lui-même: Ouvrage dans lequel, outre le récit des souffrances de l'Auteur depuis 1700 jusqu'en 1713, on trouvera diverses Particularités curieuses, relatives à l'Histoire de ce Temps-là, & une Description exacte des Galères & de leur Service* (Amsterdam, 1757).

   René Duguay-Trouin (1673–1736), a famous Breton privateer who fought at sea against the English and the Dutch. Educated by the Jesuits, he knew how to write; his terse, vivid autobiography is a minor classic.

   Louis Garneray (1783–1857), a distinguished painter (seascapes and naval battles). He ran away from home and went to sea at age thirteen; served as a privateer under the great Surcouf; lived through countless extraordinary adventures—battles, mutinies, shipwrecks—before eventually being captured by the English (age twenty-three) and spending nine years on the notorious and barbaric prison-ships of Portsmouth. Finally freed in 1814, he wrote of his early adventures at sea (*Voyages, aventures et combats*) and of his ordeal in captivity (*Mes pontons*). Garneray, as a memorialist and story-teller, is simply fabulous!

2. Alain Gerbault (originally a tennis champion), Bernard Moitessier (yachtsman of genius) and Éric Tabarly (originally a navy officer) all became famous for their solitary voyages under sail. Alain Bombard is a medical doctor who, in 1952, crossed the Atlantic Ocean on an inflatable raft, without any supplies of water or food, to demonstrate scientifically the possibility of survival at sea. The author of *Naufragé volontaire*, his visionary daring decisively modified traditional practices

which, for centuries, had needlessly condemned countless shipwreck victims to death.

3. Joseph Conrad, for instance; one of his letters is featured. Interesting, though not exactly his greatest literary work, it was originally written in French (like a significant part of his correspondence) and it provided me with a good pretext to include his irreplaceable presence in the anthology.

4. I am thinking first and foremost of Jonathan Raban, *The Oxford Book of the Sea* (Oxford University Press, 1992).

5. "This could have occurred nowhere but in England, where men and the sea interpenetrate, so to speak—the sea entering into the life of most men, and the men knowing something or everything about the sea, in the way of amusement, of travel, or of breadwinning." Thus begins *Youth*, one of Conrad's most perfect sea narratives. Before him, R.L. Stevenson developed the same notion, in a different mode: "If an Englishman wishes to have such a patriotic feeling, it must be about the sea…The sea is our approach and bulwark; it has been the scene of our greatest triumphs and dangers, and we are accustomed in lyrical strains to claim it as our own. The prostrating experiences of foreigners between Calais and Dover have always an agreeable side to English prepossessions. A man from Bedfordshire who does not know one end of the ship from the other until she begins to move, swaggers among such persons with a sense of hereditary nautical experience…We should consider ourselves unworthy of our descent if we did not share the arrogance of our progenitors, and please ourselves with the pretension that the sea is English. Even where it is looked upon by the guns and battlements of another nation, we regard it as a kind of English cemetery, where the bones of our seafaring fathers take their rest until the last trumpet; for I suppose no other nation has lost as many ships or sent as many brave fellows to the bottom." (*The English Admirals*, 1881, quoted by J. Raban, *op. cit.* p. 284.)

6. "Neither Out Far Nor In Deep," in *A Further Range* (New York: Holt, 1936).

7. "Things I Consider Overrated," in *From the Uncollected Edmund Wilson* (Ohio University Press, 1995), pp. 120–21. Wilson ends his diatribe with the observation that sea literature is unreadable. Well before him,

Théophile Gautier made the same point, with much more wit (see my anthology, Vol. 1, pp. 501–3). Americans often consider Wilson as a prince of modern criticism; he seems to me a rather vulgar mind.

8. Boswell, *Life of Johnson* (entry of March 1759). And again: "A ship is worse than a gaol. There is, in a gaol, better air, better company, better conveniency of every kind; and a ship has the additional disadvantage of being in danger. When men come to like a sea-life, they are not fit to live on land" (Boswell, *Life of Johnson*, entry of 19 March 1776). And this conversation between Johnson, Boswell and William Scott (entry of 10 April 1778):

> *Johnson*: As to the sailor, when you look down from the quarter deck to the space below, you see the utmost extremity in human misery; such crowding, such filth, such stench!
>
> *Boswell*: Yet sailors are happy.
>
> *Johnson*: They are happy as brutes are happy, with a piece of fresh meat,—with the grossest sensuality…
>
> *Scott*: We find people fond of being sailors.
>
> *Johnson*: I cannot account for that, any more than I can account for other strange perversions of the imagination.

9. Johnson was a landlubber to an almost Continental degree. He was from Lichfield, one of the very few English cities that are located more than 100 miles from the nearest shore. Though he became a Londoner quite early in his career, it is only at age fifty-nine that he saw the sea for the first time in his life—during an excursion to Plymouth, on which he had been dragged by his old friend, the painter Joshua Reynolds.

10. Letter to Sidney Colvin, written from Tahiti, 16 October 1888. See *Selected Letters of Robert Louis Stevenson* (Yale University Press, 1997), p. 382.

11. Éric Tabarly, *Mémoires du large* (Paris: Editions de Fallois, 1997), p. 126. Also in the same book, these lines of equally refreshing sincerity: "One often asks lone sailors what they think about when out at sea, and their answers are nearly always awkward. As for myself, I don't think at all. Or rather, I only think of the boat; my ears are attuned to its every sound; my only concern is to make it sail as fast as possible. All the time, I only think of the boat, because on board the tasks are absorbing. Contrary to what most people believe, a boat is not synonymous with free-

dom. To sail means to accept constraints one has freely chosen. It is a privilege: most people must bear with the constraints which life is imposing on them." (*Ibid.*, p. 122.)

12. "I must go down to the seas again, to the lonely sea and the sky / And all I ask is a tall ship and a star to steer her by / And the wheel's kick and the wind's song and the white sail's shaking / And a grey mist on the sea's face and a grey dawn breaking. / I must go down to the seas again, for the call of the running tide / Is a wild call and a clear call that cannot be denied; / And all I ask is a windy day with the white clouds flying, / And the flung spray and the blown spume and the seagulls crying. / I must go down to the seas again, to the vagrant gypsy life, / To the gull's way and the whale's way where the wind's like a whetted knife; / And all I ask is a merry yarn from a laughing fellow rover, / And quiet sleep and a sweet dream when the long trick's over."

13. Quoted in David Hays and Daniel Hays, *My Old Man and the Sea* (New York: Anchor Books, 1996), p. 197.

14. Joseph Conrad, "The *Torrens*: A Personal Tribute," in *Last Essays* (London & Toronto: Dent & Sons, 1926).

15. Joseph Conrad, "The Secret Sharer," in *'Twixt Land and Sea* (London & Toronto: Dent & Sons, 1912). Conrad repeatedly evoked this paradoxical feeling of security: "The peace of the sea . . . a sailor finds a deep feeling of security in the exercise of his calling. The exacting life of the sea has this advantage over the life of the earth, that its claims are simple and cannot be evaded." Joseph Conrad, *Chance* (London: Methuen & Co., 1914), Chap. 1.

16. Hilaire Belloc, *The Cruise of the "Nona"* (London: Century Publishing, 1983), new edition with an introduction by Jonathan Raban. The original edition was published in 1925.

IN THE WAKE OF MAGELLAN

1. *Deus escreve direto por linhas tortas.*

INDEX

OTHER NEW YORK REVIEW CLASSICS

For a complete list of titles, visit www.nyrb.com or write to:
Catalog Requests, NYRB, 435 Hudson Street, New York, NY 10014

* Also available as an electronic book.